SAMUEL FOOTE

by Jean François Colson

A BIOGRAPHICAL DICTIONARY

OF

ACTORS, ACTRESSES, MUSICIANS, DANCERS, MANAGERS & OTHER STAGE PERSONNEL IN LONDON, 1660–1800

Volume 5: Eagan *to* Garrett

by

PHILIP H. HIGHFILL, JR., KALMAN A. BURNIM
and
EDWARD A. LANGHANS

SOUTHERN ILLINOIS UNIVERSITY PRESS
CARBONDALE AND EDWARDSVILLE

Publication of this work was made possible in part through a grant from the National Endowment for the Humanities.

PN
2597
H5
v. 5

Library of Congress Cataloging in Publication Data (*Revised*)

Highfill, Philip H., Jr
  A biographical dictionary of actors, actresses, musicians, dancers, managers & other stage personnel in London, 1660–1800.

  Includes bibliographical references.
  CONTENTS: v. 1. Abaco to Belfille.—v. 2. Belfort to Byzand.—v. 3. Cabanel to Cory.—v. 4. Corye to Dynion.—v. 5. Eagan to Garrett.
  1. Performing arts—London—Biography. I. Burnim, Kalman A., joint author. II. Langhans, Edward A., joint author. III. Title.
PN2597.H5   790.2′092′2   [B]   71–157068
ISBN 0–8093–0832–0 (v. 5)

List of Illustrations

VIEWS AND DRAWINGS OF PROVINCIAL THEATRES

Acknowledgments

SINCE the publication of the first two volumes of this *Dictionary* the authors have been the grateful recipients of information and assistance from a number of individuals and institutions. We acknowledge thankfully our indebtedness to:

The National Endowment for the Humanities for a third—and extremely generous—grant for time, travel, and secretarial help.

The Folger Shakespeare Library for summer fellowships and grants-in-aid and for continuing logistical support to the project.

The George Washington University for a summer grant-in-aid.

The National Library of Scotland and its Librarian, Dr. E. F. D. Roberts, for a Theodore Stewart Fellowship.

Mrs Norma Armstrong for gracious permission to employ information in her invaluable manuscript calendar of eighteenth-century theatrical performances in Edinburgh.

Mrs William S. Clark, II for generously giving access to her extensive notes, and to those made by the late Professor William S. Clark, II, concerning the Irish stage in the eighteenth century; and Professor Peter Verdurmen for guidance and assistance in exploiting those and his own notes on the subject.

The Library of the University of Cincinnati for access to, and permission to publish from, manuscript notebooks of W. J. Lawrence.

Mr Harry Greatorex for his generosity in making available his transcripts of theatrical news accounts on the Lincoln circuit and for his warm hospitality.

Miss Jeanne Newlin, Curator, Harvard Theatre Collection, for indispensable assistance in assembling pictures, and for many other acts of kindness.

Miss Kathleen M. D. Barker for further valuable information on performers of the Bristol theatre.

Professor Joyce Hemlow for access to and assistance with the Burney materials at McGill University.

Mr Ira Burnim for photographic work in Volumes I through VI.

For various courtesies, warm thanks are due also to: Professor Denis Arnold, Faculty of Music, Oxford; Mr Geoffrey Ashton; Miss Yolande Bird, the National Theatre; Professor William Beattie; Bild-Archiv und Porträt-Sammlung, Österreichische Nationalbibliothek, Wien; Mr D. H. B. Chesshyre, Rouge Croix Pursuivant, College of Arms; Mr Oliver Davies, Keeper of Portraits, Royal College of Music; Mr David Dyregrove; Miss Gareth Esersky; Mr Martin Harvey, Secretary, The Garrick Club; Miss Pauline Hewitt; Institute für Theatergeschichte, Wien; Dr Jamie Kassler; Dr Michael Kassler; Mr Iain Mackintosh, Arts Council of Great Britain; the Raymond Mander and Joe Mitchenson Theatre Collection; Professor Jennifer Martin; Miss J. M. Nichol, Publications Officer, National Portrait Gallery; Lord Olivier; Mr James Osborn; Mr Patrick Pigott; Mr Alvero Riebaro; Rev David Sharpe, St Peter Mancroft, Norwich; Dr Lola Szladits, Curator, Berg Collection, New York Public Library; Mr Edward Telesford, Photographic Service, British Museum; and Mr Alick Williams.

P. H. H., *Jr.*
K. A. B.
E. A. L.

Volume 5

Eagan *to* Garrett

= E =

Eagan. *See also* EGAN.

Eagan, Mr [*fl. 1767*], *dancer.*
A dancer named Eagan was a member of the Drury Lane company as of 24 January 1767 at a weekly salary of £1. He was probably not the "Eagan" who acted at the Haymarket Theatre in 1775 with Foote's troupe; that performer was very likely William Egan the elder.

Eagle, Master [*fl. 1740–1741*], *actor.*
Master Eagle played Puck in *Robin Goodfellow* at Drury Lane on 15 October 1740 and at subsequent performances through 9 January 1741.

Eagles. *See* ECCLES.

Eaglesfield, Mr *d. c. 1700, dancer, choreographer.*
Mr Eaglesfield was the dancing master at Christopher Rich's Drury Lane Theatre during the 1699–1700 season, but he died before 6 July 1700. On that date a new entry composed by him appeared and he was cited as the late Mr. Eaglesfield.

Eales. *See* ECCLES.

Ealy. *See* ELEY.

Eames, William [*fl. 1672*], *musician.*
William Eames was one of 17 musicians ordered arrested on 2 October 1672 for playing music without a license.

Earl, the Messrs Joseph [*fl. 1794*], *singers.*
Doane's *Musical Directory* of 1794 listed two men named Joseph Earl, both living at No 4, Gray's Inn Lane. Joseph the elder was a *basso* (or possibly a bass player) who participated in the Handel concerts at Westminster, and Joseph the younger sang in the oratorios at Covent Garden.

Earle, William Benson [*fl. 1795–1800?*], *singer, actor?*
William Benson Earle was a principal performer in the musical spectacle *Veluti in speculum* at the Royal Circus on 17 April 1795. On 19 October 1796 he sang in the chorus of soldiers in *Richard Coeur de Lion* at Drury Lane, and the following 7 January 1797 he was in the chorus of *The Honey Man*. Possibly he was the "Earl" who played Orano in *Pizarro* at Chesterfield on 17 January 1800.

Earnshaw, Mr [*fl. 1776–1777*], *dresser.*
Mr Earnshaw was one of the Drury Lane dressers earning 9s. weekly during the 1776–77 season.

Eason, Mr [*fl. 1794*], *singer?*
Doane's *Musical Directory* of 1794 listed a Mr Eason of New Peter Street, Westminster, as a participant in the Handel performances at Westminster Abbey. Doane described Eason as a bass—probably a *basso,* though perhaps he was a player on the bass viol.

Eastland, Mrs [*fl. 1661–1671*], *actress.*
The Lord Chamberlain's accounts show Mrs Eastland as a member of the King's

Company at the Vere Street Theatre on 27 March 1661, so it is probable that the prompter John Downes was correct in saying she was one of the original seven actresses in the company. The Eastland who had a role in *The Royal King* about 1661–62 was probably the actress rather than Edward Eastland, whose career was restricted to the 1670s but who may have been related to Mrs Eastland. Only two roles are known for Mrs Eastland, both of them minor: Cydnon in *Tyrannick Love* on 24 June 1669 and Halyma in both parts of *The Conquest of Granada* in December 1670 and January 1671 at the Bridges Street Theatre.

Eastland, Edward   ₁*fl. 1670–1679*₁, *bookkeeper, actor.*

Edward Eastland, doubtless related to the Mrs Eastland active in the 1660s, was a bookkeeper (probably, that is, the prompter's helper) in the King's Company at the Bridges Street Theatre in 1670–71. A warrant in the Lord Chamberlain's accounts dated 14 July 1671 so cited Eastland, but the entry was cancelled for some reason; a second, but uncancelled, warrant of the same date also listed Eastland as a member of the troupe. On 14 March 1673 he was sued by Thomas Humphryes, and over a year later he and Robert (or Rupert) Eastland were sued by the same creditor. On 5 January 1678 Daniell Maedeus petitioned against Edward Eastland for £9 10s.

In addition to serving the King's Company as bookkeeper, Eastland acted, though the only role known for him is Garbato, a small part in *The Amorous Old Woman.* The play was presented between December 1673 and February 1674 when the troupe was playing at the Lincoln's Inn Fields Theatre. The last mention of Eastland in the records was on 23 June 1679, when he was still listed by the Lord Chamberlain as a member of the King's Company.

Eastland, Rupert   ₁*fl. 1674–1675*₁, *actor?*

Rupert Eastland, possibly an actor, was mentioned in a list of King's Company members on a warrant dated 23 March 1674. On the following 3 June Thomás Humphyres sued Edward and "Robert" Eastland for debt; perhaps "Robert" was a slip for "Rupert." Rupert Eastland was a member of the King's Company during the 1674–75 season, according to *The London Stage.*

Eaton, Mr   ₁*fl. 1716–1717*₁, *actor.*

On 4 December 1716 Mr Eaton played a Servant in *Woman is a Riddle* when it was first performed at Lincoln's Inn Fields, and he shared a benefit with Cook when the work was presented again on 28 May 1717.

Eaton, Mrs   ₁*fl. 1736*₁, *actress.*

On 26 April 1736 at the Haymarket Theatre Mrs Eaton played Sylvia in a performance of *The Female Rake,* according to the 1736 edition of the work.

Eaton, Charles   ₁*fl. 1786*₁, *proprietor.*

In 1786 Charles Eaton was the proprietor of the Adam and Eve Tavern, near the west end of St Pancras Church, when he advertised the attractions of his gardens and pleasure grounds.

Eaton, Henry   ₁*fl. 1660*₁, *actor?*

On 12 May 1660 Henry Eaton, Anthony Turner, and Edward Shatterall were charged with putting on plays illegally at the old Red Bull playhouse.

Eaton, Jer₁emiah?₁   *d. 1739, actor, dancer.*

Mr Eaton was first noticed in the playbills on 8 September 1726, when he played Lord Lovewell in *The Unnatural Parents* at Spiller and Egleton's booth at Southwark Fair. He was not cited again in London advertisements until 29 January 1728, when he was Harry Paddington in *The Beggar's Opera* at Lincoln's Inn Fields. In July and August at the same house he danced, and the following 18 January 1729 Eaton acted a Sicilian and a Gardener in *The Rape of Proserpine*. He turned up at Blackheath Fair on 30 September 1729 to play Grigg in *The Beggar's Wedding* and Hob in *Flora*, after which he joined the Goodman's Fields troupe for the 1729–30 season. There he danced and essayed such roles as the Welsh Collier in *The Recruiting Officer*, Dicky in *The Constant Couple*, Pierot in *The Fashionable Lady*, Sir Hugh Evans in *The Merry Wives of Windsor,* and Dorcas Guzzle in *The Cobler of Preston.*

In the summer of 1730 Eaton was at Tottenham Court and Southwark Fair, and then he returned to Goodman's Fields for the 1730–31 season to appear as Foigard in *The Stratagem*, in some of his old parts, and as a dancer. After putting in his usual stint at Southwark Fair, he was back at Goodman's Fields in October and November 1731 dancing a *Peasant Dance* and *Scotch Dance* and repeating Dicky in *The Constant Couple.* The playbill on 8 October 1731 provided a clue to his Christian name: he was cited as "Jer." Eaton. He did not complete the season, it seems. Eaton died eight years later and was buried in November 1739 at Carmarthen, Wales.

Eaves, Mr ₁*fl. 1786*₁, *house servant?*
Mr Eaves, possibly one of the house servants, had his benefit tickets accepted at Covent Garden on 27 May 1786.

Eball. *See* **ABELL.**

Ebelin, Christopher ₁*fl. 1732–1754*₁, *violinist.*
The Mr Ebelin who held a benefit concert at Hickford's Music Room on 6 March 1732 was probably Christopher Ebelin, one of the original subscribers to the Royal Society of Musicians on 28 August 1739. The Ebelin who was paid 8*s.* for playing

tenor violin in the performance of the *Messiah* at the Foundling Hospital in May 1754 was very likely the same person.

Eberardi, Teresa ₁*fl. 1760–1762*₁, *singer.*
Teresa Eberardi (or, incorrectly, Eleardi) was first noticed in London documents when she was announced as one of the singers engaged by Signora Mattei for the King's Theatre in the Haymarket. As second *buffa* in the company in 1760–61 and 1761–62 she sang Clarice in *Il mondo nella luna* on 22 November 1760 for her first appearance. During the rest of her stay at the King's Theatre she sang Alcestes in *Arianna e Teseo*, Lena in *Il filosofo di campagna*, Decio in *Tito Manlio,* Nerina in *La pescatrici,* Timagenes in *Alessandro nell Indie,* and Brigida in *Il mercato di Malmantile.* She also appeared at the Great Room in Dean Street, Soho, in the oratorio *Isaac* on 21 January 1761, and, for her last appearance, at the concert for the benefit of decayed musicians and their families at the King's Theatre on 11 May 1762. Dr Burney said that Signora Eberardi "gave great pleasure in the *simplicetta* and *innocente* way, both in the serious and comic opera of these times."

Eberlin, Mr ₁*fl. 1726*₁, *scene painter.*
Mr Eberlin, along with his fellow scene painters Devoto, Tillemans, and Dominick, prepared the scenery for John Thurmond's *The Miser,* which was presented at Drury Lane on 30 December 1726.

Eccles, Miss. *See* **EDMEAD, ELIZABETH.**

Eccles, Henry *c. 1652–1742?,* *violinist, composer.*
Henry Eccles the younger, born about 1652, was the brother of the more famous John and son of the eccentric musician and religious fanatic Solomon. Perhaps some of the musical activity recorded for the elder

Henry Eccles (possibly an uncle of the younger Henry) should be assigned to our subject, for Grove suggests that the younger man was a player in the royal band from 1674 to 1710. The Lord Chamberlain's accounts contain frequent references to one or another Henry Eccles in the King's Musick. On 17 July 1689 our subject was, according to John Jeffreys's *The Eccles Family,* appointed to the King's private music.

An entry in *The London Stage* dated 27 July 1702 refers to music composed by John Eccles for the coronation, but the late Emmett Avery's notes indicate that that may be an error for Henry Eccles the younger. Only on 2 January 1705 does *The London Stage* report a reference to Henry Eccles "Jr." On that date he played several Italian sonatas on the violin for his own benefit at Hill's Dancing Room in Crosby Square, Bishopsgate Street.

A letter of 1 March 1706 concerning a contract with "The Baroness" at the Queen's Theatre refers to a "Mr Eccles" who was present at conferences concerning the matter but who could not bear witness to the conversations since he did not understand the (Italian?) language. That may have been another Eccles, as also may have been the Eccles who was proposed "to oversee ye Musick" at £40 annually in a company organized (on paper only) in the early years of the eighteenth century. A violinist "Echel" was cited with others in documents in the Coke papers at Harvard in connection with the Queen's Theatre in November–December 1710, and the same person, but with his name spelled "Igl," was one of the second violinists at the Queen's about 1711.

An Eccles, identified as "Musician to His Grace, the Duke d'Aumont, Ambassador extraordinary from France," was given a benefit at Stationers' Hall on 15 May 1713, and that was very likely the younger Henry, who had thought himself neglected in England and who had gone to Paris

sometime after 1710 to serve in the French King's band. A song by Henry Eccles Junior, "No more let Damon's Eyes," was published in *Wit and Mirth* in 1719 in London, and in 1720 Eccles published in Paris two books of *Twelve Solos for the Violin,* parts of which were cribbed from Giuseppe Valentini's *Alletamenti.* Eccles was still in Paris in 1735 and is said to have died in 1742.

Eccles, Henry [fl. 1675–1702], violinist, singer?

The elder Henry Eccles was possibly an uncle of the younger Henry and of the more famous John. Perhaps it was he who was one of the violinists in the production of the court masque *Calisto* in February 1675. Like the other members of the Eccles family, Henry's name was frequently spelled "Eagles." On 31 August 1685 Henry Eccles was listed as a bass (singer, presumably) in the private music of James II, and documents in the Lord Chamberlain's accounts refer to Eccles regularly through 1702. In January 1691 he was one of the royal musicians who accompanied William III on a trip to Holland, but of his other activities in the King's Musick the records tell us little more than that Eccles was paid £40 annually. The accounts usually cited Eccles's first name, but possibly some of the references could be to the younger Henry Eccles, who is said to have been a musician at court from 1689 on.

Eccles, John 1668–1735, composer, violinist?

John Eccles was born in 1668, one of the sons of the eccentric Solomon Eccles the elder. By 1690 John had turned to writing music for the theatre, an activity which absorbed much of his time for the following 15 years. On 22 June 1694 he was appointed to the King's Musick, but without fee until Thomas Tollett's place should become vacant. On 2 September 1696 Eccles

Folger Shakespeare Library

Song by JOHN ECCLES

was waiting for Tollett to die, for a warrant in the Lord Chamberlain's accounts stated that John was to receive Tollett's wages and livery upon the latter's decease. By 1697 Eccles had evidently succeeded to a salaried post, for he was listed as a member of the instrumental music at court at an annual salary of £40 plus livery. The instrument he played was not specified, but everyone else in the Eccles family was a violinist.

When Nicholas Staggins died in 1700 the King and the Lord Chamberlain considered abolishing the position of Master of the King's Musick, but the post was continued, and on 3 June 1700 John Eccles was appointed to it at a fee of £250 annually—plus livery, presumably, for Congreve spoke of the position as being worth £300 a year. In his new office Eccles fulfilled his duties by composing music for New Year and birthday odes while continuing his prolific outpouring of theatre works.

In March 1701 his music for Congreve's *The Judgment of Paris* was heard at the old Dorset Garden playhouse, but Eccles lost to John Weldon in the musical contest that was held and took the second prize of £50. After 1705 the rate of his theatrical composing diminished, but he continued writing music for court celebrations, for which he usually received special fees (in 1715–16 he was paid £22 for compositions for New Year's Day and the King's birthday, for instance).

In time Eccles gave up his musical career and retired to Kingston, where he spent his days angling on the Thames. He died on 12 January 1735. Eccles had written his will on 30 July 1728, cutting off his three daughters, Ann, Bridget, and Mary, with a shilling each. He had warned them: "I do hereby request that my three daughters shall not presume to dispute this my will the said one shilling being the whole that I will them to have." His estate, of undetermined worth, went to his servant Sarah Gainor. A codicil written on 27 December

1734 provided an additional £30 to Sarah for five years of wages due her. The will was proved on 13 January 1735.

The names of Eccles's daughters and those of his brothers Thomas and Henry would suggest that the following entries in the parish registers of St. Giles in the Fields concerned the musician: Henry-Thomas, son of John Eccles, gentleman, and his wife Ann, was baptized on 2 September 1702; their daughter Bridget was baptized on 29 August 1703; and their daughter Eleanor was baptized on 30 December 1705. The daughters Ann and Mary, named in Eccles's will, have not been traced.

John Eccles's reputation rests not on his performing, of which we know almost nothing, but on his work as one of the most facile and melodic composers of his day. Many of his songs were individually printed, as the *Catalogue of Printed Music in the British Museum* attests. He also published three volumes called *Theatre Music* in 1699 and 1700 and a collection of almost 100 of his songs in 1710. In 1704 *A Collection of Songs for One, Two, and Three Voices* was issued; *Mercurius Musicus,* issued in 1700 and 1701, included many Eccles songs; and *Wit and Mirth* in 1719 contained the lyrics of a number of songs which Eccles had set to music. Grove provides a very useful and complete listing of all of Eccles's work for the stage.

Eccles, Solomon [*fl.* 1685–1702], violinist?, composer?

Solomon Eccles was presumably the son of the religious fanatic and musician-turned-shoemaker Solomon Eccles (1618–1683), and some of the information in *Grove's Dictionary of Music and Musicians* concerning late compositions by the elder Eccles should perhaps be assigned to Solomon the younger or to the more eminent John. The elder Solomon Eccles seems not to have performed during the Restoration period.

The Solomon Eccles who married Rebecca Clifton at Temple Church on 7 June 1677 was probably our subject. On 12 November 1685 Solomon "Eagles" (a common variant spelling of the name) was paid 3s. daily for attending the King and Queen at Windsor and at Hampton Court, a chore which he repeated in the summers of 1686 and 1687. By 25 March 1689 he was earning £30 annually plus livery, a salary that probably remained constant for a few years, but by 1697 he was receiving £40. In the late summer of 1689 he attended the King at Newmarket, and in January 1691 he followed him to Holland for a short visit. Eccles was petitioned against by Dr Fisher Littleton for £400 on 9 March 1694, but details of the case have not been discovered. Solomon Eccles was still a member of the King's Musick in 1702.

Grove assigns the music for *The City Heiress* and *Venice Preserv'd,* both performed at the Dorset Garden Theatre in 1682, to the elder Solomon Eccles, but it is doubtful the older man would have resumed his musical activities at that late date, and, considering his Quakerism, it seems unlikely that he would have engaged in so frivolous an activity as writing music for plays. Solomon the younger may have been the composer.

Eccles, Thomas *1672–c.1745, violinist.*

Thomas Eccles, brother of the more famous John, was born in 1672, studied under his brother Henry, and with him went to Paris at some time after 1710. He returned to London, played for Handel, performed in taverns, and died about 1745.

Echel. *See* **ECCLES.**

Echelis, Mr [*fl.* 1778], *actor.*

Mr Echells played Pedro in *The Spanish Fryar* at the Haymarket Theatre on 26 January 1778, after which he was not mentioned in the London bills again.

Ecnad. *See* **DANCE.**

Eddis, [**William?**] [*fl.* 1766–1770], *office keeper.*

The first gallery office keeper at the Covent Garden Theatre from 1766 to 1770 was named Eddis—or possibly, as in a few references to him, Ellis. He was first cited in the accounts as a member of the company in 1766; his salary was 2s. nightly according to an account entry dated 14 September 1767. In 1768 and 1769 Eddis shared benefits with two of the theatre's boxkeepers, and he was mentioned as a friend of William Powell in the Colman lawsuit of 1770. That last reference suggests that Eddis was probably the subject of the following entry in the baptismal registers of St Paul, Covent Garden: on 26 October 1768 William Eddis and his wife Elizabeth christened a daughter Elizabeth Powell Eddis.

Eddleston or **Edelston.** *See* **EDLESTON.**

Eden, Mr [*fl.* 1749–1756?], *actor.*

In the summer of 1749 Mr Eden was a member of the company playing at Twickenham. He shared a benefit with Mrs Burnet on 15 August when *The Busy Body* and *Miss In Her Teens* were played, but no casts were listed in the bill. On 26 September Eden acted Mat o' the Mint in *The Beggar's Opera*. At the Haymarket Theatre in London on 17 April 1750 he attempted Macheath in *The Beggar's Opera*. It is probable that he was the Eden who appeared as Bonniface in *The Beaux' Stratagem* at Canterbury on 27 July 1756. In that performance Mrs Eden played Lady Bountiful, but she seems not to have acted in London.

Eden, Mr [*fl.* 1769?–1782], *actor.*

A Mr Eden played Brief in *Don Quixote in England* at the Haymarket Theatre on 4 March 1782. Perhaps he was the Eden

who was in Miller's company at Derby in
February 1769, in Carleton's troupe there
in November 1772, and in Whitley's band
in December 1779.

Edenborough, Mr _[fl. 1794]_, _bas-
soonist._

Doane's _Musical Directory_ of 1794 listed
Mr Edenborough of Nottingham as a
bassoonist who played in Handelian concerts at Westminster Abbey.

Edes, Thomas _[fl. 1672]_, _musician._

On 2 October 1672 Thomas Edes and
several others were ordered arrested for
playing music without licenses.

Edeter, Mr _[fl. 1707]_, _house servant?_

Mr Edeter's position at the Queen's
Theatre in the Haymarket is not certain,
though he would appear to have been one
of the office staff. The Coke papers at
Harvard contain a bill dated 1707 from a
Mr Sherman for £7 13s. which was paid
by Mr Edeter's order.

"Edgar, Sir John." _See_ STEELE, RICH-
ARD.

Edge, Miss _[fl. 1788–1793?]_, _actress._

Miss Edge acted in August and September 1788 at the Theatre Royal, Plymouth,
playing Donna Rodriguez in _Barataria_ on
18 August, Miss Le Blond in _The Romp_ on
22 August, and Lady Sneerwell in _The
School for Scandal_ and Phoebe in _Rosina_
on 27 August. She repeated Phoebe on 11
September, the last night of the season.

On 4 March 1793 at Covent Garden
Theatre, advertised as "A Young Lady,"
Miss Edge attempted Zara in _The Mourning Bride_ for one performance. The _Euro-
pean Magazine_ identified her by name and
commented that she "appeared to possess
some requisites for the stage, but her performance scarcely deserves to be distinguished from the numerous failures we are
bound to record."

Perhaps our subject was the "Mrs" Edge
who acted (as "A Young Lady") at the
Crow Street Theatre in Dublin on 30 April
1793. The name of the actress was revealed
in _Democratic Rage_ on 12 June.

Edgerton. _See also_ EGERTON.

Edgerton, Miss _[fl. 1744–1772?]_, _ac-
tress._

The London Stage lists a Miss Edgerton
as acting at Drury Lane in 1744–45, though
no roles are recorded for her. Possibly she
was the Miss Egerton who belonged to
Price's company in Ireland and was
drowned crossing the Boyne in the spring
of 1772.

Edleston, Mr _d. c. 1778, doorkeeper._

A doorkeeper at Drury Lane Theatre, Mr
Edleston shared a benefit with three other
employees on 22 May 1776, but the house
was small, and he lost £18 4s. Edleston
was mentioned in the theatre accounts as a
member of the staff in 1776–77, but on
22 May 1778 tickets delivered by his
widow were accepted. Precisely when Edleston died is not known.

Edmead, Elizabeth, née Hull? _[fl.
1786–1832]_, _actress._

Advertised simply as "A Young Lady,"
Elizabeth Edmead played Belvidera in
Venice Preserv'd in Tate Wilkinson's
troupe at Doncaster on 28 September 1786
and received warm applause. She remained
with that company at York and Hull
through 25 May 1787, playing as "Miss
Eccles." Wilkinson recalled in _The Wandering Patentee_ in 1795 that she had come
to him strongly recommended by the actors
Mr and Mrs Thomas Hull. "She is made
equal in proportion, as to limbs, to that of
any female figure I ever saw," observed
Wilkinson; "her features are by no means
handsome, and her mouth is not one of the
least apertures. . . . She is a sensible well-
bred woman. . . ."

In June 1787 Elizabeth came to London and moved into lodgings at No 13, King Street, Covent Garden. On 19 July, again cited only as "A Young Lady," she acted Belvidera at the Haymarket Theatre. The *European Magazine* identified her as Miss Eccles from the York Theatre. From London she went to Manchester, where she played Belvidera again on 14 November. On 30 January 1788 she acted the title role in *Julia* there. "Miss Edmeads" made her first appearance at Richmond on 26 July 1788 for her benefit, giving her address as at Mr Travers in Old Court Road, Richmond. At Cheltenham on 30 September she played Imogen in *Cymbeline*.

She made her first appearance in Dublin on 1789–90 at the Crow Street Theatre, and when she acted at Norwich for the first time on 3 January 1791 she was hailed as from the Irish capital. At Norwich Elizabeth performed under her own name, as she continued to do for the remainder of her career. She startled Norwich audiences with Hamlet in 1791, for they had not seen an actress play the Dane before, and in 1793 she acted the title role in *Alexander the Great*. Two of her other roles at Norwich were mentioned in a poem by a local admirer, probably in the early 1790s:

> WITH *mirth to delight, or with sorrow to move,*
> *See Edmead step forward, whom all must approve;*
> *Her sense-beaming eyes can the passions controul,*
> *Can move to gay laughter, or harrow the soul:*
> *Her form should the painter attempt to pourtray,*
> *He wou'd soon in despair throw his pencil away,*
> *Since to make her resistless the grace combin'd,*
> *And fashion'd her person, and brighten'd her mind:*
> *When Rosalind's beauties she brings to our view,*

> *Not only Orlando she designs to subdue,*
> *With him each spectator is fix'd in amaze,*
> *Their hearts beat with rapture as silent they gaze:*
> *Mark sad Belvidera, lost, wretched, forlorn,*
> *Bereav'd of all comforts, with agony torn,*
> *Her sighs pierce our bosoms, and spight of our will,*
> *Our tears flow spontaneous, a proof of her skill.*
> *But 'tis vain of her merits thus singly to tell,*
> *Who always can charm us, in all can excel.—*
> *May the warmth of applause still attend her endeavour,*
> *May pleasure and fortune pursue her forever;*
> *May genius and fancy still marshal her ways,*
> *And joy guide her footsteps wherever she strays.*

While at Norwich Elizabeth Edmead wrote a comedy, *The Events of a Day*, which was acted there in 1795 but seems not to have been printed.

Miss Edmead received instruction in acting from George Steevens. On 26 May 1795 she wrote him from Norwich beseeching his aid:

Sir

ever most gratefully bearing in mind the honour conferr'd on me by your notice of my small talents, and really feeling more flatter'd by it than by any other circumstance of my theatric life, I venture to hope that if you shou'd see Mr Harris, and think me not unworthy to fill the vacancy which, I hear, will be made at Covent Garden by Miss Wallis's marriage, you will have the goodness to name me to him: — you once said "let me know of any engagement you make;" — this were an engagement "devoutly to be wish'd"; and therefore I hope will plead my excuse for the liberty of addressing you: — let me entreat you, Sir, to add to the great favours already conferr'd, that of believing,

I am with the most perfect respect
your obedient servant
Elizabeth Edmead

She did not, however, receive a London offer until some years later.

Miss Edmead left the Norwich troupe in
1798, and on 26 February 1799 made her
Drury Lane debut as Mrs Oakley in *The
Jealous Wife*. She is not known to have
played any other roles at that theatre. The
Monthly Mirror in June said her performance "discovered intelligence, sensibility and
professional skill, but she appeared to want
powers of voice and of expression to give
full efficacy to a character that required a
considerable portion of both, in a theatre
of this vast extent."

Elizabeth stayed in London, it would
seem, though she may have retired temporarily from the stage. On 17 October
1803 she wrote to Lord Chedworth, the
benefactor of the Norwich theatre, in
Ipswich, commenting on her personal difficulties and the London theatre scene:

My Lord
The great distress in which I have been involved prevented me from thanking your
Lordship for sparing a piece of time to write
when you were hurried; the Edinburgh proposal, of which you favor me by inquiring
the result, had too much certain expence at
the outset for me to undertake; but all debate
with myself was soon terminated by a most
perplexing circumstance—a quarrel between
the two landlords of 40 Portland St was so
revengefully follow'd up that we were turn'd
out at one nights notice:— our furniture
broke to pieces— My poor aunts nearly insane
with fright and helplessness and everything
resting on me. even strangers were interested
for us—but tho courtesies cheer the hart a
little, a million of 'em can't repair a great
evil:—in the haste oblig'd to call in any help
that I cou'd, and every imposition that cou'd
take place was practis'd: the immoderate price
which for both houses and lodgings is now
demanded made it impossible to settle till
two or three days since, (at N° 109 Titchfield

St) and my aunts were all laid up with illness. —I think a hundred miles wou'd not
measure my walks in pursuit of a residence
within our compass; and the weather was so
unfavorable that I was generally twice or
thrice drench'd and after all we are merely
hous'd for 2 or 3 months:— that persons so
quiet—so punctual in payment—so inoffensive shou'd so severely suffer from nearly a
stranger is amongst the dispensation of things
one can't account for: —but I shall tire your
lordship I fear; tho no words can describe
what I have suffer'd.

I have not been to the theatre's at all this
season: Miss Brunton has, I am told, exactly
the faults that your lordship remark'd her
father might be likely to teach her—the family manner— Mr Kemble's artful humility
entertains me—Cook must play second to him
now or there is a fair pretence for not re-
engaging him at the end of the season. I am
little of a politician, but it appears to me, as
if the French consul's plan was win us by the
enormous expence we are put to, rather than
make any bold attempt; but either way tis a
dismal prospect. —your Lordship [*sic*] goodness will forward the enclosed to Mr Ryley,
Theatre Liverpool, and permit me to subscribe myself with the highest respect—My
Lord your oblig'd and obedient Servant

Eliza Edmead

When Lord Chedworth died in 1804 he
left Eliza £1300; he made similar generous
bequests to other Norwich theatre folk.

Perhaps Elizabeth Edmead returned to
the stage somewhere in England, but in
1832 Genest wrote that "she has retired
from the stage for several years."

Charles Beecher Hogan owns a letter
from the actor Thomas Hull dated only
"Friday 26 June"—probably 1801 or 1807
—which leads him to believe that Miss Edmead may possibly have been Hull's natural
daughter.

Edmonds, Mr [*fl.* 1754], *boxkeeper.*
Mr Edmonds, a boxkeeper at the Haymarket Theatre, received a benefit on

17 September 1754 at "Mrs Midnight's" (Christopher Smart's) concert.

Edmonds, Mr *d. c. 1801, house servant.*

Mr Edmonds worked in the first gallery at Drury Lane from 1798 through 1801. His benefit tickets were accepted on 16 June 1798, 2 July 1799, and 13 June 1800, and the account books cite him vaguely in 1801. A widow "Edmunds," very likely his wife, was in the company in 1802–3, so we may guess that Edmonds died about 1801.

Edmunds, Mr ⌊fl. 1776–1777⌋, *dresser.*

Mr Edmunds was a dresser at Drury Lane in 1776–77 at a weekly salary of 9s.

Edrid, Mr ⌊fl. 1794⌋, *singer?*

Doane's *Musical Directory* of 1794 listed a Mr Edrid of Crayford as a participant in the Handel performances at Westminster Abbey. Doane called Edrid an "alto," by which he probably meant alto singer (countertenor), though Edrid may have been a horn player.

Edward ⌊fl. c. 1797⌋, *performing horse.*

James De Castro in his *Memoirs* (1824) spoke of a performing horse named Edward who "amongst the rest of his tricks, used to run away with a living boy in his mouth without injuring him in the least,—we believe the first and last instance of an act of this kind." Though De Castro was vague in his references, Edward was apparently one of Hughes's trained horses at the Royal Circus about 1797.

Edward, Mrs ⌊fl. 1797–1799⌋. *See* GRANGER, JULIA.

Edward, Miss ⌊fl. 1724⌋, *actress.*

Miss Edward played Manto in *Oedipus*

at the Bullock-Spiller booth at Bartholomew Fair on 24 September 1724.

Edwards, Mr ⌊fl. 1728⌋, *singer.*

A Mr Edwards sang the role of Hopkins in *Penelope* at the Haymarket Theatre on 8 May 1728.

Edwards, Mr ⌊fl. 1737–1742⌋, *dancer.*

A Mr Edwards (or Edward) played a Drawer in *Hymen's Triumph* at Lincoln's Inn Fields Theatre on 1 February 1737 and was apparently the Edwards who danced on 27 December 1742 at the New Wells, London Spa, Clerkenwell.

Edwards, Mr ⌊fl. 1738–1745⌋, *office keeper.*

Mr Edwards was an office keeper at Drury Lane from 1738–39 through 1744–45. He shared benefits or had his benefit tickets accepted every spring, the first mention of him being on the benefit bill of 19 May 1739 and the last on that of 9 May 1745. A "Widow Edwards" who may have been the actress Mrs Edwards (fl. 1735–1746?) received on 22 December 1746 from the Covent Garden Theatre £3 1s. in full payment of her late husband's arrears. Possibly our subject left Drury Lane for Covent Garden just before he died, but we cannot be certain.

Edwards, Mr ⌊fl. 1744–1750?⌋, *actor.*

At May Fair on 1 and 3 May 1744 a Mr Edwards played Marquis in *Harlequin Sclavonian* at Hallam's theatre. On the latter date he also appeared as Philotas in *The Captive Prince.* He was probably the Edwards who played Blunt in *1 Henry IV* at the Goodman's Fields Theatre on 29 October 1746 and Piercy in *Anna Bullen* at the James Street playhouse in December of the same year. At the Haymarket Theatre on 9 February 1750 a Mr Edwards—perhaps the same actor—acted Oronte in *L'Officier en recrue,* a translation into French of *The Recruiting Officer.* For the same troupe he played the Gueux in *L'Opéra du gueux* on 16 February, Valère in *L'Avare* on 26 February, and Belamy in *Arlequin fourbe Anglois* on 13 March. He was probably the "Edward" for whom a benefit performance of *Venice Preserv'd* was presented at James Street on 28 March 1750.

Edwards, Mr [fl. 1767?–1771], actor.

Mr Edwards acted Ratcliffe in *Jane Shore* on 16 November 1770 and Stukely in *The West Indian* on 15 April 1771 at the Haymarket Theatre. Possibly he was the Mr Edwards who had played at Chester with Austin and Heatton's troupe in 1767.

Edwards, Mr [fl. 1781?–1782], harpist.

On 27 April 1782 at Covent Garden Theatre a dance and vocal piece called *St David's Day* was performed after the mainpiece, with the harpist Mr Edwards accompanying the vocalists. The offering was supposedly the same as that given on 13 December 1781, though on the earlier date Edwards was not mentioned in the bill.

Edwards, Mr [fl. 1786–1820?], boxkeeper.

The earliest mention of an Edwards who may have been our subject was on 27 May 1786 at Covent Garden, when the benefit tickets of a Mr Edwards were accepted at the theatre. He was similarly cited there on 30 May 1787. By 15 June 1792 he was working for the Drury Lane company at the King's Theatre, where he served also in 1792–93. At the new Drury Lane on 6 June 1795 Edwards shared a benefit with 11 other boxkeepers, as he did on 13 June 1796, 16 June 1797, and 14 June 1798. The Edwards who shared a benefit at Drury Lane on 4 July 1799 was more likely John Edwards, another boxkeeper. The theatre accounts refer to Edwards the boxkeeper

(but which one it is hard to tell) through 1819–20. Our subject, then, may have worked at the theatre up to the end of that season.

Edwards, Mr [fl. 1794], singer.

Doane's *Musical Directory* of 1794 listed a Mr Edwards of No 24, Angel Street, St Martin le Grand, as a bass who had sung in the oratorios at Westminster Abbey and Drury Lane. A second Mr Edwards, who sang tenor in the oratorios at the Abbey, we take to have been the actor and singer John Edwards (fl. 1774–1805). Perhaps the subject of this entry was a son of John.

Edwards, Mrs [fl. 1735–1746?], actress.

A Mrs Edwards made her first stage appearance on 29 December 1735 at the Haymarket Theatre playing the Queen in *The Spanish Fryar.* Perhaps it was she who appeared as Juno in *The Judgment of Paris* at Drury Lane on 12 March 1742 and was the "Widow Edwards" who on 22 December 1746 received £3 1s. from Covent Garden Theatre as full payment of her late husband's arrears. In what capacity Widow Edwards's husband had served the theatre we do not know; the only Mr Edwards who was active theatrically in the early 1740s was a Drury Lane office keeper (fl. 1738–1745). It is possible that that Edwards left Drury Lane and joined the Covent Garden company shortly before his death, but there is not sufficient evidence to be certain.

Edwards, Mrs [fl. 1779], actress.

On 13 October 1779 a Mrs Edwards played Mrs Prim in *A Bold Stroke for a Wife* at the Haymarket Theatre. She seems not to have acted again in London.

Edwards, Mrs [fl. 1786–1794], actress, singer.

The Secret History of the Green Room in 1790 retailed the story that the actress-singer Mrs Edwards was the daughter of a housekeeper in Bow Street. She sold matches in Covent Garden and became known as "Match Matilda." Her parents set her on the road to prostitution, but she became independent and captured the heart of an auctioneer who, in 1790, was still keeping her. By that time she had already begun her stage career.

Mrs Edwards's first appearance on any stage was at the Haymarket Theatre on 7 July 1786, when she played Macheath in *The Beggar's Opera;* she was advertised only as "A Lady," but the *European Magazine* that month identified her by name and commented that "This lady is not young and has the disadvantage of an unwieldly figure. Her performance did not want ease but was on the whole not of sufficient excellence to excuse the impropriety of a female performing a man's character."

She returned to the Haymarket in the summer of 1787 to perform Goody Muzzy in *Harvest Home* on 16 May, followed by Pallas in *The Golden Pippin,* a Bacchante in *Comus,* some songs and the title part in *The Intriguing Chambermaid* for William Jewell's benefit on 14 August, and Kate in *The Village Lawyer.* Her involvement in Jewell's benefit suggests that Mrs Edwards may have been related to Jewell's wife, Ann Edwards Jewell. In the summer of 1788 Mrs Edwards is known to have played only two new parts at the Haymarket: Floretta in *The Quaker* and Patty in *Inkle and Yarico.*

The Secret History implied that Mrs Edwards used artifice to induce Wrighten, the Drury Lane prompter, to obtain for her a place at that playhouse, and that she employed similar practices to persuade Kelly to give her singing lessons. In any case, on 9 March 1789 she made her first appearance at the patent house, playing Alice in *The Strangers at Home.* During the remainder of the season she acted such roles as Peggy in *The Lord of the Manor,* Biddy in *The Divorce,* and the Mother in *The*

Harvard Theatre Collection

MRS WEBB as Lucy, and MRS EDWARDS as Captain Macheath in *The Beggar's Opera*

artist unknown

Recruiting Serjeant, and she sang in the chorus in *Macbeth.* In the summer she returned to the Haymarket to play Parley in *The Constant Couple,* Mary in *The Prisoner at Large,* a vocal part in *The Battle of Hexham,* Inis in *A Wife Well Managed,* and the Mayoress in *Peeping Tom.*

The 1789–90 season was her busiest and most successful. She began it at Drury Lane by playing Lucy in *The Beggar's Opera,* which brought praise from *The Secret History;* the description of her as short "and very lusty," with a "face pretty, though her eyes are very small," and a voice lacking compass but good in low comedy suggests that she should have been well suited to the role. During the rest of the season at Drury Lane and then in the summer at the Haymarket Mrs Edwards added to her repertoire such parts as the Abbess in *The Island of St Marguerite,* Cicely in *The*

Quaker, Audrey in *As You Like It,* Marinette in *Try Again,* Fringe in *The Agreeable Surprise,* and Mindora in *Daphne and Amintor.*

At £3 weekly Mrs Edwards continued at Drury Lane in 1790–91, trying such new parts as Katharine in *Don Juan,* Lucy in *The Recruiting Officer,* and Ghita in *The Siege of Belgrade.* Then she played her last summer season at the Haymarket, acting Evans in *The Next Door Neighbours,* a vocal role in *The Surrender of Calais,* and Gymp in *Bon Ton.* The Drury Lane troupe performed at the King's Theatre in 1791–92 and 1792–93, and there Mrs Edwards attempted such new parts as Dorothy in *No Song No Supper,* Lucy in *The Country Girl,* Wishwell in *The Double Gallant,* Mrs Larron in *The Fugitive* (substituting for Miss Pope; the *Thespian Magazine* in January 1793 said that Mrs Edwards "showed no want of spirit in her performance"), Tag in *Miss in Her Teens,* Toilette in *The Jealous Wife,* and Tippit in *All in the Wrong.* Her last recorded appearance was on 10 June 1793, when she played Cicely in *The Quaker.* Kemble noted in March 1794 that Mrs Edwards was then retired.

Of Mrs Edwards's family very little is known. She had a sister, Mrs Topple, from Bury St Edmund's, who died in Charlotte Street, Rathbone Place, London, on 25 January 1790, according to *The Diary, or Woodfall's Register.*

A caricature of Mrs Edwards as Macheath, with Mrs Webb as Lucy, was published by Thomas Cornell in 1786.

Edwards, Mrs *[fl. 1794–1804], wardrobe keeper.*

The Covent Garden Theatre accounts for the 1794–95 season cite a Mrs Edwards who was paid 15*s.* weekly for working in the wardrobe department. A Mrs Edwards, doubtless the same woman, was assistant wardrobe keeper at the Haymarket Theatre in the summer of 1804.

Edwards, Miss *[fl. 1737–1769].* See **MOZEEN, MRS THOMAS.**

Edwards, Miss *[fl. 1792], actress.*

At the Haymarket Theatre on 15 October 1792 a Miss Edwards played Miss Doiley in *Who's the Dupe?*

Edwards, Ann. See **JEWELL, MRS WILLIAM.**

Edwards, Edward *1738–1806, scene painter.*

Prefacing the *Anecdotes of Painters* by Edward Edwards is a "Life" from which we learn that Edwards was born on 7 March 1738 in Castle Street, Leicester Fields, the first son of a chairmaker and carver from Shrewsbury who had settled in London. Young Edward, a sickly and crippled child, was sent to a protestant school for Huguenot children, where he learned French, but at 15 he withdrew and began to work with his father at the shop of the upholsterer Hallet at the corner of St Martin's Lane, Longacre. Edward continued there for three years, and though his father intended him for a career as a carver and gilder, Edward objected and went to a drawing school. In 1759 "he was deemed qualified to be admitted a student at the Duke of Richmond's gallery, which contained excellent casts of many of the first antique statues."

The elder Edwards died in 1760, leaving Edward, then 22, to support his mother, brother, and sister. He had lodgings in Compton Street, Soho, where he taught art to young men interested in becoming ornamental furniture makers. Though the "Life" does not mention it, Edwards spent the latter part of 1760 working at the Smock Alley Theatre in Dublin for Mossop, painting scenery and decorations. *Faulkner's Dublin Journal* of 21–25 October reported that "the decorations are designed and executed in a very elegant Taste, and in a Manner different from any Thing ever yet seen in this Kingdom."

In London in 1761 Edwards was admitted a member of the Academy in Peter Court, St Martin's Lane, where he studied figure drawing. One of his drawings won "a premium proposed by the Society established for the encouragement of Arts, Manufactures, and Commerce. . . ." Boydell employed Edwards to make drawings of celebrated pictures of old masters from which engravers were to work. The following year he won a prize from the Society of Arts for "the best historical picture in chiaro oscuro." He became an exhibitor and a member of the Incorporated Society of Arts, but he resigned his membership in 1770 and was employed by the President and Council of the Society of Antiquaries. For that group he spent six months (earning only 110 guineas) making a drawing "from an old picture in the Castle at Windsor, representing the interview between Henry VIII. and Francis I. at Calais." In 1771 he began exhibiting at the Royal Academy, his first work shown there being "The Angel appearing to Hagar and Ishmael."

Edwards was elected an associate of the Royal Academy in 1773 and soon after was commissioned to repair a ceiling, which had been painted by Sir James Thornhill, at Lord Bessborough's Roehampton. The publisher John Bell also hired Edwards to do book designs, and Robert Udley employed Edwards and gave him money to go to the Continent for further study. Edwards went to France in July 1775, studied in Rome, toured Italy, and returned to London in September 1776. Back to work he went to support his mother and siblings, but his successes were meager, and he never had a sufficient income.

In 1781 he won a prize for a landscape painting and delivered a paper before the Royal Society on the storm at Roehampton, accompanied by his drawings of the storm's effects. The following year he began painting three arabesque ceilings for Charles Hamilton; the commission occupied him

By permission of the Houghton Library, Harvard University

EDWARD EDWARDS

self-portrait, engraving by Cardon

until March 1783, after which Walpole engaged him at Strawberry Hill. He and Walpole had a falling out in 1784 over an exorbitant fee charged by a cabinetmaker Edwards had recommended.

Edwards was appointed a teacher of perspective at the Royal Academy in 1788, a post he held to the end of his life. In January of that year, though the "Life" does not mention it, Edwards painted scenery for the new Theatre Royal in Newcastle-upon-Tyne for total fees amounting to £607 6s. 7d. In 1792 he completed a collection of 52 etchings on various subjects, and the following year he exhibited a representation of "the Commemoration of Handel in Westminster Abbey, in which he introduced a multitude of figures, many of them portraits." For the *Macbeth* production which was the first dramatic offering at the new Drury Lane playhouse on 21 April 1794 Edwards painted the interior view of the palace at Forres ("a very fine Gothic apartment," according to *The World* of 22 April), and it is likely that he served as one of the scene painters for other Drury Lane productions that season. That employment the "Life" also neglected to mention.

In 1799 Edwards's friend Boydell commissioned him to paint a scene from *The Two Gentlemen of Verona*. He painted a number of subjects from the bard's works for Boydell's *Shakespeare Gallery,* and he provided some portraits of actors for Lowndes's *New English Theatre*. In 1800 his mother died at the age of 93; she had apparently been in his care the previous 40 years.

Edwards published *A Treatise on Perspective* in 1803 and spent his last years preparing *Anecdotes of Painters who Have Resided or Been Born in ENGLAND; with Critical Remarks on Their Productions*. Edward Edwards died on the evening of 19 December 1806 (some sources say the tenth). He was buried in St Pancras churchyard. His *Anecdotes* came out in 1808, a portrait of the late artist serving as a frontispiece. The "Life" called him a gentle, friendly, and virtuous person; "he sometimes in a pleasant vein, wrote verses to his friends; but his hours of leisure were for the most part occupied in practising on the violin."

Edwards, John *d. 1706, jester.*

Though a quack horse doctor during most of each year, John Edwards was William Pinkethman's Merry Andrew at Bartholomew Fair. When Edwards died in Castle Street, St Giles, in 1706, an *Elegy on the Much Unlamented Death of John Edwards* was published.

Edwards, John [*fl. 1774–1805*], *actor, singer.*

On 21 February 1777 at Drury Lane Theatre a Mr Edwards made what was advertised as his first public appearance, sing-ing in *Judas Maccabaeus*. If he was John Edwards the singer and actor, the billing was incorrect, for John had performed at the Smock Alley Theatre in Dublin in the summer of 1774. The careers of John and of the Mr Edwards who performed in London in the late 1770s and early 1780s mesh so neatly that it is very likely that they were one and the same.

Mr Edwards sang in most of the oratorio offerings at Drury Lane in February and March 1777, and during the 1777–78 season he was one of the singers in *Macbeth*. On 24 March 1778 he appeared as Tyrrell in *Richard III* at the Haymarket Theatre, and, significantly, on 31 March he was dropped from the list of singers in *Macbeth* at Drury Lane. He was back at Drury Lane for the 1778–79 season, apparently, for the accounts show a payment to him on 6 October 1778 of £17 4s. for 12 weeks' work, but his name did not appear in any bills during the season (perhaps the payment was for appearances the previous season). On 27 November 1779 Edwards played Mervin in *The Maid of the Mill* at Drury Lane, and during the 1780–81 season he was mentioned as a singer in *Macbeth* and *Romeo and Juliet* and a member of a group that offered "Rule Britannia." On 18 May 1781 his benefit tickets were accepted at the theatre.

John Edwards, who, we are guessing, was the Mr Edwards we have been following, played at Smock Alley in 1781, advertised as from Drury Lane, according to W. S. Clark's *The Irish Stage in the County Towns*. John also acted in Cork in August 1781 and in Limerick in August 1782.

The *Hibernian Journal* on 14 July 1784 reported the marriage of John Edwards and a Miss Emerson at Portarlington, Offaly, Ireland. Both were described as "of the theatre," and after their marriage they pursued parallel acting careers. The Mr Edwards who had been active in London from 1777 to 1781 disappeared from the playbills there during the early 1780s, when we know John Edwards was busy in Ireland.

On 10 February 1785 a Mr Edwards, again probably John, acted a principal role in *The Fair Refugee* and Young Cape in *The Author* at the Haymarket Theatre in London. Mr and Mrs Edwards performed at Hull in October 1785, hailed as from Dublin; in 1786–87 they appeared at Norwich and York; in 1787–88 they were again at Norwich; 1788–89 found Edwards (if not his wife as well) at Manchester; and Mr and Mrs Edwards acted at the new theatre in the market place at Ashley in 1792. They were probably the couple of that name playing at Margate in September 1794. A notice from Margate that month stated that "A Mr and Mrs Edwards have been chiefly distinguished by public Approbation, the former in the higher sing^g Parts & in genteel Comd. the latter a Votary of the Melancholy Muse who is said to make a very creditable Fig.^r in the heroic & tender province."

That description would support the conjecture that John Edwards was the Mr Edwards listed in Doane's *Musical Directory* of 1794 as a tenor who had sung in the oratorios at Westminster Abbey. Doane gave Edwards's address as No 24, Angel Street, St Martin le Grand, where lived also a bass named Edwards, possibly a son of John. However, there is no other evidence of John Edwards working in London in the early 1790s.

Mr and Mrs Edwards were at Wolverhampton in December 1801 and in 1802. (Could Mrs Edwards also have been the woman of that name who was on the Covent Garden payroll in London at £1 10s. in 1801–2 and 1802–3?) By 1805 Mr and Mrs Edwards were at Worcester. According to the *Thespian Dictionary,* John was

formerly a pupil of the late Mr. Linley. When young he possessed a clear, strong counter tenor voice, with some sweetness, but his pipe has of late been fumigated too much with

tobacco and ale. He is now with the Worcester company, where he has been some years. His wife was a Miss Emerton [*sic*], whom he married in Ireland. She is a good speaker, and has merit in many parts, but is too fond of the young and tender line, not recollecting it is impossible to pass for a girl at her age.

Edwards, John   [*fl. 1777–1794*], *musician.*

John Edwards of No 62, Old Bailey, became a freeman in the Worshipfull Company of Musicians on 12 September 1777. On 19 June 1794 his son John was bound apprentice to him for seven years. The Guildhall manuscripts concerning the Company contain an entry dated 10 July 1805 that may concern our subject, but the information it contains is confusing: John Edwards, the son of John Edwards, late of Seymour Court, Chandos Street, musician, deceased, was bound apprentice to Neville Butler Challoner, musician, of No 25, Greek Street, Soho. Possibly the John Edwards who died before 10 July 1805 was our subject, but it is most unlikely that he would have had two sons named John, both of whom would have to have been alive in 1794.

Edwards, John   [*fl. 1797–1820*], *house servant.*

John Edwards was first cited in the Drury Lane playbills on 15 June 1797, when his benefit tickets were accepted. On 15 June 1798 he shared a benefit with eight other boxkeepers, and he was similarly cited on 4 July 1799 (unless the other boxkeeper named Edwards was meant) and 17 June 1800. The Drury Lane account books named him in June 1800 as an office keeper at a salary of £19 7s. 6d. for 155 days' work, but account entries in 1802 spoke of Edwards as a doorkeeper, and in later years he was described again as a boxkeeper. John was probably the J. Edwards to whom Richard Brinsley Sheridan referred in a letter to Richard Peake sometime after June 1803: "Give my £31.10.0 to J. Edwards before you sleep for God's sake." Very likely Sheridan owed Edwards some back pay. The Drury Lane accounts cited an Edwards who was a boxkeeper as late as the 1819–20 season and it seems likely that John was the man.

Edwards, Joseph *d. 1697, singer.*

The Westminster Abbey registers record the burial of Joseph Edwards in the cloisters on 20 September 1697. He was, according to the registers, a chorister and, according to the notation of the Harleian Society's editor in the printed registers, possibly the father of Thomas Edwards. He was not, however, mentioned in any of the Lord Chamberlain's accounts concerning the King's Musick and the Chapel Royal. There is a possibility that Joseph was the Edwards who sang at royal birthday celebrations and in the theatres in the 1690s, though we have credited those appearances to Thomas.

Edwards, Thomas *1659?–1730, singer.*

A Mr Edwards was one of the singers of Purcell's "Hail Bright Cecilia" on 22 November 1692, and on 30 April 1693 he sang at court to celebrate the Queen's birthday. He was at Drury Lane Theatre singing in *Bonduca* in September 1695, and perhaps in November at Dorset Garden playhouse he sang in *3 Don Quixote*. He had a part in *The Younger Brother* at Drury Lane in February 1696 and sang in *Brutus of Alba* on 26 October 1696. When the 1719 edition of *Wit and Mirth* was published, songs with Edwards's name cited as singer were included, indicating, perhaps, not only the popularity of the songs but of Edwards as well.

The identity of that singer is not certain, but it is probable that he was Thomas Edwards, who was admitted to the Chapel Royal as an Epistler on 2 March 1700, a few years after references to Edwards the popular singer ceased. Thomas Edwards

spent the rest of his musical career as a member of the King's Musick. He was, perhaps, the son of the chorister Joseph Edwards, who died in 1697. Thomas Edwards died on 18 August 1730 (at the age of 71, says the editor of the Westminster Abbey registers), and was buried four days later in the North Cloister of the Abbey. He was remembered as one of the *bassos* of the Abbey and of St Paul's Cathedral.

Thomas Edwards had made his will on 18 June 1724; it was proved by his widow Mary on 28 August 1730. Edwards left £1000 in trust to his wife and John Edwards, citizen and farrier of London (doubtless a relative), for the benefit of the two Edwards children, Thomas and Mary, who must have been in their minority when the will was made. To his daughter Mary, the singer left £500, the remainder of his estate being marked for his son Thomas. It is probable that Edwards had provided for his wife before his death, for she was named in the will only as executrix. Perhaps young Mary Edwards became the popular singer Miss Edwards of later years.

We have questioned Thomas Edwards' year of birth in the headnote to this entry, since there is a possibility that it could be ten years too late. If Thomas Edwards died at 81 rather than 71, then it is highly probable that he was the Thomas Edwards who was from 1660 to 1664 one of the Children of the Chapel Royal under Henry Cooke and who was for a while a servant of Samuel Pepys. According to Pepys, young Tom Edwards played the lute and "would, with little practice, play very well," and sang. His voice broke in 1664 and he left the Chapel Royal. That would suggest a birthdate about 14 or 15 years earlier.

Edwards, William [*fl. 1663–1670*], *scenekeeper.*

The London Stage lists William Edwards as a scenekeeper in the King's Company in 1663–64, but the first mention of him in the Lord Chamberlain's accounts seems not to have occurred until 20 February 1665. *The London Stage* notes Edwards as still serving the troupe in 1669–70.

Edwin, David *1776–1841, actor, engraver.*

David Edwin, one of the numerous offspring of the twenty-year liaison between John Edwin the elder and Sarah Walmsley, was born in Bath in 1776. The first certain record of his activity was when a "Master D. Edwin" appeared in the part of the Child in Garrick's alteration of Southerne's *Isabella; or, The Fatal Marriage* at Drury Lane on 30 April 1784 for the benefit of Becky Wells. He repeated the part at Drury Lane on 11 May and at the Haymarket on 5 August. In the summer of 1790 Master Edwin acted at Richmond.

Young David's theatrical career was brief. He was listed ("Mr D. Edwin") in the playbills for the private theatricals of Lord Barrymore at the Wargrave Theatre in December–January 1791–92. He was probably the Edwin who drew 7s. 6d. payments in March and May of 1792 for dancing at Drury Lane. He was then apprenticed to Christian Jossi, a Dutch engraver, who took him to Amsterdam in 1796.

He is said to have disagreed with his master and to have worked his way across the Atlantic before the mast. But he had already nearly finished his apprenticeship, and when he came to Philadelphia in December 1797 he was 21 and an accomplished engraver. T. B. Freeman, a Philadelphia publisher, gave him a job, and soon he was receiving commissions from many painters and publishers for his careful stipple engravings of portraits and scenes. Dunlap called him "the first good engraver of the human countenance that appeared in this country."

David Edwin left letters which Dunlap employed in his *History of the Arts of Design* (1834). Mantle Fielding's *Catalogue of the Engraved Works of David Edwin*

(1905) and the short biography by Joseph Jackson in *The Dictionary of American Biography* (1931) should be consulted for his career as an engraver.

Edwin, Elizabeth, called Mrs Williams *[fl. 1784–1797], actress, mountebank.*

James Winston recalled in "The Manager's Note-Book" that "In November, 1788 [*recte* 1784] a preparatory paragraph appeared in the newspapers, saying that a sister [Elizabeth] of [the elder John] Edwin's was about to appear at the Haymarket Theatre." The bill of the evening of 10 February 1785 gave the part of Mrs Cadwallader in Foote's *The Author* to "A Young Lady," who was said to be appearing for the first time at the Haymarket and for the second time "on any stage." Tickets could be obtained from her at the Artificial Flower Warehouse, Store Street, Bedford Square. That address would seem to prove the debutante to have been Miss Edwin, as will appear below.

There is no further record of Elizabeth Edwin's theatrical activity, under either her own name or the assumed one of Mrs Williams. But Winston tells us something more about this most eccentric member of a rather eccentric family:

Mrs Cadwallader was no other than Edwin's sister, who was at that time so universally known by the name of Williams, to whose house in Store Street more crowds of fashionable females resorted in a day to inquire into the events of fate and futurity than ever attended the ancient temple of the famous oracle of Delphos. She repeatedly advertised her artificial flower-shop, but, "bolder grown," in 1789, she advertised her trade in the following unequivocal terms: —
"Mrs. Williams respectfully informs those ladies who did her the honor to call, during her absence, that she is returned from France, and may be consulted with as usual, from eleven in the morning till six in the evening at her house, the artificial flower-warehouse, Store Street, Bedford Square.

"N.B. Ladies will please to observe it is a small house, with green rails."

In February, 1797, she was had up before Justice Nares. After this she altered her advertisements, but continued to advertise still, from Store Street, that, having formerly studied the occult sciences, ladies may still consult her on nervous and consumptive cases, every day from eleven till three. Her Batavian Tincture might be had at five and ten shillings a-bottle. After 1797 she was heard of no more.

It is not known what relationship, if any, she bore to the Miss Edwin who was on the list of the Drury Lane Company from 1809–10 until at least 1814–15 or to the Miss Edwin who played with Hallam's company at Albany, New York, in November 1810.

Edwin, John *1749–1790, actor, singer, composer.*

John Edwin "the elder" was born on 10 August 1749 in Clare Market, St Clement Danes, the only son and the eldest of three children of the watchmaker John Edwin and his wife Hannah, who was a daughter of Henry Brogden, a sculptor of York. John, our subject, had two sisters, Mary and Elizabeth. The second, noticed above, acted briefly and told fortunes under the assumed name "Mrs Williams." Their parents, though in only moderate circumstances, were people of some cultivation, the father particularly possessing good taste and some abilities in music, which he passed along to his son. At the age of nine the boy was sent to relatives in the country near Enfield and there schooled until he was 15. While he was at Enfield he is reported to have acted in amateur performances in a stable.

When John was 15, a post was obtained for him at the pension office of the Exchequer, a near-sinecure requiring his attention for some two hours a day only. Much of the rest of his time during 1764 he spent enthralled by the amateur declamation at the "spouting club" which perennially held forth at the French Horn tavern in Wood Street. Up to that time John had given no serious thought to the stage as a career, but the admired performance, at the club, of William Woodfall in the role of Old Mask in *The Musical Lady* seems to have settled his future. He began to practice acting in earnest at the Falcon, another spouting club in Fetter Lane. There he became one of the "managers," along with Francis Godolphin Waldron (who later became a well-known actor and prompter). There also, apparently, Edwin first encountered the great Ned Shuter, upon whose general style he afterwards modelled his comic action. Shuter is reported to have told him, "My boy, You will be an excellent actor when I am laid low."

John Lee, then active at Drury Lane, saw Edwin's performances with the amateurs and engaged him for the following summer, 1765, to perform at Manchester at a guinea a week, a substantial salary for any provincial actor at that period but a princely sum for a boy of 16. Edwin is said by James Winston to have performed once, "at a private benefit," as Quidnunc in *The Upholsterer,* though the extant bills do not confirm that appearance. At nearly the same time died a wealthy distant relation, John Edwin of George Street, Hanover Square, who had raised great financial expectations in the family of the young actor, but who had left his entire estate, some £50,000, to various charities. Perhaps as a balm for his disappointment, young John Edwin was appointed to another sinecure, the secretaryship of the trust which was set up to disburse funds to the charities, by which he is said to have realized some £200 during the year that he kept the office. The executors appear also to have given him £500 outright, most of which he gave to his father before launching forth into the professional theatre.

During John Edwin's initiate summer at Manchester he acquired several prominent roles in farce, principally those of old men, despite his youth. He also gained the affec-

Courtesy of the Garrick Club

JOHN EDWIN

attributed to Gainsborough

tions of the pliant Sophia Baddeley, whose husband was that summer forty miles distant, playing at Liverpool.

Mossop engaged the young man for Smock Alley, Dublin, in the fall of 1765 at 30s. per week. He appeared first as Sir Philip Modelove in *A Bold Stroke for a Wife* and then as Lord Trinket in *The Jealous Wife*. He steadily gained ground with the audiences, but his pay was so irregular that he was driven finally to the expedient of having himself "arrested" by a friendly bailiff in order that he might send a desperate message from the sponging house to his manager that "nothing less than ten pounds would liberate him" to play that night. The ruse was effective.

Edwin next was engaged briefly by Ryder at Waterford. He went then to Preston and then, apparently in January 1767, joined Joseph Austin's company to play successively at Bewdley, Shrewsbury,

Bridgenorth, and Chester. Soon thereafter, Edwin determined to leave the profession, went to London, and took lodgings at No 8, Hemmings Row. Before long, however, at the urging of John Lee, who needed someone to replace the recently deceased John Arthur, he joined the Bath company, arriving at his lodgings at the Bear, Cheap Street, Bath, on 2 October 1768. On 7 October he appeared as Periwinkle in *A Bold Stroke for a Wife.* He remained at Bath, becoming a great favorite with the audiences, in the winter seasons of 1776–77, 1777–78, and 1778–79. There also (sometime before 1769) he met Mrs Sarah Walmsley, "a respectable milliner in Horse Street," who assumed his name and bore his children. She remained faithfully his common-law wife for twenty years.

Edwin's first professional London appearances were at the summer theatre in the Haymarket in 1776, when, according to the bills, he played at least eight times, beginning in an unspecified part in *The Cozeners* on 19 June. He repeated the role on 1 July, along with Jobson in *The Devil to Pay,* and followed during the rest of the summer with Diego in *The Padlock,* Minnikin in *The Capuchin,* Robin in *The Waterman,* and unspecified parts in *The Maid of Bath, The Orators,* and *The Rehearsal.*

The Haymarket changed hands after the death of Samuel Foote in October 1777, and the new proprietor George Colman evidently set about cutting salaries. For in a letter to Colman from Bath dated 4 March 1777 Edwin protested that Foote had paid him a guinea a week and that the expenses of travelling and of London living were so great that he could not consider Colman's offer. He needed to bring a wife, his son Jack, and another child (evidently the "Richard, son of John & Sarah Edwin" christened at Bath Abbey on 11 August 1774). Mrs Edwin's services were also proffered; she "pretends to no great merit, but as numbers are sometimes wanted, she had a very good study & might upon an

Harvard Theatre Collection

JOHN EDWIN, as Jerry Blackacre

engraving by Angus, after Ryley

The Suicide, Pantaloon in *The Portrait,* the original Carlo in Charles Dibdin's *The Gipsies,* the original Davo in O'Hara's *April-Day,* the original Tipple in Bate's *The Flitch of Bacon,* one of the Witches in *Macbeth,* Lazarillo in *The Spanish Barber,* Justice Woodcock in *Love in a Village* (filling in for Parsons and playing it "with great pleasantry," according to the *Gazetteer* of 8 June 1777), Jerry Sneak in *The Mayor of Garratt,* the original Etiquette in M. P. Andrews' *Summer Amusement,* and the original Splash in *A Widow and No Widow.*

He played Scrub in *The Stratagem* for his benefit on 17 August 1779, when tickets could be had of him at No 9, St Martin's Street, Leicester Fields. On that occasion the song "Ted Blarney" was sung at the end of Act IV of the mainpiece and a monologue was spoken before the afterpiece by "Master Edwin," who was John Edwin the younger, then about ten years of age. He had first appeared in London on 30 July 1778 at the Haymarket as Hengo in *Bonduca.* The elder Edwin played also at Bristol in the spring and summer of 1779.

Harris at Covent Garden offered Edwin a contract of £5 per week for 1779–80, which he refused, demanding £7. After some weeks Harris complied. For his first appearance at Covent Garden, on 24 September 1779, Edwin chose Touchstone in *As You Like It.* The *London Chronicle* found him "unintelligible and too rapid." On 27 September he was the first Canteen in Frederick Pilon's new afterpiece *The Device* and on 1 October Master Stephen in *Every Man in His Humour.* In addition, that season he played Gracculo in *The Bondman,* Sir Harry Sycamore in *The Maid of the Mill,* Francis in *1 Henry IV,* Old Mirabel in *The Inconstant,* Sir Hugh Evans in *The Merry Wives of Windsor,* the original Mercurius in *The Widow of Delphi* by Richard Cumberland on 1 February 1780, the original Silvertongue in Hannah Cowley's *The Belle's Stratagem* on 22 February,

emergency supply the place of a better actress." Young Jack, who had sung upon the stage since Colman last saw him and had gained some reputation, could also assist. The whole family would perform for five guineas a week.

The Edwins alternated Bath in the winter with London in the summer for the following three years. The *London Magazine* of June 1777 thought that "Edwin, in spite of his thin voice and disgusting articulation, is at least equal to half his London contemporaries, and exhibited proofs that neither his conception, nor style of playing is limited to a particular cast of parts, or mode of acting." He added to his Haymarket repertoire Launcelot in *The Merchant of Venice,* Butler in *Piety in Pattens,* the title part in *Midas,* the original Snip in *Buxom Joan,* the original Wingrave in Colman's

Dogberry in *Much Ado About Nothing,* and the original Woolwich in Pilon's *The Siege of Gibraltar* on 25 April. He lived at the time of his benefit on 22 April 1780 at "No 76, the corner of Long Acre, Drury Lane."

John Edwin the elder was a chief attraction at Covent Garden in the winters and at the Haymarket in the summers until his death in 1790. His winter salary increased from an initial £7 per week to £12 in his last season, 1789–90, and his benefits were generally large. He was immobilized for a few days in July 1786 when *A Beggar on Horseback* was postponed "on account of Edwin's being unluckily hurt by a fall from his horse." Occasionally he slipped out of town for short engagements with provincial managers. He was briefly at Dublin in 1783; he accompanied William Palmer's company to Stourbridge Fair in Cambridge to oppose the Norwich company's monopoly in 1786; he acted at Crow Street, Dublin, in the summer of 1788; and he acted at Brighton during some part of the season of 1789. In the summer of 1789 Edwin rented the theatre at Richmond, Surrey, and there assembled a notable company for a successful season.

In Passion Week of 1790 Edwin went to Rochester to play to a full house for the benefit of his close friend Lee Lewes. The morning after, in a spirit of celebration, he and Lewes left for Paris, where they were "seen in the Café Chartres, and parading the Palais Royal with National cockades, larger than ordinary," according to James Winston in "The Manager's Note-Book," and where Edwin's comical manner and rough bearskin greatcoat were admired by the Dauphin as they promenaded in the Tuileries. On 7 April following, Edwin took his last benefit at Covent Garden, playing Dromio of Syracuse in *The Comedy of Errors.* At the end of the mainpiece he spoke his "Comical, Whimsical, Operatical, Farcical Rhapsody *Lingo the Butler's Opinion on Men and Manners.*" During the

evening he also sang "Four and Twenty Fiddlers all in a Row," which he had sung, said Winston, at his first "and every other of his benefits, and it never failed to produce the most rapturous applause."

Edwin returned to the Haymarket in the summer of 1790, acted the part of Gregory Gubbins in *The Battle of Hexham* on 15 June, the title role of the afterpiece *Peeping Tom* on the next night, and presented his famous Jerry Sneak in *The Mayor of Garratt* on 22 June. On the twenty-third, twenty-fifth, and twenty-eighth of the month the bills carried announcements of his illness, and plays in which he was scheduled to appear were postponed. On 5 July Edwin played both Bowkitt in *The Son-in-Law* and Lingo in *The Agreeable Surprise.* On the fifteenth he was again Peeping Tom, on the twenty-second Lingo, and on the thirty-first Gregory Gubbins.

Harvard Theatre Collection

JOHN EDWIN

artist unknown

On 2 August, he struggled again through Gregory Gubbins. He was never heard again in any theatre. On 11 August 1790, according to Gilliland, Lord Barrymore performed Scaramouch in *Don Juan* and the swordsman and socialite Harry Angelo was Mrs Cole in *The Minor* for Edwin's benefit.

Edwin's breakdown had been coming on gradually for some years. James Boaden in his *Life of Bannister* called him "the absolute victim of sottish intemperance." He was often thrust onstage drunk, yet "his acting seemed only the richer for the bestial indulgence that had overwhelmed him." In May of 1790 his physicians, Drs Brocklesby and Garthshorne, sent him to lodgings at the Reindeer in Epping Forest, for rest and fresh air. But he would stay only three weeks away from London. On 13 June he married Miss Mary Hubbard at St. John's, Westminster.

Three weeks before his death a consultation of physicians was held at his residence, and their decision was, that unless he was immediately removed to Nice he must die; Harris [proprietor of Covent Garden] volunteered to advance any money that was necessary for the voyage, and a vessel was engaged, but he was too far gone to undertake it: he was cheerful to the last, and two days before his death he felt confident he would recover when on board the vessel; he could not be persuaded to keep his bed. On the 30th of October he lay on a couch before the fire, and continued there until a quarter past four the following morning unable to express his wishes; he attempted to rise, but could not — put out his hand to his wife — looked up — and died in his forty-second year.

On 8 November 1790, between seven and eight in the evening, Edwin was buried in the north side of St Paul, Covent Garden, between Dr Arne and Ned Shuter. His pallbearers were the chief suppliers of his musical comedies, the playwright John O'Keeffe and William Shield the composer, along with the actors Lewis, Hull, Quick, Wilson, Holman, and Johnstone. (John Philip Kemble's notations in the British Museum inform us that "All the low strumpets in Town were there, and behaved very indecently.") In February 1791 a tombstone was erected by Edwin's friend Henry Reading, with lines supplied by "Anthony Pasquin":

*Each social need which honours human
    kind,
The dust beneath this frail memorial
    bore;
If pride of excellence uplift thy mind,
Subdue the weakness and be vain no
    more.*

*A nation's mirth was subject to his art
Ere icy death had smote this child of
    glee;
And care resumed his empire o'er the
    heart,
When Heaven isued — Edwin shall not
    be.*

Even worse verses appeared occasionally in newspapers and magazines during several months following.

John Edwin the elder was a variously talented comic actor with an original manner. By 1780 he had emerged from the shadow of his infatuation with the devices of his admired mentor, Ned Shuter. Reynolds the dramatist recalled that Edwin "established a sort of entre-nous-ship . . . with the audience, and made them his confidants." Colman called him the best burletta singer that the theatre had ever seen, adding:

Nature in gifting him with the *vis comica* had dealt with him differently from low comedians in general, for she had enabled him to look irresistibly funny, with a very agreeable, if not handsome, set of features, and while he sung in a style which produced roars of laughter, there was a melody in some of the upper tones of his voice that was beautiful.

Carl Philipp Moritz, the German visitor to London in 1782, was captivated by him:

"[He], in all his comic characters, still preserves something so inexpressibly good tempered in his countenance, that notwithstanding all his burlesques and even grotesque buffoonery, you cannot but be pleased with him." John Bernard in his *Retrospections* called Edwin the "greatest genius" he had ever known and "the most original actor" in "the old world or the new." John Bannister, his close friend, deplored the brevity of his service: "His career was short and brilliant. He was a firework—a sort of squib; bright, dazzling, sputtering, and off with a pop."

Among Edwin's many characters, besides those enumerated above, were the following, arranged chronologically: Skirmish in *The Deserter*, Jacky Minim in *The Separate Maintenance*, the original Ambuscade in M. P. Andrews's comic opera *Fire and Water*, Francisco in *The Tailors*, the original Jacob in Sophia Lee's *The Chapter of Accidents*, the First Gravedigger and Polonius in *Hamlet*, Gomez in *The Spanish Fryar*, Colonel Oldboy in *Lionel and Clarissa*, Lord Grizzle in *Tom Thumb*, the original Goose in Pilon's farce *The Humours of an Election*, Lopez in *The Mistake*, the original Plummet in Henry Knapp's farce *The Excise Man* (on 4 November 1780, in a performance which, the *London Chronicle* said, "was not suffered to proceed to its conclusion; . . . the actors, when [the second act] was not more than half gone through, were driven from the stage by the clamours of . . . the spectators"), the first Gil Perez in Charles Dibdin's comic opera *The Islanders*, Robin in *The Waterman*, the first Bronze in Hannah Cowley's comedy *The World As It Goes*, Jeremy in *Barnaby Brittle*, the original Serjeant Shirtless in Richard Wilson's prelude *Seventeen Hundred and Eighty One*, Judas in *Bonduca*, the original Motley in *The Dead Alive*, Sir Andrew Aguecheek in *Twelfth Night*, a transvestite Lucy in *The Beggar's Opera*, the original Thimble in James Cobb's musical entertainment *Kensington Gardens*, the original

JOHN EDWIN, as Lingo
benefit ticket

artist unknown

Grinder in Charles Stuart's interlude *Damnation*, the original Timid in Thomas Holcroft's comedy *Duplicity*, Momus in *The Golden Pippin*, the original Mercury in Charles Dibdin's burletta *Jupiter and Alcmena*, Bullock in *The Recruiting Officer*, Corporal Trim in *Tristram Shandy*, Solomon in *The Quaker*, Don Manuel in *She Wou'd and She Wou'd Not*, and Precipe in *Retaliation*.

Also Autolycus in *The Winter's Tale*, Dr Last in *The Devil Upon Two Sticks*, Don Vincentio in *A Bold Stroke for a Husband*, Ubaldo in *The Magic Picture*, Rupee in *The Positive Man*, Sir Marvel Mushroom in *More Ways Than One*, the Town Clerk in *Much Ado About Nothing*, the Hunchback Barber in *Harlequin Rambler*, Speed in *The Two Gentlemen of Verona*, the original Ruttekin in Leonard Macnally's *Robin Hood*, Sir Amorous La Foole in *Epicoene*, Tokay in *The Wives Revenged*, Diggery in *All the World's a Stage*, Hob in *Hob in the Well*, Dame Turton in *The Genius of Nonsense*, the first Dicky Ditto in George Colman's *Two to One*, the original Fool in Holcroft's *The Noble Peasant*, the original Billy Bristle in Knapp's *Hunt the Slipper*, Mawworm in *The Hypocrite*, Lissardo in *The Wonder*, Gregory in *The Mock Doctor*, the original Antonio in Holcroft's *The*

Follies of a Day, Daphne in *Midas*, the original Sir Simon Lollop in the anonymous afterpiece *The Israelites*, the original Nicholas in Macnally's *Fashionable Levities*, Penurio in *Women Pleas'd*, the original Peter in William Pearce's *The Nunnery*, the Drunken Man in *Lethe*, Gregory (or Tippoo) in *The Campaign*, a Sailor in *Harlequin Teague*, the original Humphry in Elizabeth Inchbald's *Appearance is Against Them*, the original Pedro in Holcroft's *The Choleric Father*, Young Clincher in *The Constant Couple*, Ben in *Love for Love*, the original Dry in the anonymous *The Peruvian*, Hunks in *The Two Misers*, Jerry Blackacre in *The Plain Dealer*, Morello in *The Bird in a Cage*, Dr Druid in *The Fashionable Lover*, the Butler in *Piety in Pattens*, Farmer Hodge in *The Ghost*, Hodge in *Love in a Village*, the original La Bruce in Macnally's *Richard Coeur de Lion*, the original Caleb in Pilon's *He Wou'd Be a Soldier*, the original Joseph in John Scawen's *The Girl in Style*, John Moody in *The Provok'd Husband*, Jobson in *The Devil to Pay*, Gardiner in *King Henry VIII*, Billy Button in *The Maid of Bath*, the original Nicholas in Mrs Inchbald's *The Midnight Hour*, Trudge in *Inkle and Yarico*, Joe in *Sir John Cockle at Court*, the original Sheepface in Colman's *The Village Lawyer*, Simon in *The Apprentice*, Humphry Gubbin in *The Tender Husband*, Timothy Shacklefigure in *The Lady of the Manor*, Young Philpot in *The Citizen*, Sir Harry Beagle in *The Jealous Wife*, La Fleur in *Animal Magnetism*, Sir Troubadour in *The Crusade*, the King of Queerumania in *Chrononhotonthologos,* and Croaker in *The Good Natur'd Man*.

Edwin's association with John O'Keeffe the dramatist was close and symbiotic and O'Keeffe in his *Recollections* acknowledged the benefit. "Anthony Pasquin" thought that "to the force of his muscles, and strength of his name, / O'KEEFE is in debt for his pence and his fame." A jest current during the 1790s was that "when Edwin

died, O'Keeffe would be damned." When Edwin actually did die O'Keeffe was ready with a doggerel elegy in which he named 20 of his characters represented by the comedian: Bowkitt in *The Son-in-Law*, Clod in *The Young Quaker*, Darby in *The Poor Soldier* and *Love in a Camp*, Lingo in *The Agreeable Surprise*, Corney in *The Beggar on Horseback*, Motley in *The Dead Alive*, Tallyho in *Fontainebleau*, Pedrillo in *The Castle of Andalusia*, Shelty in *The Highland Reel*, Philip in *The Czar*, Tom in *Peeping Tom*, Jemmy Jumps in *The Farmer*, Rupee in *The Positive Man,* Metheglin in *The Toy*, Cricolo in *The Siege of Curzola*, Muns in *The Prisoner at Large*, Bob Dobbin in *The Man-Milliner*, Savetier in *The Grenadier*, Toddy in *Tantara Rara*, and Otho in *The Blacksmith of Antwerp*. The verses conclude:

This hand which held the pen that made
  the strokes,
That gave thy native humour those
  prime jokes,—
Once held thy pall—thy funeral moved
  along—
Abreast of me walk'd Shield, who gave
  thee song:
To Covent-Garden Church-yard flam-
  beaux light
Gleam on the sacred Duty—solemn rite.

Edwin was celebrated as fully for his occasional songs "in character," and his entr'acte singing, as for his acting. He was much in demand for convivial gatherings in homes of fashion and at clubs like the Anacreontic Society. The *Catalogue of Printed Music in the British Museum* lists some of the many songs printed under Edwin's name, but the words to most of them were by O'Keeffe.

Edwin's domestic life had begun to show signs of strain after 1785 and Winston said that in 1789 he had brought a new mistress to his residence in Bedford Street. (His benefit bills gave his address as No 19,

Piazza, from 1784 through April 1789.) When the intrusion was resented by his common-law wife, he "forced her and her eldest son John out of doors, because [the son], very naturally espoused his mother's cause, and advertised them in the newspapers, as not being his wife and son, and insisted on their being discharged from every theatre in which he was engaged."

An unedifying exchange between the elder John Edwin and his common-law wife and son over the extent of Edwin's financial support of his family occurred in August and September of 1790, during Edwin's final illness.

The number of offspring of Edwin's long but irregular connection with the actress Sarah Walmsley (who continued to act under Edwin's name until her death in 1794) is not surely known. Young John was well known as a performer and is separately noticed, as are David Edwin and Sarah Edwin, both of whom acted briefly in London. "Four Sons of the deceased" are listed in the "Order of Funeral" published after the obsequies of the elder Edwin. An obituary of the common-law Mrs Edwin, printed in the *European Magazine* after her death on 8 January 1794, stated that the loss of her daughter, "a short time since," was supposed to have hastened her death.

As with many comic personalities John Edwin's name was posthumously fastened to compilations with which he had nothing to do. The undated *Edwin's Jests* is in a tradition which stretches at least as far back as the Elizabethan comedian Tarleton. More extensive (and somewhat repetitive of the first) was *Edwin's Pills To Purge Melancholy* (second edition in 1788). *The Eccentricities of John Edwin, Comedian. Collected from His Manuscripts, and enriched with Several Hundred Original Anecdotes and Digested by Anthony Pasquin, Esq.*, published in two volumes in 1798, is the only authority for Edwin's early life. "Anthony Pasquin" (John Williams) seems to have been a friend and an admirer of Edwin and presumably the vital facts are substantially correct. But the "Several Hundred Original Anecdotes" are, as is usual with such volumes, highly suspect. A copy in the Folger Shakespeare Library is lightly annotated by Edwin's close associate the actor Waldron, who ridiculed some of the stories. The spurious *The Last Legacy of John Edwin* (c. 1790) contains an engraved portrait of the actor.

Other portraits of John Edwin the elder include:

1. By Henry Edridge. Watercolor. In the Garrick Club. Engraving by W. Ridley as a plate to the *Monthly Mirror*, 1805.

2. By Thomas Gainsborough. Painting. In the Garrick Club.

3. By J. Roberts. Pencil drawing; wearing cocked hat. In the Garrick Club.

4. By J. Roberts. Pencil drawing; three-quarters to left. In the Garrick Club.

5. By unknown artist. Pencil drawing. In the British Museum.

6. Engraving by J. Heath, after T. Beach. Published by S. Watts, 1786.

7. By unknown engraver, after Rider. Plate to Edwin's *Pills to Purge Melancholy*.

8. By unknown engraver. Published by J. Aitken.

9. As Autolycus in *The Winter's Tale*. Engraving by C. Grignion, after H. Ramberg. Plate to *Bell's British Theatre*, 1785. A copy was engraved by Woodman and published by John Cawthorn, 1806.

10. As Bob in *Man Milliner*. Anonymous engraving published by William Holland, 1787.

11. As Caleb in *He Would Be a Soldier*, holding hat in right hand. Pencil drawing by unknown artist. In the British Museum.

12. As Caleb. Anonymous engraving. Published by S. W. Fores, 1786. Based on No 11.

13. As Caleb. Anonymous engraving published by William Holland, 1786.

14. As Croaker in *The Good Natured Man*. Engraving by C. Taylor, after C. R.

Ryley. Published by Lowndes as a plate to *New English Theatre*, 1788.

15. As (Gomez?) in *The Spanish Fryar*, with Henderson and Mrs Mattocks. Anonymous pencil and wash drawing. At the Folger Shakespeare Library.

16. As Jemmy Jumps, with Mrs Wells as Betty Blackberry, in *The Farmer*. Anonymous engraving published by Laurie & Whittle, 1794.

17. As Jemmy Jumps, with Johnstone as Captain Valentine. Anonymous engraving published by J. Aitken, 1791.

18. As Jerry Blackacre in *The Plain Dealer*. Engraving by W. Angus, after C. R. Ryley. Published by Lowndes as a plate to *New English Theatre*, 1788.

19. As Jerry Blackacre. Colored drawing on vellum by J. Roberts. In the British Museum.

20. As Justice Woodcock in *Love in a Village*. Painting by Thomas Beach. In the Garrick Club.

21. As Justice Woodcock. Colored drawing by J. Roberts, 1775. In the British Museum.

22. As Lingo in *The Agreeable Surprise*. Engraving by C. J. Hodges, after J. Alefounder. Published by T. Bradshaw, 1784.

23. As Lingo, with Mrs Wells as Cowslip. Engraving by E. Scott, after H. Singleton. Published by I. Birchall, 1788.

24. As Lingo, with Mrs Wells as Cowslip. Anonymous engraving published by W. Holland, 1789.

25. As Peeping Tom in *Peeping Tom*. Painting by Thomas Beach. In the Garrick Club.

26. As Sir Troubadour in *The Crusade*. Anonymous engraving published by J. Aitken, 1790.

27. As Skirmish in *The Deserter*. Engraving by Barlow, after I. Cruikshank. Published by J. Roach, 1791.

28. As Spouting Dick in *The Apprentice Before a Country Manager*. By unknown engraver.

29. Broadside sheet of verses for "Mr Edwin's New Four and Twenty Fiddlers," with crude anonymous engraving in oval inset: Edwin center-stage, flanked by a row of women on either side, with violinists in pit.

30. Benefit ticket, showing Edwin in character, with quotation, "Jupiter was a fine God he swam on a Bull to Europe."

31. Caricature, "What Nature Ought to Be." Engraving by A. Scratch. A satire on Edwin's Lingo, published by Bentley & Co, in *Attic Miscellany*, 1790.

Edwin, Mrs John, Sarah, née Walmsley *d. 1794, actress, singer.*

Sarah Walmsley was "a respectable milliner in Horse Street," Bath, when she met the rising young comedian John Edwin, probably sometime after his arrival in the Bath company in 1768. They set up housekeeping together, she took his name, and their association lasted for some 20 years and produced at least five children. They were never married. Their son, the well-known actor and singer John Edwin the younger (d. 1805), generally is said to have been born in 1768, but very likely that date is incorrect by at least a year. "Richard, Son of John & Sarah Edwin," was christened at Bath Abbey on 11 August 1774. Another son, David, born in 1776, abandoned acting for engraving and died in 1841. A daughter, Sarah, sang and danced in London in 1791 and 1792 and died, apparently quite young, in September 1793. An "Order of Funeral" for the elder John Edwin published in 1790 alluded to "Four Sons of the deceased."

Evidently Sarah Walmsley had no acting experience when she took up her relationship to Edwin. But, on the evidence of a letter from Edwin to George Colman dated 4 March 1777, from Bath, she was by then acting at Bath at least occasionally: she "pretends to no great merit, but . . . she had a very good study & might upon an emergency supply the place of a better actress."

Edwin had already played at the Haymarket, beginning in the summer of 1776, but there is no record of any London appearance for Mrs Edwin (as she was then known) until 9 July 1781, when she came on at the Haymarket as Grootrump in the first offering of Miles Peter Andrews's farce *The Baron Kinkvervankotsdorsprakengatchdern*. She was Mistress Quickly in *The Merry Wives of Windsor* at the theatre on 24 August and then appeared no more that season. The rate of two roles a summer (which may have been a sop to her increasingly valuable husband) was resumed in 1783 and maintained in 1784. She appeared only once in 1785, but in 1786 she was allowed to act seven times, in 1787 again seven times, and in 1788 five times. The modest increase in the frequency of her appearance may have reflected the domestic disquiet which was soon to grow to an open breach between Mrs Edwin and her common-law husband. It may have been that Mrs Edwin was then the principal support of her children, and that consequently the Haymarket management was responding to her need. At any rate, according to James Winston's rather feverish account, Edwin's intemperance and neglect grew, until

In the spring of 1789 [Edwin] renewed an intimacy with a notorious woman of the town. To force her to return to him, he threatened to charge her with stealing his watch, a practice not uncommon with her. This threat reconciled the amiable couple, and he actually brought her to his residence in Bedford Street. This was resented by Mrs. Edwin. He forced her and her eldest son John out of doors, because [John] very naturally, espoused his mother's cause, and advertised them in the newspapers, as not being his wife and son, and insisted on their being discharged from every theatre in which he was engaged.

On 13 June 1790 the elder John Edwin, already sinking toward death, married a Miss Mary Hubbard, and during the summer the newspaper war between Edwin and "the *soi-disant* Mrs Edwin" intensified, with charge and countercharge: that young John was the sole support of his mother and siblings; that the elder John had, according to him, "very lately settled an account" with "Mr Milne, of Salvador House Academy, Tooting . . . of more than seventy pounds for the board and education of two children by that unhappy connexion, which, to restore my peace of mind, I was obliged to put an end to"—and so on. John Edwin the elder died, in his forty-second year, on 30 October 1790.

Sarah Walmsley continued to appear in the summer Haymarket bills (and in 1789–90 and 1791–92 occasionally also at Drury Lane during the regular season) as "Mrs Edwin." There, according to a British Museum manuscript, she was a soprano singer in the chorus at £2 per week. Her last appearance was at the Haymarket on 19 November 1793 in an undesignated "vocal part." She died on 8 January 1794. The *European Magazine* reported that the loss of her daughter (young Sarah, who had died in September 1793) had caused her death.

Mrs Edwin's talents were small; she acted and sang tertiary comedy parts and sometimes smaller ones, and she did so infrequently. Her salary never rose higher than the weekly £2 which she received from Drury Lane from 1789–90 onward, and there is some doubt that she received that salary during many weeks when she did not act. Her named roles, in addition to those already mentioned, were: the Wife in *The Triumph of Honor*, the Aunt in *The What D'Ye Call It*, Garnet in *The Good Natur'd Man*, Juno in *Midas*, Ursula in *The Widow's Vow*, a Waiting Maid in *Summer's Amusements*, a Housemaid in *Here, and There, and Everywhere*, Mrs Slammekin in *The Beggar's Opera*, Judith in *The Young Quaker*, Dolly in *The Ghost*, Lady Pedigree in *Gretna Green*, Mrs Starch in *Sir John Cockle at Court*, Mrs Gobble in *The Sword of Peace*, Fadladinida in *Chrononhotonthologos*, Mrs Sturdy in *Half an Hour After Supper*, the Actress in *The Manager in Distress*, a Lady in *The Belle's Stratagem*, a Villager in *The Battle of Hexham*, a Priestess in *The Cave of Trophonius*, as Mrs Edwin herself in *Poor Old Haymarket*, the Mayoress in *Peeping Tom*, Dorcas in *Richard Coeur de Lion*, the Nurse in *The Chances*, Mrs Cheshire in *The Agreeable Surprise*, Candy in *Piety in Pattens*, a Bacchant in *Comus*, a Lady in *The London Hermit*, a Bridesmaid in *Royal Clemency*, and Mrs Clagget in *The Confederacy*. She also sang undesignated "Vocal Parts" and made one of the chorus in a number of musical pieces.

Edwin, John   *1769?–1805,   actor, singer.*

John Edwin "the younger" was the eldest son and one of at least five children born to the notable comic actor and singer John Edwin and his common-law wife, the milliner-turned-actress Sarah Walmsley of Bath. Evidently his mother and father did not meet until his father entered the Bath theatrical company in October of 1768; thus the date 1768 usually given as the year of young John's birth is probably inaccurate. It rests perhaps on James Winston's recollection in "The Manager's Note-Book" that "Young Edwin, who was always called Jack, made his first appearance at the Haymarket in Hengist, in 'Bonduca,' in 1778, being then ten years old." The part was actually Hengo and the date was 30 July 1778.

Young Jack Edwin had already tasted provincial applause by the time he joined his father and mother at the Haymarket. The elder John had offered Jack's acting to Colman as a part of a whole-family deal in a letter from Bath dated 4 March 1777. (The proposed combined salary of five guineas a week had been too high for the Haymarket manager, and the elder Edwin,

Harvard Theatre Collection

JOHN EDWIN, the younger, as Zekial Homespun

engraving by Page, after De Wilde

who had acted for Colman in the summer of 1776, returned to London alone in 1777.) Jack had already received instruction from his talented father, also. Both tutelage and experience were apparent in his Haymarket debut, and both were commented on by newspaper critics. Le Texier, in the *Morning Post* of 28 August 1778, after *Bonduca* had played five times, greatly praised that "sweet child" Master Edwin but remarked that

he had unluckily been taught to wind up his voice to a very disagreeable pitch. They make him speak, as it were, by jerks; and the poor little fellow strains himself in such a manner that all his little frame is in a state of convulsion. Such a promising youth needs no teaching; he only wants a guide; for it may be observed that he is never more interesting than when he is permitted to be himself. His father, I suppose, instructs him; the child cannot be in better hands; – but Mr. Edwin should take care not to force that tender plant, lest he should pay too dear for the untimely fruits he may gather from it.

The advice was evidently followed faithfully. *Bonduca* ran only three more nights that summer and little Jack was not listed in any other offering. He repaired with his family to the Bath-Bristol alternation in September 1778, but his roles that year are not known. He helped open the Haymarket on 31 May 1779, again as Hengo, but was named in no other bills that summer except on 17 August, when, for his father's benefit bill, he sang "Ted Blarney" at the end of Act IV of the mainpiece and offered the monologue "Bucks Have at Ye All" after Act V. The Edwins were then living, according to the benefit bill, at No 9, St Martin's Street, Leicester Fields.

The elder Edwin came onto Covent Garden's roster for the next season, beginning a decade of memorable association with that house on 24 September 1779, but not until toward the season's end, on 22 April 1780, did Master Jack begin his Covent Garden service. Again for his father's benefit he spoke a special prologue, written by Samuel Foote. The family then lodged at No 76, the corner of Longacre, Drury Lane. The younger Edwin accompanied his father once more to the Haymarket in the summer of 1780 but played only three times, so far as the bills show. One appearance was as Hengo, but he also played the Duke of York in *Richard III* and on 2 September sang as the original Head Boy of the Marine Society in the elder George Colman's new and "Original, Whimsical, Operatical, Pantomimical, Farcical, Electrical, Naval, Military, Temporary, Local Extravaganza" *The Genius of Nonsense.*

He appeared at Covent Garden on 3 October 1780 as the title character in *Tom Thumb*, and the following 30 April the bills named him again, once more speaking an occasional prologue on his father's benefit night. He was called upon to play at the Haymarket five times during the summer of 1781, so far as the bills show, and that was the pattern for the next five years. Until he was about 17 years old young John Edwin's parts were few, insignificant, repetitive, and invariably juvenile, and his appearances were infrequent. When he appeared at Covent Garden, which was sometimes no more than twice a year, he earned (by 1782–83) £1 5s. a night, but that would surely have been little more had he been employed weekly. His first adult part was as Dick in Murphy's afterpiece *The Apprentice*, for his father's benefit on 26 March 1788. In the summer of 1788 he acted at Richmond.

On 15 August 1788 and again on 15 September he "supplied the place of his father," in the words of the *London Chronicle,* as Trudge in *Inkle and Yarico*, billed as "Edwin junior." From that point on until the elder Edwin's death in 1790, it is sometimes difficult to distinguish between the Edwins, father and son, when the playbills do not specify "the younger."

Edwin's puberty and young manhood had been traumatized by increasingly stormy weather in the household of the elder Edwins. The father had finally deserted his common-law wife of twenty years, at one point denying his parentage of the children. He had quarrelled violently with his wife in the public prints and his drunkenness was often uncontrollable. In the latter matter the young Jack Edwin was an early and diligent imitator of his father.

Edwin had met the sixteen-year-old actress Elizabeth Rebecca Richards when both were engaged at Richmond in July 1790 and in 1791 he married her. In February 1791 he had taken her from her engagement with Tate Wilkinson at York to assist, with himself, his father and his brother David, in the theatricals at War-

Harvard Theatre Collection

JOHN EDWIN, the younger, as Tom Thumb

artist unknown

grave, sponsored by his boon companion the Earl of Barrymore. (She had overstayed her allotted time and quarrelled with Wilkinson in consequence.) The Edwins signed on with the Haymarket again in the summer of 1792.

Advertised as "a London performer," Edwin joined Stephen Kemble's company at Sheffield in September 1792 and soon found himself at loggerheads with Kemble over salaries and benefit nights for himself and Mrs Edwin. Appeals to the public were published by both Edwin and Kemble from Newcastle in June 1793. Edwin played at the Edinburgh Theatre Royal from January to May 1793.

In 1794 Edwin and his wife were briefly

at Brighton. They performed on the York circuit (York, Wakefield, Hull, Pontefract, Doncaster, and Leeds) in the seasons of 1795, 1796, and 1797. From 1797–98 through 1803–4 they played in Bath at the Orchard Street Theatre and at the Theatre Royal, Bristol, making side excursions to Doncaster, Weymouth, and other country towns. Edwin, while at Bath, was made an honorary professional member of the Harmonic Society and in 1801, according to the *Theatric Tourist,* was principally responsible for establishing the Theatrical Fund at Bath, the only such institution except those of London and Norwich.

The Harvard Theatre Collection contains a note from Edwin dated 13 February 1801 from Caroline Buildings, Bath, to a Mr Shaw (probably the band leader) at London: "Not knowing who is acting Manager of Margate, I have taken the liberty to write to you for an engagement for myself & wife." The enquiry is the last certain word of John Edwin the younger which we have until the year of his death. He evidently accompanied his wife to Dublin in 1804 and probably acted until near the time of his demise in 1805.

In 1804 John Wilson Croker, the Irish politician and essayist, published a *Rosciad*-like poetic satire on the Dublin stage which created a small local furor. In it he called Edwin the "lubbard spouse" of Mrs Edwin and compared him unfavorably with his father. Upon reading those lines Edwin is supposed to have written to a friend: "Come and help me to destroy myself with some of the most splendid cogniac [*sic*] that I have ever exported to cheer a broken heart." Surely the remark was jocular, and Jack Edwin had already enthusiastically followed the bibulous example of his father in dissipation. The probability is that he drank himself to death, but not because of Croker's illiberal remark.

But Mrs Edwin caused the following lines to be incised on his tombstone in St Werburgh's churchyard, Dublin (the transcription is from the *Monthly Mirror* of March, 1810):

Here lie the remains of Mr. JOHN EDWIN, of the Theatre-Royal, who died Feb. 22, 1805, aged 33 years. His death was occasioned by the acuteness of his sensibility. Before he was sufficiently known to the public of this city, to have his talents properly appreciated, he experienced an illiberal and cruel attack on his professional reputation, from an anonymous assassin. This circumstance preyed upon his mind to the extinction of life.

While in apparently bodily vigour, he predicted his approaching dissolution. The consciousness of a brain rending with agony, accounts for this prescience, and incontrovertibly establishes the cause of his death.

This stone is inscribed to the memory of an affectionate husband, as a tribute of duty and attachment, by her, who, best acquainted with the qualities of his heart, can best record their amiability.

Like his father, Jack Edwin was a type much esteemed by the British public in the last quarter of the century: a fine comic actor of eccentric and hearty melodic roles, a singer of glees and patriotic songs, a merry public man, bumper-lifter, and trencherman. He found no secure footing on the London patent stage, playing almost exclusively at the Haymarket while in the metropolis and maturing his career and finding most favor before provincial audiences. A selected listing of the adult roles he consolidated will suggest how near his talents were to his father's: Spatter in *The English Merchant*, Blister in *The Virgin Unmask'd*, Motley in *The Dead Alive*, Drawcansir in *The Rehearsal*, Jacob Gawky in *The Chapter of Accidents*, the Drummer in *The Battle of Hexham*, Tipple in *The Flitch of Bacon*, Dicky Ditto in *Two to One*, the Music Master in *Catherine and Petruchio*, Remnant in *The Volunteers*, Scaramouch in *Don Juan*, Moses in *The School for Scandal*, Dick in *The Apprentice*, Trappolin in *A Duke and No Duke*, and Skirmish in *The Deserter*. Tate Wil-

kinson singled out for special praise his Lenitive in *The Prize*, his Nipperkin in *The Sprigs of Laurel*, and his Mr Tag in *The Spoil'd Child*. "Mr Edwin," he vowed, "dresses his characters better and more characteristic than any comic actor I recollect on the York Stage."

The *Catalogue of Printed Music in the British Museum* credits Edwin with the composition of the song *From the County of Cork* (1800?).

Edwin was pictured at age 12 by an anonymous engraver as the title character in Fielding's *Tom Thumb* for an edition of the play published by J. Harrison in 1780. A watercolor ascribed to Georgiana Keate, in the Westminster Public Library, shows Sarah Siddons in an unidentified play with an actor identified as the senior John Edwin but probably his son. The picture is inscribed "Bath" on the back, and the elder Edwin was with Mrs Siddons at Bath only on occasions from 1780 to 1782, when Georgiana Keate was between seven and nine years old. In the Harvard Theatre Collection is an engraving by Page, after De Wilde, of Edwin as Zekial Homespun in *The Heir at Law*. It is not listed in the Hall catalogue.

Edwin, Mrs John, Elizabeth Rebecca, née Richards   *1771?–1854, actress, singer.*

Elizabeth Rebecca Richards was a daughter of William Talbot Richards (d. 1813), an actor in the Dublin, Edinburgh, and provincial English theatre, and of his first wife, an actress and singer. Joseph Knight, in *The Dictionary of National Biography*, tentatively assigns the birth year 1771 to Miss Richards. But William S. Clark, in *The Irish Stage in the County Towns*, says that she was born in 1773; that date seems less likely to be the correct one.

There is considerable conflict in the surviving evidence about the chronology of her theatrical service and other events of her life. How early she was introduced to the theatre is not really known. One Miss Richards played the juvenile Duke of York in *King Charles the First* at Edinburgh on 5 April 1777. A vague and verbose piece, "Memoirs of Mrs Edwin" in the *Monthly Mirror* for February and March 1810 (an undated letter in her hand now at Harvard nevertheless endorses it as "the most correct" of several such thumbnail biographies) said that "in the last year of Mr Crawfords management, Miss Richards, then only six years of age, made her first effort upon the stage, for her mother's benefit, in the character of the Romp." But the last year of Billy Crawford's management of Crow Street, Dublin, was apparently 1782, which fact would mean that (if the debutante was indeed only six) she must have been born in 1776. However, Clark in his index fixes her for the first time at Crow Street in 1780. The Drury Lane account books list her at 10*s.* for "1st 3 days" on 30 September 1780. A Miss Richards shared in tickets at Drury Lane on 23 May 1783 and 15 May 1784. The *Monthly Mirror* account asserted that, because "her health became, in a degree, impaired from her public exertions at those tender years," she was for a time withdrawn from acting. "Her next theatrical career [*sic*] commenced at York, where, at the age of fifteen, she took the lead in comedy; from thence she went to the Theatre Royal at Richmond, in Surry, where she became acquainted with her future husband. . . ." There was certainly a Miss Richards on the Richmond roster in the summer of 1790. But if she was born in 1773 she cannot have been only 15 when she went to York. For she did not appear on Tate Wilkinson's company list until 1790–91, and he is said to have dismissed her for overstaying her "leave" after her new husband Edwin had taken her to the Wargrave Theatre of the Earl of Barrymore in March 1791. Wilkinson recalled that "she went with her mother to the Margate Theatre" in the late spring of 1791.

But she was certainly married to Edwin by late 1791, and she appeared at the Haymarket Theatre in London on 20 June 1792, for the first time under her new name. The *European Magazine* rather coolly noticed her portrayal that night of Lucy in *The Virgin Unmask'd*: "This lady has been some time one of Lord Barrymore's troop of comedians and if not excellent, showed talents enough to preserve her from censure. Her fears seemed to overcome her powers, and prevented her from displaying the full extent of her abilities." She probably was the Mrs Edwin who sang once or twice in supporting choruses for the rest of the summer of 1792 (rather than her "mother-in-law," the "widow" of John Edwin the elder, who was a character-actress at that house at the time).

Mrs Edwin and her husband joined Stephen Kemble's company at Sheffield in September 1792, played with his troupe at Edinburgh in February and March 1793, and left him in Newcastle before June, when there was a flurry of published charges and countercharges over salaries and benefits between the manager and the Edwins. At some point between 1792 and the summer of 1794 Mrs Edwin was also associated with the private theatre opened by Lord Westmeath and Frederick Jones in Fishamble Street, Dublin. The couple turned up at Brighton in the summer of 1794. They rejoined Wilkinson on the York circuit at Doncaster in October 1794 and remained with him in 1795, 1796, and 1797. In 1801 George Wilson named her with other notable female performers who had been on the York stage, paying her a compliment in his *Retort Courteous*. From 1797–98 through 1803–4 the Edwins were at Bath and Bristol and in Southampton, Cheltenham, and several other country towns.

The *Monthly Mirror* account speaks of the assiduous patronage which the Duchess of York gave Mrs Edwin during her tenure at Bath and of Mrs Edwin's "just delineation of the *haut ton*" and the consequent loud praise from "the Irish nobility," which led Frederick Jones to invite the Edwins again to Ireland in 1804. John Edwin died, probably of cumulative dissipation, in Dublin on 22 February 1805. His widow attributed his death to an anonymous attack by John Wilson Croker in *Familiar Epistles* (1804). In his *Histrionic Epistles* (1807) Croker also attacked Elizabeth Rebecca. The following year she was wounded in the face during an inept bit of swordplay in *Ella Rosenberg* in March 1808 and was out of action for five days.

Mrs Edwin was given a benefit at Crow Street, Dublin, on 5 May 1808. She was next recorded at the Theatre Royal, Shakespeare Square, Edinburgh, on 3 December 1808 and remained through the 1808–9 Edinburgh season playing a wide variety of parts, including Albina Mandeville in *The Will*, Alexina in *Tekeli*, Angela in *The Castle Spectre*, Antonio in *Richard Coeur de Lion*, Beatrice in *Much Ado About Nothing*, Bisarre in *The Inconstant*, Charlotte Rusport in *The West Indian*, Desdemona in *Othello*, Dinah Primrose in *The Young Quaker*, Donna Olivia in *A Bold Stroke for a Husband*, Donna Violante in *The Wonder*, Eliza Ratcliffe in *The Jew*, the title part in *Ella Rosenberg*, Emma in *The Birthday*, the Female Prisoner in *Such Things Are*, Flora in *The Midnight Hour*, Helen Worrett in *Man and Wife*, Julia in *The Way to Get Married*, Juliana in *The Honeymoon*, Juliet in *Romeo and Juliet*, Lady Amaranth in *Wild Oats*, Lady Racket in *Three Weeks After Marriage*, Lady Teazle in *The School for Scandal*, Lady Townly in *The Provok'd Husband*, Letitia Hardy in *The Belle's Stratagem*, Lydia Languish in *The Rivals*, Maria in *The Citizen*, Marianne in *The Dramatist*, Miranda in *The Busy Body*, Miss Hardcastle in *She Stoops to Conquer*, Miss Peggy in *The Country Girl*, Mrs Oakly in *The Jealous Wife*, Rosalind in *As You Like It*, Roxa-

lana in *The Sultan*, Sophia in *The Road to Ruin*, Widow Belmour in *The Way to Keep Him*, and Widow Cheerly in *The Soldier's Daughter*.

At the recommendation of Sheridan Mrs Edwin was engaged at Drury Lane for the fall of 1809. Before she reached the theatre it burned, and on 14 October she appeared with the Drury Lane company at the Lyceum, as the Widow Cheerly. By the spring of 1810 she had moved to No 13, King Street, Covent Garden, near the Drury Lane Theatre, which she served until 1814–15. A British Museum manuscript account dated 24 July 1812 records a contract for three years by which she was to realize £15 per week plus £50 at the end of each season, the latter sum doubtless in lieu of a benefit. In 1813–14 she was raised to £16 per week. Arnold, her manager, selected her to recite his verses in commemoration of Waterloo on 3 July 1815.

In 1815 Mrs Edwin returned to the Crow Street Theatre, and thereafter news of her professional activity is scarce. In 1817 Dublin managers were scolded for not employing her, by the playwright Leonard MacNally, in a newspaper encomium to her talents. On 16 October 1818 she was at the Olympic, speaking the opening address by Moncrieff. In the 1819–20 season she returned to the company at Drury Lane where, according to the account books, she was paid £15 per week.

For the next few years Mrs Edwin continued to act, in short engagements at Covent Garden, Drury Lane, the Adelphi, the Olympic, and the Surrey in London, and at many provincial towns. She had saved her money with the expectation of retirement but was disappointed in that aim because of the defalcation of a stock broker, who made off to America with over £8000 of her money. Her last years were lived in obscurity. She died at her lodgings in Chelsea on 3 August 1854.

Elizabeth Edwin, widow, of the Strand, later of Sloane Street, and then of Cadogan

Harvard Theatre Collection

ELIZABETH EDWIN, as Juliana

engraving by Cardon

Julia Faulkner in *The Way to Get Married*, Miss Blandford in *Speed the Plough*, the title part in *Ella Rosenberg*, the Princess in *Jean de Paris*, Lucy in *Past Ten O'Clock*, Victoria in *A Bold Stroke for a Husband*, Miss Prue in *Love for Love*, and Geraldine in *The Foundling of the Forest*.

Tate Wilkinson held a high opinion of Mrs Edwin when she was Miss Richards, a fledgling actress on his York circuit, although he had discharged her for disciplinary reasons. She was his "Euphrosyne."

Her face is more than pretty, it is handsome and strong featured, not unlike [George Anne] Bellamy's: Her person is rather short, but take her altogether she is a nice little woman. She was then . . . in full and equal spirits: She played a variety of characters with great success; and the contrast was such and so happily hit on, that when not suited to her person and powers, yet by the aid of youth and spirits, were to a degree pleasing, and in the [Dorothy] *Jordan line* the best, ay, the very best I have seen.

Street, Chelsea, had written her will on 3 May 1852. She had left all her property, unspecified, to Alice Wallace, wife of Martin Wallace of Gloucester House, Sloane Street, Knightsbridge, on the condition that she should see her "buried as a Gentlewoman should be in the All Souls Catholic Canetory [*sic*; cemetery? cantatory?] Chelsea where I have purchased a grave." An annuity of £100 was to provide £25 for funeral expenses.

Among the roles of her maturity reflected in a manuscript Drury Lane casting book in the Folger Library are the following: Beatrice in *Much Ado About Nothing*, Charlotte in *The Hypocrite*, Lydia Languish in *The Rivals*, Flora in *The Midnight Hour*, Violante in *The Wonder*, Mrs Rivers in *Sons of Erin*, Clara in *Matrimony*, Corinna in *The Confederacy*, Fanny in *The Clandestine Marriage*, Helen Worrett in *Man and Wife*, Lady Trapwell in *First Impressions*,

Portraits of Elizabeth Rebecca Edwin include:

1. Engraved portrait by H. R. Cook, after W. Foster. Published by G. Cowie & Co, 1813.

2. Engraved portrait by S. Freeman, after De Wilde. Plate to the *Monthly Mirror*, 1810.

3. Engraved portrait by unknown artist. Plate to *Ireland's Mirror*.

4. As Albina Mandeville in *The Will*. Painting by De Wilde. In the Garrick Club.

5. As Beatrice in *Much Ado About Nothing*. Engraving by J. Carver, after J. Partridge. Plate to the *Theatrical Inquisitor*, 1815.

6. As Eliza in *Riches*. Painting by De Wilde. In the Garrick Club. (May be wrongly identified; Mrs Orger was the original Eliza. Mrs Edwin was probably always Lady Traffic. See No 11, below.)

7. As Fanny in *The Clandestine Mar-*

riage. Engraving by Alais. Published by J. Roach, 1812.

8. As Miss Hoyden in *The Relapse.* Engraving by Alais. Published by J. Roach, 1811.

9. As Juliana [in *The Honeymoon*]. Engraving by Cardon. Published by John Bell, 1812.

10. As Juliana in *The Honeymoon.* Engraving by J. Rogers. Plate to Oxberry's *Dramatic Biography,* 1826. A copy of No 9, above.

11. As Lady Traffic in *Riches.* Watercolor by De Wilde. In the Garrick Club.

12. As Letitia Hardy in *The Belle's Stratagem.* Engraving by Woolnoth, after Wageman. Plate to Oxberry's *New English Drama,* 1819.

13. As Lydia Languish in *The Rivals.* By unknown engraver. Plate to *Hibernian Magazine,* 1805.

Edwin, Sarah *d. 1793, singer, dancer?*
Miss Sarah Edwin, a daughter of John Edwin the elder and his common-law wife Sarah Walmsley, was first noticed in the playbill of 31 December 1791 when she appeared as one of the Spirits in the elaborate alteration and revival of Garrick's *Cymon* by the Drury Lane company playing at the King's Theatre.

She was then a juvenile, for her companion Spirits—Master and Miss D'Egville and Miss Gaudry—were small children. They were also dancers. Sarah probably then sang as well as danced, as she did in her second appearance, on 23 May 1792, when she was one of the Voices in the chorus at the first presentation of Prince Hoare's alteration of Metastasio's *Didone abbandonata* called *Dido Queen of Carthage.*

Sarah was carried in the bills again as a chorus member for the premiere of James Cobb's comic opera *The Pirates* on 21 November 1792. She probably assisted in three more performances of it that season, the last of which was on 11 June 1792, but

her name was not in the bills. During her brief time on the stage she earned 15*s.* per week. The last payment to her recorded in the manuscript account books of Drury Lane Theatre was 17*s.* for seven nights, on 9 March 1793. She was buried at St Paul, Covent Garden, on 1 October 1793.

Edzard, Mrs [Gustavus-Jacobus, Astrea?] [*fl. 1722?–1724*], *actress.*
Mrs Edzard played Rose in *The Recruiting Officer* on 22 May 1723 at Lincoln's Inn Fields for her shared benefit with Lanyon. The pair took in a total of £54 4*s.* Though no further parts are known for her, she shared a benefit with two others on 25 May 1724 which brought in £80 14*s.* Perhaps she was Astrea, the wife of Gustavus-Jacobus Edzard; they christened a son Gustavus at St Paul, Covent Garden, on 1 September 1722.

Eensley. *See* **BENSLEY.**

Effert. *See* **EIFFERT.**

Egan. *See also* **EAGAN.**

Egan, Miss [*fl. 1764–1769*], *dancer.*
With Walker, Miss Egan danced a double hornpipe for her first appearance at Drury Lane Theatre on 14 May 1764. She remained in the company through 1768–69, apparently, though she was rarely cited in the bills and, at a salary of 2*s.* 6*d.* nightly (in 1765), was in the bottom rank of dancers. In the summer of 1767 she danced with Atkins at Richmond; on 26 April 1768 the Drury Lane bills noted that she was added to a cotillion; and on 17 May 1769 she danced a solo hornpipe.

Egan, Catherine Ann. *See* **ACHMET, MRS.**

Egan, Timothy [*fl. 1740*], *performer?*
Timothy Egan wrote a letter to the *Daily Post* on 5 December 1740 concerning his

benefit at the New Wells, Goodman's Fields, but nothing else is known of the benefit or of Egan.

Egan, William *d. 1785, actor.*

William Egan married Elizabeth Paul at St Paul, Covent Garden, on 31 August 1766 and by her had a daughter, Sarah Elizabeth, who was baptized there on 15 July 1767. Egan may have been the actor of that name who played Perdicas in *The Rival Queens* on 8 August 1768 at Bristol and the Egan who was discharged from the Norwich company on 24 August 1772. On 15 May 1775 William Egan appeared at the Haymarket Theatre in London in *The Devil upon Two Sticks*, probably as O'Sasafras or Sligo. On 22 May he was in *The Nabob*, on 5 June *The Bankrupt*, on 16 August *The Orators*, and on 4 September *A Trip to Portsmouth*. In the summer of 1776 he returned there to perform in *The Cozeners* as well as in revivals of *The Devil upon Two Sticks*, *The Orators*, and *The Bankrupt*.

The summer of 1777 provided Egan with a greater opportunity to show his abilities, according to the playwright Sarah Gardner, for when John Palmer and Charles Bannister gave up some of their roles at the Haymarket, Egan fell heir to them. As a result, between May and September Egan played a part in *The English Merchant*, Zacharydes in *The Tailors*, a role in *The Nabob*, Sligo in *The Devil upon Two Sticks*, Solanio in *The Merchant of Venice*, Hacker in *Polly*, Guildenstern in *Hamlet*, Wealthy in *The Minor*, Alonzo in *Rule a Wife and Have a Wife*, Polixenes in *The Sheep Shearing*, Westmoreland in *1 Henry IV*, Ratcliff in *Richard III*, Jasper in *Miss in Her Teens*, Captain O'Conner in *The Advertisement* (Sarah Gardner's play, in which, she said, Egan "displayed such genuine humour and ability in the performance as did credit to himself, and was a great support to the piece"), Decius in *Cato*, Colonel Tivy in *Bon Ton*, a role in

The Rehearsal, the Lord Chamberlain in *Henry VIII*, Alcade in *The Spanish Barber*, and Lord Rake in *The Provok'd Wife*. Many of the parts he was assigned that summer he kept to the end of his career.

Egan returned to the Haymarket in the summer of 1778 to add to his repertoire such parts as Snarl in *Man and Wife*, Frank in *Tony Lumpkin in Town*, a Waiter in *The Suicide*, and the Irishman in *The Apprentices*. His winter activities until 1778–79 are unaccounted for; perhaps he acted in the provinces.

From 1778–79 through 1782–83 Egan acted at Covent Garden in the regular season for £3 weekly and was a regular in the summer company at the Haymarket. His first role at Covent Garden was Teague in *The Twin Rivals* on 21 October 1778. During the rest of his first season there he played Roger in *The Invasion*, a role in *The Lady of the Manor*, Eumenes in *Alexander the Great*, Captain Jamy in *Henry V*, a part in *The Touchstone*, Foigard in *The Stratagem*, Decius in *Cato*, Balthazar in *The Comedy of Errors*, Bardolph in *1 Henry IV*, and Bulgruddery in *Dr Last in His Chariot*. He shared a benefit with three others on 12 May 1779. At the Haymarket in the summer he revived a number of his old roles and added such new ones as Curius in *Bonduca*, Heeltap in *The Mayor of Garratt*, Captain O'Kite in *A Widow and No Widow*, and Sir Patrick O'Neale in *The Irish Widow*.

From 1779–80 through 1782–83 at Covent Garden and the Haymarket Egan continued to expand his repertoire. Among his many new roles during this period were Captain MacMorris in *Henry V*, the Mad Parson in *The Pilgrim*, Lodovico in *Othello*, an Irishman in the Pit in *The Manager in Distress*, the leading role of Lt O'Connor in *St Patrick's Day*, Pistol in *The Merry Wives of Windsor*, the title role in *Harlequin Teague*, the Irishman in *Rosina*, Bernardo in *Hamlet*, Charles in *As You Like It*, and Tipperary in *Gretna Green*. As of 1780

Egan was living at No 2, Martlet Court, Bow Street.

He was not at Covent Garden in 1783–84 for, according to the *Thespian Dictionary* (1805) he was "engaged for Giordani's English Opera House, Capel Street [in Dublin]; though like several others who belonged to that theatre, [Egan was] incapable of rendering it any service in the vocal line." He very likely entertained Dubliners with some of his Irish roles. Egan's Dublin debut was on 27 December 1783 (not, as Gilliland reported, in 1779). He suffered an indisposition while in Ireland which may have led to his death. Egan returned to London for the summer season at the Haymarket and essayed such new parts as Lory in *The Man of Quality*, Selim in *A Mogul Tale*, and Traverse in *The Clandestine Marriage*.

He began the 1784–85 season at Covent Garden but did not complete it. In addition to some of his old parts he played Francisco in *The Chances* on 21 September 1784, Oxford in *Richard III* on 11 October, the Prince of Tanais in *Tamerlane* on 4 November, the Drunken Butler in *Fontainebleau* on 16 November (but the role was "expunged" before the second performance), Montague in *Romeo and Juliet* on 29 December, Borachio in *Much Ado About Nothing* on 21 January 1785, and the Officer in *Venice Preserv'd* on 24 January. His last appearance was in *Rosina* on 1 February; four days later Bates replaced Egan in that piece, and on 21 April 1785 William Egan died.

His widow became wardrobe mistress and costume designer at Covent Garden. A Miss Egan who danced at Drury Lane from 1764 to 1769 may have been a relative; George Egan, who died at Bath, may have been William's brother; and William Egan the actor (1762–1822) may have been William's son (but he was born four years before the elder Egan's marriage in 1766, at which time Egan declared himself to be a bachelor).

Egan, Mrs William, Elizabeth, née Paul *d. 1807, wardrobe mistress, costume designer.*

Elizabeth Paul married the actor William Egan on 31 August 1766 at St Paul, Covent Garden. They had a daughter, Sarah Elizabeth, who was baptized at the same church on 15 July 1767. William Egan died in 1785, and his widow was given benefit tickets to sell for a Covent Garden performance on 2 June 1786. Perhaps this was merely a charitable gesture on the part of the management, but it is likely that soon after William's death (or perhaps even before) Elizabeth had become wardrobe mistress at the theatre—a post she certainly held in later years. Every spring from 1786 through 1792 Mrs Egan's benefit tickets were accepted at the playhouse. (*The London Stage* lists her in some years as "Egan" rather than "Mrs Egan.") She was not mentioned in the spring of 1793, but her tickets were accepted again on 4 June 1794, when her name was paired with that of Mr Dick the tailor.

The account books mentioned Mrs Egan in 1794–95 as a mantua maker at a salary of £1 11s. 6d. weekly. She also managed the wardrobe at Covent Garden and paid the women dressers. On 6 April 1795 the playbill for the afterpiece *Windsor Castle* noted that the dresses for the spectacle were by Lupino, Dick, and Mrs Egan. Thereafter she was cited regularly as a costume designer, some of the productions for which she prepared costumes being *Merry Sherwood* and *Harlequin's Treasure* in 1795–96; *Olympus in an Uproar*, *Harlequin and Oberon*, and *Raymond and Agnes* in 1796–97 (Mrs Egan, Dick, and Goostree were cited as being in charge of dresses *and* decorations in *Raymond and Agnes*); *The Round Tower*, *Harlequin and Quixotte*, *Joan of Arc*, and (at the Haymarket Theatre) *Cambo-Britons* in 1797–98; *Ramah Droog*, *Albert and Adelaide*, *The Magic Oak*, *A Gallimaufry*, and *An Egeirophadron* in 1798–99; *The Volcano*, *Joanna*, and (at the Haymarket) *Obi* in 1799–1800; and *Corsair* at the Haymarket in 1801. The accounts show Mrs Egan to have worked again at the Haymarket in 1802.

According to the *European Magazine,* Elizabeth Egan died on 27 April 1807. She had made her will at her house in Great Russell Street, Covent Garden, two days before her death, leaving about £200 (the will is ambiguous) in 4 percent annuities to her daughter Sarah Elizabeth Folthorpe, wife of Stephen Folthorpe of Walthamstowe, Essex. To her sister, Ann Paul, Elizabeth left £50. The rest of her estate she bequeathed to the two women jointly. They proved the will on 15 July 1807.

A Miss Egan, probably a relative of Elizabeth Egan, worked at Covent Garden from 1811 to 1814, apparently in the wardrobe.

Egan, William *1762–1822, actor, dancer.*

Perhaps the William Egan who was born in 1762 was the son of William Egan the actor (d. 1785), but when the elder Egan was married in 1766 he was recorded in the parish registers of St Paul, Covent Garden, as a bachelor. The younger Egan may have been illegitimate, or his birthdate, which is based on the report that he was sixty when he died in 1822, could be in error. It may be significant that the younger Egan played some roles which the elder Egan had essayed.

William the younger was acting at Bath as early as 1780, according to Penley in *The Bath Stage;* he was certainly there from 1786–87 through 1788–89. At Plymouth on 17 August 1789 he played Aimwell in *The Beaux' Stratagem* and the Lieutenant of Marines in the ballet *The Death of Captain Cook.* At a salary of £1 10s. weekly he acted at Covent Garden Theatre in London, his first role being Tressel in *Richard III* on 25 September 1789. After that he played Donalbain in *Macbeth,*

Douglas in *1 Henry IV,* Salerio in *The Merchant of Venice,* Rossano in *The Fair Penitent,* a Sportsman in *Harlequin's Chaplet,* Acreless in *The Gamesters,* an Officer in *Eudora,* Slip in *The Czar,* Hortensio in *Catherine and Petruchio,* a Shepherd in *Cymon,* an unspecified character in *Arden of Feversham,* Don Quixote in *Barataria,* and Belville in *The Country Girl.* (The Egan who, according to *The London Stage,* sold benefit tickets for 12 June 1790 was probably Elizabeth Egan, the widow of William the Elder.)

Egan performed at Richmond from July to September 1790, one of his parts there being Sir George Wealthy in *The Minor* on 11 August, and he is reported to have acted at Bath (and, presumably, Bristol) from 1792 until his death. But he also played at the Theatre Royal, Edinburgh (as did his wife, the former Miss Bennet) in 1793, 1795–96, 1796–97, and 1800–1801. Some of his roles at Edinburgh were Arviragus in *Cymbeline,* Bassanio in *The Merchant of Venice,* Belmour in *Jane Shore,* Castalio in *The Orphan,* Charles Dudley in *The West Indian,* Claudio in *Much Ado About Nothing,* Colloony in *The Irishman in London,* Courtall in *The Belle's Stratagem,* the title role in *Douglas,* Edmund in *King Lear,* Gayless in *The Lying Valet,* Hephestion in *The Rival Queens,* Laertes in *Hamlet,* Lothario in *The Fair Penitent,* Merlin in *King Arthur,* the Prince in *Romeo and Juliet,* Prince Edward in *Richard III,* Romeo, Sir Lucius O'Trigger in *The Rivals,* and Wilson in *A Peep Behind the Curtain.*

Mrs Egan, according to the *Monthly Mirror* in 1801, was "at times successful in old maids." Some of her Edinburgh roles were Caroline in *The Irishman in London,* Dorinda in *The Beaux' Stratagem,* Lavinia in *The Fair Penitent,* the Maid in *The Rivals,* Miss Alton in *The Heiress,* Miss Godfrey in *The Lyar,* Miss Neville in *She Stoops to Conquer,* Miss Ogle in *The Belle's Stratagem,* Nerissa in *The Merchant* of *Venice*, and a Sea Nymph in *King Arthur*.

William Egan was seen in Manchester as Marlow in *She Stoops to Conquer* on 9 January 1797, Pisanio in *Cymbeline* in 1799, and a role in *Pizarro* in February 1800. Mrs Egan also acted in Manchester. A Shrewsbury bill for 6 October 1801 listed Egan as Modish in *The East Indian*, with his wife as Mrs Blaball, and Egan as Richard in *The King and the Miller of Mansfield*, with Mrs Egan as Kate. In 1801 Egan was also at Liverpool, and he acted second leads at Bristol in 1801–2. He appeared at Brighton in 1805 and shared the management of the Tenley theatre in the summer of 1810. He is known to have played Teague in *The Twin Rivals* at Bath on 31 March 1812, with Mrs Egan as Mrs Midnight. His activity at Bristol can be traced as late as 1816–17, but if he played at Bath until his death he may have continued to appear at Bristol, too. His wife seems not to have acted in London.

The Drama in 1822 reported that William Egan died in November 1822. Only one comment has been found about his acting: while he was in Edinburgh in the late 1790s, the local correspondent to the *Monthly Mirror* reported that Egan had "a good figure, a good voice, but further this deponent sayeth not."

Egerson, Mrs. *See* CUSSANS, MRS.

Egerton. *See also* EDGERTON.

Egerton, Mr [*fl.* 1734], *actor.*

On 28 August 1734 at York Buildings *The Orphan* was performed with Castalio played by a Mr Egerton, who boasted that he had acted the role some time before at the Haymarket Theatre. No previous or later appearances are known for him.

Egerton, Mrs [*fl.* 1728?–1758], *actress.*

Mrs Egerton—unless in the bill the printer made a mistake for "Egleton"—was first mentioned on 19 July 1728 when she played Aurelia in *The Wife's Relief* at the Lincoln's Inn Fields Theatre. The following 12 May 1729 she was at Drury Lane playing Arabella in *The Committee*—again, assuming no error in the bills. Not until 1733–34 was Mrs Egerton mentioned again. From April to August 1734 she acted at the Haymarket Theatre, her first part there being Mrs Sneak in *Don Quixote in England* on 5 April. Her other roles were Mother Punchbowl in *The Covent Garden Tragedy*, Minerva in *Penelope*, Mrs Chaunter in *The Beggar's Wedding*, Lady Bountiful in *The Beaux' Stratagem*, and the intriguing character of Mrs Buffskin in *The Humorous Election*.

Mrs Egerton turned up again in the summer of 1735 at Lincoln's Inn Fields and the Haymarket to play Lady Graveairs in *The Careless Husband*, the Doctor's Wife in *The Anatomist*, Mrs Motherly in *The Provok'd Husband*, Sukey in *The Beggar's Opera*, and the Steward's Wife (Mrs Clearaccount) in *The Twin Rivals*. The rest of the 1730s found her similarly trying to gain attention by playing at the minor houses, but her appearances were sporadic. Her more interesting roles were Mrs Mayoress in *Pasquin*, Constance in *The Twin Rivals*, Lucy in *The Recruiting Officer*, and Emilia in *Othello*.

In 1740–41 she was engaged by Drury Lane, her first role there being the Nurse in *Love for Love* on 9 September 1740. She stayed at that theatre through 1743–44 playing such roles as Mrs Sealand in *The Conscious Lovers*, the Nurse in *The Relapse*, Audrey in *As You Like It*, Mrs Wisely in *The Miser*, Mrs Security in *The Gamester*, and the Nurse in *The Fatal Marriage*. During this period she put in an appearance at Bartholomew Fair to play the Queen in *Darius* on 22 August 1741.

Mrs Egerton's name disappeared from the London playbills for several years. She was at the Jacob's Wells Theatre in Bristol in the summers of 1746 and 1747, and perhaps she did other performing in the provinces that we know not of. Advertisements in Bristol papers show that she acted Mrs Day in *The Committee* on 9 June 1746, the Aunt in *Sir Courtly Nice* on 14 July, and Lady Darling in *The Constant Couple* and a Lady of Pleasure in *The Harlot's Progress* on 20 August. She shared a benefit with two others in September 1746 and enjoyed a solo benefit in August 1747.

Years later, on 22 June 1758 at Drury Lane, *The Beggar's Opera* was performed for the benefit of a number of distressed actors and actresses, Mrs Egerton among them. Her share came to a pitiful £5 5*s*.

Egerton, Mrs ɪ*fl. 1770–1785*ɪ. *See* **AMBROSE, MISS, LATER MRS KELF.**

Egerton, Daniel *1772–1835, actor, manager.*

Daniel Egerton was born in London on 14 April 1772 and, though bred to the law, went into business near Whitechapel. He is said to have made his first stage appearance at the Royalty Theatre, probably in 1787. On 16 January 1792 he was at the Crown Inn, Islington, acting Inkle in *Inkle and Yarico*, and on the following 15 October at the Haymarket Theatre he appeared as Harcourt in *The Country Girl*. A Mrs Egerton, probably his wife, acted with him occasionally from that time until 1802. Not until 1796–97 did Egerton's name turn up in the London bills again. On 28 September 1796 at the Haymarket he acted Faulkland in *The Rivals*, and he was there again in January 1797 as Alfred in *The Battle of Eddington* and Lovemore in *Barnaby Brittle*.

On 5 June 1797 Egerton made his first appearance at Covent Garden, playing Milford in *The Road to Ruin*. The following 18 September he was in *The Country Girl* again at the Haymarket, and he returned there on 26 March 1798 in four roles: Rat-

Harvard Theatre Collection

DANIEL EGERTON, as Clytus

engraving by Thomson, after De Wilde

cliffe in *The Jew*, Tom Grog in *A Naval Interlude*, Major Sturgeon in *The Mayor of Garratt*, and Farmer Harrow in *The Ghost*. He made his second appearance at Covent Garden on 28 April as Horatio in *Hamlet*, then, advertised for some reason as making his first appearance at the Haymarket, Egerton played Bulcazin in *The Mountaineers* on 6 September.

He was at Birmingham on 4 June 1799, acting Captain Absolute in *The Rivals*. He acted at Edinburgh in 1799–1800, playing Ataliba in *Pizarro*, Captain Ambush in *The Young Quaker*, Frederick in *The Miser*, and Old Belfield in *The Brothers*, then he returned to Birmingham for the summer of 1800. He acted at Newcastle for the first time on 28 November 1801 (when he played Millamour in *Know Your Own*

Mind), and at Shields and Newcastle-upon-Tyne in 1802. When he acted Frederick in *The Poor Gentleman* on 17 May 1803 at Bath, he was described as from Newcastle and Edinburgh. He played Jaffeir to Miss Smith's Belvidera in *Venice Preserv'd* at the last performance at the old Orchard Street Theatre in Bath on 13 July 1805 and was in the cast of *Richard III* at the opening of the new Theatre Royal on Beaufort Square on 12 October. At Bath Egerton also offered such parts as Mr Oakley in *The Jealous Wife*, Rolla in *Pizarro*, and Lord Townly in *The Provok'd Husband*.

On 28 October 1809 he returned to Covent Garden to commence a long association with that house which by 1814–15 paid him £11 weekly. His roles there included Henry VIII, Tullus Aufidius in *Coriolanus*, Syphax in *Cato*, Clytus in *Alexander the Great*, and Lord Avondale in *The School of Reform*. About 1810 he married the actress Sarah Fisher (his second wife?), with whom he had acted at Bath for several years. Both Egertons performed at Covent Garden for many years, and without giving up his duties there Daniel played at Edinburgh in 1818–19 and became involved in 1821 in the management of the Olympic Theatre in London and from 1821 to 1824 in the management of Sadler's Wells. Mrs Egerton acted at the Olympic and at the Wells, though Daniel did not. The Olympic venture was not successful, but that did not deter Egerton in 1833 from joining William Abbot in the management of the Victoria Theatre (formerly the Coburg). Again, the venture was unsuccessful.

The *Observer* of 2 August 1835 reported the actor-manager's death on 22 July at the age of 64 (*recte* 63):

Mr. Egerton, for many years a most useful member of the Covent Garden Company, and Secretary of its Theatrical Fund, did not long survive his discharge from the Fleet prison, where he had been confined for several weeks in consequence of embarrassments created at

Harvard Theatre Collection

DANIEL EGERTON, as Hassarac

artist unknown

the Victoria Theatre. He lost the whole earnings of a long, frugal, and industrious life in his speculation at the Victoria. His mortal remains were buried on Wednesday [at St Luke, Chelsea] by the side of those of poor Blanchard, who preceded him only a few weeks . . . Egerton's personation of Henry the Eighth and Clytus will not soon be forgotten.

Despite the kind remarks on his acting by the *Observer*, other reports described Egerton as a portly 5' 10" man who was listless in his performances. Henry Crabb Robinson saw Egerton play Stukely in *The Gamester* on 21 April 1811 at Covent Garden and found him "below all criticism. . . . The putting such a man in such a character is an affront to the public."

Portraits of Daniel Egerton include:

1. As Clytus in *Alexander the Great*.

Watercolor by De Wilde. At the British Museum. Engraving by J. Thomson was published in *The Theatrical Inquisitor*, 1817.

2. As Clytus. Engraving by H. R. Cook after T. Wageman. Published in Oxberry's *New English Drama,* 1818.

3. As Hassarac in *The Forty Thieves*. Twopence-colored engraving published by O. Hodgson.

4. As Hassarac. Twopence-colored engraving published by J. L. Marks.

5. As Henry VIII. Engraving by J. Rogers after R. Page. Published in Oxberry's *Dramatic Biography*, 1825.

6. As Henry VIII. Engraving by Waldeck after De Wilde. Published by H. Berthoud in 1822.

Egerton, [**Mrs Daniel the first?**] [*fl.* 1792–1802], *actress.*

The Mrs Egerton whose career paralleled that of Daniel Egerton from 1792 through 1802 was probably his wife. She acted Lucy in *The Country Girl* at the Haymarket Theatre on 15 October 1792, Mrs Brittle in *Barnaby Brittle* there on 26 January 1797, and two parts at the same house on 26 March 1798: Mrs Sneak in *The Mayor of Garratt* and Dolly in *The Ghost*. She and Daniel were acting in the winter of 1802 at Shields and Newcastle-upon-Tyne, but her career cannot be traced after that year.

Egissielli and **Egizzieli.** *See* "Gizziello."

Egleton, John 1698–1727, *actor, manager.*

Born in 1698, John Egleton, Chetwood tells us, was "commonly call'd Baron Egleton, for taking that Title upon him in France, where he squandered away a small Patrimony. His Person was perfectly genteel, and [he was] a very pleasing Actor. . . ." It was presumably after his trip to France that Egleton began to follow a theatrical career in London. The earliest mention of him seems to be in the cast of the 1717 edition of *The Perjuror*, in which Egleton was named for Joseph Idle. The work was performed at the Lincoln's Inn Fields playhouse on 12 December 1717. The manuscript cast for *The Lady's Triumph*, a work presented at that house on 22 March 1718, listed Egleton as one of two Gentlemen, and the 1718 edition of *The Coquet*, a work performed on 19 April, cited him as Le Grange. He shared a benefit with three others on 3 May.

Egleton remained at Lincoln's Inn Fields throughout his career except for summer work at the fairs. Some of his roles over the years were Florio in *The Traytor*, Horatio in *The Younger Brother*, Pedro in *The Spanish Fryar*, Hemskirk in *The Beggar's Bush*, the Mad Scholar in *The Pilgrim*, Salisbury in *Richard II*, Malcolm in *Macbeth*, Polladore in *Cymbeline*, Easy in *The Fair Quaker of Deal*, Vernon in *1 Henry IV*, Stanmore in *Oroonoko*, Cheatly in *The Squire of Alsatia*, Dick in *The Confederacy*, Muley Zeydan in *Don Sebastian*, Fenton in *The Merry Wives of Windsor*, Diomedes in *Troilus and Cressida*, Froth in *The Double Dealer*, the Provost in *Measure for Measure*, Cornwall in *King Lear*, Catesby in *Richard III*, Roderigo in *Othello*, Gibbet in *The Stratagem*, Tinsel in *The Drummer*, Clodio in *Love Makes a Man*, Brazen in *The Recruiting Officer*, Antonio in *The Merchant of Venice*, Sir Novelty in *Love's Last Shift*, Renault in *Venice Preserv'd*, Razor in *The Provok'd Wife*, Harlequin in *The Emperor of the Moon*, Marplot in *The Busy Body*, Osric and Laertes in *Hamlet*, Sparkish in *The Country Wife*, Antonio in *The Rover*, and Mockmode in *Love and a Bottle*.

Egleton's activity at the summer fairs began on 5 September 1720, when he played an unnamed part in the droll *Friar Bacon* at the Leigh-Hall booth at Southwark Fair. He seems not to have returned until the summer of 1723, when he appeared at Bartholomew Fair and Southwark Fair—in both places acting at booths operated by

William Pinkethman, at whose theatre in Richmond Egleton may also have performed during the summer. On 8 September 1726 he was at Southwark Fair again, this time sharing the management of a booth "down the Queen's Arms Tavern Yard" with Spiller and playing Dame Strike Fire in *The Unnatural Parents*. He styled himself for the occasion "Baron Egleton." He had his own booth at the Fair on 27 September of the same year, at the lower end of Mermaid Court, next to the Marshalsea Gate, where he acted Marplot in *The Busy Body*—his last known appearance —for his own benefit; he advertised that he had been for three months under confinement, presumably for debt.

Other facts known about Egleton are few. In 1721 he married the actress Jane Giffard; in 1722, when Christopher Bullock died, Egleton inherited some of his foppish parts; and in 1724–25 Egleton's salary was £1 daily (?) plus a benefit which, as in other seasons, he shared with his wife. According to Chetwood, Egleton, "through a wild Road of Life . . . finish'd his Journey in the 29th year of his Age." John Egleton died early in 1727 and was buried at Dulwich on 19 February, according to a note in Lysons's "Collectanea" at the Folger Shakespeare Library.

Egleton, Mrs John. *See* GIFFARD, [MRS THOMAS?], JANE.

Egville. *See* D'EGVILLE.

Eichner, Ernst *1740–1777, instrumentalist, composer.*

Ernst Eichner was born at Mannheim on 9 February 1740. He became a proficient organist and harpsichordist and excelled on the bassoon. At a concert in Frankfurt-am-Main on 28 February 1771 he styled himself "Ducal Konzertmeister of Pfalzzweibrücken." Eichner spent some time in Paris, where some of his compositions were published, and came to England in 1773. On 19 April he played the harpsichord (and, possibly, the bassoon) at a concert at the Haymarket Theatre. After his London visit Eichner served at Potsdam as a member of the chapel of the Crown Prince (later Frederick William II). Eichner died at Potsdam early in 1777.

Eiffert, [Peter?], Philip [*fl. 1754–1785], *oboist.*

The oboist Eiffert who was active at Oxford from 1754 to 1773 and played in London occasionally from 1765 to 1785 was probably Peter Philip Eiffert, the executor and residuary legatee of the flutist and oboist Charles Weideman, whose will was written on 24 January 1781 and proved on 5 June 1782. The Faculty of Music at Oxford owns a portrait of Eiffert painted by Teeds and identifies the oboist as

Courtesy of the Faculty of Music, Oxford

PETER PHILIP EIFFERT

by Teeds

J. Philip Eiffert; the J may have been a scribal error for P. In the 1760s in London a printer's error turned Eiffert's name into "Eisent" on playbills.

Eiffert performed in concerts held in the Holywell Music Room at Oxford between 1754 and 1773, and perhaps during that period he presented his portrait to the Music School. In 1765–66 a Mr Eisent (or Esient), whom we take to be Eiffert, was an oboist in the band at the King's Theatre in London, and on 10 April 1766 he was featured in a *"Concerto on Oboe."* A decade later, on 8 June 1776, Eiffert accompanied Signora Gabrielli in a song introduced into the second act of *Antigono* at the King's. He is known to have again (or perhaps still) held a post as oboist in the band at the King's Theatre in 1783. Eiffert played in the Handel Memorial Concerts at Westminster Abbey and the Pantheon, in May and June 1784. He was a member of the Court of Assistants of the Royal Society of Musicians in 1785, the last mention of him in the Society's records being on 6 March that year.

Eisent. *See* **EIFFERT.**

Elard. *See* **ALLARD.**

Elcock, Mrs [fl. 1785], *actress.*
Mrs Elcock played Mrs Vixen in *The Beggar's Opera* at the Haymarket Theatre on 15 March 1785.

Eld, Mrs. *See* **ROGERS, MISS, LATER MRS ELD.**

Elderton. *See* **ELRINGTON.**

Eldred, Mr [fl. 1695–1696], *actor.*
At the Drury Lane Theatre under the management of Christopher Rich a Mr Eldred acted Decius in *Bonduca* in September 1695. He moved to the Lincoln's Inn Fields playhouse to act with Betterton's troupe in 1696, playing Dodge in *The City*

Bride in March and Humdrum in *Love's a Jest* in June.

Eleardi. *See* **EBERARDI.**

Eleonore, Mlle. *See* **SIMONET, LÉONORE.**

"Elephant Smith." *See* **UNDERHILL, CAVE.**

Eley, Christoph Friedrich *1756–1832, instrumentalist, composer.*
Christoph Friedrich Eley (or Ealy) was born in Hanover in July 1756. By 1787–88 he was principal violoncellist for the Academy of Ancient Music in London at a season salary of £12 12s. On 3 March 1793 he was proposed for membership in the Royal Society of Musicians, at which time he declared he was engaged as first violoncellist at Covent Garden Theatre and also played the violin, flute, and clarinet and taught other instruments. He stated that he was married and had two children: Ann, born on 18 June 1787, and Harriet, born on 18 October 1791. Later Christoph and his wife Ann had other children, according to the registers of St Paul, Covent Garden: Elizabeth Henrietta, born on 5 June and baptized on 30 June 1797; Rosenna, born on 22 April and baptized on 21 May 1795; and John Peter, born on 26 June 1800, baptized three days later, and buried on 22 January 1801.

Eley was unanimously elected to the Society on 2 June 1793. In 1793–94 he earned £105 for performing at the Drury Lane oratorios, and Doane's *Musical Directory* of 1794 indicated that Eley also played for the New Musical Fund, in the band of the Guards' Second Regiment, and at Covent Garden Theatre. He was living in 1794 at No 15, Russell Court, Drury Lane. From May 1794 through 1804 (with the exception of 1801) he played cello at the St Paul's concerts; on 17 November 1794 some of his music was used in *Her-*

cules and Omphale at Covent Garden; at
the Haymarket on 4 March 1795 he played
in *The Thespian Panorama*; and on 29 January 1799 some of the pantomime music
in *The Magic Oak* at Covent Garden was
composed by him. By the 1799–1800 season at that playhouse he was earning 8*s.*
4*d.* nightly. Eley died in 1832, and on
4 March of that year the Royal Society of
Musicians granted £12 for his funeral expenses. The fate of his wife and children
is not known.

According to Michael Kelly's *Reminiscences* there was a second musician named
Eley flourishing during C. F. Eley's time. In
preparing the extravaganza *Blue Beard* for
production at Drury Lane on 16 January
1798 Kelly, "not sufficiently conversant with
wind instruments" but wishing to insert a
passage of martial music, "therefore went
to Mr. Eley, a German, and Master of the
band of the guards. I took my melody to
him, and he put the parts to it most delight-
fully." The Eley in question was not
Christoph Friedrich. Many years later, a
dispute arising between Kelly and some
acquaintance as to the proper attribution of
the melody, Kelly asked the bandmaster to
settle the matter. He received a circumstantial reply, signed *R. T.* Eley of 48 Frith
Street, Soho, dated 21 July 1821, recalling
the incident and awarding the invention of
the melody to Kelly.

Elezinti, Signora   [*fl. 1761–1762*],
singer.

Signora Elezinti was, according to *The
London Stage*, a singer in the opera company at the King's Theatre in the Haymarket in 1761–62, but no roles are known
for her.

Elford, Mrs   [*fl. 1700–1706*], *dancer.*

Mrs Elford was first noticed in London
playbills on 5 July 1700 when she danced
an entry at the Lincoln's Inn Fields Theatre, though the records for the early years
of the eighteenth century are very incom-

plete, and she may have performed earlier
and more frequently than we know. She
was mentioned as dancing at the same playhouse on 21 October 1701, and beginning
with the 1702–3 season she was regularly
cited. That season she danced a popular
Wedding Dance with L'Abbé and *Blouza-
bella* with Prince and appeared also in unnamed numbers. A document in the Public
Record Office concerning the establishment
of a performing company about 1703 included Mrs Elford among the dancers at a
salary of £40 yearly.

In December and January of 1703–4
she performed at Drury Lane, but she completed the season back at Lincoln's Inn
Fields and appeared there off and on
through 1705. One of her students, Mrs
Bruce, danced there in September 1705.
The spring of 1706 found Mrs Elford dancing at the new Queen's Theatre in the Haymarket, one of her last notices there being
on 13 June 1706 when she was seen in
a *"Chacoon"* and a *"Passacail."* Though
Mrs Elford may have been related in some
way to the singer Richard Elford, she was
apparently not his wife.

Elford, Richard   *c. 1676–1714, singer,
composer.*

Richard Elford was born about 1676. He
was trained as a chorister at Lincoln Cathedral and when his voice changed to
countertenor, he was appointed to the choir
of Durham Cathedral. He is said to have
come to London about 1700 to attempt a
stage career, but his ungainly figure and
clumsy actions ruined his chances. There is
no record of any roles for him, but the
documentation for this period is sparse.
Elford did, however, compose a number of
popular songs which were sung at the theatres, one being *Ah! cruel Damon, cease to
teaze*, which Mrs Hodgson sang at Lincoln's
Inn Fields and which was published about
1700. Another of his songs, untitled, was
sung by her in a production of *Tamerlane*
and published about 1702.

Elford was sworn a Gentleman of the Chapel Royal, appointed a vicar-choral of St Paul's, and made a lay vicar of Westminster Abbey. The *Diverting Post* of 25 November 1704 reported that he had gone to Winchester to sing in a concert with Richardson, and in December 1706 he and Leveridge sang, somewhere, "A New Ode, or Dialogue, between Mars the God of War and Plutus" and "From Glorious Toyls of War"—both published in *Wit and Mirth* in 1719. At court on 6 February 1713 Elford sang in a presentation of Handel's birthday ode for Queen Anne.

Richard Elford died at the age of 38 on 29 October 1714 at his house in Queen Street, Westminster; he was buried in the West Cloister of Westminster Abbey on 1 November. Administration of his estate was granted on 9 November to John Peachey for Elford's infant children Anne and Bridget, Elford's wife Catherine renouncing. Elford had married Catherine, the daughter of George London, on 10 December 1706 in the Chapel of London House, Aldgate Street. She followed Elford to the grave on 15 December 1715. As late as 1730 Elford's anthems were being published and he was still remembered as "the late Famous Mr. Elford," singer and composer.

Eliot. *See* ELLETT, ELLIOT, ELLIOTT.

Elisi, Filippo ₁*fl.* 1760–1766₁, *singer.*
On 25 August 1760 Signora Mattei announced her opera performers for the coming opera season at the King's Theatre; among them was Filippo Elisi, "the first singer in Italy." Elisi became ill shortly after his arrival in England and was not heard until 16 December, when he sang Teseo in *Arianna e Teseo.* On 21 January 1761 Thomas Gray wrote about him in a letter:

Elisi is finer than anything, that has been here in your memory: yet, as I suspect, has been finer than he is. he appears to be near forty, a little-pot-bellied & thick-shoulder'd, otherwise no bad figure; his action proper & not ungraceful. we have heard nothing, since I remember Operas, but eternal passages, divisions, & flights of execution. of these he has absolutely none, whether merely from judgement, or a little from age, I will not affirm. his point is expression, & to that all the graces, & ornaments he inserts (wch are few and short) are evidently directed. he goes higher (they say) than Farinelli, but then this celestial note you do not hear above once in a whole Opera; & he falls from this altitude at once to the mellowest, softest, strongest tones (about the middle of his compass) that can be heard.

Elisi's only other known role during 1760–61 (casts were not always listed in the bills) was the title part in *Tito Manlio* on 7 February 1761.

In 1761–62 he sang Poro in *Alessandro nell' Indie* on 13 October 1761, used *Arianna e Teseo* (with alterations) for his benefit on 1 March 1762, and participated in the benefit concert for "decay'd" musicians and their families on 11 May. He returned to the King's Theatre for the 1765–66 season (the Duchess of Northumberland wrote that Elisi "has lost his Voice & is grown fat as a porpoise") and sang in *Eumene* on 23 November 1765, possibly in *Sofonisba* on 25 January 1766, and *Eumene* (altered) for his benefit on 13 March. He also appeared in the benefit concert on 10 April for impoverished musicians.

Elkins, Sarah, née Miller ₁*fl.* 1794₁, *singer.*
Doane's *Musical Directory* of 1794 listed Mrs Sarah Elkins, late Miss Miller, as a singer living in West Street, Seven Dials. She participated in Handelian performances at Westminster Abbey and concerts presented by the Longacre Society.

Ellard, Thomas ₁*fl.* 1760–c.1795₁, *actor.*

Thomas Ellard acted at the Smock Alley Theatre in Dublin in 1760–61, at the Crow Street Theatre there in 1761–62, 1763–64, and 1764–65, and at Cork in 1761, 1762, and 1763. He appeared with Foote's company at the Haymarket Theatre in London during the summer of 1767, playing Albany in *King Lear* on 15 July and Gratiano in *Othello* on 24 July. Ellard performed in Norwich in 1767 either before or after his London engagement. The Ellard who acted clown parts and other small roles at Bristol in 1768, 1770, and 1771 was probably Thomas. A Mrs Ellard, presumably Thomas's wife, acted in Dublin from 1761 to 1766 but seems not to have appeared in London.

Charles Lee Lewes in his *Memoirs* said that Ellard was a useful performer and told a tale of how Ellard married a young lady from Exeter and built for her at Teignmouth a fine house. Ellard was still living at Teignmouth about 1795.

Ellen. *See* ELLETT.

Ellerson, Mrs ₁fl. 1714₁, *actress*.

Mrs Ellerson played Dorothea in *Injured Virtue* at Richmond in the summer of 1714 with a troupe styled the Duke of Southampton and Cleaveland's Servants. The same group, apparently, performed the play again on 1 November 1714 at the King's Arms Tavern in Southwark.

Ellett. *See also* ELLIOT *and* ELLIOTT.

Ellett, Jone ₁fl. 1671–1672₁, *tirewoman*.

Jone Ellett was readmitted to the King's Company on 4 July 1672, according to warrants in the Lord Chamberlain's accounts. She was apparently discharged at some earlier date, but the circumstances are not known. *The London Stage* records her in the 1671–72 season as Mrs "Jane Ellen."

Elliot. *See also* ELLETT *and* ELLIOTT.

Elliot, Mr ₁fl. 1746–1759₁, *house servant*.

Mr Elliot (or Elliott) was a house servant at Covent Garden Theatre from the 1746–47 season through 25 May 1759, his last mention in the bills. His benefit tickets were regularly accepted in May of each year, and we know his income on two such occasions: on 22 May 1747 he received two-thirds value for a total of £3 17s. 6d., and on 7 May 1750 he received half-value for a total of £4 12s. 6d. His daily salary was not recorded, nor was his job at the theatre specified. He was apparently not the Elliott who worked at Drury Lane in 1747; for their two careers appear to overlap.

Elliot, Mr ₁fl. 1778?–1784₁, *actor*.

Though Mr Elliot was billed at Covent Garden on 16 December 1779 as "A Young Gentleman" making his first appearance on any stage in the title role in *Oroonoko*, he may have been the actor of that name who appeared at Kilkenny in Ireland on 18 February 1778. The only other reference to Elliot in the London bills was on 20 August 1784 when he played Kirk, the Lieutenant of the Tower, in *Lord Russell* at Drury Lane.

Elliot, Mr ₁fl. 1799–1814₁, *singer, actor*.

Mr Elliot sang in the chorus of Villagers in *Feudal Times* on 4 February 1799 at Drury Lane Theatre and in the chorus of *Pizarro* at the same house on 24 May. At the Haymarket Theatre on 28 August, advertised as making his first appearance (first in a speaking role, presumably), Elliot played Dermot in *The Poor Soldier*. In the 1799–1800 season at Drury Lane he sang in the choruses of *Blue-Beard*, *The Tempest*, *Pizarro*, *Lodoiska*, *The Egyptian Festival*, and *De Montfort*. The *Monthly Mirror* in September 1799 identified Elliot as "brother to the little boy so well known in the musical world" — the Master Elliot who sang often in the years from 1795 to 1801. The brothers sang at Willis's Rooms about February 1801, and Mr Elliot was again in the chorus at Drury Lane in the 1800–1801 season. Elliot was a Georgian Guard in *Shamacda* at the Royal Circus on 11 April 1814.

Elliot, Mrs   [*fl.* 1716–1726]. *See* **Aylett, Mrs.**

Elliot, Mrs   [*fl.* 1780–1794], *actress.*
Mrs Elliot, described as "A Lady" making her first appearance on any stage, played Lady Townly in *The Provok'd Husband* at Drury Lane on 20 January 1780. On 11 November 1782, advertised as making her second appearance on any stage, she acted at the Crow Street Theatre in Dublin. In 1785 she performed at Brighton, and she was almost certainly the Mrs Elliot who played Harriet in *The Guardian* and Touchwood in *The Belle's Stratagem* at the Theatre Royal in Edinburgh in March 1791. In 1794 she acted Catherine in *The Siege of Belgrade* at Woodbridge. She was probably not the Mrs Elliot who had appeared at Kilkenny on 18 February 1778, though the two women may have been related.

Elliot, Master   [*fl.* 1795–1801], *singer, composer.*
Master Elliot was one of the principal singers in the Handel oratorio concert at Covent Garden on 20 February 1795. He sang again on 11 March in the *Messiah* and offered "Happy Iphis" from *Jeptha* in the concert on 25 March. On 12 February 1796 he performed in *Alexander's Feast* and on 17 February he sang "Come and trip it" in *L'Allegro ed il Penseroso*. He continued appearing regularly in the oratorios at Covent Garden through 1800.

He also played Henry in *The Chimney Corner* at Drury Lane on 7 October 1797 and was at Ranelagh Gardens with Miss Capper on 18 May 1798. Master Elliot sang in the first performance of Thomas Busby's

The Prophecy at the Haymarket on 29 March 1799, and he "displayed great merit," said the *Monthly Mirror*, when he sang in *Ruth* in the Concert Rooms at the King's Theatre on 22 April 1799. He participated in the first performances of Haydn's *Creation* on 28 March and of Busby's *Britannia* on 16 June 1800 at Covent Garden. He and his brother sang in the concerts at Willis's Rooms about February 1801. The Master Elliot we have been following is said to have become a glee composer in later years.

Elliot, Ann   1743–1769, *actress, singer.*
Ann Elliot was born on 16 November 1743, according to her tombstone inscription at Tunbridge. Her father Richard was a sexton there, and her mother's name was Mary. Ann used the name Miss Hooper when she first came to London, and it is probable that she had turned prostitute before she attracted the attention of the actor-author Arthur Murphy about 1760 or 1761. He seems certainly to have made her his mistress, tutored her in acting, and brought her onto the stage for the first time.

On 22 June 1761 Garrick wrote to Murphy about a young actress, apparently Miss Elliot. She had received a hearing from Garrick on Murphy's recommendation, but Garrick wrote him afterwards that "She does not appear to Me to have a Genius for ye Stage. . . ." Garrick found her powers weak, her voice indifferent, her pronunciation erroneous, and her face formed to create passion (which it certainly did in Murphy) but not to express it. He advised her not to appear on the stage at all; yet if her heart was fixed on it and she had Murphy's favor, he said he would consent to giving her a trial at no salary in the fall but could make no commitments for the winter.

That response dampened hopes for the fall of 1761 but did not deter Murphy from bringing out Ann as Maria in his play *The Citizen* on 2 July 1761 at Drury Lane, rented for the summer by Murphy and Foote. She was advertised simply as a "young gentlewoman," but the bill for 9 July, when she repeated the role for the fourth time, told the town that she was Miss Elliot. The only other part she played that summer was Colombine in *The Wishes* on 27 July. She was given a solo benefit on 5 August, for which she chose *The Citizen.*

Murphy said his farce gained its success from Ann's performance, but whether that was because of her natural talent or because he tailored the role of Maria to suit her abilities is not certain. She gained much attention, however, and played Maria frequently throughout her career. Edward Thompson in *The Meretriciad* in 1761 included her among the notorious women of London:

> Behold, what's here! a lovely form of
> joy,
> A fairer hellen, for a greater Troy;
> How could pollution such a Genius wed?
> A genius worthy of the chastest bed.
> How came she lost in ignorance and
> rust?
> A common prostitute, to common lust;
> Mur—y if e'er thy deeds, or Summer
> plays,
> Deserv'd encomiums, or the publick's
> praise,
> 'tis now, for introducing to the light,
> The peerless Elliot, for the Town's de-
> light. . . .

Then Thompson described "majestic Elliot" seen "Above the rest" in a procession of sluts.

After her success in the summer of 1761 Miss Elliot went to Dublin, with Murphy's recommendation. Cumberland recorded the fact and noted that though Ann was uneducated, she had "great natural talents, and played the part of Maria in her patron's farce of The Citizen with admirable spirit and effect." She acted at the Crow Street Theatre and then returned to London for the end of the summer season in 1762

Harvard Theatre Collection

ANN ELLIOT

engraving by Sherlock, after Kettle

at the Haymarket under the management of Samuel Foote. There she played Mrs Harlowe in *The Old Maid* on 10 August, the title role in *Polly Honeycomb* on 30 August, and, for her benefit on 7 September, her favorite part of Maria.

John Beard offered Ann an engagement at Covent Garden for 1762–63. She began with Cherry in *The Stratagem* and Mrs Harlowe in *The Old Maid* on 20 September 1762. During the season she was seen in a number of important comedy roles: Phillis in *The Conscious Lovers*, Edging in *The Careless Husband*, Miss Biddy in *Miss In Her Teens*, Bizarre in *The Inconstant*, Lady Betty in *The Careless Husband* (for her benefit on 16 April 1763), and Berinthia in *The Relapse*. Critical response was favorable. The *Theatrical Review* in 1763 said that Miss Elliot "has infinite vivacity: She is admirably adapted to the pert and sprightly parts of comedy; but

ANN ELLIOT, as Juno

engraving by Watson, after Kettle

with respect to delicacy and deportment, we can by no means allow her equal to those of a nature more elevated and refined." The *Smithfield Rosciad* in the same year called her "flutt'ring Elliot, wanton Hen,/ One Thousand paramours attend her train,/ Who from her piercing eye receive disdain."

Except for a season off in 1765–66, when Ann made only a single appearance (at Drury Lane in *The Citizen*), she stayed at Covent Garden through the 1766–67 season. To her repertoire she added Estifania in *Rule a Wife and Have a Wife*, Flora in *The Country Lasses*, Lucinda in *No One's Enemies But His Own*, Lady Rockett in *What We Must All Come To*, Prue in *Love for Love*, a role in *False Concord*, Kitty Carrot in *The What D'Ye Call It* (with a song, " 'Twas when the seas were roaring"), Mrs Sullen in *The Stratagem*, Millamant in *The Way of the World*, Termagant in *The Upholsterer*, Calista in *The Fair Penitent* (her only attempt at tragedy), and Ann in *The School for Guardians* (Murphy's version of *The Country Wife*, which he gave to Ann in 1766).

Ann Elliot's Calista brought a friendly comment from *The Court Miscellany* in 1766. The critic said that not much that season was "worth mentioning except Miss Elliot in the character of Calista; who, to the reserve of voice, which may be got the better of, has, we think, very great merit as a tragic actress." In 1766–67 Ann received two benefits: one on 13 January 1767 which netted her only £24 9s. 6d. and one on 18 February, when *The School for Guardians* was performed, which brought her only £66 4s. The devoted Murphy had given Ann his benefit night and his play, but to little avail. To compensate for her low receipts at her benefits the Covent Garden management took some of the house charges and gave her a gift of £21 on 24 March. It was, perhaps, a going-away present, for her last appearance on the London stage seems to have been on 7 April 1767, when she played Maria in *The Citizen*.

It was a bit late for the critics to offer comments, but Kelly's *Thespis* in 1767 called Miss Elliot attractive, soft, and delicate but "circumscrib'd in voice." *The Rational Rosciad* in the same year predicted that "Elliot, no subterfuge will need / merit like her's is certain to succeed." The irony was doubtless apparent to all. Ann had established a liaison as early as 1766 with the Duke of Cumberland.

Murphy's "heart was exhausted of Love by Miss Elliot," according to *Thraliana*. Yet he and Ann seem to have remained friendly. The charitable Duke arranged matters so that Murphy could visit Ann on occasion; he also provided for Ann during her last years, when she was in poor health, and gave her most of the money she later distributed in her will. But the *Town and Country Magazine* (1769) informs us that the Duke deserted her shortly before she died.

Ann is said to have offered Murphy most of her money, but he refused it. He was willing, however, to serve with George Garth as one of her executors when she drew up her will on 3 April 1769. Ann gave her address as Greek Street, Soho, in the parish of St Ann, Westminster. Her will mentioned a mortgage given her by Cumberland and his brother, the Duke of Gloucester. Some of the principal had already been paid, and "in consequence thereof the sum of one thousand pounds has been invested in the funds to my use by my good and worthy friend George Garth." She also owned "a considerable quantity of household furniture," which was given to her by Cumberland. She requested that after the Duke discharged the rest or any part of his indebtedness to her, the money should be invested in the funds by her executors for the benefit of her estate. To her father and stepmother she left interest on £500; to her sister Mary Elliot she gave £500 and all her household furniture except jewelry; to her "sister" Mary Clarke she gave the interest on £500; to her aunt Elizabeth Searle of Deptford she left £100; and to her nephew Augustus Corke (Clarke?) she left £500—when he should reach the age of 21—for educational purposes. She asked her executors to apprentice her nephew to a trade. The rest of her estate was to be divided between her niece Nancy Corke (Clarke?) and Elizabeth Garth of New York. In a codicil Ann bequeathed her clothes to her sister Mary Elliot, £50 to Margaret Gallon of Piccadilly, and £20 to her maid Betty Stevens.

A clipping in Lysons's "Collectanea" at the Folger Shakespeare Library states that Ann Elliot died at her house in Greek Street, Soho, at about 10:30 in the morning of 30 May 1769 after a long and painful illness. The Duke of Cumberland followed a dying request by Ann that her mother's remains should be removed from their burial place in Tunbridge and the remains of mother and daughter be interred together in the same vault in the churchyard of the Tunbridge parish church in Kent. Her epitaph read:

> Of matchless form, adorn'd with Wit
>   refin'd,
> A feeling heart, and an enlighten'd Mind,
> Of softest Manners, Beauty's fairest
>   bloom,
> Here Elliot lies, and moulders in her
>   tomb!

Murphy helped prove her will on 15 June 1769. The following 7 December at Covent Garden a benefit was held for Ann's creditors. Either Ann had exaggerated the value of her estate when she drew up her will, or the Duke had not discharged his indebtedness to her. In any case, it is clear that Ann was not possessed of the money she tried to give away.

T. Kettle painted at least three portraits of Ann Elliot. A miniature after Kettle is in the Garrick Club, and an engraving of it by Sherlock was used in Foote's *Life of Arthur Murphy* in 1811. Another portrait, showing Ann as Juno, was engraved by J. Watson and published by R. Sayer. A third, picturing her as Minerva, was engraved by J. Saunders and published in 1772. The Saunders engraving is incorrectly listed in the *British Museum Catalogue of Printed Engravings* as after a painting by R. Cosway.

Elliot, John ₁fl. 1783–1823₁, *singer*.
Ita Hogan in *Anglo-Irish Music* states that John Elliot (or Elliott) sang at concerts in Dublin from 1783. Doane's *Musical Directory* in 1794 listed Elliot as living in London at No 25, Little Newport Street, Soho, and as a tenor who sang for the Choral Fund and the Longacre Society. By the 1801–2 theatrical season Elliot was singing in the chorus at Drury Lane for £1 5s. weekly, a fee he continued receiving until the fall of 1807. Hogan places him again in Dublin after that, serving as the master of the choristers at Christ Church until 1823.

Elliot, Thomas ₁fl. 1795–1815₁, *singer, organ builder*.
Doane's *Musical Directory* of 1794 listed Thomas Elliot, of No 10, Sutton Street, Soho Square, as a bass singer and builder of organs. Elliot sang for the New Musical Fund, the Choral Fund, the Longacre Society, the Cecilian Society, the Surrey Chapel Society, and in the oratorios at Westminster Abbey and Drury Lane Theatre. He was still a subscriber to the New Musical Fund in 1815.

Elliot, William ₁fl. 1794–1800?₁, *singer*.
Doane's *Musical Directory* of 1794 listed William Elliot of No 9, St Martin's Court, St Martin's Lane, as a tenor who sang for the Handelian Society and at the oratorios at Westminster Abbey and the Covent Garden Theatre. About 1800 the song *Oft let me wander* was published with the notation that it had been sung by W. Elliott—probably our subject.

Elliott. *See also* **ELLETT** and **ELLIOT**.

Elliott, Mr ₁fl. c. 1698?–1715₁, *actor*.
The Mr Elliott who was active in Dublin about 1698 was perhaps the Elliott who acted Jack Stanmore in *Oroonoko* at Lincoln's Inn Fields Theatre on 3 February 1715.

Elliott, Mr [*fl. 1747*], *house servant?*

A Mr Elliott, apparently not the same person as the Elliot who worked at Covent Garden at this time, shared a benefit at Drury Lane with six others on 18 May 1747.

Elliott, Miss [*fl. 1786*], *actress.*

All that is known of Miss Elliott is that on 28 October 1786 she appeared in an unnamed new pantomime at the Royal Circus.

Elliott, Nicholas [*fl. 1669*], *musician.*

Nicholas Elliott and four other musicians were ordered apprehended on 17 December 1669 for performing music without licenses.

Elliott, Susanah [*fl. 1671–1674?*], *actress?*

The London Stage lists Susanah Elliott as a member of the King's Company in 1671–72. A warrant in the Lord Chamberlain's accounts shows that she was readmitted to the troupe on 5 March 1673, apparently after having been discharged for some reason. It is likely that the following entry in the St Paul, Covent Garden, registers explains Susanah Elliott's disappearance from theatrical accounts after 1673: on 13 May 1674 a John Ratie married a Susaña Elliott.

Ellis. *See also* EDDIS.

Ellis, Mr [*fl. 1767–1771*], *house servant.*

Mr Ellis was paid £1 4s. 6d. on 19 February 1767 for scouring the men's dressing room at Covent Garden. Thereafter, every May through 1771, Ellis was listed in the bills as one of several whose benefit tickets would be accepted at the door. In most years he received only half value; and his income from this supplementary source was pitifully slender (£2 2s. in 1768, for instance, and £2 1s. in 1770). His weekly salary is not known, but it would have been a pittance, considering his lowly job. His name was last mentioned on 27 May 1771 when his benefit tickets were accepted.

Ellis, Mr [*fl. 1789–1814*], *dresser.*

The Drury Lane accounts show occasional payments of 9s. weekly to Mr Ellis, one of the men's dressers, from 1789–90 through 1813–14.

Ellis, John *d. c. 1812, puppeteer, scene painter, writer.*

In 1776 in Abbey Street, Dublin, string puppet performances were presented by Kane O'Hara with the assistance of the scene painter John Ellis. Ellis had been apprenticed to a cabinet-maker, but had shown skill in perspective painting and had devoted his career to designing scenery for puppet shows. The Dublin Society awarded him a silver palette for his work. He married the daughter of a grocer, against her father's will, and came to England in 1776. He presented shows at the Patagonian Theatre, Exeter 'Change, the Strand, with the help of the Drury Lane comedian Stoppelaer.

Ellis was the subject of a letter from T. Wilkes to Garrick on 7 September 1776:

Macklin made an offer to Ellis of a piece of his writing for his puppet-show, provided he would let him be a *partner*, which he refused, and in a few days after, Mr Harris returned Ellis's plan of the pantomime, &c., and has, I am told, refused to pay him a shilling of what he agreed with him. . . . Macklin was most certainly the occasion of this.

Thus Ellis, it would seem, also wrote entertainments for live actors, as a sideline.

On the death of his father-in-law, Ellis returned to Dublin. By 1790 he had opened a shop in Mary Street where he exhibited works by Irish artists. He had a son who made a career in London forging Canalettos. Someone named Ellis—perhaps John or his son—had a company of puppeteers at

Bartholomew Fair in London in 1800–1801. John Ellis died about 1812 or soon thereafter.

Ellis, Rebecca, later Mrs James Burney *c.1681–c.1720, actress?*

Fanny Burney's grandfather, James Burney (1678–1749), married Rebecca Ellis about 1697 when he was 19 and she 16. Fanny stated that Miss Ellis had been an actress at Goodman's Fields Theatre, but that playhouse did not open until 1729, and perhaps Fanny was thinking of the Lincoln's Inn Fields playhouse, which was in use from 1695 to 1714 before being rebuilt. Tradition has it that James Burney was disinherited by his father for marrying Miss Ellis and that by her he had several children. According to the "Worcester" Journal of Henry Edward Burney, Rebecca Ellis was "a genteel and handsome young lady . . . who brought [James Burney] fifteen children" and died shortly before Burney's second marriage in 1720.

Elliston, Robert William *1774–1831, actor, singer, manager, playwright.*

One of the most diversified talents and one of the most perplexing personalities of his time, Robert William Elliston was born on 7 April 1774 in Orange Street, Bloomsbury. His father, Robert Elliston, a watchmaker, was the son of a farmer of Gedgrave, near Orford, on the Suffolk coast. Little is known of Robert William's mother, except that she died of "a consumption" on 27 November 1798, in her forty-sixth year. His father's eldest brother, William Elliston, who received his degree from St John's, Cambridge, in 1754, and in 1760 was elected Master of Sidney College, Cambridge, was to become a most important influence in his young nephew's education and care. Another brother of his father had been a naval commander, and a sister was married to the Rev Thomas Martyn, also of Sidney College and professor of botany.

National Portrait Gallery

ROBERT W. ELLISTON

by Harlow

At the age of nine, Robert was placed in St Paul's School by his uncle William Elliston, who recognized the boy's intelligence and was determined to salvage him from an environment dominated by an indolent and sottish father. About the same time, Robert's father moved the family to Charles Street, Covent Garden, where the boy continued to lodge during school months. During holidays he visited his uncles at Cambridge or traveled with them. Although he was intended for the clergy, Elliston's talents and ambitions for the stage began to become irrepressible. In 1790, at the age of 16, he received great applause for his original thesis oration at school. He took tuition in French at an evening academy kept by a Madame Cotterille in the Strand, near Bedford Street, where he met a fellow student, the young Charles Mathews, and where students were allowed to act plays, in English, several times a year. In December 1790, in Madame Cotterille's rooms over a pastry shop, he acted Pyrrhus and Mathews acted Phoenix in *The Distrest Mother*; several months later he played Chamont and Mathews played the Chaplain in *The Orphan*. Soon Elliston became a favorite in private theatricals at the Lyceum Rooms, where he performed Young Norval in *Douglas* and Pierre in *Venice Preserv'd*.

In his *Memoirs of Robert William Elliston* (1845), George Raymond tells of Elliston, in the early morning hours of a day in the spring of 1791, sneaking from his father's house to take the coach to Bath, determined to launch a professional stage career. The same story is told in earlier biographical notices of Elliston which appeared in the *Monthly Mirror* in September 1796 and in the *Theatrical Inquisitor* for April 1813. Perhaps the details of Raymond's account are romanticized, but there is no doubt that Elliston went to Bath, leaving behind his schooling and probably the good will of his uncles. His introduction to Dimond, then manager of the Bath theatre, failed to obtain him an immediate engagement, so the seventeen-year-old lad took a job as a clerk in a lottery office. Before long, however, he got his opportunity and on 21 April 1791 made his "first appearance upon any stage," as Tressel in *Richard III*. The local press reported:

A young gentleman, whose name we are not yet in possession of, but whose connections, we understand, are of the highest respectability in the University of Cambridge, sustained the character of *Tressell*. He displayed considerable ability—far greater, indeed, than could have been anticipated from his age. . . .

Elliston acted the role again at Bristol on 25 April, and three days later he played Arviragus in *Cymbeline* at Bath. Impressed by the performances, Mr Wallis, the father of the Bath actress Elizabeth Wallis (later Mrs Campbell), recommended the boy to Tate Wilkinson, manager of the York circuit, who engaged him immediately and put him on as Eumenes (not Dorilas as Raymond states) in *Merope* at Leeds on 30 May 1792. In a letter to Wallis, cited by Raymond, the circuit manager gave his endorsement:

He is already very generally liked, and, being a sensible youth, gives the best evidence of becoming an improving actor. His features and voice are very pleasing, and his legs and arms good, but his powers are not extensive. He is of service to me; and if he always behaves as well as he has conducted himself with me, he will be an acquisition wherever he goes. He has not the common fault of young people—rant, rant. A little more energy and variety would do him no harm.

For three seasons, 1791, 1792, and 1793, Elliston remained a member of Wilkinson's company at York. He showed no extraordinary distinction, but received excellent schooling in playing about 44 different roles. Dissatisfied with his progress, he returned to London in May 1793, having made it up with his uncle William Elliston, and through Dr Richard Farmer and George Steevens he was introduced to John Philip Kemble in July. Kemble sent him off to study Romeo in preparation for the opening of the new Drury Lane Theatre, which was scheduled for the spring of the following year. Elliston applied to Dimond, who then happened to be playing at Richmond for the summer, for a Bath engagement, and in September 1793 he began an uninterrupted association with Bath which lasted until 1804. He played Romeo during race week, September 1793, with "sound and well-cultivated understanding," according to the *Bath Herald* of 28 September 1793. His voice was full of "force and melody." Quickly he became a favorite of Bath audiences, and at his benefit on 6 March 1794 he made £102, compared to totals of £77 for Dimond, £81 for Mrs Keasberry, and £92 for Blisset at their re-

Harvard Theatre Collection

ROBERT W. ELLISTON, as Falstaff

engraving by Gear

spective benefits. In that first season with Dimond's company, Elliston had acted more than 40 parts.

Elliston did not go to Drury Lane in 1794 but remained a Bath regular. According to the *Monthly Mirror* of September 1796, Elliston had turned down an offer from Kemble of 40s. per week, having decided that Bath offered more opportunity for experience. During those early years at Bath he played a variety of first-line roles, including Macheath in *The Beggar's Opera*, Horatio in *The Fair Penitent*, Meadows in *The Deaf Lover*, and the title roles in *Oroonoko* and *King Lear*. He also acted at Bristol in 1793–94, 1794–95, and 1795–96.

On 1 June 1796 Elliston was married at Bath Abbey to a teacher of dancing who is given in the marriage register as Elizabeth Randell, of Walcot, Bath, but whose surname in various memoirs of Elliston is given as Rundell. She was an assistant at a dancing academy at Bath which was operated by Catherine Flemming, who, according to Raymond, also had a strong interest in Elliston. Elliston's marriage had originally been intended for midsummer, but was rescheduled because he had agreed to play for Colman at the Haymarket Theatre in London during June. On the night of the marriage day the actor Murphy interrupted the performance of *The Wheel of Fortune* on the Bath stage to congratulate Elliston and drew thunderous applause.

With the approval of Dimond, his Bath manager, Elliston made his London debut at the Haymarket on 25 June 1796 as Octavian in *The Mountaineers* and Vapour in *My Grandmother*. The reviewer for the *Monthly Mirror* said that "his reception was highly flattering," and that "Louder applause never resounded within the walls of a theatre." In a full critique of the debut by the *Monthly Mirror*, Elliston was described as having a figure of medium build and of fine proportions, a voice perfect in gradations of tone, and mature judgment. His action, however, was "too liberal, but by no means inelegant," and his deportment was too "unrestrained" for that particular character. He was judged as better suited for the playfulness and vivacity of comedy than for "the loftier and more forcible exhibitions" of tragedy which required "a flexibility of feature, especially of the *eyebrow* not possessed by Mr. Elliston." "On the whole," concluded the critic, Elliston would be "a vast addition to the London stage, increasing both its professional and moral reputation." Another reviewer in the *How Do You Do?* (27 August 1796) also found Elliston to be an actor of "superior merit." Although he lacked polish, he possessed "the strong features of professional discrimination to point him out as an actor of great promise." Compared to Kemble,

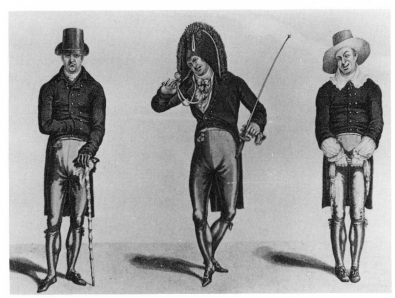

Harvard Theatre Collection

ROBERT W. ELLISTON, as three characters in *Three and the Deuce*

artist unknown

who had originally created the role of Octavian, and had "wanted speed occasionally" during the last act, Elliston had the opposite fault of hurrying along too rapidly.

After repeating Octavian on 28 June, Elliston acted Sheva in *The Jew* on 30 June with enormous success. He played Octavian again on 1 July and Sheva the following night and then returned to play at Bath and Bristol for the rest of July and most of August, clearing £100 at his Bristol benefit. Colman, who was anxious to have Elliston return to the Haymarket as soon as possible, wrote to him on 14 July 1796 a most flattering letter: "I shall be very happy to see you again the moment your engagement will permit you to return. I will either defer settling terms till we meet, or fix them with you by letter. If you prefer the latter, pray propose, and nothing that I am able to effect shall be left undone to meet your wishes." He offered to coach Elliston in Hamlet—"of whom you seem a little afraid"—which he felt was well within Elliston's abilities.

Elliston returned to the Haymarket to act Octavian again on 12, 15, and 22 August. That month he wrote to his uncle at Oxford of his preparations to play Sir Edward Mortimer in *The Iron Chest*, Colman's musical drama. It had been a failure on its first appearance at Drury Lane on 12 March 1796, according to the author's acrimonious charge in the preface to the printed edition, because Kemble had played the role so badly. Elliston told his uncle:

It is thought by many a bold attempt, but by none more so than myself. If this succeeds, it will do greatly for me; if it fails, the blame will remain where the public voice has already declared it—on the play and the author. Young Bannister, eaten up with spleen, has positively refused my repeating *Sheva*, which he claims his unalienable own; and as I do not think it prudent to perform *Hamlet*, or indeed anything I could not confidently offer to the public, I am at a stand. The 'Iron Chest' engages all my attention – I am already in the stirrup of my purpose – wish me, dear sir, success.

The Iron Chest was revived at the Haymarket on 29 August 1796, and of Elliston's performance one journal wrote, "We must set it down as one of the first exhibitions of the day." The *Gazetteer* called it "a masterful performance, though he occasionally rants a little too much." And the critic of the *How Do You Do?* on 10 September 1796 proclaimed Elliston an actor "who promises to make his competitors, of the highest stamp, shake in their shoes," and who possessed "powers of judgment uncommon in so juvenile a candidate for professional fame."

In his portrayal of Sir Edward Mortimer the raw youth from Bath, scarcely 22 years old, had established himself as a performer of the first class. He repeated the role on 31 August and 11 times in September, and on 7 September he acted Romeo for his own benefit, when tickets could be had of him at No 3, Frith Street, Soho. On 16 September he acted Octavian in *The Mountaineers* once more.

Immediately the managers of both winter houses solicited Elliston's services. Oddly enough, the critic of the *How Do You Do?* (10 September 1796) who had been so enthusiastic over Elliston's talents, warned him that he might not be ready for "struggling against the established favourites of either house," for although his voice was strong for the small Haymarket Theatre it might fail in the bigger houses. Elliston, however, could not be released from his articles for the coming season at Bath. Moreover, his wife had settled into a business partnership there with Miss Flemming, under a bond of £500. Sheridan, then manager of Drury Lane, did not agree to Elliston's steep terms of £1000 to cover the forfeit sum for his articles at Bath and his wife's bond penalty, plus a large weekly

salary. So Elliston came to an arrangement with Harris at Covent Garden by which he agreed to perform 12 nights during the season for a total remuneration of £200. Thus he acquired the nickname of "The Fortnight Actor," playing at intervals at Covent Garden while regularly engaged at Bath.

Elliston's debut at Covent Garden occurred on 21 September 1796 in the role of Sheva before an audience reported to have been one of the largest ever assembled in a winter house so early in the season. "He played with great correctness, and considerable force of effect," wrote his admiring reviewer in the *How Do You Do?* of 24 September 1796. "His enunciation, his deportment, and his action, were all appropriate to the character, and assumed and supported with as much ease and truth of colouring as if he had been in the habit of exhibiting before a collection of connoisseurs, more crowded and capable of comparing merit with its opposite, than his youthful eye had ever before experienced."

He repeated Sheva on 28 September, 3 and 12 October, and 16 November. On 26 October 1796 he attempted Young Norval in *Douglas* but without the success he had enjoyed in previous roles. The *How Do You Do?* on 5 November 1796 reported that he had come out in the role without a rehearsal at Covent Garden (he had played the role at Bath several seasons earlier, on 6 November 1794) and duly criticized him for being unprepared in "the duty he had undertaken here." The critic also made a bigotted reference to Elliston's greed – he "can perform the Jew as well off the Stage, as on it" – in consequence of his demanding 10 guineas to play for Haymes's benefit at Richmond, which was much more than could be afforded, and £15 to play in Cross's benefit at the same place, on a night when only £30 was taken in. When requested by Cross's friends to abate a portion, Elliston firmly announced he would not leave Richmond without the money in full, though at the last minute he re-turned £2.

His next role at Covent Garden was Philaster on 24 November 1796. His only other performance in 1796–97 at that thea-tre was as Sheva again on 19 May 1797. He returned to the Haymarket in the summer of 1797 to play for Colman in the roles of Octavian on 9 August, Sir Edward Morti-mer on 14 August, Walter in *The Children of the Wood* on 19 August (a role he had performed at Bath on 25 February 1796), Shylock on 28 and 29 August, Othello on 4 September (which he had acted at Bath on 8 June 1797), and Sheva on 8 Septem-ber. The *Monthly Mirror* of August 1797 reported a considerable maturation in his playing of Octavian, to the degree that memories of Kemble's excellence in the role were now "forgotten." Depending "en-tirely on his own genius," Elliston's Oc-tavian was in no way a copy of Kemble's. As Shylock, according to the *Monthly Visi-tor* of September 1797, after the discovery of Jessica's flight Elliston was "more noisy than impressive," and the speech "Hath not a Jew eyes?" was delivered with a dreadful rant. At the time of his benefit as Othello on 4 September, his London lodging was still at No 3, Frith Street.

After the summer of 1797, Elliston did not return to play in London until 1803, though he evidently made frequent visits and was a member of various drinking clubs, such as the "Court of Comus" in Wych Street; he also developed a taste for gambling. But most of his time was spent at Bath, where he first took a large house in Pulteney Street. Later he took up resi-dence in Bathwick Street. He acted regu-larly at Bristol, and when the theatre at Bath was dark he engaged with other pro-vincial houses. He also managed small theatres at Wells and Shepton Mallet.

As a member of Stephen Kemble's com-pany at Edinburgh in April 1799 he was praised by "Timothy Plain" for his per-formance as Henry IV: "His figure is tol-erably genteel, and suited to the part; con-sequently he looked the part well." But as Dr Pangloss in *The Heir at Law* he was denounced as "a caricature of a caricature," loud, vulgar, and overdone. An Edinburgh critic found him "egregiously wrong" as Macbeth, especially in respect to figure: "He is too short, boyish, and insignificant to play the hero and the tyrant," and his manner, "composed of ranting, grinning, and whining," diminished the tragic effect. Elliston was also advised to leave off imi-tating John Philip Kemble.

During the late summer seasons of 1799 and 1800 he also played at Birmingham. In August of 1799 he alternated between Bristol and Windsor, acting in the latter city six times. Five of those performances were before the King, who presented El-liston with 25 guineas at his benefit. For his Windsor efforts he cleared 100 guineas in a fortnight. He also recited occasional verses in the character of Merlin at a fete given at Frogmore on 7 August 1799 in honor of the birthday of Princess Amelia and supervised the royal festivities at Radi-pole on 1 August 1801. At Weymouth in the summer of 1801 he was a chief attrac-tion to audiences frequently graced by the presence of their Majesties, and on one oc-casion (so the story goes), while practicing on the violin one afternoon Elliston dis-turbed the King, who had retired to the royal box for a nap. At Reading in 1803, according to a notation in one of Winston's manuscripts now in the Folger Library, El-liston played six nights at 10 guineas per night and together with his clear benefit realized a total of 100 guineas.

During that period Elliston also made unsuccessful attempts to obtain a patent for a new theatre in London and for permission to open a playhouse in Oxford. Those fail-ures delayed, but only for a while, his pro-pensity for plunging into reckless adven-tures of management.

At the Orchard Street Theatre in Bath Elliston's career continued to prosper. At his benefit in 1800 he had grossed over £150. In March 1800, the *Monthly Mirror* announced that he was "to sway the theatrical sceptre" in the stead of Dimond, who was to retire, but the managerial position, through John Palmer's influence, went to Charles Charlton. Styled as "the very Proteus of the theatre," Elliston enjoyed success as Richard III, Henry V, Sylvester Daggerwood, and Lord Aimworth. By 1802 the Ellistons were lodging at No 31, Milson Street, Bath. At his benefit at Bristol on 28 June 1802, Mrs Elliston and her sister danced in the ballet. (Mrs Elliston maintained dancing academies at both Bristol and Bath from as early as August 1802.)

Elliston was engaged by Colman at the Haymarket for approximately £14 per week in the summer of 1803, returning to act there on 16 May 1803 in a prelude of his own called *No Prelude*, and then in such roles as Hotspur, Captain Beldaire in *Love Laughs at a Locksmith*, Young Wilding in *The Lyar*, Peregrine in *John Bull*, Le Gloire in *The Surrender of Calais*, Henry V, Ben Block in *The Maid of Bristol*, and Richard III (for the first time in London). He also served Colman as acting manager and received two benefits, one as actor and the other as manager.

After the season of 1803–4 at Bath, Elliston left his West Country career for London, where his principal successes, both acting and managing, were still ahead of him. He joined the Haymarket company to assume such roles as Orlando in *As You Like It*, Felix in *The Hunter of the Alps*, Abednego in *The Jew and the Doctor*, the title part of George Barnwell, and Rolla in *Pizarro*. So many people wished to attend his benefit when he played Rolla on 10 September 1804 he was obliged to rent the King's Theatre. So great was the crush, that many people pushed in without paying, and when the curtain drew up spectators were even sitting on the stage. There was an uproar, but riot was averted when Elliston appealed to the audience that as "Madame

Bouti, a foreigner, had been allowed to place her friends on the stage, surely he, as an Englishman, might be allowed to do so." Pointing out the loss he might suffer, he sent men around the house with plates to collect the unpaid entrance fees, and in the end he cleared £600. (He also acted at the Haymarket in 1805 and 1811.)

On 20 September 1804 he made his debut as Rolla at Drury Lane Theatre, where he had been engaged at £20 per week. He acted Doricourt in *The Belle's Stratagem* on 25 September and Rolla again two nights later and then took a short leave to Weymouth to supervise a fete which took place on the royal yacht on 29 September. By 5 October he was back at Drury Lane to play Archer in *The Beaux' Stratagem*; during the remainder of the season there he acted Charles Surface in *The School for Scandal*, Don Felix in *The Wonder*, Young Devil in *The Conscious Lovers*, Beverley in *All in the Wrong*, Romeo, Richard III, and Hamlet, among other parts. For his benefit on 26 April 1805 he produced a dramatization of his own composition, *The Venetian Outlaw*, in which he acted the role of Vivaldi. The piece was actually an adaptation of Lewis's *The Bravo of Venice* and Pixérécourt's *L'Homme à trois masques*.

Elliston remained at Drury Lane for four seasons, through 1808–9. In 1805–6 and 1806–7 his salary was still £20 per week, but it rose to £28 in 1807–8. His benefits were usually excellent: £132 7s. 3d. in April 1805; £299 18s. 10d. in May 1806; £343 6s. 8d. in May 1807; and £308 17s. 7d. in 1808 (all, presumably, less house charges). In 1807 Elliston also received £300 from the estate of his uncle William Elliston of Cambridge. In the summer of 1807 he performed at Liverpool and Buxton, and in 1807–8 he was at Edinburgh. His roles at Drury Lane during this period were varied. In 1805–6 he played Macbeth, Sir Harry Wildair in *The Constant Couple*, Lord Townly in *The Provok'd Husband*, Sir Charles Racket in *Three Weeks after*

Marriage, Alexander in *Alexander the Great*, and Valentine in *Love for Love*. In 1806–7 he played the title roles in *Tekeli* and *Mr. H*, Anson in *The Vindictive Man*, Durimel in *Point of Honour*, Sir Harry in *Assignation*, Inkle in *Inkle and Yarico*, Fitzharding in *The Curfew*, and Lothair in *Adelgitha*. In 1807–8 he acted the title roles in *Percy, Faulkner*, and *The Earl of Warwick*, Romeo, Blandford in *Time's a Tell-tale*, Young Mirabel in *The Inconstant*, and Don John in *The Chances*. In 1808–9 he was Charles Austincourt in *Man and Wife*, Captain Absolute in *The Rivals*, and Puff in *The Critic*.

On 24 February 1809 Drury Lane Theatre burned nearly to the ground. Its chief proprietor Sheridan resignedly watched the progress of the disaster from the Piazza Coffee House across the way. Questioned about his philosophic calm he is said to have replied, very much in character, "Surely man may take a glass of wine by his own fireside." Elliston was less composed, and, according to Raymond, dashed into the building to salvage some of his possessions, only to discover when he emerged to safety that he had dropped his gold watch, a bequest from his late uncle. The company played at the King's Theatre for a week before moving to the Lyceum Theatre, which was to remain their home for another two seasons.

On 23 February 1809, the day before the fire at Drury Lane, the Royal Circus Theatre in Blackfriar's Road across the river had been advertised for sale or lease. Elliston eventually negotiated a lease for its use at £2100 per year for seven years, and announced on 23 March that the theatre would reopen on Easter Monday under his management. The refitted and redecorated house was opened on 3 April 1809 with a melodrama entitled *Albert and Adela; or, the Invisible Avengers* and the pantomime *Harlequin's Resource; or, the Witch of Ludlam*.

Because of his commitments to the Drury Lane company at the Lyceum, Elliston did not perform in his own house until 15 June 1809, when he played Macheath in a burletta version of *The Beggar's Opera*. An immediate success, the piece ran for over 50 nights throughout the summer and was followed in September by a burletta version of *Macbeth*. On 22 September 1809 Elliston advertised his feeling that it would be improper for a proprietor to take a benefit on his own account, but that he had reserved the performance on 27 September to render his special gratitude to all his supporters. On that night he acted Macbeth and delivered an address, a ploy which filled the house and the treasury. Although evidently the season was intended to end on 4 November, an additional performance was given on 6 November "as a General Benefit for the Performers free of Expence."

Now fully taken up with his new enterprise, Elliston proceeded to extricate himself from his obligations to the Drury Lane company by arguing that he had no responsibility to be with them now that they were playing at the Lyceum. The management reminded him of his articles, dated 10 March 1807, which obliged him to perform for a total of five years, and ordered him to report to play at the Lyceum by 27 October 1809, the agreed-upon date which would allow him to wrap up his season at the Royal Circus. Elliston replied that he "would not play at the Lyceum under the arrangement which then existed." Sheridan began a law suit but eventually abandoned the action. Elliston's association with the patent house was discontinued for the following three years.

Meanwhile, in August 1809, Elliston purchased the freehold of the Croydon Theatre for £940. He paid another £100 for the scenery, wardrobe, and properties. In December 1809 he took over the management of the Manchester Theatre, which he opened on the fourth of that month. Elliston now had three theatres, and there were more to come, as he added one after another during the next few years.

His original license for the Royal Circus

did not authorize Elliston "to present any Entertainment therein in which Dialogue can be used, excepting with an accompaniment of Music throughout." Determined eventually to gain a patent allowing the Royal Circus to perform "legitimate" drama, he petitioned the House of Commons for a license which would make it possible for him to take an important step in that direction. As he explained in a published broadside-letter to the Prime Minister, Spencer Perceval, dated 1 March 1810, he was presently obliged to restrict dialogue to the nature of recitative. He did not ask for the common patent rights to comedy, tragedy, or farce, but to perform musical pieces with dialogue in the "ordinary way," together with pantomimes and ballet. Percival replied that Elliston's request could not be granted, "except upon a ground which would go to alter the whole principle upon which theatrical entertainments are at present regulated within the metropolis, and twenty miles round it." Undaunted, Elliston appealed to the Crown through the Privy Council for a royal patent to a third theatre but failed there also, largely through the opposition of the incumbent patentees, who suggested that Elliston was already operating illegally. The fruitless petitions to the House and to the Privy Council cost Elliston £101 and £31, respectively.

The disappointed Elliston rashly told an audience at Manchester on 24 March 1810 that he would never again step on a London stage, "except a new Theatre should be built or Drury Lane should rise from its ashes." But he had already been busy preparing the Royal Circus for a new phase in its history. On Easter Monday, 23 April 1810, Elliston reopened the Royal Circus under its new name, the Surrey Theatre, having converted the equestrian arena into a pit for spectators and the stables into salons, at the cost of some £2000. The opening piece was the popular burletta taken from *The Beggar's Opera*. Early in the sea-

son a musical version of *The Beaux' Stratagem* was brought out in which Elliston played Archer, and Sally Booth, making her first appearance on the London stage, played Cherry. The music was written by Elliston's wife. Soon afterward, Mrs Elliston provided music for an adaptation of *A Bold Stroke for a Wife*.

In the year following the opening of the Surrey, while continuing with his several established enterprises, Elliston purchased a freehold property in John Street, Bristol, for £1600 and set up a trade in second-hand books. In the back apartment, which he styled "The Lyceum," he opened a "Literary Association." But the project, which he placed under the supervision of a former schoolmaster named Brick, soon failed.

In the summer of 1811 Colman persuaded Elliston to act at the Haymarket for £40 per week with two clear benefits. The strong company included Holman, Mathews, Liston, Mrs Glover, and Munden. Elliston's roles included Welford in *Trial by Jury*, Florian in *The Foundling of the Forest*, Charles in *The Royal Oak*, Selico in *The Africans*, Batho in *The Quadrupeds of Quedlinburg*, Pierre in *Venice Preserv'd*, Job Thornberry in *John Bull*, Lothario in *The Fair Penitent*, Zarno in *Zorinski*, Welford in *Darkness Visible*, Robert in *Travellers Benighted*, Frederick in *Of Age Tomorrow*, Captain Absolute in *The Rivals*, and Don Vincentio in *A Bold Stroke for a Husband*. Elliston was then under engagement to act for five nights in November 1811 at the new Theatre Royal in Beaufort Square, Bath, but was obliged to leave in the middle of the run because of the death of his infant daughter Mary Juliet.

At the Surrey in 1812, Elliston acted in a mélange of farces, melodramas, burlettas, and pantomimes, which included *The Mayor of Garratt, Days of Old, False and True, Blank Cartridge*, and *Seven Wonders of the World*. At times his stage was graced as well with trained dogs, elephants, and camels. Added to his company was S. T.

Russell, who also took on the job of stage manager. (It was Russell who stood as Elliston's second in a duel with Vincent De Camp which resulted after a fistfight. The combatants met on 9 September 1812, on Dulwich Common; shots were exchanged, no one was hurt, and the parties were persuaded to shake hands.)

The offer by Richard Wilson to the committee of the new Drury Lane Theatre to take a lease on that house jointly with Elliston for 21 years at a rent of £20,000 per year was declined. Arnold was appointed manager, and on 30 June 1812 Elliston signed articles for five years, renewable at the option of the management after the end of three years, at £30 per week for three nights of playing per week, plus £5 per night above three nights. The new theatre opened on 10 October 1812, with an address written by Lord Byron and spoken by Elliston, who also acted Hamlet. His roles at Drury Lane that season included Leon in *Rule a Wife and Have a Wife*, Don Alva in *Remorse*, Joseph in *The School for Scandal*, Captain Daverscourt in *Recrimination*, Belville in *The School for Wives*, Orloff in *The Russian*, and Lackland in *Fontainbleau*. His benefits for the season totalled £702 3s.

Elliston continued as an actor at Drury Lane through 1814–15. At the same time he kept busy expanding his own theatrical empire. Still operating the Surrey, Elliston bought the Olympic Pavilion in Wych Street from Philip Astley for £2800 and an annuity to the seller of £20. Under the name of Little Drury Lane, the theatre was opened on 19 April 1813 for burlettas and other musical pieces, with a license, passed from Astley, to operate the year round. Within a month the proprietors of Drury Lane and Covent Garden had the place closed by the Lord Chamberlain, on a technicality, but in December Elliston was able to reopen it, calling it now the Olympic.

Seemingly possessed by a territorial imperative, Elliston almost succeeded in obtaining Vauxhall Gardens from Barrett at a price of £35,000, but negotiations broke down at the last moment. He gave up schemes to purchase the Crow Street Theatre in Dublin and the theatre in Edinburgh, but in 1813 he took the lease on the theatre in Birmingham for five years, agreeing to open it for 20 weeks each year and to play there himself at least 12 nights per season. In 1816–17 he leased the Leicester Theatre for a short season for £157. And in 1818 he managed the theatre at Northampton for a brief period. About that time he also established a circulating library in the name of his sons William and Henry at Leamington, where he had a fashionable apartment. To his Leamington properties he added a baby theatre for his own amusement. An attempt at a "provincial Vauxhall" at Leamington, complete with ballrooms, singers, suppers, and fireworks, failed.

Elliston salvaged time enough from those multifarious activities to become an ornament of London clubs and to assure his reputation for hard drinking. More than one contemporary observer accused him of being a dabbler in everything but a master in nothing. As early as 1813 the *Theatrical Inquisitor* lamented his "unprofitable bustle" at the cost of his real potential for distinguished acting: "With powers, that properly cultivated might render him the first ornament of the legitimate drama, he is content to bustle through his parts in a manner that exercises the patience of the audience . . . ; to disgust by a degree of negligence, hurry and grimace, for which no examples of occasional excellence can atone; and to grin, and stamp, and roar for the amusement of the rabble."

In August 1819 Elliston achieved his central ambition by securing the lesseeship of Drury Lane Theatre against stiff competition from S. T. Arnold, Thomas Dibdin, and Edmund Kean. The agreement was for 14 years at a yearly rent of £10,200, with the lessee responsible for all taxes and

Harvard Theatre Collection

ROBERT W. ELLISTON

engraving by Picart, after Wivell

rates. He was also obliged to lay out £1000 in decorating the house prior to opening his first season and £6000 in maintenance and decoration prior to the second season. The terms also prevented Elliston from engaging professionally in any other theatre in London. On 13 June 1820, the Olympic Theatre was put up for auction by Mr Robins, auctioneer, at the Auction Mart opposite the Bank of England. In the bill of particulars describing the property and the terms of sale it was stated that Elliston had spent just short of £30,000 in 1819 for remodelling and rebuilding the property.

He opened Drury Lane on 4 October 1819 with *Wild Oats*, in which he acted Rover. Although he could not entice Mrs Siddons from retirement, he gathered into the company Pope, Dowton, Munden, Harley, Knight, Braham, Mrs West, Mrs Egerton, Mrs Edwin, and, not least of all, Ed-

mund Kean, who played Lear and Jaffeir for the first time during that season. Eventually he engaged Madame Vestris, who produced dramas by Sir Walter Scott and also Byron's controversial *Marino Faliero* on 25 April 1821. His support of his scene designers Clarkson Stanfield and David Roberts prepared London for the great investment in scenic effects which was to come within another decade. Much credit for the survival of his management for six years must be given to his chief assistant James Winston; on 23 December 1819, soon after Elliston took over, R. B. Peake wrote to George Bartley in Boston, Massachusetts (letter in Harvard Theatre Collection), that "Elliston is the luckiest man in the World—he is *not yet ruined*! His management is *beastly*. I have only to say that Winston has influence & control & that, I presume, is sufficient. . . ." In the summer of 1821 Elliston produced on the Drury Lane stage a replica of the Coronation of George IV, in which he played the monarch, which ran for 104 performances to February 1822.

By the end of 1825–26, according to his own testimony, Elliston had lost a personal fortune of some £30,000 and was obliged to return Drury Lane to a committee of proprietors. On 10 December 1826 he was declared a bankrupt, his property having been put under the hammer at his premises, No 9, Stratford Place, Oxford Road, the previous 26 November. (He had maintained the house since 1808. About 1804 he had lived at No 6, Great Russell Street, Covent Garden, and from 1805 to 1808 at No 13, North Street, Westminster.)

By the time of his latest business misfortunes Elliston was quite ill, having suffered an epileptic seizure in January 1823 and a second attack—probably a stroke—in August 1825. According to Raymond the second seizure left him "a helpless, decrepit, tottering old man." After his last performance at Drury Lane on 11 May 1826, when he acted Falstaff in *1 Henry IV*,

Elliston was so exhausted that he fell flat on the stage.

Despite his failures in business and health, Elliston became involved in a scheme to rebuild the burned-out Royalty Theatre in Chamber Street, Lemon Street. The negotiations advanced to the drawing of a lease for the new speculation in March 1827, but the matter was dropped when the backers became apprehensive. Elliston had been spared a tragic involvement, for the theatre was finally built by other parties and opened on 25 February 1828; but three days later, on 28 February, the roof fell in killing at least 15 persons.

Elliston meanwhile had retreated to Leamington. His final examination before the Commissioners of Bankrupts occurred in March 1827. In *The Times* for 18 May 1827 he read that the Surrey Theatre, his old stamping ground in St George's Fields, was up for rental. With money advanced by friends he again became its proprietor in 1827 (although the lease was made to his son Charles Robert) and enjoyed success, especially in his performances of *The Three Singles*, in which he played the characters of a collegian, a Frenchman, and a fool. In 1829 he produced Douglas Jerrold's *Black-Eyed Susan*. While acting Sheva in *The Jew* at the Surrey on 24 June 1831, Elliston clearly was the picture of a dying man. The afterpiece was the two-hundred-and-twenty-first performance of *Black-Eyed Susan*.

During an early morning ride on 6 July 1831 to visit his married daughter Frances Maria Wilson, Elliston suffered a stroke on the road and was brought back to his house at No 84, Great Surrey Street, Blackfriars, into which he had moved in June 1828. After lingering for two days, Elliston died at 6:30 on the morning of 8 July, at the age of 57. By instructions in his will, made a year earlier on 8 July 1830, Elliston was put into a lead and oak coffin, with black nails, bearing no ornament except a center plate with an inscription of his own composition (with a space left for the date of his

death): "ROBERTUS GULIELMUS ELLISTON / Natus Septimo die Aprilis, 1774; Obit Octavo die Julii, 1831." After a "walking" funeral procession, his body was put to rest in a vault under St John's Church, Waterloo Road, near the coffin of the actor Henry Bengough. In August 1833 a marble tablet was placed by the south side of the altar of the church, containing a Latin epitaph in Elliston's memory written by his son-in-law, Nicholas Torre, of Cheltenham.

In his will, which was proved at London on 6 August 1831 by James Winston, one of the executors ("the other named William Moore having renounced"), Elliston directed that all his estate in securities and money should be divided equally among his nine children by his wife Elizabeth Elliston, but he named only six: William Gore Elliston, Henry Twistleton Elliston, Charles Robert Elliston, Albina Jane Martyn Elliston, Lucy Ann Elliston, and Mary Ann Elliston.

However, Elliston is known to have had at least ten children. The eldest son, William Gore Elliston, was born by 1801; he emigrated to Australia but returned to establish the County Library at Leamington in partnership with his brother Henry Twistleton. The second son, Henry Twistleton Elliston, was born on 14 January 1802 and resided most of his life at Leamington. He was a sound professional musician and served as organist of the parish church. He also built a music hall and became lessee of the royal assembly rooms. He died at Leamington on 19 April 1864. (He is noticed in *The Dictionary of National Biography*.) The third son, Charles Robert Elliston, was born on 5 November 1804; he assisted his father in his second management of the Surrey Theatre. A fourth son, Edmund Elliston, born on 17 September 1813, was not mentioned in his father's will, and little is known of him, except that in 1829, at the age of 16, he had accompanied his eldest brother William Gore Elliston to Australia.

The first daughter and eldest child, Eliza

Elliston, was born at Bath on 22 May 1797 and was not mentioned in the will. Probably she was the wife of Nicholas Torre. She had appeared in a ballet divertissement with her sister Frances Maria for her father's benefit at Bristol on 27 October 1816. The second daughter, Frances Maria, born in 1800, married the musician Marmaduke Charles Wilson (b. 1796) on 1 October 1821. The third daughter, Albina Jane Martyn Elliston, was born on 10 March 1808. The fourth, Mary Juliet Elliston, was born on 21 July 1809 and died in the fall of 1811. The fifth, Lucy Ann Theresa Elliston, was born on 21 December 1811 and died on 28 January 1831, about eight months before her father. The sixth daughter, Mary Ann Elliston was born on 10 November 1817. Elliston also seems to have had a bastard child by a woman named Douglas who had applied for an engagement at Drury Lane in July 1823.

A Mr and Mrs Elliston were members of W. Adamson's company of players which acted in Spanish Town, Jamaica, and other places in the Caribbean, in 1816–17, but there is no evidence that they were related to our subject.

Elliston's wife Elizabeth had died at London on 31 March 1821 of "a spasmodic attack," at the age of 46, and had been buried in St George's burial ground, Bayswater. On the day of her funeral the bells at Bath Abbey had tolled. Elliston's father, Robert Elliston, had died at his son's house in Bathwick Street, Bath, on 17 June 1800.

In addition to the dramatic pieces already cited (*No Prelude*, 1803; *The Venetian Outlaw*, 1805; *The Coronation*, 1821), Elliston wrote a preface to *The Flying Dutchman*, published in Richardson's *New Minor Theatre*, 1828; an alteration of *Coriolanus*, published in 1820; and a preface to an edition of *Love in a Village*, published 1821. A quantity of material relating to Elliston may be found in No. 75 of the "Register of Playbills, Programmes and Theatre Cuttings" at the British Museum and in an extra-illustrated set of *Actors and*

Actresses in the Harvard Theatre Collection. The latter collection contains a news cutting describing his theatrical wardrobe, which was sold in September 1831.

Raymond's claim that "As a comedian, Elliston was, perhaps never excelled, and it may be, he will never be equalled," is obviously exaggerated. He was certainly, however, an excellent actor, one of great diversity who never fulfilled the potential of his natural powers. He possessed a comic genius of irresistible quality which shone in the gentlemanly comedy of such roles as Vapid in *The Dramatist*, Ranger in *The Suspicious Husband*, and Charles Surface in *The School for Scandal*. In later years his "coarse buffoonery of manner" served Falstaff with distinction.

Elliston was not well suited for tragedy. Henry Crabb Robinson called him "A wretched Tragedian—his attempts at dignity are ludicrous." Robinson saw his Hotspur on 7 January 1813 and judged him "unworthy." When he saw Elliston later as Nourjahad in *The Illusion*, Robinson wrote in his diary that "his untragic face can express no strong emotions." Yet Leigh Hunt proclaimed Elliston "the only genius that has approached the great Garrick in universality of imitation," as well as "the second tragedian on the stage" and the "best lover . . . both in tragedy and comedy." Lamb honored him with high praise in "To the Shade of Elliston," and Charles Mathews, his friend since childhood, characterized him as "A most fascinating, brilliant actor."

In person Elliston was charming and facile; at one time he considered standing for Parliament on the strength of his handsome and bright qualities. He lacked prudence and temperance, but he was generous and convivial. He had an aversion to cats and a great weakness for drink. By the testimony of Winston's *Diaries*, Elliston was frequently so drunk he was irrational and threatened suicide. His addiction to alcohol certainly hastened his death. He was an erratic husband who could shower affection and regard upon his wife impulsively, yet treat her for long periods with neglect. He frequently consorted with whores and compromised the actresses under his control. In 1821 he brought Miss Cubitt, the actress, to live with him for a while at Stratford Place. Yet one cannot quarrel with Raymond's affirmation that for all his pretensions, absurdities, and faults, Elliston's "energy and activity were truly wonderful."

Elliston's career as a manager—"the great Lessee"—has recently been detailed by Christopher Murray in *Robert William Elliston, Manager* (1975).

Portraits of Elliston include:

1. By George Harlow. In the National Portrait Gallery.

2. By George Harlow. In the Garrick Club, similar to the version in the National Portrait Gallery. An engraving by C. Turner was published by J. P. Thompson, 1808.

3. By George Harlow. Pencil drawing in the Garrick Club, signed "G. H. H. March 20th, 1814." An engraving by I. J. Penstone was published by Cunningham and Mortimer, 1843.

4. Miniature by unknown artist, c. 1807. In the Mander and Mitchenson Collection.

5. Engraving by Cardon, after Bennett. Published by Jenkins, 1810.

6. Engraving by Cooper, after Harlow. Published by Dean & Munday as a plate to the *Lady's Monthly Museum*, 1828.

7. Engraving by Picart, after Wivell. Published by Lawford, 1825.

8. Engraving by Read.

9. Engraving by Ridley, after Drummond. Published by Bellamy as a plate to the *Monthly Mirror*, 1796.

10. Engraving by Thomson, after Drummond. Published by Asperne as a plate to the *European Magazine*, 1819.

11. Engraving by unknown engraver. Published by Chappell & Son as a plate to the *British Stage*, 1820. The same picture, on the same plate with a picture of Mrs Jordan, marked "E. Smith, del.," was published in Holcroft's *Theatrical Recorder*, 1805.

12. Engraving by an unknown engraver. Published by Phillips, 1805.

13. As Ben Block in *The Maid of Bristol*. Engraving by Alais.

14. As Beverley, with Mrs Jordan as Belinda, in *All in the Wrong*. Engraving by Alais. Published by Roach, 1808.

15. As Colonel Feignwell in *A Bold Stroke for a Wife*. Engraving by Rogers, after Page. Published by Virtue as a plate to Oxberry's *Dramatic Biography*, 1825.

16. As Doctor Pangloss, with Blisset as Duberly, in *The Heir at Law*. Drawn and engraved by Caldwell.

17. As Don Felix in *The Wonder*. Engraving by Alais. Published by Roach, 1805.

18. As Don Felix. By unknown engraver. Published by Hodgson & Co, 1823.

19. As Duke Aranza in *The Honeymoon*. Painting by De Wilde. In the Garrick Club. An engraving by Hopwood was published as a plate to *The Cabinet*, 1807. A similar, but full-length watercolor by De Wilde, dated July 1808, is in the British Museum; an engraving of it by Scriven was published by Bell & DeCamp in 1808 and another by Tegg in 1810. An original watercolor version by De Wilde, dated December 1807, is in the Harvard Theatre Collection, and another original by De Wilde, this in pencil and wash, dated 1808, is in the Victoria and Albert Museum.

20. As Duke Aranza. Drawn and engraved by I. R. Cruikshank. Published by Duncombe as a plate to *The Theatre, or Literary and Dramatic Mirror*, October 1819.

21. As Aranza. Engraving by Warren, after Singleton. Published by Longman, 1807.

22. As Falstaff. Engraving by John W. Gear. Not listed in Hall's catalogue but is in the Harvard Theatre Collection.

23. As Falstaff. Engraving by T. Wageman, 1826. In the Folger Shakespeare Library.

24. As Falstaff. By an unknown engraver. Published by Dyer. Not listed in Hall's catalogue but is in the Harvard Theatre Collection.

25. As Frank Heartall in *The Soldier's Daughter*. Painting on wooden panel, by Thomas Wageman. In the Players Club. An engraving by Woolnoth, after Wageman, was published by Simpson & Marshall as a plate to Oxberry's *New English Drama*, 1818.

26. As George IV in *The Coronation*. By unknown engraver. Published as a twopence-colored and penny-plain by W. West, 1821.

27. As Hotspur in *1 Henry IV*. Watercolor by W. Loftis, 1805. In the Folger Shakespeare Library.

28. As Macbeth. Engraving by Billing.

29. As Mercutio in *Romeo and Juliet*. Engraving by Findlay. Published by Duncombe as a plate to the *Mirror of the Stage*, 1822.

30. As Nourjahad in *Illusion*. By unknown engraver. Published as penny-plain by W. West, 1814.

31. As Octavian in *The Mountaineer*. Painting by Henry Singleton. In the Garrick Club. An engraving by H. R. Cook was published by Chapple as a plate to the *Theatrical Inquisitor*, 1813.

32. As Octavian. Engraving by Bond, after Singleton.

33. As Ranger in *The Suspicious Husband*. Engraving by Page, after Wageman. Published by Elvey as a plate to *The Drama*, 1823.

34. As Richmond in *Richard III*. Drawn and engraved by I. R. Cruikshank. Published as a plate to the *British Stage*, December, 1819.

35. As Richmond. By an unknown engraver. Published as a twopence-colored.

36. As Rochester in *Rochester*. Engraving by Robinson. Published by Cumberland as a plate to Cumberland's *Minor Theatre*. The same picture by an unknown engraver was published by Richardson, 1830.

37. As Rosenberg, with Mrs Siddons as Ella, in *Ella Rosenberg*. By unknown engraver. Published by Scales as a plate to an edition of the play.

38. As Rover in *Wild Oats*. Watercolor by De Wilde. In the Harvard Theatre Collection.

39. As Rover. By unknown engraver. Published by Roach as a plate to the *Dramatic Censor*, 1820.

40. As Pertinax, Peregrine, and Percival in *The Three and the Deuce*. By unknown engraver. Published by Walker & Knights, 1812.

41. As Sylvester Daggerwood, singing "Bonaparte" at the Surrey Theatre. Drawn and engraved by G. Cruikshank. Published by Laurie & Whittle, 1811.

42. As Walter in *Children in the Wood*. Engraving by Woolnoth, after Wageman. Published by Cumberland as a plate to Cumberland's *British Theatre*, 1827.

43. Caricature entitled "Elliston and the Flower of Knockmele-down." Drawn and engraved by G. Cruikshank. Published as a plate to Raymond's *Life*, 1857.

44. Caricature entitled "The King and the Player." Drawn and engraved by G. Cruikshank. Published as a plate to Raymond's *Life*, 1857.

45. Caricature entitled "Alas, poor Ghost." Drawn and engraved by G. Cruikshank. Published as a plate to Raymond's *Life*, 1857.

Ellys. *See* ELLIS.

Elmes, Richard ₁*fl. 1679–1682*₁, *singer.*

John Blow was paid £30 a year beginning 21 May 1679 to clothe and maintain Richard Elmes and one other former boy singer in the Chapel Royal. Warrants in the Lord Chamberlain's accounts as late as 16 August 1682 refer to Elmes as a former Chapel boy whose voice had changed.

Elmy, Mrs ₁**William?**₁, **Mary, née Morse** *1712–1792, actress.*

Mary Morse (sometimes "Moss") was born in 1712. She may have been the Miss Morse who played La Guiol in *The Wanton Jesuit* at the Haymarket Theatre on 17 March 1732. There was a Mrs Morse acting regularly at that playhouse, however, and the billing may have been meant for her. Miss Morse was not mentioned in any other bills for a year and a half. On 8 October 1733 at Drury Lane Miss Morse played Charlotte in *Oroonoko*; then on 23 November she was Chloe in *Timon of Athens* (*The London Stage* assigns the role to "Mrs" Morse, apparently in error). Advertised again as Miss Moss, our subject acted Lucy in *The Livery Rake* at Drury Lane on 8 January 1734. Between 14 and 31 January she became Mrs (William?) Elmy. On the latter date, under her new name, she played Charlotte again, after which she finished the season as Pallas in *Cupid and Psyche*, Amanthe in *The Fatal Falsehood*, and Araminta in *The Confederacy*. Her benefit tickets were accepted on 3 May at Lincoln's Inn Fields (where some of the Drury Lane players performed) and on 13 May at Drury Lane. On 24 August at Bartholomew Fair she played the title role in *The Fair Rosamond*.

During the rest of the 1730s Mrs Elmy's activity was sporadic. She played Mrs Foresight in *Love for Love* at Drury Lane on 20 May 1735; in 1736 she acted the title role in *Jane Shore* on 11 February and Mrs Slammekin in *The Beggar's Opera* on 26 June at the Haymarket Theatre; in 1737 she made her first appearance at Covent Garden as Florinda in *The Rover* on 11 April and repeated Mrs Slammekin at Lincoln's Inn Fields on 2 August; and in 1738 she played Araminta in *The Old Bachelor* at her benefit shared with three others at Covent Garden on 18 May. It is not possible to tell whether or not she was acting regularly in unadvertised parts at various theatres during those years.

Having made little headway in London, Mrs Elmy tried her fortune in Dublin. In October 1738 she was at the Aungier Street

Theatre, where she made her first appearance in Ireland as Mrs Sullen in *The Stratagem*, hailed, curiously, as from Drury Lane. The following 11 December she made her Smock Alley debut. Mrs Elmy remained in Dublin through 1743–44. Roles known for her include Mrs Townly in *The Provok'd Husband*, Lady Betty in *The Careless Husband* (both at Smock Alley), Flareit in *Love's Last Shift*, and the Lady in *Comus* (both at Aungier Street).

Upon her return to London in the fall of 1744 she appeared as Phyllis in *The Conscious Lovers* at the Haymarket Theatre with Theophilus Cibber's "Academy" group. On 11 February 1745 she was at Drury Lane to act Lady Dainty in *The Double Gallant*. Again she made little progress in London, and perhaps George Anne Bellamy in her *Apology* was correct in assessing Mrs Elmy's talents at that time: "she was a humourist and possessed of a great good sense, but by her want of powers, was prevented from making a conspicuous figure upon the stage." In 1745–46 Mrs Elmy acted at the Aungier Street Theatre and at Smock Alley again, serving as a supporting actress during Garrick's engagement.

On 3 January 1747 she was acting Lady Grace in *The Provok'd Husband* back at Drury Lane, and there she remained to the end of the 1740s. Some of her roles became associated with her for many years: the Lady in *Comus*, Indiana in *The Conscious Lovers*, Belinda in *The Man of Mode*, Desdemona in *Othello* (for her benefit on 4 April 1747, tickets for which were available from her at the Star in Bow Street, Covent Garden), Selima in *Tamerlane*, Queen Elizabeth in *Richard III*, Mrs Strictland in *The Suspicious Husband*, Lavinia in *The Fair Penitent*, Amanda in *The Relapse*, Mrs Frail in *Love for Love*, Angelina in *Love Makes a Man*, Dorinda in *The Stratagem*, Hero in *Much Ado About Nothing*, Lady Charlotte in *The Funeral*, and Octavia in *All for Love*. She also acted, for the occasion, Lady Macduff in *Macbeth* at her solo benefit on 2 April 1748, tickets for which she made available at the corner of Tavistock Street, next to Southampton Street, Covent Garden. Her benefit brought her a profit of £86.

Mrs Elmy's career had taken a turn for the better, and the critics began commenting on her work. In 1749 Chetwood wrote in his *General History* that she had a weak voice but was well-meaning on stage. But "She seems to have more Spirits *off* the Stage, in a Chamber, than she has *in* the public Theatre. . . ." Chetwood also noted that her husband, whose whereabouts were unknown to both Chetwood and Mrs Elmy, was from Norwich. Mrs Elmy, he said, had started her career in a provincial company and been on the stage about 17 years. Hill in *The Actor* (1750) spoke of her as "an actress of great judgment, endowed with a sweet voice and a pleasing deportment, [who] obtain'd a merited applause in the Character of Lavinia in the *Fair Penitent*; so great that it startled the *Calista* [Mrs Cibber]." Hill felt that the "sweetness of disposition, tenderness, affection, and fidelity of that part suited extremely well with the peculiar turn of this actress," so much so that "many were in doubt whether they should declare her the second, or the first actress of the present stage." But in other characters she wanted "that Promethean heat, that fire" which she sometimes had as the Lady in *Comus* but lacked in other roles.

On 16 October 1750 she played Belinda in *The Provok'd Wife* at Covent Garden, incorrectly advertised as making her first appearance on that stage. There she remained for the rest of her career in the second rank of actresses in the troupe. Between 1750 and her last appearance in 1762 Mrs Elmy continued playing most of her old characters and added some new ones: the Duchess of Suffolk in *Lady Jane Gray*, Queen Elinor in *King John*, Selima in *Zara*, Mrs Marwood in *The Way of the World*, Belinda in *The Old Bachelor*, Ger-

trude in *Hamlet*, Lady Touchwood in *The Double Dealer*, Lady Brute in *The Provok'd Wife*, Lady Easy in *The Careless Husband*, Lady Woodville in *The Non Juror*, the Duchess of York in *Richard III*, Regan in *King Lear*, and Portia in *Julius Caesar*—but many of those parts she acted only for a season, and her repertoire in 1761–62 was not greatly changed from that of 1750–51.

Some of her roles, such as Lavinia, she performed to perfection, and *The Monitor*, commenting on her Desdemona in 1753, allowed that "no part has been better represented in our memory, and indeed we scarce knew what it was before she acted it." The more typical reaction of the time, however, was not unlike the comment in *The Present View of the Stage* in 1753: when "good Sense, Ease and Gentility, are the distinguishing Characteristics few appear to more Advantage." In 1757 the *Theatrical Examiner* cautioned her: "Mrs. E——y should not chuse, at this time of day, to play the gentle Desdemona; she is generally allowed to *do* Lady Grace, and I think she is inferior to no person in the play, when she does Octavia in the World Well Lost."

Her financial record also reflected her status. Though she had solo benefits yearly, the accounts show that by the late 1750s she was not drawing well. In 1758 there was a deficit at her benefit, and though the tickets she sold covered the loss, she was left with only £62 2s. In 1760 she suffered a loss of £30 13s. 6d. Her salary at Covent Garden as of 22 September 1760 was 13s. 4d. daily; the next year she was paid £3 weekly or a total of £158 for the season. Happily, her 1761 benefit brought her a profit of £103 6s. 6d., but by that time the end of her career was near. In 1761–62 she played Lady Grace, Isabella, Gertrude, Selima, Mrs Foresight, Cynthia (in *The Wife's Relief*), the Duchess of York, Queen Elinor, and the Lady in *Comus*. She chose *Comus* for her last benefit on 29 April 1762, after which she retired from the stage.

The Rosciad of C–v–nt G–rd–n (1762) commemorated her in verse:

> *See ELMY slow advance, with decent grace;*
> *A modest diffidence mark'd in her face:*
> *She is not envious of another's praise,*
> *Nor by their fall desires herself to raise.*
> *How well, how just, she plays! in GER-*
> *   TRUDE's part!*
> *When injur'd HAMLET wrings her*
> *   guilty heart;*
> *Her glowing features burning rage ex-*
> *   press,*
> *Temper'd with filial love, and deep dis-*
> *   tress:*
> *Action and mein, their various merits*
> *   join;*
> *And when she speaks, with force united*
> *   shine.*

On 1 April 1792, according to the *European Magazine*, Mary Morse Elmy died at Knightsbridge at the age of 80. She had made her will on 12 October 1780 and had added a codicil on 28 April 1789. The will was proved on 19 April 1792. She described herself as a widow and left £100 each to four cousins in Norwich: Charles Frint, Thomas and John Jarvis, and Mrs Sarah Ferguson. To her cousin Mrs James Steward of the parish of St Clement Danes in London she left £20. To each of the children of her cousin Daniel Dey of Norwich she left £10. To Ann Williams she bequeathed her best diamond ring. The rest of her goods, plus £1000 in stock, she left to her cousin Sarah Smith of Norwich. The codicil to her will added a bequest of £50 to Spranger Barry's widow, Anne Crawford,

Courtesy of the Garrick Club

MARY ELMY (?) as Gertrude, and SPRANGER BARRY as Hamlet
by Hayman

"though now call'd Mrs. Brown at Colney near St. Albans. . . ."

Mrs Elmy may have been the actress pictured playing Gertrude to Spranger Barry's Hamlet in a painting by Francis Hayman now at the Garrick Club. The identification was made in the catalogue for the Harris sale in 1819 and is not certain; but between 11 October 1751 and 28 February 1758 she did indeed play Gertrude to Barry's Hamlet and was praised for the role. No better authenticated portrait of Mrs Elmy is known.

Elrington, Mr *[fl. 1794]*, *oboist, violinist.*

Doane's *Musical Directory* of 1794 listed a Mr Elrington of No 34, Tufton Street, Westminster, as an oboist and violinist who played in the Westminster Abbey concerts and was a member of the band of the Second Regiment of Guards. Doane identified him as Elrington Junior to distinguish him from the Mr Elrington, composer and flutist of the same address, who was the master of the band of the First Regiment of Guards.

Elrington, Miss *[fl. 1781–1782]*, *singer.*

Miss Elrington sang in performances of *Macbeth* at Covent Garden during the 1781–82 season, the first being on 17 December and the last on 27 May. On 10 May 1782 she was one of many minor members of the company whose benefit tickets were accepted at the theatre.

Elrington, Ralph *d. 1761*, *actor, dancer.*

On 15 May 1717 at the Lincoln's Inn Fields playhouse "Elrington Junior" shared with others a benefit performance of *Oedipus*. Thomas Elrington was with the company at that time, but he was not the person referred to. His younger brother Ralph may have been Elrington Junior, though he is not otherwise known to have performed

in England. The billing would suggest that the beneficiary was a minor member of the troupe who played no named roles during the season.

Elrington certainly performed in Dublin from 1717 onward and in the 1730s became a noted harlequin. Unfortunately, the Irish playbills frequently cited R. Elrington, and since both Ralph and his brother Richard were active at the same time, it is often difficult to make role assignments. In the following list we can be fairly sure that the R. Elrington in the harlequin parts was Ralph; the rest of the roles are certain, for the bills cited his Christian name. The roles belong to the period from 22 March 1731 through 7 February 1745 at Smock Alley (unless otherwise noted): Buckingham in *Richard III*, Lysimachus in *The Rival Queens*, Springlove in *The Jovial Crew*, George Barnwell in *The London Merchant*, Samur in *Love and Ambition*, Arcas in *Damon and Phillida*, Edgar in Tate's version of *King Lear*, Harlequin in *The Necromancer* (on 8 March 1733 – though he may have played such parts earlier), Trivoltio in *All Vows Kept*, Valentine in *Love for Love*, the Copper Captain in *Rule a Wife and Have a Wife* (at Aungier Street), John in *Don John* (at Aungier Street), Osmyn in *The Mourning Bride* (at Aungier Street), Harlequin in *The Hussar*, Harlequin in *The Squire of Alsatia*, Harlequin in *The Rival Sorcerers*, and Torrismond in *The Spanish Fryar* (with the United Company). Ralph Elrington was with the Smock Alley company through the 1757–58 season.

Chetwood in his *General History* in 1749 wrote that Ralph

was admired some years ago as a good executing Harlequin, Agility and Strength being two main Ingredients in the Composition of that motley Gentleman, where Heels are of more Use than the Head. In one of his Feats of Activity he was much hurt, and was in some danger of breaking his Neck to please the Spectators, the Ears having little to do in such Entertainments; yet this unlucky Spring met with universal Applause.

Chetwood implied that Elrington gave up playing harlequin; the latest date we have found for him in such roles is 1742. The registers of St Peter and St Kevin, Dublin, contain the baptismal record of Ralph, son of Ralph and Catherine Elrington on 15 January 1743. That son must have died in infancy, for a second Ralph was christened on 24 March 1744. We assume the father was our subject.

Faulkner's Dublin Journal on 27 January 1961 reported that Ralph Elrington (the performer) had died the previous week.

Elrington, Richard   *d. 1770, actor.*

Richard Elrington, one of the sons of the actor-manager Thomas, is said by Clark in *The Irish Stage in the County Towns* to have appeared at the Smock Alley Theatre in Dublin as early as 1729. There are a number of references in Dublin playbills to R. Elrington, but some of them could concern Richard's brother Ralph, who was active about the same time. The bills make clear, however, that Richard acted the Duke of York in *Richard III* on 22 March 1731 at Smock Alley, and Chetwood stated in his *General History* that Richard played Brazen in *The Recruiting Officer* at the Aungier Street playhouse when it opened on 9 March 1734. Dublin bills cited Richard as Bellamour in *Wit Without Money* at Aungier Street on 26 January 1738 and Hal in *1 Henry IV* with the United Company on 29 April 1745.

As early as 1746 Richard Elrington "married" Elizabeth Martin. She was either born Elizabeth Grace or took that name and was later attached to Christopher Martin. At Oswestry, Shropshire, in 1746 Elrington acted Iago in *Othello* and she, as Mrs Elrington, played Desdemona. By May 1750 Master Richard Elrington, presumably Richard's son by an earlier marriage or

liaison, was performing at Smock Alley with him.

Elrington was with a touring company in England in 1749, was back in Dublin in the spring of 1750, and was in London for the 1750–51 season at Covent Garden. His first notice there was on 25 October 1750, when he played Bernardo in *Hamlet*. During the remainder of the season he acted a number of other small roles: Oxford in *Richard III*, Blunt in *1 Henry IV*, Coleville in *2 Henry IV*, Decius Brutus in *Julius Caesar*, Westmoreland in *Henry V*, Mat in *The Beggar's Opera*, Essex in *King John*, and Abergavenny in *Henry VIII*. On 9 May 1751 he shared a benefit with four others, not having made much of an impression on London audiences.

According to the Bath *Journal* of 11 November 1751 Elrington acted at the Orchard Street Theatre in that town, but the length of his engagement is not known. In the winter of 1753–54 he ostensibly managed a troupe of players who proposed opening a new playhouse in Manchester, but he ran into difficulties with the local authorities and returned to Ireland.

Faulkner's Dublin Journal on 8 October 1754 may have confused Richard Elrington with one of the other members of the family when it announced his debut at Smock Alley for 9 October, for he was certainly at that theatre in earlier years. In the winter of 1754–55 Elrington's company played at the Vaults in Belfast. In the troupe were Richard's "wife" Elizabeth, his brother Joseph, his sister Nancy (Mrs Thomas Ward), and Master Richard Elrington. On 3 January 1755 the group showed Belfast audiences *Harlequin Amazed*, the first pantomime ever performed there, and while in Belfast Elrington appeared as Hamlet, Romeo, and Brutus in *Julius Caesar*. About mid-March the company performed in Derry.

It is very likely that Richard Elrington's relationship to Elizabeth Martin was informal, for by 1760 she had gone off to "marry" a Mr Workman, and Elrington was said to have married a woman named Katherine. *Faulkner's Dublin Journal* reported on 17 April 1770 that Richard Elrington had died lately at Ballyboughbridge. His will was proved on 11 April.

Elrington, Mrs Richard, Elizabeth, earlier Mrs [Miss?] Grace, then Mrs. Barnes, then Mrs Christopher Martin; later Mrs Workman, then Mrs Richard Wilson the first *b. 1716, actress, singer, dancer.*

Mrs. Richard Elrington discarded so many "husbands" that tracing her progress accurately is most difficult. She may have been born Elizabeth Grace, though Charles Lee Lewes took Grace to be either the name of a man to whom she was attached, or a name she gave herself. According to Lewes's figures, Elizabeth was born in 1716, and he said she was the original Jenny in *The Provok'd Husband*. But the 1728 edition of that play listed Mrs Cibber (Theophilus's first wife, Jane) as Jenny; Lewes was thinking, probably, of the Mrs Grace who played Myrtilla, and she was not Elizabeth but the Mrs Grace who later became Mrs Macklin.

By 1732 Elizabeth Grace had become Mrs (sometimes Miss) Barnes and was acting at the Rainsford Street Theatre in Dublin. Bills transcribed by the late W. S. Clark show a Miss Barnes to have acted Prue in *Love for Love* on 5 February 1733 and Jaculine in *The Royal Merchant* on 13 November 1735. She was at that playhouse in the intervening seasons and served as a dancer at Smock Alley in 1736–37. Related to her, perhaps, were the Mr and Master Barnes in Mme Violante's troupe at the Dame Street Theatre, Dublin, in 1731–32.

Elizabeth's association with Mr Martin began in 1741 (Lewes made all of her attachments "marriages," but it is likely that none were legal). Christopher Martin posed as a man of good family and prospects, but he was a younger brother and had no prospects at all. Martin lived off Betty's salary, in Dublin apparently; the Mrs Martin who acted in London at the Covent Garden Theatre in the 1730s and 1740s was another woman. Christopher Martin ended up in prison on a robbery charge, during which time Betty gave birth to his son Thomas. Thomas in time became a musician and was with Stanton's company of players in Bridgnorth late in the eighteenth century.

Richard Elrington, according to Lewes, inherited his father Thomas's theatrical properties if not his talent. He performed in Dublin in the 1730s and early 1740s, and about the time that Betty Martin found Ireland an undesirable place to stay, Elrington recruited her for a tour to England. His alliance with her may have begun as early as 1746, when she is known to have sung between the acts and played Desdemona in *Othello* as Mrs Elrington in Ward's troupe at Oswestry, Shropshire. Lewes claims that in addition to the child Betty had by Martin, she also brought to England with Elrington a daughter she had had by a Dublin sadler named Davis. That daughter, Lewes said, married respectably in 1756 and was in 1805 an eminent London actress—left unnamed.

Lewes had it that upon their arrival in England Betty took over the reins of management of the strolling players, though the company belonged ostensibly to Richard. Lewes did not date the couple's original trip to England, though we know that Elrington was in England in 1749, after which he returned to Dublin in the spring of 1750 and then came back to England for the 1750–51 season. Betty, on the other hand, performed in London in the spring of 1750. She appeared as Lady Froth in *The Double Dealer* on 19 April at Covent Garden, advertised as "a Young Gentlewoman who never appeared on this stage before." She was paid £5 5s. on 25 April for her acting and was identified as Mrs Elrington in the account books. Possibly she was the "Elrington" who received half-value for benefit tickets at Covent Garden on 7 May and collected a miserable £1 5s. Richard Elrington is not known to have performed in London that spring, though he did appear the following fall. Betty seems not to have acted in London again.

The Elrington company played at Buxton at some point, and in Manchester in December 1753 they encountered considerable resistance from the law. Lewes melodramatizes their encounter with the authorities and pictures Betty putting on a mad scene for their benefit:

"Yes," said the artful Betty, "let me be instantly manacled, shackled, or closed up in such a brazen bull, as the infernal Phalaris used, as recorded in Grecian story."

She had no sooner said this, than she rose and tore a valuable wig from her bald pate, which had long before been despoiled by a cruel disorder of its flaxen locks. Thus in a state of affected distraction she ran like a fury about the room.

The justices still insisted that the troupe leave town in 24 hours. The company left Manchester for Liverpool where they embarked for Belfast.

The Elringtons acted at the Vaults in Belfast in 1754–55, one of Betty's roles there being Juliet (to Richard Elrington's Romeo) on 28 February 1755. Betty also performed at Lisburn and Derry before the end of the winter season. Lewes added that the company went to Lough and then to the Maze races, after which, he said, they were persuaded by Betty to attempt Carmarthen, Wales. Lewes claimed that Elrington was on the tour to Wales, though we can find no corroborating evidence. While in Wales, Lewes stated, Elrington was lured back to Dublin by his mother to marry the daughter of an old gentleman of great property whom his own mother had married. Elrington left money with a clergyman in Caernarvon for his natural son Richard and departed for Ireland. Betty

followed him to Dublin to no avail and in time returned to her theatrical property in Caernarvon. Lewes said that she was deserted by Elrington in 1760, when she was 44 years old.

From Lewes too we get the story that she found a miserable company of players at a village near Caernarvon, took them over, and formed an alliance with a Mr Workman, who was a painter and player and had the bad luck to die of lead poisoning not long afterward. Betty was then left, said Lewes, with her son by Christopher Martin and also with young Richard Elrington, whom Lewes took (in error, we think) to have been a child of hers. Shortly after Workman's death "Dancing Dicky" Elrington reached his majority, received the £100 that his father had left for him, and may then have gone off on his own. By 1766 Betty was a manager at Mansfield.

She then joined Whitley's company and met the young Richard Wilson. They acted as husband and wife for a few months, and then joined the Leeds company under Leister, where they were in 1767. Sometime after that Wilson left Betty. Since we do not hear of her again, she may have given up her theatrical career.

Elrington, Thomas [*fl. 1663–1670*], *scenekeeper, stagekeeper.*

The London Stage lists Thomas Elrington as a member of the King's Company in 1663–64, though his name seems not to have appeared in the Lord Chamberlain's accounts until 3 March 1665, when he was described in one warrant as a scenekeeper and in another as a stagekeeper—variant terms for the same job, perhaps. According to *The London Stage* Elrington was still in the company in 1669–70.

Elrington, Thomas *1688–1732, actor, manager.*

Thomas Elrington was born in June 1688 near Golden Square. His father served the Duke of Montagu and may have been (or been related to) the Thomas Elrington who was a scenekeeper in the King's Company in the 1660s. The younger Thomas's brothers, Francis (1692–1746), Joseph (died 1755), and Ralph (died 1761) all became actors.

Thomas was not at first destined for the theatre. According to Chetwood, he was apprenticed to a French upholsterer in Covent Garden, in whose shop he and Chetwood used to act plays when the master was not around. One day, when they were doing a scene from *Sophonisba*, the master walked in, and young Thomas in consternation and fear thrust his playbook inside a cushion he was working on and sewed it up to prevent discovery. Later Thomas organized an amateur production of *Hamlet* in which he played the Ghost. His master discovered him, beat him into the street, and was stopped from further abusing the lad only by sympathetic members of Elrington's audience. The master made the boy swear never to act again, but in time he relented, and during the last year of Tom's apprenticeship (which would have been about 1708) he allowed him to do some amateur performing. Theophilus Keene the actor spotted Elrington and introduced him to the professional stage.

Elrington's first professional appearance was on 2 December 1709 at Drury Lane when he played the title role in *Oroonoko*, billed (probably through a printing error) as Elderton. His years of amateur acting stood him in good stead, for he went on to act Plume in *The Recruiting Officer* on 15 December 1709, the Ghost of Laius in *Oedipus* on 14 January 1710, Carlos in *The Successful Strangers* on 31 January, Proculus in *Valentinian* on 1 February, Don Lorenzo in *The Mistake* on 11 February, Cribidge in *The Fair Quaker of Deal* on 25 February, and Lovewell in *The Gamester* on 23 May. Elrington received two benefits at Drury Lane: one shared with Corey on 7 March 1710 and one shared with Powell on 26 May. At Pinketh-

man's theatre in Greenwich during the summer of 1710 Elrington played, in addition to some of his earlier roles, the Governor in *Love Makes a Man*, Belford in *The Fatal Marriage*, Spinosa in *Venice Preserv'd*, the Ghost in *Hamlet*, Clytus in the burlesque *The Rival Queens*, Don Lopez in *The Libertine Destroyed*, Ferdinand in *The Tempest*, Malcolm in *Macbeth*, Woodly in *Epsom Wells*, Cinthio in *The Emperor of the Moon*, Sir George Airy in *The Busy Body*, and Ranger in *The Fond Husband*.

He may have spent the full 1710–11 season at Drury Lane, but he was recorded for roles only from March 1711 onward. His new parts included Cecil in *The Albion Queens*, Surefriend in *Injur'd Love*, Valerio in *The City Ramble*, and Winwife in *Bartholomew Fair*. In 1711–12 he added, among other characters, Trasiline in *Philaster* and Slur in *The Wife's Relief*. The 1719 edition of *The Heroick Daughter* listed Elrington as Don Sanchez, but it is doubtful that he played the part at the premiere on 28 November 1712 at Drury Lane, for he is said to have been in Ireland at that time.

The manager Joseph Ashbury invited Elrington to Dublin in 1712, and though the actor may have returned to London for appearances the following year or two, his main activity from 1712 to 1715 appears to have been in Dublin, where he shared the management of the Smock Alley Theatre with Ashbury, Evans, and Griffith. In 1713 he toured with the company to Cork, playing in a room they refurbished there. Sometime in 1713 he made his position secure by marrying Ashbury's daughter Frances (b. 1697). Elrington's parts in Ireland included the title role in *Timon of Athens*, Bajazet in *Tamerlane*, Colonel Blunt in *The Committee*, and Lord Townly in *The Provok'd Husband*.

He returned to London for the last half of the 1714–15 season at Drury Lane, one of two "uncelebrated Actors" from Dublin mentioned by Cibber in his *Apology*. On

24 January 1715 he played Cassius in *Julius Caesar*, after which he appeared as Torrismond in *The Spanish Fryar* (against Cibber's wishes), Hotspur in *1 Henry IV*, Orestes in *The Distrest Mother*, Sylla in *Caius Marius*, the title role in *Mithridates* (for his benefit on 21 March), and the Earl of Pembroke in *Lady Jane Gray*. Robert Wilks was apparently instrumental in bringing Elrington over, and when he arranged Elrington's benefit behind the backs of his colleagues Doggett and Cibber, Doggett became most "untractable." The benefit showed a deficit of £10, which Wilks and the reluctant Cibber covered.

Elrington again went to Ireland, but he was back in London for the 1716–17 season, playing for John Rich at the new theatre in Lincoln's Inn Fields. He began with Hamlet on 6 October 1716 and continued with such other parts as Essex in *The Unhappy Favorite*, Morat in *Aureng-Zebe*, the title role in *Don Sebastian*, Cortez in *The Indian Emperor*, Varanes in *Theodosius*, Alexander in *The Rival Queens*, and Macduff in *Macbeth*. Also in the playbills at Lincoln's Inn Fields during the season was an "Elrington Junior," probably Thomas's brother Ralph. In 1717–18 Thomas was again in Ireland, but in 1718–19 he returned to Drury Lane to play a number of his old roles: Hotspur, Torrismond, Macduff, Bajazet (which Barton Booth much admired), and Cassius. He also appeared as Chamont in *The Orphan*, the King in *The Mourning Bride*, and Busiris in *Young Busiris*.

Joseph Ashbury died in the summer of 1720, and Elrington succeeded not only to the managership of the Smock Alley company but also to Ashbury's deputy Mastership of the Revels in Ireland and stewardship of the King's Inns of Court. He also held two sinecures: a position in the Quitrent Office and a post as gunner to the Train of Artillery. By this time he had probably started his family. He and Frances had a daughter Nancy, who became Mrs

Wrightson and then Mrs Thomas Ward and who acted, though apparently not in London. They also had a son Joseph, who seems to have confined his acting to Ireland, and a son Richard, who had a career as actor and manager in both Ireland and London. Their son Thomas became a professional soldier in Flanders.

Most of Elrington's time in the 1720s was spent in Ireland, acting, training actors, managing Smock Alley, and increasing his theatrical empire. Among the extensive list of parts he played at Smock Alley from 1720–21 to 1731–32 were the title role in *The Rover*, Othello, Torrismond, Bajazet, Clerimont in *The Tender Husband*, Lovemore in *The Amorous Widow*, Varanes in *Theodosius*, Macbeth, Courtwell in *Woman is a Riddle*, Plume in *The Recruiting Officer*, Biron in *The Fatal Marriage*, Archer in *The Beaux' Stratagem*, Essex in *The Unhappy Favorite*, Myrtle in *The Conscious Lovers*, Brutus in *Julius Caesar*, Oroonoko, Don Carlos in *Love Makes a Man*, the King in *The Mourning Bride*, Oedipus, Herod in *Mariamne*, Hotspur, Cato, Hamlet, Dumont in *Jane Shore*, Chamont in *The Orphan*, the title role in *The Pilgrim*, Orestes in *The Distrest Mother*, Sir Hugh in *The Merry Wives of Windsor*, Antony in *All for Love*, Morat in *Aureng-Zebe*, Alexander in *The Rival Queens*, Barnwell in *The London Merchant*, and Townly in *The Provok'd Husband*.

One of Elrington's most promising protégés was Dennis Delane, who made a considerable career for himself in London. And one of Thomas's real estate purchases was the yard of the Three Crowns Inn, which he bought from Richard Ashbury.

Elrington came to London again during the late 1720s, despite his heavy obligations in Ireland. In 1728–29 he supplied the place of the ailing Barton Booth, an actor he much admired. On 10 September 1728 at Drury Lane he played Hotspur once again, after which he revived a number of other old roles and essayed Osmyn in *The*

Mourning Bride, Othello, the King in *Henry IV*, Lothario in *The Fair Penitent*, Melantius in *The Maid's Tragedy*, Antony in *All for Love*, Cato, and Edgar in *King Lear*. He received two benefits during the season, one on 9 November 1728 and a second on 29 March 1729. He faced audiences that inevitably compared him with Booth, and the author of Booth's *Life* (1733) wrote that

so famous as Mr. *Elrington* was, and had been, the Town could scarce relish him when he came over to *England*, and play'd the Season after Mr. *Booth* was oblig'd to quit the Stage. There was none whenever the *Distrest Mother* was perform'd, but would think upon what they had seen; and tho' they justly applauded Mr. *Elrington*, would still think upon the lost Mr. *Booth*.

Booth, however, probably would have responded warmly to Elrington, for he had been generous in his praise of him in earlier years. Elrington, for his part, always stood in awe of Booth, who had, he thought, a power quite beyond his own. The Drury Lane managers were certainly pleased with Elrington's 1728–29 engagement, for they asked him to become a permanent member of the troupe. Elrington refused, according to Davies, on the grounds that he was well-established financially and socially in Ireland.

He was back in Ireland in 1730 and during the year was taken to task by someone calling himself Elrington's "unknown trusty Friend" in *An Epistle to Mr. Thomas Elrington, Occasion'd by the MURDER of the Tragedy of CATO Last Monday Night*. The critic criticized Elrington for "bellowing" as Cato and admonished him for using for that character the same costume he used "in the Parts of Alexander, Varanes, and Orestes, &c. . . . and no doubt if this Proves not a caution, he may wear it in the part of *Julius Caesar*." During the Senate debates in *Cato*, the author said, Elrington

being enraged to see a little extraordinary Tricks of [a] *Monikee* in the Pit, started from his Chair to drive her out, which added a particular Lustre to the Play . . . [but the monkey got on the stage] midst Pails of Claps [and] The Servants were so stupefied with their Storming, Scolding Master, they neglected bringing in the Chair to expire in . . . [H]e gave up Life, amidst as much Spleen, as if he were Bajazet, instead of Cato

> . . . *mocking all the Grimly Starts of Death,*
> *Fell back and snored the last of* Cato's *Breath.*

By 20 June 1732 Elrington was engaged with John Evans and others in a project to lease the great cellar of the malt house in Cork. On the following 22 July he was at his house in Drumcondra Lane in Dublin, discussing plans for a new Dublin playhouse based on Drury Lane, when he died of a malignant fever attended with violent convulsions. He was buried at St Michan's, Dublin. After his death his estate was managed by his widow, and the records show that funds for a new playhouse in Cork (presumably the one planned by Elrington a month before he died) came from the actor-manager's estate. On 11 August 1741 Frances Elrington sold the theatre on Dunscomb's Marsh in Cork and the theatre in Waterford to the proprietors of the Aungier Street Theatre in Dublin. Those properties had been developed by Elrington. From the sales Frances Elrington was able to establish an annuity for herself of £277 10*s*. She was still alive on 9 May 1752 when her benefit tickets were accepted at Smock Alley.

After his death Thomas Elrington was called "the most celebrated Tragedian" and "the ornament and delight of the Irish Stage." Reed in his "Notitia Dramatica" quoted a contemporary obituary:

His perfections as a player are so well and universally known both here and in England (whither he has been often by the managers of both theatres in London with very advantageous offers invited) that it would be impertinent to insert here. Nature certainly formed him as an actor, and to his amazing genius for representing such a variety of grand characters gave him a voice and person scarce ever equalled and never excelled by any of his contemporaries or predecessors of the Stage, and it is to be feared will never be rivalled by any of his successors. All who are lovers of the most polite and rational entertainment must be sensibly concerned at the loss of a man so eminent in his profession.

Chetwood in 1749 was a bit more specific about Elrington's talent and person. He called him "a true copy of Mr. Verbruggen" but noted that Elrington also had "an infinite Fund of (what is called Low) humour upon the Stage. I have seen him perform Don Cholerick in the Fop's Fortune [i.e. *Love Makes a Man*] with Infinite Pleasure." His voice, according to Chetwood, was strong and manly, but sweet, and his figure tall and well proportioned. In manner he was honorable, humane, good natured, and polite. But even from these comments, Elrington the man and actor is somehow missing. One would wish for the kind of precise critical description of his work that Colley Cibber gave for so many actors, for judging from what little we know, Thomas Elrington one of the most important actors alive during the transitional period between Betterton and Garrick.

Elsam, Mrs [fl. 1716–1730], actress.

Mrs Elsam played Necessary in the first performance of *Woman is a Riddle* at the Lincoln's Inn Fields Theatre on 4 December 1716. On 15 May 1717 she shared a benefit there. In 1717–18 (once styled in error "Miss" Elsam) she was seen as Prudence in *The Amorous Widow* on 4 January 1718 and then Laetitia in *The Fair Example*, an unnamed character in *Tartuffe*, and Pert in *The Lucky Chance*. The summer of 1718 found her in William Pinketh-

man's troupe at Richmond in August playing Chat in *The Committee*, the Nurse in *Love for Love*, and Mrs Security in *The Gamester*.

She returned in the fall of 1718 to Lincoln's Inn Fields and performed there in John Rich's troupe through the 1720–21 season, adding to her repertoire such new roles as Hob's Mother in *Hob's Wedding*, Ruth in *The Squire of Alsatia*, and Mrs Mopsus in *The Cheats*. On 8 September 1721 she was Olinda in *The Noble Englishman* at Lee's booth at Southwark Fair, after which her name disappeared from the bills until 8 September 1726, when at Southwark Fair she acted Lady Wealthy in *The Unnatural Parents*. On 15 October 1728 she was at the Haymarket Theatre playing Martina in *The Metamorphosis* and Widow Speedy in *The Craftsman*. Her last known role was Lady Bountiful in *The Stratagem*, which she played at the Haymarket on 18 September 1730 and at Southwark Fair on the twenty-fourth.

Elvin, Mons [fl. 1795], actor, dancer.

A press clipping in the Percival Collection in the British Museum indicates that Mons Elvin played Discord in the pantomime *Pandora's Box* at Sadler's Wells on an unspecified date in 1795.

Elwart, Mr [fl. 1707], musician.

Mr Elwart and several other court musicians were given leave on 1 December 1707 to perform at the Queen's Theatre in the Haymarket.

Elworth. *See* ALEWORTH.

Ely, Mrs [fl. 1724–1726], dresser?

The Lincoln's Inn Fields accounts twice mention a Mrs Ely, possibly one of the theatre's dressers. On 7 December 1724 she was paid 18s. for 12 days, and on 17 October 1726 she received £1 1s. on account for dresses.

Emanuel. *See* EMMANUEL.

Emberton, Mr [*fl.* 1746–1747], *stage doorkeeper.*

Mr Emberton, the Drury Lane stage doorkeeper, received shared benefits on 9 May 1746 and 8 May 1747.

Emery, John 1777–1822, *actor, singer, violinist, composer, poet, painter.*

John Emery, the son of country actors, was born on 22 December 1777 at Sunderland, near Durham. His father, Mackle Emery (c. 1742–1825), never performed in London, but his mother (c. 1747–1827) appeared at the Haymarket Theatre on 6 July 1802 as Dame Ashfield in *Speed the Plough* and then acted at Covent Garden. John received "a scanty portion" of school learning at Ecclesfield, in the West Riding of Yorkshire, but while there he mastered the dialect which later was to support his delineation of northern characters with such superiority. Having been instructed on the violin, he was able at the age of 12 to play in the orchestra at the Brighton Thea-

National Portrait Gallery

JOHN EMERY

by Raven

tre and also in the orchestras of Plymouth, Exeter, and other theatres to which the family toured. When John was a mere boy, Michael Kelly saw him leading the band at Plymouth with excellent ability. In January 1790 John sang two songs for his father's benefit at Sheffield, the first a comic song "describing the tailors, gluttons, cooks, sots, lawyers, parsons, landlords, soldiers, sailors, lovers, bullies, misers, managers, and players' dogs," and the other called "Fat Dolly the Cook; or, a Sop in the Pan."

At Brighton in 1792 he made his first appearance as an actor, playing Old Crazy in the farce *Peeping Tom*; the role of a feeble old man may have been an odd one for a lad, but his favorite roles in the future were to be such portrayals. In this year and in the summer of 1793 he toured with his parents in John Bernard's company to Dover, Plymouth, and Teignmouth, going on in such country boys as Diggory in *She Stoops to Conquer*. By 1795, he was playing low comedy leads in Wilkinson's company on the York circuit. He made his first appearance at Hull as Caleb in *He Would be a Soldier*, and Wilkinson, soon realizing that Emery's real *forte* at the time was neither old men nor low comics, persuaded him to play rustics. During the four years he remained with the York company he became "universally allowed to have no equal in the representation of Yorkshire rustics."

Emery's northern reputation in such roles earned him a three-year contract at Covent Garden, where he made his debut on 21 September 1798 as Frank Oatland in *A Cure for the Heartache* and as Lovegold in the afterpiece *The Miser*. The reviewer in the *Monthly Mirror* judged that as Oatland Emery had acquitted himself nobly in comparison to Fawcett, who had created the role (many thought Emery to have exceeded the original), and that as Lovegold he exhibited *"great"* acting for so young a performer. On the basis of his *"original genius"* it was predicted that Emery would prove to be a most important acquisition to Covent Garden. Emery was not a copy of any other actor and showed no bad habits of random gestures and coarse muggings which candidates from the provinces commonly picked up—"he does not disdain, however, the mechanical usages of actors, but makes them secondary and subordinate to more important considerations." For the critic of the *Monthly Mirror* Emery had "conveyed the full intention of the author":

it was a portrait of rustic simplicity, blended with the shrewd cunning which is frequently its concomitant—of strong brotherly affection, filial duty, and attachment to his master:—of a man, whose family wants are most pressingly urgent, thrown into a trying situation, which, while it shews the acuteness of his sensibility, evinces the triumph of principle over strong and artful temptation. While we have no occasion to disconnect the author and the actor, we are pronouncing the eulogium that ought to be most gratifying to the feelings of the latter: but a still narrower investigation will be expected from this work, and, luckily, the performer will bear it.

Mr. Emery reminds us of that child of nature Blanchard, whose habitual excesses precipitated him into an early grave; he acts from his own feelings, and they direct him to the right application of his powers; his simplicity is without effort; and his stage habits are such only as the purposes of stage representation require. The theatre will always demand something beyond what real life can furnish; but Mr. Emery makes no extravagant sacrifice to purchase this *desideratum*. He does not think the mere assumption of the rustic habiliments constitutes the character, but his *countryman* is faithfully sketched from nature, and his own experience and observation have no doubt assisted him in preparing the draught; he seems more attentive to character than effect, and this, at a time when effect is every thing, is no mean praise. If we had not seen his *Frank Oatland*, in which his performance of the *purse scene* displayed great feeling and originality; his *second recruit* [in *The Recruiting Officer*] had been sufficient to stamp him in our opinion an actor of the

first promise. If it was not *absolutely* Nature, it was as *near* it as the author would allow him to approach.

Described as of middle height, without features "peculiarly and positively *comic*" in themselves, Emery could elicit humor without seeming to labor or distort. His one objectionable trick, thought the *Monthly Mirror*, was the use of a lisp in playing the old man, Lovegold, in an attempt to suggest the lack of teeth which was "too palpably assumed." He next played Silky in *The Road to Ruin* on 3 October 1798, in which he showed his talents "to much advantage." Except for acting Abel Drugger in *The Tobacconist* on 21 November, Emery passed the remainder of his first season in numerous supporting roles, mostly old men, which included a Recruit in *The Recruiting Officer*, Mr Pickle in *The Spoil'd Child*, a vocal character in *The Mouth of the Nile*, M'Gilpin in *The Highland Reel*, Nicholas in *Secrets Worth Knowing*, Oldcastle in *The Intriguing Chambermaid*, Bromley in *The Jew and the Doctor*, a Witch in *Macbeth*, Old Vizorly in *The Votary of Wealth*, Mr Morgan in *The Old Cloathsman*, Sir Simon Flourish in *Abroad and at Home*, Orson in *The Iron Chest*, Toby Allspice in *The Way to Get Married*, Gurnet in *Who is She?*, Vinegar in *The Son-in-Law*, Ferret in *The Horse and the Widow*, Record in *The Adopted Child*, Sir Gregory in *Hartford Bridge*, Doctor Butts in *Henry VIII*, Snacks in *Fortune's Frolics*, Dickins in *Life's Vagaries*, Matthias in *The Midnight Hour*, Blister in *The Virgin Unmask'd*, and a principal character in *Albert and Adelaide*.

After spending the summer at Brighton, Emery returned to Covent Garden at a salary of £2 10s. per week to perform a similar list of roles, to which he added many others. In the part of Gibbet in *The Beaux' Stratagem*, which he first acted on 11 October 1799, he had "the art of making up his face, and twisting himself into

Farquhar's . . . travelling Captain, with so much address, that an auditor would scarcely suppose it was possible for him to soften himself into any part in which simplicity and innocence of habit were its leading features" (*Theatrical Inquisitor*, April 1814). Thomas Hutton in the *Dramatic Censor* (1800) followed Emery through his numerous new roles that season: as Diego in *Paul and Virginia* on 1 May 1800, he looked and acted the part of "a stern, savage, unrelenting taskmaster," and his portrayal of Farmer Grouse in *Liberal Opinions* on 12 May entitled him "to great commendation." That was a role which went to him only because Thomas Knight was ill, a somewhat fortuitous circumstance for Emery, who was so aptly suited to the character.

On 28 May 1800 Emery shared £326

JOHN EMERY, as Stephen Harrowby
engraving by Bond, after De Wilde

(less house charges) in benefit receipts with Mrs Johnson and Mrs Thomas Dibdin. For the event he acted Lord Priory in a revival of *Wives As They Were*, and Hutton wrote that "Mr Emery is a young, but very promising performer." During the season Emery experienced a narrow escape with his life when in March 1800 Chapman's "New Eidophusikon" exhibition in Panton Street, Haymarket, was consumed by fire. During the fire "A sergeant of the 2d regt. of guards, of the name of Poole, stepped on a skylight, belonging to the roof of an adjoining house, and falling through, was killed upon the spot," reported the *Monthly Mirror* in March 1800. "In falling he made an effort to lay hold of Mr. Emery, the comedian, who stood next to him, but, fortunately for the actor, the attempt was unsuccessful."

In the summer of 1800 Emery was engaged at the Haymarket, where he made his debut on 13 June as Zekiel Homespun in *The Heir at Law*; at the end of the play George Colman, the author of the piece as well as the manager, proclaimed in the green room that he had never seen the role so well acted. On that night Emery also acted Bromley in *The Jew and the Doctor*. Emery's other roles at the Haymarket that summer were Germain in *The Castle of Sorrento*, Don Gortez in *'Tis All a Farce*, Sir Christopher Curry in *Inkle and Yarico*, Crazy in *Peeping Tom*, Abel Drugger in *The Tobacconist*, Sheepface in *The Village Lawyer*, Rawbold in *The Iron Chest*, Juan in *What a Blunder*, Sir Charles in *The Guardian*, Shenkin in *Cambro-Britons*, Captain Bertram in *The Birth Day*, Jabal in *The Jew*, and a character in *The Review; or, the Wags of Windsor*.

Although obliged in these early years to act mostly inferior characters, Emery was slowly establishing a line of old men and country rustics. In the latter he was eventually to hold "an absolute and undisputed supremacy." On 11 February 1801 at Covent Garden he was the original Stephen Harrowby in Colman's *Poor Gentleman*, a role especially written for him by the author. Again with Colman at the Haymarket in the summer of 1801 he played Clod in O'Keeffe's *The Young Quaker* and Farmer Ashfield in *Speed the Plough*, a role which went to him at Covent Garden when Knight left several years later and which Emery made "a great feature."

Emery continued as a favorite actor at Covent Garden for another 21 years until his death. His salary was £6 per week in 1800–1801 and £7 in 1801–2 and 1802–3. Receipts at his benefits over the years were a substantial testimony to his popularity: £439 12s. on 5 June 1804; £536 6s. 6d. on 31 May 1805; £556 12s. 6d. on 29 May 1806; £569 19s. 6d. on 27 May 1807; £490 17s. 6d. on 31 May 1808; £599 13s. 6d. on 13 June 1810; and £502 4s. 6d. on 19 June 1811—presumably less £160 in house charges in each instance.

Emery's original roles at Covent Garden included Dan in Colman's *John Bull* on 5 March 1803; Tyke in Morton's *School of Reform* on 15 January 1805—"He astonished the town by a display of feeling and passion, nearly approaching to the most thrilling tragedy . . . . His archness, his villainy, his presumption, his agony, and his repentance, were all finely given"; Ralph Hempseed in Colman's *XYZ* on 11 December 1810; Dandie Dinmont in Terry's *Guy Mannering* (from Walter Scott) on 12 March 1816—"His excellent and very natural delineation . . . materially strengthened the piece"; Sam Sharpset in Morton's *The Slave* on 12 November 1816—his singing of "York, you're wanted" was superb and unforgettable; Ratcliff in Terry's *Heart of Midlothian* on 17 April 1819; and Fixture in Morton's *A Roland for an Oliver*—"one of his truest delineations." When he played Fixture at Liverpool in the summer of 1819, the audience would not permit the play to continue until he had repeated his principal scene.

One role in which Emery was not suc-

Harvard Theatre Collection

JOHN EMERY, as John Moody

engraving by Woodman, after De Wilde

cessful, it being totally out of his line, was Ennui in *The Dramatist* which he acted only once, on 29 April 1806; in that season, however, he shone as Caliban in *The Tempest* and Barnardine in *Measure for Measure*. In the latter role Genest said he "looked and acted inimitably." He also acted Sam in *Raising of the Wind* (1803–4), Silence in *2 Henry IV* (1803–4), Giles Woodbine in *Blind Bargain* (1803–4), Ralph in *The Maid of the Mill* (1809–10), Tom Tough in *For England Ho* (1813–14), Lockit in *The Beggar's Opera* (1813–14), and Dougal in *Rob Roy* (1818–19).

By 1821–22, his last season at Covent Garden, Emery's salary was £13 per week. He gave his last performance in that theatre on 29 July 1822 as Edie Ochiltree in *The Antiquary*. He engaged at the English

Opera House for the summer of 1822, playing on 1 July Giles in *The Miller's Maid*, a role he had introduced there the previous summer. He repeated the role on the third, his last performance on the stage. He was announced for the same role for the fifth, illness prevented his playing, and the character was undertaken by T. P. Cooke.

After three weeks of illness, on 25 July 1822 at the age of 45, Emery died about 8:00 in the evening at his home at No 12, Hyde Street, Bloomsbury, of pneumonia brought on by a disease of the liver. A "decay of nature," evidently caused by cold brandy and water—"he studied [with] a new part in one hand and a glass in the other, he took in alternately the words and the liquor"—brought about a premature old age. In his *Diaries* for July 1822, James Winston noted that "Emery became latterly incapable of fulfilling his duty. He drank excessively, was in a public house great part of his time." Emery was buried in a vault in St. Andrew, Holborn, on 1 August. In December 1822 the administration of his estate, valued at £300, was granted to Ann Emery (née Thompson) his widow and relict, the daughter of a tradesman in the Borough, whom he had married in May 1802.

When still a young actor in the provinces before coming to London, Emery had intended to marry the actress Maria Rebecca Duncan (d. 1858), but for some reason the wedding never occurred: "the wedding clothes were bought," reported Winston in his *Diaries*, and "the disappointment hung upon him through his life." She later married James Davison in 1812 and had a considerable acting career on the nineteenth-century stage.

Soon after Emery's death a meeting of his friends was advertised for 29 July—before he was buried—at the coffee room of the English Opera House "to adopt the most prompt and efficient means for relieving his distressed widow, and seven orphans, left totally unprovided for by his

sudden death." The youngest of the children was 18 months old. Also surviving him were his elderly parents, who had relied on him for support. A subscription was solicited and a public theatrical benefit, under the patronage of the Duke of York, was held on 5 August 1822 at Covent Garden, where Emery had acted for some 24 years. Arnold closed the English Opera House on that night, and Elliston closed Drury Lane. *The Rivals* was played with a stellar cast: Munden as Sir Anthony Absolute, Charles Kemble as Captain Absolute, Liston as Acres, Mrs Davenport as Mrs Malaprop, and Mrs Edwin as Lydia Languish. Principal singers and dancers, including Madame Vestris, participated in a concert, and the English Opera company played *Belles Without Beaux*. The following lines, written by George Colman, were spoken in eulogy by Mr Hartley:

Friends of the Muse! who, in a polish'd
    age,
Support the morals of our British stage;
Who, when a public favourite gives birth
To feelings of respect for private worth,
With generous and equal ardour scan
The merits of the actor and the man;
Need we, to-night, express our grief? or
    tell
Sorrows in which you sympathise so
    well?
Poor Emery is gone! who play'd his part,
Each day he breathed, home to the very
    heart.
True to the drama's as to friendship's
    call,
He charm'd us—for 'twas honest nature
    all.
How oft, when scarce an effort would
    appear,
He drew the giant's bow of genius here!
Seem'd like a random shooter in the dark,
But never, never fail'd to hit the mark:
Various his range, but, in the pleasant
    vein,
'We n'er may look upon his like again.'
'Twas his, well studied in the rustic
    school,

To show the arch, the vicious, and the
    fool;
'Twas his, with matchless humour, to
    portray
The Lumps or Dundie Dinmonts of his
    day;
'Twas his, in Tyke, with truth's resistless
    force,
To fill the lowly villain with remorse;
'Twas his to feel, too, with becoming
    pride,
How talent can support its own fire-side;
Till in his prime, also! of life bereft,
Life's dearest objects shelterless were left.
Patrons of genius! guardians of distress!
Friends of the destitute and fatherless!
For you his widow will her prayer re-
    peat —
For you his children's grateful bosoms
    beat; —
And may his spirit now look down to
    view
The succour they obtain this night from
    you.

On 8 August 1822 James Ackland, "ora-torical lecturer and professor of the science of mnemonics," delivered a funeral oration at the City of London Tavern, for which the proprietors had given free use of the rooms. A single-sheet *Ode on the Death of John Emery Comedian, By T. Greenwood* was published in this month. On 7 December 1822 the trustees of the benefit and subscription funds, John Calcroft, M.P., John Rowland Durrant, Esq, and George Henry Robins, Esq, announced that the benefit night had brought in £946 18s. 6d. and the subscriptions and donations had reached £2372 8s. 6d., for a total of £3319 7s. Contributors included the Dukes of York, Devonshire, Bedford, and Sussex; the Marquis of Hartford, Lord Egremont, the Earls of Essex, Fitzwilliam, Glengall, and Spencer, Lord Carlisle, Lord Cholmondley, and a host of actors, politicians, knights, businessmen, and other patrons of the arts. An anonymous donor, who was later dis-covered to have been the former actress Harriot Mellon, then Mrs Thomas Coutts

and later Duchess of St Alban's, subscribed £100. She also settled a guinea per week upon Mr and Mrs Mackle Emery, John's elderly parents, for the rest of their lives.

In person, Emery cut an awkward figure, looking ever so much like one of the farm-ers he so expertly portrayed. Being a robust and very strong five feet nine inches in stature, he kept up an active interest in field sports and in driving four-in-hand; re-putedly the Brighton coachmen often gave him the reins. He frequented the boxing matches at the Five Courts, enjoyed the fel-lowship of jockeys and boxers, and some-times presided at their public dinners. He also made regular calls at the Rose and Crown in Little Russell Street. "If he was a drunkard, he never forgot his public du-ties," observed a London journal; "if he was a sporting man, he was also a fond husband, if he was a friend to prize-fighters, he was also a kind father."

By the testimony of Wilkinson, Emery was a sound musician and a good violinist. He sang in a low tenor voice and often composed comic songs and verses which he delivered at his own benefits or at those of others. Evidently he really did not like to sing on the stage, though his roles fre-quently required it. Emery was also a tal-ented artist who exhibited between 1801 and 1817 some 19 pictures (mostly sea-scapes) at the Royal Academy, as an hon-orary member. Many of his pictures were sold for "a good price," and it was reported that once at Sunderland while waiting in the wings he sketched a likeness of John Kemble which later brought a very high figure.

The *New Monthly Magazine* (October 1821) called Emery "one of the most real, hearty, and fervid of actors." Of his acting Hazlitt wrote, "It is impossible to praise it sufficiently because there is never any op-portunity of finding fault with it." In Emery's rustic characters Leigh Hunt pro-claimed him to be "excellent and almost perfect." A comprehensive tribute to his tal-

JOHN EMERY, as Andrew

self-portrait

ents appeared in "The Manager's Note-book":

In most of his characters, Emery was with-out a rival. His look, dress, voice, and action, were in general so completely identified with the character he represented, that the *ars ce-lare artem* was constantly realized in his per-formance. He never had recourse to stage trick, buffoonery, or quackery: his acting was chaste, original, humorous, and powerful. It was not, however, to the mere delineation of your "countryman," *per se*, that his talent was confined; there were characters which only lived, and which, in all probability, died with him. We may have a thousand actors of York-shiremen, and yet not one that can play Tyke, Fixture, or Giles. Emery was a Yorkshireman, acting any character he pleased: his *lourde* figure, slouching gait, and provincial dialect, stood merely for the back-ground of the pic-ture which he drew. They were but the canvas upon which he painted; and his design was grotesque, or terrific, his colouring sombre or gay, as the fancy of the author by chance had dictated, or the need of the scene might hap-pen to require. Till Emery came to London, all our stage countrymen were from "Zum-merzetshire," or rather from no shire at all, but of a bastard breed, a mongrel mixture of all. He introduced that fine, broad, rich, York-shire phraseology, with a *naiveté* so unac-countable, and effect so irresistibly ludicrous, there was hardly on the stage his equal—his superior, none.

John's father, Mackle Emery, died on 18 May 1825, aged 83, and his mother died on 6 April 1827, aged 72. Ann Emery, John's wife, survived him by 45 years; she died on 24 January 1870, aged 89. Little is known to us about their seven progeny. A son, John Felix Emery, was baptized at St Paul, Covent Garden, on 4 April 1803. John and three other sons, Horatio, Robert, and Wil-liam, were chief mourners at their father's funeral. Another son, Samuel Anderson Emery, was born in Hyde Street, Blooms-bury, on 10 September 1817, acted in the London theatres in the middle of the nine-teenth century, and died in King William Street, Strand, on 19 July 1881. (He is noticed in *The Dictionary of National Biog-raphy*.) The birth of a child in February 1806 was the cause of Emery's late arrival at the theatre one night to play Sentinel in *Pizarro*: he gave a most humorous apology which charmed the indulgent audience: "my wife has lately been in that state to which most men that are married are lia-ble; . . . this is a *family complaint*." A Miss Emery who acted at Philadelphia in 1828 perhaps was related. The Rebecca Emery who married James Bannister (pos-sibly the son of the actor of that name who flourished 1771–1783) at St George, Han-

WILLIAM BLANCHARD as Dr Camphor, JOHN EMERY as Andrew, JOHN LISTON as Lubin Log, and CHARLES MATHEWS as Flexible in *Love, Law, and Physic*

engraving by Lupton, after Clint

over Square, on 3 April 1809 perhaps was John Emery's sister.

Portraits of John Emery include:

1. By Samuel Raven. Miniature painting. In the National Portrait Gallery.

2. By John Turmeau. Watercolor. In the Garrick Club.

3. By John Varley. Pencil sketch. In the Garrick Club.

4. Portrait engraving by T. L. Bushby,

after Arrowsmith. Published in 1822 by Ferguson with a dedication to the Committee and Subscribers of Emery's benefit.

5. By an unknown engraver. Published as a plate to *The Gazette of Fashion*.

6. As Andrew in a scene from *Love, Law, and Physic*, with William Blanchard as Dr Camphor, John Liston as Lubin Log, and Charles Mathews as Flexible. Painting by G. Clint. In the Garrick Club. Engraved and published in 1831 by T. Lupton.

7. As Andrew. A vignette of Emery's picture of himself. Published in 1822 by Smart.

8. As Dan in *John Bull*. Painting by DeWilde. In the Garrick Club. Engraved by W. Ridley for the *Monthly Mirror*, 1803.

9. As Dan. A vignette engraving by "P. R." Published by Hodgson in 1822.

10. As Dan. A rare engraving by an anonymous artist. In the Harvard Theatre Collection.

11. As Dandie Dinmont in *Guy Mannering*. Engraving by I. Cruikshank as a plate to *The British Stage*.

12. As Dandie Dinmont. Watercolor by DeWilde. In the Harvard Theatre Collection. Engraving by Jenkins, printed by J. Brain.

13. As Dandie Dinmont. By unknown engraver. Published by Jameson in 1822.

14. As Davy in *Bon Ton*. Watercolor by Stothard, in the Harvard Theatre Collection. Engraved by T. A. Dean, and published in Oxberry's *New English Drama*, 1822.

15. As Farmer Ashfield in *Speed the Plough*. Watercolor by DeWilde. In the Garrick Club.

16. As Farmer Ashfield. Engraving by J. Rogers, after J. Kennerley. Published in Oxberry's *Dramatic Bibliography* in 1825.

17. As Giles in *The Miller's Maid*. By unknown engraver. Published in *The Mirror of the Stage* in 1822.

18. As John Lump in *The Review*. Painting by DeWilde. In the Garrick Club.

Engraved by R. Woodman and published by M. Emery, 1815.

19. As John Lump in *The Wags of Windsor* (*The Review*), with J. H. Johnstone as Looney. Emery's own picture, engraved by J. and H. Caulfield.

20. As John Moody in *The Provok'd Husband*. Engraving by Woodman, after DeWilde. Published in Oxberry's *New English Drama* in 1822.

21. As Robert Tyke in *The School of Reform*. Painting by DeWilde. In the Garrick Club. A second version of this painting, probably the original, was exhibited at the Royal Academy in 1806, and was lent to the National Portrait Exhibition of 1868 by W. C. Cater. The latter painting was purchased by Somerset Maugham and is now in the possession of the National Theatre; this was the painting which was engraved by Turner and by Woodman, both in 1808.

22. As Robert Tyke in *The School of Reform*. Watercolor by Samuel DeWilde. In the National Theatre.

23. As Robert Tyke. Engraving by J. Rogers, after T. Wageman. Published in *The Drama*, 1822.

24. As Sam in *Raising the Wind*. Pencil drawing by C. Linsell, 1815. In the Garrick Club.

25. As Stephen Harrowby in *The Poor Gentleman*. Engraving by W. Bond, after DeWilde. Published in *The Theatrical Inquisitor* in 1814. The same engraving was also published by Bell and DeCamp.

26. Singing at Covent Garden, 1806. By unknown engraver. With text of song. Published by Laurie and Whittle, 1806.

Emery, Thomas *d. 1774, sceneman.*

According to testimony which he delivered in the litigation in 1768–69 between Harris and Colman, Thomas Emery began working at the Covent Garden Theatre as a carpenter about 1756. On 12 June 1764, when he proved the will of Thomas Thorne, who had been the chief sceneman at the theatre, Emery described himself as from the parish of St Giles (in the Fields?). By September 1767 he was cited in the theatre accounts as a scene painter and was paid £3 14s. 7d. daily, which sum he distributed among the scenemen. His own salary, by 1768–69, was £1 10s. weekly, and he contracted with Colman about that time to remain at Covent Garden for another two years. Surely he was the Thomas Emery who was buried on 20 March 1774 at St Paul, Covent Garden. A Widow Emery shared benefit receipts at the theatre on the following 7 May.

Emery, [Mrs Thomas?] [fl. 1774–1779?], house servant?

Thomas Emery the sceneman probably died in March 1774, and it was presumably his widow who was one of several whose benefit tickets were admitted at the Covent Garden Theatre on 7 May that year. She was similarly cited on 4 May 1776 and 14 May 1778. Though those may have been charity benefits for the widow of a deceased employee, it is quite possible that after her husband's death Mrs Emery worked at Covent Garden as a house servant. Perhaps she was the Mrs Emery who was a member of the company at York in 1779, though that woman more probably was Mrs Mackle Emery, John Emery's mother.

Emmanuel, Mr [fl. 1790–1793], scene painter.

Mr Emmanuel (or Emanuel, Imanuel) served the Earl of Barrymore as a scene painter at his private playhouse at Wargrave in 1790. The *Thespian Magazine* of January 1793 stated that Emmanuel fitted up and decorated a private theatre for Lord Petre at Thorndon Hall, Essex, in 1792. The Covent Garden accounts indicate that "Imanuel" worked 121 nights during the 1792–93 season and with his fellow scene painters Mc Quoid and Loyde received £25 6s. 6d.

Could Mr Emmanuel have been the scene painter and machinist Emanuel Jones, who on 29 August 1793 began working at the Federal Street Theatre in Boston for £450 yearly? The last record of Mr Emmanuel in England and the beginning of Jones's work in America match so well that the possibility can be raised. Emanuel Jones was a native of Frankfurt, Germany, and was a topographical, scene, and decorative painter. He worked in Charleston, South Carolina, from 1806 until his death in 1822.

Emmet, [John?] [fl. 1736?–1748], pit doorkeeper.

The Covent Garden bills show shared benefits for Mr Emmet, the pit doorkeeper, on 11 May 1744, 14 May 1745, 6 May 1746, 19 May 1747, and 5 May 1748. The manuscript accounts mention him only once: on 20 May 1747 Emmet was paid (apparently) £5 on account by Mr Bell.

It is at least conceivable that the Covent Garden functionary was the John Emmett who had served as box office keeper at York around 1736.

"Emperor of Horseflesh, The." *See* DUCROW, ANDREW.

English, Mr [fl. 1752], actor.

Mr English was an actor in the summer company at Richmond, Surrey, in 1752. He played Watchal in *A New Way to Pay Old Debts* on 15 August, Boxkeeper in *The Gamester* on 17 August, Perez in *The Mourning Bride* on 22 August, Bardolph in *Henry IV* on 26 August, Charon in *Lethe* on 16 September, Melidore in *Zara* on 20 September, and the Constable in *The Provok'd Wife* on 23 September. He shared a benefit with Miss Moore on 25 September, two days before the season ended.

English, William d. 1795, instrumentalist.

On 6 October 1776 William English was recommended for membership in the Royal

Society of Musicians, but not until 3 August 1777 was he admitted. He was probably the Mr English who played horn in the Handel Memorial Concerts at Westminster Abbey and the Pantheon in May and June 1784, and it is likely that he was the W. English, violinist, who was receiving a season salary of £4 4s. from the Academy of Ancient Music during 1787–88.

William English played at the Haymarket Theatre on 4 March 1795 when *The Thespian Panorama* was presented, and shortly after that he died. The Royal Society accounts show that he had paid his subscription through June 1795 and that in January 1796 his childless widow asked the Society for £31 10s. in aid. The Governors declared that English had left his wife well provided for and that she was in a respectable line of business (which they did not describe), so that on 7 February 1796 they rejected her plea. They relented later, however, for on 7 January 1798 she was granted the "usual allowance." On 7 December 1800 her allowance was stopped, but on 3 June 1804 a petition from her, signed Sarah English, was granted, and from that time forward she was the recipient of £2 12s. 6d. monthly. By 5 February 1826 she had died, for her niece was given £12 for funeral expenses for Mrs English on that date.

"English Aristophanes, The." See FOOTE, SAMUEL.

"English d'Eon, The." See CHARKE, MRS RICHARD.

"English Girl, The." See DAVIES, CECILIA.

"English Hunter, The" [fl. 1790–1791], *performing horse.*
At Astley's Amphitheatre on 22 October 1790 several "surprising leaps" were performed by "The English Hunter." That animal was apparently young Astley's horse, which was described on 6 May 1791 as performing the same feats.

"English Mercury, The." See MATHEW, MR [fl. 1784–1786].

"English Orpheus, The." See PURCELL, HENRY c. 1659–1695.

"English Rose, The." See ASTLEY, JOHN PHILIP CONWAY.

"English Rossignol, The." See ADAMS, MR [fl. 1782–1800].

"English Sampson, The." See JOY, WILLIAM.

"English Sappho, The." See ROBINSON, MRS THOMAS, MARY.

Enoe, Mr [fl. 1780–1783], *house servant?*
Mr Enoe was first mentioned in theatrical records on 17 May 1780 when his benefit tickets were accepted at Drury Lane. He received a shared benefit with four others on 26 May 1781 and was granted similar benefits on 30 May 1782 and 29 May 1783. Judging by the names of those who shared with him, Enoe was probably a house servant. On 15 May 1784 tickets delivered by Mrs Enoe were accepted at the theatre; unless the bill should have read "Mr," the reference was probably to Enoe's wife, possibly also a house servant.

The marriage registers of St Marylebone contain entries for two men named Enoe who may have been related to the Drury Lane employee: William Enoe, widower, married Gwyn Jones, spinster, on 22 June 1762; Spencer Enoe, bachelor, married Ann Hopkins of St James, Westminster, spinster, on 7 September 1794.

Enoe, Mrs [fl. 1784], *house servant?* See ENOE, MR.

Enslen, Mr (fl. 1786), exhibitor.

An exhibition of "air figures" by Mr Enslen was advertised for presentation at the Pantheon on 7 March 1786.

Entwisle, Thomas 1764–1819, instrumentalist, music copyist, actor.

Thomas Entwisle was born in 1764, the son of a German musician who had come to England with the band of George II. Thomas's mother was an orphan, the dowerless daughter of Sir Fleetwood and Lady Betty Haversham, according to Mrs Baron Wilson in *The Memoirs of Harriot Mellon* (1839). Thomas joined Kena's touring company in Lancashire as a violinist and met Sarah Mellon (Harriot's mother), the dresser, wardrobe keeper, and money taker in Kena's troupe. Thomas and Sarah were married on 14 July 1782, by which time Entwisle had become the leader of the company's band. The Entwisles were at Leigh, Lancashire, in February 1789 and then joined Bibby's strollers at Ulverstone, where Harriot Mellon made her debut and where, on 12 December 1789, Thomas Entwisle is known to have acted Duke Frederick in *As You Like It*. The family joined Stanton's company and, in 1795, came to London.

Thomas worked as a music copyist (and probably as a member of the band) at the Drury Lane Theatre as early as 28 October 1795, nine months after Harriot Mellon had made her London debut. There is no record of Mrs Entwisle's having worked in a theatre in London. On 5 March 1797 Thomas as proposed for membership in the Royal Society of Musicians. He was described in the Society's Minute Books as proficient on the violin, viola, and violoncello. He had been married for 14 years and had no children, and he had had engagements at Drury Lane and in Liverpool. Admission was refused him by a vote of seven to four, but on 4 February 1798, when he was proposed again, he was accepted almost unanimously. For the Society Entwisle played viola in the St Paul's benefit concerts in May 1800, 1802, 1803, 1804, and 1806. He continued working at Drury Lane through 1803–4 as a member of the band at a weekly salary of £1 15s.

In March 1804 Thomas and his wife moved to Cheltenham and opened a music house in the High Street. He served (ineffectively, it is reported) as the postmaster at Cheltenham and returned periodically to London for his duties in the May concerts at St Paul's. The success of Harriot Mellon allowed her to take care of her family in their old age, but Thomas is said to have grown sedentary, corpulent, and addicted to low acquaintances. His wife died on 6 May 1815 at 63, and Thomas Entwisle died on 6 June 1819 at 55; both were buried at St Mary's in Cheltenham. Harriot Mellon Coutts erected a memorial tablet to Thomas and Sarah in the south aisle of the church.

Eon. *See* **D'ÉON.**

Epine. *See* **DE L'ÉPINE.**

"Equestrian Mercury, The." *See* **CROSSMAN, JOHN,** and **"LITTLE FLYING MERCURY, THE."**

Erakine, Mr (fl. 1795), house servant?

The bills preserved for the Richmond theatre show a Mr Erakine (Erskine?) to have been a member of the company there in the summer of 1795. Perhaps he was one of the house servants.

Erard, Mr (fl. 1736), singer.

Mr Erard sang the bass part in the first performance of Handel's oratorio *Alexander's Feast* at Covent Garden on 19 February 1736. He also sang Haman in *Esther*, probably the same year.

Ernst, John Gotfrid (fl. 1700–1714), trumpeter.

The Lord Chamberlain's accounts for 5

January 1700 listed John Gotfrid Ernst as a replacement for Thomas Barwell, trumpeter, in the King's Musick. He was probably the John Conret Ernst who was listed in the royal musical establishment in 1702. Ernst was still one of the Queen's trumpeters in 1714.

Errington, Mr d. 1810, actor.

Mr Errington acted Tubal in a performance of *The Merchant of Venice* at the Haymarket Theatre on 23 March 1775. He was probably the Errington who acted with his wife at Norwich in 1779, played at Manchester in 1790 and 1791, and who died, probably at Sunderland, in 1810.

Erskin, John [fl. 1787?–1794], oboist, flutist.

Doane's *Musical Directory* of 1794 listed John Erskin of York as an oboist and flutist who played in concerts sponsored in London by the New Musical Fund. Perhaps he was the John "Erskine" who had been cited in the Irish Musical Fund books earlier. On 1 January 1787 he had begun his subscription by paying the annual fee of 13s. He made his last payment on 8 March 1789 and was expelled the following July.

Erskine. *See also* JOHNSTON, HENRY ERSKINE.

Erskin[e], Mr [fl. 1794–1800], oboist.

Doane's *Musical Directory* of 1794 listed Mr "Erskin" of Manchester as an oboist who participated in the Handelian concerts at Westminster Abbey. The Mr Erskine who played the oboe at the Birmingham theatre in the summers of 1796, 1799, and 1800 was probably the same musician.

Erwin, Mr [fl. 1737], house servant?

Mr Erwin's benefit tickets were accepted at Drury Lane on 30 May 1737. He was possibly one of the house servants.

Erwin, Mrs [fl. 1695–1715], singer, actress.

As a member of Christopher Rich's company at Drury Lane and Dorset Garden, Mrs Erwin played the Daughter in *The Mock Marriage* in September 1695, the Maid in *The Cornish Comedy* in June 1696, and Diana in the masque in *The Pilgrim* on 29 April 1700. She is also known to have sung in *Achilles* in December 1699, *The Grove* on 19 February 1700, and *The Reformed Wife* in March 1700.

Perhaps her stage career ended after the 1699–1700 season, for no other specific appearances are known for Mrs Erwin, yet many songs were published during the first 15 years of the eighteenth century with her name (sometimes spelled Unwinn, Urwin, Irwin) cited as the singer. She sang Daniel Purcell's *In a Grove's forsaken Shade* (published about 1697) from John Hughes's *Amalasont*, a work not otherwise known to have been performed, and she was apparently in a production of *Iphigenia*—perhaps the one in December 1699 at Lincoln's Inn Fields—and sang Daniel Purcell's *Morpheus thou gentle God* (published in 1700). Other Daniel Purcell songs she is cited in the *Catalogue of Printed Music in the British Museum* as having sung include *With Horns and with Hounds* from *The Pilgrim*; *Fond Woman with Mistaken Art* from *The Reformed Wife*; *Cease your am'rous Pipes and Flutes*, *Happy Mansions pleasant Shades*, and *In vain you tell me* from *The Grove*; and *We with Coldness and Disdain*—apparently a specialty song not connected with any play but sung by Mrs Erwin at one of the theatres.

Esbury, Mr [fl. 1760], dresser.

On 22 September 1760 Mr Esbury was earning 1s. daily as a men's dresser at the Covent Garden Theatre.

Esch. *See* VON ESCH.

Escoelil, Mlle [fl. 1775–1776], dancer.

Mademoiselle Escoelil was one of the dancers at the King's Theatre in the Haymarket in 1775–76.

Esient. *See* EIFFERT.

"Espagnole, La Belle." *See* REDIGÉ, MME PAULO.

Espini. *See* DE L'ÉPINE.

Esser, Miss [*fl. 1771*], *singer, violinist, harpist.*
Though *The London Stage* roster for 1770–71 lists Miss Esser as a harpist, the calendar shows her to have been a singer who occasionally accompanied herself on the violin. She performed at Marylebone Gardens from 6 July through 17 September 1771.

Esser, Karl Michael [*fl. 1736–c. 1795*], *violinist, composer.*
Karl Michael, Ritter von Esser, was born at either Aachen or Zweibrucken in 1736. He played in the orchestra at Kassel, but beginning in 1759 he spent most of his time touring Europe as a violin virtuoso. In 1763 at Mainz young Mozart, then a lad of seven, remonstrated with Esser for adding too many embellishments and not sticking to the music as written. Esser served as concertmaster at Kassel, then toured again, going to Rome in 1772, where he was made a knight of the papal Order of the Golden Spur. He was in Paris in 1774 and, according to van der Straeten in *The History of the Violin*, Esser performed in London in 1775–76. We have found no evidence of performances by Esser in London, however, and there is a possibility that the "Ritter" who appeared in England was not our knight but Georg Wenzel Ritter the bassoonist, who was in London in 1774 and Dublin about 1775.
Esser appeared at Berne in 1777, Basle in 1779, and Spain in 1786. In addition to the violin, Esser played the viola d'amore.

He composed some symphonies, violin duets, quartets, a concerto, and a ballad opera. Esser died about 1795.

Essex, Mr [*fl. 1697*], *actor.*
A Mr Essex played Charinthus in *The Humorous Lieutenant* at Drury Lane in late July 1697.

Essex, Mr [*fl. 1771*], *singer.*
Mr Essex sang at Marylebone Gardens in the summer of 1771.

Essex, Mr [*fl. 1782–1786*], *actor.*
Mr Essex played Catesby in *Richard III* at the Haymarket Theatre on 4 March 1782; the performance was a benefit for Mrs Lefevre, who essayed the title role. On 25 November of the same year Essex turned up again at the Haymarket as Francisco in *Wit Without Money*, and in the summer of 1786 he appeared at Hammersmith as Harry Stukely in *All the World's a Stage* on 19 July and Silvertongue in *The Belle's Stratagem* on 26 July.

Essex, Mrs [*fl. 1696*], *actress.*
Mrs Essex played Patience in *The Female Wits* at Drury Lane Theatre in the summer or early fall of 1696.

Essex, Miss. *See* ROCK, MRS EDWARD ANTHONY.

Essex, Miss J. [*fl. 1776*], *actress.*
Miss J. Essex, probably the sister of the Miss Essex who became Mrs Edward Anthony Rock, played Wheedle in *The Miser* on 18 September 1776 and Dorinda in *The Beaux' Stratagem* on 23 September—both at the Haymarket Theater, where Foote's summer company was holding forth.

Essex, John d. 1744, *dancer, choreographer, author.*
John Essex was first mentioned in theatrical advertisements at Drury Lane Theatre

on 20 August 1702, when he danced *Tollet's Ground* with Mrs Lucas. The following 5 February 1703 he performed at York Buildings. On 24 February he complained to the Lord Chamberlain that the manager of Drury Lane, Christopher Rich, had stopped 32 days of his salary "for no Reason, but not performing a Dance when I was so lame I had not the Power to do it." Essex requested either a discharge from the company or his lost wages, and since his name disappeared from the Drury Lane bills, he was doubtless dropped from the roster.

His activity during the years that followed seems to have been confined to teaching and writing. In 1710 he published his translation and augmentation of Feuillet's *Chorégraphie*, calling it *For the Further Improvement of Dancing*; it appeared in a new edition in 1715. In 1721 *A Collection of Minuets, Rigadoons, & French Dances* included compositions by Essex, and perhaps he was the John Essex who published *The Young Ladies Conductor; Rules for Education, with Instructions for Dress and Advice to Young Wives* in 1722. Essex was cited by John Weaver in 1721 as one of England's dancing masters, and by that time William Essex, John's son, had also established himself as a teacher of dance.

In 1724–25 Essex was back on stage at Drury Lane, performing entr'acte specialties and playing a Shepherd in *Apollo and Daphne*. Though he remained affiliated with Drury Lane, two of his students—Mrs Anderson and Thomas Burney—danced in 1725–26 at Lincoln's Inn Fields. Essex was again at Drury Lane in 1726–27, where he remained (except for a portion of the 1733–34 season when he joined Cibber's rebels at the Haymarket) until the end of his career. His pantomime roles over the years included Mercury in the masque in *Harlequin Doctor Faustus*, a Sylvan in *Apollo and Daphne*, a Statue in *The Miser* and in *Harlequin's Triumph*, a Bridesman in *Harlequin Happy and Poor Pierrot Mar-*

ried, Acis in *Acis and Galatea*, Mercury, Jupiter, and a Triton in *Perseus and Andromeda*, a Diety of Pleasure, Sea God, and Gormogon in *Cephalus and Procris*, Colin in *The Country Revels*, one of *Les Capricieux* in *The Harlot's Progress*, Colin in *Harlequin Restored*, and the Ethiopian in *The Fall of Phaeton*. He participated in such specialty dances as *The Cobler's Jealous Wife*, *The Masques*, *Les Bergeries*, *Les Amants constants*, *La Bagatelle* (with Miss Latour), *Revellers*, *Les Ombres des amants fidèles*, a *Polish Dance*, *Rover*, and the *Sleepy Dutchman and his Frow*.

He continued his teaching, one of his students being the younger Miss Robinson, who first appeared on 5 January 1728 and went with Essex and other dancers to perform in Paris in the summer of 1732. In the mid–1730s Essex received regular solo benefits each spring. His address in 1736 was next door to the Bedford Tavern in Covent Garden and in 1737 at Mrs Holt's near the Playhouse Passage in Bow Street— where he apparently lived for the rest of his career.

On 2 December 1736 he was dancing in *The Fall of Phaeton* and had some accident which curtailed his career, for the following 7 December he was replaced by Muilment, and on 23 April 1737 at his benefit Essex advertised: "many of my Friends may not be appris'd of the hurt I receiv'd in my Performance on the Stage at the beginning of this Season, which still continues." Drury Lane allowed him benefits through 1741 even though he did not perform in most seasons; it is probable that he still served the theatre as a dancing master. At his benefit on 2 May 1739 he played Vulcan in *Mars and Venus* ("Being the first Time of his Appearance on the Stage these two Years"). Not until 1740–41 did he try dancing again, and then he appeared only in a comic ballet which was infrequently performed. His benefit on 18 April 1741 was his last at Drury Lane. Covent Garden gave him a benefit on 5 April 1743.

Essex made his will on 29 March 1743, naming his brother-in-law Malachi Hawtayne his executor. From the dancer's £2000 capital stock in the new South Seas annuities he gave £500 to his son William and £1500 to his daughter Elizabeth. Other bequests were £20 each to his cousins William Legan and Elizabeth Ingram, £20 to the dancer John Weaver of Shrewsbury, and £20 to Hawtayne. The rest of his estate was to be divided equally between his son and daughter. John Essex died less than a year later. He was buried at St Dionis Backchurch on 6 February 1744, and his will was proved the next day.

The registers of St Dionis Backchurch contain other references to Essex. He was identified as a music master in the records in the early years of the century, but since all dancing masters were musicians, the references are surely to Essex the dancer. John's wife was named Catherine (Hawtayne?). Their daughter Catherine was born on 27 August 1707, baptized on 2 September, and buried on 6 September. A daughter, Frances, was born on 20 September 1710 and baptized on 6 October; she presumably died before the dancer made his will in 1743. A son, John, was born on 28 June 1712, baptized the following day, and buried on 13 July. A daughter, Elizabeth—presumably the one cited in Essex's will—was born on 18 November 1713 and baptized on 6 December. Another son, Charles, was born and baptized on 11 March 1715 and buried on 27 March. Mrs Essex, identified in the registers as the wife of John the "Dan. Masʳ:," was buried on 9 March 1721. The registers contain no mention of William Essex, so perhaps he was christened before his parents became residents of the parish.

In addition to the publications already mentioned, John Essex published (and with J. Brotherton, sold) *The Dancing Master . . . Done from the French of Monsieur Rameau, by J. Essex* in 1728. Humphries and Smith's *Music Publishing in the British*

Isles gives the address of Essex as Rood Lane, Fenchurch Street.

Essex, Timothy [*fl. 1794–1815*], *violinist, harpsichordist.*

Doane's *Musical Directory* of 1794 listed Timothy Essex, of No 2, Newman Street, as a violinist and harpsichordist who performed at concerts presented by the New Musical Fund. He was doubtless related to the Timothy Essex of Coventry who was a composer, flutist, and violinist in the early nineteenth century. In 1805 and 1815 our subject was a member of the Court of Assistants of the New Musical Fund.

Essex, William *d. 1747, dancer.*

William Essex was the son of the dancer John; both were cited by John Weaver in his 1721 lectures in Chancery Lane as dancing masters active in England. William was doubtless the Essex Junior who made his first stage appearance on 26 September 1724 dancing with Mrs Anderson at Drury Lane. He stayed with the company for the 1724–25 season, after which he seems to have concentrated on teaching. In 1744 he figured in his father's will, receiving a bequest of £500. Probably he was the Essex who appeared as Vulcan in *The Loves of Mars and Venus* and danced in *The Revellers* at Covent Garden for his benefit on 17 April 1746. Possibly some audience members recalled that William's father had performed the same role and participated in the same dance years before.

Essex died at Horncastle, Lincolnshire, about 15 September 1747. He had made his will on 12 September, describing himself as of Stamford and leaving his estate to his wife Charlotte Maria. The will was proved before the end of September.

Estcourt, Richard *1668–1712, actor, playwright, lyricist.*

According to W. R. Chetwood's possibly unreliable account in his *General History* in 1749, Richard Estcourt was born in

Tewksbury, Gloucestershire, in 1668 and educated at the Latin grammar school there. He left home at the age of 15 to join a company of strolling players and appeared in Worcester as Roxana in *The Rival Queens*. His father sent after him, but Richard escaped detection by staying in costume and going to Chipping-Norton, 25 miles away. His father caught up with him and apprenticed him to an apothecary in Hatton Garden in London. The boy stayed there until the expiration of his indenture, went into business, tired of it, and returned to the stage.

The earliest theatrical notice of Estcourt was in 1693, when he spoke an epilogue upon Lord Sydney's leaving Ireland. That was presumably in Dublin, though Estcourt is not otherwise recorded there until 1694. He played at the Smock Alley Theatre (and probably elsewhere in Ireland) through 1704, though he may have made a trip or two to England in connection with his publications. Three roles for him in the 1698–99 season in Dublin were Sir Joslin Jolly in *She Wou'd If She Cou'd*, Wheedle in *The Comical Revenge*, and Old Bellair in *The Man of Mode*. He wrote the words to the song *As I was walking, I heard a maid talking*, which was published in London about 1700. His first play, *The Fair Example: or The Modish Citizens*, was performed at Drury Lane on 10 April 1703 and published in 1706.

Though Colley Cibber thought that he had first acted in London in 1696, Estcourt was billed as making his first appearance in England on 18 October 1704 at Drury Lane, when he played Dominic in *The Spanish Fryar*. Cibber was correct in his recollection of Estcourt's first role in England, however, and noted that though the newcomer

had remembered every Look and Motion of the late *Tony Leigh* so far as to put the Spectator very much in mind of him, yet it was visible through the whole, notwithstanding his Exactness in the Outlines, the true Spirit

that was to fill up the Figure was not the same, but unskilfully dawb'd on, like a Child's Painting upon the Face of a *Metzo-tinto*: It was too plain to the judicious that the Conception was not his own, but imprinted in his Memory by another, of whom he only presented a dead Likeness.

Since Leigh had died in 1692, perhaps Estcourt may be forgiven for not remembering more than the outlines of the earlier actor's characterization.

The audiences were pleased even if Cibber was not. In the *Diverting Post* of 28 October 1704 it was noted that Estcourt had signed with Christopher Rich the manager to play ten times at Drury Lane and that he was doing so with great applause. In fact, the new actor stayed the entire 1704–5 season, acting Blunt in *The Rover*, Sir Thomas Calico in *Sir Courtly Nice*, Bluff in *The Old Bachelor*, Teague in *The Committee*, the Gravedigger in *Hamlet*, Antonio in *Venice Preserv'd*, Sir William Belfond in *The Squire of Alsatia*, Bayes in *The Rehearsal*, Falstaff in *1 Henry IV*, Scaramouch in *The Emperor of the Moon*, Bulfinch in *The Northern Lass*, Palmer in *The Comical Revenge*, Old Mr Holdfast in *Farewell Folly*, Yeoman Woodcock in *Tunbridge Walks*, Harry in *The Quacks*, and Higgen in *The Royal Merchant*, plus his old role of Sir Joslin.

Cibber admitted that Estcourt's defects were "not so obvious to common Spectators; no wonder, therefore, in by his being much sought after in private Companies, he met with a sort of Indulgence, not to say Partialty, for what he sometimes did upon Stage." Cibber was clearly jealous of Estcourt's quick success, and others in London also had misgivings. The *Diverting Post* on 10 March 1705 published an anonymous poem, "On Mimmick, the Irish Actor," which was probably a jab at Estcourt:

Self-Love does Mimmick's Breast inspire,
It seems with Reason good;
For did he not himself admire,
No other Mortal wou'd.

The Town damns Mimmick's Acting,
*   Why?*
Well has he Play'd his Part,
To gain so good a Salary
Without the least Desert.

A similar view was expressed in the 21 April 1705 issue by another unknown versifier in "The Player's Litany":

From Irish Players without Desert,
Whose Acting is not worth a Fart,
Yet they must have vast Salaries for't,
*   Libera nos &c.*

Christopher Rich, on the other hand, placed a high value on Estcourt. He hired the actor, apparently at a handsome salary, for a second season at Drury Lane, during which Estcourt added to his list of roles such parts at Kite in *The Recruiting Officer*, Trinculo in *The Tempest*, the title role in *Sir Solomon Single*, Hearty in *The Basset Table*, Henry VIII in *Vertue Betray'd*, and Lady Addleplot in *Love for Money*. The actor's Kite drew much attention. John Downes the prompter wrote in 1708: "Mr. Estcourt, Histrio Natus; he has the Honour (Nature enduing him with an easy, free, unaffected Mode of Elocution) in Comedy always to Laetificate his Audience, especially Quality, (Witness Serjeant Kyte) He's not Excellent only in that, but a Superlative Mimick." On 25 May 1709 in the *Tatler* Sir Richard Steele commented that ". . . Mr. Estcourt's proper Sense and Observation is what supports the Play. There is not, in my humble Opinion, the Humour hit in *Sergeant Kite*, but it is admirably supply'd by his Action. If I have Skill to judge, that Man is an excellent Actor." Much later Chetwood remembered that Estcourt as Kite "every night of performance entertained the audience with a variety of little catches and flights of humour, that pleased all but his critics."

Estcourt continued to busy himself with occasional writing. For the opening performance of *Camilla* at Drury Lane on 30 March 1706 he wrote an epilogue for Anne Oldfield to speak, and about that time he penned the lyrics for the song *Lard how man can Claret drink*, which was published about 1707. He wrote a ballad on the Battle of Almanza sometime after April 1707. Some of his later works included the song *Dearest Philip my Grandson of Spain*, printed about 1710, *Our Ordnance Board* (about 1712), *You Tell me Dick you lately read* (about 1712), and *Let's be Jolly, fill our Glasses* (about 1720, posthumously). He also wrote the interlude *Prunella*, which was first performed at Drury Lane on 12 February 1708 with Estcourt as Ayres; it was published the same year.

Estcourt's 1706–7 season was spent outside London. He played Kite at Bath on 16 September 1706 and perhaps strolled with the Duke of Grafton's Servants under John Power during the season. In 1707–8 he was back at Drury Lane, acting most of his old roles and adding Mercury in *Amphitryon*, Pounce in *The Tender Husband*, Sir Sampson in *Love for Love,* Puzzle in *The Funeral*, and Otter in *The Silent Woman*. Estcourt's success was so great that on 31 March 1708 he joined Cibber and Wilks as a deputy manager of the theatre.

He was at Drury Lane in 1708–9 and at the Queen's Theatre in 1709–10. During those two seasons his stock of characters did not change greatly, though he tried such new parts as Sir Epicure Mammon in *The Alchemist*, Mustapha in *Don Sebastian*, Quack in *The Country Wife*, Sir Francis Gripe in *The Busy Body*, Pandarus in *Troilus and Cressida*, the Mad Priest in *The Pilgrim*, and Sullen in *The Stratagem*. His salary as of 8 July 1709 was £5 weekly or £112 10s. for the season, but the *Advertisement Concerning the Poor Actors* (1709) noted that to his salary in 1708–9 he added £51 8s. 6d. at his benefit plus £200 "besides" (probably in gifts), bringing his total income for the season to £363 18s. 6d. for acting only 52 times.

By 1709 Estcourt counted among his

friends Parnell, the Duke of Marlborough, Addison, and Steele. Steele seems not to have tired of writing of Estcourt in the *Tatler*, and the actor was certainly good copy. On 5 August 1709 Steele used Estcourt (in the guise of "Tom Mirrour" the mimic) to launch into a discourse on how little we know how we appear to others; on 7 February 1710 he commented that his old apothecary Estcourt, now afflicted with stone and gout, was having a benefit which no one should miss; and on 25 May 1709 he praised the actor's portrayal of Kite.

Estcourt acted at the Queen's Theatre in October and November 1710 but was back at Drury Lane for the remainder of the 1710–11 season. He essayed no new roles that season or the next, and in December and January 1711–12 he advertised in the *Spectator* the opening of his Bumper Tavern in James Street, Covent Garden, whence he had moved from his lodgings in Tavistock Row. He promised that the best wines from Brook and Hellier would be delivered by "trusty Anthony"—probably the strolling player Tony Aston. By the end of the 1711–12 season Estcourt had decided to retire and devote his full time to the tavern. He acted Palmer in *The Comical Revenge* on 12 June 1712 and then left the stage. But he did not live to enjoy his new enterprise.

About 25 August 1712 Richard Estcourt died. He was buried at St Paul, Covent Garden, on 27 August, on which day his old friend Steele paid him a final tribute:

I am very sorry that I have at present a circumstance before me which is of very great importance to all who have a relish for gaiety, wit, mirth, or humour. I mean the death of poor Dick Estcourt. I have been obliged to him for so many hours of jollity, that it is but a small recompense, though all I can give him, to pass a moment or two in sadness for the loss of so agreeable a man. Poor Estcourt! the last time I saw him, we were plotting to show the town his great capacity for acting in its full light, by introducing him as dictating to a set of young players, in what manner to speak this sentence, and utter t'other passion —he had so exquisite a discerning of what was defective in any object before him, that in an instant he could show you the ridiculous side of what would pass for beautiful and just, even to men of no ill judgment, before he had pointed at the failure. He was no less skilful in the knowledge of beauty; and, I daresay, there is no one who knew him well but can repeat more well-turned compliments, as well as smart repartees, of Mr. Estcourt's than of any other man in England. This was easily to be observed in his inimitable faculty of telling a story, in which he would throw in natural and unexpected incidents, to make his court to one part, and rally the other part of the company. Then he would vary the usage he gave them, according as he saw them bear kind or sharp language. He had the knack to raise up a pensive temper, and mortify an impertinantly gay one, with the most agreeable skill imaginable. There are a thousand things which crowd into my memory, which make me too much concerned to tell on about him.

. . . .

It is an insolence natural to the wealthy to affix, as much as in them lies, the character of a man to his circumstances. Thus it is ordinary with them to praise faintly the good qualities of those below them, and say it is very extraordinary in such a man as he is, or the like, when they are forced to acknowledge the value of him whose lowness upbraids their exaltation. It is to this humour only that it is to be ascribed that a quick wit in conversation, a nice judgment upon any emergency that could arise, and a most blameless inoffensive behaviour, could not raise this man above being received only upon the foot of contributing to mirth and diversion. But he was as easy under that condition as a man of so excellent talents was capable; and since they would have it that to divert was his business, he did it with all the seeming alacrity imaginable, though it stung him to the heart that it was his business. Men of sense, who could taste his excellencies, were well satisfied to let him lead the way in conversation, and play after his own manner; but fools, who provoked him to mimicry, found he had the indignation to let it be at their expense who called for it, and he would show the form of conceited heavy fellows as jests to the company at their own request, in revenge for interrupting him from being a companion to put on the character of a jester.

What was peculiarly excellent in this memorable companion was, that in the accounts he gave of persons and sentiments, he did not only hit the figure of their faces and manner of their gestures, but he would in his narration fall into their very way of thinking, and this when he recounted passages wherein men of the best wit were concerned, as well as such wherein were represented men of the lowest rank of understanding. It is certainly as great an instance of self-love to a weakness, to be impatient of being mimicked, as any can be imagined. There were none but the vain, the formal, the proud, or those who were incapable of amending their faults, that dreaded him; to others he was in the highest degree pleasing; and I do not know any satisfaction of any indifferent kind I ever tasted so much, as having got over an impatience of seeing myself in the air he could put me when I have displeased him. It is indeed to his exquisite talent this way, more than any philosophy I could read on the subject, that my person is very little of my care; and it is indifferent to me what is said of my shape, my air, my manner, my speech, or my address. It is to poor Estcourt I chiefly owe that I am arrived at the happiness of thinking nothing a diminution to me, but what argues a depravity of my will.

It has as much surprised me as anything in Nature to have it frequently said that he was not a good player: but that must be owing to a partiality for former actors in the parts in which he succeeded them, and judging by comparison of what was liked before, rather than by the nature of the thing. When a man of his wit and smartness could put on an utter absence of common sense in his face, as he did in the character of Bullfinch in the 'Northern Lass,' and an air of insipid cunning and vivacity in the character of Pounce in the 'Tender Husband,' it is folly to dispute his capacity and success, as he was an actor.

Poor Estcourt! let the vain and proud be at rest; they will no more disturb their admiration of their dear selves, and thou are no longer to drudge in raising the mirth of stupids, who know nothing of thy merit, for thy maintenance.

. . . .

But I must grow more succinct, and, as a Spectator, give an account of this extraordinary man who, in his way, never had an equal in any age before him, or in that wherein he lived. I speak of him as a companion, and a man qualified for conversation. His fortune exposed him to an obsequiousness towards the worst sort of company, but his excellent qualities rendered him capable of making the best figures in the most refined. I have been present with him among men of the most delicate taste a whole night, and have known him (for he saw it was desired) keep the discourse to himself the most part of it, and maintain his good humour with a countenance, in a language so delightful, without offence to any person or thing upon earth, still preserving the distance his circumstances obliged him to; I say, I have seen him do all this in such a charming manner that I am sure none of those I hint at will read this without giving him some sorrow for their abundant mirth, and one gush of tears for so many bursts of laughter. I wish it were any honour to the pleasant creature's memory that my eyes are too much suffused to let me go on—

Actually, Steele did go on; the following appeared in the periodical issue but not in the collected edition and concerned Estcourt in his last illness:

It is a felicity his friends may rejoice in, that he had his senses, and used them as he ought to do, in his last moments. It is remarkable that his judgment was in its calm perfection to the utmost article, for when his wife out of her fondness, desired she might send for a certain illiterate humorist (whom he had accompanied in a thousand mirthful moments, and whose insolence makes fools think he assumes from conscious merit) he answered, *"Do what you please, but he won't come near me."* Let poor Estcourt's negligence about this message convince the unwary of a triumphant empiric's ignorance and inhumanity.

The "illiterate humorist" has not been identified.

Colley Cibber was one of those few who thought Estcourt not always a good player:

. . . I have seen upon the Margin of the written Part of *Falstaff* which he acted, his own Notes and Observations upon almost every Speech of it, describing the true Spirit of the Humour, and with what Tone of Voice, Look, and Gesture, each of them ought to be delivered. Yet in his Execution upon the Stage he seem'd to have lost all those just Ideas he had form'd of it, and almost thro' the Character labour'd under a heavy Load of Flatness: In a word, with all his Skill in Mimickry and Knowledge of what ought to be done, he never upon the Stage could bring it truly into Practice, but was upon the whole a languid, unaffecting Actor.

Perhaps Cibber was being unfair, but he was a remarkably keen observer of the faults and virtues of actors, and he was willing to compliment Estcourt as well as damn him:

This Man was so amazing and extraordinary a Mimick, that no Man or Woman, from the Coquette to the Privy-Counsellor, ever mov'd or spoke before him, but he could carry their Voice, Look, Mien, and Motion, instantly into another Company: I have heard him make long Harangues and form various Arguments, even in the manner of thinking of an eminent Pleader at the Bar, with every the least Article and Singularity of his Utterance so perfectly imitated, that he was the very *alter ipse*, scarce to be distinguished from his Original.

For Cibber, Estcourt's mimic skill was not enough, yet Estcourt pleased so discerning a critic as Steele both onstage and off. Since the actor's art is ephemeral, we may never know which critic was right.

Very little is known of Estcourt's personal life. *Who's Who in the Theatre* (eleventh edition) provided a series of genealogical charts for the Lupino family which show that Richard Estcourt had a daughter Charlotte Mary (1688–1754)

who became a dancer and actress and married George Charles Luppino (1683–1725) the dancer on 3 August 1709. Charlotte Mary Estcourt's mother's name is not known. Luppino and his wife had three children, one of whom carried on the Estcourt name. He was George Richard Estcourt Luppino (1710–1787) who became a dancer and married the dancer Rosina Violante. The Estcourt name was not continued into the following generation.

Este, Charles *1752–1829, actor.*

According to Rev Charles Este's autobiography, *My Own Life* (1787), he was on the stage, apparently with Samuel Foote, for about eight months in 1768–69. Foote played at the Haymarket Theatre in the summer of 1769, but the bills contained no mention of Este. Este was one of the editors of *The World,* a periodical which appeared from 1 January 1787 to 30 June 1794, and he published *A Journey Through Flanders, Brabant, etc., in* 1795.

Este, Thomas *d. 1745, actor, singer.*

From April through August 1734 Thomas Este performed in London, now at one theatre, now at another. His first notice was on 26 April, when he acted Poudre in *The Harlot's Progress* at Drury Lane. He stayed there less than a month, also appearing as Jack Stocks in *The Lottery* and Pierrot in *The Harlot's Progress.* At Lincoln's Inn Fields on 23 May he was Friendly in *The School Boy*; then on 29 May at James Street he played Frederick in *The Miser.* In June and July he was holding forth at the Haymarket Theatre as the King in *The Humours of Sir John Falstaff,* Leander in *The Mock Doctor,* Lovemore in *The Lottery,* Altamont in *The Fair Penitent,* Mat in *The Beggar's Opera,* Woodvil in *The Non Juror,* Ulysses in *Penelope,* and an unnamed character in *The Humorous Election.* At Lincoln's Inn Fields on 20 August he was seen as Basset in *The Provok'd Husband*; two days later he returned to the Haymarket as Harry Pyfleet in *The Cobler's Opera*; and on 24 August he appeared at Bartholomew Fair as Face in *The Imposter*.

After that restless perambulation Este settled down a little in 1734–35 — except for an excursion to the Haymarket — and became a member of the Drury Lane troupe in the winter. In the summer he was at the Haymarket — except for a brief transfer to Lincoln's Inn Fields. He repeated many of his old parts and added some new ones, among which were Tattle in *Love for Love*, Gadshill in *1 Henry IV*, Charles in *The Busy Body*, Frederick in *The Fatal Marriage*, Dorilant in *The Country Wife*, Horatio in *Hamlet*, Surly in *The Alchemist*, Leon in *Rule a Wife and Have a Wife*, Foppington in *The Careless Husband*, Fenton in *The Merry Wives of Windsor*, and Aimwell in *The Stratagem*. He remained at Drury Lane in 1735–36, playing such parts as Mustacho in *The Tempest*, the Captain of the Galley in *The Fall of Phaeton*, and Flash in *Harlequin Restored*. At the end of the season he received two benefits, one at Lincoln's Inn Fields, shared with Mrs Cantrell, at which he was Damon in *Damon and Phillida*, and the other at Drury Lane, shared with Wright, at which he took the male leads in *The Livery Rake* and *The Country Lass*.

His last season in London was 1736–37 at Drury Lane. Among his new parts were Trueman in *The Squire of Alsatia*, Hephestion in *The Rival Queens*, Marcus in *Cato*, Filch in *The Beggar's Opera*, and Vainlove in *The Old Bachelor*. He also sang in the chorus accompanying *Macbeth*. Este shared a benefit with Turbutt on 21 May 1737, advertising that tickets would be available from him at his lodgings in Wild Street.

By 14 November 1737 Este was playing at the Smock Alley Theatre in Dublin; on that date he acted Trueman in *The Squire of Alsatia*, one of his Drury Lane parts. During the rest of the 1737–38 season he was seen as Manly in *A Cure for a Scold*, Melefont in *The Sharpers*, Polly in *The Beggar's Opera*, Lord Sparkish in *Polite Conversation*, and Maskwell in *The Double Dealer*. In 1739–40 at Smock Alley, after a season's absence, Este appeared as Lovemore in *The Lottery* and Feignlove in *The Relapse*. On 18 March 1740 his unpublished ballad farce, *A Cure for Jealousy*, was performed at Smock Alley for his benefit.

Este turned up next at Edinburgh, where from as early as 21 December 1741 until his death on 10 February 1745 he led a troupe of players at Taylors' Hall, Cowgate. He circumvented a restriction against plays by styling his offerings concerts with free theatricals, but his chief protection against the authorities seems to have been the patronage of the Duke of Hamilton, several members of whose family participated in Este's productions. We know of two performing assignments Thomas Este gave himself: on 16 January 1744 he played Lord Townly in *The Provok'd Husband*, and on the following 6 and 9 March he delivered a humorous epilogue in the character of Nobody.

The *Caledonian Mercury* of 12 February 1745 reported that Thomas Este had died "about 6 in the evening" two days before. Este was lauded as having "for these 4 years past most agreeably entertained the town with his excellent performances on the stage. As he was a most indulgent and affectionate husband, a tender father, a sincere friend, and a facetious and agreeable companion, his death is greatly lamented by all who had the pleasure of his acquaintance."

In Edinburgh, Este and his wife, also a performer, had lived at "Mr Munro's the musician in the Cowgate, near Taylor's Hall."

Este, Mrs Thomas ₍*fl.* 1741–1746₎, *actress, singer?*

Mrs Thomas Este performed with her

husband at the "concerts" with free theatricals which he offered at Taylors' Hall, Cowgate, Edinburgh, from as early as 1741. Dibdin's *Annals* and the *Fragmenta Scoto-Dramatica* are at variance in the dating of events in Edinburgh concerning Mrs Este. On either 21 or 17 February 1743 a benefit was held at Taylors' Hall for Mr and Mrs Este, but the bill announced that "As Mrs Este's present condition will not admit of personal application, she hopes the ladies, notwithstanding, will grace her concert." Perhaps she was pregnant (by 1745 she apparently had had at least one child), but she was able to deliver "an humorous epilogue, in the character of Nobody" at her solo benefit on 2 March 1743 (Dibdin dated that 6 March 1744; old style/new style dating may have contributed to the confusion).

Thomas Este died on 10 February 1745. On 22 March 1746 a Mrs Este, probably

Harvard Theatre Collection

HARRIET ESTEN

artist unknown

our subject, made her first appearance in London playing Lady Brumpton in *The Funeral* at Goodman's Fields. That, however, seems to have been her only attempt on the London stage.

Este, Mrs [William?] [*fl.* 1735–1743], *actress.*

The Mrs Este who appeared in London in the summer of 1735 was probably the wife of William Este, a Dublin actor. On 1 July she played Charlotte in *The Mock Doctor* at Drury Lane, advertised as making her first appearance on any stage. The same claim was made on the following 14 August when she played Edging in *The Careless Husband* for her benefit. She seems not to have remained in London, and since William Este died in 1743, she was probably the widow Este who received a benefit on 9 March 1743 at the Smock Alley Theatre, Dublin.

Esten, Mrs James, Harriet Pye, née Bennett, later Mrs John Scott-Waring 1765?–1865, *actress, pianist, singer, dancer.*

The actress who played in London in the 1790s as Mrs Esten was born Harriet Bennett, the daughter of Agnes Maria Bennett (d. 1808), author of several popular novels including *Anna; or Memoirs of a Welch Heiress* (1785), *Juvenile Indiscretion* (1786), and *The Beggar Girl and her Benefactor* (1797). *The Dictionary of National Biography* states that Mrs Agnes Maria Bennett was "a married lady with many children, who survived her," and claims that "there is no evidence of her birth, her parentage, or her condition." But in his *Memoirs* (1805) the actor Charles Lee Lewes identified Agnes Maria as the daughter of Mr Evans, a grocer of Bristol. The Bennett she married was said by Lewes to have been a tanner at Brecknock, though Gilliland in *The Dramatic Mirror* (1807) claimed that both Mrs Bennett's husband and her father were custom-house officers.

The tanner and his wife soon separated, according to Lewes, and Mrs Bennett then became a slop-seller in Wych Street, London, afterwards working in a chandler's shop in Borough High Street. There she met Admiral Sir Thomas Pye, who was so charmed by "her polite attention" that he soon "elevated [her] to the post of his housekeeper, at Tooting, in Surrey." It seems clear that Agnes Maria Bennett lived as the Admiral's mistress for some time and had at least two children by him: Thomas Pye Bennett, a naval officer, and Harriet Pye Bennett, the subject of this entry. In 1793, after she had become Mrs Esten, Harriet signed "Harriet Pye Esten" to legal papers relative to the management of the Edinburgh Theatre.

On 24 February 1784 "Harriet Bennett" was married at the church of Lower Tooting Graveney, Surrey, to James Esten, with the consent of her mother, who was then living in Bath. Esten, who had been introduced to Harriet by her brother Thomas, was a lieutenant in the Royal Navy, a purser in the man-of-war *Quebec*. Harriet was then about 19 years old. Two children were born to this couple over the next several years, but Esten suffered severe financial losses (either by the decommissioning of his ship, or according to another report because of adventures "in some undertakings which proved unsuccessful") which required him to seek refuge in France from his creditors. In order to support her children, Mrs Esten turned to the stage. That, at least, is the version of their separation told both by Gilliland and *The Secret History of the Green Room* (1792). W. J. Lawrence reported that her husband remained with her during the early years of her stage career (which began in 1786) and that in 1788 they were living in apartments at No 42, Grafton Street, Dublin, while Mrs Esten was engaged at the Smock Alley Theatre. The profligate manager Richard Daly had designs on her and lured Mr Esten to the gaming tables, where he

was ruined. Esten then, according to Lawrence, applied to Mrs Bennett to clear him of debt, which she did, contingent on his promise forever to foreswear connection with her daughter Harriet and the two children and to leave the country. Whichever version is nearer the truth, Esten eventually secured an appointment on a ship bound for the Caribbean. He settled at Santo Domingo and prospered. In July 1789, during the period when she was acting at Dublin, Mrs Esten obtained a deed of separation from him.

Mrs Bennett was probably instrumental in launching her daughter's career. She arranged through a barrister named Dawes (Manasseh Dawes who died in 1829?) to have Harriet introduced to Thomas Harris of Covent Garden, who counseled her to gain provincial experience before thinking of a London career. Subsequently she was engaged for the Bath-Bristol company by William Dimond, who took her on, it was said by *The Secret History of the Green Room*, because he preferred petite actresses, he himself being short. Described as a young lady from London making her first appearance on any stage, Mrs Esten made her debut at Bristol on 19 June 1786 as Alicia in *Jane Shore*. On 26 June she acted Letitia Hardy in *The Belle's Stratagem*. When the company moved to Bath in the fall she again acted Letitia Hardy on 14 October 1786, billed as making her first appearance at Bath and her third on any stage. For her benefit at Bath on 11 January 1787 she played Widow Belmour in *The Way to Keep Him* and Miss Tittup in *Bon Ton*. On 3 March she acted Roxalana in *The Sultan*, on 21 April Beatrice in *Much Ado About Nothing*, and on 1 May Lady Morden in *The Seduction*. When, at Bristol on 2 July 1787, she acted Roxalana and the title role in *Isabella*, her benefit receipts only amounted to a disappointing £45, whereupon Mrs Esten in an address to the audience accused the managers of deliberately arranging her night to coincide with a sailing match of great local interest. During that summer at Bristol she also acted Belvidera in *Venice Preserv'd*, Lady Bab Lardoon in *The Maid of the Oaks*, Juliet in *Romeo and Juliet*, Maria in *The Citizen*, Mrs Oakly in *The Jealous Wife*, and Alicia in *Jane Shore*. Supported by her great beauty, Mrs Esten made a most favorable impression upon audiences at Bath and Bristol, to the extent that the local press dubbed her "the Bath Abington." A combative disposition and ill-will toward Dimond, however, caused her to quit Bath for Ireland, where she took up an engagement at Smock Alley, Dublin, in 1788–89 under Daly's management. At Cork in August and September of 1788 she played Lady Macbeth and Beatrice. After returning to Cork the next summer she went on to Waterford to play Juliet, Rosalind, Desdemona, and Belvidera.

Harvard Theatre Collection

HARRIET ESTEN, as Lady Flutter
engraving by Leney, after De Wilde

A most successful engagement followed at Edinburgh where on 19 January 1790 she made her debut as Juliet and fast became a popular and lasting favorite with the public. She acted Beatrice on 13 March, and on 29 March in the character of Widow Belmour she introduced a song and accompanied herself on the "*Forte-Piano*," the first instance known of that instrument being played in the Edinburgh Theatre. Having joined Wilkinson's company for the summer, she acted Monimia in *The Orphan* at York on 19 May 1790 and was advertised for five nights in August at Pontefract. According to Wilkinson, at her York debut "Mrs Esten's peculiar neatness and elegance prepossessed the audience in her favour, and she had not finished her first scene before they, with one consent, adopted 'the orphan,' and wished to secure her as their own." Wilkinson, himself, found her to be "truly captivating . . . blessed with a set of features uncommonly lovely and expressive; [with] a voice at once powerful and plaintive, cheerful and mellow, her merit . . . is nearly equal in the grave and the gay."

Her work at Edinburgh and York soon gained her a London engagement. Earlier, in May of 1789, the Covent Garden management had made enquiries about her Dublin performances, but had been put off by the Irish playwright Robert Jephson, who reported that "With her borrowed manner and her general faintness, she could only suggest the idea of Mrs Siddons in a consumption." Harris, who had sent her out for seasoning, finally engaged her for the season of 1790–91. Genest reported that "Jackson of the Edinburgh theatre was sorry to lose her, but Harris's offers were too advantageous to be refused." Gilliland may have been correct, however, in his assertion that so anxious was Mrs Esten to come to London that she played the whole first season without a salary but with a clear benefit; for her name does not appear in the Covent Garden pay list for 1790–91.

Most critics were captivated by Harriet's beauty and grace at her debut as Rosalind in *As You Like It* on 20 October 1790. *The World* found that "She looked and acted divinely." "She played the character with great ease, great spirit, and great archness," wrote the reviewer in *European Magazine*—"The applause she met with was unbounded . . . and we declare her performance entitled her to it." In the audience was Henry Crabb Robinson who wrote in his *Diary*: "her face may be fairly pronounced pretty, and her figure engaging. Her voice, in the pathetic tones, resembles that of Mrs Siddons, but is more clear and articulate." An especially complete account of the quality of her debut performance was provided in the *Biographical and Imperial Magazine* (October 1790):

Her figure, though not tall, is genteel and majestic, and her countenance elegant and expressive; in her attitudes she was generally graceful, though, at times, rather too artificial, and in the management of her features, though we were sometimes displeased with the appearance of affectation in the rolling glances of her eyes, the skill of an ingenious and discriminating actress were well displayed. The embarrassment at her *entré*, though not excessive, was natural and interesting; but threw a veil over her merits during the first act. When this was pretty well overcome, the actress blazed upon us, and we were presently induced to conclude her a valuable acquisition to the theatre, and the town. As a breeches figure, though of better Nature, she is perhaps inferior to Mrs. Jordan; being in fact more finely formed with the characteristic flow and delicacy of her own sex, and consequently less calculated to appear with advantage in the semblance of the other. But this cannot be esteemed as a defect, since, though in the garb of Ganymede, Shakespeare still designed his audience to keep in mind that it was Rosalind was before them. The spirit of her performance in the scenes with Orlando was particularly conspicuous, and her manner of singing the cuckoo song was delightful. Holman seemed to catch fire from her performance, and was more respectable

in Orlando than we ever remember to have seen him.

For her second appearance, on 23 October, she offered Indiana in *The Conscious Lovers*, and again the *Biographical and Imperial Magazine* commented:

Her figure is well calculated for elegant comedy, and she has learned the art of expressing all the fine feelings of the heart, and entering into the deep pathos of sentiment and affection. Though, perhaps, more the child of art than of native sensibility, yet our feelings sufficiently evinced how well she has acquired the power to touch the tender chords of the heart. We, however, advise her to correct the posture and motions of her arms a little, and to dismiss much of that stiffness, which betrays labour and exertion. The elbow squared, the hands turned back, and the wide extended fingers, have a stiff and unnatural, consequently an unpleasant appearance.

As Roxalana in the afterpiece of *The Sultan* on the same evening, she demonstrated her versatility in a character widely different from the one she acted earlier in the evening, and although not possessing the vivacity and romping hilarity of Mrs Jordan (then playing at Drury Lane), she showed "the spirit and design of her author" and exhibited "a degree of characteristic dignity, and British elevation of soul . . . in which her Drury rival is certainly rather deficient."

Other roles played by Mrs Esten in her first season at Covent Garden included Monimia in *The Orphan,* Lady Bab Lardoon in *The Maid of the Oaks*, Belvidera in *Venice Preserv'd*, Ophelia, Lady Townly in *The Provok'd Husband*, Rutland in *The Earl of Essex*, and the title role in *Isabella* (11 February—"The performance was highly meritorious," wrote the *Gazetteer* on the following day). For her benefit on 15 February 1791 she acted her favorite role of Letitia Hardy (with a song and minuet by her) and after the play she recited Collins's *Ode on the Passions*. Tickets could be had of Mrs Esten at No 5, Nassau Street,

Soho, where she lived with her mother Mrs Bennett. Presumably the total evening's receipts of £353 18s. were hers in a clear benefit, in lieu of salary.

In August she returned to play at York in her familiar roles. Notwithstanding her success in the previous season at Covent Garden, Harris was not inclined to reengage her. Some highly placed influence, however, worked in her favor. The banker Thomas Coutts asked the Duke of Clarence to intervene with Harris in her behalf, so the Duke, after consulting with his Mrs Jordan, who supported the request, put severe pressure on the Covent Garden management. Mrs Esten was offered £11 per week for the ensuing season. Mrs Esten's relationship with Douglas, the Eighth Duke of Hamilton, was already established at that time. The author of *The Secret History of the Green Room* observed that despite an income from acting which did not exceed £600 or £700 per year, she was able "to keep her carriage, footman, &c and live in very splendid style."

In 1791–92, her second season at Covent Garden, Mrs Esten added to her London repertoire Biddy Tipkin in *The Tender Husband*, Estifania in *Rule a Wife and Have a Wife*, Honoria in *Notoriety*, Pauline in *A Day in Turkey*, and Clara in *The Fashionable Levites*. For her benefit on 14 April 1792, at which she cleared £206, she offered Moggy (for that night only) in *The Highland Reel* and the recitation again of Collins's ode. On 28 August 1792 she made a single appearance at the Haymarket Theatre, as Roxalana in *The Sultan*. She also acted at Richmond.

That summer of 1792 Mrs Esten won the lease of the Edinburgh Theatre which Jackson had had to give up because of financial problems. In 1791, Jackson had negotiated with both Mrs Esten and Stephen Kemble, and had finally given the lease to Kemble, who had run the theatre in 1791–92. As a result of the influence of the Duke of Hamilton, who had caused himself to be ap-

pointed, along with Henry Dundas, as patentees of the theatre, Kemble soon had found himself without authority to perform, and of course Mrs Esten and her mother had then been given the lease of the patent. Accounts of the political hocuspocus, litigation, and general excitement caused by the dispute can be found in James Dibdin's *The Annals of the Edinburgh Stage* (1888), the *Memoirs of Charles Lee Lewes* (1805), and a *Memorial for Robert Playfair, writer in Edinburgh, Trustee for the Creditors of John Jackson, late Manager of the Theatre-Royal, Edinburgh; and for Mrs. Harriet Pye Esten, Lessee of the said Theatre-Royal* (1793).

Put out of the Theatre Royal, Kemble arranged to have Jones's Circus in Edinburgh fitted up as a theatre. After a few weeks of playing Kemble's theatre was interdicted on 6 February 1793, to the joy of the manager of the Theatre Royal, whose box office had suffered from the competition. No longer permitted to perform plays at the Circus, Kemble pitifully struggled on with concerts of vocal and instrumental music.

After winning the lease, Mrs Esten left the responsibilities of the management of the Edinburgh Theatre to her mother while she herself played her third season at Covent Garden. The press, indeed, pointed out the "absurdity of appointing, as the Manageress of the Edinburgh Theatre, a Lady, who, while she should be at her post in Scotland, is to be performing in London." In 1792–93, Mrs Esten acted her usual repertoire, to which she added Lady Betty Modish in *The Careless Husband*, Nelti in *Columbus*, Julia in *The Rivals*, Sophia Strangeways in *Notoriety*, Violante in *The Wonder*, Clarinda in *The Suspicious Husband*, and Luciana in *The Comedy of Errors*. At her benefit on 17 April 1793 she took £146 7s. 6d. after house charges. Harriet then went back to Edinburgh to make her first appearance since becoming lessee, as Indiana in *The Conscious Lovers* and

Roxalana in *The Sultan* on 22 June 1793. In July she acted Juliet, Beatrice, and Rosalind. When the Edinburgh season closed on 20 July Mrs Esten gave up the lease to Stephen Kemble for a consideration of £200 per year.

In her next and last season at Covent Garden, 1793–94, she was still earning £11 per week. A pay sheet for that year indicates she received a total of £300 13*s*. 4*d*. On 11 October 1793 she played Fanny in *The Clandestine Marriage*, her first appearance in that character; other new characters for her at London in that season were Widow Belcour in *The Way to Keep Him*, Rosa in *How to Grow Rich*, Marianne in *The Dramatist*, Lady Harriet in *Grief-a-la-Mode*, Lady Dainty in *The Double Gallant*, Louisa in *The World in a Village* (with an original epilogue written by her), Miss Wooburn in *Every One has his Fault*, Paulina in *Love's Frailties*, Cordelia in *King Lear*. On 3 May her name was no longer carried on the pay list. At Edinburgh in July 1794 she gave birth to Anne Douglas Hamilton, the Duke's daughter. Mrs Esten's only appearance at Covent Garden in the next season was on 29 April 1795 when, for Mrs Mattocks's benefit, she played Indiana in *The Conscious Lovers* and gave Dryden's *Ode on St Cecilia's Day*.

Having for the moment retired from the stage, Mrs Esten settled into an elegant house in Half Moon Street, Piccadilly, supported by an allowance reported to have been £1000 per year from the Duke of Hamilton, by which "the virtuous receiver exalts in the splendour," jibed *The Secret History of the Green Room*, "if not the credit of high life." Her mother had left her lodgings in Nassau Street to share in Harriet's "magnificent elevation." In 1797 James Esten returned from St Domingo possessed of a fortune reputed to have been £200,000 (*Morning Post*, 2 September 1797) and he was granted a divorce from Harriet in the Consistory Court of the Bishop of London on 4 July of the same

year. He tried to have the marriage dissolved as well by the House of Lords but the bill was rejected on 2 March 1798, presumably by the influence of the Hamilton family who feared that if the dissolution passed then the Duchess might follow Esten's example, thereby opening the way for the Duke to marry Harriet. The Duke of Hamilton died on 1 August 1799, leaving Harriet, it was said, an annuity of £3000.

Mrs Esten ventured once more to the Edinburgh Theatre in 1802–3, at £50 per night, in a short engagement which proved very successful, after which she seems never again to have returned to the stage. On 15 October 1812 she became the third wife of Major John Scott-Waring. His second wife had been the actress Maria Hughes, and his marriage to her had prompted the epigram: "Although well known for ages past, / She's not the worse for Waring."

Waring died at Harriet's house in Half Moon Street on 5 May 1819. Harriet lived on for another 46 years until 29 April 1865, when she died at No 36, Queen's Gate Terrace, Kensington, reputedly at the age of 100. Notice of her death was carried in the *Gentleman's Magazine* for June 1865.

One of her children by James Esten, Harriet Hunter Wildman Esten, married Thomas Darby Coventry of Henley-on-Thames at St George, Hanover Square, on 21 December 1809. In her will Mrs Esten evidently left the Coventry family a considerable sum of money. Anne Douglas Hamilton, her daughter by the Duke, married the third Baron of Rossmore on 25 June 1820; she died childless on 20 August 1844. Lt John T. Scott-Waring and the Miss Scott-Waring who became Mrs Fry were evidently Mrs Esten's children.

In the flowering of her career Mrs Esten was a beautiful and agreeable actress. She presented a small neat person, and was "the perfect mistress of the use of a fine pair of eyes" which she exploited "by the exercise of art upon her eye-brows and eyelashes, and the languishing rollings of which every one who has been near her must acknowledge the charm." Her voice, possessing the qualities of "huskiness and hollowness" was better fit for tragedy than comedy and was "plaintively monotonous." F. G. Waldron in *Candid and Impartial Strictures on the Performers* (1795) nevertheless placed her "next to Miss Farren in the elegant walks of comedy." She was to Waldron "A little enchanting made-up manufactured piece of elegance," whose only blemish was a little twist in the hip, "that inclines to be *crooked*," a physical defect also noted in *The Secret History of the Green Room*. The tenor of the description of Mrs Esten found in the latter publication suggests that she was not greatly intelligent but had been promoted by her mother's shrewdness and indiscriminate puffing on her behalf.

A portrait of Mrs Esten was engraved by the younger Hibbert, after Plimer, at Bath in 1797; a variation of this portrait was engraved by Mackenzie for the *Monthly Mirror* in 1804. In 1793 the *Thespian Magazine* published a portrait of her by an unknown engraver. An engraving by Thornthwaite, after De Wilde, of her as Belvidera in *Venice Preserv'd* was published in *Bell's British Theatre* in 1791. De Wilde's painting of Mrs Esten in the character of Lady Flutter in *The Discovery* is at the Garrick Club; it was engraved by W. Leney for publication in *Bell's British Library* in 1793.

Estrange. *See* L'ESTRANGE.

Etherington, Mr ₁*fl. 1746–1761₁, house servant.

A Mr Etherington was paid £15 12s. on 12 November 1746 for 39 nights' arrears as lamplighter at the Covent Garden Theatre. The Mr Etherington earning 2s. daily in 1760–61 as an assistant in the Covent Garden office or as a lobby doorkeeper was probably the same person.

"Eunuch, The." *See* FERRI.

Evance. *See* EVANS and EVENS.

Evans. *See also* EVENS.

Evans, Mr ₁*fl. 1703–1706₁, equestrian, acrobat, rope dancer.

At Drury Lane Theatre on 27 April 1703 Mr Evans, lately arrived from Vienna, vaulted on a managed horse, and "he lyes with his Body extended on one Hand in which posture he drinks several Glasses of Wine with the other, and from that throws himself a Sommerset over the Horses Head, to admiration." Three days later he appeared at the disused Dorset Garden playhouse. Evans was back in London on 18 September 1704 at Southwark Fair, according to the *Daily Courant* of that date (a notice not in *The London Stage*), with Pinkethman's company. He performed on the managed horse with Baxter, "And also Mr. Evans Walks on the Slack Rope, and throws himself a Somerset through a Hogshead hanging eight Foot high, with several other Entertainments too tedious to insert here."

On 11 October 1705 Evans was at the Lincoln's Inn Fields Theatre, doing his wine-drinking exhibition again and specifying in the bills that the number of glasses he would consume would be nine. With Findley and the Widow Barnes, Evans operated a booth at May Fair on 1 May 1706.

Evans, Mr ₁*fl. 1723–1735?₁, actor.

Graspall in *A Wife to be Let* on 12 August 1723 at Drury Lane may have been played by the Mr Evans cited in the 1735 edition of the work; he was certainly at the theatre that month. On 16 August 1723 *The Impertinent Lovers* was performed, and the 1723 edition of the play has Evans down for the part of Fropish. Since the actor's name also appeared in the 1735 edition of the first play, perhaps he was then still active, but *The London Stage* lists no more performances by him—unless the dancer-actor-singer Evans (fl. 1730–1734) was the same man.

Evans, Mr ₁fl. 1730–1734₁, *dancer, actor, singer.*

On 28 October 1730 at Drury Lane Mr Evans appeared as a Sea God in *Cephalus and Procris*. During the rest of the 1730–31 season he was a Triton in the same work, an Infernal Spirit in *The Tempest*, and Crowdero in *Bayes's Opera*. Then he played Plausey in *The Banished General* and danced at the Mills-Miller-Oates booth at Bartholomew Fair on 26 August 1731. He was back at Drury Lane in 1731–32 to repeat his role of Triton and play a Bridesman in *Perseus and Andromeda*. It is probable that he also danced regularly in smaller parts that were not named in the bills.

In 1732–33 he joined the company at Goodman's Fields to appear as a Follower in *The Amorous Sportsman*, Punch in the dance *Masquerade*, Punch in *The Tavern Bilkers* (and in its retitled version, *The Cheats*), Trebonius in *Julius Caesar*, and Rochford in *Vertue Betray'd*. On 11 May 1733 he shared a benefit with Miss Cole. In 1733–34, his last recorded season in London, he was again at Goodman's Fields. He performed in such entr'acte turns as *A Pyrrhic Dance*, a *Rural Dance*, and a *Tambourine Dance*, as well as appearing as a Bravo in *The Inconstant*, a Follower in *The Happy Nuptials*, a Grenadier in *Britannia*, and a Companion in *Diana and Acteon*. The "Mrs" Evans listed by *The London Stage* as participating in a *Milk Pail Song and Dance* on 8 January 1734 we take to be Mr Evans. He shared a benefit with Miss Cole on 8 May 1734.

Evans, Mr ₁fl. 1742–1743₁, *actor.*

A Mr Evans shared a benefit with Baumgartner at the James Street Theatre on 25 January 1742 when *The Virgin Unmask'd* was performed by "persons for their own diversion." At the same house on 31 May he shared a benefit with Bostock, who played the title role in *Ulysses*. No roles were mentioned for Evans in these productions; perhaps he was the organizer. It is likely that he was the Evans who appeared as Barnardine in *Measure for Measure* on 25 November 1742 and as Alberto in *A Duke and No Duke* on 26 April 1743 at Covent Garden.

Evans, Mr ₁fl. 1753₁, *wire walker.*

At Bartholomew Fair on 3 September 1753 at the Lower Booth in George Inn Yard, wire walking was exhibited by a Mr Evans.

Evans, Mr ₁fl. 1766–1775₁, *wardrobe keeper?*

On 5 November 1766 and on other occasions, 1771 through 1775, a Mr Evans was paid £10 10s. on the wardrobe account at Drury Lane. Though Evans may have been a supplier of costumes rather than a theatre employee, one account book note suggests that he was a house servant: on 11 November 1774 the standard sum was paid Evans and described as the season's wardrobe "allowance." Perhaps, then, he was the keeper of the company's wardrobe.

Evans, Mr ₁fl. 1770–1772₁, *actor.*

A Mr Evans played the King in *The Mourning Bride* at the Haymarket Theatre on 19 December 1770. A notation in the Drury Lane company books on 18 March 1772 indicated that Evans had been engaged for the Haymarket Theatre (for the summer of 1772, one supposes). That entry in the Drury Lane books suggests that perhaps Evans had worked at that playhouse during the 1771–72 season. In any case, no playbills at any theatre mentioned the actor after his December 1770 billing.

Evans, Mr ₁fl. 1776₁, *candleman?*

The Drury Lane accounts show a payment of £5 to one Evans for spermacetti candles on 25 March 1776. He was probably a candleman at the theatre, though he may have been a supplier.

Evans, Mr [*fl.* 1776–1784?], *bassoonist.*

The Mr Evans who played bassoon in the Drury Lane band in 1776–77 was perhaps the Evans who was a bassoonist at the Handel Memorial Concerts at Westminster Abbey and the Pantheon in May and June 1784.

Evans, Mr [*fl.* 1777–1806], *actor, dancer, singer.*

There were so many performers named Evans active during the last quarter of the eighteenth century that distinguishing among them is most difficult. The following account may unintentionally treat more than one Evans.

On 18 August 1777 a Mr Evans was paid 1s. nightly as an extra at the Liverpool theatre. Perhaps he was the Evans who was in the cast of *The True-Born Irishman* at the Haymarket Theatre in London on 9 October 1777, and he may have been the Evans who, with his wife, was a member of Phillips's company in Worcestershire in 1778. That Evans was in *The Clandestine Marriage* and played Charon in *Lethe* in Ludlow in January 1778 and was Soup Maigre in *The Fairy Revels* at Bewdley on 6 March. An Evans was a member of the company at the Richmond theatre in 1791 and 1792; in the latter year he danced in *The Rustic Villagers* on 13 July, played Amiens ("with a song") in *As You Like It* on 18 July, was a Servant in *The Road to Ruin* on 20 July, had parts in *A Day in Turkey* and *The Highland Reel* on 23 July, and appeared in *Wild Oats* and *Rosina* on 31 August. The same Evans was at Richmond again in September 1796 and was probably the Evans who acted an unnamed character in *The Battle of Eddington* at the Haymarket Theatre in London on 23 January 1797.

An Evans played Villars in *The Belle's Stratagem* and the Lover in the pantomime *Harlequin Will o' the Whisp* (*sic*) on 30 July 1798 at the Theatre Royal, Plymouth. Evans was at the Birmingham theatre in 1799. Hob in *Hob in the Well* was played by a Mr Evans at Bath on 16 May 1805, and Genest later reported that the Bath Evans "had a considerable degree of low humour, and played some parts, particularly old men, very well—but to please the gallery, he frequently inserted so much nonsense in his part, that his acting was abominable." On 12 October 1805 at the new theatre in Beaufort Square, Bath, the same Evans had a role in *Richard III*. At Drury Lane Theatre in London on 18 November 1805 a Mr Evans (apparently not the old-timer Benjamin Evans) played Barber in *The Weathercock* and then repeated the role at Manchester on 8 March 1806.

Evans, Mr [*fl.* 1778], *actor.*

A Mr Evans made his first appearance on any stage on 28 December 1778 at the Haymarket Theatre playing an unnamed role in *The Macaroni Adventurer* and the Chairman in *The Covent-Garden Tragedy*. Perhaps he was the Evans (fl. 1777–1806?) who appeared at the same theatre in 1796–97, but there is not sufficient evidence to make a satisfactory identification.

Evans, Mr *d. 1789?, harper.*

At Beard's benefit on 29 March 1758 at Drury Lane a Mr Evans played a piece on the harp. He appeared on 5 May 1759 at Roberts's benefit at Covent Garden to play a number on the "Welch" harp, and in 1760 at the same house he performed twice: on 17 March at Mrs Hamilton's benefit he offered several pieces, including the Irish ballad "Ellen-a-Roon," and on 6 May at Roberts' shared benefit Evans accompanied Roberts in a song and played "A Lass that was Laden with Care" with variations. Twice more, on 6 May 1761 and on 4 May 1762, Evans appeared to support Roberts's benefits. On 7 January

(1763, apparently) he played at the Music Room in Prince's Street, Bristol.

He was probably the Evans who played the Welsh harp at the Oxford Music Room about 19 May 1770 and the triple harp at Covent Garden on 24 April 1771. In June 1787 he performed again in Bristol, at Coopers' Hall. The *Biographical and Imperial Magazine* reported on 24 September 1789 the death "At Fisherwick-hall, the seat of the Earl of Donnegal, of Mr. Evans, of Bath, the celebrated performer on the triple harp." The *European Magazine* reported in October 1791 that Mr Evans, harper of Bath, had died "lately in consequence of a fall from two pair of stairs window, at Fakenham, Norfolk." Whether the first report was erroneous or there was another Evans, harper of Bath, is not now known.

Evans, Mrs [*fl.* 1678–1688?], *singer.*
The Mrs Evans who sang Manto in *Oedipus* in September 1678 for the Duke's Company at the Dorset Garden Theatre may have been the Mrs Evans who is listed in *The London Stage* as a member of the United Company in 1686–87 and 1687–88.

Evans, Mrs [*fl.* 1705–1708], *dancer.*
A student of Siris, Mrs Evans was first mentioned as a dancer on 23 November 1705 when she performed at Drury Lane. She danced with the company regularly through 1706–7, receiving benefits each spring. She began the 1707–8 season at Drury Lane, transferred to the new Queen's Theatre in the Haymarket by 7 February 1708, and then was mentioned no more in the bills. At the Queen's she was earning £1 3s. 4d. daily but was at the bottom of the roster of dancers. A Miss Evans, possibly her daughter, danced at the same theatre that season and had been active since 1703.

Evans, Mrs [*fl.* 1734]. *See* **EVANS, MR** [*fl.* 1730–1734].

Evans, Master [*fl.* 1755], *actor.*
Master Evans played a Fairy in *The Fairies* at Drury Lane on 3 February 1755.

Evans, Miss [*fl.* 1703–1708], *dancer.*
On 21 December 1703 Miss Evans danced at a concert at the Lincoln's Inn Fields Theatre. About that year her name was listed in a proposal for a performing troupe at a yearly salary of £20. She was cited sporadically in the Lincoln's Inn Fields bills through 26 June 1704, on which date she danced a *Scotch and Irish Dance* for her shared benefit with Miss Mountfort. Miss Evans turned up at Drury Lane on 16 October 1704 dancing a chaconne at her shared benefit, and perhaps she remained there throughout the 1704–5 season. In 1708 she was among the minor dancers at the Queen's Theatre in the Haymarket. At the Queen's also was a Mrs Evans, possibly her mother.

Evans, Miss [*fl.* 1734–1735], *dancer.*
The London Stage lists Miss Evans as one of the dancers at Drury Lane during the 1734–35 season, but no trace of her has been found in the bills. She doubtless was one of the minor members of the *corps de ballet* who never achieved notice in the advertisements.

Evans, Benjamin *d. 1820, actor, singer.*
Benjamin Evans was first mentioned in the bills on 26 December 1793, when he played the Lover's Servant in *Harlequin Peasant* at the Haymarket Theatre. In the spring of 1794 he was a member of the Drury Lane company receiving £1 weekly for singing in the *Macbeth* chorus, playing the Cryer in *Henry VIII*, acting a Countryman in *The Quaker*, and swelling the Horde in *Lodoiska*. From that time through the 1818–19 season Evans worked at Drury Lane, seldom playing roles of much size. He seems always to have been on hand when an extra member of a soldier's chorus was required or when a small servant's role

needed filling. Occasionally he was given individualized parts, such as James in *The Provok'd Husband*, William in *The Wedding Day*, Harry in *The Man of Ten Thousand*, Bob in *The Deaf Lover*, Gibson in *The Belle's Stratagem*, Vasquez in *The Wonder*, Peter in *Catherine and Petruchio*, Lopez in *Aurelio and Miranda*, or Seville in *The Child of Nature*. But to indicate the pace of his progress: over the years he worked his way up in *Hamlet* from a Gentleman to Francisco. Perhaps his most important roles before the end of the eighteenth century were Wat Dreary in *The Beggar's Opera* and Leonardo in *The Merchant of Venice*.

From £1 weekly in 1794 he rose to £1 5s. by 1799–1800 and £2 by 1808–9. He remained at £2 through 1815–16, still playing mostly servants, but he dropped to £1 weekly in 1816–17, by which time he was apparently getting on in years and perhaps not able to perform regularly. The record book of the Drury Lane retirement fund indicated that Evans had subscribed 10s. 6d., beginning in 1794–95, and that he died on 31 May 1820.

Evans, Charles [fl. 1660–1684], harper.

On 9 June 1660 Charles Evans was appointed Harper in ordinary in the King's Musick, replacing Phillip Squire. The accounts made frequent mention of Evans over the years, though in most instances he was simply granted £5 (almost yearly) for strings for his harp. His salary in January 1669 was £46 10s. 10d., in addition to which he presumably received an annual livery allowance. Once, on 7 October 1674, he was petitioned against by Ambrose Henbrough for a £200 bond, possibly connected with a debt. The last mention of him in the accounts was on 22 February 1684 when he was ordered to receive his usual £5 for harp strings. One account, of 1663, listed Evans among the violins, but that was probably a matter of administrative con-

venience rather than an indication that he was also a violinist, since on many warrants the royal band was rather arbitrarily divided into violins and wind instruments.

Evans, Charles *c. 1756–1823, harpsichordist, violinist, violist, organist.*

Born about 1756, Charles Evans was recommended to the Royal Society of Musicians on 7 October 1781 at the age of 25. At that time he was proficient on the harpsichord, violin, and tenor (viola), and played in the band at Drury Lane. He was admitted to the Society the following year. He was probably the Mr Evans who played second violin at the Handel Memorial Concerts at Westminster Abbey and the Pantheon in May and June 1784. He played violin at the St Paul's benefit concerts in May of 1789, 1790, and 1794 (and probably in other years), and perhaps he was the Mr Evans who played a solo on the harpsichord at a concert on 28 April 1791 at the Kingston theatre.

Doane's *Musical Directory* of 1794 listed Charles Evans as an organist as well as violinist and noted that he participated in concerts sponsored by the Academy of Ancient Music and in Handel performances at Covent Garden. He was then living in Stangate Street, Lambeth.

On 1 June 1800 Evans was granted £7 19s. by the Royal Society of Musicians, for he had broken his arm and could no longer follow his profession. At that time he had a wife and five children under 14 years of age to support. By 3 August, Evans informed the Society that he had somewhat recovered and could relinquish his claim, but testimony delivered by his surgeon showed that Evans still required medical attention. The Society granted him £7 17s. 6d. for medical assistance. Perhaps his arm never healed properly, for the records of the Society for the following 23 years show constant applications by Evans for financial assistance to cover medical expenses. On 6 May 1821, at which time Evans was living at Ludlow, the Society received a letter from Mr Foxton, a surgeon, describing Evans's physical condition as "deplorable." The Society sent Foxton £15 for Evans's benefit. Assistance was continued for two more years. A grant of £20 was made on 2 February 1823 to Evans and his family, but by 6 April he had died. His widow Sarah was given a grant of two and a half guineas. On 1 January 1837 she was described as an aged widow and was sent a donation from the Society of £1.

Evans, Charles ₍fl. 1794₎, *singer.*

Doane's *Musical Directory* of 1794 listed Charles Evans, of No 24, James Street, Westminster, as a singer in the Chapel Royal and a participant in concerts presented by the Academy of Ancient Music. He was not the singer Charles Smart Evans, whose career began later, nor was he Charles Evans the harpsichordist and violinist.

Evans, Ephraim *d. 1740, proprietor.*

Ephraim Evans was the proprietor of Cuper's Gardens, across the Thames from Somerset House, from 1738 to 1740. He had previously kept the Hercules Pillars, a tavern opposite St Dunstan in the West. He improved Cuper's Gardens by erecting a bandstand and installing an organ; then he offered concerts from six to ten in the evening featuring such performers as the blind Welsh harper Jones and music composed by Handel and Corelli. Care was taken to prevent liveried servants from entering the gardens, and special watchmen were hired to protect patrons who left the premises late at night by way of the back gate leading to St George's Fields. As in earlier years, most customers came to Cuper's (or Cupid's, as it was often called) by water. Evans died on 14 October 1740, according to the *Gentleman's Magazine*, after which the gardens were overseen by his widow.

Evans, Mrs Ephraim ₍fl. 1740–1753₎, *proprietress.*

Upon the death of her husband in 1740 Mrs Ephraim Evans took over the management of Cuper's Gardens, on the south bank of the Thames near where Waterloo Station now stands. Described as "a woman of discretion" and "a well-looking comely person," Widow Evans presided at the bar in the evenings when the gardens were open and provided her patrons over the years with first-rate musical entertainments and elaborate fireworks. During the 1740s the music of Burgess, Handel, Hasse, Corelli, and Arne was heard, and performers like Master Mattocks, Mrs Mattocks, Signora Sibilla, and Maria Bennett sang. After the musical offerings came the fireworks. On 28 June 1743 it was announced that "this night will be burnt the Gorgon's head . . . in history said to have snakes on her hair and to kill men by her looks, such a thing as was never known to be done in England before." On 30 April 1750 an exact replica of the Hague was displayed, from which the fireworks were shot off. In 1752 the curtain drew to reveal a perspective of the city of Rhodes, complete with a model of the Colossus. Neptune rose from the sea to set fire to a pyramid, dolphins spouted water, and water-wheels and rockets threw up balloons. A spectator in a tree became so excited at the finale that he lost his hold and fell into the crowd below.

After the passage of the Licensing Act of 1752 the Widow Evans was refused a license, and though she complained bitterly and accused her competitors of spreading false rumors about the respectability of Cuper's Gardens, she was forced to settle for reopening the place as a tea garden in July 1753. It is not clear how long Widow Evans remained proprietress of Cuper's Gardens. The name of Benjamin Clitherow, her pyrotechnist, appeared with increasing frequency in the bills, and control of the Gardens may have passed to him after 1753. By 1755, under the masquerade of subscription concerts, entertainments of the old kind were revived, but by 1759 Cuper's Gardens ceased to exist as a pleasure spot.

Evans, Erasmus *[fl. 1697–1700], actor.*

Erasmus Evans, the father of the dancer Susanna Evans (d. 1699), played Gusman Junior in *The Imposture Defeated* at Drury Lane Theatre in September 1697. The following February 1698 he was Segerdo in *The Fatal Discovery*, and in March he played Lepidus in *Caligula.* He concluded the season acting Prince Landevile in *The Campaigners* in June. Perhaps he was the "Evance" from Drury Lane Theatre who affronted a Mr Norton and was ordered apprehended on 27 March 1698.

In November 1698 Evans played the King of Tidore in *The Island Princess*, and, according to a note provided us by the late Emmett Avery, Evans was still advertised for that part on 5 December 1700. In February 1700 Evans was Richmond in the Cibber version of *Richard III.* He doubtless acted far more than the scanty records of the time reveal.

Evans, John *c. 1677–1718, actor, manager.*

Clark's *The Early Irish Stage* states that John Evans joined the Smock Alley troupe in Dublin in the fall of 1699 after having gained some experience acting in London. What that experience was is not certain, for though there were actors named Evans working in London in the late Restoration period, none seem to have been John. Evans worked in Dublin through the end of 1709 and was associated with Elrington, Griffith, and Ashbury in the management of Smock Alley. His Dublin activity has not yet been chronicled, but he is known to have played Friar Andrews in *The Spanish Wives* in 1707–8 and to have received a benefit in Dublin on 2 December 1709 just before coming to England.

On 16 March 1710, billed at lately arrived from Dublin, Evans played Kite in *The Recruiting Officer* at the Queen's Theatre in the Haymarket. On 14 April he took the title role in *The Spanish Fryar*, and for his benefit on 4 May he played Falstaff in *1 Henry IV.* He returned to Dublin for the following four years. In the summer of 1714, according to Chetwood's *General History*, Evans toured with the Dublin company to Cork, where he raised the ire of a group of army officers by proposing the Queen's health at a party. A duel ensued with one of the officers, and it speaks well for Evans's theatrical training that he disarmed his opponent. After the company returned to Dublin, however, Evans's antagonist tried to create a riot when Evans was playing Alexander in *The Rival Queens.* "Kneel, you Rascal!" cried a voice from the pit. "I'll kneel to none but God, and my Queen!" said Evans, whereupon he kneeled, thus satisfying himself and his opponents, and the performance was allowed to go on.

In 1715 Evans returned to London for an engagement at Drury Lane (along with Elrington and Griffith). On 22 January he played Claudius in *Hamlet*, after which he revived his earlier roles of Kite, the Spanish Fryar, and Falstaff. On 21 March he acted Aquilius in *Mithridates*; for his benefit on 28 March he chose King Harry in *Vertue Betray'd*; and on 19 April he acted Bonniface in *The Stratagem.* In Dublin during the rest of 1715 he played Alcibiades in *Timon of Athens*, Axalla in *Tamerlane*, and Lieutenant Story in *The Committee.* He was seen in *Irish Hospitality* at Smock Alley Theatre in 1717. Evans returned to London once again in the fall of 1718 to play at Lincoln's Inn Fields, his first appearance there being on 26 September as Dorax in *Don Sebastian.* He once more revived Kite, the Fryar, and Falstaff and then went on to play Flip in *The Fair Quaker of Deal*, Alexander, Tamerlane, and Cato. His last appearance was as Tamerlane on 4 November 1718.

On his way back to Ireland Evans became ill at Whitchurch, Shropshire, and was taken to Chester for medical care. He died there in November or December 1718 at the age of 41. Chetwood later described Evans as an actor of good repute who had a harmonious voice and just delivery but who was inclined to be gross and too indolent.

Evans, John *d. 1792, instrumentalist.*

John Evans, an instrumentalist, was one of the Court of Assistants in the Royal Society of Musicians in February and March 1785. On 3 May 1789 he informed the Society that he was going to Wales and that Mr Schubert would take his place in the band at Vauxhall Gardens where he had been playing. Though the Society records are somewhat ambiguous, Schubert apparently agreed to pay Evans 10s. weekly for the position at Vauxhall, and the Society granted Evans an allowance of three guineas a month, probably because he was in poor health. On 5 August 1792 the Society was informed that John Evans had died at the beginning of July.

Evans, John [*fl. 1794*], *singer.*

Doane's *Musical Directory* of 1794 listed John Evans as a singer living at No 24, James Street, Westminster, where Charles Evans lived; they were surely related, perhaps as brothers. John Evans was a member of the Academy of Ancient Music and of the Chapel Royal.

Evans, Lewis *d. 1666, lutenist, harper.*

On 26 November 1633 Lewis Evans the lutenist was sworn to one of the places previously held by Robert Johnson in the King's Musick at a salary of 1s. 8d. daily plus a livery allowance of £16 2s. 6d. per year. On 9 November 1660 Pepys received instructions on the lute from Evans, who had been reappointed to the King's Musick at the Restoration. On 15 October 1666 Henry Brockwell replaced Evans, who must have been dead by then. Indeed, the harper

Evans to whom Pepys referred in his *Diary* on 19 December 1666 was surely Lewis. One of the court musicians, Hingeston, had told Pepys of the poverty of many of his colleagues, some of whom were still waiting for wages from five years before. ". . . Evens, the famous man upon the Harp, having not his equal in the world, did the other day die for mere want, and was fain to be buried at the almes of the parish, and carried to his grave in the dark without one linke, but that Mr Hingston met it by chance, and did give 12d. to buy two or three links."

Evans, P. [*fl. 1776?–1794*], *organist.*

Doane's *Musical Directory* of 1794 listed P. Evans as the organist of St Giles Church, Holborn. It seems probable that he was the P. Evans cited in Humphries and Smith's *Music Publishing in the British Isles* as a music seller and publisher at No 102, High Holborn from 1776 to about 1786. They state that Evans had previously been with Longman, Lukey and Company.

Evans, [S.?] *d. 1780, boxkeeper.*

Mr Evans shared a benefit with three other boxkeepers at the Haymarket Theatre on 25 April 1735, after which he moved to Covent Garden to spend the rest of his long career. Over the years the Covent Garden bills show regular benefits for Evans, usually shared with from one to three others. His income from them varied from year to year, of course, but the records that have survived show that even when the performance lost money, Evans sold more than enough benefit tickets to cover his share of the deficit. It would appear that he could probably depend upon making from £25 to £50 in most years. This was in addition to his salary, which was £10 annually in 1746–47 and had risen to 12s. weekly by 1776–77. He must have had other employment.

An entry in the theatre accounts on 29 September 1749 showed a payment of 3s.

4*d.* for two days to a Mr. S. Evans; he may have been the boxkeeper, though there is no certainty. Evans was probably the house servant of that name who served for 10*s.* 6*d.* at the *Messiah* performances at the Foundling Hospital in May 1758 and 1759. On 22 September 1760 he was listed on a Covent Garden payroll at 2*s.* daily but designated a lobby doorkeeper—certainly an error, for his benefit bills through the years identified him as a boxkeeper (the salary, in any case, was the same for both positions). Evans's last benefit was on 20 May 1780 when he and two other boxkeepers shared £104 16*s.* 4*d.* profit. On 26 August 1780 Evans was reported as having died a few days before.

Evans, Susanna *d. 1699, dancer.*

Possibly the "fine Danceing Girle" referred to on 20 July 1695 in a document in the Kent Archives Office as a member

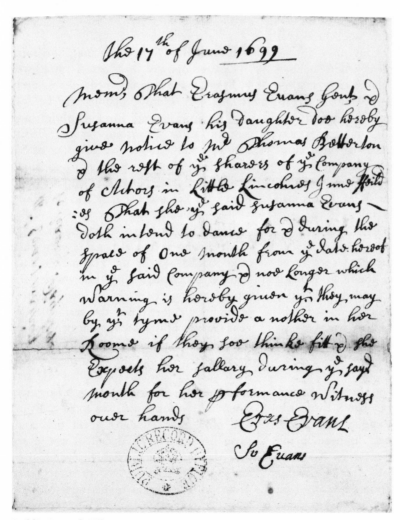

Public Record Office

Letter of ERASMUS and SUSANNA EVANS

of Betterton's troupe at Lincoln's Inn Fields was the talented young Susanna Evans. She was certainly a member of the company in 1698–99, for her father Erasmus gave the following notice to the manager on 17 June 1699:

Know, That Erasmus Evans Gent, and Susanna Evans his daughter doo hereby give notice to Mr Thomas Betterton and the rest of ye sharers of ye Company of Actors in Little Lincoln's Inne ffeild That she ye said Susanna Evans – doth intend to dance for ye during the space of One month from ye date hereof in ye said Company & noo Longer which Warning is hereby given y^t they may by y^t tyme provide a nother in her Roome if they may be fitt & she Expects her sallary during ye sayd month for her performance witness our hands
Eras Evans
Su Evans

Perhaps she danced in a performance of *Don Quixote* at some point, for she was so advertised, in error, on 5 July 1700, a year after she died.

In the Hatton correspondence is a letter from Alice Hatton written in September 1699: "I believe shall be on Munday at a ball at St. James, where, as they tell me, ther is a famose new danser to apere, which is to charme us all, but not make amends for ye loss of Mrs Ibbings [i.e. Evans] who danced at Lincolns Inn Feild and is lately dead." Vanbrugh, in a letter to the Earl of Manchester dated 25 December 1699, wrote, "Miss Evans the dancer at the New Playhouse is dead too; a feaver Slew her in eight and forty hours. She's much lamented by the Towne as well as the House, who can't well bare her loss; Matters running very low with 'em this Winter. . . ."

Evans, Susanna   *b. 1735.* See **MULLART, SUSANNA.**

Evans, Thomas   [*fl. 1762–1803?*], *treasurer.*

Thomas Evans shared a benefit with Lee at Drury Lane on 9 May 1764, the first mention of him in the playbills; he was identified as the sub-treasurer of the company. But *Trials for Adultery* (1779) recorded Evans's testimony during the court case of W. Earle vs K. Earle which indicated that Evans had been employed in the theatre's treasurer's office since 1762 or earlier. Evans received annual benefits during the rest of the 1760s, sometimes solo but usually shared with another – frequently Miss Rogers. His pay was 5s. daily or £1 10s. weekly, and though some of his benefits may have augmented his income, the records show that in 1767 he and Miss Rogers had to pay a deficit of £28 18s. 6d. His last benefit was on 13 May 1771, shared with Mrs Dorman, after which he was paid a salary plus a flat fee (in lieu of a benefit) each year – usually £42 to £45. His position in the company was important, however, and he was frequently called upon to witness wills (as he did in 1767 for David Garrick, in 1768 for James Lacy, and in 1799 for William Shrubsole) or to handle large sums of money.

Richard Cumberland in his *Memoirs* told a story about Evans bringing him his benefit proceeds:

My property in the piece was reserved for me with the greatest exactness; the charge of the house upon the author's night was then only sixty pounds, and when Mr. Evans the Treasurer came to my house in Queen-Ann-Street in a hackney coach with a huge bag of money, he spread it all in gold upon my table, and seemed to contemplate it with a kind of ecstasy, that was extremely droll; and when I tendered him his customary fee, he peremptorily refused it, saying he had never paid an author so much before, I had fairly earnt it, and he would not lessen it a single shilling, not even his coach-hire, and in that humour he departed.

At some point, perhaps beginning in 1771–72 when he switched from a benefit to a flat yearly fee, Evans was promoted to be treasurer of Drury Lane, a post he held at least until 1779. The last mention of him—unless it was a reference to a different Thomas Evans—was on 30 December 1799 when he witnessed Shrubsole's will. By that time he had long retired from Drury Lane.

Perhaps the theatre employee was the Thomas Evans, bookseller and publisher of Paternoster Row from 1770 to 1803, listed in Humphries and Smith's *Music Publishing in the British Isles.*

Evans, [Thomas?] [*fl.* 1784], *singer.*

A "Mr Evance" Junior sang tenor in the Handel Memorial Concerts at Westminster Abbey and the Pantheon in May and June 1784. Also singing at those performances was Thomas Evans, listed by Burney as "Mr Evance" Senior, presumably the younger singer's father.

Evans, Thomas [*fl.* 1784?–1794], *singer.*

The "Mr Evance" who sang tenor in the Handel Memorial Concerts at Westminster Abbey and the Pantheon in May and June 1784 was probably the Thomas Evans listed in Doane's *Musical Directory* of 1794. Doane described Evans as a member of the Choral Fund, the Longacre Society, and the Surrey Chapel Society and a participant in the oratorios presented at Westminster Abbey and Drury Lane Theatre. The *Catalogue of Printed Music in the British Museum* cites a serenata, *Look ere you Leap,* published in 1792, as having been sung by Evans and others at Vauxhall Gardens. Evans's address as of 1794 was No 80, Snow Hill. A Mrs Thomas Evans was granted £20 by the Royal Society of Musicians on 3 March 1816 for the benefit of the family of Thomas Evans; if that reference was to our subject's family, then he had evidently died prior to that date. One member of the family, perhaps, was the "Mr Evance" Junior who sang with his father in the 1784 Handel concerts.

Evants, Mrs [*fl.* 1781–1782], *actress.*

Mrs Evants was the "Young Lady" who played Princess Huncamunca in *Tom Thumb* at the Haymarket Theatre on 22 August 1781. She repeated the role on 24 August, but the work was not presented again. The *Public Advertiser* on 23 August noted that "Huncamunca was very well performed by a Lady who resembled Mrs Kennedy in her voice." On 23 October 1782 at the Covent Garden Theatre, again described in the bill only as "A Young Lady" and again said to have been making her first appearance on any stage, Mrs Evants played Phillis in *The Conscious Lovers.* She acted Fanny in *The Maid of the Mill* on 25 October, but she was given no further roles in London. A manuscript note on one of the Kemble playbills identified the woman who played Phillis as Mrs Evants, and a letter from Robert Baddeley to a Mrs Caulfield in Dublin identified Mrs Evants as the actress who played Huncamunca:

I went to see the part of Phillis in the Conscious Lover play'd by a Lady being the first appearance on any Stage, when lo! & behold! it prov'd to be a Lady who play'd Huncamunca in Tom Thumb, for Willson's Benefit the Summer before last at the Hay-Market. Her Phillis was no wonderful performance one way or another. She is rather too plump, & good Face week speaking voice & affects Mrs Wrighten's Manner. She made her second appearance last night in Nanny in the Maid of the Mill. I have not yet heard with what success, but I think she met with applause in her singing at the Haymarket.

Evatt, Robert [*fl.* 1787–1809], *actor.*

The *Thespian Dictionary* in 1805 stated that Robert Evatt had been a shopman, or perhaps an apprentice, to Mr Dyde the haberdasher in Pall Mall before making his first stage appearance somewhere in the provinces. In 1787–88 Evatt began an association with the Covent Garden company in London which lasted until 8 March 1794. His initial salary was £1 weekly, and the roles he played during his first season were mostly small. On 29 October 1787 he was the Officer in *Venice Preserv'd*, after which he appeared as a Servant in *The Careless Husband*, a Brother in *Comus*, Tomlins in *The Man of the World*, the Upholsterer in *The Miser*, Towha in *Obi*, John in *The Jealous Wife*, the first Scholar in *The Padlock*, John in *The Foundling*, the second Shepherd in *Cymon*, Thessalus in *Alexander the Great*, Hali in *The Mourning Bride*, and Philip in *The Brothers* (on 30 May 1788, when his benefit tickets were honored at the theatre). In the summer of 1788 he played at Richmond.

Evatt was one of the workhorses of the Covent Garden troupe who acted heavy schedules season after season, seldom played large roles, and were paid little for their efforts. He was raised to £1 10*s.* in 1788–89, and there he stayed for years; in his last season, 1793–94, Covent Garden paid him £2 per week. He augmented his income by acting again at Richmond in the summer of 1789, and from 1790 through 1793 he performed heavy schedules at the Haymarket Theatre in the summers. His Haymarket weekly pay, at least in 1793, was £3.

Evatt's roles improved somewhat over the years, though some of the parts he played in his first Covent Garden season he was still playing in his last, such as a Shepherd in *Cymon*, a Brother in *Comus*, and the Officer in *Venice Preserv'd*. But during his period of service at Covent Garden and the Haymarket he acted dozens of roles, often learning as many as 30 a season. A sampling includes Don Manuel in *The Revenge*, Lovelace in *Three Weeks After Marriage*, Hortensio, Pedro, and Biondello in *Catherine and Petruchio*, Brunetto in *A Duke and No Duke*, Sylvius in *As You Like It*, Sparkle in *The Miser*, Cadi in *The Little Hunchback*, Jeremy in *She Stoops to Conquer*, Mercury in *Poor Vulcan!*, Sir Charles Freeman in *The Beaux' Stratagem*, Oxford, Norfolk, and Ratcliff

in *Richard III*, Pistol in *The Merry Wives of Windsor*, Jemmy Twitcher in *The Beggar's Opera*, Bernardo, Marcellus, and Rosencrantz in *Hamlet*, Trueman in *The Clandestine Marriage*, Simon in *The Suspicious Husband*, Cornwall and the Physician in *King Lear*, Solanio in *The Merchant of Venice*, Beaufort in *The Citizen*, the Prompter in *The Manager in Distress*, Paris, Balthazar, and the Prince in *Romeo and Juliet*, Trap in *Wild Oats*, Douglas in *1 Henry IV*, Don Lewis in *She Wou'd and She Wou'd Not*, Don Manuel in *Love Makes a Man*, Omar in *A Mogul Tale*, Rossano in *The Fair Penitent*, Meanwell in *Tit for Tat*, Cuto in *Columbus*, and innumerable supernumerary parts.

The *Secret History of the Green Room* (1792) mentioned Evatt: "he certainly renders himself useful, though in very trifling characters." He was generally perfect in his lines and paid attention to his duties, and "his assiduity and modesty deserve reward." But, the critic noted, Evatt had a "coldness, and apparent bashfulness, together with a certain awkwardness of person and deportment."

Since we know that Evatt was married by 1798, perhaps the following entry in the registers of St Paul, Covent Garden, concerns him: on 29 December 1792 a Robert Evatt of that parish married Elizabeth Cludd of St Marylebone, spinster. One of the witnesses was Sarah Evatt.

Evatt acted regularly during the first half of the 1793–94 season at Covent Garden, but on 8 March he was dropped from the paylist. The following 14 or 16 June he made his first appearance at the Theatre Royal, Edinburgh, as Frederick in *The Jew*. The *Monthly Mirror* correspondent spoke cryptically of Evatt, "whose conduct on a late occasion remains to be cleared." Only one other part in Edinburgh is known for Evatt in 1794: Aboan in *Oroonoko* on 25 July. Though Edinburgh became Evatt's home through the 1808–9 season, much of his performing until 1804 seems to have been done elsewhere. In May

1797 he was at Newbury; in September of that year he played at Richmond and Kingston; in 1798 he and Mrs Evatt were at Richmond; in September 1799 they performed at Eastbourne; and in 1801 they were at Richmond again.

The *Monthly Mirror* in September 1797 commented on the Kingston theatre and referred to Evatt: "There is a little barn fitted up at Kingston, in which the Richmond company performs once a week. The Stadtholder now and then takes his seat among the cobwebs, and enjoys a comfortable nap with his *cara sposa*. The heads of the gallery people brush the tiles. *Nosey Evatt* is the Roscius." On 12 September 1799 the Evatts were in *Lovers' Vows* at Eastbourne, and the *Monthly Mirror* reported that "Evatt, formerly of Covent-Garden theatre, performed the part of Frederick with considerable ability."

The research of Norma Armstrong has uncovered a large number of roles Evatt played at Edinburgh from 1804 through 1809, among which were Antonio in *The Merchant of Venice*, the Duke in *As You Like It*, Banquo in *Macbeth*, Bellamy in *The Suspicious Husband*, Biondello in *Catherine and Petruchio*, Buckingham in *Richard III*, Captain Duretête in *The Inconstant*, Cloten in *Cymbeline*, Don Pedro in *Much Ado About Nothing*, Don Vincentio in *A Bold Stroke for a Husband*, Gloucester in *Jane Shore,* Exeter in *Henry V*, Flutter in *The Belle's Stratagem*, Gratiano in *The Merchant of Venice*, Hastings in *She Stoops to Conquer*, Horatio in *Hamlet*, Lissardo in *The Wonder*, Lord Ogilby in *The Clandestine Marriage*, Lord Randolph in *Douglas*, Manly in *The Provok'd Husband*, Marplot in *The Busy Body*, the title role in *Pizarro*, Hal in *1 Henry IV*, Priuli in *Venice Preserv'd*, Sir Benjamin Backbite in *The School for Scandal*, Sir Lucius O'Trigger in *The Rivals*, the title role in *Sylvester Daggerwood*, and Young Philpot in *The Citizen*.

A Miss Evatt acted at Edinburgh on 29 June 1805; she was perhaps Robert's daughter.

Evatt, Mrs Robert, ₁Elizabeth, née Cludd?₁ ₁*fl. 1792?–1806*₁, *actress.*

Perhaps the wife of Robert Evatt the actor was Elizabeth Cludd, a spinster from the parish of St Marylebone who married a Robert Evatt at St Paul, Covent Garden, on 29 December 1792. *The Thespian Dictionary* in 1805 reported that Mrs Evatt had acted at Richmond in 1798 with Evatt and after that had "assisted at a private theatre." In 1799 the couple were hero and heroine at the Eastbourne Theatre. The *Monthly Mirror* reported that at Eastbourne on 12 September 1799 Mrs Evatt played Agatha Fribourg in *Lovers' Vows* and was "a very beautiful woman, who, had she attended to correctness in her delivery, should have had our approbation." Mrs Evatt acted with her husband at Richmond again in 1801.

A number of her roles at the Theatre Royal, Edinburgh, are known for the seasons 1803–4 through 1805–6, among which were Augusta in *Gustavus Vasa*, Bridget in *The Chapter of Accidents*, Cora in *Pizarro*, Dorinda in *The Beaux' Stratagem*, Flora in *The Wonder*, Lady Randolph in *Douglas*, Lady Restless in *All in the Wrong*, Louisa in *Love Makes a Man*, Lydia Languish in *The Rivals*, Mrs Belville in *The School for Wives*, Gertrude in *Hamlet*, Mrs Strickland in *The Suspicious Husband*, the Queen of France in *Henry V*, Volante in *The Honeymoon*, and Zaphira in *Barbarossa*.

Evenel, Mr ₁*fl. 1742*₁, *actor.*

Mr Evenel played Trick in *The Indian Merchant* on 25 August 1742 at the Phillips-Yeates Bartholomew Fair booth.

Evens. *See also* EVANS.

Evens, Henry ₁*fl. 1672*₁, *musician.*

Henry Evens was one of a large group

of musicians ordered arrested on 2 October 1672 by the Lord Chamberlain for playing music without a license.

Everard, Edward Cape b. 1755, actor, dancer.

By his own account in his autobiography, *Memoirs of an Unfortunate Son of Thespis* (1818), Edward Cape Everard was born on 3 February 1755 in a public house operated by his parents called the Hare and Hounds Inn at Tottenham High Cross, about five miles from London. His father Edward Everard (1728–1755) had been an under steward to Governor Stevenson, near Edmonton, some eight miles from Whitechapel, London, where he met and married Ann Sowerby, housekeeper in the Stevenson family. The father died on 9 December 1755, at the age of 27, in the year of Edward's birth, and was buried in the churchyard near his inn.

Edward's younger brother John was taken by his mother to her native city of Carlisle, but Edward was left at London under the care of his mother's relative, Mr Cape, a native of Durham. Cape, Edward's godfather, was a men's dresser at Drury Lane Theatre at that time and also owned a house in the Little Piazza, Covent Garden, where lodged the actors Charles Holland, Joseph Austin, and Michael Atkins. As a small child Everard was taught dancing by Atkins, and then one day, at the age of four, he was introduced by Austin to the great Garrick, who on that day just happened to need some extras for fairies and Lilliputians. Garrick asked the child, "what can you do, my little man?" "Oh, Sir," replied Edward, "I can dance a hornpipe." Whereupon, recounted Everard, Garrick said:

"Ay, indeed, my little fellow . . . pray let's see you."— Accordingly, I began and shuffled as well as I could, which pleased him so highly that he gave me, I think, half a crown, and took a fancy to me, I believe, immediately. I made my humble appearance soon after with a vast number of others, but I was the young-est of all, and the least of all the little ones; and, as I remember well, the very first night, in forming a large fairy-ring, they hauled me so, that I fell *down* upon the stage; it proved a bad omen, for never since, have I been able to *rise* on it!

Everard claimed that the above encounter and debut occurred when he was scarcely four years of age, or in 1759. Everard's recollections generally are phenomenally accurate for one writing in 1818, some 58 years after the events, and his *Memoirs* accordingly are very reliable in contrast to numerous others of the kind. His memory in this particular, however, may have been fallible. It is, of course, possible that he had appeared on the Drury Lane stage by 1759, but the first time his name was given in the bills was on 28 December 1761, when as "Master Cape" he danced in *The Genii*, "An Arabian Night's Entertainment" by Henry Woodward. During the 1761–62 season he appeared in a total of 40 performances of *The Genii*. On 20 March 1762, he was introduced as one of the children in Garrick's *The Farmer's Return*, in a scene immortalized by Zoffany's painting showing Garrick, Mrs Bradshaw, and Master Cape. (A reproduction of that painting can be found in Vol. II, p. 287 of this dictionary.) At his shared benefit on 18 May 1762 he danced a hornpipe, at which time he was noted as a scholar to John Walker, who also had been Nancy Dawson's dancing instructor. Everard credited Walker with teaching him a proper hornpipe and claimed that he was much noticed by George II and the nobility—but that those in the gallery "from their distance, used to think me a puppet!"

In 1762–63, which was the second season his name appeared in the bills, Everard performed only about 15 times in *The Genii*, and the bills made no mention of his hornpipe, despite his claim that he had danced above 50 nights. In 1763–64 he again made regular appearances in the same piece and on 23 November 1763 he made his debut as an actor when he played Puck in the Garrick-Colman version of *A Midsummer Night's Dream*. Only three days later, on 26 November, he danced as one of the Fairies in *The Fairy Tale*, yet another, but vastly reduced, version of Shakespeare's play by Colman. On 23 May 1764, Master Cape shared in a benefit for all the children who had performed that season in *The Fairy Tale*, at which time he offered a double hornpipe with Miss Rogers.

Young Edward continued at Drury Lane for another nine years under the name of Master Cape, regularly playing such roles as: Puck in Woodward's pantomime of *Queen Mab*, a Boy in *Wit's Last Stake*, a Boy in *The Contrivances*, Young Clarence in *Henry IV,* a Servant in *The Widow'd Wife*, Cupid in *A Trip to Scotland*, Jack in *The Committee*, a Boy in *The Chances*, Donalbain in *Macbeth*, Varro in *Timon of Athens*, the Black Boy in *The Irish Widow*, a Messenger in *Philaster*, a Sailor in *The Fair Quaker*, a Servant in *The School for Wives*, and characters in *The Jubilee* and *The Pigmy Revels*.

In the summer of 1769, Master Cape acted at the Haymarket Theatre, where he played the Duke of York in *Richard III* on 6 May and Prince Edward in the same play on 14 August. He also danced at Bristol in the summers of 1765 and 1766, during which times he lodged in King Street with the actor William Powell (1735–1769). Sometime in 1766, Edward, Miss Collett, and Miss Giorgi, with some musicians from Drury Lane, were summoned to entertain the Prince Regent and the Duke of York at Ancaster House. Everard claimed that he practiced his dances, as a sailor, for two months before, and that all the entertainers were liberally rewarded, but that he received the smallest remuneration. His dancing master at that time was Jean Georges Noverre.

In his early years, according to his *Memoirs*, Edward came under the influence and tutelage of Garrick, whom he writes about frequently and with reverence. Indeed, in his *Theatric Tourist* (1805), James Winston spread the gossip that Everard was the illegitimate child of Garrick, but there seems to be no validity to this rumor. Everard told the story of Garrick directing him at a rehearsal of *2 Henry IV* in which he wished Everard as young Clarence to "give with a little more feeling," whereupon the youngster, but 12 years of age, replied, "Oh yes, sir, I intend to do so at night." "At night," shot back Garrick, "why, can you speak or play better at *night* than in the *morning*?" Edward explained that when he was dressed for the part, before a real audience, he would be able to rise to the role. "Then, you are no actor!" admonished Garrick, "If you cannot give a speech, or make love to a table, chair, or marble, as well as to the finest woman in the world, you are not, nor ever will be a great actor!" Garrick's judgment proved to be prophetic.

Toward the end of the season 1770–71, Edward requested that his godfather Cape should bind him apprentice to some trade. He wished, he said, to be a compositor or bookseller, but Cape would not oblige, claiming that Garrick objected. Edward believed, however, that the objection proceeded from his guardian's "own private views," inasmuch as the boy was bringing money into the house for his work at the theatre. In the summers of 1771, 1772, and 1773, Edward was engaged at the Plymouth Theatre, under the management of Jefferson, a Drury Lane actor.

At the end of his second summer at Plymouth, Edward, now age 17, decided to get rid of his "godfather's shackles," as he put it, and assert his independent manhood. He had, of course, been raised from infancy by Cape, and had come to regard him, as everyone else did, as his real father. To everyone in the theatre district he was known as Cape's son and was commonly called "the Cape of Good Hope." But evidently Cape was becoming overbearing, and, as Edward characterized him, "more indolent, more extravagant, and of course more necessitous." When they met behind the scenes at Drury Lane at the opening of the 1772–73 season, Cape took him by the hand, and "with almost a tear in his eye," said, "What, will you leave me, Ned?" Edward softened his resolve, went home with him again, "and lost another winter." When he returned to Plymouth for the summer season of 1773, however, he had "fully quitted" his godfather, and, determined to shed the name of Cape as well, he requested that Jefferson put his name on the bills as Everard. Jefferson reluctantly complied, cautioning that he already enjoyed credit with the Plymouth audience as Cape. But Edward danced on the first night under his new name. "I never danced *there* so well in all my life," he reported, "but, yet, I rather lost than gained ground." For, as he put it, the press complimented the earlier Cape at the new Everard's expense:

Though Everard's feet
So true did beat
To music sweet,
And dress'd so neat,
Was thought a cheat
I' th' dancing feat
Compared to Cape's, so trim, so fleet;
To th' Galleries it was grog—fresh meat;
To Pit and Boxes, quite a treat.

Ironically, Everard was not allowed to be as good a dancer as Cape—"numbers of the town would by no means give credit that he and Everard was one and the same person."

When he returned to Drury Lane for the beginning of the season of 1773–74, however, his name again appeared in the bills as Master Cape. He was so billed when he played a Sailor in *The Fair Quaker* on 9 November 1773 and a Servant in *The School for Wives* on 11 December. But on 31 December, in the latter role, he was called Mr Everard. Master Cape was ir-

revocably behind him. The management also decided that he had now grown too big for boy's parts, though "yet not quite competent to the men's," so he was assigned a series of servants and grooms and was also asked to assist in the figure dances, with an addition to his salary. In that season he played Prince Henry in *King John*, Spinner in *The Male Coquette*, a Jockey in *The Note of Hand*, and roles in *The Swindlers* and *Phaedra and Hippolitus*. In the summer of 1774 he joined Foote's company at the Haymarket, where he performed Beau Trippit in *The Lying Valet*, James in *the Mock Doctor*, a Scholar in *The Padlock*, Dick in *The Minor*, a Footman in *The Devil to Pay*, Pedro in *Catherine and Petruchio*, the Printer's Devil in *The Author*, John in *The Patron*, Catesby in *Richard III*, and roles in *The Devil Upon Two Sticks*, *The Cozeners*, and *A Trip to Portsmouth*. He remained at Drury Lane through the season of 1776–77. He acted again at the Haymarket for Foote in the summers of 1775 and 1776. His salary at Drury Lane in 1774–75 was £1 5s. per week, but by his last season there, 1776–77, it was £1 10s. per week. At the time he was hardpressed for money: on 1 June 1776 he repaid Drury Lane £5 15s. 6d. for his "debt and costs," but soon after, on 10 June 1776, he borrowed £21 by note from the theatre treasury.

In addition to those listed above, Everard's other roles at Drury Lane during this period included Le Beau in *As You Like It*, Hone in *The Cobbler*, Donalbain in *Macbeth*, Balthazar in *Romeo and Juliet*, Crib in *Harlequin's Invasion*, and a host of servants, soldiers, and minor miscellaneous walk-ons in such pieces as *The School for Lovers, Braganza, The Earl of Warwick, The Runaway, The Orphan, The Spleen,* and numerous others. His roles at the Haymarket were in the same vein. In his *Memoirs*, Everard described what it was like to be a journeyman actor in a major London theatre during the eighteenth century:

The porter, or call-man, used to come to my lodging of a morning, and, knocking at my door, this little dialogue use to pass: — "Mr. Everard. . . . At ten o'clock, if you please, to As You Like It. . . . At eleven in the Green Room, to the reading the New Play. . . . At twelve, to Much ado about Nothing, Mr Garrick will be there. . . . At one in the practicing room below, Mr Grimaldi's dances in the Tempest. . . . At two, on the stage, Mr Slingsby's dance, the Savage Hunters. . . . At half-past two, Signior Dagueville's Double Festival. . . . At three o'clock, Mr Atkins's Sailor Revels. . . . At half-past three, Signior Galli's practice . . . from ten till four in the afternoon, and having perhaps to dress and begin the play, from five to nearly twelve.

By his own account, Everard acted at Brighton with Roger Johnstone's company in the summer of 1775. His usual line, of course, was comic characters in comic plays. At Brighton, however, he appeared in some tragedies, but in essentially comic roles such as Polonius and the Gravedigger (the first "old" parts that he ever performed), Mercutio, and Roderigo in *Othello*. There he also acted Davy in *Bon Ton* for 14 nights, "with much credit," or at least so he wrote in the *Memoirs*. The Brighton manager tried to persuade Everard to remain at his theatre after the summer, but the actor, though not pleased with his situation at Drury Lane ("it was unprofitable, humiliating, and fatiguing") would not offend Garrick by failing to return to London. Johnstone made a difficult situation by scheduling Everard's benefit at Brighton very late in the season on the very night that Drury Lane was to open. Everard made a public appeal to the audience about the injustice, and the manager was pressured to advance the benefit night, for which Everard netted £40 when he acted Richard III and Mungo in *The Padlock* and danced a hornpipe.

Everard returned to Drury Lane for 1775–76. In the summer of 1776 he was back in Brighton, again for Johnstone. Garrick had retired in June 1776, and Everard himself intended to leave his engagement at Drury Lane at the same time. Reluctantly, however, he returned to play for the new management under Sheridan in 1776–77, at the end of which season he did leave that theatre. Everard claimed he had quit because his roles and wages failed to improve, despite expectations to the contrary, but it is also possible that the new managers decided to let him go. He played the summer of 1777 at Brighton under the new management of Joseph Fox. On 23 March 1778 he acted Sir Harry Beagle in *The Jealous Wife* and Grumio in *Catherine and Petruchio* in specially-licensed performances at the Haymarket. Playing the chambermaid in the former piece was Mrs Everard, née Ann Gibson, whom Everard had married about 1776.

In the summer of 1778, Everard joined some actors for performances at the China Hall Theatre, Rotherhithe, a few miles east from London Bridge. He made his first appearance there on 1 June 1778 with a hornpipe, and on 3 June played the Butler in *The Devil to Pay* and Whisper in *The Busy Body*. His other roles at the China Hall included Canton in *The Clandestine Marriage*, Paris in *Romeo and Juliet*, Elliot in *Venice Preserv'd*, a Servant in *High Life Below Stairs*, Raleigh in *The Earl of Essex*, Doctor Druid in *The Fashionable Lover*, Chapeau in *Cross Purposes*, Clerimont in *The Miser*, Whittle in *The Irish Widow*, and the major role of Barnwell in *The London Merchant*. After the performance on 26 June, in which Everard danced a hornpipe, the theatre burned down. The actors rigged up a temporary booth in which on 30 July Everard acted Launcelot in *The Merchant of Venice*. Everard recalled that the booth had been operated for about six weeks, and that in August he had acted Lear three times to G. F. Cooke's Edgar.

According to the *Memoirs*, Garrick had promised to use his influence to get Everard an engagement at Covent Garden for 1778–79. But the negotiations became complicated, and before the matter could be resolved Garrick died, in January 1779. While waiting around London, Everard acted occasionally at the Haymarket, playing Squire Richard in *The Provok'd Husband* and the Squire in *Piety in Pattens* on 18 September 1778, Marmozet in *The Prejudice of Fashion* and Faddle in *The Foundling* on 22 February 1779, and Martin Sly in *Wit's Last Stake* on 8 March 1779.

Except for some occasional engagements at London, Everard passed the next 39 years as an itinerant actor, during which time he was with practically every provincial company, large and small, throughout England and Scotland. His difficult and somewhat anonymous life as "An Unfortunate Son of Thespis" in the provinces is laid out at length in his autobiography. He returned to London briefly in 1783 to play, by his account, some 40 performances of Mungo in *The Padlock* at the Apollo Gardens near Westminster Bridge. Subsequently he joined Thornton's circuit of 16 theatres in such places as Cowes, Arundel, Reading, Guildford, and Chelmsford.

At a special benefit for Lee Lewes, under the patronage of the Royal Family, Everard played a single performance as Charles in *The Busy Body* at the Haymarket on 7 March 1791. Several years later, on 22 April 1795, he himself was given a benefit at the Haymarket, for which he performed Canton in *The Clandestine Marriage*, a character in *Mrs Doggerell in her Altitudes*, and Cadwallader (with the original Prologue) in *The Author*. Tickets could be had of him at Mr Shade's, Woburn Street, near the Drury Lane Theatre. He acted at Covent Garden in 1801–2.

Sometime in 1804 Everard returned to London, not as an actor but as a tutor to the son of Colonel M'Neale, at a salary of a guinea per week. He took up lodgings near Hans Square, by Sloane Street, and

soon became re-acquainted with Lord Erskine (then the Lord High Chancellor), who Everard claimed was a friend of his wife's parents. As Everard tells the story, one day in April 1805, Erskine became impatient at Drury Lane's failure to respond to his solicitations on behalf of Everard and finally insisted to Mr Justice Graham, the president of the theatre's board of management, that the actor be engaged immediately. That very evening, presumably, Everard was hustled onto the stage as one of the anonymous characters in *Forty Thieves* and was engaged for the remainder of the season at 25*s.* per week. The engagement was resumed in 1805–6; on 14 June 1806 he had benefit tickets as Lord Ogleby in *The Clandestine Marriage*.

He continued at Drury Lane in 1806–7 and 1807–8 at a salary of £2 per week, but his position evidently was in constant jeopardy, and he was finally discharged. He returned to the provinces but experienced difficulty in retaining engagements, took up temporarily the teaching of dancing at Leek, and wandered about to Buxton, Macclesfield, Knutsford, and other places giving recitations. In the *Memoirs* he claimed to have quit the stage by 1808, except for two benefit performances he enjoyed in Edinburgh—one on 24 January 1817 as Lord Ogleby and the other on 14 April 1818 as Sir Handy in *Speed the Plough* and Sir Felix Friendly in *The Agreeable Surprize*. But Egerton manuscript 2299 at the British Museum lists an Everard at £1 5*s.* per week at Covent Garden between 1811–12 and 1814–15. And the bills for the Theatre Royal, Edinburgh, reveal that there on 7 June 1819 he acted Shylock and Jerry Sneak (in *The Mayor of Garratt*), his last recorded performances.

Between 1808 and 1818 Everard survived hand-to-mouth by giving recitations in various halls and rooms about the countryside. Despite the fact that he was one of the earliest subscribers to the Drury Lane fund (he had subscribed 10*s.* 6*d.* in 1775), he was rendered ineligible for assistance when, according to his story, he was struck off the fund after 21 years of membership because he came one day late with his payment to Robert Baddeley, one of the committee. Throughout his autobiography Everard related his attempts to be reinstated and bemoaned that he was made to suffer so during his life by Baddeley's cruel officiousness. There was perhaps another side to the story; the Drury Lane Fund Book in Winston's hand (now at the Folger Library) shows that in 1779 Everard had "neglected payment." When Everard published his *Memoirs* in 1818 he sent a copy to Mrs Garrick, with a letter (in the Harvard Theatre Collection), written from No 58, Drury Lane, in which he persisted with his accusation of injustice at Baddeley's hands. "My case is peculiarly hard," he wrote, and he submitted himself to her generous consideration.

Everard wrote his *Memoirs of an Unfortunate Son of Thespis* while in Edinburgh. He hoped by its publication in 1818 to procure "a bit of bread for myself and wife for the short time we shall be allowed to trouble the world." He was at the time 63 years old and had spent most of those years, since the age of four, upon the stage. It is understandable that he was "so contented, rather indeed so tired of my travels" that he wished no more of them. Despite so long a stage career, of which about 20 years were spent in the employ of London theatres, Everard was essentially a theatrical anonym. Except for the several major roles he played at his own benefits in the early nineteenth century, in London he seldom rose above the rank of journeyman actor or figure dancer. It is his autobiography, one of the best and most detailed of its kind, which holds for us such great interest because of its accounts of the strolling life at the time.

How long Everard lived after 1818 is not known to us. His wife, who was still alive in 1818, is entered separately in this volume. They had at least two children,

one of whom died in infancy. Edward Cape Everard's mother was buried at Carlisle. His brother, John Everard, an "oil and colour man" who lived at No 19, Houndsditch, London, died about 1816. A Rev Edward Everard, son of Edward's brother, was living in Kent in 1818, the actor's only living relation.

The only known picture of Everard is the above-mentioned painting by Zoffany showing him with Garrick and Mrs Bradshaw in *The Farmer's Return*.

Everard, Mrs Edward Cape, Ann, née Gibson *b. 1756, actress.*

The wife of the actor Edward Cape Everard was born Ann Gibson in a house in the High Street, Edinburgh, in 1756. She was one of 21 children of Peter Gibson, a native of Dundee, and Ann Lumsden Gibson, of Dumfries. When her parents lost their lands and property, forfeit to the Crown in the aftermath of the 1745 rebellion, they moved to London, where Everard made their acquaintance some years before he married Ann. In her infancy Ann suffered smallpox, an affliction which rendered her blind for over three years. She regained partial sight in her childhood, but her vision remained impaired to the extent that Everard, writing in 1818, reported her to be then half-blind and moving about "by feel and guess."

Ann Gibson wed Everard about 1776. As Mrs Everard she made her first recorded professional appearance at the Haymarket on 23 March 1778 in the role of the Chambermaid in *The Jealous Wife*. Her husband played Sir Harry Beagle. On 18 September 1778 she played Mrs Motherly in *The Provok'd Husband* and on 8 March 1779 Mrs Watchly in *Wit's Last Stake*, both at the Haymarket. She acted in London on one other occasion only, twelve years later, when she played an unspecified character in *The Advertisement*, a farce afterpiece by James Fennell which was produced at the Haymarket on 7 March 1791.

Perhaps Mrs Everard worked as a very

minor supporting actress in the provinces during her husband's long career as an itinerant player, but his *Memoirs of an Unfortunate Son of Thespis* (1818) does not settle the point. His affectionate references to her are usually concerned with their travels to join one another somewhere in the provinces. She evidently spent her later years in Newcastle, while he toured.

The Everards had more than one child, but their names are not known to us. One child, born at Stowmarket, died young and was buried at Carlisle. After her first accouchement, about 1778, "a dropsical complaint" attacked Mrs Everard; it rested principally in her legs, leaving her lame and ill for the rest of her life—"indeed she has been so severely and uncommonly afflicted in various parts of England and Scotland, that if the humane gentlemen of the faculty who have in different places so gratuitously assisted her," wrote Everard, "if they were to make a proper demand . . . for advice, attendance, and medicines, I am certain that two hundred pounds could not pay them."

Mrs Everard was still alive when her husband wrote his *Memoirs* in 1818, at which time she was 62 years of age. Her father Peter Gibson had died in 1794 at the age of 96, and her mother died in 1806 at the same age, according to Everard.

Everard, Nathaniel [fl. 1794], singer.

Nathaniel Everard was listed in Doane's *Musical Directory* in 1794 as an alto, a member of the Handelian Society, and a performer in the Handel Memorial Concerts at Westminster Abbey who was then living at No 2, Snow's Fields, Southwark.

Everett, Mr [fl. 1796–1800], singer.

Mr Everett sang in the chorus at Covent Garden from 1796–97 to the end of the century, his first mention in the bills being on 6 October 1796 when he was one of the musical characters in *The Mountaineers*. His assignments were seldom described very specifically: he was an Irish Peasant in *Bantry Bay*, a vocal character in *Harle-*

quin and Quixotte, an Indian Soldier in *Ramah Droog*, and a member of the singing chorus in *Joanna* and *Raymond and Agnes*. Perhaps Everett was either William or Henry Everett, both singers of the period.

Everett, Henry [fl. 1794], singer, bassoonist.

Doane's *Musical Directory* of 1794 listed "Henery" Everett of No 5, Bunhill Court, Bunhill Row, as a bassoonist and "tennor" (singer, presumably). He was a member of the Choral Fund and participated in oratorio performances at Drury Lane and Westminster Abbey.

Everett, John [fl. 1672–1676?], musician.

On 2 October 1672 John Everett and 16 others were ordered apprehended for playing music without licenses. Possibly he was the John "Everet" who married Ann Wallace at St Marylebone on 31 December 1676.

Everett, William [fl. 1794], singer.

Doane's *Musical Directory* of 1794 listed William Everett, of No 21, Gray's Inn Lane, as a tenor singer and a member of the Choral Fund.

Eversman, John Christian [fl. 1724–1739], violinist, harpsichordist.

The Mr Eversman who played the harpsichord at the end of the second act of *Titus Andronicus* at Lincoln's Inn Fields on 19 March 1724 was probably the violinist Eversman of later years and very likely the John Christian Eversman who joined the Royal Society of Musicians on 28 August 1739. In 1724 Eversman was also noted in the bills as having been given a benefit concert at Hickford's Music Room on 18 March and as playing the harpsichord again at Lincoln's Inn Fields Theatre on 25 April. By 16 September 1726 he was being paid 5s. (probably for one night's work) at Lincoln's Inn Fields, and he appears to have been a regular employee, presumably playing in the band, throughout the 1726–27 season. On 3 May 1728 the playhouse permitted him a benefit, which brought in over £130. That would suggest that Eversman had held an important post in the band during the 1727–28 season.

On 28 March 1729 he had a benefit at York Buildings, and on 12 March 1731 he had another. In between, on 15 May 1730, he shared a benefit at the playhouse. Eversman played a solo on the violin at Lincoln's Inn Fields on 12 May 1731, and just a year later he shared a benefit with Petit that brought in over £120. For the 1732–33 season he joined the troupe at the Goodman's Fields Theatre, regularly appearing as a violin soloist. His scholar, Master Cutting, sang at the theatre on 28 and 30 November 1732. Eversman again appeared as a soloist at Goodman's Fields during the 1733–34 season; at his benefit on 13 May 1734, when he performed "The Cuckow Concerto," he was cited as the theatre's first violinist. With Prelleur he wrote the music for *Jupiter and Io*, presented at Goodman's Fields on 24 January 1735, and he appeared as an occasional soloist during the season. In 1735–36 he seems only to have played a solo on the occasion of his benefit, on 27 April 1736, after which he left Goodman's Fields. On 17 December 1737 Eversman held a benefit concert at the Swan Tavern, and in 1739 he joined the newly organized Royal Society of Musicians.

Eves, Mr ₍fl. 1774–1784₎, *dancer.*

Mr Eves, a scholar of Fishar, made his first appearance on 15 April 1774 at Covent Garden dancing a triple hornpipe with Miller and Miss Matthews. On 23 May 1780 he executed the same dance with Ratchford and Miss Lings; on 10 May 1782 he danced in a number called *The Waterman*; and on 11 May 1784 he and Mrs Ratchford entertained with a *Caledonian Reel*. At each of his appearances in the 1780s his benefit tickets were accepted, which suggests that, though only on those occasions did his

name appear in the bills, Eves may have been a regular member of the Covent Garden *corps de ballet* throughout the years.

Eves, Mr ₍fl. 1794–1795₎, *dresser.*

In 1794–95 at Covent Garden Theatre Mr Eves was paid 9s. 6d. weekly as one of the male dressers.

Evison, Miss ₍fl. 1779₎, *actress.*

Miss Evison made her first and last appearance on the London stage on 27 December 1779 when she played Sukey Ogle in *The Rival Milliners* at the Haymarket Theatre.

Ewin, Mr ₍fl. 1774₎, *treasurer.*

Mr Ewin, identified as the Sadler's Wells treasurer, shared a benefit there with Miss Valois on 27 September 1774.

Excell, James ₍fl. 1730–1741₎, *singer, actor.*

James Excell made his first stage appearance on 13 May 1730 at Drury Lane Theatre playing Jolt, the coachman, in *The Stage Coach Opera*, and he repeated that role and also sang "Some Songs" for his benefit at Goodman's Fields on 17 July. On 20 August he appeared as Davy in *The Generous Free Mason* at the Oates-Fielding Bartholomew Fair booth, a role he played at their booth again on 9 September at Southwark Fair. He sang at the Haymarket Theatre on 18 September before joining the Drury Lane company for their 1730–31 season. His roles were few, though he is known to have been a Forester and a Triton in *Cephalus and Procris*, a Beggar in *The Jovial Crew*, and Jupiter in *Bayes's Opera*. The summer of 1731 found him at Tottenham Court on 4 and 12 August offering songs, at Drury Lane on 11 August playing a role in *The What D'Ye Call It*, at the Hall-Hippisley-Fielding Bartholomew Fair booth on 24 August singing and playing Smart in *The Emperor of China*, and at the same trio's Southwark Fair booth on 8

September singing "Chimes of the Times" with Mrs Egleton. After playing a Beggar in *The Jovial Crew* at Drury Lane on 25 September 1731, he joined the troupe at the Goodman's Fields Theatre, which house became his home base for the rest of his career.

His chores at Goodman's Fields in 1731–32 included playing Moody in *The Lover's Opera* (on 5 November 1731, his first appearance there that season), a Witch in *Father Girard*, Isaac in *The Footman*, Genius in *Harlequin's Contrivance*, and a Sailor in *The Fair Quaker of Deal*. He also sang a "Bacchanalian Song" several times and shared a benefit concert at the Sun Tavern, behind the Royal Exchange, on 30 November 1731. For his Goodman's Fields benefit on 15 May 1732 Excell sang and played Rovewell in *The Contrivances*, a part he enjoyed for several years. In 1732–33 he added to his repertoire such roles as Bagshot in *The Beggar's Opera*, an Attendant and the Jolly Huntsman in *The Amorous Sportsman*, and Bacchus in *The Contending Deities*. He returned to Bartholomew Fair on 23 August 1733 to play Gibbet in a burlesqued *Jane Shore* and a Follower of Cupid in *The Gardens of Venus* at the Mills-Miller-Oates booth. His 1733–34 Goodman's Fields season consisted of repetitions of some of his earlier pantomime roles plus singing in *Macbeth*, playing a Citizen and a Grenadier in *Britannia*, being a Follower in *Diana and Acteon*, and singing a *Chacon à Boire*. He also shared a benefit concert at the Swan Tavern with his fellow musician Prelleur on 22 March 1734 in the middle of his Goodman's Fields season and sang a new dialogue with Mrs Fitzgerald at Southwark Fair on 7 September.

In 1734–35 at Goodman's Fields Excell played a Basket Woman and a Grenadier in *Britannia* and roles of the same descriptions in *Harlequin in the City*, Inachus in *Jupiter and Io*, and his old role of Rovewell in *The Contrivances*. At his shared benefit

with two others on 21 April 1735 he sang a new song entitled "Goodman's Fields Theatre." After that season his name disappeared from the bills until 29 April 1741, when he and his brother Mason Montgomery shared a benefit at Goodman's Fields. Excell wrote the words for a new song, "Advice to the Sons of Bacchus," which he sang for the assembled Masons. After that he seems to have left the stage.

Exon, Mr [*fl. 1792–1810*], *puppeteer.*
Speaight's *History of the English Puppet Theatre* lists a Mr Exon as a puppeteer at Bartholomew Fair between 1792 and 1810.

Eyford, Mr [*fl. 1754–1758*], *oboist.*
Mr Eyford (or Eyferd) played oboe in a performance of the *Messiah* at the Foundling Hospital in May 1754 for 10s. and on 27 April 1758 for 10s. 6d.

Eyre, Edmund John *1767–1816, actor, playwright.*
Edmund John Eyre was born on 20 May 1767, the son of the Rev Ambrose Eyre (d. 1796), rector of Leverington and Outwell in Cambridgeshire. At the age of ten Edmund entered Merchant Taylors' School, and though he later went to Pembroke College, Cambridge, he did not take a degree. Before making a brief appearance on the stage in London, he gained some experience acting at Windsor in 1789 and then at Shrewsbury. On 28 May 1791, when his play *The Dreamer Awake* was given its second (and last) performance of the season at the Covent Garden Theatre, Eyre played Standfast, advertised as "A Young Gentleman" making his first appearance on any stage. That was Eyre's only London performance in the eighteenth century.

Most of his acting in the 1790s was done in the provinces. In June 1794 he was at Leominster, and from 1794–95 through 1803–4 he played at Bristol (and Bath as well, probably). He appeared at the Theatre Royal, Edinburgh, in 1803–4, was at

Bath in 1804–5, and at Edinburgh again in 1805–6. Eyre acted also at Newcastle and Worcester. After performing at Drury Lane in London from 1806–7 through 1808–9 and at the Lyceum with the Drury Lane troupe in 1809–10 and 1810–11, he returned to Edinburgh to act in 1811–12 and from 1813–14 through 1815–16. Many of his Edinburgh roles have been found by Norma Armstrong, who kindly shared with us her findings. Among his roles there were Adam in *As You Like It*, Aegeon in *The Comedy of Errors*, Antonio in *The Merchant of Venice*, Banquo in *Macbeth*, the title role in *Barbarossa*, Buckingham in *Henry VIII*, Casca in *Julius Caesar*, Colonel Britton in *The Wonder*, Dionysius in *The Grecian Daughter*, the Duke of Milan in *Two Gentlemen of Verona*, Kent in *King Lear*, Earl Osmond in *The Castle Spectre*, Faulkland in *The Rivals*, Friar Lawrence in *Romeo and Juliet*, Hamlet, Hubert in *King John*, Iago in *Othello*, Leonato in *Much Ado About Nothing*, Lord Townly in *The Provok'd Husband*, Malvolio in *Twelfth Night*, Menenius in *Coriolanus*, Ford in *The Merry Wives of Windsor*, Strickland in *The Suspicious Husband*, Old Norval in *Douglas*, Pierre in *Venice Preserv'd*, Pizarro, Sir Oliver in *The School for Scandal*, Stockwell in *The West Indian*, Thorowgood in *The London Merchant*, and Woodville in *The Wheel of Fortune*.

While in London in 1810 Eyre and other actors unsuccessfully petitioned the King for a patent for a third theatre.

Much of his career was devoted to playwriting. His works were *The Dreamer Awake* (1791; performed at Covent Garden 1791), *The Maid of Normandy* (1793 or 1794; acted at Dublin and elsewhere), *The Consequences* (1794; acted at Worcester), *The Fatal Sisters* (1797), *The Discarded Secretary* (1799), *The Caffres* (unpublished; acted at Covent Garden 1802), *The Tears of Britain* (1805), *The Vintagers* (1809; acted at the Haymarket 1809), *High Life in the City* (1810; acted at the

Haymarket 1810), *The Lady of the Lake* (1811; acted at Edinburgh 1811), *Look at Home* (1812; acted at the Haymarket 1812), *The Fates* (unpublished; acted at the Royalty 1813), *Hyde Park in an Uproar* (unpublished; acted at Drury Lane 1813), and *The Savage Chieftain* (unpublished; acted at the Surrey Theatre 1814).

Little is known of Eyre's personal life. *The Dictionary of National Biography* claims that he had a large family of doubtful legitimacy. He was married to the former Mrs Bolton as of 1791, and she continued acting as Mrs Eyre through 1799–1800. But Eyre is said to have eloped with a Miss Smith in 1804 when he was acting at Bath and to have married her at Stratford le Bow in July of that year. Presumably she was the Henrietta Eyre who performed in Edinburgh from as early as the spring of 1805 and acted there with Eyre until his death in 1816 and remained a member of the Theatre Royal company at Edinburgh to at least 1820. Among her many Edinburgh roles were Alithea in *The Country Girl*, Calpurnia in *Julius Caesar*, Desdemona in *Othello*, the Duke of York in *Richard III* (she must have been petite), Lady Capulet in *Romeo and Juliet*, Lady Macbeth, Lady Sneerwell in *The School for Scandal*, Millwood in *The London Merchant*, Mrs Page in *The Merry Wives of Windsor*, Patch in *The Busy Body*, the Queen in *Cymbeline*, Gertrude in *Hamlet*, and Yarico in *Inkle and Yarico*.

Edmund John Eyre died in Edinburgh in April 1816. *The Dictionary of National Biography* dates his death on 11 April, but the O. Smith papers at the British Museum contain a note to the effect that Eyre died on 23 April.

Eyre, Mrs Edmund John the first, formerly Mrs Bolton *[fl. 1784–1800]*, actress.

According to a manuscript note in the Huntington Library copy of Edmund John Eyre's *The Dreamer Awake* (1791), the playwright's wife was the former Mrs Bolton. Mrs Bolton acted Mrs Goodman in *The English Merchant* at the Haymarket Theatre for one performance only on 22 March 1784. She reappeared there on five other occasions: on 10 February 1785 in unspecified roles in *The Fair Refugee* and *A Musical Interlude*, on 12 February 1785 as Mariana in *The Miser*, on 26 April as Jacintha in *The Suspicious Husband*, on 29 April 1788 as Biddy in *Miss in Her Teens*, and on 30 September 1788 in that role again and also Mrs Brittle in *Barnaby*

Brittle and Maria in *The Citizen*.

She performed at Richmond and Brighton in 1785 and was probably the Mrs Bolton who acted a Chambermaid in *Hobson's Choice* at the Royalty Theatre in London on 3 July 1787. After becoming Mrs Eyre she appeared with her husband at Bristol (and, presumably, at Bath) from 1794–95 through 1799–1800. In 1804 Eyre eloped with a Miss Smith, so perhaps by then the first Mrs Eyre had died.

Eyres. *See* **AYRES**

= F =

F., Mrs. *See* WEAVER, MRS JAMES.

Fabian, Mrs [*fl.* 1781], *actress.*

Mrs Fabian played Lucy in *The Recruiting Officer* and the title role in *The Old Maid* at the Crown Inn, Islington, on 15 March 1781.

Fabiani, Michele *d. 1786, dancer, choreographer.*

According to the catalogue of the Instituti di Storia e d'Arte, Milan, Michele Fabiani was a choreographer in Milan in 1781–82. Fabiani made his first appearance in England dancing in a new *Divertissement* at the King's Theatre in the Haymarket on 11 March 1786. He served as ballet master and dancer for the season of 1785–86, appearing in *L'Amour jardinier, Le Premier Navigateur, Les Deux solitaires, Les Amans surpris, Ninette à la cour,* and other specialty dances. His last appearance was on 11 July 1786, after which he went to Paris. Fabiani died there shortly before 30 October of the same year. The Milan catalogue lists a picture of him inscribed "Al sublime merito del Signor Michele Fabiani celebre inventore, e direttore de' balli nel nobile Teatro a Torre Argentina, Carnevale 1791." Since Fabiani died in 1786, the date must be that of the picture.

Fabiano, Luca [*fl.* 1759–1762], *dancer.*

Though no mention has been found in London records of the dancer Luca Fabiano, when he made his first appearance in Ireland, at the Crow Street Theatre on 10 October 1759, he was said to be from Covent Garden. He seems to have remained in Dublin for the 1759–60 season, one of the entertainments in which he danced being *Mountain Goat Herds*. He appeared with Whitley's company at Manchester in 1760, and beginning 28 October of that year he used the theatre as a dance studio on days the troupe did not perform. According to Hodgkinson and Pogson's *The Early Manchester Theatre*, Fabiano advertised in the *Mercury* for students, saying that he could teach young ladies and gentlemen the "Minuet or Hornpipe, in the most elegant and genteelest Taste. . . ."

By January 1762 Fabiano had moved his operation to Mr Henry's Boarding School, according to the *Manchester Mercury*. But in December he advertised that he "purposes having his Ball on Wednesday, the 22nd instant at the Theatre, the Upper End of King Street. . . ."

Fabres, [Lucia?] [*fl.* 1742–1761?], *dancer.*

On 8 January 1742 a Mlle Fabres received her first notice in the Covent Garden bills when she danced the *Old Woman* and *Air* in *The Rape of Proserpine.* During the remainder of the 1741–42 season she appeared as a Shepherdess in *Rural Assembly* (a dance introduced into *The Winter's Tale*) and a Follower in the ballet *Mars and Venus.* On 11 May, when her benefit tickets were accepted, she danced a minuet with Villeneuve.

In 1742–43 Mlle Fabres was at Drury Lane, where she danced in *Les Amant volages* within *The Dragon of Wantley,* a *Tyrolean Dance,* and *Comus.* Back at Covent Garden in 1743–44, where she was occasionally cited in the playbills as "Mrs"

Fabres, she repeated some of her earlier pantomime roles and also played an Aerial Spirit in *The Royal Chace* and three small parts in *Orpheus and Eurydice*. On 26 April 1744 she shared a benefit with three others, but she did not return the following season. Perhaps she was the Mlle Fabre who danced in Destouche's troupe at Bordeaux in 1748, and there is certainly a possibility that she was Lucia Fabris, who danced in Milan in 1761 and was that year pictured in an engraving by Marc'Antonio Dal Re.

Fabri, Annibale Pio *1697–1760, singer, composer.*

Annibale Pio Fabri, sometimes called "Balino" or "Il Bolognese," was born in Bologna in 1697 and studied music under Pistocchi. He probably made his debut as a tenor in 1716 in *L'Alarico* at the Teatro Formagliari in his native city. He became a member of the Accademia Filarmonica of Bologna, serving as a composer, and he was named president of the society in 1725, 1729, 1745, 1747, and 1750.

In July 1729 Handel recruited Fabri and his wife for the opera season in London. Fabri was described in the *Daily Journal* of 2 July as "a most excellent Tenor, and a fine Voice," and Jean Jaques Zamboni wrote to Count Manteuffel that Fabri kept "excellent time." The tenor's first appearance in England was as Berengario in Handel's *Lotario* on 2 December 1729 at the King's Theatre. Mrs Pendarves had attended a rehearsal a few days before the opening and wrote to her sister that "Fabri has a tenor voice, sweet, clear and firm, but not strong enough, I doubt, for the stage: he sings like a gentleman, without making faces, and his manner is particularly agreeable; he is the greatest master of musick that ever sang upon the stage."

Fabri's other roles during his stay in London were Emilio in *Partenope* on 24 February 1730, the title role in *Ormisda* on 4 April, Araspe in *Tolomeo* on 19 May, the title role in *Scipione* on 3 November, Ales-

Courtesy of Civica Raccolta delle Stampe Achille Bertarelli, Castello Sforzesco, Milan

MICHELE FABIANI

artist unknown

sandro in *Poro* on 2 February 1731, and Goffredo in *Rinaldo* on 6 April. Fabri was to sing Atone in *Adelaide* in 1730, but the production never materialized.

Much in demand at continental courts, Fabri was a special favorite of the Emperor Charles VI. He was appointed to the royal chapel in Lisbon, and it was there that he died on 12 August 1760.

Fabri, Signora Annibale Pio *[fl. 1729], singer.*

The *Daily Journal* of 2 July 1729 reported that Handel had recruited Signora Annibale Pio Fabri, "who performs a Man's Part exceeding well," for the 1729–30 opera season at the King's Theatre in the Haymarket. Her husband was recruited at the same time and sang in London for two seasons, but Signora Fabri's name did not appear in any of the bills. Possibly she did not perform, or perhaps she settled for a position in the chorus.

Fabris, Jacoppo c. 1689–1761, scene painter.

Jacoppo Fabris was in London from 1730 to 1740, and Ifan Kyrle Fletcher conjectured in *Theatre Notebook* that he may have painted scenes during his stay. The bills for that decade made no mention of Fabris, but it would have been odd if so experienced a designer had not worked in the London theatres during so extended a visit. Fabris was born in Venice about 1689, worked in Baden from 1719 to 1721 and at Hamburg from 1724 to 1730. At the latter city he painted scenery for at least 25 operas. He was in Berlin from 1740 to 1747 working for Frederick the Great, after which he went to Copenhagen to continue his career. He died there on 16 December 1761.

Fabris Monari, Signora [fl. 1766], dancer.

The *Public Advertiser* on 25 January 1766 spoke of the "elegant agility of Sga *Fabris Monari*," who danced at the King's Theatre.

Fabrizzi, Orsola [fl. 1796–1797], singer.

Signora Orsola Fabrizzi made her first appearance in England as Lenina in *I Traci amanti* at the King's Theatre on 16 February 1796. The *Morning Chronicle* the next day said, "Her voice is strong and clear rather than sweet, and she sings with very fine taste and science. Her comic powers were very admirably displayed in this opera, which is full of laughable incident, and she was encored in two of her songs." She was also described as "a diminutive figure, full of animation and address, possessing considerable science, with some few tones

of very full body, and peculiar sweetness." But the *Times* on 17 February found her voice "loud and penetrating, but neither mellow nor full."

During the rest of her first season at the King's Signora Fabrizzi sang a principal character in *I due gobbi*, Madama Perlina in *La modista riggiatrice*, a principal character in *La buona figliuola*, and Limpida in *Il tesoro*. On 5 May 1796 she was granted a solo benefit which was not successful, and during her second year Taylor, the manager, gave her a present of £150 in lieu of a second benefit. In the 1796–97 season she was heard as Cascolina in *L'amor fra le vendemmie*, Giannina in *Il consiglio imprudente*, Diana in *L'albero di Diana*, and Giannina in *Le gelosie villane*.

Faideric. *See* FREDERIC.

Faigel. *See* GARRICK, MRS DAVID.

Faini, Anna Maria [fl. 1737], singer.

Signora Anna Maria Faini sang principal roles in four *intermezzi* produced at the King's Theatre in the Haymarket in early 1737: *Il marito giocatore* on 1 January, *Monsieur de Porsugnac* on 25 January, *Grullo, e Moschetta* on 19 February, and *L'impresario* on 26 March.

Fairbank, Charles d. 1729, dancer, choreographer, composer.

Charles Fairbank was the son of the actor Henry Fairbank. Though his birth date is not known, he introduced some of his dancing students to the public as early as 1704, so it is likely he was almost out of his minority on 12 February 1702, when he signed the following articles with Thomas Betterton at Lincoln's Inn Fields: "M[r] Firbanks son is to have 40[s] pr week & a play in March paying 30[£] for ye charges of y[e] house." The agreement was "for a year certain & after yt either party may give six monthes notice." Since Charles Fairbank was not referred to by his own name, the elder Fairbank and Betterton may have worked out the agreement.

The earliest notice of Charles Fairbank's performing was on 28 April 1703, when he danced at Lincoln's Inn Fields. From then through 1705–6 he appeared regularly in entr'acte dances and entries in plays, and he introduced some of his scholars to playgoers. On 3 February 1704, for example, he danced with "his boy"—probably just one of his pupils, though possibly a son—and on the following 8 June Charles danced with one of his scholars. He seems to have moved with Betterton and his troupe to the new Queen's Theatre in 1705, but after the 1705–6 season there he left the stage and confined his activities to teaching and choreographing dances for others.

John Weaver wrote in 1712 that Fairbank had "arrived at true Skill and Taste of Genteel Dancing," and in the 1717 edition of *The Loves of Mars and Venus*, as Jennifer Martin has pointed out to us, Weaver said

Mr. Firbank was for some time Competitor to Mr. de la Garde; for he was strong and active in his Way of Dancing, yet very taking and genteel which he kept so long as he performed on the Stage. The World must allow him an extraordinary Genius in Musick; and his happy Compositions in several Dramatick Entertainments by their great Success confirms this to a Demonstration.

Fairbank had composed "the musical Airs of the Dancing Parts" for that work, which was revived at Drury Lane on 2 March 1717 with Weaver dancing Vulcan.

Periodically the playbills noted dances by Fairbank which were presented by others. In November 1718 at Drury Lane, for instance, his *Maggot* was danced by Topham and Miss Tenoe. In 1721 was published *A Collection of Minuets, Rigadoons, & French Dances*, which included pieces by Fairbank. He was still teaching in 1724, two of his students being Miss Robinson

and young Rainton, both Drury Lane performers.

Charles Fairbank died on 29 October 1729 and was buried on 3 November at St Paul, Covent Garden, though he was from the parish of St Giles in the Fields. On 3 December 1729 administration of his estate was granted to Giles Sayer, guardian of Anne Fairbank, a minor. Fairbank was cited as a widower at his death.

Fairbank, Henry ₍*fl.* 1697–1710₎, *actor.*

Henry Fairbank's first notice in the records of the late seventeenth century was in late July 1697 when he played Timon in *The Humorous Lieutenant* at Drury Lane. Before the end of the century he was also cited as Van Scopen in *The Campaigners* in June 1698, and Brush in *Love and a Bottle* in December 1698. The early years of the eighteenth century are similarly innocent of detailed records, but Fairbank is known to have added to his repertoire at Drury Lane between 1700 and 1706 such parts as Oxford in *Richard III*, Shark in *Sir Harry Wildair*, Tom in *The Funeral*, Clearaccount in *The Twin Rivals*, Ferret in *The Royal Merchant*, and Appletree in *The Recruiting Officer*. Though associated with Drury Lane during this period, Fairbank appears to have been instrumental in arranging with Thomas Betterton at Lincoln's Inn Fields a contract for Fairbank's son Charles. It was signed on 12 February 1702.

Henry Fairbank left Drury Lane to join the troupe at the Queen's Theatre in the Haymarket at the beginning of the 1706–7 season, his first role there being Appletree in *The Recruiting Officer* on 14 November 1706. He remained at the Queen's through January 1708, playing such new roles as Day in *The Committee*, Kite in *The Recruiting Officer*, Otter in *The Silent Woman*, Jaqueline in *The Fatal Marriage*, Tranio in *The Taming of the Shrew*, Bomilcar in *Sophonisba*, Nightingale in *Bartholo-*

mew Fair, and Higgen in *The Royal Merchant*.

At Drury Lane from February 1708 onward he acted Setter in *The Old Bachelor*, Stratocles in *Tamerlane*, Jack Stanmore in *Oroonoko*, Ventosa in *The Tempest*, Cheatly in *The Squire of Alsatia*, Priam in *Troilus and Cressida*, and Alphonso in *The Spanish Fryar*. After a benefit on 18 March 1710 Fairbank seems to have left Drury Lane. The only other record of him is on 24 August of that year when he played the Surgeon in *The Sea Voyage* at Greenwich.

Fairbrother, Robert *1769–1841, actor, dancer, acrobat, prompter, singer, swordsman.*

A Fairbrother danced a hornpipe in Act III of *The Beggar's Opera* at the Haymarket Theatre on the occasion of a special benefit for Dighton on 13 December 1784. It was the first occurrence of the name in any extant playbill and the only one that sea-

Harvard Theatre Collection

ROBERT FAIRBROTHER

engraving by P. Roberts

son. He was probably the same Fairbrother who was a tumbler at Sadler's Wells on 15 September 1785, was called an "acrobat" in the Bristol theatrical records of 1785–86, tumbled again at Sadler's Wells on 23 April 1787 and 12 May 1788, danced in a ballet there on 13 September 1788, then on 22 December 1788 had an unspecified part in *Robinson Crusoe; or, Harlequin Friday* at Drury Lane Theatre. On 22 May 1789 he was a Fisherman in *Don Juan; or, The Libertine Destroyed* also at Drury Lane.

Fairbrother was in the regular Drury Lane dance company in 1789–90, drawing £1 per week and dancing and taking small parts in farces and harlequinades several times during the season. But on 12 April 1790 he was also at Sadler's Wells, dancing and singing in *The Incas of Peru*.

In 1790–91 Fairbrother's salary at Drury Lane was advanced to £2 per week for the same sort of service—tailors, waiters, valets, "Scaramouch" or "Harlequin" or "Clown." James Winston's Folger transcript of the Drury Lane fund book shows "Rob. Fairbrother" paying in his 10s. 6d. to join the Fund in 1791.

In the years following Fairbrother was occasionally given petty named roles—Signor Ritornello in *The Critic*, Sebastian in *Lodoiska*, Perdiccus in *Alexander the Great*, Castor in *The Triumph of Hymen*—but was usually confined to such unnamed roles as a Gaoler (in D'Auberval's ballet *The Deserter*) or an Indian Warrior (in the melodic spectacle *The Cherokee*). He was carried on the Drury Lane company list as a dancer in 1791–92, and a bill of 9 April 1792 shows him also of the ballet company at Sadler's Wells, dancing in *Medea's Kettle*. Neither the magnitude nor the frequency of his stage duties would have justified the £4 weekly he was earning at Drury Lane by 1792–93. Before that season, then, the first on which we have evidence about his salary, he may already have entered on those services as a sort of confidential general factotum and secretarial handyman to

Richard Brinsley Sheridan, Drury Lane Theatre's patentee and manager, services which are vaguely alluded to in a number of accounts. There are occasional entries in the Drury Lane account books as late as 1808–9, when his salary was still £4, and in September 1807 he was described as "2nd Clown" in a Folger manuscript. But after that, payments cease until 1816.

The Letters of Richard Brinsley Sheridan reflect Fairbrother's indispensability to Sheridan as trusted go-between in dealings with Richard Peake, undertreasurer, Charles W. Ward, Secretary to the Board of Management of Drury Lane, and others, particularly in delicate financial negotiations. Fairbrother seems to have been custodian of a separate and secret bank account for the financially perplexed manager. On one occasion he arranged bail bond for a jailed friend of Sheridan's. On the morning after the calamitous fire of 24/25 February 1809 leveled Drury Lane Theatre, Sheridan sent Fairbrother with the letter breaking the news to Mrs Sheridan. An anonymous manuscript in the Folger Library gives an interesting glimpse of the relationship between Fairbrother and Sheridan:

When I was a member of the Coburg Theatre, old Bob Fairbrother, our Prompter, told me a singular Anecdote. . . . Sheridan after the destruction of Drury Lane Theatre was often distressed for money. . . . Early one morning he sent for Fairbrother and accompanied by him and some workmen went into the ruins of the Theatre and after searching and digging for some time found the remains of a peal of bells, once belonging to the Theatre, which they dug out and sold to a Bell founder in Whitechapel for £90.

Sheridan wrote in 1815 to Thomas J. Dibdin, then assistant stage director at Drury Lane:

Dear Sir,

This is the first application I make to your new Directory; I am very earnest in urging it:

it is in favour of Robert Fairbrother, an old and true servant to me and to the theatre, though latterly discountenanced. I will pledge my life for his zeal, integrity, and ability in whatever he may be employed. What the line is in which he may be made most useful, Mr. Ward is most competent to explain. I say nothing of his large family, many of whom are qualified to give fair assistance to the theatre. I have only to add that your kind attention to this will oblige me more than I can express.

The next references to Fairbrother occur in the Folger's Drury Lane account books, and they are puzzling, though they at least show that he was connected somehow to the theatre. There is an entry for 20 April: "Mr. Fairbrother Composition [*sic*] according to Act of Parliament 20/0/0." The following week, on 27 April: "Mr. Fairbro' Compensation accord^{g} to Act of Parliament 20/0/0." On 4 May: "Fairbrother on Account Composition 20/0/0." On 18 May: "Fairbrother Compensation 20/0/0."

Charles Dibdin the younger, in recounting in his *Memoirs* his assumption of the management of the Surrey Theatre in March 1825, gave us later news of Robert Fairbrother:

My Prompter was, my old acquaintance, *Bob* Fairbrother (as he is familiarly called by the Profession) a veteran in the service of the Stage of more, I think, than 50 years standing, when he left it (in 1826). He had originally been a superior Mimist, and broad sword player: and was many years attached, confidentially, to the late R. B. Sheridan, Esq. in the Theatre Royal, Drury Lane: and was subsequently attached to the directorship of the West London, or Tottenham Street Theatre. He has a married Daughter, (Mrs. Ebsworth) who has written, or translated, some pieces for the Stage, which have been successfully performed; and a son of his is prompter at the Surrey Theatre now. I found among the company also two of his Daughters: the eldest a principal Dancer; a very clever, and what is much better, a very correct girl; she is now a principal dancer of the Caledonian Stage: her sister, as well conducted as herself, was also a Dancer; she is now married, and where, I know not.

Fairbrother joined George Wathen and James Winston in witnessing Robert William Elliston's will on 8 July 1830. Fairbrother died in 1841, aged 72.

His wife, a Miss Bailey, had been introduced to him by Joe Grimaldi. According to Findlater she was the daughter of Grimaldi's landlady, who invited her new son-in-law into her business, a fur brokerage. Fairbrother was also at one period an undertaker.

A genealogical chart published in older editions of Parker's *Who's Who in the Theatre* brings the Fairbrother family connections into the twentieth century. It shows the oldest daughter, Mary Emma Fairbrother (1794–1881), as having married Joseph Ebsworth (1788–1868) the actor, dramatist, and musician. Ebsworth was at Drury Lane in the chorus from 1812–13 until at least 1817–18. She was probably there as a child—"M. Fairbrother" in the company list for the 1807–8 season —and she joined both chorus and ballet corps as Mrs Ebsworth in 1817–18. From the Ebsworths a number of performers were descended. Robert Fairbrother's second child, Samuel Glover Fairbrother, was a theatrical publisher; his third, Benjamin Smith Fairbrother (1802–1878), was a stage manager; and his fourth, Robert, was a theatrical printer. The junior Robert's daughter, the dancer Louisa Fairbrother (1816–1890), was the morganatic wife of the Duke of Cambridge.

An engraved portrait of Robert Fairbrother by P. Roberts was published by his son S. G. Fairbrother.

Fairchild, Charles [fl. 1794–1815], *bassoonist.*
According to Doane's *Musical Directory* of 1794, Charles Fairchild, of Stamford,

Lincolnshire, played the bassoon in London in performances sponsored by the New Musical Fund. He was still a subscriber to the organization in 1815.

Fairclough, Mr [fl. 1798–1804?], *singer.*
Mr Fairclough sang at Covent Garden during the 1798–99 and 1799–1800 seasons as a member of the chorus. He was one of the Europeans in *Ramah Droog* on 12 November 1798 and subsequent dates, and he sang in *Albert and Adelaide* beginning on 11 December. His activity the following season was limited to chorus work in *Joanna* from 16 January to 7 February 1800, though he may have sung in other productions without being named in the bills. The Mr Fairclough who appeared at Sadler's Wells on 28 May 1804 may have been the same performer.

Fairlamb, Miss [fl. 1770–1771], *actress.*
Miss Fairlamb played a number of roles at the Haymarket Theatre during the 1770–71 season, beginning with Charlotte in *The Apprentice* on 1 October 1770. Following that she appeared as Patch in *The Busy Body*, Corrina in *The Citizen*, Anna in *Douglas*, Peggy in *The Miller of Mansfield*, Leonora in *The Mistake*, Dollallolla in *Tom Thumb the Great*, Kate in *The King and the Miller*, Lady Rusport in *The West Indian*, and, at her last appearance on 20 April 1771, Serina in *The Orphan*.

"Fairy, The Corsican." *See* TERESIA, MME.

"Fairy, The Windsor." *See* "MORGAN, LADY."

"Fairy of the Wells, The" [fl. 1787], *singer.*
A three year old singer, sex unspecified, sang the popular air "Fal de ral Tit" in the

character of Jack Ratlin at Sadler's Wells in 1787, billed as "The Fairy of the Wells."

"Fairy Queen, The" [fl. 1700], dancing dwarf.

At Bartholomew Fair in July 1700 was exhibited, according to the advertisements recorded in Morley's *Memoirs of Bartholomew Fair,* a three-foot-tall black dwarf called "The Black Prince" and his "*Little Woman,* NOT 3 foot high, and 30 years of Age, straight and proportionable as any woman in the Land, which is commonly called the *Fairy Queen*, she gives a general satisfaction to all that sees her, by Diverting them with Dancing, being big with child." Their two-foot-high "*Turkey-Horse,*" the puff said, was kept in a box, and the trio were the "least Man, Woman, and Horse that ever was seen in the World A-live."

Falck, John Christian [fl. 1794], instrumentalist.

According to Doane's *Musical Directory* of 1794, John Christian Falck, of No 16, Pavement, Moorfields, played the violoncello and double bass for the Choral Fund, Cecilian Society, Handelian Society, and in Salomon's concerts. This person may actually have been a member of the Flack family of musicians.

Falkner. *See also* FAULKNER.

Falkner, Mr [fl. 1745?–1755], actor.

A Mr Falkner was a member of the company acting at Richmond and Twickenham in the summer of 1750. At Richmond he played Don Lorenzo in *The Mistake* on 16 June, Altamont in *The Fair Penitent* on 23 June, Fantome in *The Drummer* on 27 June, Aegan in *Damon and Phillida* on 7 July, Euricles in *Merope* on 14 July, the Duke of Norfolk in *Richard III* on 28 July, Ambrosio in *Don Quixote* and Jasper in *Miss in her Teens* on 30 July, Clerimont in *The Tender Husband* on 18 August,

Dugard in *The Inconstant* on 27 August, Horatio in *Hamlet* on 5 September, and Bedamar in *Venice Preserv'd* on 12 September. At Twickenham he acted Pharamond in *Philaster* on 3 July and Tressel in *Richard III* on 11 September.

Perhaps he was the Mr Falkner who had acted at Norwich in 1745. No doubt he was the Falkner who was at Smock Alley, Dublin, in 1750–51 and 1751–52, where among other roles he performed Freeman in *A Bold Stroke for a Wife*, Mellefont in *The Double Dealer*, Blunt in *1 Henry IV*, Horatio in *A Man of Taste*, Lord Rake in *The Provok'd Wife*, Sir Charles in *The Stratagem*, and Bedamar in *Venice Preserv'd*. Falkner was at the Bath theatre between 1750 and 1755; he is known to have played Beverly in *The Gamester* there on 27 February 1753 and at the Jacob's Wells Theatre, Bristol, on 29 March 1755.

Falkner, Anna Maria, later Mrs William Donaldson, then Mrs Charles Lumm [fl. 1745?–1784], singer, dancer.

Anna Maria Falkner was the niece and adopted daughter of George Faulkner (1699?–1775), whom Swift called "the prince of Dublin printers." Anna Maria preferred spelling her name Falkner. That is how it was rendered in the bills most of the time and how she signed herself. She was probably the "Young Gentlewoman" who was announced as making her first appearance on any stage as Eurydice in *Orpheus and Eurydice* at Covent Garden Theatre on 23 November 1745, since her name was later listed in the bills for that role at the next performance of that pantomime afterpiece on 20 March 1746. Curiously, when it was repeated on 5 April 1746, Eurydice was again by "A Young Gentlewoman." On 8 January 1746 Miss Falkner had joined with a number of singers to accompany Beard's rendition of a new English ballad called "The English

ANNA MARIA FALKNER

by A. von der Myn

Hero's Welcome Home," and on 29 April, when she shared tickets with Paddick and Messink, she herself sang Handel's "Come let us Trip."

Although her name did not appear on any bills in 1746–47, possibly she was a chorus singer at Covent Garden. In the summer of 1747 she appeared at Marylebone Gardens, where she continued as a principal singer every subsequent summer through at least 1752. In August 1747 Garrick wrote to the bookseller Andrew Millar of his possible interest in engaging her at Drury Lane: "If Miss Faulconer will keep herself disengag'd till I come back I will go to Marylebone & talk about next Winter: If you will speak to her upon this head." In 1747–48, however, Anna was not at Drury Lane but back at Covent Garden where her name appeared in the bills on 13 February 1748 as singing four songs in Italian and English: "Ah Se amanti fasti mai," "Felice Belve," "O Sleep, Why dost thou leave me?" and "Tis Liberty, dear Liberty alone." On 15 February she sang "Chi nacque alle pene" and "Lusingo piu cara."

Throughout the remainder of the season she rendered similar songs between acts of the main pieces. On 3 March she performed Diana in the revival of *Apollo and Daphne*, "A Dramatic Entertainment of Dancing, not performed these eight years," a piece which was repeated numerous times before the end of the season. For her benefit on 14 April 1748, when tickets could be had of Anna Maria at her house in Leicester Fields, she played Polly in *The Beggar's Opera*, for the first time and "by Particular Desire." The listing of a Miss E. Faulkner as dancing a minuet with Villeneuve on 21 April 1748 must give us pause. That is the only notice we find of a Miss E. Faulkner, so possibly there was a printing error in the bills. If, however, the bills were correct, and a different Miss Faulkner was intended, then all the assignments for dancing given herein to Anna Maria may really have belonged to Miss E. Faulkner.

On 19 May 1748 Anna Maria, listed as of St Ann's parish in Soho, married William Donaldson, the son of a linendraper, at St George's Chapel, Hyde Park Corner. She continued, however, to perform at Covent Garden Theatre under her maiden name through 1751–52. Her roles included Sabrina in *Comus*, Andromeda in *Perseus and Andromeda*, the title role in *Phebe*, Venus in *The Judgment of Paris*, Flora in *A Cure for a Scold*, Margery in *The Dragon of Wantley*, and vocal parts in *Macbeth*, *The Maid of the Mill*, and *Henry VIII*. In the late summer of 1749 she played Polly at Richmond on 13 September and at Twickenham on 26 September.

In the season 1751–52 she performed little: Andromeda on 30 September and Diana in *Apollo and Daphne* on 4 December, playing the latter role in the advanced stage of pregnancy. On 14 January 1752, John Donaldson, son of William and Anna Maria Donaldson, was baptized at St Paul,

Covent Garden. She reappeared on 17 March to sing in *Macbeth*. For her benefit on 3 April she sang in *The Conscious Lovers* and delivered the epilogue, and on 18 April she played the character of Peace in the first London performance of Pasquali's masque *The Triumphs of Hibernia*.

After her regular engagement at Marylebone Gardens in the summer of 1752, Anna Maria did not return to Covent Garden Theatre but engaged with Thomas Sheridan at the Smock Alley Theatre, Dublin. When she made her first appearance on that stage on 16 October 1752 as Polly, she was said to be from the Theatre Royal, Covent Garden. When she repeated the role on 9 November she appeared in the bills as Mrs Donaldson, her married name, under which she appeared throughout the remainder of the season. Although presumably engaged for singing roles, she took on several major straight characters apparently for the first time: Ophelia on 6 November, Jessica ("with the songs") in *The Merchant of Venice* on 13 December, and Ariel ("with the Songs in Character") on 17 January 1753. Her other roles at Dublin included Arabella in *The Honest Yorkshireman* on 22 December 1752, Sabrina in *Comus* on 17 February 1753, Philidel in *King Arthur* on 20 March, Laura in *The Chaplet* on 29 March, and Patience (with a song in character) in *Henry VIII* on 23 April.

Anna Maria made only one more appearance on the stage of a London theatre when on 2 April 1755 at Covent Garden, billed as "Mrs Donaldson (late Miss Falkner)," she sang "Ellen a Roon" after Act II of *The Stratagem*. By then her husband, an extravagant and idle fellow, had consented "to a base arrangement" whereby his wife could live with George Montague Dunk, the second Earl of Halifax (1716–1771). Admired for her voice and beauty, she had numerous suitors, among them Lord Vane and Sir George Saville, and by 1753 she had become the mistress of Lord Halifax (one report claims that first she was the governess of his daughter). Halifax's wife, Anne Richards, who had brought him a fortune of £110,000, died prematurely in 1753, thereby clearing the way for a more open relationship between Halifax and Anna Maria. He provided her with a house at Hampton Court Green where she lived for some years. At a later date, when Halifax was considering marriage to the daughter and heiress of Sir Thomas Drury of Northamptonshire, he was surprised in front of his friends at Vauxhall Gardens one evening by Anna and was persuaded to break off the engagement. She accompanied Halifax to Ireland "and became notorious" there and elsewhere as a "placemonger." Anna Maria had two children by him, one of whom, Anna Maria Montague, when a young child, visited Garrick at Hampton in July 1769 and played and danced in his Shakespeare Grotto.

Lord Halifax died in 1771 and by 1784 William Donaldson had also died. Little is known of Anna Maria after Halifax's death except that on 17 July 1784, identified as Anna Maria Donaldson, widow, she married Colonel Charles Lumm at St Marylebone.

Numerous songs published as sung by her when a principal singer at Marylebone Gardens are listed in the *Catalogue of Printed Music in the British Museum*. A collection of songs and dialogues by Master Arne and Miss Falkner at Marylebone Gardens, as set by Mr Arne, was published in Book III of *Vocal Melody* in August 1751.

Caricature portraits of her and Lord Halifax were printed in the *Town and Country Magazine* in 1769. A portrait of her was published with one of "Le Comte des Lunettes" in the *Town and Country Magazine* in 1777, and an engraving of her by A. vr. Myn, which depicts her seated and holding an open music book, is in the British Museum.

Falkner, Robert [fl. 1760–1780],

musician, instrument maker, author, music seller and publisher.

According to the *Dictionary of Musicians* (1824), Robert Falkner was a German musician, resident in London by about 1760. He authored and published in 1770 a work entitled *Instructions for playing the Harpsichord, Thorough-Bass fully explained, and exact Rules for tuning the Harpsichord*, and issued a second edition in 1774. As early as 1763, according to *Mortimer's London Directory*, Falkner lived at No 45, Salisbury Court, Fleet Street, where he also published until about 1775; then he lived at No 3, Peterborough Court, Fleet Street, until about 1780. About 1775 he also had a shop at No 159, the Strand, near Somerset House, and during that period he purchased the printing plant and type of the music publisher Henry Fougt.

Probably Robert was the father of Henry Falkner who was a partner with Charles Christmas in a music sales and publishing concern at the Opera Music Warehouse, No 9, Pall Mall, from about 1811 to 1814 and then at No 36, Pall Mall, until 1816. In 1816 the partnership was dissolved and Henry Falkner conducted business independently at No 3, Old Bond Street, until 1844.

Fallowfield, William [fl. 1794], singer.

According to Doane's *Musical Directory* of 1794, William Fallowfield of Bagshot, Surrey, was an alto who sang for the Choral Fund, the Handelian Society, and in the Westminster Abbey Handel concerts.

"Falstaff, Sir John." *See* STEELE, RICHARD.

Falwood. *See* FULLWOOD.

"Famous Spaniard, The." [fl. 1789], acrobat.

Hodgkinson and Pogson in *The Early*

Manchester Theatre cite an advertisement for a performance in Manchester on 20 March 1789 that featured "The Famous Spaniard from Sadler's Wells, who will perform feats, throw a somerset backward and discharge two pistols at the same time."

Farci. *See* **FERZI.**

Farebrother. *See* **FAIRBROTHER.**

Farey, John *1766–1826, singer, geologist.*

John Farey was born in Woburn, Bedfordshire, in 1766, went to school in Halifax, Yorkshire, and in 1792 was made the Duke of Bedford's agent for the Duke's estates in Bedfordshire. Doane's *Musical Directory* of 1794 listed Farey as a tenor and his wife Sophia as a soprano; both were members of the Choral Fund. Though he lived in Woburn, John sang in London for the Cecilian Society, the Surrey Chapel Society, and in the oratorios performed at Drury Lane Theatre.

Farey's career, however, was not music but geology. His profession took him to all parts of England, and he amassed a large collection of rocks and minerals and drew up many geological sections and maps. He wrote a large number of scientific papers, contributed to Rees's *Encyclopaedia*, and wrote books on geology. Some of his articles dealt with music. He and his wife had a large family. Their son John (1791–1851) had a distinguished career as a civil engineer. The elder John Farey died in 1826 in London, where he had moved in 1802.

Farey, Mrs John, Sophia ⟨*fl. 1791–1794*⟩, *singer. See* **FAREY, JOHN.**

Farinel, Michel *b. 1649, violinist.*

Michel Farinel, the son of Robert Farinel and reputed uncle of the famed male soprano Farinelli, was baptized in Grenoble on 23 May 1649. His travels took him to Spain and Portugal, and between 1675 and 1679 he was in England, supposedly in the employ of Charles II as a violinist. Roger North reported that one of the musicians with whom the elder Nicola Matteis played in contest was Farinel, "whom he made stand still, and stare at him." As late as 1690 he was described as a "gentleman pensioner" of the King of England. He became intendant of music to the Queen of Spain and, after his retirement, singing master to the nuns of Montfleury near Grenoble. There he published a volume of sacred music in 1696. Today his fame rests on his "Les Folies d'Espagne," known in England as "Farinel's Ground."

Farinella, Signora ⟨*fl. 1772?–1775*⟩, *singer.*

Signora Farinella sang principal roles at the King's Theatre in the Haymarket during the 1774–75 season, but only one of her parts is known: Lisinga in *Montezuma* on 7 February 1775. The other operas in which she participated from November 1774 to May 1775 were *Armida, Alessandro nell'Indie*, probably *La buona figliuola, La finta giardiniera, I viaggiatori ridicoli, La difesa d'amore*, and *La donna di spirito*.

It is probable that Signora Farinella was one of two singers named "Farinelli" from Bath who sang at Bristol in 1772 and 1773. The two ladies took principal vocal parts in a "Concerto Spirituale" at the Assembly Room in Prince's Street on 11 June 1772 and were praised by a local critic: "both sung with elegant Judgement and perfectly in tune, adding to this the most refin'd Voices and each a most delicate Shake." During Passion Week in 1773 in Bristol the Signoras Farinella participated in a performance of the *Messiah*.

"Farinelli," stage name of Carlo Broschi *1705–1782, singer, instrumentalist, manager.*

Carlo Broschi was born on 24 January 1705 at Andria in Apulia, one of the two sons of the musician Salvatore Broschi (d. 1717). In a letter to John Alcock (in the Osborn Collection at Yale) Dr Burney said that Carlo was born in Naples, the son of a musical baker, and that the nickname "Farinelli" derived from the Italian word *farina*, or wheat flour. Both Carlo and his brother Riccardo came to be called Farinelli, so the nickname was for the family rather than for Carlo alone. Salvatore Broschi, in addition to his activities as a composer and music teacher, served as governor of the towns of Maratea and Cisternino from 1706 to 1709. Young Carlo's early musical training was with his father, after which he was sent to Naples to study under Porpora.

Carlo may have left his native Andria for Naples when very young, for he always thought of Naples as his birthplace (hence Dr Burney was not really mistaken). There he went through a rigorous musical training under Porpora for many years. A possibly apocryphal anecdote was published in the nineteenth century in a newspaper article (now at the Huntington Library) called "Good Words" describing Farinelli's early training:

The drudgery of singing two notes and no more for the space of three years was imposed upon him; the story seems incredible, but there is no doubt of its truth. The two notes were F and B, the interval between which constitutes the most perilous passage for a singer, and nearly always suffers from inaccuracy of intonation. After declaiming this interval for three years Farinelli asked his master what was the next interval he should learn. 'You know all intervals,' replied Porpora. 'You need practice no other.' His fourth year of study was devoted to learning the trill. . . .

After a year perfecting his trill the boy studied poetry, composition, and harpsichord, and he was also made to practice before a mirror to overcome "a natural inelegance of bearing and sternness of feature." By the time he was 15 Carlo was

dubbed *il ragazzo* (the boy) and was famed in southern Italy for his singing. He studied under Porpora, according to "Good Words," for seven years in all, and by the age of 17 his

voice was a soprano of the most extraordinary compass. He could ascend to the E on the ledger line above the staff, and could sink to the E in the middle of the bass clef. He was quite unconscious of his powers, and was still in the midst of exercises and studies, blindly pursuing and achieving day by day the task that was set him with methodical accuracy, till at last the day arrived when, according to the legend, he came to Porpora and said: 'Master, what more shall I do to attain perfection?' Porpora replied: 'Go, my son; you have no further need of me. You are the greatest singer in the world.'

Farinelli's debut was at Naples in 1720 in *Angelica e Medoro*, a *serenata* by Porpora with words by Metastasio. The event led to a lifelong friendship and extensive correspondence between the librettist and the singer. In 1722 Porpora took Farinelli to Rome where he sang in his master's *Flavio Anicio Olibrio*. Burney left a description of the singer's dazzling contest with a German trumpeter in Rome:

He was seventeen when he left [Naples] to go to Rome, where during the run of an opera, there was a struggle every night between him and a famous player on the trumpet, in a song accompanied by that instrument; this, at first, seemed amicable and merely sportive, till the audience began to interest themselves in the contest, and to take different sides: after severally swelling a note, in which each manifested the power of his lungs, and tried to rival the other in brilliancy and force, they had both a swell and shake together, by thirds, which was continued so long, while the audience eagerly waited the event, that both seemed to be exhausted; and, in fact, the trumpeter, wholly spent gave it up, thinking, however, his antagonist as much tired as himself, and that it would be a drawn battle; when Farinelli, with

Courtesy of the Royal College of Music

CARLO BROSCHI FARINELLI

by Bartolommeo Nazari

a smile on his countenance, shewing he had only been sporting with him all that time, broke out all at once in the same breath, with fresh vigour, and not only swelled and shook the note, but ran the most rapid and difficult divisions, and was at last silenced only by the acclamations of the audience. From this period may be dated that superiority which he ever maintained over all his contemporaries.

Farinelli left the tutelage of Porpora in 1724 and journeyed to Vienna. In 1725 he

Harvard Theatre Collection

"The Opera House, or the Italian Eunuch's Glory"

artist unknown

was in Venice to appear in *Didone abbandonata,* after which he returned to Naples to sing with Vittoria Tesi. He appeared in *Ciro* in 1726 in Milan and then made a second visit to Rome. In 1727 he was in Bologna singing in *La fedelta coronata* with Bernacchi, a singer with an especially florid style who seems to have influenced Farinelli in that direction and is known to have passed on to the younger singer some of his technical secrets. The following year found Farinelli in Vienna again, after which he toured to Venice, Rome, Naples, Piacenza, and Parma. He sang with the best singers of the day—Nicolini, Faustina Bordoni, Francesca Cuzzoni—and everywhere he was showered with praise and gifts.

In 1731 he was again in Vienna and came under the influence of the Emperor Charles VI, who urged him to forsake mere brilliance and work for more pathos in his singing. In the years immediately following he visited Venice and Rome again and

made appearances in Ferrara, Lucca, and Turin. In September 1734 he came to London to sing for the Opera of the Nobility.

Farinelli's old master Porpora was the impresario and composer for the company at the King's Theatre which the singer joined; Handel's rival troupe performed at Covent Garden. Though Farinelli was astonishingly successful during his stay in London, he arrived at a time when the rivalry between the two opera troupes was playing havoc with finances. Porpora's venture ultimately lost £19,000 and had to be abandoned. Part of the reason for the failure was certainly the outrageously high salaries paid the singers. Farinelli, for example, was given 2,000 guineas per season. But for a moment in history London heard the most stunning quartet of singers of the eighteenth century: Farinelli, Senesino, Faustina, and Cuzzoni.

The first London appearance of Farinelli was as Arbace in *Artaserse* on 29 October 1734 at the King's. The *Daily Advertiser* the following day reported that "All the Royal Family were at the Opera, when Signior Farinelli perform'd . . . with prodigious Applause. The Theatre was exceedingly crowded." Burney described the performance: "Senesino had the part of a furious tyrant, and Farinelli that of an unfortunate hero in chains; but in the course of the first air, the captive so softened the heart of the tyrant, that Senesino, forgetting his stage-character, ran to Farinelli and embraced him in his own." When *Artaserse* was repeated on 2 November Lord Hervey wrote to Henry Fox, "No place is full but the Opera; and Farinelli is so universally liked, that the crowds there are immense."

Farinelli joined other musicians to perform at the Crown and Anchor on 27 November 1734. His next opera role was Aci in *Polifemo* on 1 February 1735, and on 15 March he advertised that he would sing in *Artaserse* for his benefit. For that occasion, reported the *Daily Advertiser* two days earlier,

'Tis expected that Signor Farinelli will have the greatest Appearance . . . that has been known. We hear that a Contrivance will be made to accomodate 2000 People. His Royal Highness the Prince of Wales has been pleas'd to give him 200 Guineas, the Spanish Ambassador 100, the Emperor's Ambassador 50, his Grace the Duke of Leeds 50, the Countess of Portmore 50, Lord Burlington 50, his Grace the Duke of Richmond 50, the Hon. Col. Paget 30, Lady Rich 20, and most of the other Nobility 50, 30 or 20 Guineas each; so 'tis believ'd his Benefit will be worth to him upwards of 2000 *l*.

For the benefit the pit was full by four in the afternoon. The stage, according to one newspaper report,

was crowded with beauty and fashion, [and] no scenes were used during the performance: gilt leather hangings were substituted, which usually adorned that part of the Theatre at Ridottos. Many of the songs in the Opera were new; that which preceded the chorus was composed by Farinelli [his brother Riccardo], and so vehemently applauded, that he sung it a second time at the request of the audience, though the chorus was over, and the musicians had retired from the orchestra. The Prince of Wales soon after presented this favourite singer with a richly wrought gold snuff-box set with rubies and diamonds, containing a pair of diamond knee-buckles, and a purse of 100 guineas.

Farinelli concluded his first London season singing at the Crown Tavern on 24 March 1735, performing Giasone in *Issipile* on 8 April at the King's Theatre and singing Achille in *Ifigenia in Aulida* there on 3 May. His income for the season was probably close to £5000. Farinelli so overwhelmed a lady in the audience at one performance that she cried out, "One God, one Farinelli!" Hogarth incorporated the phrase in plate two of "The Rake's Progress" and depicted a small Farinelli on a pedestal with two hearts burning at his feet.

Dazzling though his voice was, Farinelli's acting seems to have left everything to be desired, despite those years of practice before a mirror. Pickering's *Reflections upon Theatrical Expression in Tragedy* (1755) described the singer's awkwardness on stage:

I shall therefore, in my farther remarks . . . go back to the Old Italian Theatre, when Farinelli drew every body to the Haymarket. What a Pipe! what Modulation! what Extasy to the Ear! But, Heavens! What Clumsiness! What Stupidity! What Offence to the Eye! Reader, if of the City, thou mayest probably have seen in the fields of Islington or Mileend—or if thou art in the environs of St. James's, thou must have observed in the Park —with what ease and agility a Cow, heavy with Calf, has rose up at the command of the Milk-woman's foot. Thus from the mossy bank sprung up the Divine Farinelli. Then with long strides advancing a few paces, his left hand settled upon his hip, in a beautiful

Harvard Theatre Collection

CARLO BROSCHI FARINELLI

engraving by Wagner, after Amiconi

Bend like that of the Handle of an *old fashion'd Caudle Cup*, his right remained immoveable across his manly breast, till numbness called its partner to supply its place; when it relieved itself in position of the other handle to the *Caudle-Cup*.

But his clumsiness did not bother the lovers of opera. Prévost wrote in 1735:

Signor Farinelli, who came to England with the highest expectations, has the satisfaction of seeing them fulfilled by generosity and favour as extraordinary as his own talents. The others were loved: this man is idolized, adored; it is a consuming passion. Indeed, it is impossible to sing better [than he does]. . . . [A] spell draws the crowd to [Farinelli]. Imagine all Senesino's and Carastino's art combined, with a voice more beautiful than those two taken together.

The English were torn between their admiration for Farinelli and their concern over what he cost them. *Fog's Journal* on 24 January 1736 contained a jocular article on "Tickling":

I must not here omit one Publick Tickler of great Eminency, and whose Titillative Faculty must be allowed to be singly confined to the Ear, I mean the great *Signor Farinelli*, to whom such Crowds resort, for the Extasy he administers to them through that Organ, and who so liberally requite his Labours, that if he will but do them the Favour to stay two or three Years longer, and have two or three Benefits more, they will have nothing left, but their Ears to give him.

Farinelli's 1735–36 season at the King's Theatre consisted of Farnaspe in *L'Adriano in Siria* on 25 November 1735 followed by Sifare in *Mitridate* and Eucherio in *Onorio*. His final season brought him out in the title role in *Siroe,* Epitide in *Merope,* Alceste in *Demetrio,* Sextus in *Tito,* Gomaspe in *Sabrina,* and Timantes in *Demofoonte.* The rivalry between the Handel and Porpora companies ended, and Farinelli left England. Grove reports that the singer departed on 11 June 1737, though *The London Stage* shows a performance of *Sabrina* scheduled for that date, and another performance of it on 14 June was apparently cancelled due to Farinelli's ill health. In any case, the singer went to France for a brief stay, during which Louis XV favored him with a gift of his portrait set in diamonds and another present of 600 louis d'or. From France Farinelli traveled to the court of Philip V of Spain, and there he remained for almost 25 years.

The singer intended returning to England, but he won so important a position in the Spanish court that he stayed on. He charmed Philip out of a fit of melancholia by singing for him and was rewarded with a yearly salary of about £3000, for which, according to the legend, he sang the same four songs nightly before the king. Farinelli became a court favorite, not unlike Rasputin in Russia in the nineteenth century. He was involved with civic and court projects far afield from music, and in 1750 the new monarch, Ferdinand VI, made him Commander of the Order of Calatrava.

Farinelli found the new Queen, Barbara of Portugal, much enamoured of opera, so he set up an Italian opera at Buen Retiro and ruled it with a firm but just hand. According to his biographer Sacchi, Farinelli allowed "no one, even of the highest rank" to visit the dressing rooms, insisted on decorous costumes for the women, permitted no ballets, and refused to allow his singers to take outside engagements that might tire their voices. As a manager he showed a great interest in scenes, machines, and special effects, especially a rain machine.

When Ferdinand was succeeded by his half-brother Charles III in 1759, Farinelli's situation in Spain deteriorated, and he moved in July 1760 to Bologna to retire to a villa he had built on land he had acquired some years before. Burney visited the singer there in 1771 and reported:

This day I had the pleasure to spend with Signor Farinelli, at his house in the country, about a mile from Bologna, which is not yet quite finished, though he has been building it ever since he retired from Spain. . . . Signor Farinelli has long left off singing, but he amuses himself still on the harpsichord and viol d'amour: he has a number of harpsichords made in different countries. . . . His favourite is a piano forte, made at Florence in the year 1730, on which is written Rafael d'Urbino. . . . He played a considerable time upon his Raphael with great judgment and delicacy, and has composed several elegant pieces for that instrument. The next favour is a harpsichord given him by the late Queen of Spain, who was Scarlatti's scholar, both in Portugal and Spain. . . .

Burney found the aging Farinelli "very conversable and communicative" about old

times in England. The singer died on 16 September 1782.

Farinelli had made his will on 20 February 1782, leaving his fortune, which must have been considerable, to Maria Carlotta Pisani, the daughter of his nephew Don Matteo Pisani and his wife Anna, née Gatteschi. Farinelli had apparently not been entirely pleased with his nephew's choice of wife, though he appears to have been generous to her while he lived, and he provided a pension for her after his death if she should be widowed.

An opera, *The Queen of Spain; or, Farinelli in Madrid* (1740), was inspired by the singer's Spanish years. Sacchi's biography of Farinelli appeared in 1784, and René Bouvier published a modern biography in 1943.

Portraits of Farinelli include:

1. By Amiconi, showing Farinelli, Metastasio, Teresa Castellini, and Amiconi. At the National Gallery of Victoria, Melbourne. Reproduced with Amiconi's entry in the first volume of this dictionary. Engraving by I. Wagner; Wagner then took the head of Farinelli from it to create an oval portrait, but reversed, which was used by Hawkins in his *General History*.

2. By Amiconi. "The Triumph of Farinelli," an allegorical tableau showing Farinelli, Cuzzoni, and Faustina. At the Museo Musicale de Bologna. Engraving by C. Grignion.

3. By Hogarth, showing Farinelli with Handel and Mrs Fox. In the collection of Mrs Gough Nichols in 1889.

4. By Bartolommeo Nazari, 1734. At the Royal College of Music. Previously attributed to Amiconi.

5. Bust, sculptured by Louis François Roubiliac. Seen by Vertue in 1738.

6. Anonymous engraving, showing Farinelli and Senesino in oval frames on pedestals.

7. Anonymous satirical print, showing Farinelli reclining on a cushion and wallowing in gifts.

8. Engraving by H. Adlard.

9. Engraving after a painting by Fedi, between 1801 and 1807, showing Farinelli with numerous other singers. At the Civica Raccolta delle Stampe Achille Bertarelli, Milan.

10. Engraving by V. Francheschini. Published in Florence in 1734.

11. Satirical print by Goupy, after Marco Ricci, 1729–30, showing a very tall and slim Farinelli, with Cuzzoni and the impresario Heidegger. Those three were not together in England in 1729, thus the artist created an amusing but fictional gathering. The Countess of Burlington's name was attached to the Goupy work as though she were the designer; she was the patron of Faustina and may have written the verses that were attached to the print, or she may have added the figure of Heidegger.

12. Engraving by G. Guzzi. In the Civica Raccolta delle Stampe Achille Bertarelli, Milan.

13. Engraving in mezzotint by A. van Haecken, after C. Lucy, 1735.

14. Engraving by Hogarth (Plate 2 from "The Rake's Progress"), showing Farinelli on a pedestal.

15. Engraving by Wagner, after Amiconi, 1735, showing Farinelli being crowned by the Muse of Music.

In an extra-illustrated set of Brayley's *History of London Theatres* at Harvard is a pen and ink sketch, printed sheet, showing a group of singers on a stage; they have animal heads, and one presumably caricatures Farinelli. The drawing is titled "The Opera House, or the Italian Eunuch's Glory," and along the left side is a statement: "A list of the rich presents Segnor Farinello ye Italian Singer Condisended to accept off ye English nobility & Gentry for one Nights Performance in ye Opera Artaxerses." Down the right side is the list of gifts.

A 1723 engraving attributed to Hogarth shows opera singers on a stage; one of them, grotesquely pictured, has sometimes been identified as Farinelli but is probably Berenstadt. Hogarth introduced into his "Masquerades and Operas" in 1724 the same scene, with variations, on a banner. Farinelli had not yet come to England when those drawings were made.

Farley, Charles *1771–1859, actor, singer, dancer, choreographer, playwright.*

Charles Farley was born in London in 1771. An anonymous manuscript in the British Museum and a notation by James Winston in the Folger Library agree that he was a callboy at Covent Garden Theatre, but there is no account-book warranty for the assertion. Certainly he appeared on stage at Covent Garden at age 13, on 11 October 1784, as Prince Edward in *Richard III*. His only other parts that season were the Page in *The Orphan* on 4 February 1785 and Abdiel, the Genius, in the musical afterpiece *The Land of Enchantment*, on 18 April 1785.

He returned to Covent Garden the following season. In his second season he earned 1s. per six-day week, in his fifth (1788–89) £1. In 1789–90 his salary was £1 10s., and in 1791–92 it had risen to £2. By the end of the 1793–94 season it was £2 10s. There it remained until the 1799–1800 season, when it advanced 5s. In 1800–1801, however, Farley was suddenly making £6 and in 1801–2 £6 10s. By that time his utility at devising ballets and pantomimes of his own or suggesting "business" for the works of others was beginning to be obvious to the management. He reached £10 weekly by 1804–5, and there he remained through at least 1821–22.

The first production identifiable as wholly Farley's in choreography and dialogue was *Raymond and Agnes; or, the Castle of Lindenbergh*, an elaborately staged ballet-pantomime at Covent Garden with music by William Reeve, its gothic-melodramatic fable taken from an episode

CHARLES FARLEY

engraving by Ridley and Holl, after Emma
Smith

But while Farley was inventing these delights he was not neglecting his own acting-
singing-dancing. In fact, by the end of his
long career he may have amassed more
roles than anyone in the theatre of his
time, if not in the history of the theatre.
Many were short roles, depending largely
on his energetic legs and voice; but many
others were substantial. In addition to his
chorus dancing and his dozens of early
anonymous footmen and shepherds, sailors
and Frenchmen, already by 1805 or 1806
—when the pace of his performances slack-
ened a little in favor of other duties—he
had played a tremendous variety of roles, as
the following selection shows:

The Welsh Collier in *The Recruiting*

in Matthew Gregory Lewis's *The Monk*.
Its 15 episodes were synopsized on the
playbill. Farley assumed the leading role,
Raymond. The work was performed 15
times in the month following its introduction on 16 March 1797, and it was frequently revived in following seasons.

Farley's second considerable success was
*The Magic Oak; or, Harlequin Woodcut-
ter*, in collaboration with Thomas John
Dibdin on 19 January 1799 and for many
nights following. It was a two-act pantomime, of the sort that Farley and all the
Dibdins were becoming identified with, to
the delight of the public and horror of dramatic purists. All the resources of a whole
corps of customers, scene painters, machin-
ists, and devisers of "tricks" were employed
for the visual backgrounds for 50 dancers
and actors. A large orchestra (plus Murphy
on the union pipes and Weippert on the
pedal harp) accompanied the 16 singers.
Farley played a character named Brisk.

CHARLES FARLEY, as Jessamy

engraving by Cooke, after De Wilde

Officer, Lopez in *The Duenna*, Oxford in *Richard III*, Balthazar in *Romeo and Juliet*, Sam in *The Man of the World*, Pedro in *The Female Pursuit*, Scarlet in *Robin Hood*, Whisper in *The Busy Body*, Dick in *Hob in the Well*, Lovelace in *Three Weeks after Marriage*, both Biondello and Pedro in *Catherine and Petruchio*, the Lieutenant in *Tippoo Saib*, Frank in *Half an Hour After Supper*, Charles in *The Village Lawyer*, Heeltap and Roger in *The Mayor of Garratt*, Morven in *Oscar and Malvina*, Ismael in *A Day in Turkey*, James in *Notoriety*, a Clerk, a Tennis Marker, a Servant, a Tradesman and a Postillion in the same performances of *A Road to Ruin*, the Prompter in *A Peep Behind the Curtain*, Quildrive in *The Citizen*, Twig in *The Young Quaker*, Crop in *All in Good Humour*, Peto, Sir Walter Blunt, and Douglas in *1 Henry IV*, a King of Brentford in *The Rehearsal*, Charles in *The Village Lawyer*, Putty in *The Flitch of Bacon*, Pompey in *Cross Partners*, William in *As You Like It*, Frill in *The Prisoner at Large*, Le Frizz in *Just in Time*, the Captain in *Columbus*, Squire Foxchase in *Harlequin's Museum*, Lopez in *The Duenna*, Lamp in *Wild Oats*, James in *The Deaf Lover*, Idle in *The Son-in-Law*, the Boatswain in *The Shipwreck*, Buckle in *The Suspicious Husband*, Bagatelle in *The Poor Soldier*, Vasquez in *The Castle of Andalusia*, Dago in *Mago and Dago*, Col Epaulette in *Fontainebleau*, Peleno in *Windsor Castle*, Harry in *The Irish Mimick*, Drummer in *The Tithe Pig*, Nab in *How to Grow Rich*, Ennui in *The Dramatist*, Peter in *Romeo and Juliet*, Signor Cygnet in *The Rage*, Bumbo in *The Poor Sailor*, Vickery in *Speculation*, Filch in *The Beggar's Opera*, Robin in *Cross Purposes*, a Persian Merchant in *Harlequin's Treasure*, La [*sic*] Jeunesse in *Bantry Bay*, Spruce in *The School for Wives*, Pacha in *The Mountaineers*, Cartridge in *Hartford Bridge*, Bronze in *A Cure for the Heart Ache*, Jeffrey in *Netley Abbey*, Oscar in *Oscar and Malvina*, Placid in *Everyone Has His Fault*,

Jeremy in *Love for Love*, Floriville in *The Dramatist*, Borachio in *Much Ado About Nothing*, Ramille in *The Miser*, Paris in *The Jealous Wife*, Sideboard in *The Way to Keep Him*, the Valet in *Secrets Worth Knowing*, Finder in *The Double Gallant*, the Herald in *England Preserved*, Captain Vain in *Lock and Key*, Clinch in *The Ghost*, Figaro in *The Follies of a Day*, Cash in *Every Man in His Humour*, John Dory in *Wild Oats*, Puff in *Reformed in Time*, both Changeable and William in *The Jew and the Doctor*, Paragraph in *Five Thousand a Year*, Glib in *What Is She?*, Leillet in *Life's Vagaries*, a Brother in *Comus*, Picard in *The School for Arrogance*, Maon in *The Round Tower*, Cymon in *The Irishman in London*, Alltrade in *Management*, Smart in *The Turnpike Gate*, Clinch in *The Ghost*, Dick in *The Belle's Stratagem*, Bluard in *The Camp*, Dangle in *The Critic*, Squire Chace in *Liberal Opinions*, Vane in *The Chapter of Accidents*, Col Belgardo in *'Tis All a Farce*, Vapour in *My Grandmother*, Captain Orford in *Obi*, Lopez in *What a Blunder*, and Valentine in *Valentine and Orson*.

Farley retired from the stage in 1834. He died at his house, No 42, Ampthill Square, Hampstead Road, London, on 28 January 1859. The address was apparently a relatively new one, for he had lived much of his life at No 3, Hart Street, Bloomsbury, and that fact was registered in his will. His effects were worth less than £4000.

A few of Farley's Shakespearean characters were unsurpassable—Cloten, Osric, Barnardine, Roderigo—but he was principally a performer of melodrama, knew it, and was content. He had an ugly face, his stage manners were emphatic, and his voice was loud. He was, in fact, sometimes called "Stentor." His appearances were frequent, his salary sufficient (in 1821–22 he was at Drury Lane making £10 per week from acting alone; his pantomime work for Covent Garden was extra), and his benefits were well attended. He was an important influence on other performers and was the instructor of the great clown Joseph Grimaldi.

John Doran wrote for *Notes and Queries* in 1859 a sentimental memoir of the Farley he had known in his youth, some parts of which bear quoting:

when he assumed men's characters he displaced old actors from favourite parts, and made [them] permanently his own. After he came, Bernard no longer played Cloten, nor the Gentleman Usher in *King Lear*, nor Sparkish in *The Country Girl*. Before him, [the elder Charles] Macready . . . possessed (so to speak) the parts of Fog, Poins, Roderigo, Osrick, and Count Basset. Farley took them, and kept them to the last. His Poins was a speaking picture; his Osrick, Cloten, and Roderigo, all fools in different ways, were charmingly discriminated by him. There are few such true bits of Shakesperian acting now to be seen,—acting in which the person represented, and not the player, stands before you. . . .

[Canton in *The Clandestine Marriage*] was one of his best French parts, of which no two were alike; and yet he was in some degree a mannerist . . . [in these] he was admirable for variety and minuteness. The same may be said for all his fops. In the representation of these his voice assisted him, for he had a curious bubbling sound, which he could less control as his very remarkable nose grew larger and larger. But he did not depend on a *defect* for an *effect*. He was great without speaking, and his . . . dumb Francisco, in *The Tale of Mystery*, was as eloquent and touching as though he had had a hundred tongues all tuned to tell with irresistible force a tale of suffering.

Doran, like many others, believed that his best characters were Grindoff in *The Miller and His Men* and the title character of *Timour the Tartar*. "As the bandit-miller [Grindoff] he was, night after night, hard at work—loving, jilting, grinding corn, singing glees, and getting blown up by a final explosion, which, with rare discrimination, injured only the wicked. . . ." Of Farley's Timour Doran testified:

People went to the doors at midday to be first in the rush towards the enjoyment that name held out to them. And surely the Timour they beheld was a much more enjoyable chief than the original Tartar! How grand, dignified, condescending, brave, yet gentle-hearted! Who could believe that Barnardine, that arch-brute in *Measure for Measure*, was identical with [the] very superb Khan? . . . [F]or many a year the afterpiece at Mr. Farley's benefit was "Timour the Tartar, with all the horses."

Doran concluded:

Jolliest of millers, most imposing of Tartars, most wicked of sorcerers, most abominable of ruffians, gayest of Frenchmen, most laughable of fops,—a score of years ago, he

Harvard Theatre Collection

CHARLES FARLEY, as Grindoff

artist unknown

laid down all, and, curiously enough, got rid, with medical assistance, of a great portion of that huge nose that used so well to serve him on the stage. He lived surrounded by troops of friends, and died regretted by them, – not altogether, we believe, unindebted to the [performers' retirement] Fund, of which he was a great promoter, a staunch supporter, and to which he was a steady contributor. . . .

Farley acted frequently at the Haymarket in the summers of his younger days and was on the Drury Lane lists in 1807–8, 1808–9, 1809–10, 1810–11, 1811–12, 1812–13, 1813–14, and 1821–22. He was in the bills of the Liverpool Theatre in 1794 and was at Birmingham sometime in 1799. He may have been the Farley who, with Abbot, succeeded John Boles Watson as a manager of Gloucester's New Theatre.

Much of Farley's creative work was selflessly submerged in enterprises to which other people's names were attached. In a note to Farley's canon in his "Hand-List," Allardyce Nicoll states: "Farley seems to have been responsible for many of the C. G. annual pantomimes. I have included . . . only those distinctly attributed to his pen. In the others probably only the effects were arranged by him." Besides *The Magic Oak*, mentioned above, Nicoll lists *The Corsair; or, The Italian Nuptials*, music by Samuel Arnold, 1801; *Harlequin and Asmodeus; or, Cupid on Crutches*, 1810; *Aladdin*, 1813; *Harlequin Munchausen; or, The Fountain of Love*, 1818; *The Battle of Bothwell Brigg* (derived from Scott's *Old Mortality*), music by Bishop, 1820; *Harlequin and Friar Bacon; or, The Brazen Head*, 1820; *The Spirit of the Moon*, 1824; *Harlequin and Mother Shipton; or, Riquet with the Tuft*, 1826; *and Harlequin Pat and Harlequin Bat*, 1830.

Portraits of Charles Farley include:

1. Portrait engraving, by Ridley and Holl, after Emma Smith. Published as a plate to the *Monthly Mirror*, 1806.

2. As Amurath in *Sadak and Kalasrade*. By anonymous engraver. Published as "Penny Plain" by W. West, 1824.

3. As Anthropophagus the Ogre, with Joseph Grimaldi as Scamperini, in *The Ogre and Little Thumb*. By anonymous engraver. Published as plate with the play by T.& R. Hughes, 1807.

4. As Canton, with William Farren (the younger) as Lord Ogleby and Richard Jones as Brush, in *The Clandestine Marriage*. Painting by George Clint. In the Garrick Club. Exhibited at the Royal Academy in 1819; represents a scene from the production at Covent Garden on 18 September 1818. An engraving was done by Henry Meyer, 1821.

5. As Cloten in *Cymbeline*. Engraving by Woolnoth after T. Wageman. Published as a plate to Oxberry's *New English Drama*, 1821.

6. As Francisco in *The Tale of Mystery*. Painting by De Wilde. Formerly in the Somerset Maugham Collection, now in the possession of the National Theatre. Exhibited at the Royal Academy in 1803.

7. As Francisco. Painting by De Wilde. In the Garrick Club. Formerly believed to be of William Farren (the elder).

8. As Grindoff in *The Miller and his Men*. Drawn and engraved by G. Cruikshank. Published as a plate to *The British Stage*, 1818.

9. As Grindoff. Anonymous engraving published by J. Fairburn.

10. As Grindoff. Anonymous engraving published by Pitts.

11. As Grindoff. Anonymous engraving published by Bailey.

12. As Grindoff. Drawn and engraved by Marks. Published by the engraver.

13. As Grindoff. Anonymous engraving, after W. West. Published by West, 1824.

14. As Jessamy in *Bon Ton*. Painting by De Wilde. In the Garrick Club. Engraving by Cooke published as plate to Cawthorn's *Minor Theatre*, 1806.

15. As John Balfour of Burley. Engraving by B. Reading, after T. Wageman. Published by John Lowndes, 1820.

16. As Kalig in *The Blind Boy*. Water color drawing by De Wilde. In the Garrick

Club. Engraving by W. Bond. Published by Bell & De Camp, 1809.

17. As Robinson Crusoe. Anonymous engraving.

18. As Timour the Tartar. Anonymous engraving. Published by W. West, 1818.

19. As the Water King in *Undine*. Anonymous engraving. Published in *Hodgson's Theatrical Portraits*.

20. As Zembuca. Anonymous engraving. Published by W. West.

Farley, Farlo, Farlow, Elizabeth. *See* **WEAVER, MRS JAMES.**

Farlow, Mr [*fl.* 1784], *violinist.*

Mr Farlow played second violin in the Handel Memorial Concerts at Westminster Abbey and the Pantheon in May and June 1784.

Farmer, Master [*fl.* 1784], *singer.*

A Master Farmer sang a principal part in a revival of Dr Arne's *Eliza* at the Haymarket Theatre on 24 March and 2 and 27 April 1784.

Farmer, Jane. *See* **POWELL, MRS WILLIAM, JANE** *d. 1831.*

Farmer, John [*fl.* 1669–1677], *violinist.*

By 8 January 1669 John Farmer was a page in the Chapel Royal, having previously been one of the Children of the Chapel under Henry Cooke. Farmer played violin in the court masque *Calisto* on 15 February 1675, but no other performing activity of his has come to light. As late as 13 November 1677 the Lord Chamberlain's accounts cited Farmer in connection with unpaid maintenance to the amount of £90 which was due him as a former Chapel boy.

Farmer, M. [*fl.* 1689], *musician.*

On 25 March 1689 a list of the musicians in the King's Musick under William III included "M. Farmer" at an annual salary of £30. This citation may refer to the violinist

Thomas Farmer if the initial was simply an abbreviation for "Mr." But there is some evidence that Thomas Farmer may have died before that date, and M. Farmer may have been another person.

Farmer, Thomas *d. 1688, violinist, singer?*

Thomas Farmer was first mentioned in the Lord Chamberlain's accounts on 4 November 1671 when he was cited as one of four court violinists who attended Charles II at Windsor for six days the previous summer. He was paid 8*s.* daily for his services. The accounts contain many similar citations over the years: attendance at Newmarket in the fall of 1674 and spring of 1675, at Windsor in the summer of 1675, at Newmarket in the spring and fall of 1677, at Windsor in the late summer of 1678 and the summer of 1679, at Windsor and Hampton Court in the fall of 1685, at Windsor in the summer of 1686, at Windsor and Hampton Court in the summer and fall of 1687, and at Windsor in the summer of 1688.

In addition to his many trips out of London in the King's service, Farmer also served as a member of the band of 24 violins at court, played in the court masque *Calisto* on 15 February 1675, and participated in play productions at court. On 15 November 1681 he was temporarily suspended for neglecting his duty when *The Rival Queens* was presented by the King's Company at court, but his record otherwise appears to have been a good one and his position in the King's Musick important.

On 4 September 1675 he was named to replace both John Strong among the violins (a permanent position; before that he may have served without fee) and Jeoffrey Aleworth among the wind instruments. The latter appointment may have been administrative, for there is no other record of Farmer's being a wind player. On 5 March 1678 Farmer was paid £12 for a treble violin, and on 6 November 1679 he may have been appointed successor, at least temporarily, to John Banister in the King's private music at a fee of £110 yearly. His normal salary as of December 1679 was £46 12s. 3d. annually plus livery. On 31 August 1685 Farmer was listed among the counter-tenors in the private music of James II (another administrative rather than actual appointment?), but on 5 July 1687 he was noted as one of the instrumentalists in the Chapel Royal at a yearly salary of £50.

Thomas Farmer was a prolific if not dis-tinguished composer. He wrote music for a number of plays: *The Citizen Turn'd Gen-tleman* in 1672, *The Cheats of Scapin* in 1677, *Brutus of Alba* and *Sir Patient Fancy* in 1678, *Troilus and Cressida*, *The Virtuous Wife*, and *Caesar Borgia* in 1679, *The Soldier's Fortune* in 1680, *Constantine the Great* in 1683, and *The Princess of Cleve* in 1681. It is not unlikely that Farmer played at the public theatres, though there is no record of such activity. His music appeared in a number of publications: Playford's *Choice Ayres* (1675) and *The Theater of Musick* (1685–1687), D'Urfey's *Choice New Songs* (1684) and Farmer's own *A Consort of Musick in four parts* (1686) and *A Second Consort of Musick in four parts* (1690).

Anthony Wood said that Farmer had been one of the Waits of London, which ex-perience would have given him a sound training in music. And it is known that Farmer managed to take a degree at Cam-bridge in 1684 despite his activity in Lon-don. He lived, according to the musician John Singleton's will in 1686, in the Cov-ent Garden area.

Notices of Thomas Farmer in the Lord Chamberlain's accounts seem to stop in 1688. On 20 October of that year an order was issued to pay Farmer and others for attendance at Windsor from 24 July to 20 September. (The "M. Farmer" listed on 25 March 1689 as a musician serving William III was probably another person.) Thomas Farmer was certainly dead by 1690, for Henry Purcell wrote an elegy upon his death about that time. It is likely, then, that the Thomas Farmer who was buried at St Paul, Covent Garden, on 5 December 1688 was the musician. That Thomas Farmer was noted in the parish register as having been from St Martin-in-the-Fields.

The musician's name was a remarkably common one and can be found in many London parish registers. Some of the entries in the registers of St Andrew, Holborn, in the 1660s may well concern our subject or his parents: Francis and Mary, twins of Thomas Farmer "Musitioner" and his wife Elizabeth, of the upper end of Robinhood Court in Shoe Lane, were baptized on 21 March 1660; Alice, wife of Thomas Farmer "Musition" of Robinhood Court in Fetter Lane, was buried on 29 March 1660; John Farmer, son of Thomas and Rease of Robin-hood Court in Gray's Inn Lane, was bap-tized on 30 April 1665; and Rose Farmer, "a Girle aged about 12 yeares of Age daughter in Lawe to Thomas ffarmer Musi-tioner in Robin Hood Court in Shoe Lane," was buried on 2 May 1665.

Farmer, William [fl. 1674], *musi-cian.*

A Lord Chamberlain's warrant dated 9 January 1675 listed William Farmer as one of the court musicians who attended Charles II at Windsor from 18 May to 3 September 1674.

Farnese, Luiggia [fl. 1776–1777], *singer.*

On 2 November 1776 Signora Luiggia Farnese sang Sidonia in *Astarto* at the King's Theatre in the Haymarket. She fol-lowed that with Lisetta in *La Frascatana* on 5 November, a principal role in *Il geloso in cimento* on 4 February 1777, Ismene in *Antigono* on 1 March, Clori in *Le ali d'amore* on 13 March (but she was re-placed by Marianna Farnese—her sister?—on 20 March), and principal roles in *La schiava* on 1 April, *Alcina* on 17 April, and

La buona figliuola on 29 April. Her last part was Argia in *Orione* on 24 May 1777.

Farnese, Marianna *[fl. 1777]*, *singer.*

Signora Marianna Farnese, possibly the sister of Luiggia Farnese, sang at the King's Theatre in the Haymarket from January to June 1777. On 21 January she was Alvida in *Germondo*, after which she sang a principal role in *Telemaco*, replaced Luiggia as Clori in *L'ali d'amore* on 20 March, was Carlina in *I capricci del sesso*, and closed the season with Tirsi in *Orione*, beginning on 24 May.

Farr, James *[fl. c.1660–1681?]*, *violinist, organ-maker.*

James Farr was appointed organ-maker to the Chapel Royal, replacing Thomas Craddock, shortly after the Restoration. On a warrant in the Lord Chamberlain's accounts dated 12 November 1663 Farr was also cited as a member of the band of violins at court. In addition to these duties, he looked after the needs of boys in the Chapel choir whose voices had changed; a warrant on 10 May 1664 granted Farr £30 yearly for keeping young Michael Wise. Farr was still the court organ-maker on 9 January 1669 but died sometime before 30 May 1681 when he was succeeded by Bernard Smith.

Farr, John *[fl. 1685–1688]*, *actor.*

John Farr (or Barr?) played the Chaplain in *The Commonwealth of Women* in mid-August 1685 at Drury Lane as a member of the United Company. Warrants in the Lord Chamberlain's accounts dated 12 January 1688 show that he was still a member of the troupe during the 1687–88 season, but no other roles are known for him.

Farrel, Mr *[fl. 1781]*, *actor.*

A Mr Farrel acted the following roles at the Crown Inn, Islington, in the spring of 1781: Justice Guttle in *The Lying Valet* and Rossano in *The Fair Penitent* on 27

March; Ratcliffe in *Richard III* on 30 March; the King in *The King and the Miller of Mansfield* and Polydore in *The Orphan* on 5 April; and Blunt in *George Barnwell*, Gregory in *The Mock Doctor*, and Linco in *Linco's Travels* on 9 April.

Farrell, Mr *[fl. 1769–1772]*, *actor.*

A Mr Farrell acted in Foote's summer company at the Haymarket Theatre regularly from 1769 through 1772. In 1769 he played Goodwill in *The Virgin Unmask'd*, Jasper in *Miss in her Teens*, a Corporal in *The What D'Ye Call It*, Mob in *The Mayor of Garratt*, Bagshot in *The Beaux' Stratagem*, Ben Bridge in *The Beggar's Opera*, Popilius in *Julius Caesar*, and Catesby in *Richard III*. Some of his other roles in subsequent summers included: the Player King in *Hamlet*, Theodore in *Venice Preserv'd*, Old Hob in *Hob in the Well*, Corydon in *Damon and Phillida*, Vulcan in *Midas*, Gratiano in *Othello* in 1770; Formal in *Every Man in his Humour*, Robin in *The Author*, Tradelove in *A Bold Stroke for a Wife*, Skiff in *The Brothers*, Antheus in *Dido* in 1771; and a Watchman in *The Provok'd Wife* and a role in *The Rehearsal* in 1772.

Although there is no evidence to connect them, Farrell possibly was Thomas Farrell, who acted in Ireland and Scotland between 1759 and 1771. If so he was married to the Irish actress, Mrs Farrell (d. 1773), the daughter of the Orfeurs who acted in London earlier in the century. She was the older sister of Elizabeth Orfeur, who married the actor Lawrence Kennedy (c. 1729–1786) and perished, as Mrs Kennedy, in a fire in King Street, Covent Garden, in 1774.

Farrell, Mr *[fl. 1783–1784]*, *actor.*

At the Haymarket Theatre a Mr Farrell acted Norfolk in *Richard III* and Bates in *The Irish Widow* on 15 December 1783 and Bruin in *The Mayor of Garratt* on 8 March 1784.

Farrell, Mrs _[fl. 1771]_, _actress._

At the Haymarket Theatre in the summer of 1771, a Mrs Farrell acted Cornet in _The Provok'd Wife_ on 5 June and Betty in _The Old Bachelor_ on 2 September. Probably she was the wife of the Mr Farrell who performed at the Haymarket between 1769 and 1772.

It is also possible that she was Mrs Thomas Farrell, née Orfeur, who acted in the Irish and English provinces from 1757 until her death in 1773 and was the elder sister of Mrs Lawrence Kennedy. According to playbills cited by W. J. Lawrence in a manuscript in the National Library of Ireland, however, Mrs Thomas Farrell and her husband were performing in Belfast at the time our subject was at the Haymarket.

Farrell, Margaret. _See_ KENNEDY, MRS MORGAN HUGH.

Farren, Elizabeth, later Countess of Derby _1762–1829, actress, singer._

Elizabeth Farren, who rose from obscurity to the highest stratum of society and wealth, was born on 6 July 1762. The place of her birth is not known. It could have been in Ireland, or in Bath, where her mother was acting in 1761, or perhaps at Southampton, where her father was associated with a theatrical company about 1761.

Elizabeth's father, George Farren (d. c. 1770), originally intended for his father's wine business in Dublin, had become a surgeon and apothecary in Cork. His brother was a Captain Farren of the 64th Foot. His sister Elizabeth lived at Cork all her life. A Thomas Farren, perhaps his uncle, became Lord Mayor of Cork in 1736, and a quay there was named after him. Elizabeth's mother, Margaret (neé Wright, c. 1732–1803), was the daughter of a wealthy brewer (some say publican) of Liverpool who eventually fell on hard times. Early in their marriage, which occurred about 1758, George and Margaret

Harvard Theatre Collection

ELIZABETH FARREN

engraving by Knight, after Lawrence

Farren lived at Cork, and soon his fondness for the bottle and bad friends brought him to financial distress. Just when or why they turned to the stage is not known. According to the _Memoirs of the Present Countess of Derby late Miss Farren, by Petronius Arbiter_ [1797], George Farren was already an actor when he met his future wife in Liverpool, and indeed he was acting with a company which played in the Town Hall in Southampton between about 1756 and 1766; he was also a member of Shepherd's strolling company, and he acted at Sligo about 1768. Lee Lewes suggests that Farren had made his debut in Dublin and then had become a stroller in England. Lewes says that Farren was rejected in his application to William Gibson, sometime manager at Liverpool in the 1750s and 1760s. A heavy drinker, Farren was evidently often drunk on stage. Mrs Farren, according to "Petronius Arbiter," had made her first stage appearance at a theatre in Lancashire. She had been acting at Dublin before she made her debut at Bath in the spring of 1761.

The death of George Farren about 1770 placed a heavy burden upon his wife, who was left with four young daughters: Elizabeth (called Eliza), Catherine (called Kitty), Margaret (called Peggy), and a fourth whose name and life remain somewhat of a mystery. Kitty, who had no special beauty or polish, acted with her sisters at Wakefield, Manchester, Liverpool, and Birmingham in the 1770s, but died early of consumption, on 10 January 1777. Peggy, the youngest, also acted with the family in the 1770s. In 1788 she married Thomas Knight, an actor who later became a lessee of the Theatre Royal, Liverpool; as Mrs Knight (d.1804) she made her debut at Covent Garden on 25 September 1795 and is entered separately in these volumes under her married name. According to an item in *Notes and Queries* in November 1884, there was a fourth daughter, who died young; and according to a notation in a manuscript at the Folger Shakespeare Library dated 22 July 1791, a Mrs Hughs, late of the Bath Theatre, who was to appear the following season at Covent Garden, was the sister of Elizabeth Farren, but that appearance seems not to have occurred, and nothing more is known of Mrs Hughs. On the other hand, "Petronius Arbiter" reported that the fourth child was a son who died young.

Just when Elizabeth Farren made her first stage appearance is also indefinite, but certainly she was very young at the time. According to James Winston, the northern manager Joseph Younger discovered Eliza delivering Stevens's "Lecture Upon Heads" in a barn when she was barely in her teens. Younger supposedly prevailed upon Mrs Farren to article her daughter to him. It seems, however, that before the Farrens became involved with Younger Eliza may

have acted children's roles at Bath. Some years after Eliza was a recognized success, a writer in the Salisbury *Country Magazine* in March 1787 boasted that "Miss Farren's first appearance was at the Salisbury Theatre." In the latter half of 1773 she was with her mother and sisters under the management of James Whitley, an eccentric and influential manager of a circuit in the Midlands, who had rented a theatre in Marsden Street, Manchester. During their stay with Whitley at Manchester, the Farrens lived successively in Bootle Street, in Yates Street, and in Jackson's Row, all in the humble area of Deansgate. They were befriended in their financial distress by the actors Mr and Mrs Stanfield, the parents of the celebrated nineteenth-century scene designer Clarkson Stanfield. In later years, according to a scarce pamphlet entitled *Biographical Gleanings of the Countess of Derby, formerly Miss Farren*, Eliza "nobly returned their hospitality when the Stanfields became reduced, and the fortunes of

By gracious permission of Her Majesty, Queen Elizabeth II

ELIZABETH FARREN

by Rivers

the Farrens had attained to the ascending scale."

Eliza's earliest performances with Whitley consisted of employing her fine soprano voice in entr'acte songs and appearing in the pantomimes. Toward the end of the season, on 8 April 1774, she sang a new song, accompanied on the guitar by Clagget, and spoke an epilogue written by Foote after a performance of *The Merchant of Venice* in which her sister Kitty acted Nerissa. Her other sister Peggy sang "Sweet Willy O," and the evening—which was for the benefit of "Mrs Farren and her three children"—was concluded with "a poetic address of thanks to the ladies and gentlemen of Manchester, written by a gentleman of the town for the occasion, spoken by Miss Betsey Farren."

With Whitley's company she also played at Wakefield in the summer of 1774 and probably at Chester and other places on the manager's circuit. But after the termination of his summer season, Whitley felt no further need for the services of the Farrens. A long letter which he wrote to Mrs Farren is worth quoting for its candid but gracious assessment of their abilities and his advice:

Madam.—I have duly considered the subject of our late conversation. & do not think there is the least chance of your deriving any permanent benefit from theatrical pursuits. Inclination does not confer talent; for the sake of yourself & children, I strenuously advise you to turn your attention to some other less dangerous & precarious line of life. I say less dangerous as applies to your daughters. I have passed a long career upon the stage, & where I have seen one person prosperous & happy, ten have failed, & many, particularly females, have been morally cast away. . . . Fix on some safe & certain occupation. Even a laundress, with tolerable plenty of work, is preferable to treading the stage as a make-weight. . . . Nature has not endowed *you* with the qualities that are necessary to ensure success: as to Betsy, although she seems to possess every natural requisite, she is yet too young,

& were she my daughter, I would sooner rear her up to go to service in a respectable family. Inclosed is a trifle of which I entreat the acceptance. When the wheel of fortune takes a more favorable turn, you may return it. I would not advise you to leave Manchester. It is a busy, thriving town. . . .

It was at that point that Eliza and her family became associated with Younger, who upon the recommendation of Whitley took the girl into the company at the Theatre Royal, Liverpool, where at barely 13 she acted Rosetta in *Love in a Village*. Among the numerous stories surrounding her is the one, told in *Walker's Hibernian Magazine* for July 1794, that so poor was she at her debut with Younger that the other actresses of the company "were obliged to subscribe each a proportion of apparel before she could be properly equipped." When she played her next role, Lady Townly, she was so successful that the manager could now procure "credit with his tradesmen for what cloaths any of the family stood in need of." With her sisters she acted at Birmingham in the summers of 1775 and 1776 and was in Younger's company playing at Liverpool and Manchester in the seasons of 1775–76 and 1776–77, in the latter season earning £1 1s. per week.

Upon the recommendation of Younger, Eliza was engaged by the elder Colman for his summer season at the Haymarket Theatre, where she made her first London appearance on 9 June 1777 as Miss Hardcastle in *She Stoops to Conquer*. Several of the reviewers found her voice to be somewhat sharp and she was also criticized for some lack of grace, energy, and force, but for the most part the debut was very successful. The *Morning Chronicle* of 10 June 1777 reported that her face was genteel, her features pretty, and her face expressive and paid her a high compliment: "Miss Farren is, in fact, more perfect than most of the theatrical ladies who have been

National Gallery of Victoria, Melbourne

ELIZABETH FARREN, as Hermione

by Zoffany

initiated into the profession in country seminaries, & has less ill habits than any we remember to have seen translated from the exalted station of heroine in a country corps to the more humble, though more respectable, rank of a candidate for Fame in a company of Royal Regulars"; to Younger praise was accorded for training her. During that summer she also took singing lessons from Jonathan Battishill.

After acting Miss Hardcastle again on 13 June, Eliza played Maria in *The Citizen* on 30 June, then during July continued in both roles. On 12 August she performed Rosetta in *Love in a Village* and on 18 August Miss Tittup in *Bon Ton*. On 20 August 1777 she was Rosina in the premiere of *The Spanish Barber*, Colman's adaptation from Beaumarchais. Smitten by her appearance in her performance of Rosina, one versifier thought he should have turned his eyes away and listened only to her voice, except, alas, that its beauty would have consumed him too. *The Spanish Barber*, for which she also spoke the epilogue, enjoyed a total of seven performances before the summer season ended in mid-September, the last performance coming on 16 September for Miss Farren's benefit. David Garrick, who had now been in retirement for over a year, had seen her perform and in a letter to Colman on 2 September 1777 called her a "most promising piece"—"t'is a Shame that she is not fix'd in London—I will venture my Life that I could teach her a capital part in Comedy, ay & tragedy too, that should drive half our actresses mad—she is much too fine Stuff to be worn & soil'd at Manchester & Liverpool."

But neither winter manager had Garrick's expert and perceptive eye for talent, it seems, for Eliza returned to play in 1777–78 at Manchester and Liverpool at a salary of £2 per week. Colman had the good sense, however, to bring her back to the Haymarket for the summer of 1778. She reappeared on 11 June as Rosina, a role she then sang several more times until she performed Miss Hardcastle on 1 July. In the premiere of Colman's comedy *The Suicide* on 11 July she played Nancy, her first breeches role, for which her profile was then not yet suited. It was reported that one of her ardent pursuers of the summer, Charles James Fox, exclaimed: "D – – n it, she has no prominence either before or behind—all is a straight line from head to foot; & for her legs, they are shaped like a sugarloaf." Nevertheless, an admiring poetaster in the press proclaimed her to be "simply a new Venus." *The Suicide* ran for 19 nights including 16 September when Miss Farren had her benefit. She also acted Lady Townly in *The Provok'd Husband* on 21 August 1778 and several other times during the summer.

Finally, in the autumn of 1778, now about 16 years of age, she had engagements at not one but both winter patent houses. The one at Drury Lane was more rightly a regular employment, but she played several nights at the beginning of the season at Covent Garden, making her first appearance there on 23 September 1778 as Clarinda in *The Suspicious Husband,* and again on 30 September as Lady Townly, on 9 October as Belinda in *All in The Wrong*, on 22 October as Evelina in *Caractacus*, and on 30 October again as Lady Townly. Her debut at Drury Lane came on 8 October 1778, when she played Charlotte Rusport in *The West Indian*, a character for which, by testimony of the *Evening Post* (10 October), "the coup d'oeuil of her figure, and the vivacity of her manner" made her particularly suited. In a comment, the irony of which the reviewer could not possibly have realized at this point in Eliza's life, he judged her performance to have fallen short of that of Mrs Abington, who had created the role, because "Grace, and polished manners, are only to be acquired by a strict observation of high life, and a judicious imitation of their example, both of which are works of time." Yet Miss

Farren had acquitted herself very well, indeed:

There was a good deal of ease in her deportment, and a sufficient share of sprightliness and good humour, both in her delivery and in the expression of her features; indeed, if any thing, too much of the latter, as she wore a smiling face somewhat too often, and by never looking serious, destroyed in part the picturesque effect of the dramatic design of the author. . . . [She] has no fault but that of being occasionally too light and flippant.

In her first season at Drury Lane, Eliza followed her Charlotte Rusport with a number of roles, most of which she was announced as playing for the first time: Lady Sash in the premiere of Sheridan's *The Camp* on 15 October 1778, the second Constantia in *The Chances* on 31 October, Berinthia in *A Trip to Scarborough* on 21 December, Mrs Knightly in *The Discovery* on 3 February 1779, Penelope in *The Gamesters* on 13 March, Nell in *The Devil to Pay* on 9 April for her benefit at which she cleared a modest £68 17*s.*, Louisa Freemore (with the epilogue) in *The Double Deception* on 28 April, Millamant in *The Way of the World* on 1 May, Clarinda in *The Suspicious Husband* on 10 May, and Ann Lovely in *A Bold Stroke for a Wife* on 21 May 1779. Acting at Drury Lane during that and subsequent seasons were William Farren (1754–1795) and his wife Mary Farren (1748–1820) to whom Eliza seems not to have been related.

Again Eliza returned to Colman's Haymarket in the summer of 1779, her new roles being Mrs Sullen in *The Stratagem* on 17 August and Lady Newbery in *The Separate Maintenance*, another new comedy by Colman, on 31 August. Eliza seemed to have acted Lady Newbery, according to the *Morning Chronicle* of 1 September 1779, with an "additional zeal," evidently aware of the challenge of replacing Mrs Abington, who originally had been announced for the part. The situation served to stir more

briskly the competition between the two actresses which the press seldom let pass unnoticed. An accusation in the papers that Miss Farren had some power over Colman was met by a rebuttal in the *Morning Post* of 17 September which pointed out that her roles at the Haymarket during that summer had not been many and dismissed the charge as groundless. Being young, she had performed Lady Newbery with "infinite justice," but it was ridiculous, suggested the correspondent, to compare her powers with those of Mrs Abington.

In 1779–80, her second season at Drury Lane, where she was to continue for an uninterrupted period of another 17 years until her retirement, Eliza's roles included Angelica in *Love for Love*, Desdemona, Bella in *The Runaway*, Lydia Languish in *The Rivals*, Hermione in *The Winter's Tale*, Belinda in *The Old Bachelor*, and Olivia (with a song) in *Twelfth Night*. For her

Harvard Theatre Collection

ELIZABETH FARREN, as Olivia

engraving by Thornthwaite, after Burney

benefit on 5 April 1780 as Maria in *The Citizen*, when tickets could be had at her lodgings, No 50, Great Queen Street, Lincoln's Inn Fields, she realized net receipts of £101 2s. 6d.

On 24 May 1780 she was Miss Loveless in the first London performance of *The Miniature Picture*, a comedy afterpiece by the beautiful Elizabeth Craven, wife of Lord Craven. The production brought out the Duchess of Devonshire, the Duchess of Richmond, Lady Harcourt, and other nobility to watch Eliza and Mrs Robinson (as Eliza Camply). Mary "Perdita" Robinson was by then a mistress of "Florizel," the Prince of Wales. No doubt it was all heady stuff for young Eliza, now about 18, but in years to come she herself would evoke similar excitement and curiosity from the nobility.

In the 1780s Eliza became an enormous favorite in roles of fine ladies, a line in which she succeeded Mrs Abington when that actress left Drury Lane in 1782 and in which she remained unexcelled during her stay upon the stage. Indefatigable in the pains she took to improve her art and station, she eventually realized upon the stage the personification of cultivation and femininity and became at once the model and toast of fashion. In her performances of over a hundred roles in comedies, tragedies, farces, and musical pieces she displayed, by the common testimony of her age, that rare combination of charm, beauty, and art which has always mesmerized audiences. The beautiful full-length portrait of her painted by Thomas Lawrence about 1790 testifies to her special attractiveness, and indeed, by virtue of that painting the 22-year old artist was catapulted into immediate fame and royal favor.

Among the numerous roles she acted at Drury Lane in the 1780s were (with the season of first appearance): in 1780–81 Miss Titup in *Bon Ton*, Macarici in *The Royal Suppliants*, Emma in *Henry and Emma*, Mrs Lovemore in *The Way to Keep Him*, Juliet in *Romeo and Juliet*, Statira in *Alexander the Great*, Cecilia in *The Chapter of Accidents*, Violante in *The Wonder*, Lady Betty Modish in *The Careless Husband*, Imoinda in *Oroonoko*, and Sophia in *The Lord of the Manor*; in 1781–82 Lady Harriet Trifle in *The Divorce*, Miss Harriet Temple in *Variety*, Rosetta in *The Foundling*, Miss Griskin in *A Trip to Scotland*, and Indiana in *The Conscious Lovers*; in 1782–83 Lady Teazle in *The School for Scandal*, Mrs Harley in *False Delicacy*, Clarissa in *The Confederacy*, Lady Sadlife in *The Double Gallant*, Ophelia Wyndham in *The School for Vanity*, Lady Rentless in *Dissipation*, Mary in *The City Madam*, Maria in *Imitation*, and Widow Belmour in *The Way to Keep Him*; in 1783–84 Miranda in *The Busy Body*, Estifania in *Rule a Wife and Have a Wife*, Mrs Ford in *The Merry Wives of Windsor*, Louisa in *The Reparation*, Leonora in *Love in a Veil*, Mrs Oakley in *The Jealous Wife*, and Alcmena in *Amphitryon*; in 1784–85 Fanny in *The Clandestine Marriage*, Emmeline in *Arthur and Emmeline*, Lady Plyant in *The Double Dealer*, Lady Paragon in *The Natural Son*, Mrs Plotwell in *The Beau's Duel*; in 1785–86 the Comic Muse in *The Jubilee*, Lady Emily in *The Heiress*, Lady Brute in *The Provok'd Wife*, Young Lady Languish in *The Widow Bewitch'd*; in 1786–87 Donna Seraphina in *A School for Grey-Beards*, Lady Morden in *Seduction*; in 1787–88 Lady Charlotte Courtley in *The New Peerage*, Beatrice in *Much Ado About Nothing*, Florinda in *Tit for Tat*; in 1788–89 the Countess in *False Appearances*; and in 1789–90 Lady Bell in *Know Your Own Mind*, Dorinda in *The Tempest*, Leonora in *The False Friend*, Susan in *The Follies of a Day*, Bisarre in *The Inconstant*, Charlotte in *The Hypocrite*, Julia in *The Rivals*.

During the 1780s she also continued to play regularly during the summers at the Haymarket in 1780, 1781, and every season from 1784 through 1788. Many of her

By permission of the Birmingham Museum and Art Gallery

Probably a scene from *Arthur and Emmeline,* with JOHN PHILIP KEMBLE as Arthur, WILLIAM BRERETON as Oswald, FRANCIS AICKIN as Merlin, and ELIZABETH FARREN as Emmeline

by Wheatley

roles there she had acted previously at Drury Lane, but those which she first played at the Haymarket included Cecilia in *The Chapter of Accidents* on 5 August 1780, Elvira in *The Spanish Fryar* on 22 August 1780, Portia in *The Merchant of Venice* on 24 August 1780, Angelica in *Love for Love* on 5 September 1780, Emelia in *The English Merchant* on 18 July 1781, Clarissa in *The Confederacy* on 21 August 1781, Mrs Ford in *The Merry Wives of Windsor* on 24 August 1781, Fanny in *The Clandestine Marriage* on 19 August 1784, Lady Harriet in *The Two Connoisseurs* on 2 September 1784, Helena in *All's Well That Ends Well* on 26 July 1785, a Young Lady in *I'll Tell you What* on 4 August 1785, the Baroness in *The Disbanded Officers* on 24 July 1786, Florinda in *Tit for Tat* on 29 August 1786, Lady Rustic in *The Country Attorney* on 7 July 1787, Beatrice in *Much Ado About Nothing* on 17 August 1787, Susan in *The Follies of a Day* on 21 August 1787, and Miss Eliza Moreton in *The Sword of Peace* on 9 August 1788.

As the popular heroine of various comedies in which she excelled—Hazlitt wrote of her "fine-lady airs and graces, with that elegant turn of her head and motion of her fan and tripping of her tongue"—Miss Farren, of course, attracted a certain amount of satire and envy. Her exquisite style was sometimes, perhaps rightly, attacked as affectation, and she does seem to have assumed in life many of the airs she portrayed on the stage. The *New Rosciad* accused her of being "affected, proud, conceited, pert, and vain / As dead to feeling, as alive to gain." She was not admired by Sylas Neville in her portrayal of Almeida in *The Fair Circassian* which he saw on 7 December 1781, and after seeing her as Rosetta in *The Foundling* on 4 April 1782 he wrote in his *Diary* that she was an "insufferable piece of affectation" but "a tollerable coquette" in the role. As Belinda in *All in the Wrong* she was taken to task by the *English Chronicle* (25/27 October 1785) for her "lolling carelessness" which she allowed to creep over her carriage, "that may rather too easily be mistaken for affectation"; it was suggested that if she had not had such fine teeth she would have laughed no more than the character required. On 29 October 1785 the *Morning Herald* besought her to walk more erectly: "Do not mistake for *grace* what an accidental spectator would call a *broken* back!"

In the summer of 1781, after performing in *The Chapter of Accidents* at the Haymarket on 7 September, she was stricken by the smallpox. She was replaced as Rosina in *The Spanish Barber* on 12 September, and on the following day the *Morning Herald* reported that she was confined with the illness at her house in Great Queen Street. Fortunately she escaped from the attack with only some six pocks on her face—which Lord Derby, "her noble inamorato," as the press styled him, "kisses with the most rapturous transports." By 26 September she was fully recovered, but it was reported that she was approaching the management of Drury Lane "with more airs than graces," with demands for a salary "almost unknown in the dramatic annals of either house!"

The report of her claim perhaps was somewhat exaggerated. Figures of her salary during the earlier part of her career are unknown, but by 1789–90 (eight years later) she was earning £17 per week, the highest salary in the London theatre save those of Mrs Billington (£26 5s. per week) and Mrs Pope (£18), at the other house. That year at Drury Lane, Baddeley was earning £9 per week, J. P. Kemble £14, Mrs Crouch £12; at Covent Garden, Charles Bannister £12, Lewis £13, Quick £12 12s., and Mrs Martyr £10. Miss Farren's salary, moreover, remained a constant £17 from 1789–90 right through 1796–97, her last season. She never profited a great deal by benefits compared to other popular performers (a net of about £117 on 23 April 1781, about £2 plus an unknown quantity of tickets out on 8 April 1782), so as early as 1783–84 she obtained an arrangement with the management which continued throughout her career for a payment of £300 (usually given in two payments of £150) each season in lieu of a benefit performance.

Her first appearance at Drury Lane after her illness was as Charlotte Rusport in *The West Indian* on 2 October 1781. This return drew hoards of the curious, especially the ladies, "the majority hoping that so promising a genius might not have suffered the least injury from the small pox," reported the press, "while some of those who live by an infamous barter of their beauty, wished that they might not continue to be put out of countenance by a person equally fair in face." Looking as charming as ever, Eliza played to great applause. Several days later a paragrapher defended her against the charge of scene-stealing in a performance of *The Lord of the Manor* on 6 October:

It having been intimated to us that Miss Farren's coughing [as Sophia], during the time Miss Prudom [as Annette] was singing some of the most admired airs in this piece, was considered by many of the audience as an unpardonable interruption, and proceeded from a gross affectation, or what is worse, an *envious* disposition. We take this opportunity of assuring the public, that the contrary is the fact, and that since her indisposition Miss Farren has been afflicted with a severe cold, which it is imagined she received in consequence of her going to the theatre rather too soon after her indisposition.

Nevertheless, like other theatrical queens, on occasion Miss Farren could be obstinate and temperamental. The notes of J. P. Kemble (in the Folger Library) record for 17 December 1788 a "Great quarrel with Miss Farren about her dress." Kemble would not change the play (evidently *The Suspicious Husband* on the following night) and "She acted, at last." On 21 October 1789 *The Beggar's Opera* had to be substituted at the last minute for the intended premiere of *The False Friend* when she was taken "violently ill" at rehearsal. *The False Friend*, an alteration by Kemble of Vanbrugh's comedy, opened on 24 October 1789 and was repeated on 28 October, on which date Kemble noted his determination never to present the play again ("Miss Farren does not like her part and acts it abominably"), a vow he kept.

Despite these instances which did her no credit, there is little question that Eliza was a lovely and accomplished talent. In his *Memoirs* Cumberland called her "exquisite," in his *Wandering Patentee* Wilkinson testified to her "infinite merit," and in his *Life of Siddons* Boaden claimed that after her retirement comedy degenerated into farce. Horace Walpole wrote of her to the Countess of Upper Ossory, in anticipation of seeing her play Donna Seraphina in the premiere of *The School for Grey-Beards* on 25 November 1786, as "the first of all actresses." "We never saw anything more naturally assumed, or more agreeably wicked, if we may so phrase it," thought the reviewer in the *Morning Chronicle* of 11 January 1786, than Miss Farren's playing of Berinthia in *A Trip to Scarborough* on the previous evening. Adolphus, in his *Memoirs of Bannister*, wrote with enthusiasm of her performances of Lady Emily in *The Heiress*, which first played at Drury Lane on 14 January 1786 with a superb cast that included King, Baddeley, Bannister, Smith, Miss Pope, and Mrs Crouch ("We never saw a play more admirably performed in all its parts," claimed the *Gazetteer* on 16 January):

Whether high and honourable sentiments, burning and virtuous sensibility, sincere and uncontrollable affection, animated through sportive reprehension, elegant *persiflage*, or arch and pointed satire, were the aim of the author, Miss Farren amply filled out his thought; and by her exquisite representations made it, even when faint and feeble in itself, striking and forcible. Add to these, the irresistible graces of her address and manner, the polished beauties of her action and gait, and all the indescribable little charms which give fascination to the woman of birth and fashion, and the power and influence of Miss Farren's performance may in some degree be appreciated.

Numerous poetasters sang her praises in bad verses, typical of which were those by John Williams in *The Children of Thespis* (1786):

> To copy her frame, where divinity's seal
>   is,
> Would beggar the talents of fam'd
>   Praxiteles.
> . . . .
> In Teazle, the springs of mild elegance
>   move her,
> But the sightless sweet Emmeline, that's
>   her chef d'oeuvre.

Some nine years later, although equally appreciative, T. Bellamy's lines on her in *The London Theatres* (1795) were not of better quality:

> With lively air, impressive face,
> A form of symmetry and grace;
> With all that speaks, (and praise apart)
> That speaks a good and gentle heart,—
> We hail thee, FARREN; winning
>   maid,—
> In Nature's ornaments array'd.

In the same year, in his *Candid and Impartial Strictures on the Performances*, F. G.

Waldron gave an anatomization which can stand for the spate of adoring notices:

Her person, excepting being rather too tall, is peculiarly well formed for the sphere of acting in which she moves, and the inexpressible graces that uniformly attend her deportment, give a luxuriant feast to the beholder, he never receives from any other performer. Her countenance is bewitchingly beautiful, with eyes of the most expressive softness, and a voice distinct, clear, and harmonious. She is in our opinion the only female on the stage, that can give us a proper idea of the real polished woman of fashion, in which she is very little inferior to any other actresses within our recollection.

During the 1790s she continued to play her familiar and successful repertoire at Drury Lane, taking on few new roles. She acted Miss Herbert in *The Fugitive* on 20 April 1792 at the King's Theatre (where the Drury Lane company performed in 1791–92 and 1792–93), the Niece in *The Tender Husband* on 20 October 1792, Louisa Ratcliffe in *The Jew* on 8 May 1794, Lady Bellair in *The Welch Heiress* on 17 April 1795, Lady Roby in *First Love* on 12 May 1795, Jane in *The Dependent* on 20 October 1795, Olivia in *The Man of Ten Thousand* on 23 January 1796, Helen in *The Iron Chest* on 12 March 1796, Melantha in *Celadon and Florimel* (adapted by Kemble from Cibber's *The Comical Lovers*, Larpent MS 1133) on 23 May 1796, and her last new role, Lady Dorville in Holcroft's *The Force of Ridicule* on 6 December 1796. The premiere of the last piece had originally been scheduled for 29 November 1796 but was suddenly postponed by Miss Farren's illness, reported by the *Oracle* on 30 November to have been feigned. The audience was offered a choice of a refund of admission or remaining to watch Mrs Siddons, who at the last minute consented to act Isabella, and hundreds left the theatre.

The *Morning Herald* the next morning claimed that Miss Farren had balked at playing because she could not get her salary from Sheridan, who had a reputation for not being able to meet his payrolls. But the *Morning Herald* of 1 December printed a letter from Miss Farren, sent from her house in Green Street, Grosvenor Square, confirming that she really had been ill. Several years earlier, she had refused to appear in the production of Mary Robinson's farce *Nobody* (Larpent MS 1046) on 29 November 1794 because, according to the *Times* on 6 December 1794, "thinking she would appear *Nobody*, gave up the character and paid the forfeit, that she might continue to be thought somebody." If her professional conduct was wanting in this instance her judgment was not. *Nobody* was hissed throughout and after two more performances was withdrawn.

Farren's charm and vivacity made her most suitable for her frequent delivery of prologues and epilogues. It was she who spoke the address written by Alexander Bicknell especially to honor the retirement of George Anne Bellamy at Drury Lane on 24 May 1785, Mrs Bellamy being unable herself to speak it. She was also chosen to deliver the long epilogue at the grand opening of the new Drury Lane Theatre on 21 April 1794, although she did not perform a role that evening.

During her two decades at Drury Lane, Miss Farren did not often venture out of London to play. She acted at Crow Street, Dublin, in 1784–85. In the summer of 1787 she acted Lady Paragon at her sister Margaret's benefit in York on 2 July, played there a week, and performed several nights at Leeds to large houses. She was again at York during race week of 1789. In June of 1789 she returned to Crow Street for 12 nights. She again was engaged at Dublin for 12 nights in July 1794 at a reported salary of £500 and a clear benefit. In October of that year, at Cork for £50 per night she acted Lady Bell, Bisarre, Estifania, Beatrice, Lady Emily, and Violante.

In July 1795 at York she acted for six nights, offering Lady Bell, Lady Paragon, Violante, Julia, Clarinda, and Beatrice. She also acted at Worthington in September 1796.

In an age when the reigning stage queens were often more celebrated for their antics off the boards than on, it is notable that Eliza's character and morals were rarely aspersed. When she was still quite young, her infatuation with the actor John Palmer seemed innocent enough. One morning in August 1779, when Palmer was late getting to rehearsal for *The Separate Maintenance*, Eliza ran into the Green Room to tell the waiting actors and author "he was arrived & coming along the stage-passage: —she knew him by his tread," whereupon she blushed at the chiding of her colleagues.

There was also a brief affair with Charles James Fox. Soon, however, she was introduced by the Duchess of Leinster to Edward, the twelfth Earl of Derby. By 1785 Eliza and the Earl had formed a liaison, though his countess was still alive. He was assiduous in his attentions to Eliza and introduced her to the best society, including Lady Dorothea Thompson and Lady Cecilia Johnson, who became her patronesses, and the Duke of Richmond for whom she evidently supervised amateur theatricals at his Whitehall residence in the late 1780s. Among her dinner companions were counted Walpole, the Thrales, Edward Jerningham, and Anne Seymour Damer, the aristocratic sculptress who did a bust of Eliza as Thalia. In 1790 Eliza's friendship with Mrs Damer—whom Hester Lynch

MARGARET FARREN, the Earl of Derby, and ELIZABETH FARREN

caricature by unknown artist

Thrale described in her diary as "a Lady much suspected for liking her own Sex in a criminal Way"—became awkward. Henry Siddons, husband of Sarah and friend of the Thrales, wrote a private verse on them:

Her little Stock of private Fame
Will fall a Wreck to public Clamour,
If Farren leagues with one whose Name
Comes near—Aye very near—to Damn
her.

Whatever the nature of the friendship, it obviously disturbed Lord Derby, who by 1795 insisted, according to Mrs Thrale, that Eliza keep Mrs Damer "at Distance."

Derby himself presumably tried to be as discreet as possible in public with Miss Farren because of his own marital circumstances, but it would be naive to believe that by no means, as one early biographer put it, was the attachment "indecorous." With his small spare figure topped by a large head, with hair tied in a long pigtail, and his attachment to short nankeen gaiters, Derby was a singular-looking figure who was a prominent subject of caricaturists. He was seen, it was said, usually escorting Eliza from the theatre to her house in Green Street, following her "puffing from want of breath and sighing his soft tale, which she, from mere wantonness, kept him on a jog-trot, and hardly deigned to give him a smile." In her *Diary of a Lady of Quality*, Miss Wynne wrote of seeing Derby leave his private box one night to steal on stage behind the screen set up in *The School for Scandal*—"of course we all looked with impatience for the discovery, hoping the screen would fall a little too soon and show to the audience Lord Derby as well as Lady Teazle." Horace Walpole was charitable about the relationship: "Miss Farren is as excellent as Mrs Oldfield because she has lived with the best style of men in England."

At length, the first Countess of Derby kindly obliged the couple by dying on 14 March 1797. Within a few weeks Eliza announced her retirement from the stage and her forthcoming marriage. At the age of 35 she was fast approaching the point where her "dimples shall to wrinkles turn," as John Williams so unchivalrously put it. On 3 April 1797 she performed Estifania in *Rule a Wife and Have a Wife*, on 4 April Susan in *The Follies of a Day*, on 6 April Bisarre in *The Inconstant*—all curiously amusing titles under the circumstances—and finally on 8 April 1797 she presented herself for her last appearance at Drury Lane as Lady Teazle in *The School for Scandal*. The house was jammed with 3656 persons who paid a total of £728 14s. 6d., the largest amount taken at that theatre on a nonbenefit night between the year it opened in 1794 and 1800. The amiable Lord Derby was applauded loudly upon his appearance in his box. Lady Teazle's valedictory speech to Lady Sneerwell took on a special emotional significance, and Eliza was reported to have been moved to tears at her delivery of it. After the play, Eliza declining to address the audience herself, Mr Wroughton spoke doggerel verses to her (written by Sheridan during the course of the performance) as she stood to the side supported by Mr King and Miss Miller. In "a state apparent of much agitation," Eliza then came forward to make her curtsies to the right, left, and center of the house.

Three weeks later on 1 May 1797 she and Derby were married, by special license, at the Earl's house in Grosvenor Square in a ceremony conducted by the Rev J. Hornby, Vicar of Winnick, Lancashire. Officially she was now the character she had sustained in her numerous stage roles. Within another three weeks, on 17 May 1797, she was one of the ladies chosen by Queen Charlotte to walk in the procession at the marriage of the Princess Royal.

On 5 June 1803 the Countess of Derby's mother, Margaret Farren, whom she had supported, died at Grosvenor Square and was buried at St. George, Hanover Square. Her obituary notice in the *Manchester Mercury* (14 June 1803) described her as "a lady whose many virtues & mild, affectionate, & placid manners will make her death a subject of deep & lasting regret to all who had the pleasure of her acquaintance."

After a long illness "of protracted suffering" the Countess of Derby died at Knowlsey Park, Lancashire, on 23 April 1829. She was buried in the Derby family vault in the Ormskirk Parish Church. A brass plaque was raised on the south wall of the nave in Huyton Parish Church, but was subsequently moved to the chancel, with the inscription:

Near the place where she loved to worship, and where her voice was so often lifted up in prayer and praise, this tribute of grateful affection is dedicated to the virtuous memory of Elizabeth Farren, Countess of Derby, wife of Edward, twelfth Earl of Derby.

From her earliest years, and through every change of her most eventful life, she made Religion Her companion and guide, while the native graces of mind and manners made her seem born for that station to which she was subsequently raised. Beneficent without ostentation, she was zealous in every good work. She visited the fatherless and the widows in their affliction. She kept herself unspotted from the world, and she died as she had lived, in the fear of and love of GOD, and in humble hope of His redeeming mercy.

She was born on July 6, 1762, and died April 23, 1829.

'Thou hast a few names even in Sardis, which have not defiled their garments; and they shall walk with me in white: for they are worthy.'—Rev. iii. 4.

Her husband survived her until 21 October 1834. They had three children: Lady Lucy Elizabeth, who died at the age of 10 in 1809; James, who died at the age of 17 in 1817; and Lady Mary Margaret, who married the Earl of Wilton in 1821.

In *The Wandering Patentee*, Tate Wilkinson wrote that he could not recall, "to my mind's eye, such fashion, ease, pleasantry, and elegance, in the captivating coquette and the lady of fashion all conjoined, as when I view the alluring, the entertaining, the all-accomplished Miss FARREN . . . Good actresses may put in their claim, but that face, with the domains that there adjacent lie—in short, the *tout ensemble* is not to be equalled."

Portraits of Elizabeth Farren include:

1. Perhaps by Richard Cosway. In the Garrick Club. Presented in 1854 by William A. Commerell as by Gainsborough.

2. By John Downman, in chalk, 1787. In the National Portrait Gallery. An engraving by J. Collyer was published by M. Lawson, 1788. A similar engraving, bust only, by Ridley was published as a plate to the *Monthly Mirror*, 1796.

3. Attributed to Horace Hone, miniature on ivory. In the Garrick Club.

4. By Ozias Humphrey, pastel drawing. In the National Gallery of Ireland.

5. By Thomas Lawrence, full-length canvas. Exhibited at the Winter Exhibition, the Royal Academy, 1790, called "Portrait of an Actress." Owned by Edward Stanley, 12th Earl of Derby, until 1829 and then by the Earls of Wilton until 1894; subsequently owned by J. Pierpont Morgan, then by Edward S. Harkness, the latter bequeathing it to the Metropolitan Museum of Art, New York, in 1940. An engraving of the portrait, with Charles Knight's name given as the engraver, was published in 1791; it was reprinted by J. P. Thompson in 1803 and as a plate to *La Belle Assemblée* in 1813. This engraving has been commonly attributed to F. Bartolozzi, but William Roberts in *Pictures in the collection of J. Pierpont Morgan at Princes Gate and Dover House* (1907) documents that the so-called Bartolozzi engraving was really by Knight. Other engravings of this Lawrence portrait were done by M. Cormack, and by Pratt in 1898.

6. By Lawrence, half-length. In the collection of Wentworth Beaumont in

1900. Perhaps this is the portrait now at Port Sunlight. A replica, sold at Christie, Manson, and Woods on 27 June 1863 for 79 guineas to a Mr Smith, is in the collection of Sir Francis Grant; this item may have been the example lent to the Art Treasures Exhibition of North Wales and border Counties, Wrexham, England, 22 July 1876, as belonging at that time to Reginald Cholmondeley.

7. By Lawrence, watercolor. Lent to the Whitechapel Art Gallery in 1910 by Mrs Aston.

8. By Lawrence, oval sketch. Lent to the 1913 Edward Gallery Exhibition of Lawrence Drawings (no 8).

9. By Lessore, drawing in pencil, dated verso "3 June 92." In the Harvard Theatre Collection.

10. By Rivers, drawing in pencil. At Windsor Castle, property of Her Majesty Queen Elizabeth II. An engraving by Ridley was published by Vernor & Hood, 1800.

11. Marble bust, as Thalia, by Mrs A. Damer. In the Collection of Rupert Gunnis. An engraving by J. Jones was published by J. Roberts, at Oxford, 1789.

12. Engraving by J. Condé. Published as a plate to the *Thespian Magazine*, 1792.

13. Engraving, with the Earl of Derby, by R. Dighton. Published by Dighton, 1795.

14. Engraving by unknown artist. Published by J. S. Jordan, 1797.

15. Engraving by unknown artist. Published by R. Cribb, 1790.

16. Engraving by unknown artist. Entitled "the Hibernian Thais," and published by T. Walker, 1777.

17. As Almeida, with Robert Bensley as Omar, in *The Fair Circassian*. A large steel engraving signed "J. P.," a caricature. In the Huntington Library. Reproduced in vol II, p. 39, of this dictionary.

18. As Beatrice in *Much Ado About Nothing*. Vignette engraving by unknown artist.

19. As Beatrice. Rare engraving by un-

known artist, in the Harvard Theatre Collection. Published as a plate to the *Hibernian Magazine*, June 1789.

20. As Clarinda in *The Suspicious Husband*. Engraving by J. Phillips. Published by E. Hedges, 1785.

21. As Creusa in *Creusa*. By anonymous engraver. Published by Harrison & Co, 1781.

22. As Desdemona in *Othello*. Colored drawing by J. H. Ramberg. In the British Museum. Evidently never engraved.

23. As Lady Emily, with Thomas King as Sir Clement, in *The Heiress*. Engraving by J. Jones, after J. Downman. Published by Jones, 1787.

24. As Lady Emily. Engraving by J. Jones, after J. Downman. Published by J. Tayleure, 1823.

25. As Emmeline, with John P. Kemble as Arthur, in *Arthur and Emmeline*. Drawing by Thomas Stothard. In the Henry E. Huntington Library. An engraving by J. Heath was published by W. Lowndes, 1786.

26. Possibly as Emmeline, with three other actors. Painting by Francis Wheatley. In the City Museum and Art Gallery, Birmingham, England. This painting has previously been thought to be of a scene in Act IV of *The Tempest*, but Phillipe Downes has suggested that it might represent the final scene of J. P. Kemble's *Arthur and Emmeline*. If so, then the other figures would be Kemble as Arthur, William Brereton as Oswald, and Francis Aickin as Merlin. The features of Miss Farren are similar to those of her as depicted by Lawrence. The painting is signed "*F. Wheatley pnx 1787*." It was in the Collection of Sir Horatio D. Davies, K.C.M.G, until it was sold at Christie's on 17 February 1913. Eventually it came into the possession of Herbert Buckmaster, who put it on loan to the Buck's Club for many years. It was purchased at auction at Christie's on 7 March 1958 by Birmingham.

27. As Hermia in *A Midsummer Night's*

Dream. Engraving by Newham, after Ramberg. Published as a plate to *Bell's British Theatre*, 1785. The same picture was engraved by Leney and printed by J. Cawthorn, 1805.

28. As Hermione in *The Winter's Tale*. Painting by John Zoffany, c. 1780. Once owned by Archibald Seton of Touch. In the National Gallery of Victoria, Melbourne. On 24 March 1961 it was purchased at Sotheby's by Agnew's, from whom it was acquired by the Australian gallery in 1966. An engraving by E. Fisher was published by Sayre & Bennett, 1781.

29. As Olivia in *Twelfth Night*. India ink and wash drawing by E. F. Burney. In the British Museum. An engraving by Thornthwaite was published as a plate to *Bell's British Library*, 1785.

30. As Olivia. Engraving by Grignion and Bartolozzi, after Ramberg. Published as a plate to *Bell's British Library*, 1785. Scriven also did an engraving of the same picture.

31. As Penelope in *The Gamester*. Engraving by Neagle, after De Wilde. Published as a plate to *Bell's British Library*, 1792. A copy was also printed by C. Cooke, 1808.

32. As the Queen in *Richard III*. Engraving by Thornthwaite, after De Wilde. Published as a plate to *Bell's British Library*, 1786.

33. Speaking the Epilogue at the opening of the New Drury Lane Theatre, 21 April 1794. By anonymous engraver.

34. Caricature, titled "A Theatrical Venus," depicting a nude Miss Farren. By anonymous engraver. Published as a plate to *Man of Pleasure's Magazine*.

35. Caricature, with the Earl of Derby, at an exhibition of pictures. By anonymous engraver, after Gilray.

36. Caricature, titled, "A Peep behind the Curtain at Widow Belmour," depicting Miss Farren naked, full-length, backstage. By anonymous engraver. Dated December 1790.

37. Caricature, titled "The Platonic Lovers, A Scene in the green Boxes between Lord Doodle and Miss Tittup, with her Mamma at a humble distance." Designed by "Fashion" and engraved by "Folly." Dated 29 March 1784.

Farren, Margaret. *See* KNIGHT, MRS THOMAS, MARGARET.

Farren, William *1754–1795, actor.*
Born in 1754 the son of a tallow chandler in Clerkenwell, William Farren spent his youth in London. According to a manuscript account of his early life (now in the Folger Shakespeare Library), he and a number of brothers and sisters were well brought up, and William—"the old man's pet"—who was a handsome and charming young man was placed in a banking office in Lombard Street. An obituary notice of William in the *Gentleman's Magazine* for June 1795, on the other hand, states that he had been apprenticed to a Mr Baylis, a tinman, in Red Lion Street, Holborn. Soon bored with his business, whatever it was, Farren determined to become a player, a decision no doubt influenced by his developing a friendship with Richard Yates, an actor at Drury Lane.

William's father by then being dead, Yates negotiated with the youth's master for his indenture and at the age of 18 William was apprenticed to Yates for seven years.

It is possible that Farren made his stage debut in London at the Haymarket Theatre on 16 September 1773 playing an unspecified role in *The Macaroni*. The name Farren was given in the bills for the day, as it also was for the Nephew in *The Irish Widow* on 18 September 1773 and Sir George Airey in *The Busy Body* and Young Wilding in *The Citizen* on 24 January 1774; but we believe that those instances were variant spellings for James Fearon, an actor at the Haymarket during that period. It is more likely that Farren made

Courtesy of the Garrick Club

WILLIAM FARREN

artist unknown

his first stage appearance as a member of the company which Richard Yates directed in Birmingham. Few bills for Birmingham have survived for that period, but Farren can be placed in that theatre in the summer of 1774. Evidently impressed by Farren's talent, Yates arranged for him to make his debut at Drury Lane Theatre on 20 March 1775, announced as a gentleman making his first appearance at that theatre, as Jason in *Medea*, a performance in which Mrs Yates played the title role on her own benefit night. The reviewer in the *Morning Post* the next day reported that Farren had a "full round voice" but one "wanting variety of tones and extent of powers." Although he lacked expressive features, he could make the most of his rather pleasing person, advised the critic, "by moving erect." Upon the whole he had made "a very decent appearance."

The following season, 1775–76, Farren began a long engagement at Drury Lane which lasted through 1783–84. Although his name did not appear on the bills until 4 November 1775, when he acted Stratocles in *Tamerlane*, from the onset of the season he had been filling supernumerary roles, for on 18 November 1775 the treasury paid him £10 for 40 nights, at the rate of £1 10s. per week. On 29 December he played Salarino in *The Merchant of Venice*, a role he repeated on 2 January 1776. Other roles for which he received billing that season included Ratcliff in *Jane Shore* on 9 January, Macduff in *Macbeth* on 19 January, Lycander in *Medea* on 11 March, Merton in *The Spleen* on 16 March, Eumenes in *Alexander the Great* on 28 March, Sebastian in *The Tempest* on 18 May, and Tybalt in *Romeo and Juliet* on 22 May.

Still being paid £1 10s. per week in the next season, 1776–77, Farren expanded his repertoire considerably. While retaining Ratcliff, Lycander, Stratocles, and Sebastian, he also played Rivers in *The Note of Hand*, Rossano in *The Fair Penitent*, Lemos in *Braganza*, Claudio in *Measure for Measure*, Guiderius in *Cymbeline*, Acreless in *The Gamesters*, Sharper in *The Old Bachelor*, Charles Stanley in *All the World's a Stage*, the Ghost in *Hamlet*, Paris in *Romeo and Juliet*, the Captain in *Macbeth*, Sir Petronal in *Old City Manners*, Charles in *The Jealous Wife*, Cassander in *Alexander the Great*, Sebastian in *Twelfth Night*, and Lt Story in *The Committee*. He was the original Careless in the first performance of *The School for Scandal* on 8 May 1777 and for 19 subsequent times before the close of the season. On 17 April he shared his benefit with Baker and Miss Abrams, when he played Lewson in *The Gamester,* and took £22 as his net portion.

In 1777–78 Farren continued in his line of supporting roles, adding among others Horatio in *Hamlet*, Buckingham in *Richard III*, Vernon in *1 Henry IV*, Westmoreland in *2 Henry IV*, Pembroke in *King John*, Wellbred in *Every Man in his Humour*, and Fenton in *The Merry Wives of Windsor*. He shared some £193 at his benefit with Katharine Sherry on 4 May 1778, when tickets could be had of him at Rumler's, Clare Court, Covent Garden. On 9 July 1778, David Garrick, who had retired from the stage after Farren's first season at Drury Lane, wrote to Hannah More that "I like Farren in the parts I have seen him Act." Indeed, after three years at Drury Lane, Farren was a well-seasoned and serviceable actor, possessing a repertoire of some 40 roles.

Over the following six seasons he added about 50 roles more, including the more substantial roles of Valentine in *Love for Love*, Young Mirabel in *The Inconstant*, Lord Randolph in *Douglas*, Freeman in *A Bold Stroke for a Wife*, Phocion in *The Grecian Daughter*, and Polydore in *The Orphan*. He acted Fainall in *The Way of the World* for the first time on 1 May 1779 when he shared £144 7s. 6d. in benefit tickets with Miss Sherry, and tickets could be had of him at No 14, Catherine Street, the Strand. For his benefit on 22 April 1780, when he was living at No 41, Great Queen Street, Lincoln's Inn Fields, he acted Granger in *Who's the Dupe?* His first attempt at Hotspur in *1 Henry IV* came on 2 October 1780, and on 11 May 1781, when tickets could be had of him at No 60, Theobald's Road, he played Lovewell in *The Clandestine Marriage* for his benefit. At his benefit on 23 April 1782, when he was living at No 13, York Street, he acted the capital role of Othello for the first time. By his next benefit, on 24 April 1783, when he made his first appearance as Zanga in *The Revenge*, he was living at No 35, Great Queen Street, an address he retained until 1787.

In 1778–79, Farren's salary at Drury Lane had been raised by 6s. 8d. per week to £1 16s. 8d. The following season, 1779–80, it was set at £4 per week, or 13s.

Harvard Theatre Collection

WILLIAM FARREN, as Orestes

engraving by Thornthwaite, after De Wilde

4d. per acting night, a level at which it seems to have stayed for the remainder of his time there.

During his tenure at Drury Lane, Farren occasionally played at Covent Garden Theatre when the management there needed someone to fill a role left unexpectedly vacant. Such performances included Cromwell in *Henry VIII* on 16 October 1778, Elwin in *Buthred* on 8, 10, and 14 December 1778 and 12 January 1779, Dollabella in *All for Love* on 19 January and 5 February 1779, and Altamont in *The Fair Penitent* on 6 April 1779 and 4 October 1779. Since Farren is not known to have played any of those three roles at Drury Lane, they must have been familiar to him from his provincial experience, which included leading roles at Bristol in the summer of 1778 and at Birmingham in the summer of 1779.

In his last season at Drury Lane, 1783–84, Farren subscribed £1 1s. to the Theatrical Fund. He acted Osmond in *Tancred and Sigismunda* for the first time on 24 April 1784 for Mrs Siddons's benefit. At his benefit on 26 April he acted Alexander in *Alexander the Great* for the first time, taking in the substantial sum of £216 19s. An assessment of Farren's abilities at that stage of his career was provided in the *Theatrical Review* for 7 October 1783, a date on which he played Myrtle in *The Conscious Lovers*:

Although we have our prejudices in favour of this gentleman's abilities in Tragedy, yet we cannot accede to their congeniality, to what are required in Genteel Comedy. His person is rather too portly, his voice too sonorous, and his manner too rigid, for that elegance, agreeableness, and pliancy, which he so particularly required for the *Bel Homme* in Comedy. His manner is peculiarly adapted to rigid, strong, and masculine parts in Tragedy. Indeed, it is our opinion, that his merits are entirely eclipsed from the notice and entertainment of the public, by not having a cast of the foremost parts in Tragedy suitable to his forte and nature. But in Myrtle, he appeared to us like a good painting in a bad light. He had the perspicuous knowledge of what the author required, and as far as his judgment, which is none of the worst, would permit him, he was accurate and discriminate.

Farren gave his last performances at Drury Lane as Othello on 21 May and as Charles in *All the World's a Stage* on 24 May 1784. The following season, discontented with his utilitarian function at Drury Lane, Farren began an engagement at Covent Garden Theatre which lasted for a decade, until his death. He made his debut there as a regular member of the company on 27 September 1784 as Othello. His lot profited somewhat by the move, with Polydore in *The Orphan*, Altamont in *The Fair Penitent*, Barnwell in *The London Merchant*, Abudah in *The Siege of Damascus*, and Jaffeir in *Venice Preserv'd* (for the first time at his benefit on 13 April 1785). He also continued in less major roles, some familiar, such as Seward in *The Hypocrite*, Tressel in *Richard III*, Axalla in *Tamerlane*, Claudio in *Much Ado About Nothing*, Cheaterly in *The Fashionable Levities*, Horatio in *Hamlet*, Lysimachus in *Alexander the Great*, and Banquo in *Macbeth*.

At Covent Garden the following season, 1785–86, during which he was paid £8 per week, Farren added a number of new roles to his repertoire, including Allworth in *A New Way to Pay Old Debts*, Charles in *The West Indian*, Woodville in *The Chapter of Accidents* for his benefit on 3 May 1786, and Teribazus in *Zenobia*. On 6 May 1786 he acted King Lear for the first time, but the press attention went to Elizabeth Brunton who was making her first attempt at Cordelia. Farren's Lear was criticized in verses by Leigh in *The New Rosciad* (1786):

With pompous gravity his accents roll,
That shew the cool emotions of his soul;
His elocution just—yet much I fear
He ne'er will rise beyond a decent Lear.
By close attention he may gain renown
From grocers, mercers, in a country town.

About the same time, he received similar treatment from John Williams writing as "Anthony Pasquin" in *The Children of Thespis*; Williams found him inflexibly turgid and rigidly dull: "Melpomene shrinks from his heroes and LEARS, And Thalia debases her smiles into snears. . . ."

Among the characters he took on during his period at Covent Garden were Alcanor in *Mahomet*, Poliphonetes in *Merope*, Lovemore in *The Way to Keep Him*, and Buckingham in *Henry VIII*. In 1786–87 his salary was £8 10s. per week; it rose to £9 in 1787–88, to £9 10s. in 1788–89, and to £10 in 1789–90. In the 1789–90 season he was still playing a repertoire of some 35 different roles in comedy, tragedy, and farce.

Although still a comparatively young man, at the age of 36, he was noticed by the *Biographical and Imperial Magazine* of May 1790 to exhibit growing signs of a poor memory. The following season, although there was no perceptible change in his status in respect to roles or his number of playing nights, his salary was reduced to £8 per week.

In the summer of 1791 Farren entered into the only engagement of his career at the Haymarket Theatre, where he made what was announced as his first appearance there on 30 July 1791 as Ribaumont in *The Surrender of Calais*, a singular role which he repeated 11 times until 29 August. Farren, it seems, had no inclination to work at acting during the summers, although on occasion he went to the north; he played Othello at Manchester during race week in August 1781, and also performed there during the same period in 1783. In 1786 he played at the Theatre Royal, Liverpool, taking £91 11s. 6d. after charges at his benefit on 7 August. He preferred to relax in a house he owned in Kingston, near the river. His professional earnings did not allow such indulgence, but the patronage of a dear friend did. According to a manuscript at the Folger Shakespeare Library which offers a brief account of the incident, one November evening upon returning to his lodgings after playing Lord Norland in *Every One Has His Fault*, Farren rescued an old gentleman from the assault of two robbers. The gentleman, immensely rich and a bachelor, showed his gratitude by bestowing a large share of his fortune upon Farren and his family, enabling the actor to purchase a fine house in Gower Street, Bedford Square, and to support a carriage, servants, and a luxurious table. The benefactor, according to the report, lived *en famille* with the Farrens until his death, whereupon Farren and his children received the remainder of his fortune.

Actually, Farren did not act Norland in Mrs Inchbald's play until 29 January 1793,

Harvard Theatre Collection

WILLIAM FARREN, as Sir Charles Easy

engraving by Thornthwaite, after De Wilde

at its premiere, although he had been living in Gower Street since the spring of 1788. For his benefit on 14 May 1789, his address was given as No 73, Gower Street. On 11 May 1791 it was listed as No 14, Lower Charlotte Street, Bedford Square, but by 2 May 1792 he was in his home at No 85, Gower Street, where he lived until his death. The account given in his obituary in the *Gentleman's Magazine* for June 1795 no doubt more closely approaches the truth about his good fortune. His benefactor seems to have been a Percival Pott, who had "had a partiality for him" since Farren's infancy. Pott lived for many years with him; he did not die before Farren but was a principal mourner at the actor's funeral.

Even without his patron, Farren did well

financially during his last years. On 2 May 1792, when he acted the role of Captain Absolute in *The Rivals* for the first time, he took a benefit profit of £256 9s. 6d. In 1792–93, he cleared £290 16s. 6d. at his benefit on 8 May, when he first played Don Felix in *The Wonder*. In the following season, at a salary of £9 per week, he took £220 when he acted Carlos in *Love Makes a Man* on 14 May 1794. While he retained a certain number of the roles he had been playing throughout his career, his repertoire during 1794–95 began to reflect his advance in years and girth. Though he continued to offer young Aimwell and Myrtle, he was also performing old Capulet in *Romeo and Juliet*.

Farren's last performance at Covent Garden was as Penius in *Bonduca* on 24 April 1795. His name was omitted from the bill of 25 April for his usual role of King Edward III in the afterpiece *Windsor Castle*, and his role of Manly in *The Provok'd Husband* was taken by Macready on 27 April. Farren died on 9 May 1795, evidently from pneumonia brought on by fishing near his retreat at Kingston. Probably he had been ill for some months, although he continued to perform, for on 4 February 1795, at the age of 41, he had drawn his will (which was witnessed by the actors William Macready and John Fawcett). A performance of *Everyone Has His Fault* was given at Covent Garden on 13 May 1795 for the benefit of his widow Mary Farren which brought her £391 6s., presumably less the usual house charges of £105. Farren was buried at St Paul, Covent Garden, two days later, on 15 May.

Farren had begun to live with Mrs Mary Orton by the middle of the 1770s. As Miss Mansell she had acted in the provinces and made her debut at Drury Lane in the role of Louisa Dudley in *The West Indian* on 26 September 1772, several years before Farren began his career at that theatre. By 1778 she was acting under the name of Mrs Farren, although there is no record of any marriage of the two performers. Before she became Farren's mistress and then his common-law wife, she seems to have been married to and separated from a Thomas Orton of Birmingham, who perhaps was a northern actor. In his will, Farren was careful to describe her as his "dear friend" Mary Orton, wife of Thomas Orton, and to specify her as the mother of his children. She survived Farren by 25 years, acting as Mrs Bell in the nineteenth century and dying at the age of 75 in Bath on 27 January 1820. See her separate notice as Mrs William Farren (1748–1820).

By Mary Mansell Orton, William Farren had eight children, four of whom died before their father did and four of whom were minors at his death. The eldest surviving child was Percival (known as Percy) Farren, born in 1780, who became a playwright and a stage manager at the Brunswick and Haymarket theatres in London in the nineteenth century. He also managed the theatre at Plymouth about 1806. He made his London debut at the Haymarket as Sir Robert Ramble on 20 April 1825. By December 1801 he was married to a Miss Perry, who acted at Edinburgh in 1800 and at Wolverhampton in 1802. She was, no doubt, the daughter of James Perry (d. 1783), a provincial actor and manager who also performed at Covent Garden in the 1750s and 1760s and is entered separately in these volumes. Her brother was James Perry (1756–1821), an actor at York and Edinburgh who is noticed in *The Dictionary of National Biography*. Percival Farren died at Brompton on 28 May 1843 at the age of 63.

The second son, William Farren, was born on 13 May 1786 and made his first appearance on the stage at the Theatre Royal, Plymouth, under his brother Percy's management, in 1806 as Sir Archy MacSarcasm in *Love à la Mode*. After acting for some years in Dublin he appeared at Covent Garden on 10 September 1818 as Sir Peter Teazle and subsequently became the leading actor of his day as well as a manager of London theatres. (See his notice in *The Dictionary of National Biography.*) In 1856 he became the second husband of Harriet Diddear Faucit (1789–1859), an actress at Covent Garden who by her first marriage to the actor Saville Faucit (d. 1853) was the mother of the well-known nineteenth-century performer Helen Faucit (1817–1898). The younger and more famous William Farren died at Brompton on 24 September 1861. By a woman whose name is not known he had two sons. One was Henry Farren (1826–1860), who acted in London and in America and is noticed in *The Dictionary of National Biography.* By his first marriage, to Ellen Smithson, he extended the dynasty of theatrical Farrens into the twentieth century through their children: Florence (d. 1878); Harriet, who married the manager Charles Moore; and Nellie (1848–1906), who married the actor Robert Soutar. The younger William Farren's other son, William (1825–1908)—the third of that name, acted in London and became the father of William Percival Farren (1853–1937), another actor.

The third son of the elder William Farren and Mary Mansell Orton was George Farren, about whom little is known beyond his father's statement in the will that his baptism was registered at St Giles in the Fields and that, according to a manuscript notation in the Folger Shakespeare Library, he became "the highly talented actuary to one of the most popular of our life insurance associations."

A fourth child, Mary, was born on 24 March 1794 and was baptized as the daughter of "William & Mary Farren" at the Kingston parish church on 4 June 1794.

At his death William Farren was reported to have been worth £800 per year independent of theatre engagements. In his will he left all his furniture, plate, jewels and other possessions to Mary Orton, as well as the income of £150 per year from his three leasehold houses at Nos 16, 41, and 73, Gower Street, for her lifetime and not liable to the control or inheritances of her husband Thomas Orton. After her death, the house at No 41, Gower Street, was to go to Percival, No 16, to William, and No 73, to George, at the attainment of their respective majorities. The four children were also to share in a sum of £500 in such proportions as their mother saw fit, and in addition Farren left £1500 to his daughter Mary, to be paid at her coming of age or on her marriage. The will was proved at London on 16 May 1795 by the trustees and executors, James Albert of Wolverhampton, druggist, and Percival Pott, his benefactor, who, it was reported, settled £6000 upon each of the Farren children.

Though not an actor of the first rank or quality, William Farren served the London theatres for over 20 years in the second walk of acting with evident sense and reliability, but without great stir. Outside the theatre he led a quiet life, one uncommonly free of travail and made comfortably agreeable by his private means and investments. His good character seems supported by the lack of scandal or attacks upon him. He enjoyed the good will and fellowship of his colleagues in a club which met regularly every Wednesday fortnight in the 1780s for dinner in the Long Room at Hampstead. Among the members were King, Quick, Mattocks, Wroughton, and Lewis. He was also a member of the so-called "School of Garrick," a group formed by old theatrical friends after the death of the great actor.

Portraits of William Farren include:

1. As a member of "the School of Garrick." By an unknown artist. In the Garrick Club.

2. In character. Painting by De Wilde. In the Garrick Club.

3. Painting by Gainsborough Dupont. In the Garrick Club.

4. Wash drawing, after Alexander Pope. In the Garrick Club.

5. Portrait engraving by W. Ridley. Published as a plate to Parson's *Minor Theatre,* 1793.

6. As Careless in *The School for Scandal*, with Smith as Charles, Yates as Sir Oliver, and Baddeley as Moses. By an unknown engraver.

7. As Sir Charles Easy in *The Careless Husband*. Engraving by Thornthwaite, after De Wilde. Published as a plate to *Bell's British Theatre*, 1791; a reversed engraving by Houston was published by William Jones, 1793.

8. As Orestes in *The Distrest Mother*. Painting by De Wilde. In the Garrick Club. An engraving by Thornthwaite was published as a plate to *Bell's British Theatre*, 1791.

Farren, Mrs William, Mary, née Mansell, later Mrs Thomas Orton, then Mrs Bell *1748–1820, actress.*

Born in Ireland in 1748, Mary Mansell may have been the sister of Dorothea "Maunsell," who at the age of 15 in 1766 entered into a notorious marriage with her singing teacher Giusto Ferdinando Tenducci. If so, then Mary's father was Thomas Maunsell, a Limerick councilman and head of "a very respectable family." In *The Irish Stage in the County Towns*, William Clark has mistakenly attributed to Dorothea Maunsell some of Mary's career and marriages.

Mary probably was the Miss Maunsell who had made her stage debut as Juliet at the Crow Street Theatre, Dublin, on 25 April 1770 and who acted Jane Shore, Cherry in *The Stratagem*, and Imoinda in *Oroonoko* at the Theatre Royal, Cork, at the end of the summer of 1770, but that person could have been Dorothea. Mary was performing at Norwich in December 1771, announced as from Dublin.

On 26 September 1772 Mary Mansell made her first appearance at Drury Lane Theatre, as Louisa Dudley in *The West Indian*. The prompter Hopkins wrote in his playhouse diary on that night: "She had a good face her figure rather Clumsey a hoarse Voice & not much simplicity." (The

Town and Country Magazine for October 1772 stated that "some years since" she had been introduced by Foote at the Haymarket as Elvira in *The Fop's Fortune*, but we find no corroboration of this report.) She next acted Juliet on 1 and 10 October, followed by Statira in *Alexander the Great* on 16 and 19 October, Charlotte in *The Gamester* on 23 October, Hero in *Much Ado About Nothing* on 3 November, Selima in *Tamerlane* on 4 November, Maria in *The London Merchant* on 9 November, and Fanny in *The Clandestine Marriage* on 16 November. Her other roles that season included Ismene in *Merope* on 13 January 1773, Teresa in *Alonzo* on 27 February, and Miss Marchant in *False Delicacy* on 16 April.

After that season at Drury Lane, in which she seems to have made no great impact on the London public, Miss Mansell acted at Bristol in the summer of 1773. She was also there in 1776 and 1777, as well as at Brighton in 1777, and at Bath in 1776–77, where she played principal roles in tragedy and serious comedy. In 1777 she left Bath to play at Edinburgh through the spring of 1778, after which she returned to Bristol. By this time probably she had already married and separated from Thomas Orton of Birmingham (who may have been the Mr Orton who worked at the Theatre Royal, Liverpool, in the summer of 1786) and had begun to live with the actor William Farren (1754–1795) who was then engaged at Drury Lane.

Evidently she had been in negotiation for an engagement at Covent Garden Theatre for 1778–79, for on 19 August 1778, Thomas Hull, acting on behalf of Harris, the manager of that theatre, addressed her as Miss Mansell at Bristol with a polite reprimand for not replying to his last letter and advised her not to trouble to make an attempt at Covent Garden for the coming season. She did, however, secure an engagement at Drury Lane—no doubt assisted by Farren—and billed as Mrs Farren she reappeared on that stage on 16 November 1778 as Zara in *The Mourning Bride*. Ironically, the management of Covent Garden called upon her in an emergency to play the Queen in *Richard III* on 7 December, and then she was back at Drury Lane on 14 December as Palmira in *Mahomet*. Her other role during the season was Leonora in *The Spanish Fryar* which she acted on 22 December 1778 and eight other times through 11 May 1779.

In the summer of 1779 Mrs Farren played at Birmingham and then joined the theatre in Glasgow for the winter of 1780. In the spring she returned to Drury Lane for a single performance on 22 April 1780 as Julia in *The Rivals*, given for Farren's benefit, in which he acted Faulkland and took net proceeds of £67 17s. 6d. During 1780–81 she made occasional appearances at Drury Lane for which she received periodic payments of £3 3s. throughout the season. Her performances included Amanda in *A Trip to Scarborough* on 17 November 1780 and 2 February and 3 March 1781, Lady Lambert in *The Hypocrite* on 26 and 31 January, Mrs Courtly in *The Generous Imposter* on 2, 5, and 13 December (in place of Mrs Baddeley), Julia in *The Rivals* on 3 April, and Melinda in *The Recruiting Officer* on 18 April.

Evidently Mrs Farren's domestic responsibilities at her comfortable home in Gower Street over the next 15 years during which she had eight children by William Farren (four of whom survived) prevented an active stage career. She did play from time to time, appearing at Crow Street in 1781–82, at Manchester in the winter season of early 1783 when she acted Portia in *The Merchant of Venice*, at Smock Alley and Fishamble Street in 1784–85, at Leeds in 1785 for Tate Wilkinson who judged her unsatisfactory, and in Mattocks's company at Manchester for the winter season beginning January 1786. She also went to play at the Stourbridge Fair in Cambridge with Palmer's company in 1786.

After acting at York in 1787–88, Mrs Farren returned to London to make her first appearance at the Haymarket Theatre on 2 July 1788 in the role of Lady Randolph in *Douglas*. That summer she also played at Richmond. Her name appeared in bills for the Brighton Theatre in the summer of 1789.

When William Farren died on 9 May 1795, at the age of 41, Mrs Farren, whom he described in his will as his "dear friend" Mary Orton, was well provided for. (See the details of the will and their children in the notice of William Farren.) At a benefit given for her at Covent Garden on 13 May 1795 she received £286.

In the nineteenth century she took the name Mrs Bell, but it is not known whether or not she remarried or performed again. She died at her lodgings in the Upper Bristol Road, Bath, on 27 January 1820 and was buried in Walcot Church, Bath, as Mary Bell, aged 72. Her obituary in the *Gentleman's Magazine* for February 1820 gave her age at the time of her death as 75 and described her generously as "Mrs Bell, formerly the celebrated and beautiful Miss Mansell, of the Bath and London theatres. She possessed a considerable share of professional merit, and in the expression of the pathetic, and the display of the higher passions, she has seldom been excelled." According to Genest she had been "latterly supported in part by the kindness of her friends," a curious circumstance in view of the comfortable income Farren had left and the substantial wealth enjoyed by her children.

Farrer, Mrs [fl. 1788–1789], *actress, singer.*

Mrs Farrer made her first appearance on any stage on 22 December 1788 at the Haymarket Theatre playing Arpasia in *Tamerlane the Great* for her benefit. She turned up at the same playhouse again on 23 February 1789 for another single performance, playing Pulcheria in *Theodosius* and Lady

Minikin in *Bon Ton* and singing "The Noon Tide Air" from *Comus*.

Farrinell. *See* FARINEL.

Farrol. *See* FARRELL.

Farusi, Zanetta. *See* CASANOVA, SIGNORA GAETANO.

Fashion, Joseph *c. 1646–1685, violinist.*

The violinist Joseph Fashion was born about 1646 and was a member of the King's Musick at least as early as 24 November 1666, when he played in the band of 24 violins under Louis Grabu. His initial appointment may have been without salary, for a warrant in the Lord Chamberlain's accounts dated 1 May 1668 granted £20 to Fashion as a replacement for Henry Smith. The records over the years show Fashion receiving extra stipends for attending the royal family outside London. On 6 November 1674, for example, he and five other musicians were paid a total of £54 for serving the Queen at Hampton Court from 17 September to 24 October 1674, and from 27 March to 17 April 1676 Fashion was paid 5s. daily for attending the King at Newmarket.

The accounts contain many other references to the violinist: on 30 March 1672 he was paid £12 for a violin; on 15 February 1675 he played in the court masque *Calisto*; on 24 March 1676 he and William Fashion (his father or brother perhaps) were named executors and residuary legatees of the estate of the musician Thomas Fitz; on 8 May 1677 he and violinists from the court who had been performing at "the playhouse" (Drury Lane, probably, but perhaps the court theatre) petitioned against Charles Killigrew for dismissing them; and on 13 December 1679 he was cited as receiving a salary of £46 10s. 10d. annually.

The parish registers of St Andrew, Holborn, contain several references to Fashion.

On 1 April 1665 Joseph "Fashen," gentleman, aged "22 & up," married Anne Terry, a spinster about 22 years old, with her mother's consent. The couple lived at Mr Hyne's house above Warwick House in Holborn when they baptized their daughter Katherine on 29 October 1668. Within a few years Anne Terry Fashion died, and Joseph remarried. On 17 July 1676, describing himself as a widower about 34 years old, Fashion married Mrs Avis Willis, a widow of about 30 from the parish of St Sepulchre. They baptized a son Benjamin on 16 August 1677 who had been born "in High Holborne neer Warwick House," and on 22 August 1678 they baptized a son Charles. By his first or second wife Joseph Fashion had other children, as his will attests, but their baptismal records have not been found.

On 26 January 1685 Fashion made his will; it was witnessed by William Fashion and Elizabeth Poole. The Lord Chamberlain's accounts stated that by 31 August 1685 he had drowned at sea and his son Joseph, a countertenor, was given a place in the private music of James II. The nature of the elder Fashion's sea voyage was not indicated in the court accounts, but it is clear that he sailed in the King's service. His will was proved on 16 March 1686 by his widow Avis. Fashion left £100 out of the arrears of his salary to each of his children: Joseph, Benjamin, Anne, Katherine, and Avis. The rest of his estate he left to his widow. He added a note to his will to the effect that if the King should bestow a place at court on his son Joseph, the £100 bequest should be divided among the other children. That, presumably, was done.

Fashion, Joseph [*fl. 1676–1688*], *singer.*

The earliest mention of Joseph Fashion the younger in legal documents was in the will of the musician Thomas Fitz, dated 24 March 1676; young Joseph was Fitz's godson and received £20. In 1685 both the elder and younger Joseph Fashion were on a sea voyage in the King's service, and the elder Fashion was drowned. On 31 August of that year young Joseph, a countertenor, was officially appointed to the private music of James II, though his presence on the sea voyage indicates that he had already been active in the royal musical service. When the elder Fashion's will was proved by his widow on 16 March 1686, young Joseph may have been cut out of a bequest, for his father had indicated that if Joseph were given a place at court, the £100 arrears in salary of the elder Fashion should be divided among the other four Fashion children, Benjamin, Anne, Katherine, and Avis, and not all five.

From 16 August to 6 October 1685 Joseph Fashion the younger attended the King and Queen at Windsor and Hampton Court; from 19 May to 16 August and from 13 September to 11 October 1687 he received 3s. daily for similar service at Windsor; and from 24 July to 20 September 1687 [sic] he received 6s. daily for singing at Windsor.

Fashion, Thomas [fl. 1689], musician.

In *The King's Musick* Cart de Lafontaine cites a Lord Chamberlain's warrant dated 25 March 1689 which lists Thomas Fashion as a court musician under William III receiving £30 annually. Since that is the only reference to Thomas, perhaps it is an error for the younger Joseph Fashion who would, indeed, have been a likely candidate for a position under the new King.

"Fat." See HALL, JOHN d. 1734, and HARLEY, "FAT."

Faucet or **Faucit.** See FAWCETT.

Faulconer. See FALKNER and FAULKNER.

Faulkner. See also FALKNER.

Faulkner, Miss E. [fl. 1748], dancer. See FALKNER, ANNA MARIA.

Faulkner, Samuel d. 1826, actor, manager.

In his *Theatric Tourist* James Winston boasted of bringing out Samuel Faulkner on the professional stage after having found him in training at the private theatre in Tottenham Court Road. Winston was no doubt referring to the fact that Faulkner had acted Douglas on 15 September 1797 at the Richmond Theatre, then under Winston's management. But Samuel had already made his professional debut on the London stage, billed as "A Young Gentleman," at Drury Lane Theatre on 21 December 1796 in the role of Orestes in *The Distrest Mother*. Faulkner's name is found for the role in a manuscript list of new performers kept by J. P. Kemble. The *European Magazine* in January 1797 reported that he was from Dublin. Despite the opinion in the *Monthly Mirror* that Orestes was an inappropriate character to select for a trial part, the writer expected that Faulkner would "attain to a very enviable rank in his profession." Received with "the loudest applause," he showed a neat, if not heroic figure, and a powerful voice, with a round and mellow tone which sometimes clouded his articulation. His action was not especially graceful.

The management of Drury Lane, however, seems not to have been impressed by Faulkner's debut, for he was not thereafter engaged by them. On 9 February 1797 he acted the title role in *The Earl of Warwick* at the Haymarket Theatre, identified as the person who had played Orestes. He made a single appearance at Covent Garden Theatre on 12 June 1799 as a principal character in *Lover's Vows*, for the benefit of the General Lying-In Hospital. He appeared once more at the Haymarket on 22 August 1799, this time as Sir Edward Mortimer in *The Iron Chest*, after which he left London for the provinces.

At Bath in January 1801 Faulkner acted King John and was called a "clever young actor" by the *Monthly Mirror*. Sometime in March 1801 he joined the Manchester Theatre where he was given some advice by the provincial correspondent for the *Monthly Mirror*, who observed that while his acting had many beauties it also had many faults:

He has an uncouth manner of speaking, upon his first entrance, or when delivering those passages which bespeak the softer or more tender emotions of the heart. When the conflicts of passion call forth the actor's exertions, a change is wrought in his utterance, that evidently shews a power, at all times, to enrich his voice with a smoothness. If Mr. F. wishes to succeed as Rolla, Richard the Third, Octavian, and Leonatus Posthumus, I recommend him to assume a loftier deportment — to hold up his head, and to tread the stage with more becoming dignity.

In the following season at Manchester, the *Monthly Mirror* provided a good account of his acting in the role of Rolla in *Pizarro*:

In the address to the soldiers, [he] is all nerve, and contrasts the motives of warfare with fine tone, and judicious point. The latter part, "The throne we honour," &c. is peculiarly glowing. In rallying the soldiers, his mode of coming on is strikingly martial, and the rebuke delivered with uncommon energy. In the prison scene, the appeal to the feelings of the centinel is forcible and pathetic, and the soliloquy, "Oh holy Nature," most judiciously varied. — With *Alonzo*, his friendly earnestness, his tender anxiety, are ably depicted, and in the scene with *Elvira* — "That soldier, mark me, is a man," &c. cannot be easily surpassed. The soliloquy in the tent of Pizarro loses none of its point; but the greatest beauty of the whole performance is his manner of pleading for Alonzo's child. The exclamation "Man, man!" and the fine and piercing transition, "Art thou a man?" — the rapid, warm, and distinct delivery of the speech, "Pizarro, thou hast set my heart on fire," and, above all, the melting, fervent pathos with which he utters the speech, "In humble agony I sue to

you," gives at once the stamp of greatness to the performance. Throughout, his manner is original, his situations naturally chosen, and his strength of intellect apparent.

In the scene where he is Pizarro's prisoner, he is natural and affecting in his manner, and sensibly spirited in his delivery. The description of the blessings of which he had been made the happy instrument, affords a sufficient proof (were there no other) of a just and strong discrimination. In the last act, his martial entrance, and earnest combat, evince Alonzo's skill.

According to a manuscript in the Harvard Theatre Collection, Faulkner had married an actress named Miss Campion (perhaps the Miss A. Campion who acted at Dublin in the 1790s and was the sister of Maria Campion, who was later Mrs Alexander Pope the second). Probably this was the woman who acted as Mrs Faulkner with him in Manchester in 1801 and 1802. Faulkner went to Birmingham by 1803 but she stayed on at Manchester acting as Mrs Reed. In commenting on her miserable representation of Cora in *Pizarro*, the *Townsman* (Manchester, 1803) called her "Mrs. Reed, last year the wife of Mr Faulkner, who is now playing at Birmingham." Faulkner later became the manager of the theatre at York.

Samuel may have been the Faulkner who acted with a Mrs Faulkner in the company at Sunderland in January 1815. Either he had become reconciled with his wife or had married (or lived with) another woman in his later years, for a woman purported to be his wife was reported by the *Edinburgh Magazine* in June 1823 to have died on 3 June 1823, probably at Edinburgh. Faulkner himself died at Leeds on 1 April 1826, according to the *European Magazine* for May 1826, an assertion which can hardly be reconciled with the notation in a manuscript at the Harvard Theatre Collection that he "committed suicide by drowning himself in the Ouse, at York." Possibly Samuel Faulkner was related to Thomas

Faulkner (1775–1847), who made his debut at Dublin in 1799 and eventually went to America in 1817, acting in Charleston, New York, and Philadelphia until his death in the last city on 6 March 1847.

Fausan, Signor *fl.* 1740–1742*,* *dancer.*

Signor and Signora Fausan danced *Le Boufon* and, with others, *Les Jardinières Suédois* at Drury Lane on 29 November 1740 and subsequent dates. In January 1741 the *Gentleman's Magazine* contained a glowing report on the Fausans:

An intimate Friend desired that I would go with him to *Drury-Lane* Playhouse to see the celebrated Comic Dancers, Signior and Signiora *Fausan,* who were become the Topic of all polite Conversation from their Performances, which are as extraordinary as they are new.

I was surpriz'd on my entring into the Pit to find it almost full, but was inform'd by my Friend, the House had been crowded ever since *Shakespear's* Play of, *As you like it,* had been acted, and these Dancers had perform'd. . . . At the end of the third Act these Foreign Dancers were to perform a Comic Dance call'd, *Le Buffon,* or the *Idiot:* My Expectation was rais'd to the height; but at their Entrance on the Stage, they alarm'd me by an inexpressive Agility and descriptive Action, Look and Motion, which were all perform'd with such mimic Variety, that I defy the most severe Cynick to say that they wou'd not at least raise in him an agreeable Surprize, to see all the Attitudes, Oddities, and mock Gesticulations of the two Idiots, who may be suppos'd to be in Love with one another. It is not any distortion of Body, or unnatural Transportation of the Limbs which they exhibit to the View, but the extravagant Idiotry, which the Passions of Love, Disdain, Joy, Resentment, would on a real Occasion actuate on the Personages they represent: Nor do they so manage their Dance that it is ungraceful; they take Opportunities to shew by Actions and Movements, that in their Comic Humour they have an Elegancy. This Performance therefore, on Reflection, appear'd to me, instead of an unnatural Extravaganza, to be founded on the nicest Observations of human Nature, and prove Signior and Signiora to be Persons of good Judgment, as well as great Agility. At the End of the Play they danced another Comic Dance, call'd the Swedish Gardiners, where there is a Courtship in Lowlife describ'd with much Humour and Expression of the Passions; for the Variations of the Countenances are so new, so comic, and at the same time so excellently adapted to the Story, that no Spectator can be so dull, as not to know what they intend should be meant, as well as if it were express'd in Words.

The Fausans continued pleasing London audiences throughout the 1740–41 season in such other specialty dances as *The Lunaticks, Le Chasse de Dian, The Enchanted Garden* (in which they appeared as a harlequin man and woman), *Les Masons, Les Matelots, Les Egyptiens,* and *L'Hydropique amoureux.*

On 9 February 1741 Signora Fausan was given a benefit, for which she advertised tickets available at Mr Cheeke's the apothecary in Bow Street; at Signor Fausan's benefit on 16 January he made tickets available at his lodgings at the corner of Martlet Court and Bow Street—apparently the same address. The Fausans made their last appearance of the season at Drury Lane on 20 May and then danced at Lee and Woodward's Tottenham Court booth on 4 August before returning to the Continent.

On 21 October 1741 they were back in London, advertised as lately arrived from Paris. At Drury Lane they revived several of their dances from the previous season and also appeared in *Le Généreux corsaire, Les Satires puni, La Foullies, Le Petit Scaramouch,* and *Arlequin petit-maître.* Their last English appearance was on 13 March 1742, by which time they had created, said the bills, 12 new dances for their London admirers.

The Fausans brought the Drury Lane

manager Fleetwood much joy. In 1743 *Queries upon Queries* asked:

Did not his Italian and French people last season stand him upwards of £70 per week? And what did they contribute to the profits of the season? . . . Did not the performances of the Fausans contribute more to the profits of a season than any actor whatsoever? And what was the condition of the theatre before their arrival, when supported by actors only?

In 1744 Fleetwood admitted that more money came into the theatre from the appearances of the Fausans than from all the plays together and thus helped to pay the actors' salaries. The Fausans, though they seem not to have returned to England after 1742, were remembered there about 1750 when music by Hasse to some of their dances was published and their names were cited in the titles.

Fausan, Signora [*fl.* 1740–1742], *dancer. See* FAUSAN, SIGNOR.

"Faustina, Signora," stage name of Faustina Bordoni, later Signora Johann Adolph Hasse *1700?–1781, singer.*

Faustina Bordoni was born, according to some sources, in 1700 at Venice; other sources date her birth in 1693 or 1689. She was from a noble Venetian family and studied singing under Gasparini. In 1716 she made her debut in *Ariodante* at the Teatro Grimani di San Giovanni Grisostomo in Venice. Her success was immediate, and in the years that followed Faustina appeared in *Eumene, Alessandro severo, Ambleto, Astarto, Ormisda,* and many other operas. She excited admiration in Florence, Naples, Bologna, and Vienna, as well as Venice, and was dubbed the "nuova Sirena."

As early as 1719 she sang with Bernacchi and Cuzzoni, and by 1724 she could command a fee of 15,000 florins in Vienna. London had heard of her fame as early as

Civica Raccolta delle Stampe Achille Bertarelli, Castello Sforzesco, Milan

SIGNORA FAUSTINA

engraving by Zucchi, after Torelli

1723, for the *London Journal* on 30 March of that year had reported the rumor that Faustina was coming to England for the following opera season. And as early as 18 March 1724 the singer was being imitated by musicians in London; on that date William Corbett played the viol de venere "after the new manner of Signora Faustina," and at the same concert Rochetti sang in imitation of her florid style. But it was not until later in 1724 that Handel began negotiations to bring her to London. She fulfilled her engagement at the Vienna court theatre, and by 31 August 1725 the *Daily Journal* in London reported that she would come from Italy the following winter to sing in London for the extraordinarily high fee of £2500.

Faustina's London debut did not come until 5 May 1726, and her salary was £500 less than had been reported. Her splendid mezzo-soprano voice was first heard in the role of Rossana in Handel's *Alessandro* at the King's Theatre in the Haymarket. The title role was taken by the eminent castrato Senesino, and Lisaura was sung by Faustina's chief rival, Signora Cuzzoni. All three singers received £2000 a year.

In the 1726–27 season Faustina sang Berenice in *Lucio Vero* on 7 January 1727, Alceste in *Admeto* on 31 January (Lady Cowper wrote in her libretto: "she is the devil of a singer"), and Ermione in *Astianatte* on 6 May (following a bout with measles in April). When *Astianatte* was repeated on 6 June a near riot occurred. The *British Journal* on 10 June reported that

a great Disturbance happened at the Opera, occasioned by the Partisans of the Two Celebrated Rival Ladies, Cuzzoni and Faustina. The Contention at first was only carried on by Hissing on one Side, and Clapping on the other; but proceeded at length to Catcalls, and other great Indecencies: And notwithstanding the Princess Caroline was present no Regards were of Force to restrain the Rudenesses of the Opponents.

The factions, led by the Countess of Pembroke (for Signora Cuzzoni) and the Countess of Burlington (for Faustina), apparently broke up performances even earlier than 6 June, and their unseemly behavior and the growing jealousy they encouraged between the two singers led to a number of satirical pamphlets. *The Devil to pay at St. James's: or, A full and true Account of a most horrible and bloody battle between Madam Faustina and Madam Cuzzoni, etc.* appeared in June 1727; it was attributed to Dr Arbuthnot, but he seems not to have written it. The following month brought forth *The Contre Temps; or, Rival Queans*, a playlet in which the singers bait one another with insults and finally engage in a hair-pulling fight, with the followers of each cheering them on with catcalls and whistles.

The warring factions were in time to lead the opera to ruin, but the rival singers continued singing together during the 1727–28 season. Faustina portrayed Zidiana

Harvard Theatre Collection

SIGNORA FAUSTINA

engraving by Grignion, after Rosalba

in *Teuzzone*, Pulcheria in *Riccardo I*, Emira in *Siroe*, and Elisa in *Tolomeo*. She also appeared at the Crown and Anchor on 22 November 1727 to participate in a St Cecilia's Day concert. On 1 June 1728 the final season of the Academy of Music operas ended, and the company disbanded. Faustina is said by Prévost to have made £1800 from her benefits.

Faustina returned to Venice, though there were attempts to lure both her and Cuzzoni back to London. Rolli in London wrote to Senesino in Venice on 21 December 1728 (or possibly 1729). Otto Deutsch in his *Handel* translated the letter:

On your return here you will be in no need of a protector: you will find two Brothers [Rolli and his brother] who will be no less friendly to you and who do not lack good behaviour and courage. If Faustina thought so also, she would meet with fewer expenses and less inconvenience, indeed also fewer complaints. But I do not want to expatiate on this subject. I know perfectly well that she has been false to me, and that I shall trim my sails according to the wind. What will she say if the dishonest Barbarian [Handel] turns the tables on her? That is what I prophesy he will do.

In another letter to Senesino on 4 February 1729 Rolli indicated that the King would provide funds in support of the opera if Cuzzoni and Faustina could be prevailed upon to return to London, and he would put up money for Cuzzoni alone but not for Faustina alone.

At the time Rolli was writing, Faustina and Senesino were singing in Venice, but their houses were inferior to those at the rival theatre where the great Farinelli was performing. Rolli hinted in his letter at the close ties Faustina had made in Vienna with the Empress, "who used to be very fond of her." But Rolli was prejudiced against Faustina, for it was she who had caused a rift between him and Handel.

Faustina married the eminent composer Johann Adolph Hasse in 1730 in Venice. They had met there in 1729, and in 1730 Hasse had written two operas for her: *Artaserse* and *Dalisa*. In 1731 Hasse was appointed director of the opera and kapellmeister at the court of Augustus II in Dresden. He was paid 500 ducats for his services, but his wife received twice that amount. As Signora Hasse, Faustina was a success in her husband's *Cleofide* on 13 September 1731. In the years that followed the couple toured to Venice, Milan, and Naples, returning frequently to their base in Dresden. On 7 October 1745 Faustina sang in Hasse's *Arminio* at the command of Frederick the Great, and though by 1747 Faustina was no longer the attraction she once had been, she still performed, and in 1750 she and her husband were a great success in Paris.

When it became necessary in 1763 for the court opera in Dresden to be curtailed to save money, the Hasses retired to Vienna. There they remained until 1775, after which they returned to Faustina's native Venice. She died there on 4 November 1781, and Hasse died on 16 December 1783.

Dr Burney wrote glowingly of Faustina:

She, in a manner, invented a new kind of singing, by running divisions with a neatness and velocity which astonished all who heard her. She had the art of sustaining a note longer, in the opinion of the public, than any other singer, by taking her breath imperceptibly. Her beats and trills were strong and rapid; her intonation perfect; and her professional perfections were enhanced by a beautiful face, a symmetric figure, though of small stature, and a countenance and gesture on the stage which indicated an entire intelligence of the several parts she had to represent . . . Apostolo Zeno [in speaking of her departure from Vienna, said] "whatever good fortune she meets with, she merits it all by her courteous and polite manners, as well as talents, with which she has enchanted and gained the esteem and affection of the whole Court."

Arteaga also admired her brilliant embellishments and mentioned the rapidity of her execution, and Tosi in his *Observations* in 1743 (translated by Galliard) commented on her "prodigious Felicity in executing."

Portraits of Faustina include a pastel by Rosalba in the Royal Gallery, Dresden; a photographic reproduction, published at Venice in 1930, is in the Civica Raccolta delle Stampe Achille Bertorelli, Milan. Engravings of the Rosalba were made by C. Grignion and an anonymous engraver. The Grignion was used by Hawkins in his *General History*. The anonymous engraving was reversed and paired with a similar one of Signora Cuzzoni and was probably the source of the picture of Faustina in the *London Magazine* of December 1777. Faustina was also pictured in an engraving by Lorenzo Zucchi, after a portrait by Stefano Torelli. In the Milan collection is a portrait by an unknown engraver.

Faux. *See also* **FAWKES** *and* **VAUX.**

Faux, John *d. 1798, doorkeeper.*

On 30 October 1790 John Faux was added to the paylist at Drury Lane as a house servant at a daily salary of 1s. 6d. He seems to have served the theatre regularly until his death in 1798 and was cited each spring as one whose benefit tickets would be accepted at the playhouse. The *Gentleman's Magazine* in November 1798 contained an obituary dated 27 October saying he died "Suddenly, while on his duty at the theatre-royal, Drury-lane, where he was a door-keeper, Mr. John Faux, of Suffolk-street, Charing-cross, formerly an eminent silversmith."

Though it seems unlikely, perhaps the following concerned the doorkeeper: on 4 November 1798 administration of the estate of a John Faux, late of Hyde, in the parish of Minchenhampton, Gloucestershire, widower, was granted to Richard Webb, husband of Martha Webb, a lunatic and the natural and lawful sister and only next of kin. The estate, valued at £5000 was to be used for the benefit of Martha Webb.

Another house servant at Drury Lane named Faux was cited in the theatre accounts in 1802–3, 1806, and 1811–12 as a ticket taker; he may have been the son of John Faux.

Favar. *See* GUIARDELE, FAVRE.

Faviere, Mimi *[fl. 1755?–1774],* *dancer.*

The managers of the King's Theatre announced on 23 October 1773 the engagement of Mimi and Nina Faviere of Florence as principal serious dancers for the 1773–74 season. Perhaps the pair were sisters, though occasionally during the season Mimi was advertised as Madame, which suggests the possibility of a mother-daughter relationship. In *The Pre-Romantic Ballet* Marian Hannah Winter says that Mimi "Favier" was the daughter of the dancer Jean Favier and was abducted by the ballet master Antoine Pitrot while on a trip to Paris (in

1755?) with her father. The child Mimi had by Pitrot was Anna Favier, called Pitrot. There is a possibility that the Nina Faviere who danced in London in 1773–74 was Mimi's daughter Anna.

On 15 November 1773 the opera at the King's Theatre in London was postponed, for the Faviere ladies had not yet arrived, and on 20 November the managers announced that the dancers were in London but too fatigued to perform. Their first appearance was on 30 November in a new "Grand Heroic-Comic-Pantomimical Ballet" called *Orfeo e Euridice*; Mimi danced Euridice and Nina portrayed an unnamed character. In addition to performances of *Orfeo*, during the rest of the season Mimi danced in a Persian pantomimical ballet entitled *Adventures of the Harem of Ispahan*, an heroic ballet called *The Tempest*, and *Les Faunes vainques*.

Nina was the more active of the pair and appeared not only in all of the pieces already mentioned but a number of others: a *Grand Serious Ballet*, a *Pastoral Ballet*, *L'Embarass du choix*, and several generally titled ballets. On 12 May 1774 she was granted a solo benefit.

Faviere, Nina *[fl. 1773–1774],* *dancer. See* FAVIERE, MIMI.

Favre Guiardele. *See* GUIARDELE, FAVRE.

Fawcett, John *d. 1793, actor, singer.*

John Fawcett the elder was born in High Wycombe and apprenticed to Dr Thomas Augustine Arne, who taught him singing and obtained for him a place at Drury Lane Theatre. There he first appeared in the juvenile role of Filch in *The Beggar's Opera* on 23 September 1760. Filch was his most recurrent part that season and for the next several years though in that first season he was allowed also to play Balthazar in *Much Ado About Nothing*, Loveless in *The Double Disappointment*, Palemon in *The Chaplet*, and a variety of unspecified "Principal Characters" and "Vocal Parts" in afterpieces. He shared his benefit on 13 May 1761 singing "A New Song, Set by Dr Arne" and "If o'er the Cruel, Tyrant Love" from Arne's oratorio *Artaxerxes*.

His roles were no more various the following season and, perhaps irritated at the lack of opportunity, he left Drury Lane after only one performance in the 1762–63 season—Loveless in the afterpiece *The Double Disappointment*, on 28 September —and apparently he left town, too. He is said by contemporary accounts to have acted at some time in Ireland and perhaps that is where he went for the summer. He was not seen again in London until 21 October 1763, at Covent Garden this time, as one of the Harvest Men in *Harlequin Sorcerer*, in which he sang or danced (or both) 30 times between October and early December, with relief only on 15 November as a member of the chorus in *Comus*.

Probably his teacher Arne's influence rescued him temporarily from those doldrums, for Arne's oratorio *Artaxerxes* was scheduled at Covent Garden on dates in December and January 1763–64 and, when after the first performance Mattocks for some reason defected, Fawcett was given his part of Rimenes, which he sang on 30 December and 1 January. After the turn of the year he sang an Aethiopian in *Perseus and Andromeda* and Damaetas in *Midas* and took an unspecified part in *The Shepherd's Artifice*.

From 21 May 1764 to 23 September 1766 Fawcett was absent from the bills of the London patent theatres, though he sang with Tenducci, Champness, Mrs Cornelys, and Miss Brent in Arne's oratorio *Judith* at the King's Theatre on 15 February 1765 and was engaged by Love for the first season of the new theatre at Richmond, Surrey, the following summer. "The Judicious Choice," as sung by him at Richmond, was published in the *Jester's Magazine* in January 1766. He sang also at Ranelagh in the

summer of 1765. Perhaps during some part of the blank period of 28 months which follows in the record he was (again?) in Ireland. He was engaged at Richmond once more in the summer of 1766, and again the *Jester's Magazine* published songs he sang there, among them some of the first songs written by James Hook. *The Catalogue of Printed Music in the British Museum* dates publication of Hook's *Come rouze Brother sportsmen* (as sung by "Fawcet" at Richmond) 1767.

Fawcett returned to Drury Lane on 23 September 1766 and subscribed his guinea to the theatrical fund. He opened with Guildenstern in *Hamlet* and on 30 September was Paris in *Romeo and Juliet* but almost immediately dropped from sight.

Fawcett had a full season at Drury Lane in 1767–68 and a much expanded repertoire. He was paid £1 10*s*. per week. He added Dorilas in *Cymon*, Quaver in *The Virgin Unmask'd*, Loveless in *The Double Disappointment*, Lord Brilliant in *The Register Office*, Lennox in *Macbeth*, Coxcomb in *The Absent Man*, Damon in *Merlin*, Freeman in *High Life Below Stairs*, and Sir Charles Freeman in *The Stratagem*. The summer of 1769 found him again at Richmond. He played at the King Street Theatre, Bristol, in the summers of 1773 and 1774 and was also in Bristol on 20 July 1774 and perhaps later that summer. In 1775–76, 1781, 1786, and probably other years he was back at Richmond. In 1780 he played for a while at York.

John Fawcett the elder, despite his good voice and evident flexibility, rose slowly and not very high. In his entire 33 years in the theatre he remained a good example of the "useful," across-the-spectrum secondary or supporting performer—always dependable, coming on season after season, now a straight dramatic performer, now a singer either in chorus or entr'acte solo, most at home in comedy but seen often in sober small parts in tragedy and melodrama, capable of oratorio but not above pantomime.

The Theatrical Review held him to be "a very glaring instance" of a "feeble" performer in 1771. In 1786 the caustic "Anthony Pasquin" in the second edition of *The Children of Thespis* sneered

> *the Great Man is rich; and he labours to*
>   *shew it,*
> *And thinks by such Madness, [foppishness] the world will all know it.*
> *Oh! bless'd independence!—for* Fawcet
>   *has clear*
> *Twelve Pounds seven Shillings and Sixpence a-year;*
> *Besides some expectancies yet in* futuro
> *From an uncle who lives by the* Tempests
>   *in* Truro.
> . . . .
> *In* Dion *he fidgets, and foams at the gallery,*
> *'Till tragedy laughs at the comic raillery;*
> *When he struts, such embargoes are laid*
>   *on his motion,*
> *You'd swear he was costive, and wanted*
>   *a potion.*

In *A Pin Basket to the Children of Thespis* (1797), "Pasquin" (John Williams) pictured Fawcett as a crowd pleaser who was always capable of being first rate but who never quite achieved it:

> *Nimble FAWCET by dashing, and*
>   *splashing, and noise,*
> *And o'ercharging his lungs, draws down*
>   *peals of applause;*
> *He spits out heroics and dramatiz'd fibs,*
> *As if he'd been gorg'd but with* crackers
>   *and squibs*
> . . . .
> *So he copies gay LEWIS's fidgets and*
>   *struts,*
> *And will steal all the husks though he*
>   *can't split the nuts:*
> . . . .
> *Yet there's strength in the soil, could his*
>   *wit give it birth,*
> *But the stones of conceit hide the fat of*
>   *the earth.*

Yet most observers agreed with the *Dramatic Censor,* which, in reviewing his benefit performance as Johnny Atkins in *A Mogul Tale* at the Haymarket on 10 September 1800, claimed that "Whenever Fawcett moves in his proper sphere, as a comic actor, he is never known to fail."

Fawcett's inventiveness evidently extended to props and costumes. A note by one O. S., in a Folger manuscript ledger reads:

Mr. Fawcett told me that, when he played Falstaff, in Henry 4th for the first time, in the country, he thought to relieve himself from the heat and fatigue occasioned by the enormous stuffed belly worn in that character. He had one made in slight basket work, which being of the usual dimensions and at the same time light and cool, seemed to answer the purpose uncommonly well, and he felt highly satisfied with the success of his invention. In the 5th Act, where he fell upon his face at the sight of Hotspur, he broke every rib in his body, and rose from the ground as flat as a pancake. His whimsical appearance, excited a burst of laughter from the audience which so confused and disconcerted him, that endeavouring to remedy the accident, he squeezed and pulled himself into such a variety of odd shapes and acute angles, as increased the mirth of the audience into shouts of laughter and applause, and finally obliged him to seek shelter in his Dressing Room, severely suffering from a disordered state of the stomach.

He seems to have pleased audiences with his comic fooleries and his pleasant tenor voice. (Burney, perhaps mistakenly, placed Fawcett among the countertenors when he sang at the 1784 Handel Memorial Concerts at Westminster Abbey and the Pantheon.) He certainly earned the £2 weekly which he seems to have been given from 1775–76 through 1792–93. He lived in the same unfashionable lodgings at No 14, Craven Buildings, Drury Lane from before 1776 until at least 1788. He seems to have saved his money and died with a competence and some property.

Among the many other roles Fawcett learned in his tenure at Drury Lane, where he was fixed until a few months before his death, were Friendly in *Flora*, Truman in *The Clandestine Marriage*, Jaques de Bois in *As You Like It*, a Knight in *The Countess of Salisbury*, Balin in *Zingis*, Mervin in *The Maid of the Mill*, the Music Master in *Catherine and Petruchio*, Eustace in *Love in a Village*, Salanio in *The Merchant of Venice*, Selim in *The Mourning Bride*, Stratocles in *Tamerlane*, Tranio in *Amphytrion*, Lord Bardolph in *1 Henry IV*, Harman in *Lionel and Clarissa*, Joe in *The King and the Miller of Mansfield*, Friendly in *Hob in the Well*, Vincent and Hilliard in *The Ladies' Frolick*, Cheatwell in *The Brave Irishman*, Towborn in *The Country Madcap in London*, Storey in *The Committee*, Merchant in *Timon of Athens*, Hymen in *The Tempest*, Captain Loveit in *Miss in Her Teens*, Littlestock in *The Gamesters*, Curan in *King Lear*, Faulkner in *The Heroine of the Cave*, Mungo in *The Padlock*, Buckingham in *The Earl of Warwick*, Simkin in *The Deserter*, Jenkins in *The Cobler*, Cabinet in *The Funeral*, Swab in *Phebe*, Noodle in *Tom Thumb*, Scapethrift in *Old City Manners*, Robin in *The Waterman*, Sir William Blunt in *1 Henry IV*, a Forester in *The Law of Lombardy*, the Soothsayer in *Julius Caesar*, Norfolk in *Richard III*, Balthazar and Montague in *Romeo and Juliet*, Mercury in *Harlequin's Invasion*, Constable in *The Critic*, Lovewit in *The Alchemist*, Sir Harry Atall in *The Double Gallant*, Linco in *Linco's Travels*, Elliot in *Venice Preserv'd*, Salisbury in *Edward the Black Prince*, Barnardine in *Measure for Measure*, Nettle in *Liberty Hall*, one of the "Advocatori" in *The Fox*, Raymond in *The Carmelite*, Furnace in *A New Way to Pay Old Debts*, Corea in *Braganza*, Gamut in *The Englishman in Paris*, Corrigidore in *She Wou'd and She Wou'd Not*, Old Matthew in *Richard Coeur de Lion*, Old Cockney in

The Romp, Formal in *Every Man in His Humour*, Sir Thomas Lovel in *Henry VIII*, Notary in *The Pannel*, Paulet in *Mary Queen of Scots*, Sir John English in *The Farm House*, Don Carlos in *Don Juan*, the Constable in *Henry V*, Miller in *Belphegor*, a Planter in *Oroonoko*, and a Taylor in *A Trip to Scarborough*.

Fawcett played 20 roles in 99 appearances in 1790–91. He acted 38 characters in 109 nights in 1791–92, speaking also many prologues; and he played 35 characters on 72 nights in 1792–93, his final season. He was Moses in *The School for Scandal* at the Haymarket (the dispossessed Drury Lane company being there temporarily) on 4 June 1793, for a benefit shared with Burton. It was his last appearance on a stage. According to Ralph Wewitzer, who was in the Drury Lane company in 1792–93, Fawcett died in October 1793, and Isaac Reed's "Notitia Dramatica" in the British Museum said the date was 9 October.

Fawcett had married Sarah Plaw at Fulham on 24 September 1767. (She was in the Richmond company in the summer of 1781 and had a benefit on 1 August. A loose page from some theatrical account book of 1795–96 records that she received £96 10s. for the season [extra-illustrated Genest in the Harvard Theatre Collection].) To the couple on 29 August 1768 was born a son John, who went on the stage at 18 and eventually far surpassed his father both in abilities and fame.

In a will signed 30 March 1792 and witnessed by Thomas Plaw, Henry Ward, and Isaac Scott, Fawcett, "Of the Theatre Royal Drury Lane and residing in Brownlow Street Long Acre in the Parish of Saint Giles in the ffields . . . Comedian," wished to be "decently interred in the Burial Ground belonging to Saint Georges Bloomsbury next to my late Grandson William ffawcett and that with as little Expence as may be. . . ."

He left freehold property, a house "with

the Outbuildings Yards Gardens and appurtenances thereunto belonging situate . . . in High Wycombe otherwise Chiping [*sic*] Wycombe in the County of Burks" and "household ffurniture jewels watches plate china prints Linnen and Wearing Apparel" to his "dear Wife Sarah Fawcett," with his son John as residuary legatee. This sequence of inheritance was requested also in regard to the income from £870 3-percent "Consolidated Bank Annuities now Standing in my name (as residing in Saint Paul Covent Garden) on the Books of . . . the Bank of England. . . ." Here occurs a curious proviso: his wife was to obtain this part of the property only if she "never lives or resides with her Mother Mary Plaw widow. . . ." Income from £365 invested in these funds went to his daughter "ffrances Elizabeth Ward wife of John Ward of Birmingham Esquire. . . ." These parts of his bequest were entrusted for administration to his son John and his "worthy" friends George Hyde and John Wood, both of Old Burlington Street in the Parish of St James, Westminster, apothecaries.

John's brother Robert Fawcett was to have a "full discharge of all monies due from him to" John. Hyde and Wood received each a guinea for a mourning ring, and Wood was bequeathed "my Silver Medal of Queen Ann the Burst [*sic*] raised and is in rare and good perfection as the last token of my Sincere and great Regard for him."

Despite his numerous roles and long career, no portraits of the elder John Fawcett are known to us.

Fawcett, Mrs John, Sarah, née Plaw
[*fl.* 1781–1796], *actress.*

Sarah Plaw married the actor and singer John Fawcett the elder at Fulham on 24 September 1767. There is no record of her as a performer before that date, and only a fragmentary one afterward. She was in the Richmond, Surrey, company in some capacity in the summer of 1781. A loose page

from some theatrical account book of 1795–96 records that she received £96 10*s.* for that season (extra-illustrated volume of Genest in the Harvard Theatre Collection.)

Sarah and John Fawcett had two children. John (1768–1837), actor and singer, and Frances Elizabeth, who married John Ward of Birmingham.

The elder John Fawcett died in 1793 leaving a considerable property to his wife. (See his entry.)

Fawcett, John *1768–1837, actor, singer.*

The second John Fawcett was born on 29 August 1768 a little over a year after the elder John's marriage to Sarah Plaw. His mother seldom performed but his father was a journeyman actor and singer on the stages and in the pleasure gardens of London, Dublin, York, and other cities for 33 years, from 1760 until near his death in 1793.

Though the elder John Fawcett opposed his son's entry to the profession and took precautions against it—enrolling him in St Paul's School on 6 February 1776 and later binding him apprentice to a London linendraper, the effort was futile. At 18 young John deserted his apprenticeship and made his way to Margate where he enrolled in Charles Mates's company under the name Foote. He made his debut at Margate, as Courtall in *The Belle's Stratagem*. Shortly afterward he came on at Tunbridge Wells, now boldly under his own name, where he attracted the notice of the playwright Richard Cumberland, who recommended him to Tate Wilkinson, manager of the York circuit.

For his York debut on 24 May 1787 the inexperienced Fawcett chose the declamatory role of young Norval in *Douglas*, and he was for some time thereafter permitted to indulge his fancy for tragedy as Romeo, Lothario, Oroonoko, and the like, despite the growing skepticism of his manager. Wilkinson "judged him promising but his

From the Collection at Parham Park, Sussex

JOHN FAWCETT, the younger

by Harlow

manner seemed rather mouthing, and did not answer my expectations. . . ." Wilkinson "rather doubted" Fawcett's "parts" as "the melting lover." But Knight, low comedian of the company, was about to be lost to Bath, and Wilkinson (perhaps remembering the talents of the elder Fawcett) determined to convert his tyro from tragedy to farce. Despite the indignation of Fawcett, who protested that he was the company's "principal tragedian," Wilkinson forced upon him the part of Jemmy Jumps in *The Farmer* on 28 April 1788. The piece played to great applause and gave considerable gratification to young John's ego. "This," Wilkinson later wrote, "made him look big

—ay, and talk big, too; for not many weeks after, when his engagement was renewed, my principal tragedian, John Fawcett, stipulated, besides an increase of salary, *never again to play tragedy*: and from that time he never did—he stuck to low comedy." The critic for the *Theatrical Register* of 1788 viewed him as Pedrillo in *The Castle of Andalusia* and thought him a little too "rustic." He also believed Fawcett should guard against "lisping," said that he "bellowed," and that his tenor voice did not carry very well—but that he was very funny withal.

The actor John Mills died at Hull in the autumn of 1787 and the actress Susan Moore, who had for some time been living with him and performing under his name, was befriended by young Fawcett. On 26 April 1788 she was carried in the York playbill as Mrs Mills. On 6 May she was called "Mrs. Fawcett late Mrs. Mills." Susan Moore, "spinster," had married Fawcett at St Michael le Belfry, York, the previous day.

The Fawcetts remained on the York circuit—York, Wakefield, Hull, Pontefract, Doncaster, and Leeds—occasionally playing engagements elsewhere (Birmingham in July 1790 and July 1791), through the summer of 1791. Fawcett performed his now-famous Jemmy Jumps on 27 September and then departed for London. A London engagement at some point was inevitable, given Fawcett's parentage (his father was still acting vigorously his line of small comic parts at Drury Lane) and his ambition. He had, moreover, learned very quickly at York, had accumulated a fine repertoire of farcical roles, and had become a considerable favorite on the northern circuit. Any performer who had succeeded that well and long with the shrewd Wilkinson was worth the £6 per week which Thomas Harris decided to risk when Fawcett was signed at Covent Garden for the 1791–92 season.

Fawcett's Covent Garden debut was in the role of Caleb in *He Wou'd Be a Soldier* on 21 September 1791. He was now in the uncomfortable situation of having to learn quickly the roles of the great John Edwin the elder, who had died in 1790, and of being compared with him at every turn. But the *European Magazine* decided that his first performance was a "very respectable" one, particularly in the song he introduced "in character." In fact, the critic prophesied, "From the merit of his first performance we derive no small expectation of the future." The immediate future bore out the prophecy, and when the actor-scribbler Francis Godolphin Waldron published his *Candid and Impartial Strictures on the Performers Belonging to Drury-Lane, Covent Garden, and the Haymarket Theatres* in 1795 he paid a high compliment:

This gentleman is . . . the best substitute for Edwin since his time. His person, by its heighth, is well suited to most of the characters he sustains, and his voice, abating a kind of snuffle, is also appropriate. He approaches very near as a burletta singer to the above performer, and we think much his superior in the delineation of artless simplicity. . . .

On 28 September 1791 Fawcett played Ruttekin in *Robin Hood*, on 30 September both Jerry Sneak in *The Mayor of Garratt* and Pedrillo in *The Castle of Andalusia*, on 13 October Humphrey Gubbin in *The Tender Husband*, on 2 November Trudge in *Inkle and Yarico*, on 25 November Gregory in *Love and War*, on 1 December Ramille in *The Miser*, on 3 December A La Grecque in *A Day in Turkey*, and on 21 December a principal character, unspecified, in *Blue-Beard*. On 2 February 1792 he was Dareall in *The Magician No Conjurer*, on 6 February Flutter in *The Belle's Stratagem*, on 26 March Lord Crop in *The Mermaid*, on 31 March Sir Macaroni Virtu in *A Peep Behind the Curtain*, on 18 April Carlos in *The Intrigues of a Morning*, and on 21 April a principal character in *The*

JOHN FAWCETT, the younger, as Falstaff

artist unknown

Irishman in London. Most of these roles he repeated several times. In addition, that season Fawcett spoke the important prologue to Thomas Holcroft's most successful comedy, *The Road to Ruin*, some 34 times.

Fawcett thus quickly entrenched himself in the favor of the pit and the regard of his fellow actors and the managers. In May of 1792 he played a brief engagement at Liverpool. In 1793–94 he was raised to £7 per week. At the expiration of his first three-year engagement he renewed for another triad, at an advancing salary of eight, nine, and ten pounds a week. He was at that time living at No 9, the Terrace, Tottenham Court Road, opposite Howland Street. In May 1794 Fawcett played four nights at Leeds for Wilkinson. On 8 July 1794 he played for the first time at the Haymarket, as Tipple in *The Flitch of Bacon* and Young Pranks in *The London Hermit*, having been recommended by Charles Ban-

nister, then departing that theatre, as the only person who could sustain his particular roles. Highly successful also at the summer theatre, Fawcett returned each year. In 1799 Colman appointed him stage manager, but a dispute caused Fawcett to leave the Haymarket in 1802. He returned, however, in 1808 and for many summers thereafter. Also in 1794 he had gone on a tour to several provincial theatres, returning in glory to his old provincial associates. It was said that Andrew Cherry, annoyed at Fawcett's reassumption of choice roles he had given up to Cherry when he went to London, returned from York to Dublin in a huff.

Fawcett's influence at Covent Garden increased year by year, though his relationship with Harris was not without difficulties. In 1800 he joined with John Johnstone, H. E. Johnston, Holman, Munden, Pope, Incledon, and Thomas Knight to publish "A Statement of Differences" between performers and management. Harris had increased benefit charges from £140 to £160, reduced the "notice" of severance from a month to three weeks, increased the fine for refusing a part to £30, and in other ways curtailed performers' privileges. The dispute was adjudicated finally by the Lord Chamberlain and in favor of management. But though Harris, in revenge of their temerity, later disposed of most of those performers, he overlooked Fawcett's indiscretion, and the salary of £12 per week Fawcett earned in 1800–1801 was raised in 1802–3 to £14. He reached £17 in 1805–6, at which salary he remained at least through 1821–22.

In 1808 Fawcett succeeded Hull, the founder of the Covent Garden retirement fund, as treasurer and trustee and at once set about energetically to increase the assets. He sometimes took engagements in the provinces. In 1803 he was with Nunn's company for six weeks at Ashbourne. In the summer of 1804 he was at Richmond, in the summers of 1809 and 1815 at Edinburgh. From about 1818 through 1828 he was the theatre's stage manager. Then, for some mysterious reason, he was thrust out of office. James Winston in "The Manager's Note-Book" said of this, cryptically: "At the commencement of the season, September, 1829, to the surprise of every one, Fawcett was superseded in the management (*he did not resign*) of Covent Garden Theatre. On this we could a tale unfold, but that would be betraying the 'secrets of the prison-house.' Immediately after, he announced his intention of quitting the stage at the end of the season."

A committee was formed among the performers of Covent Garden "to make," says Winston, "the last night of his appearance as brilliant as his professional talent and private worth had been conspicuous." He took his leave of his public on 30 May 1830, playing Captain Copp in the afterpiece *Charles II*. His farewell address was witty and affecting and at its conclusion scores of leading players from all of the theatres crowded the stage to bid him goodbye.

But Fawcett was not yet done with the profession. He retired "to a very pretty little cottage at Botley, near Southampton." But at the insistence of the governing committee of the Covent Garden Fund he continued in his dual office as trustee and treasurer at a salary of £100 a year, coming to town four times a year to pay annuitants and again to make his annual address at the Fund dinner.

Winston, who, as the sometime stage manager at Drury Lane and the Haymarket, well knew both Fawcett and his managerial problems, testified that: "In private life Mr. Fawcett's conduct was irreproachable, although his manner was rather blunt, and perhaps to those who were not acquainted with his goodness of heart apparently harsh. He was like the pineapple, rough outside, but full of sweetness within."

But it was not Fawcett's managerial or fiduciary accomplishments for which gen-

erations of London playgoers esteemed him. For nearly forty years he was one of the leading portrayers of low comedy, rustic, and eccentric characters especially those which required singing. He occasionally gave monologues and could deliver prologues and epilogues with excellent effect. Thomas Dutton in *The Dramatic Censor* (1800) asserted "Broad farce and caricature are well adapted to [his] genius; but in the sentimental walk he is entirely out of his element." In his "mouth sentiment infallibly converts into farce and ridicule." Neither did Dutton like "the coarse Grubstreet ballads" Fawcett sang, though he admitted they were "tumultuously encored." Certainly many of them were published "as sung by" him.

But Fawcett softened as the years went on, and the *Theatrical Inquisitor* of 1814 found that he had played "a wide and opposite cast of characters, which he sustains

National Portrait Gallery

JOHN FAWCETT, the younger

Painting started by Lawrence, finished by unknown artist

with the happiest effect" and that he was capable of "a chaste and classical colouring." By the time of the appearance of his Job Thornberry in 1803 he was able, indeed, to satisfy every yearning of that sentimental era for "affecting" comedy:

The physical properties of this gentleman are certainly highly advantageous to his line of acting, which, though in no way singular or disagreeable as a private gentleman, make a very effective figure, either as a countryman, pedant, old man, Quaker, or Jew, &c. His voice too, has an agreeable harshness, which well accords with the whimsical sentiments of the comic muse, without lessening the force of a pathetic passage. In confirmation of this opinion, we mention Colman's beautifully drawn portrait of Job Thornberry, in the comedy of John Bull. The transition of feelings, which so naturally animates the bosom of an aggrieved father, Mr. Fawcett depicts in the most masterly colours, and is particularly great in the scene where he throws off the waistcoat which his supposed disobedient daughter had worked for him. He looks the character, and pourtrays its minutest shades with all the feelings of a fond parent for the sufferings of a lost child.

Fawcett had begun somewhat slowly, but gradually, season after season, he added roles, many of which he "created," until he had one of the most extensive repertoires of any British comedian: Bowkitt in *The Son in Law*, Sir Harry Beagle in *The Jealous Wife*, Dr Grigsby in *The World in a Village* (after which he delivered a monologue called "Jeu d'Esprit"), Frank Millclack in *Heigho for a Husband!*, Motley in *The Dead Alive*, and Lingo (with a new song) in *The Agreeable Surprise* (Edwin's great part), were all added in the spring and summer of 1794.

A selection of his roles thereafter includes: Clod (singing "There was a littel woman I've heard tell") in *The Young Quaker*, both the Serjeant and La Gloire in *The Surrender of Calais*, Ennui in *The*

Dramatist, Gunnel in *Netley Abbey*, Gratiano in *The Merchant of Venice*, Witski in *Sorinski*, Lucy in *The Beggar's Opera*, the title role in *Peeping Tom* (singing "The Little Farthing Rushlight"), Robin in *No Song No Supper,* Goldfinch in *The Road to Ruin*, Jacob in *The Chapter of Accidents*, Adam Winterton in *The Iron Chest*, the title role in *Sylvester Daggerwood*, Scout in *The Village Lawyer*, Bob Handy in *Speed the Plough*, Don Ferolo Whiskerandos in *The Critic*, Johnny Atkins in *A Mogul Tale*, Young Sadboy in *The Young Quaker*, Caleb Quotem in *The Review*, Edward in *The Irishman in London*, Ferret in *Arrived at Portsmouth*, Cartridge in *Hartford Bridge*, Etiquette in *Summer Amusement*, La Fleur in *Animal Magnetism*, Jack Scamper in *How to be Happy*, Thomas in *Rule Britannia*, Comte Fripponi in *The Travellers in Switzerland*, the Honorable Mr Savage in *The Rage*, a Witch in *Macbeth*, Verges in *Much Ado About Nothing*, Tom in *The Conscious Lovers*, Fancourt in *The Town Before You*, Trim in *Grief à-la-Mode*, Sir John Bull in *Fontainebleau*, Cloddy in *The Mysteries of the Castle*, Muns in *The Prisoner at Large*, Joey in *Modern Antiques*, Sir Paul Peckham in *The School for Arrogance*, Nimble in *Crotchet Lodge*, Leveret in *Windsor Castle*, George Burgess in *Life's Vagaries*, Colin in *The Irish Mimic*, Ned Dash in *The Bank Note*, Latitat in *How to Grow Rich*, and Matthew Blubber in *Who Pays the Reckoning?*

There were also a Gravedigger in *Hamlet*, Humphrey Grizzle in *The Three and the Deuce*, John Dory in *Wild Oats*, Deputy Dimity in *The Wives Revenged*, Jack Arable in *Speculation*, Dick Dashall in *The Way to Get Married*, Ralph in *Lock and Key*, Thady in *The Lad of the Hills*, Napkin in *The Point at Herqui*, Sancho in *Lovers' Quarrels*, Rupee in *The Positive Man*, Bullock in *The Recruiting Officer*, Batch in *Bannian Day*, Jacky Item in *The Married and Un-Married*, Old Shepherd in

A Peep Behind the Curtain, Oliver in *Wives as They Were, Maids as They Are*, Nicholas in *The Midnight Hour*, Young Flourish in *Abroad and at Home*, Frank Oatland in *A Cure for a Heart Ache*, Valentine in *Italian Villagers*, Jack Rattling in *The Surrender of Trinidad*, April in *Secrets Worth Knowing*, Sharpset in *The Votary of Wealth*, Pisani in *A Day at Rome*, Jack Junk in *The Birthday*, Lord Sands in *Henry VIII*, Doctor Scarecrow in *Sunshine after Rain*, Acba in *The Princess of Georgia*, Metheglin in *The Lie of the Day*, Robin Roughhead in *Fortune's Frolick*, Sheva in *The Jew*, Megrim in *Blue Devils*, Blinval in *The Castle of Sorrento*, Sambo in *Laugh When You Can*, Mist in *Management*, Joe Standfast in *The Turnpike Gate*, Ephraim in *Liberal Opinions*, Numpo in *'Tis All a Farce*, Totum in *Sighs*, Valcour in *The Point of Honour*, Dashington in *What a Blunder*, and the original Bartholo in *The Barber of Seville* (not Rossini's).

Fawcett was greatly fortunate to attract the attention, early in his career, of Colman, who wrote for him a series of pieces built around his special abilities. On 15 July 1797 at the Haymarket, Colman produced *The Heir-at-Law* in which Fawcett succeeded greatly as Dr Pangloss. Other great hits were *Throw Physic to the Dogs*, at the Haymarket on 6 July 1798 in which he played the eccentric Caleb Quotem to great effect (Colman later revived Quotem in *The Review*); *The Poor Gentleman*, at Covent Garden on 11 February 1801 in which he played the droll Ollapod; *John Bull*, at Covent Garden on 5 March 1803 in which he captivated audiences as the rustic Job Thornberry; and *Who Wants a Guinea?* at Covent Garden on 18 April 1805 in which he was much admired as Solomon Gundy.

Fawcett himself turned author in 1800, and his bewitching pantomime *Obi; or, Three-fingered Jack* was produced at the Haymarket on 2 July, with music by Dr Arnold and with Charles Kemble in the

Harvard Theatre Collection

JOHN FAWCETT, the younger, as Robin Roughhead

by De Wilde

title role. He also devised the pantomime *Perouse; or, The Desolate Island* for showing at Covent Garden on 28 February 1801; a ballet, *The Fairies Revels; or, Love in the Highlands*, at the Haymarket on 14 August 1802; a ballet, *The Enchanted Island*, with music by Condell, at the Haymarket on 20 June 1804; the melodrama *The Secret Mine*, at Covent Garden on 24 April 1812 (in collaboration with Thomas John Dibdin); and *The Barber of Seville*, in collaboration with Daniel Terry, the music by Bishop, at Covent Garden 13 October 1818. *The Old Miner Ousted*, produced at Caernarvon in 1841 was probably a rewriting of *The Secret Mine*.

John Fawcett the younger had married Susan Moore in 1788. She had for some years lived with the actor John Mills, had borne him children and had acted at York and elsewhere, appearing in the bills as "Mrs Mills." She continued to perform after her marriage to Fawcett. She died in July 1797. In 1799 Fawcett was rumored engaged to the actress Anne Biggs. About 1806 he married the actress and singer Anne Gaudry, daughter of the actor Joseph Gaudry. Shortly after her marriage she retired from the stage and became wardrobe mistress at Covent Garden. Apparently she worked in that capacity at Drury Lane as late as the 1821–22 season. She died in 1849. After his retirement to the tiny village of Botley near Southampton, early in the 1830s, he raised a subscription for the erection of a new church in his neighborhood. He was the first person buried in it after his death on 13 March 1837 from an infection in his foot.

In a will dated 14 January 1837, "John Fawcett of Curdridge Common Bishops Waltham in the County of Hants [Hampshire] Esquire" directed that his household furniture, china, implements, and plate, including "the Garrick Medal presented to me by the Covent Garden ffund," go to his "dear wife Anne," for her use during life. Moreover, he devised "to my said wife for her own use and benefit all government ffunds which I have already placed in our joint names." Residuary legatee for this property was John Turner Colman Fawcett "of Owersby in the County of Lincoln Clerk." The cleric was very probably a son, for he was to receive also a portrait of Fawcett's "dear ffriend" Robert Vernon painted by Bradley "and also the portrait of myself and Wife painted by Harlowe." "And as to any shares I may die possessed of in the Provincial Irish Banks I give the same to the said John Turner Colman Fawcett for his absolute use but as he values my memory I desire He will always (as far as it is in his power) protect and assist my dear Widow." Robert Vernon was appointed executor and the will was proved at London on 20 April 1837.

Portraits of John Fawcett include:

1. By George Dance, pencil drawing. In the Garrick Club.

2. By Samuel De Wilde, painting. In the collection of Lady Leicester. Probably this is the portrait engraved by H. R. Cooke, after De Wilde, which was published as a plate to the *New Myrtle and Vine*.

3. By G. H. Harlow, painting. At Parham Park, Sussex. An engraving by W. Say was published by the engraver in 1815. Another engraving by T. Blood was published as a plate to the *European Magazine*, 1816.

4. By John Hoppner, painting. Present location unknown to us. A photograph is in the Art Reference Library of the Henry E. Huntington Art Gallery.

5. By C. Jagger, miniature on ivory. In the Garrick Club.

6. By Thomas Lawrence. In the National Portrait Gallery. The painting was begun by Lawrence and finished by an unknown artist. An engraving by W. J. Edwards was published as a plate to the *Art Journal*, 1854.

7. Engraving by W. T. Fry. Published on a sheet with the portraits of six other performers. In the Harvard Theatre Collection.

8. Engraving by K. Mackenzie, after R. Dighton. Published as a plate to the *Thespian Dictionary*.

9. Engraving by W. Ridley, after M. A. Shee. Published as a plate to *Parson's Minor Theatre*, 1794.

10. As Autolycus in *The Winter's Tale*. Watercolor by Thomas Charles Wageman, 1828. In the Victoria and Albert Museum.

11. As Caleb Quotem in *The Review*. Painting by Samuel De Wilde. In the Garrick Club. Engraving by T. Cheesman, published by C. Chapple, 1807.

12. As Caleb Quotem. Engraving by R. Page, after T. Wageman. Published as a plate to Oxberry's *New English Drama*, 1822.

13. As Caleb Quotem. Engraving by

Thomas. Published as frontispiece to *The Stage*, by W. A. Wright.

14. As Caleb Quotem. By unknown engraver. Published with the words of the song *The Waiter*, by Laurie & Whittle, 1806.

15. As Caleb Quotem. By unknown engraver. Published by H. Lee, Taunton, 1808.

16. As Captain Copp, with Charles Kemble as the King, in *Charles II*. Painting by George Clint. In the Garrick Club. Engraving by T. Lupton.

17. As Captain Copp. Engraving by J. Kennerley. Published by Duncombe. Another copy was issued by the same publisher as a plate to *The Review*, 1825.

18. As Captain Copp. Engraving by J. Rogers, after R. Page. Published as a plate to *Dramatic Magazine*.

19. As Dashall, with John Quick as Toby Allspice, in *The Way to Get Married*. Painting by De Wilde. In the Mander and Mitchenson Collection.

20. As Dr Pangloss in *The Heir at Law*. Engraving by T. W. Annis, after De Wilde. Published by B. Pym, 1803.

21. As Falstaff. By unknown engraver. Published as a twopence-colored by Hodgson & Co., 1823.

22. As Frank Oatland in *A Cure for a Heart Ache*. Painting by unknown artist. Reported by the *Monthly Mirror* to have been in the Royal Academy exhibition of 1797 (No 329).

23. As Hardy in *The Belle's Stratagem*. Engraving by I. Cruikshank. Published as a plate to *The British Stage*, 1817.

24. As Jack Nightshade in *The Choleric Man*. Engraving by Corner, after De Wilde. Published as a plate to *Bell's British Theatre*, 1793.

25. As Job Thornberry in *John Bull*. Watercolors by De Wilde. One in the Garrick Club and another in the National Theatre, both dated 1807; a third in the Harvard Theatre Collection. Engraving by Woodman, published as a plate to *The Cabinet*, 1808.

26. As "Lobskey." By unknown engraver, after "W. L."

27. As Mawworm in *The Hypocrite*. Engraving by P. Audinet, after De Wilde. Published as a plate to *Bell's British Theatre*, 1792.

28. As Paris in *Two Faces Under One Hood*. Engraving by I. Cruikshank, entitled "Three Goddesses in Pursuit of Paris," published as a heading to the verses of a song sung by Fawcett.

29. As Razor in *The Provok'd Wife*. By unknown engraver.

30. As Robin Roughhead in *Fortune's Frolic*. Pencil and watercolor drawing by De Wilde. In the British Museum. Engraving by Woodman, published as a plate to Cawthorn's *Minor Theatre*, 1806.

31. As Robin Roughhead. Watercolor by De Wilde, dated 1815. In the Harvard Theatre Collection.

32. As Servitz in *The Exile*. Watercolor by De Wilde. In the Garrick Club. Engraving by E. Scriven, published by Bell & De Camp, 1809; another by an unknown engraver, published by Tegg, 1810.

33. As Servitz. Satirical engraving by either Isaac or George Cruikshank, entitled "Mr Lobski; or the River Sprat-Catcher," as heading to verses sung by Fawcett. Published 4 November 1808.

34. As Servitz. Engraving by either Isaac or George Cruikshank, entitled "Theatrical Faux Pas." Published in *The Satirist*, 1 March 1814.

35. As Servitz. By unknown engraver, heading verses to song *Russian Nuptials*, as sung by Fawcett. Published 1 December 1808.

36. As Touchstone in *As You Like It*. Engraving by W. Ridley, after M. A. Shee. Published as a plate to the *Monthly Mirror*, 1799. Another copy by an unknown engraver, after Shee, also appeared.

37. As Touchstone. Engraving by J. Rogers, after R. Page. Published as a plate to Oxberry's *Dramatic Biography*, 1825.

38. As Touchstone. Engraving by

T. Woolnoth, after T. Wageman. Published as a plate to Oxberry's *New English Drama*, 1819.

39. As Whimsiculo in *The Cabinet*. Pencil and watercolor drawing by De Wilde. In the National Theatre. Engraving by Wageman, published by Clark, 1808. Another by an unknown engraver was published in the *Theatrical Inquisitor*, 1814; the same engraving was published, undated, with the quotation, "But what, my valiant tail of a lion?"

40. As Whimsiculo. Painting by De Wilde. In the Garrick Club. A half-length version of the De Wilde watercolor above, No 39.

41. One of a series of anonymous satirical theatrical woodcuts of 1819, this one entitled "This is THE MAN who engaged." Fawcett sits at a table weeping over a volume with blank pages headed "Bank Book."

42. A second satirical print in the 1819 series, "This is THE MAN who all men scorn." A savage attack on Fawcett as actor-manager.

43. Satirical print: "Bernard Blackmantle Reading his Play in the Green Room of Covent Garden Theatre." Undated; 27 figures, among whom Fawcett and Charles Kemble are most prominent.

Fawcett, the first Mrs John the younger, Susan, née Moore, formerly called Mrs John Mills *1761?–1797, actress, singer.*

Susan Moore Fawcett's antecedents are unknown. Apparently Miss Moore was correctly advertised as making her first appearance on any stage when she appeared at Covent Garden Theatre on 23 May 1778 as Statira in *The Rival Queens*. Her age was said by the *London Chronicle* to be 17.

By August 1778 Susan was playing in the York company, whence she returned in the summer of 1779 after wintering in Edinburgh, where she had assumed a variety of leading and secondary roles including Angelina in *Love Makes a Man*, Bel-

videra in *Venice Preserv'd*, Charlotte in *The Gamester*, Clarinda in *The Suspicious Husband*, Eleanor in *The Countess of Salisbury*, Fidelia in *The Foundling*, Imogen in *Cymbeline*, the title role in *Jane Shore*, Julia in *The Rivals*, Lady Fanciful in *The Provok'd Wife*, Lady Sash in *The Camp*, Lady Teazle in *The School for Scandal*, Lavinia in *The Fair Penitent*, Louisa Dudley in *The West Indian*, Miss Hardcastle in *She Stoops to Conquer*, Miss Jenny in *The Provok'd Husband*, Miss Neville in *Know Your Own Mind*, Miss Sterling in *The Clandestine Marriage*, Queen Dollalolla in *Tom Thumb*, Selima in *Zara*, Violetta in *The Brothers*, and Widow Delamour in *The Way to Keep Him*.

She may have returned later to the Scottish capital, for on 18 February 1783, advertised as from the theatre in Edinburgh, she took the role of Imogen in *Cymbeline* at Covent Garden, repeating it on 25 February. She was then called "Mrs Mills." She had attracted the admiration of the actor John Mills, who had deserted his wife and children to cleave to Susan Moore. There was almost certainly no formal marriage, but the informal union produced, nevertheless, at least one and probably two children. The 1795 edition of *The Secret History of the Green Room* alleged that Mills and Miss Moore had alienated the Scots audiences by their liaison.

Susan had earned the professional esteem of the manager of the York circuit, Tate Wilkinson, and she returned to him at Doncaster in race week, 24 September 1783, and was also at York in 1784, 1785, and 1786. John Mills died suddenly at Hull in October 1787 and young John Fawcett, then just 19, fell at once under Susan's spell. On 26 April 1788 she was still "Mrs Mills" in the playbills. She and Fawcett were married at St Michael le Belfry, York, on 5 May, and on 6 May Susan was called "Mrs Fawcett late Mrs. Mills" in the bills.

Susan's reviews in the *York Theatrical Register* were few and unflattering. She was not "consequential" enough as Mrs Strictland in *The Confederacy*. In *The Poor Soldier* she was "insipid" and her inattention was "unpardonable." She was accepted in her *chef d'oeuvre*, Flippanta in *The Confederacy*, but she "misconceived" Cowslip in *The Agreeable Surprise*, for that character was "designed for unaffected simplicity" and Susan was either "arch" or "vacant." Nevertheless, when in the fall the Fawcetts were translated to London, Wilkinson was indignant. He was, he later wrote, deprived of his "right-hand lady." He praised her for her unselfish service on benefit nights and in all sorts of emergent situations: "I should enter into some fulsome panegyric were I to do no more than justice to the numberless good actions and sleepless nights she must have undergone for the service of our state . . . her study was rapid, her will was great; . . . for the laws of wit and humour, she was my only woman."

On 3 October 1791, for the first time in eight seasons, Mrs Fawcett stepped onto a London stage, again at Covent Garden (and incorrectly said to be appearing there for the first time). She was the Countess of Nottingham in *The Earl of Essex*. The *European Magazine* wounded her with one of the most measured criticisms on record: "As this lady is hardly intended for any higher than secondary characters, it will be sufficient to say that she acquitted herself neither with excellence much to commend, nor yet in a manner to deserve blame."

Susan Fawcett was paid £2 per week for her efforts through 1793–94, when she was raised to £3. Though *The Secret History of the Green Room* viewed her in 1795 as "only a third or fourth-rate Actress" and "a piece of lumber, inseparably attached to" her husband, she was assigned a list of varied and often important supporting roles: Laura in *Tancred and Sigismunda*, Patty in *Inkle and Yarico*, Louisa in *Love Makes a Man*, Paulina in *The Winter's Tale*, Grace in *Fashionable Levities*, Adriana and Luciana in *The Comedy of Errors*, Cubba in *The Irishman in London*, Jenny and Trusty in *The Provok'd Husband*, Emilia in *Othello*, Margaretta in *Rule a Wife and Have a Wife*, Lady Graveairs in *The Careless Husband*, Jane in *Wild Oats*, Dimity in *Three Weeks after Marriage*, Miss Ogle in *The Belle's Stratagem*, Mrs Peachum in *The Beggar's Opera*, Mrs Bellevue in *The World in a Village*, Alicia in *Jane Shore*, Mrs Tempest in *The School for Wives*, Lady Louisa Compton in *Love's Frailties*, Mrs Wilkins in *He Would Be a Soldier*, the Widow Wadman in *Tristram Shandy*, the title character in *The Widow of Malabar*, the Queen in *Cymbeline*, Urganda in *Cymon*, Regan in *King Lear*, Mrs Casey in *Fontainebleau*, Lady Loverule in *The Devil to Pay*, Fringe in *The Agreeable Surprise*, Mary in *The Prisoner at Large*, Lucy in *The Country Girl*, and Queen Margaret in *The Battle of Hexham*. In July 1792 she was briefly at the Theatre Royal, Liverpool. On 8 August 1796 she played at Birmingham. On 28 August 1794 she made her first appearance at the Haymarket and on 19 June 1797 her second and last one there. The *Morning Herald* of 1 August 1797 announced: "An apology was last night made [at the Haymarket] for the absence of Fawcett, occasioned by a severe domestic affliction—the death of his wife. . . ."

A Miss Mills who was said to be her daughter by John Mills married the actor James Barnard and made her debut on 2 July 1819 at the Haymarket as Mary in *The Rival Soldiers*, according to a manuscript in the Harvard Theatre Collection. An anecdote by Tate Wilkinson in his *The Wandering Patentee* mentions a son by John Fawcett. A portrait of three "Masters Fawcett" by G. H. Harlow, now at Parham Park, may be of her children, but are perhaps those of the second Mrs Fawcett, née Gaudry.

Fawcett, the second Mrs John the younger. *See* GAUDRY, ANNE.

Fawkes. *See also* FAUX.

Fawkes, Mr *b. c. 1710, posture-maker, manager, conjurer, puppeteer.*

Mr Fawkes was the son of the famous conjurer, Isaac Fawkes, and his wife Alice. The lad's first notice was on 3 October 1722 at Southwark when "Fawks's famous Boy" displayed tumbling acts. He was doubtless the "Little Boy, of 12 Years of Age" who performed for Isaac Fawkes at the Haymarket Theatre about December of that year, heralded as displaying

the surprising Activity of Body . . . turning his Body into so many various Shapes, that surpasses Humane Faith to believe without seeing, for which he has received considerable Rewards from the Nobility . . . N.B. Besides these performances, he shows every Night a great Many curious Fancies by Dexterity of Hand before his Master begins, being different from what his Master performs.

By April 1723, when the elder Fawkes was exhibiting at a booth in Upper Moorfields, the advertisements made it clear that the boy of 12 was still with him, and a second lad, age nine, also performed, but "all different from what [Fawkes's] own Boy performs."

After Isaac Fawkes died in 1731 the younger Fawkes formed a partnership with Edward Pinchbeck and continued the tradition his father had begun. In 1733 Fawkes exhibited sleight of hand at the James Street Theatre; in 1734 he and Pinchbeck displayed a waxworks and puppet show at the same playhouse; and it is likely that the pair were active throughout the 1730s either at the London fairs or in the provinces.

Fawkes, Pinchbeck, and Terwin had a booth at Bartholomew Fair on 23 August 1740 where "Punch's Celebrated Company of Comedians, formerly Mrs Charke's" were seen in *Britons Strike Home*, a puppet show. The following year Fawkes and Pinchbeck had another puppet show at Bartholomew Fair and also exhibited a clockwork machine that showed "the true and exact Siege of Cartagena." They again had a "curious machine" on display on 7 September 1741 at Southwark Fair. When Charlotte Charke produced the puppet play *Tit for Tat* at the James Street Theatre on 16 March 1743 she may have employed Fawkes as one of her manipulators (but there is a possibility that she used live actors in that production).

Mr and Mrs Fawkes were at the Jacob's Wells Theatre in Bristol in the summer of 1743, but Fawkes returned to London for Bartholomew Fair. There on 23 August Fawkes and Pinchbeck produced *The Ephesian Duke* and *The Battle of Dettingen*, and on 25 August 1746 at the same fair Fawkes joined Warner to put on *The Happy Hero*, *All Alive and Merry*, and *Harlequin Incendiary*. After that Fawkes's activity seems to have ceased.

Hogarth's "Southwark Fair" (January 1734) shows Fawkes's booth, but the picture may depict the exhibition as it was before the death of the elder Fawkes.

Fawkes, Mrs [*fl. 1742–1743*], *actress.*

A Mrs Fawkes replaced Miss Short as a Country Lass in *The Rape of Proserpine* at Covent Garden on 28 December 1742 and played the Barmaid in *The Fair Quaker of Deal* on 4 May 1743. From 17 June to 6 September 1743 she was paid 4s. per performance at the Jacob's Wells Theatre in Bristol; during most of her stay there Mr Fawkes, apparently the conjurer and manager (b. c. 1710) and her husband, also performed.

Fawkes, Isaac *d. 1731, conjurer, puppeteer, manager.*

Isaac Fawkes (or Faux, Vaux) first came to the attention of Londoners on 3 October 1722 when his son did a tumbling act at Southwark Fair. About December of that year Fawkes advertised himself as a con-

BARTHOLOMEW FAIR. 1721. (Vaux the Conjuror's Booth.)
From a Painted Fan of that date.

By permission of the Henry E. Huntington Library and Art Gallery

Booth of ISAAC FAWKES

artist unknown

jurer and announced performances "in the fore Room of the French Theatre" (the Haymarket). His puff stated that he would perform "his most surprizing Tricks by Dexterity of Hand, with his Cards, Eggs, Corn, Mice, curious India Birds, and Money . . . Likewize the surprising Activity of Body perform'd by his Little Boy, of 12 Years of Age. . . ."

By April 1723 Fawkes had moved to a commodious booth in Upper Moorfields where he performed at three, five, and seven o'clock daily. In September 1724 he exhibited at the Queen Anne's Tavern in Southwark at the fair, and he seems to have appeared regularly during the late 1720s at Bartholomew Fair as well. His advertisement in the *Daily Post* of 23 August 1726 was typical:

first his surprizing Dexterity of Hand, in which he far exceeds all that ever pretended to the same Art, with his Cards, Eggs, Mice,

Money, and several curious Birds from divers Parts of the World that never were seen here before. 2d. His famous Posture Master, who is allowed to be the best in Europe of that kind. 3d. His Musical Clock that plays Variety of Tunes on the Organ, Flute and Flagelet, with Birds whistling and singing as natural as Life. 4th. His Puppet Show, with the Comical Humours of Punch and his Wife Joan: Likewise a Court of the richest and largest Figures ever shown in England, being as big as Men and Women.

In 1726 Fawkes and Powell produced a puppet show at the James Street playhouse, which was for a while called "Fawkes's Theatre," and he was there when the *British Journal* on 20 February 1731 reported:

On Monday Night their Excellencies the Algerine Ambassadors, with a great many Persons of Quality and Distinction, went to *Fawkes's* Theatre, where they saw his Performance with a great deal of Pleasure and Surprize; and, according to their Desire, Mr. Fawkes shew'd the Prospect of *Algier* amongst the other Views; which, they said, was exactly like the Place. The whole Company express'd their Satisfaction with the Entertainment, especially with his raising up an Apple-Tree which bore ripe Apples in less than a Minute's Time, which several of the Company tasted of; but none of the Algerines would touch any Thing belonging to Mr. Fawkes.

Fawkes had a booth in 1731, and an alarm of a fire in the next booth frightened his wife into a premature confinement.

That must have been early in the year. Isaac Fawkes died on 25 May 1731 and was buried in a vault in St Martin's Church on 28 May. The papers of the day noted that "he had honestly acquired a fortune of above ten thousand pounds, being no more than he really deserved for his great ingenuity, by which he surpassed all that ever pretended to that art." Fawkes left his estate to his widow Alice who, according to the

From the collection of Edward A. Langhans

"Masquerades and Operas, Burlington Gate," showing the sign of FAWKES ("Faux")

by Hogarth

Daily Advertiser of 17 November 1732, married the exhibitor Edward Pinchbeck.

Though no formal portrait of Fawkes seems to have been painted, he and his fair booth were pictured in a fan painting of Bartholomew Fair in 1721, and Hogarth depicted the conjurer's booth in "Masquerades and Operas" in February 1724. Hogarth's "Southwark Fair" (January 1734) shows Fawkes's booth, but by that date the conjurer's son was managing the enterprise; nevertheless, the figure in the picture sitting at a table performing a trick may well represent Isaac.

Fay, Mr [*fl. 1774–1783?*], *dancer.*
A dancer named Fay portrayed Boree in *Le Baillet de fleur* at the King's Theatre in the Haymarket on 8 November 1774. Perhaps he was the performer of the same name who was in Dublin in 1782–83.

Fearon, James *1746–1789, actor.*
The inscription on James Fearon's memorial in the Richmond churchyard indicates he was 43 when he died in 1789, dating his year of birth in 1746. Of his life prior to his debut in London in 1771 little is known except that he evidently came from Richmond and acted in Edinburgh and Glasgow between 1768 and 1771. At the New Concert Hall in Edinburgh he played Robin O'Bagshot in *The Beggar's Opera* on 23 March 1768 and Bellamy in

The Suspicious Husband several weeks later on 13 April. In the spring of 1769 at the same place he acted Charles in *The Jealous Wife* on 13 March and Vizard in *The Constant Couple* on 23 March. In 1770–71 at the new Theatre Royal in Edinburgh he played Bellmour in *The Old Bachelor*, the Butler in *The Devil to Pay*, Don Juan in *Rule a Wife and Have a Wife*, Dugard in *The Inconstant*, Duke Frederick in *As You Like It*, Giles in *The Maid of the Mill*, Harry in *The Mock Doctor*, Knowlife in *The Tobacconist*, Macduff in *Macbeth*, Major Oakly in *The Jealous Wife*, Sprightly in *The Author*, Trusty in *The Funeral*, and Valentine in *The Intriguing Chambermaid*.

In the summer of 1771, Samuel Foote, who had managed the Edinburgh theatre the previous winter season, brought Mr and Mrs Fearon to London to play at the Haymarket. Fearon made his first appearance there as Kitely in *Every Man in his Humour* on 17 May 1771. "His person and voice are well suited to this walk of acting," reported the *Town and Country Magazine* in May 1771 and he "displayed much judgment and great natural feeling." By the time the summer season at the Haymarket ended on 16 September, Fearon had played over 20 supporting roles, mostly in light comedies and farces, a repertoire suggesting considerable experience in the provinces. His second appearance was as Bruin in *The Mayor of Garratt* on 20 May 1771. Some other roles which he performed during this first engagement in London were Sir Jealous Traffic in *The Busy Body*, Fungus in *The Commissary*, Constant in *The Provok'd Wife*, Peter Poultice in *The Maid of Bath*, Knowlife in *The Tobacconist*, Antonio in *Love Makes a Man*, and Hawthorn in *Love in a Village*.

After the summer at the Haymarket, Fearon passed the season 1771–72 playing minor characters at the Crow Street Theatre, Dublin. Between November 1772 and April 1773 he acted with a strolling company which played at Coopers' Hall in King Street, next to the Bristol theatre. This company went to Richmond, Surrey, for the summer of 1773, but without Fearon, who rejoined Foote at the Haymarket, where he continued to be engaged every summer through 1777. Among the numerous roles he acted there were Townly in *Taste*, Harry in *The Mock Doctor*, Dorilas in *Cupid's Revenge*, Buckingham in *Richard III*, Resource in *The Bankrupt*, Gullwell in *The Register Office*, Old Incle in *A Trip to Portsmouth*, Petruchio in *Catherine and Petruchio*, George Bevil in *Cross Purposes*, Cunningham in *The Rival Fools*, Torrismond in *The Spanish Fryar*, and Sullen in *The Beaux' Stratagem*. He also made a single appearance at Drury Lane on 2 June 1774 as Gullwell in *The Register Office* for the special benefit of Bannister.

In 1774–75 Fearon began a winter engagement at Covent Garden Theatre which was to last 14 years. Despite the fact that he acted in London for a total of 18 years, his history may be told, for the most part, only through the many roles he performed. He made his first appearance at Covent Garden on 19 September 1774 as the Steward in *All's Well That Ends Well*. He played Sir Charles Marlow in *She Stoops to Conquer* on 21 September, the Uncle in *George Barnwell* on 26 September, and Cassander in *Alexander the Great* on 4 October. On 17 January 1775 he played the Coachman in the first performance of *The Rivals*. Although he filled the lighter roles he was accustomed to playing at the Haymarket, he also appeared in a number of more serious roles including Stanley in *Richard III*, Leicester in *King Henry II, or, the Fall of Rosamond*, and Arcas in *The Grecian Daughter*.

A typical season of employment at Covent Garden for Fearon may be illustrated by a list of his roles in 1777–78, at which time he was being paid £2 10s. per week: Serjeant Kite in *The Recruiting Officer*, Fungus in *The Commissary*, Escalus in *Ro-*

JAMES FEARON, as Captain Driver

engraving by W. N. Gardiner, after S. Harding

meo and Juliet, Sir John in *The Conscious Lovers*, the Friar in *Much Ado About Nothing*, the Duke in *The Merchant of Venice*, Maclaymore in *The Reprisal*, Sir John in *Know Your Own Mind*, Gratiano in *Othello*, Octan in *The Orphan of China*, Stanley in *Richard III*, Arcas in *The Grecian Daughter*, Sir Theodore Brumpton in *Love Finds a Way*, Sir John Buck in *The Englishman in Paris*, Sir Charles Marlow in *She Stoops to Conquer*, the Uncle in *George Barnwell*, Kent in *King Lear*, Jonathan in *The Brothers*, Heeltap in *The Mayor of Garratt*, Loader in *The Minor*, Governor Cape in *The Author*, Duke Frederick in *As You Like It*, Old Wilding in *The Lyar*, Ernesto in *The Orphan*, the Surgeon in *Love's Last Stake*, Ulysses in *Iphigenia*, Sir Ardolphe in *The Countess of Salisbury*, Elliot in *Venice Preserv'd*, Blanford in *All in the Wrong*, Cassander in *Alexander the Great*, Gibby in *The Won-*

der, Champernel in *The Little French Lawyer*, Cardic in *The British Heroine*, the Governor in *Love Makes a Man*, unnamed roles in *The Rehearsal* and *The Reprisal*, the King of France in *Henry V*, and Cardinal Perigort in *Edward the Black Prince* — a total of 37 roles.

On 15 May 1778, when he acted Cardinal Perigort, he shared net benefit receipts of £68 16s. 6d. with Booth and L'Estrange. In his earlier years at Covent Garden his benefit proceeds, always shared with two or three other performers, were similarly modest. For example, on 12 May 1780 he shared net receipts of £72 3s. with Booth and Egan and on 16 May 1781 £160 18s. with three others. In his last years he was not required to share, taking net receipts of £139 6s. on 11 May 1787, £76 19s. 6d. on 7 May 1788, and £41 7s. for his last benefit on 9 June 1789. Fearon's salary was £2 10s. per week between 1776–77 and 1781–82. In 1782–83 it was raised to £3, and then in 1783–84 to £3 10s., in 1786–87 to £4, and in 1787–88 to £4 10s.

On 8 May 1781 Fearon acted Governor Harcourt in *The Chapter of Accidents* at Drury Lane for the benefit of John Bannister, and on 5 June 1783 he acted Wingate in *The Apprentice* at the same theatre. Surviving playbills indicate he acted at Richmond in the summers of 1781, 1785, 1788, and 1789. In 1776–77 Fearon's lodgings were at Clay's, the cabinetmaker in Princess Street, Soho. By 1787–88 he was living at No 1, Broad Court, Bow Street, also his address at his last benefit in June 1789.

In 1788–89, his final season at Covent Garden, Fearon was still a most active performer who played nightly and in a wide variety of roles, his final ones being the Prisoner in *Such Things Have Been* and Matthias in *The Midnight Hour* on 17 June 1789. He played at Richmond during the ensuing summer but did not return to London for the beginning of the next season. He died during the evening of 30 September 1789 at his house in English Street, Richmond. The press (clipping in the Richmond Public Library) eulogized him as "a very useful performer, & much admired by those of the attendants on the theatre, who by education & real feeling could distinguish between affectation & grimace & pure simple nature." It had earlier been reported in the same newspaper that "on the death of poor [Cockran Joseph] Booth, in June last, who was of the same theatre & an intimate crony, he shook his head, & said, he should not long survive his friend." Fearon was buried in the Richmond churchyard on 6 October 1789; the inscription on his memorial reads:

This Memorial is inscrib'd
to M^r. James Fearon
late of the Theatre Royal
Covent Garden who paid the
Debt of Nature Sep^r: 30th 1789
Aged 43
In dramatic Life he held the Mirror
up to Nature
In Private life he fulfilled the Duties
Relative and Social
And as he lived respected
he died lamented.

Seven years later, the following lines written by Francis G. Waldron in praise of his deceased friend were printed in the *How D'Ye Do* on 8 November 1796:

> *On seeing Mr. Fearon perform*
> *in the Play of Such Things Are.*
> FEARON! *accept the praise thy skill*
>   *deserves*
> *Of one, whose pen from strictest truth*
>   *ne'er swerves;*
> *Not even Garrick play'd with greater art*
> *Than thou dost in the wretched captive's*
>   *part:*
> *Art do I call it? no, 'tis merely nature*
> *Speaks with thy voice, looks in thy ev'ry*
>   *feature!*
> *Thou hast a wife whom truly thou dost*
>   *love;*

> *Children thou hast, thy tenderest care*
>   *who prove!*
> *When in the mimic-prison thou art pent,*
> *And for lost family thy heart is rent;*
> *Thou, sure, forget'st thou'rt acting on a*
>   *stage;*
> *Thine own fire-side doth all thy*
>   *thoughts engage!*
> *Oh,* INCHBALD! *write a play, full of*
>   *such parts;*
> *Let* FEARON'S *act them too; then shall*
>   *all hearts*
> *Yield thee the palm from all who went*
>   *before;*
> *And Shakespeare's self be rank'd the first*
>   *no more!*

Fearon's widow Mary, who had acted occasionally in London in the 1770s, and her eight children were accorded a benefit at Richmond Theatre on 22 October 1789 when the play performed was appropriately *The Distrest Mother*. The profit to her, according to the *Oracle* on 26 October 1789 was over £100, and the Duke of Clarence also sent 20 guineas. Another benefit for the "Widow Fearon, and her Eight Orphan Children" was given at Covent Garden on 16 June 1790; the performers included Mrs Jordan, Mrs Martyr, and Mrs Crouch. Tickets could be had of Mrs Fearon at No 6, Spur Street, Leicester Fields; receipts for the night are not known.

Two of the eight Fearon children are known to us. A son, first name unknown, who was the commander of an East-Indiaman, attempted the role of Richard III at Drury Lane on 17 January 1803 to the loud cheers of his brother sailors. Soon afterward he failed as Shylock and evidently returned to the sea. Another child, Helen Fearon, at "about three months old," had been baptized at St Paul, Covent Garden, on 17 January 1779.

The Susanna Fearon who married George Soules at Richmond on 11 June 1769 was probably James Fearon's sister.

James Peter Fearon, the author of *Theatrical Criticism, a Critique on the School of Reform*, 1805, may have been related, as may possibly have been the M. Fieron who was on the Philadelphia stage between 1796 and 1798. There was no evident relationship to the nineteenth-century singer, Elizabeth Fearon (1795–1853), who married the manager Joseph Glossop (d. 1835) and as Madame Feron performed in London, New York, and Philadelphia.

An engraving by W. N. Gardiner, after S. Harding, of Fearon as Captain Driver in *Oroonoko* was published by Mrs Fearon in 1790. The original drawing by Harding is in the Widener Collection, Harvard University.

Fearon, Mrs James, Mary ₁*fl. 1770–1790*₁, *actress.*

Mary Fearon was acting with her husband James Fearon (1746–1789) as a member of Samuel Foote's company at the Theatre Royal in Edinburgh in 1770–71. Her roles that season at Edinburgh included Charlotte in *The Intriguing Chambermaid*, Charlotte in *The Mock Doctor*, Clara in *Rule A Wife and Have a Wife*, Corinna in *The Citizen*, Lucy in *The Devil to Pay*, Mrs Simple in *The Lame Lover*, Phoebe in *As You Like It*, Tattleaid in *The Funeral*, and Toilet in *The Jealous Wife*.

Accompanying her husband to London to join Foote's company for the summer, Mrs Fearon made her debut at the Haymarket Theatre on 26 June 1771 as Lady Catherine Coldstream in *The Maid of Bath*. That part of a Scottish woman was most fitting for her, for Mrs Fearon, reported the *Town and Country Magazine* in June 1771, "never till within these three months crossed the Tweed." She acted the role, her only one of the summer, 21 times through 14 September. The following summer at the Haymarket she again played that part and also acted Dolly in *The Commissary* (8 June 1772), Madge in *Love in a Village* (18 September), and delivered the epilogue to *The Nabob* on 29 June.

Mrs Fearon continued to make occasional appearances at the Haymarket through 1777. In 1773 she acted Jenny in *The Commissary* on 2 July, Lady Lochiel in *A Trip to Portsmouth* on 1 August, and Lady Catherine in *The Maid of Bath* for the benefit which she shared with Aickin on 20 September, when she was granted a special license for the performance. In 1774 she played Lady Catherine on 6 June, Jenny on 17 June, and Lady Lochiel on 5 and 6 September. She repeated those roles several times in the summers of 1775 and 1776. The following summer she made only a single appearance, as Lady Catherine on 30 July 1777, the occasion of Samuel Foote's last appearance on the stage.

On 4 November 1775 she had made her first appearance at Covent Garden Theatre in the role of Dolly in *The Commissary*, her only performance there that season. She repeated the role at Covent Garden on 24 September 1777. Her last performance on record was as Lady Catherine (for that night only) for her husband's benefit at Covent Garden on 11 May 1787.

Mrs Fearon's husband died at Richmond on 30 September 1789, and she and her eight children were given benefits at Richmond on 22 October 1789 and at Covent Garden on 16 June 1790. On the morning after the latter benefit she advertised her gratitude to the public in the press, from No 6, Spur Street, Leicester Fields, signing her name as Mary Fearon. For information on those benefits and on her children see the entry for her husband James Fearon.

Featherstone, Miss ₁*fl. 1751*₁, *performer.*

Miss Featherstone, with Master Phillips, entertained at Phillips's booth at Southwark Fair on 9 September 1751 with singing and dancing. It is difficult to tell whether she sang or danced or did both.

Fede, Signor ₁*fl. 1687–1688*₁, *musician.*

Though Signor Fede seems not to have served in the royal musical establishment long, his position was considerable. He was master of the Chapel Royal at a salary of £200 yearly from at least as early as 19 May 1687. He attended the royal family at Windsor and Hampton Court in the summer and fall of 1687 and the summer of 1688, and on 26 June 1688 he composed music for John Abell's extravagant musical celebration on the Thames. The last mention of him was on 20 October 1688 in the Lord Chamberlain's accounts, when he and others were to be paid 6s. (daily, presumably) for their attendance at Windsor the previous summer.

Fedeli. *See* FIDELI.

Federici, Vincenzo *1764–1826, composer, harpsichordist, music director.*

Born at Pesaro in 1764, Vincenzo Federici studied harpsichord and harmony with Angelo Gadani of Bologna. Orphaned at the age of 16, he came to London where he earned a living by giving music lessons. Very little is known of him until 29 April 1789, when a new pantomime ballet by Noverre, *Annette et Lubin*, with music by Federici, was given at the King's Theatre. Perhaps he returned to Italy for a brief period, for his first opera *L'Olimpiade* was produced at Turin on 26 December 1789. Several months later he was the musical director for *La villanella rapita*, by Bianchi (with two additions by Mozart), which was performed on 27 February 1790 at the Haymarket Theatre, where the opera company played after the King's Theatre burned the previous year. On 6 April 1790 *L'usurpatore innocente*, composed by Federici himself, was given at the Haymarket; the *Public Advertiser* on 7 April reported that the music had "many claims of approbation." The libretto, however, was severely criticized: "We could not see without surprise the Opera of *Demophoonte* disguised under the Appellation of *L'Us-*

urpator Innocente. Such an insult, from the hand of some botching pruner, to . . . Metastasio, the first poet of the Italian stage, should not have been tolerated." Other operas that season for which Federici was listed as director of music were *La generosità d'Alessandro* on 29 April, *Gli schiavi per amore* on 27 May, and *Andromaca* on 28 May.

Federici remained as a composer and director of music and harpsichordist (maestro al cembalo) at the opera for ten years; in those capacities he also directed the orchestra. His salary from 1794 through 1800 was £300 per season.

A new overture in the tragic style and an entire new cantata were written by Federici for a concert of vocal and instrumental music at the King's Theatre on 19 May 1791. For a similar entertainment on 4 June 1791 he composed a new sextette. In 1793 he contributed new airs to *I giuochi d' Agrigento*, *Teodolinda*, and *Odenato and Zenobia*. With other composers he provided additions to the tragic-comic operatic afterpiece *Don Giovanni* on 1 March 1794. He played the harpsichord for the oratorio *Debora and Sisara*, which was produced as a grand event, with over 200 vocal and instrumental performers under the direction of Dr Arnold, at the King's Theatre on 20 February 1795. He adapted Sacchini's *Evelina* for performance on 10 January 1797 and with Benelli and Guglielmi provided additional airs to *Didone* on 30 May 1799. On 15 April 1800 he supplied additions for the first performance in London of Sarti's *Alessandro e Timoteo*. He collaborated with Cesare Bossi on music for the ballet *Alonzo the Brave and the Fair Imogene* on 26 March 1801. Federici was also leader of the band at Ranelagh Gardens in 1792. From the memoirs of Lorenzo Da Ponte, who in one instance called Federici "monkey-face," it is also clear that the maestro did not escape embroilment in the intrigue which characterized life in the King's Theatre.

Federici left England in 1802 for Italy, where between 1803 and 1815 he wrote operas for the theatres in Milan, Turin, and Rome, including *Castore e Polluce* (La Scala, January 1803), *Oreste in Tauride* (La Scala, January 1804), *Sofonisba* (Turin, 1805), and *La conquista delle Indie Orientali* (Turin, 1808). For a more detailed account of his continental career see his entry in the *Enciclopedia dello spettacolo*. He should not be confused with his contemporary Francesco Federici whose works are often incorrectly attributed to Vincenzo, especially *Zaira*, which was produced at the Teatro Carcano, Milan, on 3 September 1803.

In 1814 Vincenzo Federici was appointed Professor of Harmony at the Milan Conservatory. He died at Milan on 26 September 1826.

Songs by him for *Alessandro e Timoteo*, as sung by Mme Banti and Signor Rosselli, which were published at London in 1800 included *Amor per tuo diletto, Bella dea, Nel seno il cor mi palpita, Odi un suon di meste note*, and *Va dove cadono in seno al Gange*. A *Pas de Deux* composed for the same opera was also published in 1800.

Federici appears in a caricature engraving by Dent entitled "High Committee, or, Operatical Contest," along with other figures representing the nobility and opera personnel who were involved in the rivalry between the two opera companies in 1791.

Feild. *See* FIELD.

Feiston. *See* FESTING.

Feldon, Daniel *d. 1832, bassoonist, organist.*
Daniel Feldon of Oxford was engaged by the Stewards of the Musical Society there in 1792 to play bassoon in the band at the Oxford Music Room, which he continued to do at least until 1808. Doane's *Musical Directory* of 1794 noted that Feldon also performed in London for the New Musical Fund and in the Handel concerts at Westminster Abbey. By 1815 he seems to have been organist of St Peter's-in-the-East, Oxford. In 1827 he was fined £25 for an assault on a Mrs Pettyfer in the parish of St Clement's. Daniel Feldon died in that parish on 14 August 1832.

Felican or **Felissent.** *See* BILLINGTON, MRS JAMES.

Felix, Sieur [*fl. 1678*], *musician.*
On 8 June 1678, according to the Lord Chamberlain's accounts, a certificate was issued making "Cir Felix alias La Montagn Cir." and two other Frenchmen musicians in the Chapel Royal.

Felix, Signor [*fl. 1786*], *mandolin player.*
At Astley's Amphitheatre on 12 May 1786 and subsequent dates through 26 August, the Venetian mandolin player Signor Felix "imitate[d] the Flagellet at the same time accompanying himself Obligato on the Mandoline, in a stile entirely new."

Fell, Abraham [*fl. 1784–1805*], *violinist, violist.*
The Mr Fell who played second violin at the Handel Memorial Concerts at Westminster Abbey and the Pantheon in May and June 1784 was very likely Abraham Fell of Benjamin Street, Clerkenwell, who, according to Doane's *Musical Directory* of 1794, was a violist for the New Musical Fund. Abraham Fell was still active in that society in 1805.

Fell, Mrs [William?] [*fl. 1755*], *actress.*
A Mrs Fell played Damaris in *The Happy Gallant* at Bence's Room at Bartholomew Fair on 6 September 1755. She may have been the wife of William Fell, one of the proprietors of the Norwich theatre in 1768.

Fellesant or Fellisent. *See* BILLING-
TON, MRS JAMES.

Fellowes, Mr ₁*fl. 1782*₁, *actor.*
At the Haymarket Theatre on 21 September 1782 Mr Fellowes played Pincet in
The Temple Beau and Dapper in *The Citizen.*

Fellows, Samuel B. ₁*fl. 1794–1815*₁,
violinist, violist.
According to Doane's *Musical Directory*
of 1794, Samuel Fellows, of No 7, Shepherd Street, Shepherd's Market, Mayfair,
was a violinist and violist for the New
Musical Fund. On the list of subscribers to
that society in 1794, 1805, and 1815 the
musician was cited as S. B. Fellows.

"Female Sampson, The." *See* "LIT-
TLE WOMAN FROM GENEVA, THE."

"Female Samson, The Italian." *See*
"ITALIAN FEMALE SAMSON, THE."

"Female Soldier, The." *See* SNELL,
HANNAH.

Fen. *See* FENN.

Fench, Mrs ₁*fl. 1776*₁. *See* FRENCH,
MRS ₁*fl. 1776–1779*₁, *actress.*

Fench, H. *See* TENCH, HENRY.

Fenell. *See* FINELL.

Fenelon, Mr ₁*fl. 1796*₁, *dancer.*
Mr Fenelon was advertised as one of
the dancers, with King and Mrs Wybrow,
in the pantomime ballet *The Strawberry
Pickers* at Sadler's Wells on 5 April 1796.
Possibly Fenelon was a misprint in the advertisements for Fialon, who was a regular
performer at Sadler's Wells in the 1790s.

Fenlin, Master ₁*fl. 1740*₁, *actor.*
Master Fenlin played Puck in *Robin

Goodfellow* on 14 October 1740 at Drury
Lane.

Fenn, John ₁*fl. 1739–1745*₁, *doorkeeper.*
John Fenn's first notice in the bills at
Drury Lane came on 14 May 1739 when
it was noted that his benefit tickets would
be accepted. He was called the assistant
stage doorkeeper, but by 1742–43, after
receiving yearly shared benefits, he was
cited as stage doorkeeper. So he remained
through 1744–45, his last benefit being on
13 May 1745. On 19 May 1746 a Mrs
Fenn's benefit tickets were accepted, but
John Fenn was not mentioned during the
season. Perhaps, if the two were man and
wife, he retired or died after the 1744–45
season, making it necessary for Mrs Fenn to
take a position at the theatre, probably as a
house servant.

Fenn, Mrs ₁John?₁ ₁*fl. 1746*₁, *house
servant?* See FENN, JOHN.

Fennell, James, stage name Cambray
1766–1816, actor, playwright.
James Fennell, one of the genuine eccentrics of the English and American
stages, was born in London on 11 December 1766, the son of an official in the pay
office of the Royal Navy named John Fennell and his wife, the former Miss Brady.
Before James was born, his father had
spent some time in New York as part of
his duty. James's mother was so indulgent
that by his own confession the lad soon
developed a streak of obstinacy by which
much of his later life was characterized.
After receiving his early schooling from
the Rev Dr French at Bow, he was sent to
Eton at about 13, and subsequently to
Trinity College, Cambridge, where his extravagant and irresponsible habits hardly
seemed appropriate to a person intended
at first for the church and then for the
law. After the university Fennell's tenure
at Lincoln's Inn was cut short when his

Harvard Theatre Collection

JAMES FENNELL

engraving by Boyd, after Wood

father discontinued his allowance and refused to help him pay his heavy gambling debts. James had already mortgaged his inheritance to his father. To recoup, James turned to the stage.

Toward the close of the summer season of 1787 Fennell presented himself to John Jackson, manager of the theatre at Edinburgh, and was allowed—in the words of Jackson, "without any introduction or recommendation but his own appearance and report"—to play the major role of Othello, assuming for his debut the stage name of Cambray. He played six times at Edinburgh, much to the pleasure of the audience, so Jackson gave him articles for the ensuing winter season, under penalty of £200 for breach of contract.

Fresh from his first triumph and having time before the new Edinburgh season be-

gan, Fennell returned to London in the autumn of 1787 to find himself disgraced in the eyes of his parents and relatives who, he said, shut their doors against him despite his consideration at having appeared on the stage under an assumed name. Presumably he had gone down to London to purchase costumes in preparation for his engagement with Jackson, but on 12 October 1787 he made his debut at Covent Garden Theatre as Othello, still employing the name of Cambray.

On 22 October he played the title role in *Alexander the Great*, with Miss Brunton as Statira and Mrs Pope as Roxana. He made his first appearance as Jaffeir in *Venice Preserv'd* opposite Mrs Pope's Belvidera on 29 October. In *The Children of Thespis*, John Williams, under the pseudonym of "Anthony Pasquin," wrote that his playing of Jaffeir, "tho' deck'd with much personal grace, / Is a part that's too vast for his skill to embrace." On 16 November he acted Young Wilding in *The Lyar* and Macbeth for his benefit (tickets to be had of him at No 18, Norfolk Street), at which he took £185 1s. 6d., presumably less the usual house charge of £105. Harris, the manager of Covent Garden, hoping to keep Fennell for the entire season, offered to buy his contract from Jackson for the penalty fee of £200 plus any reasonable sum for further damages, but Jackson refused.

Leaving London after his performances of 16 November, Fennell returned to Edinburgh in time to play the winter season for Jackson, who in his *History of the Scottish Stage* expressed appreciation for the actor's honor in not breaking the engagement: "Mr Fennell continued the winter with me in Edinburgh; and I must do him the justice to say, that he attended his business in every instance with the nicest punctuality. He was never absent at *one* rehearsal, and cheerfully undertook, at the shortest notice, every part assigned to him." Now using his real name, Fennell acted Othello on 3 February 1788, Macbeth to great applause on 6 February, and then a series of leading parts until the close of the winter season on 2 June. When the theatre reopened for the summer on 5 July he played Douglas, another leading role.

Fennell's career had started in a favorable and promising manner, but suddenly he found himself involved in a bizarre altercation with certain members of the Edinburgh public over the casting of *Venice Preserv'd*. On the evening of 8 July 1788, he was shown a letter signed anonymously "The Public" which threatened to stop the performance of the play scheduled for the next night if he persisted in acting Jaffeir, a role normally in the possession of Woods, who was announced for Pierre. The letter was disregarded, and at the performance a disturbance was raised in response to which Fennell addressed the audience, using the phrase "a scene of villainy." Disturbances followed on two more nights, and other letters were received, one of which threatened, "if you Take any more, of Mr Woods Parts . . . I, will Brick every Bone in Your Bodey" (signed "A Gentleman"). At a performance on 14 July—in which he played Montevole and Mrs Siddons Julia in *The Italian Lover*—Fennell explained that he had used the phrase about villainy only in reference to the writers of the first letter, and he was approved by the audience. The issue continued to be controversial, however. A letter to Fennell, dated 15 July, signed by about 130 prominent citizens, including lawyers, writers, and the Solicitor and Dean of Faculty at the Parliament House, demanded an apology from Fennell or his dismissal; otherwise "neither we nor our families will henceforth frequent your theatre."

Fennell brought action against his detractors, demanding damages of £15,000, and rather than apologize he announced he was quitting the stage. In a pamphlet dated from Walker's Hotel, 24 August 1788, entitled *A statement of facts occasional of*

and relative to the late disturbances at the Theatre Royal, Edinburgh, Fennell wrote his version of the controversy and further explained that Jackson, not he, was responsible for the casting. Genest called the attack on Fennell "a vile conspiracy" brought on by the offense he had given to some gentleman by presuming to intrude upon their society at the balls. Later Fennell withdrew his suit, and in a compromise he received £500 from his adversaries who also agreed to support his benefit when he appeared once more as Othello in the following summer.

In 1789 he acted at Newcastle and York and then returned to Covent Garden in the role of Othello on 16 October 1789.

Folger Shakespeare Library

JAMES FENNELL, as Macbeth

by Loftis

He repeated the role on 26 October, and then played Hotspur (his first appearance in that character) in *1 Henry IV* on 2 November, Edmund (also for the first time) in *King Lear* on 23 November, and Othello again on 15 May 1790 at which he took £200 6*s.* (presumably less house charges of £105). The reviewer in the *Biographical and Imperial Magazine* for May 1790 regretted that the benefit did not bring Fennell a better house, which his "great merits as a performer" deserved, and provided a useful account of his performance:

His representation of the jealous and high-spirited Moor, was characteristic, feeling and dignified, especially in those scenes where the turbulence of passion, the struggles of savage jealousy, and soothing fondness, and the overwhelming anguish of his soul, are so finely sketched by our immortal bard. In these parts, indeed, we may say, that Mr Fennell gave full colouring and animation to the sublime draught of his author: and, though in some of the more tender passages, it was evident (notwithstanding his feeling and just discrimination) that *his* modulations of voice are not calculated to affect, in the keenest degree, the softer sympathies; yet his deep, but not ranting tones of fury and anguish, roused all the passions congenial to the character, and shewed him to be indeed the Moor. Another attention to the decorum of nature did him equal credit. Instead of deliberately searching for new and fanciful readings, in the very tempest of his wrath (*like the puff-raised Roscius of the other house*) he poured rapidly forth the torrent of his fury, as is the nature of such passions, and seemed more intent to paint the fervour of his soul, than to impress particular syllables on the minds of his hearers. And yet the justice of his choice, in disputed readings, did conspicuous credit to his judgment, especially in the last act, where preparing to smother Desdemona, he makes the well-known apostrophism to the candle, and which he delivered thus: "Put out the light, and then" — (*pausing suddenly, and turning round, as though recollecting the horror of that act which was to follow*) "Put out the *light*!" In short, Mr. Fennel's Othello displays talents which ought not to be lost to the stage, because at present they are as unrivalled as the dramatic majesty of his person.

Fennell acted at Richmond in the summer of 1790. At Covent Garden again in 1790–91, now earning £4 per week, Fennell played Castalio in *The Orphan,* Othello, Edmund, Laertes in *Hamlet,* Don Duart in *Love Makes a Man,* and Young Cape in *The Author.* On 20 December he played Douglas, his first performance of that role in London. The afterpiece on that night was a new spectacular pantomime called *The Picture of Paris Taken in the Year 1790* which Joseph Knight in *The Dictionary of National Biography* credited to Fennell but could not date. The piece was written by Charles Bonnor and Robert Merry (not published but to be found at the Huntington Library as Larpent MS 886) and received a total of 36 performances that season. On 11 January 1791 Bonnor was paid £200 by the treasury of Covent Garden. The author of the prologue is unknown, but may have been Fennell, who was a friend of Robert Merry and who confessed in his autobiography to having been in love with Merry's wife, the former Elizabeth Brunton.

On 7 March 1791, a benefit for Lee Lewes was given at the Haymarket Theatre by special permission of the Lord Chamberlain and under the patronage of their highnesses the Prince of Wales, the Duke of York, and the Duke of Clarence, at which a two-act farce written by Fennell entitled *The Advertisement; or, A New Way to Get a Husband* (not published; Larpent MS 924) was performed for the first and only time, with the author in one of the principal roles. Another piece by Fennell, a three-act comedy called *Lindor and Clara; or, the British Officer,* was played at Richmond, probably in 1791, the year in which it was published in London in a five-act version. Fennell is said to have been the editor of a periodical called the *Theatrical Guardian*, which came out in London in six weekly numbers in March and April 1791, and *The Prompter*, which had been published in 19 numbers between 24 October and 10 December 1789.

On 10 May 1792 Fennell married Barbara Harriet Porter and took his bride to Paris, where he lived in great style, "at the expense of all who trusted his specious manners and fine appearance," wrote Dunlap in his *History of the American Theatre*. While in Paris Fennell met the Merrys, who proposed that he go to America, a suggestion he did not then act upon. Evidently he opened "a school of declamation" in Paris, but he was forced to flee France, it was said, when he was denounced by a revolutionary fanatic as a spy for William Pitt. Upon Fennell's return to London he published *A Review of the Proceedings at Paris during the last Summer* (1792).

Having contracted in May 1793 to appear in Thomas Wignell's company at the new Chestnut Street Theatre in Philadelphia. Fennell arrived in America in the summer, but his debut was delayed by an epidemic of yellow fever. He made his first appearance with Wignell's company at Annapolis, Maryland, on 19 February 1794 as Biron in *Isabella*. During the winter he gave some public lectures on natural philosophy which brought him a reputation as a scientist.

In the autumn of 1794, after playing in Baltimore, Fennell—as he tells the story in his *Apology*—was persuaded by General Knox and Governor Mifflin to leave the stage and engage in a venture of extracting salt from sea water, an enterprise which he induced many influential Philadelphians to support and which ended in financial disaster for him after several years.

In 1796, while Wignell was in England seeking recruits, Moreton engaged Fennell to play 12 nights at the end of the Baltimore season, at $30 per night, but upon his return Wignell cancelled the engagement. Fennell was with Wignell's Chestnut Street company, however, when it played in New York in August 1797, acting Zanga in *The Revenge*, among other roles. In 1799 he was engaged by Dunlap at the Park Theatre in New York where he played Othello, perhaps the best role of his career. Over the next decade, he played at Philadelphia, Boston, and New York with some regularity.

In his prime Fennell was one of the most promising actors in America, as well as one of the most popular. When he acted at Philadelphia in 1806 for 13 nights the receipts totalled $13,000, an amount termed by Clapp as representing the greatest patronage to be seen in an American theatre to that time. Fennell's lack of discipline and his penchant for extratheatrical schemes and projects prevented him, however, from achieving the high position as an actor which his potential promised. At Snow's Long Rooms in New York he gave a series of recitations from 5 January 1799. In the spring of that year he offered plays at the Pantheon in Greenwich Street, playing the *Roman Father* on 1 July, and despite the lack of audience he kept the place open through 15 July. He also gave readings and recitations in College Hall, Philadelphia.

At Boston, where he acted for the first time at the Federal Street Theatre in 1806-7, he gave readings ("with remarks") from Shakespeare at the Exchange Coffee House, and for a time he kept an academy in the Barrell House at neighboring Charlestown, having previously tried to maintain a boys' school on the Eton model in Philadelphia. In March 1810, according to Clapp, he edited a magazine in Boston called *Something edited by Nemo Nobody*. All this disparate activity was punctuated by assorted lectures on scientific and metaphysical topics, an attempt at a concordance to Shakespeare, and the writing of verse epistles.

Fennell also persisted in establishing

saltworks along the eastern shore. One of his plants was built about 1807 near Sabin's Point, a few miles down the river from Providence. Another was erected at the same time near New London. While in Providence he had duped a foreign widow named Suzman, whose property he had involved in his schemes. He had then dismissed her, according to Blake in *The Providence Stage*, "with contumely." It was reported that Fennell had become engaged to the woman, although his wife was still alive and in America at the time. Dunlap treated him harshly, denouncing him for his "career of Fraud." Fennell, who confessed his shortcomings in his *Apology*, claimed that he had had no real intent to defraud and that he was always the heaviest loser, having been jailed numerous times, once for 16 months. In his *Retrospections of America*, John Bernard attributed Fennell's mutability to that "arrant jade, Fancy," which ever lured him into speculations, after which his "sober spouse, Judgment, would lead him back to the stage and a subsistence."

After acting in Baltimore in October 1810, he was announced for six performances in November at the Park Theatre. On the third of November he played Pierre with difficulty, and then acted Richard III on the fifth. Although announced for Macbeth on the seventh and again on the fourteenth of November, he was too ill to play. Thereafter he sank into a senility which was all too apparent when he played a single performance, his final one, at the Chestnut Street Theatre on 14 April 1815, by which time his powers and memory were gone. The role was, ironically, King Lear.

Fennell died in Philadelphia on 13 June 1816, at the age of 50. (Blake claimed, incorrectly, that he died on 23 September 1815, on the day of the storm which destroyed the remains of his saltworks near Providence.) Administration of his estate, stated as less than £100, was recorded at London on 3 November 1817 as being granted to Barbara Harriet Fennell, widow, "formerly of New York but late of Philadelphia in North America." Their son, James Fennell, who had been born in 1793 just before their departure for America, acted in Philadelphia, New York, Boston, and Providence between 1811 and 1815, and from 1816–17 through 1819–20 he was with the theatre in Charleston, South Carolina. Ireland claimed "he did not betray the slightest spark of his father's talent, being, in fact, a mere cypher."

In person, the elder James Fennell was about six and a half feet tall; his towering figure, combined with a commanding voice, served him to advantage in his playing of Othello, Zanga, and Glenalvon. Although lacking in flexibility of voice and movement, he was "an excellent reader" and could express great cultivation, as well as, in Bernard's words, "a spirit the most light and mercurial." But his facial features were not handsome, his face being very heavy, his nose thick, and his eyes very light grey, with yellowish lashes and brows. As an actor, though he had no claim to genius, he was gifted.

In 1814 he published at Philadelphia *An Apology for the Life of James Fennell, written by himself*, dedicated to "Mimosa Sensitive," presumably his wife; in the self-indulgent preface he wrote of being in poverty. In addition to the works mentioned above, Fennell was the author of *The Wheel of Truth*, an unpublished farce which was played at the Park Theatre in New York on 12 January 1803.

A portrait of Fennell engraved by Boyd, after Wood, was published as frontispiece to his *Apology*. A portrait engraved by Snyder, after Doyle, was published as a plate to the *Polyanthus*, in Boston, March 1807. In the Folger Shakespeare Library is a watercolor of Fennell, full length, as Macbeth at Covent Garden, November 1787, done by W. Loftis.

Fenny, Mr [*fl.* 1794–1798], *trumpeter*.

According to Doane's *Musical Directory* of 1794, Mr Fenny, of Benjamin Street, Clerkenwell, was a trumpeter in the guards horse regiment and played in the Handel concerts at Westminster Abbey. He was still active in 1798 when, on 15 January at the Haymarket Theatre, he was one of the instrumentalists in a performance of the *Messiah*.

Fenton, Miss [*fl.* 1786], *actress*.

Miss Fenton made her first appearance, billed as "A Young Lady," at Hammersmith on 5 July 1786 when she played Belvidera in *Venice Preserv'd*. Following that she acted Lady Emily in *The Heiress* on 10 July, Donna Olivia in *A Bold Stroke for a Husband* on 19 July (when she was named in the bill), and Mrs Racket in *The Belle's Stratagem* on 26 July.

Fenton, Lavinia, née Beswick, later the Duchess of Bolton *1708–1760, singer, actress, dancer*.

In 1728 was published *The Life of Lavinia Beswick, alias Fenton, Alias Polly Peachum*, a scurrilous and probably untrustworthy work which, unfortunately, is the only source for much of our information about the original Polly in *The Beggar's Opera*. According to the *Life*, she was born in 1708, the bastard daughter of a Navy Lieutenant named Beswick. Her father was lost at sea, and her mother married a Mr Fenton in the Old Bailey. Fenton set up a coffeehouse in Charing Cross and sent Lavinia, at the age of eight, off to boarding school. Lavinia's mother, who had a succession of lovers, designed to sell her daughter to any likely prospect and in 1725 was just about to do so when Lavinia made her own bargain with "a Portuguese Nobleman." He ended up in Fleet Prison after having squandered everything he had on Lavinia, but she remained faithful to him, despite an opportunity to take up with a young merchant with good prospects. By selling her jewelry Lavinia "purchas'd [the Portuguese's] Inlargement."

Tate Gallery

LAVINIA FENTON, as Polly

by Hogarth

The *Life* further tells us that Lavinia attracted the attention of a certain nobleman who used his influence to get her on the stage. After a brief stay at the Haymarket Theatre in the spring of 1726, which won her much applause and the favor of several noblemen, she acted successfully with a company of young players at Lincoln's Inn Fields in the summer of 1726. The following fall John Rich engaged her at 15*s*. weekly at that playhouse and, to secure her, raised her quickly to twice that salary. After her success as Polly she had a succession of lovers, among them a Duke and a Knight of the Garter. She did not forget her stepfather, Mr Fenton, however, and provided him with a decent maintenance. Nor did she neglect her Portuguese nobleman, with whom in 1728, according to the *Life*, she was once again living.

Certainly some of the information contained in the *Life* is reliable, but many of the details may be exaggerated or false. Later works, such as the 1766 *Life of Quin* and the 1804 *Memoirs of Charles Macklin*, repeat the essence of the 1728 biography and provide little new or corrected information. We learn only that Lavinia had a natural talent for singing and speaking, possessed a simple, melodious voice well suited to the English ballad, and that after her success in *The Beggar's Opera* the "fan and print shops exhibited her figure every day."

The theatrical records of the 1720s are more reliable. Lavinia was possibly the "Gentlewoman who never appear'd on any Stage before" who played Serina in *The Orphan* on 24 February 1726 at the Haymarket Theatre. Perhaps she was the Miss Beswick who shared a benefit there on 12 April. As Miss Fenton she played Lucilla in *The Man's the Master* at Lincoln's Inn Fields on 15 July 1726, and she followed that with Lucia in *Epsom Wells* on 22 July and Ginnet in *The Wits* on 19 August.

The Lincoln's Inn Fields accounts show that on 16 September 1726 she was paid 5s., which, if it was a daily wage, would corroborate the statement that Rich granted her a salary of 30s. weekly. During the 1726–27 season under Rich she acted Mrs Squeamish in *The Country Wife*, a Country Lass in *The Rape of Proserpine*, Cherry in *The Stratagem,* and Lucy in *Tunbridge Walks.*

Miss Fenton's 1727–28 season was her last and most spectacular one. In addition to her earlier parts she played her most famous role, Polly Peachum, beginning on 29 January 1728. But in addition to repeated performances of that role she acted between March and May Nanny in *The Fortune Hunters*, Alinda in *The Pilgrim* (her first breeches part), Ophelia in *Hamlet*, Leanthe in *Love and a Bottle*, Betty in *A Bold Stroke for a Wife*, Marcella in *2 Don Quixote*, and Jaculine in *The Royal Merchant*. She was also featured as an entr'acte singer and dancer and offered songs within plays when the roles so required.

During that busy spring she was granted two benefits; the first, on 29 April, at which she played Cherry in *The Stratagem*, brought her £95 19s. 6d., and the second, on 4 May, when she played Polly for the forty-eighth time, brought her £155 4d. On 19 June 1728 Lavinia was replaced by Miss Warren in the role of Polly, and the *Craftsman* of 22 June reported that Miss Fenton had retired from the stage.

After *The Beggar's Opera* opened, Lavinia Fenton was the subject of much scribbling. The *Craftsman* contained a letter, written as though by her:

Whereas the Town having been imposed on by Pamphlets published in the Name of Polly Peachum; this is to inform the Publick, that I never knew of any Pamphlet made publick, save my Opera and Life, which were wrote by a Person that perform'd in the B—— O——; and in Justice to the Author and Myself, am obliged to make this Publication, in hopes to put an end to all scandal rais'd by those who are unacquainted with the Life and Character of POLLY PEACHUM.

P.S. Both which Pamphlets are to be had at all Pamphlet Shops in London and Westminster, and hope those who buy my Life will judge without Partiality.

Cheek by jowl with the letter was an advertisement for a "Beggar's Opera Screen . . . on which is curiously engrav'd in Copper-Plates, the principal Captives of the All conquering Polly, plainly describ'd by Hieroglyphicks; and on the Reverse their Amorous Letter and Declarations to that celebrated Warbler of Ribaldry. . . ."

A letter to Thomas Tickell in March 1728 stated: "Polly a Wench that acts in the Beggars Opera is the publica Cura of our noble Youth; She plays her Newgate Part well & shews the great Advantage of being born & bred in the Mint; which was really the Case. She, 'tis said, has raised her Price from one Guinea to 100, tho she cannot be a greater whore than she was before, nor, I suppose a younger." Not all the town thought that badly of her. In the *Craftsman* on 13 April one poet offered a left-handed defense:

POLLY PEACHUM
A new Ballad. To the Tune of,
Of all the Girls that are so smart.

I.

Of all the Belles that tread the Stage,
There's none like pretty Polly,
And all the Musick of the Age,
Except her Voice, is Folly.

II.

Compar'd with her, how flat appears
Cuzzoni *or* Faustina?
And when she sings, I shut my Ears
To warbling Senesino.

. . . .

V.

Some Prudes indeed, with envious Spight
Would blast her Reputation,
And tell us that to Ribands *bright*
She yields, upon Occasion.

VI.

But these are all invented Lies,
And vile outlandish Scandal,
Which from Italian *Clubs arise,*
And Partizans of Handel.

But most scribblers had a jolly time satirizing Lavinia. A mocking advertisement appeared in the *Craftsman* of the same date (13 April 1728):

Whereas P–ll–y P—ch—m *hath of late received innumerable Letters of* Love *and* Gallantry *from all Quarters of the Town, this is to give Notice that, the week after* Easter *she designs to have them printed by* Subscription, *with the Names of the Authors, in two neat Pocket Volumes. The Price to Subscribers is Two Guineas. But if any Gentlemen are apprehensive that their Amours should come to the Ears of their Wives, and endanger their*

Harvard Theatre Collection

Detail of scene from *The Beggar's Opera,* showing LAVINIA FENTON, as Polly

by Hogarth

own; or are fearful that their Passion *or* Falsespelling *should be exposed to the Publick, they may be excused upon the following Terms. For a L—d Ten Guineas; but if he have a Place or Pension regularly paid, it must be Twenty. For a B–r—t, if he be married, Eight. For a Citizen, Six. For a Toupèe, within the Precincts of Pall-Mall, Three. For all Gentlemen of the Inns of Court, provided they be under Five and Twenty, half a Guinea. Attendance is given, twice a-week, behind the Scenes, when Subscriptions are taken in and Hush-money received. N.B. The Books will be in French Binding, gilt and letter'd on the Back, and those who wou'd have her Works in Sheets must make a particular Bargain.*

And some commentators could not see what all the fuss was about. Part of a poem published on 19 April in the *Daily Journal* read:

All mankind agree to own,
That when they praise ye most,
They know not whence ye rapture flows,
Or, why thy name's their Toast.

So Coarse a Voice, so Stiff a mien,
A Face so poor in Charms!
Can ne'er demand a just applause,
Or lure us to thy Arms.

The notoriety Lavinia Fenton achieved did not deter the third Duke of Bolton. In July 1728, soon after Lavinia had quit the stage, Swift wrote that the "Duke of Bolton has run away with Polly Peachum, having settled four hundred per year on her during pleasure, and, upon disagreement, two hundred more." No serious disagreement developed, and Lavinia lived happily with her paramour for 23 years, waiting for the death of the Duchess. When that came in 1751, the Duke married Lavinia in Aix-la-Chapelle and gave her a title. She had lived in Old Bond Street in 1730 (set up there by the Duke, apparently); after their marriage the couple lived in Tunbridge Wells because of the Duke's failing health.

Joseph Warton drew a flattering picture of Lavinia in her retirement:

She was a very accomplished and most agreeable companion; had much wit, good strong sense, and a just taste in polite literature. Her person was agreeable and well made; though I think she could never be called a beauty. I have had the pleasure of being at table with her, when her conversation was much admired by the first characters of the age, particularly old Lord Bathurst and Lord Granville.

In this happy state the pair remained until the Duke of Bolton's death at Tunbridge Wells in 1754.

The Duke bequeathed all of his real and personal estate to Lavinia and made her his executrix. By the Duke she had had three sons, but they were not born at a time to make any of them eligible for the dukedom, which passed to the Duke of Bolton's brother in 1754. Lavinia stayed on at Tunbridge Wells for a year or two after her husband's death and then moved to Greenwich. According to Horace Walpole, Lavinia, late in life, married an Irish surgeon and left her fortune to him rather than to her sons.

The Duchess of Bolton died on 24 January 1760 at West Combe Park, Kent, and was buried with considerable ceremony on 3 February in a vault at St Alphege, Greenwich. The inscription on the top of her coffin read:

The Most Illustrious
Lady Lavinia Dutchess of Bolton
Dowager of the Most High
Puissant and Noble Prince
Charles Powlett late Duke of Bolton
Marquis of Winchester Earle of Wiltshire &c
Died 24th Jany 1760
Aged 49 Years

Portraits of Lavinia Fenton include:

1. By Joseph Highmore. A painting by Highmore has been supposed to show actors in the Drury Lane Green Room, 1728–1732, watching Spranger Barry rehearse Romeo. Supposedly pictured is Lavinia Fenton, huddling behind James Quin. But since neither Miss Fenton nor Quin belonged to the Drury Lane troupe, and since Barry did not make his first stage appearance until 1744, the identification of the performers must be seriously questioned. The picture, which once belonged to Sir Charles Tennant, is now in the Mellon collection at Yale University.

2. Engraving by H. R. Cook, after J. Ellis. Published by I. W. H. Payne, 1813.

3. Engraving by J. Faber, Jr, after J. Ellis. Published by J. Bowles.

4. Engraving by J. Tinney, after J. Ellis (not, as in Hall's catalogue of the Harvard collection, Ellis, after Ellis), showing Lavinia Fenton with a staff. Published by J. Bowles.

5. Satirical print, anonymous, 1728, titled "The Stage Medley."

6. As Polly in *The Beggar's Opera.* Painting by Hogarth. In the Tate Gallery. Engraving by C. Apostool. Published by S. Ireland, 1797. Engraving by T. Cook, reversed. Published in Nichol's *Genuine*

Works of Hogarth, 1808. The Faber engraving, after Ellis, noted above, is very similar to the Hogarth painting at the Tate.

7. As Polly, with other characters in the Newgate scene, with audience members watching. Painting by Hogarth. In the Tate Gallery. In the audience, among other notables, is the Duke of Bolton. Hogarth painted six versions of the scene; the other five are noted below.

8. As Polly, with other characters in the Newgate scene. Painting by Hogarth for John Rich. In the collection of W. S. Lewis, Farmington, Connecticut.

9. As Polly, with other characters in the Newgate scene. Painting by Hogarth. In the Mellon collection.

10. As Polly, with other characters in the Newgate scene. Painting by Hogarth. In the collection of Nigel Capel Cure, Esq.

11. As Polly, with other characters in the Newgate scene. Painting by Hogarth. In the collection of the Hon Lady Anstruther-Gough-Calthorpe.

12. As Polly, with other characters in the Newgate scene. Painting by Hogarth. Location unknown.

13. As Polly, with other characters in the Newgate scene. Chalk drawing by Hogarth; a sketch for the Tate painting. In the collection of Her Majesty the Queen.

14. Satirical print, 1728, by Hogarth, depicting the characters in *The Beggar's Opera* with animal heads. Polly has a pig's head, Macheath an ass's.

Fentum, John ₁*fl. 1784–c. 1835*₁, *violinist, violist, music seller.*

John Fentum was probably the son of Jonathan Fentum, the owner of a music shop at No 78, the Strand. By 1784 he had succeeded Jonathan and he continued at the same address until about 1835, when he was in turn succeeded by a relative, Mary Ann Fentum. The business flourished under John, and about 1810 he opened a second shop at No 2, St George's Place, near Camberwell Green.

Fentum was not only a music publisher and seller; he was a violinist and violist and in 1787–88 he received £4 4*s.* for playing violin in concerts of the Academy of Ancient Music that season. About 1794, according to Doane's *Musical Directory*, he played for the New Musical Fund and in the Handel performances at Westminster Abbey. He was a member of the Court of Assistants of the New Musical Fund in 1795 and 1805 and possibly in other years as well. At his shop in the Strand Fentum sold tickets for entertainments, such as for the 6 November 1803 performance at the Royal Circus.

Fenwick, Mr ₁*fl. 1760*₁, *dresser.*

Mr Fenwick was listed on a Covent Garden payroll dated 22 September 1760 as one of the men's dressers receiving 1*s.* daily.

Ferbridge, Miss. *See* **FERGUSON, JANE.**

Ferci. *See* **FERZI.**

Fereri. *See* **FERRÈRE.**

Ferg, Master ₁*fl. 1737–1744*₁, *dancer, drummer, actor.*

Master Ferg, a scholar of Liviez, danced *The Flanderkins* with Miss Wright on 7 November 1737 at Drury Lane, the pair being called "two of the Lilliputians." Their dance was frequently repeated during the rest of the 1737–38 season, and the pair also appeared in such other specialty turns as a *Punch* dance, *French Peasants*, and *Tambourine*. On 19 November Master Ferg played the title role in *The Burgomaster Trick'd*, a piece performed by the children in the company, and on 28 February 1738 he showed another side of his talent by beating a preamble on the kettledrums. At his benefit on 3 March he offered his preamble again and performed a solo *Wooden Shoe Dance*. On 23 August at Bartholomew Fair the Lilliputians acted

The Dragon of Wantley at Hallam's booth. Master Ferg was the Dragon and also danced.

He remained a member of the Drury Lane company through 1740–41, making occasional appearances elsewhere. At the patent house over the years he repeated his old specialties, played Oberon in *Robin Goodfellow*, and was seen in a number of entr'acte dances, often with Miss Wright, such as *Burgomaster and Frow*, *Pierrots*, *Drunken Peasant*, and *Miller's Dance*. He put in a dancing appearance at Covent Garden on 2 August 1739 and played Cupid in *Cephalus* at the Lee-Phillips booth at Bartholomew Fair on 23 August 1740.

He began the 1740–41 season at Drury Lane (where a Miss Ferg, probably his sister, also performed), but he joined the Covent Garden troupe on 18 November 1740 at 1s. 8d. daily. A Mrs Ferg (his mother?) was advanced £4 4s. from the Covent Garden treasury on 27 December 1740. At his new house Master Ferg was Harlequin in *Harlequin Barber* and danced in *The Metamorphosis of the Windmills* on 20 April 1741, and on 12 May he shared a benefit with three others. His activity seems to have been slight compared with that of earlier seasons. On 22 August 1741 the young dancer played Cupid in *The Wrangling Deities* at the Lee-Woodward booth at the Fair. If he returned full time to Covent Garden in 1741–42, the bills do not reflect it. The only mention of him after that season was on 14 February 1744 when, billed as "young Ferg," he played a Woman Dwarf in *Orpheus and Eurydice* at Covent Garden.

Ferg, Miss [*fl.* 1739–1740], *actress*.
Miss Ferg played Mustardseed in *Robin Goodfellow* at Drury Lane on 10 October 1739 and Peas Blossom in the same pantomime on 14 October 1740 and subsequent dates through December. She and Master Ferg were probably brother and sister and the children of Mary Ferg.

Ferg, Mary [*fl.* 1734–1735], *messenger*.
Mary Ferg was a Drury Lane messenger in 1734–35. On 26 February 1735 she came to the aid of the manager, James Quin, by printing an affidavit in the papers supporting Quin's stance in the case of Poitier and Mme Roland, two dancers who had refused to perform on 7 December 1734. The Mrs Ferg who was advanced £4 4s. on 27 December 1740, probably for Master Ferg the dancer, may well have been Mary Ferg and the mother of Master and Miss Ferg, both of whom performed in the late 1730s and early 1740s.

Ferguson, Mr [*fl.* 1734–1750], *dancer, actor*.
Mr Ferguson was mentioned as a Countryman in *The Rape of Proserpine* at Covent Garden on 30 December 1734, and the accounts at that house for 1735–36 show him receiving £43 for 172 days of work. His appearances that season were not significant: he was a Peasant in *Apollo and Daphne* and a Country Lad in *The Royal Chace*, and at the company's second playhouse, Lincoln's Inn Fields, Ferguson offered audiences a solo hornpipe which proved popular enough to be given frequently at Covent Garden in 1736–37. After that season he seems to have left the troupe.

In 1740 Ferguson and Hendrick (Kerman?) appeared in Paris in a *Fête anglaise*, and the pair played minor roles with the Grande Troupe Étrangère there for some years. With that company under Restier and the elder Lavigne, according to Campardon, Ferguson performed at the fairs, three of his roles being Pierrot in *Arlequin et Colombine captifs* on 3 February 1741, the Father of Colombine in *A Trompeur, trompeur et demi* on 3 February 1742, and Mynheer Vangelt in *Diable boîteux* on 15 February 1742.

One of Ferguson's scholars in Paris came over to London to appear at Bartholomew Fair on 22 August 1741, puffed as a "surprising little Posture-Boy." Ferguson himself seems to have returned from the Continent and joined the Covent Garden company for the 1746–47 season, though the only record of him is a note in the accounts on 25 April 1747 showing that he was taken off the roster for the rest of the season. His name appeared in no bills.

He was probably the Ferguson who acted Shadow in *The Imprisonment of Harlequin* at Phillips's Southwark Fair booth on 7 September 1750.

Ferguson, Mr (*fl.* 1785), *actor.*

Mr. Ferguson played Colonel Tomlinson in *King Charles I* when it was presented for one night only at the Haymarket Theatre on 31 January 1785.

Ferguson, Mrs (*fl.* 1735–1750), *actress.*

On 21 March 1735 Mrs Ferguson acted Stormandra in *The Covent Garden Tragedy* at York Buildings. The following 7 April she played Melinda in *The Recruiting Officer* at Southwark Fair; on 29 May she probably played Zara at York Buildings; and on 17 July at York Buildings she was Amanda in *The Relapse* when "little Miss Ferguson," probably her daughter, spoke the epilogue. It is likely that the Mr Ferguson who danced in London from 1734 to 1737 was related.

For the following several years Mrs Ferguson struggled to establish herself in London but with little success; Miss Jane Ferguson had somewhat better luck. On 28 February 1736 at Drury Lane Mrs Ferguson was a China Woman in *The Fall of Phaeton*; on 9 May 1740 at Covent Garden she played Jaqueline in *The Royal Merchant*; in 1740–41 she was receiving 1*s.* 8*d.* daily at Covent Garden but was not mentioned in the bills; and in 1746–47 she was at the same house at 7*s.* 6*d.* weekly but again received no notices. It is probable

that she was regularly employed during the 1740s as a minor actress even if the bills rarely cited her.

The playbills of the period occasionally confused Mrs Ferguson and Miss Jane Ferguson, and it is possible that some of the roles assigned in this dictionary to Jane belonged to Mrs Ferguson. Two entries in the Covent Garden accounts in 1749–50, however, almost certainly refer to our subject: on 29 September 1749 she was paid 5*s.* for two days, and on 21 April 1750 her name was dropped from the pay list.

Ferguson, Mrs, née Vincent (*fl.* 1788–1799), *actress, singer.*

On 29 March 1788 an anonymous young lady appeared as Polly in *The Beggar's Opera* at Covent Garden Theatre; the *Gazetteer* identified her as Mrs Ferguson. She was making her second appearance on the stage, but the paper did not say where she had made her first. Perhaps it was at Richmond, for the *European Magazine* in 1790 said that about 1788 Mrs Ferguson, the daughter of the Drury Lane actress Mrs Vincent, had performed at Richmond. Our guess is that the woman who acted Polly and the daughter of Mrs Vincent were one and the same. Mrs Ferguson was hailed as from Richmond when she made what the bills called her debut at Covent Garden as Rosetta in *Love in a Village* on 11 December 1790. The *European Magazine* said she was small and neither elegant nor interesting in her action and deportment. Her voice was tolerable though not powerful, and she sometimes sang out of tune. Yet she was successful in "Love should you meet a fond pair" and greatly applauded. The critic felt that possibly as a second-rate singer she might be of some use to the theatre, and perhaps she was, but the Covent Garden management did not see fit to name her again in the playbills in 1790–91.

During the 1792–93 season Mrs Ferguson sang in the oratorios at Drury Lane, and on 6 March 1793 she sang "Sweet bird" in *L'Allegro ed il Penseroso* and an Italian song at the Haymarket Theatre. She tried Polly in *The Beggar's Opera* (again) at Covent Garden on 10 May, for that night only. Two years later, on 21 May 1795, she sang a song at Drury Lane, incorrectly advertised as making her first appearance on that stage. After another lapse of two years she received billing on 9 May 1797 at Covent Garden at Yarico in *Inkle and Yarico* (with additional songs for that night only) at Johnstone's benefit. Again the critics were cool: the *Monthly Mirror* in June commented that "the audience did not seem to welcome her with much warmth. As a singer she has some little merit; but her dramatic talents (confidence excepted) are very indifferent indeed." On 12 June 1799 at Covent Garden Mrs Ferguson, perhaps with intentional irony, sang "Hope told a flattering tale."

Ferguson, Jane [*fl.* 1735–1773], actress.

Perhaps Jane Ferguson was the daughter of the Mr and Mrs Ferguson who performed in London in the 1730s. Tracing her career is sometimes difficult, for the bills seem occasionally to have confused her with her mother, and the "Miss Ferguson Junior" who was named in a bill in 1736 may have been either Jane or a second young lady (her sister?). In the 1760s Jane styled herself *Mrs* Ferguson, but by then her mother had left the stage.

Jane's first appearance may have been on 29 May 1735 when *Zara* was performed by amateurs at York Buildings. The actress playing Zara was not identified in the press, but Davies in his *Life of Garrick* said Miss Ferguson took the part. It is more likely that she spoke the prologue and epilogue and Mrs Ferguson played Zara. On 17 July at York Buildings "little Miss Ferguson" spoke the epilogue to *The Fatal Extravagance*; that night Mrs Ferguson acted Amanda in *The Relapse*. "Miss Ferguson Jr" played the Genius of Gin in *Tumble-*

Down Dick at the Haymarket on 29 April 1736, and "Miss Ferguson" was Gipsey in *The Beaux' Stratagem* at Lincoln's Inn Fields on 16 June, played Basset in *The Provok'd Husband* at the Haymarket on 29 June, and spoke a prologue and epilogue in boy's clothes at the Haymarket on 14 July. The April reference to Miss Ferguson Junior may well have been to Jane, for Mrs Ferguson was also active at the time, and the "Jr" may have been a simple method of distinguishing the two.

Jane began an association with Covent Garden Theatre and its manager John Rich in 1737–38 that continued to the end of her career, though the only known role for her that season was the Page in *Henry V* on 23 February 1738. She is said to have acted in a production of *The Orphan* at York Buildings in 1738, a performance in which David Garrick is supposed to have played Chamont, but there is no clear record of that.

Miss Ferguson's career at Covent Garden grew slowly. At benefit time each spring for several years she was merely one of many players whose tickets were accepted. She seldom acted more than one new role of any significance each season, and she augmented her income by appearing at Bartholomew Fair in the late summers. By 1745 the additions to her repertoire included such forgettable roles as Finisher in *The Comical History of Don Quixote*, Prudential in *The Devil of a Duke*, Joyce in *The What D'Ye Call It*, Charlotte in *The Indian Merchant*, Jenny in *The Glorious Queen of Hungary*, and Jenny in *The Lottery*. But she also played a few parts she continued acting for many years, such as Scentwell in *The Busy Body*, the Fool in *The Pilgrim*, Advocate in *The Fair Quaker of Deal*, and Mrs Coaxer in *The Beggar's Opera*.

In the summer of 1746 and every summer through 1750 she appeared at Richmond and Twickenham. There her parts were larger and more numerous, and she received regular benefits. She played, for instance, Isabella in *The Conscious Lovers*, Parly in *The Constant Couple*, Laura in *Tancred and Sigismunda*, Lucy in *The Recruiting Officer*, Melissa in *The Lying Valet*, Trusty in *The Provok'd Husband*, Diana Trapes in *The Beggar's Opera*, the Duchess of York in *Richard III*, and Lucilla in *The Fair Penitent*. At Covent Garden during those years she added Milliner in *The Suspicious Husband*, Mrs Anne in *Love's Last Shift*, Foible in *The Way of the World*, Situp in *The Double Gallant*, Tag in *Miss in Her Teens*, and Cornet in *The Provok'd Wife*—among other parts.

In the 1750s and 1760s Jane Ferguson clung to many of the roles she had previously acted and tried such new ones as Wheedle in *The Miser*, Delia in *Theodosius*, Mrs Clearaccount in *The Twin Rivals*, Lady Wronghead and Mrs Motherly in *The Provok'd Husband*, Callis in *The Rover*, Mrs Page in *The Merry Wives of Windsor*, Betty in *A Bold Stroke for a Wife*, Elvira in *Love Makes a Man*, Mariana in *All's Well That Ends Well*, and Lady Faulconbridge in *King John*. Many of the roles she had first acted at Richmond and Twickenham also became part of her Covent Garden repertoire. She advanced to shared benefits during those years, though she usually had to divide the receipts with three or four others, and in some years she was simply listed as having her tickets accepted. After more than 20 years at Covent Garden she was making only £1 10s. weekly.

In 1759, according to Winston's *Theatric Tourist*, Jane played at Plymouth, probably during the summer, one of her roles there being Mrs Sealand in *The Conscious Lovers*. She seems otherwise to have done little touring of the provinces. In the 1760s Jane (now calling herself Mrs Ferguson) was still playing most of her old parts: Mrs Coaxer, Wheedle, Trusty, the Duchess of York, Scentwell, Lady Faulconbridge, and a few others. By

September 1767 her salary had dropped from 5s. daily to 3s. 4d. and she was appearing less frequently. In 1772–73 she was cited as playing only the Duchess of York in *Richard III* and Isabella in *The Conscious Lovers*. On 4 October 1773 she began the new season in *Richard III*, but when the play was repeated on 9 December the Duchess of York was acted by Mrs. P. Green. Jane Ferguson apparently did not perform again.

Ferlendis, Alessandro ₁*fl.* *1783–1795*₁, *oboist, English horn player.*

Alessandro Ferlendis came to London in 1793, though not until 1795 do we find references to his performing. Dr Burney wrote on 8 May 1795 to Susanna Burney Phillips that he had attended a Haydn benefit concert and had heard the new oboist Ferlendis, who pleased Burney "more than any performer on that instrum^t. has done since Fischer was at his best." Burney noted that Ferlendis was not a young man and that his concentration was on "expression and refinements of execution. . . ." On 16 June 1795 Ferlendis played the English horn at the King's Theatre, accompanying Mme Banti. For the oboe he composed a number of pieces.

Ferlendis had a son, Alessandro, who was born in Venice in 1783 and followed in his father's footsteps. The Mme Camilla Ferlendis (b. c. 1778) who sang at the King's Theatre in 1813 was presumably the wife of the younger Ferlendis; according to Grove they married in 1802. The elder Ferlendis is said to have settled in Lisbon after his stay in London.

Ferlotti Rinaldi, Teresa ₁*fl.* *1794–1795*₁, *dancer.*

Mentioned in the *Morning Herald* of 20 November 1794 as from St Petersburg, Mme Teresa Ferlotti Rinaldi danced at the King's Theatre in the Haymarket from 6 December 1794 through 13 January 1795. She participated in two works, the heroic pantomime ballet *Giustino I* and *L'Espiègle soubrette*. References to her as Mlle Rinaldi appear to be in error.

Fern, Mr [fl. 1749–1750], *actor*.

Mr Fern was one of a group of English actors who presented a number of works in French at the Haymarket Theatre in the springs of 1749 and 1750. He first appeared as the Beggar and Delature in a French version of *The Beggar's Opera* called *L'Opéra du gueux* on 29 April 1749. On 9 February 1750 he acted Balance in *L'Officier en recrue*; on 16 February he repeated his role of Delateur; and on 26 February and 13 March he played Harpagon in *L'Avare*.

Feron. *See* FEARON.

Ferrand, Mr [fl. 1734–1744], *instrumentalist*.

On 19 November 1743 at a St Cecilia's Day concert in Bristol a Mr Ferrand from Portugal played the "Pariton, an Instrument never heard in England before, and German flute." On the program with him was the violinist Knerler. In the Harvard Theatre Collection is a clipping stating that Ferrand played the "baritone" at Marylebone Gardens in 1744.

Ferrare. *See* FERRÈRE.

Ferrarese, Signora, stage name of Adriana Gabrielli, later Signora Luigi del Bene *b. c. 1755, singer*.

The soprano Adriana Gabrielli was born about 1755 at Ferrara and thus was first known professionally as "La Ferrarese" and later as Signora del Bene after her marriage to Luigi del Bene, the son of an Italian diplomat who had taken her from the Conservatorio dei Mendicanti in Venice.

Announced as from the Opera in Turin, and advertised as Sga Ferrarese, she sang at the King's Theatre in London on 8 January 1785 in *Demetrio*, probably in the role of Barsene. The performance had been postponed twice, first on 1 January 1785 and again on 4 January, on account of the "sudden Indisposition of Sga Ferrarese." On 26 February she appeared as Beroe in the first London performance of Anfossi's *Nitteti*, and on 16 April she sang Mandane in *Artaserse*. For a revival of Gluck's *Orfeo* (with additions by J. C. Bach, Handel, and Anfossi) on 12 May she was Euridice. She made her first appearance in a comic role as Bettina in *I viaggiatori felici* on 28 May 1785. When she sang Bettina again for her benefit on 9 June, for which tickets were available from her at No 19, Oxendon Street, Haymarket, she advertised: "Sga Ferrarese, whose long and grievous Indispositions have been an Obstacle to the Success she ardently wished to obtain, cannot plead any Merit of her own, and only depends for Patronage on that well-known Liberality of a Public, equally disposed to allow for involuntary Deficiencies as to reward even an Attempt to captivate their Benevolence."

In a letter dated 17 November 1785, Giovanni Andrea Gallini, the proprietor of the King's Theatre, advised the Lord Chamberlain that although Signora Ferrarese was to be paid only £500 for the season, her contract had been drawn to show a salary of £650, "purposely to prevent her losing credit in Italy, should it be known she had engaged for so small a sum." Her first performance of the 1785–86 season was as Vespina in *Il marchese di Tulipano* on 24 January 1786, when her name appeared in the bills as Sga Ferrarese del Bene. On 11 March she sang Ernestina in the London premiere of Salieri's comic opera *La scuola de gelosi*. At her benefit on 30 March she was Epponina in the premiere of Cherubini's *Giulio Sabino*; tickets at 10s. 6d. could be had from her at No 232, Piccadilly. She also sang Nancy in the first performance of Anfossi's comic opera *L'Inglese in Italia* on 20 May. Her last performance in London was as Bettina in *I viaggiatori felici* on 17 June 1786.

Traveling through Milan, where she sang in *Il conte di Saldagna*, and Trieste, where she sang in *Giulio Sabino*, Signora Ferrarese then made her debut at Vienna on 13 October 1788 as Diana in *L'arbore di Diana*. For a revival of *Figaro* in August 1789 Mozart wrote a new aria "Al desio di chi t'adore" which she sang in place of "Deh vieni." She was the first Fiordiligi in *Così fan tutte* on 26 January 1790. In the spring of 1791 she was discharged from Vienna, probably because of her relationship with Lorenzo Da Ponte, who mentioned her often in his memoirs. By 1797 she was at Venice and Trieste. Her last performance was at the Teatro Communale, Bologna, on 11 August 1799 when with Antonio Brizzi she sang Tritto's cantata *Marte e la Fortuna* on the occasion of an imperial victory celebration. For additional details of her continental career see her entry in the *Enciclopedia dello spettacolo*. Salieri's air *Partiro dal caro* from *La scuola de gelosi* was published at London in 1786 as "Signora Ferrarese del Bene's Favorite Song."

Ferrari, Signora Giocomo Gotifredo, Victoire, née Henry *b. 1785, pianist.*

Victoire Ferrari, the daughter of the dancing master (Luigi?) Henry, was born on 24 June 1785, according to information supplied to Sainsbury for his dictionary. She was presumably born in London. Having become Kreusser's pupil by the age of seven, Victoire was proficient enough on the piano by the age of nine to play for Haydn. At 11 she performed at Raimondi's concerts in the presence of the Prince of Wales, who, according to Sainsbury's informant, "expressed his approbation" of her talent. Taken to Brighton "by a Lady," Victoire was heard at practice by Barthélemon, who sent for his violin in order to join her, and thereafter they often appeared

together in concerts. Afterwards, she was instructed by J. B. Cramer.

Grove says that Victoire Henry married the composer Giacomo Gotifredo Ferrari on 28 October 1804 in London. Ferrari was resident in London between 1792 and 1812. The couple had a son Adolfo Angelico Gotifredo (1807–1870) who became a pupil of Crivelli, married the singer Johanna Thomson, and had a career as a singer. Grove seems to say that the younger Ferrari and his wife had a daughter Sophia, but according to the Sainsbury manuscripts in the Glasgow University Library, Sophia was the daughter of Giacomo and Victoire Ferrari. Sophia was also a singer.

Giacomo and Victoire seem to have separated. By 1823 he was living in Edinburgh and she had by then "resided for many years at Brighton," where she was teaching "with great success."

Ferre. See CUZZONI.

Ferrère, Mons [*fl. 1752–1753*], *dancer.*

On 3 October 1752 the comic dancer Monsieur Ferrère was announced as lately arrived in London from Paris, and on 5 October he made his first English appearance dancing *The Matelot Basque* at Drury Lane. On 17 October he and his fellow traveler Devisse were in a dance called *Les Bûcherons*, and on 25 November he and Madame Auretti performed *The Hungarian Peasants*. Ferrère was busy throughout the 1752–53 season offering specialty dances, and he also appeared in *Comus*, *The Genii*, and *Harlequin Enchanted*.

Ferrère, [Master] [*fl. 1785*], *dancer.*

"Ferrere Jr." participated in a pantomime dance with other young performers at Astley's Amphitheatre on 27 September 1785. He was doubtless the son of (Auguste Frédéric Joseph?) Ferrère and his wife, who were performing in London at the time, but the records give no hint of the lad's age.

Ferrère, [Auguste Frédéric Joseph?] [fl. 1782?–1794], *dancer, choreographer.*

References in English bills in the 1780s and 1790s to Ferret, Ferrera, Fereri, and Ferrare all seem to concern the dancer Monsieur or Signor Ferrère, and it is quite possible he was August Frédéric Joseph Ferrère, who was active as a choreographer at Valenciennes in 1782. Marian Hannah

Bibliothèque de l'Opéra, Paris

Le Peintre amoureux de son modelle, ballet

by Auguste Ferrère

Winter in *The Pre-Romantic Ballet* discusses a manuscript at the Bibliothèque de l'Opéra named after Ferrère. It dates from 1782 and is the earliest known recording in Feuillet notation of a *ballet d'action.* Ferrère choreographed a number of works at Valenciennes and may have worked there for several years. Among the ballets in the collection are *Le Peintre amoureux de son modelle, Les Trois Cousines,* and *Les Boucherons et les sabbotiers.*

The Drury Lane bill of 18 September 1783 cited Ferrère as dancing *The Pastoral Lovers* with Miss Stageldoir. At the same house on 13 October he was in *The Triumph of Mirth,* but though he was occasionally noticed in the bills thereafter, he may not have stayed at Drury Lane for the full 1783–84 season.

In the spring of 1785 Ferrère was at Astley's Amphitheatre with Madame Ferrère. There he appeared in *The Merry Negroes* and offered a solo *Tambourine Dance.* He was again at Drury Lane on 22 May 1786, substituting for Williamson in a dance called *The Lucky Return.* The following 4 September at Astley's he was a dancing Shepherd in *Love from the Heart,* and from January through June 1787 he performed regularly at Drury Lane in such pieces as *The Village Archers* and *The Irish Fair.* During April he also served as a principal dancer at the Royal Circus.

Ferrère appeared again at Drury Lane in the fall of 1787, but a notation in the account books on 29 December indicates that he was dropped from the roster, and his daily salary of 6s. 8d. was stopped. In 1788 he and Madame Ferrère were again at Astley's, where he danced and also choreographed a number for himself and Madame Fuozi in the characters of an Indian Prince and Princess. May 1789 found him at the Royal Circus where, on the twelfth, he was a principal dancer in a ballet titled *The Morris Dancers* and on the fourteenth brought forward a new ballet of his own composition.

Ferrère danced in *Double Fidelity* at the Royalty Theatre on 5 April 1790, and he (possibly) and his wife (certainly) worked in the opera company at the Haymarket Theatre in London that year. Ferrère was at Norwich in 1790 as well. The Ferrères were at the Royal Circus in 1794, when they had principal parts in his dance called *The Croatian Merchants.*

The Ferrères had a son who performed at Astley's in 1785.

Ferrère, Mme ₁**Auguste Frédéric Joseph?**₁ ₁*fl. 1785–1794*₁, *dancer.*
In 1785 Madame Ferrère, her husband (Auguste Frédéric Joseph?), and their son were dancing at Astley's Amphitheatre. Monsieur and Madame Ferrère were members of that troupe again in 1788, but in May 1789 they were at the Royal Circus. On 5 April 1790 they danced in *Double Fidelity* at the Royalty Theatre. In May and June of the same year a "Mlle" (error for "Mme"?) Ferrère danced at the Haymarket Theatre, where the opera company was performing. Madame Ferrère appeared in *Les Mariages Flamands* on 25 May, a divertissement on 29 May, and *The Generous Slave* on 1 June. As a member of the Drury Lane company playing at the King's Theatre on 22 May 1792 she was Louisa in the pantomime *The Deserter of Naples.* She and her husband were at the Royal Circus again in 1794, where both of them danced and Monsieur Ferrère served as a choreographer.

Ferrers, Mr ₁*fl. 1725*₁, *dancer, singer.*
Mr Ferrers danced the Priest of Apollo in *Apollo and Daphne* on 20 February 1725 at Drury Lane, and for his solo benefit on 11 May he sang.

Ferret. *See* FERRÈRE.

Ferri, Baldassare *1610–1680, singer.*
Baldassare Ferri was born in Perugia on 9 December 1610 and entered the service

of Cardinal Crescenzi at Orvieto as a chorister at the age of 11. In 1625 Prince Ladislas of Poland took Ferri off to the Polish court, where he remained until at least 1655, though he may have visited Venice in 1643 when he was made a knight of St Mark's. While in Poland the male soprano was much admired for his singing, and it is said that Queen Christina of Sweden, though at war with Sigismund III of Poland, requested the services of Ferri. A brief armistice was arranged so that the singer could pass safely through the battle lines. Sweden received Ferri with as much enthusiasm as had Poland.

According to Heriot, Ferri left Poland for Vienna and the court of Emperor Ferdinard III in 1655, but Grove dates the singer's departure for Vienna 1665. The succeeding monarch, Leopold I, was so enthralled with Ferri that he caused a portrait of the singer to be hung in his bedroom, inscribed, "Baldassare Ferri, Re dei Musici."

The eunuch who sang in London in 1668 and 1669 was probably Ferri, though his nationality was said to be French, and he was not identified by name. Pepys heard "a Frenchman, but long bred in Italy" at the Bridges Street Theatre on 10 October 1668 and called him the "famous eunuch." "Such action and singing," the diarist wrote, "I could never have imagined to have heard . . . ." On 14 October Pepys went to the theatre again (*The Faithful Shepherdess* was being repeated), "that we might hear the French Eunuch sing, which we did, to our great content; though I do admire his action as much as his singing, being both beyond all I ever saw or heard." Perhaps the same singer was Zephyrus in *Psyche; or, Love's Mistress* at Bridges Street on 24 May 1669. He is also said to have performed at Whitehall on 3 June.

Ferri retired in 1675 to Perugia, a wealthy man. He left 600,000 scudi to charity when he died on either 8 September or 18 November 1680. He is said by Grove

to have had a tall, handsome figure and a soprano voice of great limpidity and agility, a brilliant shake, inexhaustible length of breath, and perfect intonation.

Baldassare Ferri was included in a large group picture by Antonio Fedi; the work was engraved between 1801 and 1807.

Ferrier. *See* FERRÈRE.

Ferries, Mr ⟨*fl.* 1794–1795⟩, *dresser.*
Mr Ferries was a men's dresser at Covent Garden in 1794–95 earning 9s. 6d. weekly.

Fery. *See* FERG.

Ferzi, Master *b. c.* 1769, *rope dancer.*
See FERZI, LAWRENCE.

Ferzi, Miss ⟨*fl.* 1766–1773⟩, *dancer.*
See FERZI, LAWRENCE.

Ferzi, Miss *b. c.* 1767, *rope dancer.*
See FERZI, LAWRENCE.

Ferzi, Lawrence ⟨*fl.* 1766–1779⟩, *rope dancer.*
Lawrence Ferzi (or Farci, Ferci, Firzi, Furzi) was a rope dancer in Placido's troupe at the Haymarket Theatre on 27 October 1766. The playbill for that night stated that Ferzi would jump "backwards and forwards over a cane, and put on and [take off] his hat"—presumably while leaping on the rope. Performing that same night was Miss Ferzi, probably Lawrence's sister. Ferzi and his sister were mentioned in an agreement of 1769 at Sadler's Wells, and Ferzi and his wife negotiated a two-year contract with the Sadler's Wells management that year. Their joint salary was seven guineas weekly plus a yearly benefit, for which they performed not only their own act but were in pantomimes, masques, and dances as well. It is possible that the Monsieur and Mademoiselle "Ferzier" who danced at the Crow Street Theatre in Dub-

LA FIGLIA del SIGNIOR FERZI.

By permission of the Henry E. Huntington Library and Art Gallery

LAWRENCE FERZI and FAMILY

engraving by Sparrow

lin in 1769–70 were Lawrence and his sister.

The Sadler's Wells bills of 1771 show that Ferzi and his wife then had a daughter four years old and a son two years younger, both of whom performed with their parents. After 1771 Mrs Ferzi and the children may have dropped out of the rope-dancing act, but Miss Ferzi, Lawrence's sister, was still at the Wells in 1773. Lawrence and some of his pupils were performing there and at Manchester in 1775, after which Ferzi was seen in Edinburgh in February and April 1776, at Birmingham for five nights in December of that year, at Derby, York, and Edinburgh in 1777, and again at Sadler's Wells in 1778 and 1779.

The Huntington Library has an engraving of Lawrence Ferzi and his children by S. Sparrow.

Ferzi, Mrs Lawrence [*fl.* 1769–1771], *rope dancer. See* **FERZI, LAWRENCE.**

Fesch. *See* **DE FESCH.**

Festing, Mr [*fl.* 1707–1708], *violinist?*

On 5 March 1707 at York Buildings a Mr Festing was given a benefit concert. Perhaps he was the father of John and Michael Christian Festing, though their parentage is not certainly known. Some sources say that the name of the boys' father was Michael Christian Festing and that he was an aide-de-camp to Prince Eugene in Germany; others say the father was a flutist in the King's Theatre band in 1727. The musician given a benefit in 1707 was probably a violinist; a painting by Mario Ricci showing Mrs Tofts and other singers rehearsing in 1708 has a note on the back saying that one "Festini" played first violin and was one of the violinists pictured. On 26 March 1708 at Stationers' Hall a Mr "Feiston" performed for Leigh's benefit; he was probably our subject.

Festing, Mr (fl. 1727), flutist.

Though *The London Stage* does not list a flutist named Festing as a member of the company at the King's Theatre in 1727, such a musician is said to have been there. He is one of three Festings who may have been the father of John and Michael Christian Festing.

Festing, Mr (fl. 1738–1739), dancer.

The London Stage lists a dancer named Festing in the Drury Lane company in 1738–39, but his name seems not to have appeared in any bills.

Festing, John d. 1772, oboist, flutist, composer, teacher.

John Festing was the brother of the violinist and composer Michael Christian Festing. Their mother's name was Elizabeth, and they had a sister, also Elizabeth who became Mrs "Duplaisey." John had a daughter named Letitia, but his wife's name is not known. John's father may have been the Mr Festing, violinist, who was active in 1707 and 1708 in London, but some accounts suggest that he was a flutist at the King's Theatre in 1727 and others identify him as the Michael Christian Festing who was aide-de-camp to Prince Eugene and who died in the battle of Blenheim in 1704.

John Festing's earliest notice in concert advertisements was on 15 March 1721, when he played at Hickford's Room for the benefit of Douglas, the "Prince." John's public appearances were sporadic, for he spent much of his time teaching flute and oboe. He played at York Buildings on 28 February 1729, at Lincoln's Inn Fields Theatre on 12 March (on the German flute), at Topham's concert room for his own benefit on 6 March 1730, at York Buildings for yearly March benefits for himself from 1731 through 1736, at Hickford's on 12 and 15 March 1736, and at York Buildings for his benefit on 5 March 1737. At Drury Lane in May 1737 a concerto for German flute composed by him was performed. On 28 August 1739 he became one of the founding members of the Royal Society of Musicians; when he subscribed, he gave his parish as St George, Hanover Square.

When John Festing died in London in 1772 he left a fortune of £8000, most of which he seems to have earned as a teacher.

On 30 November 1741 Hogarth published "The Enraged Musician." The original painting, which differs in some details from the same artist's engraving, is a monochrome oil sketch now in the Ashmolean Museum, Oxford. An engraving of that sketch was also made by E. Stalker. Pictured leaning out of a window, stopping his ears from the din in the street, is a musician; he has been variously identified as Cervetto, Castrucci, Arne, Foster, and John Festing. There is no certainty about the identification, but there is a story, supposedly told by Festing himself to Hogarth, that matches the picture. Festing, while waiting upon an acquaintance, became annoyed at an oboist outside the window who was playing tunes in return for onions a tradesman kept offering him. " 'I could not bear it; it angered my very soul — Z——ds,' said I, 'stop here! This fellow is ridiculing my profession; he is playing on the hautboy for onions!' " But the musician

From the collection of Edward A. Langhans

JOHN FESTING, "The Enraged Musician"

engraving by Stalker, after Hogarth

in the window has a violin, and that convinced Dr Burney that the subject was the
violinist Castrucci.

Waterhouse in *A Checklist of Portraits
by Thomas Gainsborough* lists a portrait of
John "Festin" (a variant spelling of Festing
found in other sources as well), but the
location of the painting is not known.

Festing, Michael Christian *1680?–
1752, violinist, composer.*

Michael Christian Festing is said to have
been born in Germany about 1680. Some
sources say his father was Michael Christian Festing, who served Prince Eugene in
Germany and died in the battle of Blenheim in 1704; other sources identify his
father as the violinist Festing who played
in London in 1707 and 1708; and still
others say his father was a flutist at the
King's Theatre in 1727. Certainly Michael
Christian had a brother John and a sister
Elizabeth, who became Mrs "Duplaisey,"
and their mother's name was Elizabeth.
Michael Christian studied under Richard
Jones, the Drury Lane band leader, and
then under Geminiani. One story has it
that the Festing brothers were patronized
by the Duke of Marlborough out of respect
for their father; that would fit with the

supposition that their father was the Festing who died at Blenheim.

The earliest mention of a public appearance of Michael Christian Festing was on 6 March 1723, when he played the violin at a concert at Hickford's Room in James Street. Subsequently he performed, often for his own benefit, at Hickford's on 26 February 1724, 11 March 1724, 30 March 1726 ("With several new Concertoes and Solos on the Violin of his own Composing"), and 15 March 1728; at York Buildings in Topham's concert room on 21 February 1729; and at the Lincoln's Inn Fields Theatre on 2 April 1731. During the 1730s Festing appeared at Stationers' Hall, Mercers' Hall, the Devil Tavern, and Hickford's, and from 1737 on he was the leader of the band at the King's Theatre.

On 4 November 1726, according to the Lord Chamberlain's accounts, Festing replaced James Moore as a member of the King's Musick at £40 annually. He continued in the royal musical establishment at least until 1750.

It was apparently the sight of the destitute orphaned children of the musician Kytch that inspired Festing and others to form the Royal Society of Musicians on 28 August 1739. At that time Festing described himself as from the parish of St James, Westminster. He served as secretary of the Society for many years while continuing to compose, appear at concert halls and theatres, serve as a member of the King's private band, play first violin for the Philharmonic Society, lead concerts at the Swan and the Castle taverns, play for the Academy of Ancient Music, and teach such students as Stephen Philpot and Thomas Augustine Arne. In addition, he served as director of music at Ranelagh Gardens beginning in 1742.

Michael Christian Festing died in London on 24 July 1752. He left a long will dated 22 April 1750 and proved on 12 February 1753. To his wife Anne he left £20 and funds sufficient to purchase and furnish two rooms for her own use. To his mother Elizabeth he left £40; to his sister Elizabeth Duplaisey, "now at Dublin," he left £10; to his brother John he left a mourning ring worth two guineas; and to the Musician's Charity Fund he left £5. To his son Michael he left such valuables as a watch, a cane, and a ring. (Michael became rector of Wyke Regis, Dorsetshire, and married a daughter of the musician Maurice Greene.) To his son Christian he left similar valuables, to be given the boy when he completed his apprenticeship—musical, apparently. To his wife Anne and sons Festing left his books, and to his wife he also gave his silver plate, some rings, pictures of his father, mother, and sons—for as long as Anne Festing remained unmarried. To Sir Joseph Hanky he left his manuscript music, and to Sir Joseph's eldest son he left his best violin bow. To his friend Thomas Pratt he gave the choice of any two of his manuscript compositions and the option to buy Festing's Stainer violin. Festing left mourning rings to a number of friends, including the musicians Maurice Greene and Charles Weidman. The rest of his estate was to be laid out in securities for the benefit of his widow. One of the residuary legatees was Letitia Festing, the daughter of his brother John.

Festing was, according to Dr Burney, noted for his "gentlemanlike behaviour," but Burney found him deficient as a musician: "Feeble hand, little genius for composition, and but a shallow knowledge of counterpoint." Hawkins, on the other hand, felt that Festing's violin solos were especially good. Festing composed a number of sonatas, concertos, songs, cantatas, and violin solos, many of which are listed in the *Catalogue of Printed Music in the British Museum*.

"Festini." *See* **FESTING**.

Fevre. *See* **DELFEVRE** and **LE FEVRE**.

Feyting, H. [fl. 1736–1737], *dancer.*

H. Feyting (or Fayting) danced in Giffard's troupe at Lincoln's Inn Fields in 1736–37 in minor or unnamed parts. He was in *King Arthur* on 30 September 1736, *The Worm Doctor* on 14 October, *Harlequin Shipwrecked* on 21 October (in three roles: a Haymaker, a Triton, and a Shepherd), *Britannia* on 7 December, and *Hymen's Triumph* on 1 February 1736. It is probable that he was related to (perhaps the father of) William Fayling or Fayting of Girdlers Hall who became a freeman in 1740 and made a career as a dancing master.

Fiala, Giuseppe Antonio [fl. 1678–1679], *actor.*

Giuseppe Antonio and Marzia Fiala, probably husband and wife, were members of the Duke of Modena's troupe of Italian players who performed six times at the court of Charles II between November 1678 and mid-February 1679. He played Capitano Sbranaleoni and she Flaminia in the company's *commedia dell'arte* productions.

Fiala, [Signora Giuseppe Antonio?], **Marzia** [fl. 1678–1679], *actress. See* **FIALA, GIUSEPPE ANTONIO.**

Fialar. *See* **FIALON.**

Fialon, Mr [fl. 1791–1803], *dancer.*

The first notice of Mr Fialon was on 17 February 1791 when he appeared as a principal dancer in a new pantomime ballet, *Amphion et Thalie*, at the Pantheon. When the ballet was given again on 26 February, his name was omitted from the bills. At the same theatre on 24 March he danced the apparently female role of the Invalid in *The Deserter*. On 9 May he performed in another new pantomime ballet, *La Siège de Cythère*, and on 10 June he danced in the ballet *La Fille mal gardée.*

Fialon was again among the dancers at the Pantheon in 1791–92. On 14 April 1792 he danced two roles, Marchand d'Esclaves and Zerbero, in a new ballet *La Foire de Smirne; ou, les Amans réunis* at the Haymarket Theatre. Also that year at Sadler's Wells he danced in *The Savages* and *The Fourth of June.* Fialon and his wife danced at the Crow Street Theatre, Dublin, in 1792–93, and then he returned to Sadler's Wells in 1793 to perform in *Sans Culottes* and *Pandora's Box.* No doubt he was the "Fialar" whose name was listed in the Sadler's Wells advertisements on 4 October 1793.

On 31 October 1794 Fialon made his first appearance on the Drury Lane stage with Aumer in a new dance composed by D'Egville. In that season he also danced the role of Darius in the ballet *Alexander the Great* 33 times between 12 February and 20 May 1795, appeared as Mountauciel in *The Deserter* on 20 May, and, with the D'Egvilles, Miss Menage, and Mrs Fialon, danced in *La Provençale* on 26 May.

Fialon's name was on the company lists as a dancer at the King's Theatre from 1795–96 through 1802–3, except in 1797–98. There in the spring of 1796 he was in the ballets *La Villageoise enlevée, The Caravan at Rest, Flore et Zéphire,* and *L'Heureux Naufrage.* His performances at King's Theatre in the next season included *L'Amour et Psiché* and Vulcain in *Sapho et Phaon.* On 22 May 1797 he was with the corps de ballet from the opera in a single performance of *Cupid and Psyche* at Drury Lane.

In 1797–98 Fialon was engaged at Covent Garden Theatre at £3 3s. per week and danced in a piece called *Peggy's Love* and in Noverre's *Cupid and Psyche.* At Drury Lane on 16 May 1798 he appeared, for that night only, in the dance *Kitty and Jemmy,* for the benefit of Mlle Parisot. Back at the King's Theatre for the season 1798–99, Fialon appeared dancing in *Tarare et Irza* on 2 May 1799 and three subsequent times. He continued at the King's Theatre at least through 1802–3. His wife was a dancer at the Pantheon in 1793 and at Drury Lane in the spring of 1795.

Fialon, Mrs [*fl. 1791–1795*], *dancer.*
In 1791, Mrs Fialon danced at the Pantheon as a follower of Amphion in the ballet *Amphion et Thalie* for 19 nights beginning on 17 February. At Drury Lane Theatre in the spring of 1795 she danced an Amazon, Thalestris, in the ballet *Alexander the Great* on 12 February and many times thereafter. Other dance characters in which she appeared at Drury Lane that season included Zephyrus in the masque *The Triumph of Hymen* and Louisa in *The Deserter*. She was also seen in a provençale on 26 May and a new reel on 1 June. Her husband appeared with her in most of the performances mentioned above.

Fichar. *See* FISCHER, FISHAR, FISHER.

"FIDDLING JOHNSON." *See* JOHNSON, SAMUEL *d. 1773.*

Fideli, Sigismondo [*fl. 1698–1699*], *singer.*
Sigismondo Fideli was brought to London by Christopher Rich to sing at Drury Lane in 1698–99 for £20 a performance; his earliest appearance in London seems to have been at York Buildings on 22 December 1698. On 28 February 1699 he sang at Drury Lane, apparently within a play, in both Italian and English, "which he never yet performed," according to the *Flying Post*. The importation of foreign artists by both Drury Lane and Lincoln's Inn Fields caused much criticism, largely because of the high salaries the entertainers commanded. The epilogue to Farquhar's *Love and a Bottle* in December 1698 had this to say about Fideli:

> *An Italian now we've got of mighty Fame,*

> *Don Sigismondi Fideli—There's Musick in his Name!*
> *His Voice is like the music of the spheres:*
> *It should be Heav'nly—for the Price it bears!*
> *He's a handsome Fellow too, looks brisk and trim,*
> *If he don't take you, then the Devil take him—*

Jo Haines spoke the epilogue at Drury Lane.

"Fidget Roscius, Esq." *See* GARRICK, DAVID.

Fie, Mr [*fl. 1748*], *actor.*
On 7 September 1748 at Phillips's Southwark Fair booth a Mr Fie played Flash in *Harlequin Imprisoned*. The name intended may have been Field.

Field, Mr [*fl. 1722*], *dancer.*
A Mr Field danced at Lincoln's Inn Fields on 13 March 1722 — apparently for that night only.

Field, Mr [*fl. 1784*], *singer.*
A Mr Field was listed by Dr Burney as a tenor vocal performer in the Handel Memorial Concerts at Westminster Abbey and the Pantheon in May and June 1784.

Field, Mrs [*fl. 1748*], *actress.*
Mrs Field appeared at the Lee-Yeates booth at Bartholomew Fair on 24 August 1748 playing Lady Worthy in *The Unnatural Parents*, and on the following 31 October she acted Maria in *The London Merchant* at the James Street Theatre.

Field, Ann, later Mrs William Forster *d. 1789, actress, singer, flutist.*
On 4 January 1777 Miss Ann Field made her first appearance on any stage as Ariel in *The Tempest* at Drury Lane. She was advertised as "A Young Lady" and described as Linley's scholar. The following

season, at a salary of 10*s*. weekly, she appeared again as Ariel on 20 September 1777 and then went on to play Prince Edward in *Richard III* on 7 October, Daphne in *Daphne and Amintor* on 22 November, Prince Arthur in *King John* on 29 November, Sabrina in *Comus* on 15 December, and Cupid in *Cymon* on 20 January 1778. Songs which she sang in *The Critic* sometime during 1778 were published that year. A notation in the account books on 10 June 1778 indicates that a Mr Booth received £8 for Miss Field's subsistence for 16 weeks, and on 3 June 1779 an identical payment was made to cover "Miss Field 16 weeks Board in advance." Booth may have been John Booth, the Drury Lane tailor and thus father (stepfather?) of Ann.

In 1778–79 Miss Field added no new roles, but she shared a benefit with three others on 18 May 1779, and her salary was apparently raised to 15*s*. weekly the following fall. The 1779–80 and 1780–81 seasons saw her in her old roles plus Jenny in *The Provok'd Husband* "(with *songs* in character)," Sylvia in *Cymon*, Nancy in *The Camp*, Venus in *Henry and Emma*, and Ophelia in *Hamlet* (on 24 May 1781, though she may have played the part as early as 1 March that year). She had been raised to £3 10*s*. weekly on 25 November 1780, and she received £8 as her summer salary in June 1781. Further evidence of her growing popularity was the publication in October 1781 in the *Hibernian Magazine* in Dublin of the song "Smiling Love, to thee belong," which she and Miss Wright sang in *Dissipation*.

When Miss Field shared a benefit on 10 May 1780 with Mrs Bradshaw and Mrs Booth, her address (and Mrs Booth's) was No 10, corner of Martlett Court, Bow Street, Covent Garden; by 16 May 1781 Ann and Mrs Booth were living at No 8, Broad Court, Longacre, where Ann lived through 1786. It is most probable that Anne Field was Mrs Booth's daughter. Mrs Booth was probably the wife of the Drury

Harvard Theatre Collection

ANN FIELD, as Ariel

artist unknown

Lane tailor John Booth; her given name was Ursula Agnes. If Anne was her daughter, then Anne's sister was the actress Elizabeth Field, who married a Dr Granger and later William Wallack.

At Drury Lane through December 1785 Miss Field added a number of new roles to her repertoire, among them Rosetta in *Love in a Village*, Philadel in *King Arthur*, Corinna in *The Confederacy*, Meriel in *The Ladies Frolick*, Gillian in *The Quaker*, Patty in *The Maid of the Mill*, Ann Page in *The Merry Wives of Windsor*, Jenny in *The Rival Candidate*, Peggy in *The Gentle Shepherd*, Lucinda in *The Conscious Lovers*, Miss Hoyden in *A Trip to Scarborough*, Leonora in *The Padlock*, the title role in *Rosina*, Inis in *The Wonder*, and Laura in

The Strangers at Home. Though a member of the Drury Lane troupe, she put in an appearance at Covent Garden Theatre on 23 March 1784, playing Sabrina and a Pastoral Nymph in *Comus.* Beginning in 1784–85 she subscribed £1 1s. to the Drury Lane fund, and by 22 April 1785 she had moved up to sharing a benefit with only one other performer—though on that occasion they split less than £60.

According to Reed, Ann Field became Mrs William Forster (perhaps in name only) on 9 January 1786. Under her new name she continued acting and singing at Drury Lane until her death, her only appearances at other houses being in the summers of 1787 and 1788, when she played at the Haymarket and on 26 March 1788, when she acted Patty in *Inkle and Yarico* at Covent Garden for Edwin's benefit.

As Mrs Forster she played at Drury Lane such roles as Laura in *The Projects,* Jessica in *The Merchant of Venice,* Jenny in *A School for Fathers,* Lucy in *The Country Girl,* Prue in *Love for Love,* Semira in *Artaxerxes,* Lauretta in *Richard Coeur de Lion,* Theodosia in *The Maid of the Mill,* and Lesbia in *Selima and Azor.* At the Haymarket she played some of her standard parts but also tried Daphne in *Midas,* Charlotte in *The Intriguing Chambermaid,* Jenny in *Lionel and Clarissa,* Narcissa in *Inkle and Yarico,* and Maria in *The School for Scandal.* In many of her roles Mrs Forster introduced songs in character, and she sang also in the *Messiah, Redemption,* and such plays as *Macbeth, As You Like It, The Winter's Tale,* and *The Captives.* She had a solo benefit on 2 May 1786 at which she made a profit of £109 5s. 6d. A year later, on 4 May 1787, she took in only £68 7s. 8d., despite the fact that she tried to lure patrons by playing Lucy in *The Country Girl* (with a song in character) and performing a "Duett on Two Flutes"—all by herself, apparently. By 1787 her address had changed to the corner of Castle Street, opposite Hart Street, Bloomsbury.

Perhaps she was the Mrs "Forrester" who in 1788–89 sang *Moggy Macbride* at Islington Spa; the song was published about 1790 and the music ascribed to Mr Forrester. Mrs Forster's last stage appearance was on 18 February 1789 at Drury Lane when she acted Theodosia in *The Maid of the Mill.* Two days later she was replaced in *As You Like It,* and thereafter her roles were taken by others. On 14 July 1789 Mrs Forster died.

Anthony Pasquin in *The Children of Thespis* in 1786 thought of Mrs Forster as a "timid nymph, who exists but in song." "Her wishes seem bent to recede from the view," he wrote, but "Tho' her merits won't bear the stern *critic's* inspection / Her gentleness tacitly calls for protection." Perhaps that was what William Forster offered her; *The Green Room Mirror* of 1786 hinted that Ann Field had been taken into keeping and had only assumed the name of Mrs Forster: "almighty love has divided her fame, and she has fell a sacrifice to *thelypthorian* artifice . . . Poor Ophelia! 'there's rue for you!' the certain inheritance of *Poly*—(what d'ye call it—*gam*—)." Perhaps the Forster in question was the oboist William John Forster, who died in 1811.

Ann Field was shown by an anonymous engraver as Ariel in *The Tempest.*

Field, Elizabeth. *See* **WALLACK, MRS. WILLIAM H.**

Field, Mr [J.?] [*fl.* 1792?–1811?], actor.

On 22 May 1794, a Mr Field acted Osmond in a specially licensed performance of *Tancred and Sigismunda* at the Haymarket Theatre for the benefit of Miss Thomas. Perhaps he was the same Mr Field who acted at Richmond in the summer of 1795. A Dublin gutterman named Field made his debut at the Crow Street Theatre on 9 February 1792 and also acted at Kilkenny in the same year, at Chester in 1794, at

Courtesy of the National Theatre, London

J. FIELD, as Frank

by De Wilde

Manchester in 1796, and at Plymouth in 1798 (with a Mrs Field).

One Mr Field was depicted as Frank in *Three and the Deuce* in a painting exhibited by De Wilde at the Royal Academy in 1812. That actor is identified by Mander and Mitchenson as J. Field, who performed small parts at the Haymarket in the summers of 1803, 1804, and 1805 and at Covent Garden from 1803–4 through 1810–11 at a salary of £2 weekly. Why De Wilde should paint this obscure actor in a role which he seems never to have played in London is unclear. The picture, owned by the late Somerset Maugham, is now in the possession of the National Theatre, London.

Field, John *1782–1837, pianist, composer.*

John Field, who was regarded as the greatest pianist of his day and was a com-poser of renown, was born in Dublin in 1782. The date of his birth has been given variously as 16 and 26 July. He was christened on 5 September (not 26 as usually stated) at St Werburgh's Church. Field, an inveterate romanticizer, invented a fictitious account of his origins, claiming that he had been born in Strasbourg, the son of a French violinist named Duchamp who had played for a while in the London theatres and then had settled in Bath, where the boy had been taken under instruction by Muzio Clementi.

A recent study by Patrick Piggott, *The Life and Music of John Field 1782–1837* (1973) disposes of numerous rumors and guesses which have marred previous accounts of the great pianist's life. John Field was indeed Irish, the eldest son of Robert Field, a theatre violinist, who was living in Golden Lane, Dublin, at the time of John's birth. John's mother was prob-ably Grace Marsh, who was perhaps the sister of a Dublin organist. Robert and Grace Field's other children included Rob-ert, born 1784 in Aungier Street (and died in infancy); Isaac, born 1785, and Robert Mark, born 1786, both in Golden Lane; Ann, born 1788, and Grace Marsh, born 1790 (and died in infancy), both in Chancery Lane; and Grace, born 1791 in Camden Street. Their paternal grandparents were probably John Fields (*sic*), a church organist, and Ann Hearne, who married at St Werburgh's in 1756.

As a child, John Field was taught piano by his father and probably also by his grandfather, who lived in the same household. Field later told Fétis, the French musicologist, that severe beatings in his childhood had caused him to run away from home, but that hunger had brought him back. In 1791, at the age of nine, John was placed with Tommaso Giordani, who, according to W. H. Gratton Flood (*John Field: Inventor of the Nocturne*, 1920), brought him out as one of the several "Musical Children" in a benefit concert for

Master Tom Cooke—another of Giordani's important pupils—at the Exhibition Rooms, William Street, on 14 February 1792. No press announcement of that appearance survives.

Field did, without doubt, play "Madam Krumpholtz's difficult pedal harp concerto . . . on the Grand Piano Forte" on 24 March 1792 in the first of three Lenten concerts, modeled on the Concerts Spirituel at Paris, that Giordani promoted at the Rotunda Assembly Rooms in Rutland Square. The *Dublin Evening Post* on 27 March 1792 reported that Master Field's playing was "really an astonishing performance by such a child, and had a precision and execution far beyond what could have been expected." At the next concert, described as a youth of eight (he was ten), he played a new concerto by his master; and at the third concert he offered a concerto and a sonata by unnamed composers.

Possibly the precocious Field was composing his own recital music by that time. David Branson in *John Field and Chopin* (1972) suggests that a piano solo of the Irish air "Go to the Devil and shake yourself" and two rondos for the piano on Giordani's songs "Since then I'm doomed" and "Slave, bear the sparkling goblet round" date from that early period. But Piggott dates them later and also discounts the likelihood that a manuscript volume in the New York Public Library containing "very simple keyboard arrangements" of well-known tunes could be by Field despite the flyleaf inscription, "John Field Junr. 1789. Duets."

All biographers of Field have indicated that the family left Dublin for England in the summer of 1793, settling first at Bath for several months. It is presumed that Robert Field took up a modest position as violinist in Rauzzini's orchestra at the elegant New Assembly Rooms, and that after the summer season at Bath the Fields came to London, where young John was apprenticed to Muzio Clementi. The chronology, it

seems, requires revision. It is likely that the Fields had left their home in Camden Street, Dublin, by 4 April 1793, the date on which Robert Field was expelled for failing to keep up payments to the Irish Musical Fund, to which he had regularly subscribed 13s. each year from 1787 through 1792. Moreover, they seem to have gone directly to London, and young John seems to have been apprenticed to Clementi by the spring of 1793. On 31 May 1793, at Covent Garden Theatre, at the end of the evening's theatre bill, was performed "a *sonata* from Op. 2, by Clementi, on one of Longman and Broderip's newly invented Grand Piano Forte Harpsichords, by the celebrated Master Field, a Child of Nine Years Old." By then John was actually almost 11. The billing as "the celebrated Master Field" does allow the possibility that he had made his London debut even earlier than that date, which itself precedes by almost a year the date previously given for his first appearance.

Perhaps the Fields did then spend the summer of 1793 at Bath. By winter they were back in London, where the father reportedly found a place in the orchestra of the Haymarket Theatre under Colman's management—although no evidence of this appointment seems to exist—and the son continued his instruction under Clementi, a most successful *maestro* whom the French called *le Pape des musiciens*, at a fee reported to have been 100 guineas. How Robert Field, with his large family and small job, managed such an enormous expense remains a mystery as does the remainder of the elder Field's life, about which nothing more is known except that he was probably the Mr Field who in 1799–1800 was earning 5s. per night in the band of Covent Garden Theatre. In 1794, Master Field's address was given in Doane's *Musical Directory* as No 8, Kennington Place, presumably his father's residence.

In April 1794, mentioned in the press

as "Master Field, the talented ten-year-old pupil of Clementi" (he was now almost 12), John was announced for a public concert in May in which he was to play a new concerto by his master and one by Dussek. He received praise from Haydn who heard him play in 1794 and wrote in his diary: "Field a young boy, which plays the pianoforte extremely well."

During these years of apprenticeship to his most demanding master, a man not celebrated for generosity, either of spirit or with money, Field also served as a sales demonstrator in Clementi's piano warehouse. Indeed, between 1795 and 1799 most of his playing seems to have occurred on those premises. On 7 February 1799, at the age of 17, Field played his first notable composition, his Piano Concerto in E-flat, at a concert given at the King's Theatre for the benefit of the New Musical Fund. Both the piece, (not published until 1815) and player were well received; the *Morning Chronicle* of 9 February stated that Field was "esteemed by the best judges one of the finest performers in the kingdom, and his astonishing ability on this occasion proved how justly he was entitled to the distinction." On 17 February Field played the concerto after a dinner party (to which he had been taken by Clementi) given by Thomas Holcroft, who noted in his diary that he "is a youth of genius, for which Clementi loves, admires, and instructs him; highly to his own honour." Field repeated the composition at the Haymarket Theatre on 27 May 1799 in a concert which was given for the benefit of another prodigy, the thirteen-year-old violinist G. F. Pinto, a pupil of Johann Peter Salomon under whom Field also may have studied the violin for a while. When he played at the Royal Circus on 6 October 1800 he was again advertised as the "celebrated Master Field."

By 1801 he had completed his apprenticeship with Clementi, but he continued to work in the warehouse at a small salary,

Courtesy of Dr Martin C. Carey

JOHN FIELD

by Lonsdale

maintaining an association with his master which would last until 1803 and beyond. He also took up some teaching on his own; one of his pupils, Master Charles Neate, only a few years younger than he, played piano for the Covent Garden oratorios in the spring of 1800. In 1801 Field published a set of three piano sonatas, Op. 1, dedicated to Clementi, and he again played his Concerto in E flat at Covent Garden on 20 February of that year.

At the turn of the century, Field stood on the threshold of a brilliant career but one which was to be passed entirely out of England except for a brief time in 1832. Clementi took him to Paris in August 1802, where the youth was a great success, playing his own compositions as well as those of Dussek, Handel, Clementi, and Bach; his performances from memory of the latter's works especially impressed the French musicians. Clementi and Field did not tarry long in Paris but set out for St Petersburg.

By permission of the Trustees of the British Museum

JOHN FIELD

artist unknown

By early autumn they had reached Vienna. Everywhere they experienced enthusiastic receptions. Clementi tried to place Field with the great contrapuntist Albrechtsberger in Vienna, but the fearful Field persuaded Clementi to take him along to Russia.

Arriving at St Petersburg in the late autumn of 1802, Clementi took inexpensive rooms at the Hotel de Paris while he prepared to establish a showroom for the sale of his pianos, again using Field as a demonstrator. Despite Clementi's evident financial success at sales and at his own concertizing, his parsimonious nature caused considerable discomfort for Field, and it was said that the master refused to purchase warm clothing to protect them against the harsh winter since they would not have need for the garments after they left that country. In his diary, the German violinist Louis Spohr had described Clementi as "a man in his best years, of an extremely lively disposition, and very engaging manners," but after he visited him and his pupil in St Petersburg, Spohr presented Clementi in an unflattering manner in his *Autobiography*:

In the evening I sometimes accompanied him after dinner to his large pianoforte warehouse, where Field was often obliged to play for hours, to display the instruments to the best advantage to the purchasers. . . . I have still in recollection the figure of the pale, overgrown youth, whom I have never seen since. When Field, who had outgrown his clothes, placed himself at the piano, stretched out his arms over the keyboard, so that his sleeves shrunk up nearly to his elbows, his whole figure appeared awkward and stiff in the highest degree; but as soon as his touching instrumentation began, everything else was forgotten, and one became all ear. Unhappily, I could not express my emotion and thankfulness to the young man otherwise than by a silent pressure of the hand, for he spoke no other language, but his mother tongue.

Even at that time, many anecdotes of the remarkable avarice of the rich Clementi were related, which had greatly increased in later years when I again met him in London. It was generally reported that Field was kept on very short allowance by his master, and was obliged to pay for the good fortune of having his instruction with many privations. I myself experienced a little sample of Clementi's true Italian parsimony, for one day I found teacher and pupil with turned up sleeves, engaged at the washtub, and Clementi advised me to do the same, as washing in St. Petersburg was not only very expensive, but the linen suffered greatly from the method used in washing it.

Nevertheless, Clementi's urbane manner and mastery of languages quickly introduced himself and his protegé into the musical and social circles of the Russian capital. John Field came into his own in Russia during the evening on which he played for a soirée at the palace of Prince Demidov, whose daughter was a pupil of Clementi. So enchanted by Field's playing were the guests that he received numerous invitations. Clementi had also introduced

Field to General Marklovsky, a wealthy music patron, who took John into his household and society in the spring of 1803, shortly before Clementi, his objective of launching a successful business having been accomplished, departed St Petersburg in June. After ten years of association with Clementi, who had given the young prodigy many advantages as well as many hardships, Field was on his own.

After passing the summer at Narva, where General Marklovsky commanded a regiment, Field took up quarters of his own at St Petersburg. In March 1804 he made his public concert debut (his previous appearances had been at private parties) in Philharmonic Hall, supported on the program by the soprano Madame Mara who was then living in Russia. His playing of his first concerto brought him glowing notices—"No other pianist can compare with him in mastery of technique and sincerity of feeling. . . . His art is inspired" —and he now became a most fashionable celebrity.

Field gave his first concert in Moscow on 2 March 1806. Between that year and 1812 he divided his time between the two Russian cities and then, for the most part, remained based in St Petersburg until 1821. As his reputation grew, he counted among his pupils many notable persons: De Kontski, the Polish prodigy; Glinka, the founder of the Russian National Opera; Charles Mayer, the German pianist and composer; and Vertowski, the Russian composer of operas. During those years, Field composed numerous pieces, including two *Divertissements* which were published in Russia in 1810 and 1811; the *Fantasie on Martin y Soler's Andante*, published in Leipzig, 1812; the *Air Russe Favori Varié Komarinskaya in B flat*, published in Russia and England, 1813; and the *Marche Triomphale en honneur des Victoires du Général Wittgenstein*. His first concerto—the one he had introduced in London in 1799—was published by Breitkopf in 1815, and his

second, third, and fourth concertos appeared in 1816. By then he had written some of those poetic piano pieces called nocturnes, a term which Field was the first to give to that type of musical romantic movement and on which, as stated by Patrick Piggott, is based "since the fading of his great fame as a pianist, his principal claim to remembrance." The first three of these "wordless love-songs" were published in 1814.

Wealth came to Field from his teaching and playing, but he was so much fêted that he fell into a pleasure-loving eccentricity, which perhaps stands as a model for the legendary Bohemian style of living to which musical artists of the nineteenth century were sometimes attracted. Although he never enjoyed robust health and in later years suffered greatly from his habits of intemperance, his creative genius seems to have been little diminished. He presumably never neglected technical practice but always had to rally his talents for the labors of composition. "Field did not work [on his composing] until forced to do so by the approach of his concerts," wrote Madame Louise Fusil in her memoirs, *Souvenirs d'une Actrice* (1841):

but it was necessary for him to be urged by his friends for a long time before he decided to sit down to the piano and begin. First he had a bowl of "grog" brought to him—to which he had frequent recourse, though without getting drunk—and he rolled up his sleeves in readiness. Then he was no longer the lazy man but the artist, the inspired composer; he wrote; he threw his pages to the winds, like the Sybil of the Oracles; and his friends gathered them together and put them in order. One had to be clever to decipher what he wrote, for he took no trouble to form the notes carefully; but his friends were used to it. As he advanced in his work his genius glowed to such a point that his copyists were almost unable to keep up with him . . . . At three or four in the morning he felt exhausted and fell upon his divan and slept. While he was sleeping his papers were put in order. The next morning, when he awoke, he would take several cups of black coffee and begin afresh. It was advisable, however, not to speak to him, even about the most urgent matter. . . .

Madame Fusil, who acted with the French company in Moscow, further described the musician as a most disorganized individual, with sloppy habits of dress and fantastic manners, but with a face that "radiated genius." Since childhood he had suffered stuttering speech, an affliction brought on presumably by early emotional conflicts and oppression.

In Moscow on 31 May 1810 Field married Adelaide Victoria Percheron, daughter of the war commissioner of the French fleet, Adrien Louis Percheron de Mouchy. Since becoming his pupil in 1807, "Percherette," as she was called, had been Field's mistress; in later years Field remarked that he had married her "because she never paid for her lessons, and it seemed the best way for him to get some return for his trouble." Their marriage was quarrelsome, and soon after their son Adrien was born in 1819 Percherette left Field, took the child, and embarked on a modest concert life of her own; for some time she taught piano at Smolensk, played for the last time in Moscow in 1842, and, outliving both her husband and child, died in 1869.

Long before his separation from Percherette in 1819, Field had found comfort with a Mlle Charpentier, about whom little is known; she may have been the Mlle Charpentier who acted with the French theatre in St Petersburg, where the Fields lived during most of the second decade of the century. In 1815 Mlle Charpentier gave him a son, Léon, who was born four years before the birth of Field's legitimate child Adrien. It seems likely that Field lived with Mlle Charpentier and Léon during the 1820s in Moscow, where the pianist had now moved. Piggott points out the curious fact that Field kept two flats in Moscow simultaneously and speculates that one was used as a residence and the other as a teaching base, social taboos preventing Field's many young female pupils from coming to a residence occupied by a mistress. Mlle Charpentier, however, remains a mystery, little mentioned in accounts of Field's later life, although the child Léon, to whom Field seems to have been devoted, brought consolation in later years.

Field remained settled in Moscow between 1821 and 1831, years which Piggott describes as "unproductive." He developed a friendship with J. N. Hummel, who had studied with Clementi in London in the early 1790s. They played together in a concert in 1822, but during the rest of the decade Field's engagements and compositions were not numerous. He continued to enjoy a good income from teaching, but the deterioration of his health was hastened by heavy drinking. He was beginning to suffer from cancer of the rectum. In 1828, and again in 1831, his death was reported. The latter report was contradicted by the Berlin paper *Iris im Gebiete de Tonkunst* on 18 April 1831: "The great piano-forte virtuoso still lives, and if he can overcome his depression and apathy . . . the rest of Europe may not be obliged to renounce the happiness of hearing . . . this extraordinary pianist."

Induced by the prospects of finding more expert medical care and of seeing his mother (to whom he had sent an annual pension of 2000 rubles since the death of his father), Field in 1831 accepted an invitation from the Philharmonic Society in London. After two farewell concerts in Moscow, accompanied by his son Léon Charpentier, Field departed the Russian capital on 15 April 1831 bound for England. After lingering at St Petersburg for several weeks, Field arrived in London sometime in the summer, after 30 years of absence. His condition was worsened when he almost immediately was maltreated for hemorrhoidal troubles by a quack barber and then was operated upon by Sir Astley

Paston Cooper, a leading surgeon. After recovering, he may have made a quick visit to Paris for the purpose of settling Léon's education. He was in London again by 21 December 1831, when he attended a concert sponsored by the Royal Academy of Music in the Hanover Square Rooms. Field himself played in London again, for the first time since his youthful triumphs, at the opening of the Philharmonic Society's season on 27 February 1832, offering his Fourth Concerto in E-Flat, a work new to the London audience. He enjoyed a cordial, if not extraordinarily enthusiastic, reception.

On 29 March 1832 Field was among the chief mourners at Westminster Abbey for the funeral of his old master Clementi. The following day, Field gave his second concert, without orchestra, in the Great Concert Room of the King's Theatre. On the next evening, 31 March 1832, after the guests had finished their Haydn Centenary dinner at the Albion Tavern, Field played Haydn's Variations in F Minor, in a program which also included performances by Cramer and Moscheles.

While in London Field met Mendelssohn at a dinner given by Moscheles and was present when the twenty-three-year-old Mendelssohn made his brilliant London debut playing his own Concerto in G Minor at the Philharmonic concert of 28 May 1832. Field's London reception had not been so dazzling, and Mendelssohn's success may have rankled. At a summer party at Charles Neate's house, before an assembly of leading foreign musicians then in London, Field sat quietly and listened while Mendelssohn played his G Minor Concerto to great applause.

After several more concerts in London, and two in Manchester, the second of which took place on 25 July 1832, Field decided to go to Paris. His mother, Grace Field, had died in early August at her home in Prince's Street, at the age of 78, and Field no doubt wished now to be reunited with

his son Léon. Moreover, he was ill again. And his success in London had been tepid by comparison to his earlier musical and social triumphs on the Continent. Moscheles, who had frowned upon his habits, claimed that "nothing can afford a more glaring contrast than a Field Nocturne and Field's manners. . . ."

His reception in Paris was full of adulation, especially from the students of the Conservatoire, despite the fact that some critics noted his failing powers. Fétis, reviewing the concerts in the Salle of the Conservatoire on Christmas Day 1832 and at the Pape Salon on 20 January and 3 February 1833, described the audience's response as "a veritable delerium," and wrote of the "marvellous mechanism of his fingers —such that the greatest difficulties appear to be the simplest things." Chopin and Liszt, however, were not greatly impressed, the former finding his playing "feeble," characterized by "no speed, no elegance," and the latter judging it "sleepy" and "lacking in vitality." Field was bitter about the successes being scored by these younger pianists who performed in a new style of excitement. His response to Liszt's vigorous and overwrought manner of performing was the quip, "Does he bite?" Of Chopin he sneered, "What has he written? Nothing but mazurkas!"

Departing Paris in June 1833, Field embarked on an extended concert tour throughout Europe. He had already played in Brussels in February, and now he went to Toulouse, Marseilles, Lyons, then to Germany and Switzerland. At Milan in November and December he was acclaimed by some critics as an unparalleled artist, but others suggested that he was no longer at the top of his form. By the time he and Léon reached Florence, Field was too ill to play; a week later he went to Genoa and by the spring of 1834 moved on to Naples, where he was hospitalized for nine months and had to rely on the beneficence of some friends who organized a benefit concert for him in Moscow and sent him the proceeds.

A compassionate noble family from Moscow named Rakhmanov, shocked at the dreadful condition in which they found him when they arrived in Naples early in 1835, took him to Vienna—where Field mustered strength enough to play two concerts in August 1835—and then on to Russia. His irreversible cancer was now ravaging his body, but it was pneumonia, contracted in December of 1836, which finally killed him on 23 January 1837, at the age of 54. It was reported by Dubek, who had been a devoted pupil, that when asked by an English clergyman, who was brought to the bedside despite Field's avowed atheism, if he was a Protestant, the dying musician replied "No." "So perhaps you are a Catholic?" —"No." "Then probably you are a Calvinist?" "Not exactly that. I am not a Calvinist, but a *Claveciniste.*" He was buried on 27 January in the Vedensky Cemetery. In 1838 a monument, subscribed by an impressive list of Russian aristocrats, colleagues, and pupils, was placed over his grave.

Field's legitimate son, Adrien, who had been a young musician of promise, became a player of dance music in taverns and ballrooms and also turned to drink. He was still alive in 1851, the year in which he sold one of his father's manuscripts, the Andante in E-flat, to the St Petersburg publisher, Bernard. Adrien was the legal heir of his father's estate, which in money consisted only of about 10,000 rubles. The illegitimate son, Léon Charpentier, had a successful career in opera under the name of Leonov until the late 1850s.

"Field's memory was kept green in Russia long after it had become faded elsewhere," writes Patrick Piggott, in his recent biography, "and the traditions of his pianistic style were handed down by his many pupils throughout the nineteenth and even into the twentieth century." In France, Field was called "the Racine of the piano." He was one of the supreme masters of the instrument even to the end of his days and is regarded by some as "one of the greatest masters of all time in his picturesque diffusion of light and shade, in perfect finesse allied to the utmost warmth of expression." His "invention" of the nocturne introduced a strong romantic flavor into music which had a far-reaching impact on the century and to which the styles of later masters are indebted. A most informative and detailed analysis of his compositions is provided by Piggott, along with a list of works.

Portraits of Field include:

1. By James Lonsdale, c. 1800. Evidently there were three versions of this portrait, all now lost. One version was in possession of the firm of Collard & Collard but was destroyed by a fire on the Bond Street premises of that business's successor, Messrs Chappell & Co, in the 1960s. It was reproduced in a history of Collard & Collard written by Edward Lamburn called *A Short History of a Great House* and on the book jacket to Piggott's biography. A second version is preserved in a photograph owned by Dr Martin Carey of Boston, Massachusetts. On the back of the photograph (reproduced here) is a notation signed by "A. F. G." which reads, "This photograph was taken for me by William Gray from the portrait of John Field in the possession of the firm of Collard & Collard. It was painted by James Lonsdale." The third version, provenance unknown, is reproduced in Professor A. Nikolayev's book on Field published in Moscow, 1960. Another painting, published as frontispiece to Nikolayev's study, is spurious.

2. Chalk drawing by Kiprensky, in the British Museum.

3. Painting attributed to M. Shee, c. 1798. Now in the possession of David McKenna, C.B.E.

4. Lithograph by Bohlens, after a portrait by an unknown artist, presumably Russian.

5. Lithograph by Engelbach, in the National Portrait Gallery.

6. Engraving by Landseer of a group of 26 musicians and singers, including Field and Clementi. The engraving is after a design by De Loutherbourg, from miniature cameos by H. de Janvry. It was published in 1801 at London by H. de Janvry and sold by Colnaghi & Co. A copy is in the Austrian National Library, Vienna.

7. Engraved portrait by unknown artist. Published by Breitkopf & Härtel, Leipzig.

8. Photographs of Field's tombstone in the Vedensky Cemetery, Moscow, are published in Piggott's biography.

Field, Robert ₁fl. 1782–1800?₁, violinist.

Robert Field, the father of the eminent composer and pianist John Field (1782–1837), was a violinist in the Dublin theatres by 1782. He was the son of an Irish organist, perhaps the John Fields (*sic*) who married Ann Hearne at St Werburgh's in 1756. Robert himself was married to Grace Marsh, who perhaps was the sister of a Dublin organist. They had at least seven children: the aforesaid John, born in 1782; Robert, born 1784 in Aungier Street; Isaac, born 1785, and Robert Mark, born 1786, in Golden Lane; Ann, born 1788, and Grace Marsh, born 1790, in Chancery Lane; and Grace, born 1791 in Camden Street.

Sometime in the spring of 1793 Robert Field took his family from their home in Camden Street, Dublin, and went to England. On 4 April 1793 he was expelled for failure to keep up payments to the Irish Musical Fund, to which he had regularly subscribed 13*s.* each year from 1787 through 1792.

The Fields seem to have gone directly to London, where young John performed at Covent Garden Theatre on 31 May 1793, and then, probably, Robert Field was engaged at Bath as a violinist in Rauzzini's orchestra at the New Assembly Rooms for the summer. In the following winter he supposedly found work at the Haymarket Theatre, although no documentation of this report exists. In 1794 the family was living at No 8, Kennington Place.

Little else is known about the life of Robert Field, except that he was probably the Mr Field who was paid 5*s.* per night for playing in the band of Covent Garden Theatre in 1799–1800. His wife Grace died at London in August 1832 at the age of 78.

Field, William ₁fl. 1671–1672₁, actor?

William Field was listed on a Lord Chamberlain's warrant dated 23 May 1672 as a member of the Duke's Company whose contract was renewed. Perhaps he was one of the troupe's minor actors.

Fieldhouse, ₁William?₁ ₁fl. 1699?–1723₁, actor.

According to the 1706 edition of *The Amorous Widow*, Mr Fieldhouse played Jeffrey. Perhaps he appeared in that work as early as 18 December 1699 when it was presented at Lincoln's Inn Fields Theatre, though most references to him date a year or more later. Those citations derive, again, from first editions of plays rather than from advertisements, so his participation in the following works cannot be assigned definitely to particular performances. At Lincoln's Inn Fields he was the Prince of Tanais in *Tamerlane* (which was performed about December 1701), Thrasolin in *Altemira* (i.e. *The General*, about December 1701), Careful in *The Beau's Duel* (about June 1702), Larich in *The Stolen Heiress* (31 December 1702), Roderegue in *Love Betrayed* (about February 1703), Gripeall in *Love at First Sight* (25 March 1704), Trick in *The Biter* (4 December 1704), and the Marquis of Hazard in *The Gamester* (22 February 1705). During that period only one reference to Fieldhouse was made in the local press: on 24 June 1704 *The Spanish Fryar* and *The Wit of a Woman* were performed for his benefit. A Mrs Fieldhouse, presumably his wife, was also in the troupe at that time.

Fieldhouse may well have acted more frequently than surviving evidence indicates, and it is possible that he moved with Thomas Betterton from Lincoln's Inn Fields to the new Queen's Theatre when it opened in April 1705. According to the first edition of *Adventures in Madrid*, Fieldhouse acted Pedro, so perhaps he was in the first performance about June 1706 at the Queen's. Nicoll reports that the Duke of Norfolk's troupe acted *The Fall of Tarquin* at Merchant Taylors' Hall in York in 1713; among the players was a William Fieldhouse who may well have been our subject. A Fieldhouse, according to Lady Bristol, acted Porcius in *Cato Burlesqued* on 6 July 1719 at Pinkethman's playhouse in Richmond. The last mention found of him is on 22 April 1723, when he played Old Gerald in *The Anatomist* at the Haymarket Theatre.

Fieldhouse, Mrs ₁William?₁ ₁fl. 1703–1705₁, *actress.*

Mrs Fieldhouse was listed in three printed casts in first editions of plays, so perhaps she acted in the premier performances at Lincoln's Inn Fields. She was Harriot in *The Different Widows* (which was first performed about November 1703), Mursa in *Abra Mule* (13 January 1704), and Mrs Topknot in *The Gamester* (22 February 1705). (William?) Fieldhouse, presumably her husband, was also in the troupe during those years.

Fieldhouse, Mr ₁fl. 1791₁, *actor.*

A Mr Fielding acted the role of Salisbury in a performance of *King Henry II* on 26 December 1791 at the Haymarket Theatre.

Fielding, Miss ₁fl. 1761–1762₁, *actress.*

Miss Fielding made her first appearance on any stage at Covent Garden Theatre on 7 January 1761 playing Bertha in *The Royal Merchant.* For her performance she received £5 5s. The following 11 April she shared a benefit with two others but received only £5 10s. 6d., half value for the tickets she had sold. In 1761–62 she was probably acting unspecified roles most of the season, but the only mention of her was on 8 May 1762, when she acted Ann Page in *The Merry Wives of Windsor* at the benefit she shared with three others.

Fielding, Henry 1707–1754, *playwright, manager, novelist, journalist.*

Twice in his life the author Henry Fielding dabbled in theatrical management, but it is difficult to determine the depth of his involvement in either instance. Since only his managerial work qualifies him for inclusion in such a dictionary as this, no attempt will be made here to cover in any

Harvard Theatre Collection

HENRY FIELDING

engraving by Basire, after Hogarth

depth his much more extensive careers as playwright, journalist, and novelist.

Fielding was born at Sharpham Park, near Glastonbury, on 22 April 1707, the son of Edmund and Sarah Gould Fielding. His first play, *Love in Several Masques*, was performed at Drury Lane on 16, 17, 18, and 19 February 1728 (while the town was agog with *The Beggar's Opera* at the rival patent house). There followed two years of study at the University of Leyden, then a return to London and seven years of playwriting. His plays, all comedies, burlesques, farces, or ballad operas, numbered 21 by 1737 when Fielding was 30; four more came out in 1742 and 1743, and one was published posthumously in 1778.

Many of his plays have been forgotten today, but since he produced some of them himself and enjoyed considerable popularity as a playwright in his day, a list of them with their publication and first performance dates and alternate titles or sources may be useful before we trace Fielding's managerial career: *Love in Several Masques* (1728), Drury Lane 1728; *The Temple Beau* (1730), Goodman's Fields 1730; *The Author's Farce* (1730), Haymarket 1730; *Tom Thumb (The Tragedy of Tragedies)* (1730), Haymarket 1730; *Rape upon Rape (The Coffee-House Politician)* (1730), Haymarket 1730; *The Welsh Opera (The Grub-Street Opera)* (1731), Haymarket 1731; *The Letter-Writers* (1731), Haymarket 1731; *The Lottery* (1732), Drury Lane 1732; *The Modern Husband* (1732), Drury Lane 1732; *The Old Debauchees (The Debauchees)* (1732), Drury Lane 1732; *The Covent-Garden Tragedy* (1732), Drury Lane 1732; *The Mock Doctor* (from Molière; 1732), Drury Lane 1732; *The Miser* (from Plautus and Molière; 1733), Drury Lane 1733; *Deborah* (never published?), Drury Lane 1733; *The Intriguing Chambermaid* (from Regnard; 1734), Drury Lane 1734; *Don Quixote in England* (1734), Haymarket 1734; *An Old Man*

From the collection of Edward A. Langhans

Benefit ticket for author's night, *Pasquin*

by Hogarth

Taught Wisdom (The Virgin Unmask'd) (1735), Drury Lane 1735; *The Universal Gallant* (1735), Drury Lane 1735; *Pasquin* (1736), Haymarket 1736; *Tumble-Down Dick* (1736), Haymarket 1736; *Eurydice* (1743), Drury Lane 1737; *The Historical Register, For the Year 1736* (with *Eurydice Hiss'd*; 1737), Haymarket 1737; *Plutus* (with W. Young; 1742), never performed?; *Miss Lucy in Town* (sequel to *The Virgin Unmask'd*; 1742), Drury Lane 1742; *An Interlude between Jupiter, Juno and Mercury* (1743), never performed?; *The Wedding-Day* (1743), Drury Lane 1743; *The Fathers* (written c. 1737; 1778), Drury Lane 1778.

Fielding was content during the early 1730s to have his plays produced by others, but in 1736 and 1737 at the Haymarket Theatre he turned his hand to management in association with James Ralph. On 5 March 1736 his *Pasquin* was first performed by "the Great Mogul's Company of English Comedians, Newly Imported." The work proved immensely popular, playing 39 times in succession and at least 62 times in all. His troupe performed 83 times in the spring and summer of 1736 and produced 11 new plays. In addition to *Pasquin*, Haymarket audiences saw *The London Merchant*, *The Female Rake*, *Tumble-Down Dick*, *The Tragedy of Tragedies*, *Chrononhotonthologos*, *The Honest York-shireman*, *The Temple Rake*, *The Noble-man*, *The Rival Captains*, *Guilt Its Own Punishment* (*Fatal Curiosity*), *The Beg-gar's Opera*, *The Mock Doctor*, *The Pro-vok'd Husband*, *The Strollers*, *A Bold Stroke for a Wife*, *The Comical Disap-pointment*, *The Stratagem*, *The Fatal Ex-travagance*, and *The Deposing and Death of Queen Gin*. Perhaps Fielding did not produce all the works cited, but even if some productions were prepared by outside groups who simply rented the playhouse

from Fielding and Ralph for a performance or two, the "Great Mogul's" season was an ambitious and successful one.

As manager, Fielding seems to have instituted a number of changes in theatrical practices. He may have been the first to offer two new plays on one night; he broke the tradition of not performing on Lenten Wednesdays and Fridays and during Pas-sion Week; he often used the curtain be-tween acts and scenes; and he revised the theatre's lighting system. He was also in-genious in his lively advertisements and changed the curtain time from six to seven in the evening.

Fielding's buoyant good humor so per-vaded some of the puffs for *Pasquin* that

From the collection of Edward A. Langhans

"Pasquin Vivetur Stultitia"

by Hogarth

one cannot be sure what to believe. The advertisement for 5 April 1736, for instance, seems to suggest that Fielding took a fling at acting, for the part of the poet Trapwit was that night to be played "by the Proprietor of the Benefit, Being the first Time of his attempting it to little Purpose." The benefit was for "Poet Trapwit. By his own particular Desire." Then:

N.B. The Spectators are desir'd to take no Notice of the Tragedy, but attend very closely to the Comedy, there being several fresh Jokes new cloath'd Second Hand for the Use of that Night. As there is little Hope of a great Demand of Tickets, or Places for that Evening, the Doors will be open'd by Six o'Clock in the Morning, and constant Attendance the whole Day given, for fear any Application shou'd be made for either.

Fielding's second and last season at the Haymarket may have begun with *The Soldier's Fortune* and *A Hint to the Theatres* on 3 December 1736, but it is unlikely that he would have been involved in the production of a pantomime, which the latter work was, in view of his satirical jabs at the form and his refusal to produce any in his spring 1736 season. On 6 January 1737 Fielding's company was certainly at work again, for *The Battle of Parnassus* was rehearsed. The next day the *Daily Advertiser* contained a puff, possibly written by Fielding:

We are inform'd, that a certain Author, tir'd with the vain Attempts he has often made in the Political Way, has taken it into his Head, as unwilling to lay down the Character of a Reformer, to explode the reigning Taste for dumb Shew and Machinery, and has declar'd open War against Harlequin, Punch, Pierot, and all the Modern Poets, viz. Joiners, Dancing-Masters, and Scene-Painters. 'Tis said, that he has dispos'd every Thing in such a manner, and is so forward in his Preparations, that he will open the Campaign next Week, having three new Pieces in Rehearsal on the Stage of the little Theatre in the Hay-Market. The Design is, no doubt, laudable, but the Chance of War is doubtful; he makes head against a powerful Alliance; and we do not hear that he is strengthen'd by any of the Auxiliaries of Parnassus.

The troupe's schedule in January and February 1737 shows Fielding's interest in revolving his repertory. After the *Parnassus* rehearsal on 6 January came a rehearsal of *The Defeat of Apollo* on 8 January; the latter was performed with *The Fall of Bob, Alias Gin* on 14, 15, and 17 January and paired with *The Rival Milliners* on 21 January. *The Mirrour*, *The Defeat of Apollo*, and *The Mob in Despair* were done on 26 January, then *The Twin Rivals* and *The Rival Milliners* were played on 9 February. Possibly a visiting troupe gave *All for Love* on 11 February, *The Orphan* on 12 February, and *Cato* on 14 February, for the advertisements lack the Fielding flavor and the plays are not typical Fielding fare.

The *Daily Advertiser* on 19 February carried a puff that sounds like Fielding:

Sir, In a late Paragraph in one of your Papers it was insinuated, that there was a Design on foot for erecting a New Theatre, which by some Wise Heads was suppos'd to come from a certain Manager, in order to revive the Playhouse Bill this Session of Parliament; I think it proper therefore, in Justice to the Gentleman levell'd at, to inform the Publick, that it is actually intended for a Company of Comedians every Day expected here, late Servants of their Majesties Kouli Kan and Theodore, who in the mean time will entertain the Town in the true Eastern manner, at the New Theatre in the Hay-Market, with a celebrated Piece call'd A Rehearsal of Kings. I am, Sir, &c. Agent for the Company.

In connection with that project, Fielding received a letter from Aaron Hill dated 28 February 1737 which cautioned him about the satire in *The Rehearsal of Kings*; Hill felt that the company might find itself in trouble. He was pleased, however, that Fielding had surrounded himself with a reliable company which included Eliza

Haywood, James Lacy, John Roberts, and Charlotte Charke.

Meanwhile at the Haymarket came a revival of *Pasquin* on 25 February, *The Parthian Hero* and *The Sharpers* on 28 February, *She Wou'd and She Wou'd Not* and *The King and the Miller of Mansfield* on 2 March, a concert on 3 March, *King John* "As originally written by Shakespear. Supervised, Read over, Revised, and Unalter'd" and *The Rival Milliners* on 4 March, *The Stratagem* on 5 March, and *Love for Love* and *The Lover His Own Rival* on 7 March.

The Rehearsal of Kings project was still in the works. On 8 March 1737 the *Daily Advertiser* reported:

We hear that the Great Mogul has acceded to the Treaty of the Hay-Market, which causes various Speculations. Our best Advices assures us, that the Town will be entertain'd there Tomorrow, by a Gentleman who never wrote for the Stage, with a new Performance call'd a Rehearsal of Kings: which will be immediately succeeded by a Dramatick Piece call'd the Historical Register, for the Year 1736, written by the Author of Pasquin. We hear this has given great Alarm to all the Pantomimical Houses in London, Southwark, Rag Fair, &c.

The scheduled performance was either disrupted or never took place; the paper reported that *The Rehearsal of Kings* "was disappointed by some Persons taking clandestinely Possession of the Hay-Market Playhouse, who were about Eight o'Clock committed to Bridewell for the same. On this Account several hundred Persons were turn'd away." The work was postponed again on 11 March but performed on the fourteenth "By a Company of Comedians dropt from the Clouds, late Servants to their thrice-renown'd Majesties, Kouly Kan and Theodore." The piece was repeated on 15 March, and on 17 March *Sir Peevy Pet* was added as an afterpiece.

Pasquin was acted again on 19 March,

and on 21 March finally came the promised *The Historical Register*, preceded by Lillo's *Fatal Curiosity*. The bill stated, among other things, that "Mr Hen gives Notice, that if any Joke is both Hiss'd and Clapp'd, such Division will be consider'd an Encore, and the said Joke be put up again." The two works were immediately successful and were repeated several times in the following three weeks. As Colley Cibber said in his *Apology*, Fielding knocked "all distinctions of mankind on the head: religion, laws, government, priests, judges, and ministers were all laid flat at the feet of this Herculean satirist!" Sir Robert Walpole was one of Fielding's chief targets, and *The Historical Register*, along with *The Golden Rump* (attributed to Fielding by Horace Walpole but probably not by him) were largely responsible for Walpole's success in pushing through the Licensing Act.

On 13 April *The Historical Register* was made the mainpiece, and another Fielding work, *Eurydice Hiss'd*, another satire on Sir Robert Walpole, was offered as the afterpiece. The pair of works played through 23 May, sometimes being augmented by other pieces, as on 25 April when *The Female Free Mason* joined them for one performance and on 2 May when *The Fatal Curiosity* was also played. On 3 May *The Sailor's Opera* replaced *Eurydice Hiss'd* for that night. *Pasquin* was given again on 4 May, with *Fame* as an afterpiece; on 5 May Fielding varied the fare again by pairing *The Historical Register* and *The Sailor's Opera*. And so the season continued, with such other pieces as *The Dragon of Wantley* and *The Lordly Husband* joining the repertory. *Macheath Turn'd Pyrate* and *The King and Titi* were scheduled for 30 May, but by then Fielding's venture had collapsed in the face of the new Licensing Act. Eliza Haywood's benefit on 23 May turned out to be the troupe's last performance.

Not until 1748 did Fielding again become involved in theatrical management. Under the pseudonym "Madame de la

Nash" he and a puppeteer—perhaps the elder Thomas Yeates—ran a puppet theatre in Panton Street. Fielding advertised his venture as a Breakfasting Room. Performances began on 28 March 1748 and ran through 2 June. Typical of the advertisements was one on 30 March:

At Ten in the Morning, and Seven in the Evening, Madame *De La NASH* Opens her large BREAKFASTING-ROOM for the Nobility and Gentry in *Panton-street* near the *Haymarket*, where she will sell the very best of TEA, COFFEE, CHOCOLATE, and JELLIES.

At the same Time she will entertain the Company Gratis with that Excellent old English Entertainment, call'd A PUPPET-SHEW, Every Day this Week will be shewn the lamentable Tragedy of BATEMAN, WHO DIES for LOVE.

With the Comical Humours of PUNCH *and his Wife* JOAN, With all the Original Jokes, F—rts, Songs, Battles, Kickings, &c Boxes 3s. Pit 2s. Gallery 1s.

☞The Tea-Kettle will boil at Eleven, and Master PUNCH will mount exactly at Twelve.

*The Tea-Kettle will boil again at Six in the Evening, and Master PUNCH will mount again exactly at Seven.

The House is fitted up in the most elegant Manner. Ladies may take Places for the Boxes at the Coffee-Room in the Passage to the Long Room, and Footmen will be admitted to keep them.

Their Ladyships are desired to send their Servants by Eleven in the Morning, and by Six in the Evening.

☞The Puppet-Play will begin every Day *precisely* at the Hours of Twelve and Seven.

In addition to *Bateman*, Fielding produced *Fair Rosamond*, *Whittington and His Cat*, and *The Covent-Garden Tragedy*. Among other targets for satire, Samuel Foote and his imitations of famous public figures came under attack, Foote being ridiculed in the character of "*Mr.* PUPPET FUT, *Esq;* Grocer and Mimick." Fielding also attacked Foote in the *Jacobite's Journal*, which he was then publishing.

TOM THUMB.

A

TRAGEDY.

As it is Acted at the

THEATRE

IN THE

HAY-MARKET.

Written by *Scriblerus Secundus*.

—— *Tragicus plerumque dolet Sermone pedeſtri.* Hor.

LONDON,

Printed: And Sold by J. ROBERTS in *Warwick-Lane.* 1730.

[Price Six Pence.]

From the collection of Edward A. Langhans

Title-page of *Tom Thumb*

by HENRY FIELDING

Eliza Haywood in *The History of Miss Betsy Thoughtless* in 1751 took a few swipes at Fielding's theatrical activity. Betsy wanted to entertain her brother, who had come to town, but

There were no plays, no operas, no masquerades, no balls, no public shews, except at the little theatre in the Haymarket, then known by the name of F——'s scandal-shop; because he frequently exhibited there certain drolls, or, more properly, invectives against the ministry: in doing which it appears extremely probable, that he had two views; the one to get money, which he very much wanted, from such as delighted in low humour, and could not distinguish true satire from scurrility; and the other, in the hope of having some post given him by those whom he had abused, in order to silence his dramatic talent. But it is not my business to point out either the merit of that gentleman's performances, or the motives he had for writing them, as the town is perfectly acquainted both with his abilities and success; and has since seen him, with astonishment, wriggle himself into favour, by pretending to cajole those he had not the power to intimidate.

Perhaps after 14 May Fielding's direct connection with Madame de la Nash's entertainments ended; on 2 June the last performance was given. After that, Fielding turned his attention to the completion of *Tom Jones* and seems not to have involved himself in theatre management again.

Henry Fielding died in Lisbon on 8 October 1754. Oddly, he did not sit for a portrait during his lifetime, but his friend

Hogarth drew him from memory in 1762 for the first collected edition of the writer's works. An engraving of Hogarth's portrait was made by James Basire, and virtually all later pictures of the writer came from the same source. Engravings were made by W. T. Fry, W. Holl, Roberts, I. H. Baker, J. Faber, J. C. Buttre, F. Baggage (after a bust by Margaret Thomas based on Hogarth's drawing, in 1883), Rogers, S. Freeman, and several anonymous engravers. The Fielding said to be pictured in the painting by Joseph Highmore, sometimes thought to be of actors in the Drury Lane Green Room, was probably Timothy Fielding. Maynadier's edition of Fielding's *Works* contains an engraving by Caxenave after (Samuel?) Reynolds, but the work

By permission of the Board of the British Library

"The Judgment of the Queen of Common Sense. Address'd to Henry Fielding Esq'."

artist unknown

probably derived from the Hogarth portrait.

In the *Times Literary Supplement* in February 1968 Esther Caspi and Benjamin Boyce discussed a portrait, once thought to be of Fielding, now at the Royal National Hospital for Rheumatic Diseases, Bath. Caspi believes the portrait is of Ralph Allen but Boyce thinks it might be of Fielding. Boyce points out that a self-portrait by William Hoare shows the artist holding a drawing in his hand, a profile of a man who is believed by some to be Fielding as he was in 1745.

Fielding, Timothy *1690–1738, actor, dancer, booth operator.*

Timothy Fielding was born in 1690 and probably made his first London appearance on 23 March 1723 dancing Scaramouch (Pan) in *Jupiter and Europa* at the Lincoln's Inn Fields Theatre. The popular work was repeated many times. Though Fielding was not cited for any other roles in the 1723–24 season, he shared a benefit with Wright at Drury Lane on 21 May 1724 and must have been active in that company. Similarly in 1725–26 and 1726–27 at the same house he shared benefits, though no roles for him were mentioned in the bills.

In 1727–28 he seems not to have been connected with either of the patent houses, but Latreille reported that on 24 May 1728 and throughout the summer Fielding was probably with the scratch company that performed *The Beggar's Opera* at the Haymarket Theatre. On 9 August at that house he acted Torrismond in *The Spanish Fryar*, and he and Reynolds produced *The Beggar's Opera* at Bartholomew and Southwark fairs in August and September.

Fielding was at Drury Lane during the 1728–29 season, playing Cepheus in *Perseus and Andromeda* on 15 November 1728 and sharing a benefit with two others on 30 April 1729. From May through July he acted Truncheon in *The Strolers*, Quorum in *Phebe* (later called *The Beg-*

gar's Wedding), Mob in *The Contrivances*, Carbuncle in *The Country Lasses*, and John in *Whig and Tory*. In August he presented *Hunter, or the Beggar's Wedding* at his Bartholomew Fair booth. His advertisement in the *Daily Post* on 23 August 1729 boasted that "The Booth is very Commodious, and the [George] Inn-yard has all the Conveniences of Coat-room, Lights, &c., for Quality and others; and shall perform this evening at Four, and every day during the time of the Fair; beginning exactly at Two o'Clock, and continuing every Hour till Eleven at Night." He promised to provide his audience with "a good Band of Instruments, accompany'd by a Chamber Organ provided on this occasion, and play'd upon by the best Hand in England."

Fielding acted at the Haymarket in 1729–30, reviving his old role of Quorum and playing such parts as Brainworm in *Love and Revenge*, Aimwell in *The Stratagem*, and the King in *Hurlothrumbo*. He was back at Bartholomew Fair again in August 1730, acting and operating a booth in partnership with Oates.

From 1730–31 through 1733–34 he performed at Drury Lane in the winter seasons and operated fair booths in the late summers. At Drury Lane he added to his repertoire such parts as Lucius in *Theodosius*, Neptune in *Cephalus and Procris*, Glaud in *Patie and Peggy*, Alonzo in *The Tempest*, Cimon in *Damon and Phillida*, Pedro's Ghost in *Don John*, the Cook in *The Devil to Pay*, Cabinet in *The Funeral*, Sir Charles in *The Stratagem*, Abergavenny in *Henry VIII*, Douglas in *1 Henry IV*, the Duke in *Rule a Wife and Have a Wife*, Furnish in *The Miser*, Cornwall in *King Lear*, Fruitful in *Aesop*, and a Countryman in *Harlequin Doctor Faustus* (his last new role at Drury Lane, which he played on 10 October 1733).

His partners at the fairs during this period varied: in 1731 he worked at both fairs with Hall and Hippisley, presenting *The Emperor of China*, but late in September he ran his own booth at Southwark Fair, offering *A Bold Stroke for a Wife*; in 1732 he and Hippisley produced *The Envious Statesman* at Bartholomew Fair; in 1733 the same pair offered *Love and Jealousy* and *A Cure for Covetousness* at Bartholomew Fair and ran a booth at Southwark Fair as well; and in 1734 Fielding and Oates presented *Don Carlos* at Bartholomew Fair.

In his zeal to celebrate the anniversary of the King's coronation, Fielding gave a party on 11 October 1732 which was reported two days later in the *Daily Post*: "Mr Fielding the Player (who keeps a Booth . . . during . . . Bartholomew Fair) gave to the Populace before his own Door in Hart-street, Bloomsbury, a Butt of the strongest Beer that could be got; also a large Bonfire." Perhaps his hospitality inspired him, a year later, to take over the Buffalo Tavern. The *Daily Post* of 15 October 1733 reported:

We hear that Mr. Fielding of Drury Lane Play House who has entertained the Town so agreeably with his company of Comedians at the George Inn in Smithfield, during the time of Bartholemew Fair, has taken that commodious Tavern at the corner of Bloomsbury Square, known by the sign of the *Buffler* and has provided good wines to entertain all Gentlemen that please to favour him with their Company.

At his tavern on 17 August 1734 he gave a public rehearsal of *Don Carlos,* which he was preparing for Bartholomew Fair. On 12 October he acted Plume in *The Recruiting Officer* at Lincoln's Inn Fields; in August 1736 he and Hippisley produced *Don Carlos* and *The Cheats of Scapin* at Bartholomew Fair; and from 7 to 18 August 1738 he and Hallam presented *The Mad Lovers* at Tottenham Court.

Early on the morning of 19 August 1738 Timothy Fielding died at his tavern. He was 48 years old. He was buried in Bloomsbury Cemetery, Brunswick Square, on 22 August, the burial register of St George, Bloomsbury, identifying him as of King Street. Fielding left no will, and on 4 September administration of his estate was granted to his widow, Christian Fielding.

Between 1728 and 1732 Joseph Highmore painted a picture of actors in the Drury Lane Green Room; the painting was once owned by Sir Charles Tennant. It is now in the Mellon collection at Yale University. It has been supposed that those pictured are Spranger Barry, Miss and Mrs Pritchard, James Quin, Lavinia Fenton, and a Fielding—more likely Timothy than Henry. But Barry did not make his stage debut until 1744, Quin and Miss Fenton were not Drury Lane actors, and the Pritchards belong to a slightly later period than that of the painting. Authorities at the Witt Library believe it to be a scene from the dramatized *Clarissa Harlowe.*

Fienzal. *See* **DURANCY.**

Fierville, Mons [*fl.* 1772–1792], *dancer, dancing master.*

Monsieur Fierville, announced as a student of the elder Leppie made his debut at the King's Theatre on 14 November 1772 in a *New Serious Ballet*. During that season he danced numerous times, and especially drew large crowds on the nights when he danced with Mlle Anne Heinel (1753–1808), whom he later married. Their first appearance together at the King's was in a pas de deux and a chaconne on 12 January 1773, selections they often repeated. On 30 March 1773, they danced as Apollo and Venus in a new grand dance, and on 3 June 1773 they introduced a new dance called *Les Sauvages.*

Fierville was re-engaged as a principal dancer at the King's Theatre for 1773–74, but although he was announced in the bills for his first performance of the season in a *Grand Chaconne* on 20 November 1773, on the previous day he sprained his ankle at rehearsal; it was necessary for him to be replaced by Mariottini, who by the mishap had the opportunity to make his first appearance in London. Fierville did not appear again until 22 February 1774, after a three-month's absence, when he danced an adagio and chaconne. For his benefit on 24 March 1774 he gave a chaconne and a Polish Ballet with Mlle Heinel, Sga Vidini, and Asselin. Fierville's name was not found in the available bills for 1774–75, but he was dancing again at the King's Theatre in 1775–76. At his benefit on 30 May 1776 he performed with Mlle Heinel and others in *Le Triomphe de la magie.* His last performance, with Helm, Mlle Sophie, and Mlle Baccelli, in *Pigmalion,* was on 8 June 1776.

After retiring from the King's Theatre, Fierville became a dancing master in London. In his *Musical Tour* (1787), Charles Dibdin related a story about Fierville, who, "wallowing in English riches," was depicted as extravagant and foolish, especially in the matter of a menagerie which he kept. One day a dealer in wild birds and beasts in the Haymarket sold him a pair of geese dyed pink, for which Fierville paid two cows and a calf in return. When the hoax was discovered, the intervention of a friend who threatened the dealer with the law retrieved £14 for Fierville.

At a date unknown to us, Fierville had married his dancing partner Anne Heinel, a very popular performer and a beautiful woman. A press clipping in the Burney papers at the British Museum relates that Fierville's face was pitted from smallpox and that his wife, "not finding herself satisfied with her match," had her marriage in the Church of England nullified by "authority of the Popish laws, which pronounce every Marriage void that has not the rites performed by a priest of the Church of Rome: She has therefore broke her matrimonial ties with Fierville, and given her hand to Signor Vestris the father. The ceremony took place about twelve days ago in Paris." The hand dating of the press

Harvard Theatre Collection

Ticket to FIERVILLE's ball

engraving by Bartolozzi, after Cipriani

notice as 6 November 1783 is manifestly incorrect. Mlle Heinel married Gaetano Vestris on 16 June 1792.

Possibly Fierville was related to Peter Fierville, the celebrated French actor who died at Munich in March 1777, aged 107.

A ticket, designed by J. B. Cipriani and engraved by E. Bartolozzi, for "Mr. Fierville's Ball" at Carlisle House, Thursday, 5 April 1781, is in the Harvard Theatre Collection.

Fife, Mr [*fl. 1734–1736*], *dancer.*

Mr Fife danced Pluto in *Cupid and Psyche* at Drury Lane on 15 April 1734 and the Park Sentinel in *Harlequin Restored* on 12 January 1736. He may well have been a member of the *corps de ballet* during the intervening years without having been cited in the bills.

Figg, James *d. 1734, pugilist, sword fighter.*

James Figg, of Thame, Oxfordshire, was one of the few pugilists who appeared at one of the London playhouses as well as at the boxing and sword-fighting amphitheatres. He was champion from 1719 until his death in 1734, fought hundreds of times, and is said to have been beaten only once, by Sutton.

On 6 June 1720 a poem was published in *Oxoniensis* on rope dancers and other entertainers at the fairs; the poet recognized that some people might prefer other, more exciting diversions:

> Let Bridewell's hardy youth resort
> To the lov'd agonistic sport,
> The cudgels flourish in the ring,
> Or try the wrestlers dangerous fling:
> Be close with sweating Butchers stow'd
> Near Islington's frequented road,
> Or Tyburn's ever famous plains,
> Where Figg the rabble entertains,
> Where bold hibernian chiefs engage,
> And fierce Viaragoes vent their rage.

Figg, described in Egan's *Boxiana* (1812) as an "extremely illiterate" fellow, was more "distinguished as a *fencer* and *cudgeller* than as a pugilist." At his Academy, known as Figg's Amphitheatre, he taught "the use of the small and back-sword, cudgelling, and pugilism. . . ."

Nothing seems to have inspired bad poets more than battles royal at the amphitheatres. Dr Byrom's lengthy but colorful verse description of one of the encounters of Figg and Sutton, in August 1725 at Figg's Amphitheatre in Oxford Road, was published in the *London Journal*:

> Long was the great Figg by the prize-fighting swains
> Sole monarch acknowledg'd of Mary-bon plains;
> To the towns far and near did his valour extend,
> And swam down the river from Thame to Gravesend.
> There liv'd Mr. Sutton, pipe-maker by trade,
> Who hearing that Figg was thought such a stout blade,
> Resolv'd to put in for a share of his fame,
> And so sent to challenge the Champion of Thame.

. . . .

> Whereupon the bold Sutton first mounted the stage,
> Made his honours as usual, and yearn'd to engage;
> Then Figg with a visage so fierce and sedate
> Came, and enter'd the list with his fresh-shaven pate.
> Their arms were encircled by armigers two
> With a red ribbon Sutton's, and Figg's with a blue;
> Thus adorn'd the two heroes 'twixt shoulder and elbow
> Shook hands, and went to't; and the word it was bilboe.

. . . .

> Figg struck the first stroke, and with such a vast fury,
> That he broke his huge weapon in twain, I assure you.
> And if his brave rival this blow had not warded,
> His head from his shoulders had quite been discarded.
> Figg arm'd him again, and they took t'other tilt,
> And then Sutton's blade run away from its hilt;
> The weapons were frighted, but as for the men
> In truth they ne'er minded, but at it again.
> Such a force in their blows, you'd have thought it a wonder
> Every stroke they receiv'd did not cleave them asunder.
> Yet so great was their courage, so equal their skill,
> That they both seem'd as safe as a thief in a mill;
> While in doubtful attention dame Victory stood,
> And which side to take could not tell for her blood,
> But remain'd like the Ass 'twixt the two bottles of hay
> Without ever moving an inch either way;
> Till Jove to the Gods signified his intention

In a speech that he made them too tedious to mention.
But the upshot of it was, that at that
very bout
From a wound in Figg's side the hot
blood spouted out;
Her ladyship then seem'd to think the
case plain,
But Figg stepping forth, with a sullen
disdain,
Shew'd the gash, and appeal'd to the
company round
If his own broken sword had not given
him the wound.
That bruises and wounds a man's spirit
should touch
With danger so little, with honour so
much!
Well, they both took a dram, and return'd to the battle,
And with a fresh fury they made the
swords rattle;
While Sutton's right arm was observed
to bleed
By a touch from his rival, so Jove had
decreed;
Just enough for to shew that his blood
was not icor,
But made up, like Figg's, of the com-
mon red liquor.
Again they both rush'd, with as equal a
fire on,
That the company cried "Hold, enough
of cold iron;
To the quarter-staff now, lads;" so, first
having dram'd it,
They took to their wood, and i'faith
never shamm'd it.
The first bout they had was so fair and
so handsome,
That to make a fair bargain it was worth
a King's ransom;
And Sutton such bangs on his neighbour
imparted,
Would have made any fibres but Figg's
to have smarted.
Then after that bout they went on to
another;
But the matter must end in some fashion
or other,
So Jove told the Gods he had made a de-
cree,

That Figg should hit Sutton a stroke on
the knee;
Though Sutton, disabled as soon as it
hit him,
Would still have fought on, but Jove
would not permit him.
'Twas his fate, not his fault, that con-
strain'd him to yield,
And thus the great Figg became lord of
the field.

The fights between Figg and Sutton drew
not only large crowds but celebrated ones:
on 6 June 1727, when the pair had a back-
sword fight, fist fight, and cudgelling match,
Sir Robert Walpole and other members of
the quality were present.

By October 1730 Figg had fought over
270 battles. It was the fashion to make
elaborate and bombastic challenges, and
when Figg and his scholar William Gill
accepted a challenge from Mathew Master-
son and Rowland Bennet, Figg assured his

Harvard Theatre Collection

JAMES FIGG

engraving by Grave

opponents in the press that "the stock and branch of superior force flourishes on Britannia's stage like the tall cedars of Lebanon" which would mourn the fate of the challengers "by shedding leaves to adorn their untimely Monuments—if any be erected."

On 3 December 1731 Figg confronted the swordsman Sparks at the Haymarket Theatre before an audience which included the Duke of Lorraine. "The beauty and judgment of the sword was delineated," said one of the papers, "in a very extraordinary manner by those two champions, and with very little bloodshed: his Serene Highness was extremely pleased, and expressed his entire satisfaction, and ordered them a handsome gratuity." In addition to his appearance at the Haymarket, at some point in his career Figg had a "Great Til'd Booth, On the Bowling-Green, Southwark, During the Time of the FAIR."

Chetwood the prompter claimed that Figg bragged that he never bought a shirt: he always had one of his scholars, some of whom were from aristocratic families, go out and borrow for him a new shirt for each match—and by the end of the fight it would be so slashed that the owner would refuse to take it back and say, according to Figg, "Damn you, keep it!"

James Figg died on 7 December 1734 leaving, according to Caulfield's *Remarkable Persons*, a widow and several children (Musgrave's *Obituary* gives his death date as 8 December). Figg was buried at St Marylebone on 11 December.

An engraved portrait of James Figg by J. Faber, Jr, after Ellis, was sold by Overton and Hoole. A copy was engraved by R. Grave and published as a plate to Caulfield's *Remarkable Persons* in 1819. Plate two of Hogarth's "The Rake's Progress" shows a quarter staff player who has been identified as Figg, and the figure in Hogarth's "Southwark Fair" sitting on a blind horse, waiting for a challenge, has also been identified as Figg. Joseph Sympson the younger engraved a ticket for Figg which shows the gladiator standing on his platform at the Amphitheatre, his head shaven and his shirt loose at the collar, ready for a challenger.

Fildew, Mr [*fl.* 1778–*c.* 1795], *actor.*

As a member of the company that played at China Hall, Rotherhithe, in the summer of 1778, Mr Fildew acted Dapper in *The Citizen* on 1 June, a Coachman in *The Devil to Pay* on 3 June, Doctor Hellebore in *The Mock Doctor* on 8 June, an Officer in *Venice Preserv'd* on 15 June, a Coachman in *High Life Below Stairs* on 18 June, a Servant in *The Fashionable Lover* on 22 June, the Taylor in *The Miser* on 24 June, and the Lord Mayor in *Richard III* on 26 July. After the last-named performance the China Hall Theatre burned down, and the company played in a temporary booth for about six more weeks.

On 13 October 1779, Fildew played Simon Pure in *A Bold Stroke for a Wife* at the Haymarket Theatre. His next known performance in London was at the Crown Inn, Islington, where he acted a Recruit in *The Recruiting Officer* on 15 March 1781. In May 1792, Fildew, his wife, and a daughter were members of Johnson's company at Barking, Essex, about nine miles from London, where they acted in the Town Hall, which had been converted to a theatre for the engagement. In a performance of *The Orphan* in the Assembly House at Kentish Town, given about September 1795 for the benefit of Mr and Mrs Fildew and Weston, Miss Fildew acted the Page and spoke the epilogue.

Mrs Fildew acted with Butler's touring company from 1788 until her death in 1815.

Fildew, Mrs *d. 1815,* actress. *See* **FILDEW, MR.**

Fildew, Miss [*fl.* 1792–*c.* 1795], *actress. See* **FILDEW, MR.**

Filiber, Mr ₍fl. 1688₎, *musician.*

Mr Filiber, one of the members of the King's Musick, was on 20 October 1688 to be paid 6s. plus 1s. 6d. daily for attending the King at Windsor from 24 July to 20 September that year.

Filizeau, Miss ₍fl. 1757₎, *dancer.*

A pupil of the dancing master Jolly, Miss Filizeau danced "Pierrotte" in *Harlequin's Maggot* at the Haymarket Theatre on 22 August 1757.

Finali. *See* FINELL.

Finch, Mrs John. *See* YOUNGER, ELIZABETH.

Finch, Katharine ₍fl. 1695–1717₎, *actress.*

Mrs Katharine Finch was a member of Christopher Rich's company at Drury Lane in 1695–96 and 1696–97. She was first mentioned as playing Flavia in *The Mock Marriage* in September 1695, after which she appeared as Quitteria in *3 Don Quixote* in November, Forge Will in *Aesop* in December 1696, the Duchess in *The Triumphs of Virtue* in February 1697, and Forge Will in *2 Aesop* in March.

Mrs Finch did not act in London again until 25 July 1705 when she played Olimpia in *The Loyal Subject* at Drury Lane. Then her name disappeared again from the bills until 19 May 1708, when she acted Alinda in *Marriage à la Mode* at Drury Lane. She stayed at the playhouse through the 1709–10 season, acting such parts as Eboli in *Don Carlos*, Elaria in *The Emperor of the Moon*, Julia in *The Fatal Marriage*, Clara in *Rule a Wife and Have a Wife*, Teresa in *The Spanish Fryar*, Bianca in *Othello* (her first recorded Shakespearean role, on 9 October 1708), Regan in *King Lear*, Octavia in *All for Love*, Scentwell in *The Busy Body*, and Advocate in *The Fair Quaker of Deal* (for her shared benefit on 18 March 1710).

Not until 14 June 1715 did Katharine Finch's London activity begin again. On that date at Lincoln's Inn Fields under John Rich she appeared as Aurelia in *Love in a Sack*. She returned to the same playhouse in 1715–16 to play the Duchess in *2 Don Quixote*, her old role of Advocate, and Celia in *The Woman Captain*. Then she was not cited until 15 May 1717 when she shared a benefit at Lincoln's Inn Fields at a performance of *Oedipus*. In 1717–18 at the same house she was seen as an Actress in *The Perjuror*, Francisca in *Mangora*, Mrs Whimsey in *The Fair Example*, an unnamed character in *Tartuffe*, and Diana in *The Lucky Chance*. At Richmond on 9 August 1718 she acted Mrs Frail in *Love for Love* and on the eleventh she played there her last known role, Favorite in *The Gamester*. Perhaps Katharine Finch was related by marriage to Elizabeth Finch, who had been born Elizabeth Younger and who performed in the early eighteenth century.

Finch, Thomas d. 1770?, *painter, proprietor.*

In 1760 Thomas Finch, a herald-painter, having inherited a house and gardens in St George's Fields, Southwark, from an aunt named Topham, fitted up the premises as a public pleasure garden. He announced on 17 May 1760 that "Finch's Grotto and Gardens are now Open'd for the reception of Gentlemen and Ladies, at the upper end of St George's Street, near St George's Fields, Southwark: there is a way from Falcon-stairs thro' Bandy-leg Walk, which leads directly to the said Grotto and Gardens." The amenities included a medicinal spring, a fountain and cascade, an orchestra stand containing an organ built by Pike of Bloomsbury, a music room, a range of tea rooms, a tavern, and promenades.

By the spring of 1764 Finch was offering concerts of vocal and instrumental music at an admission charge of 6d., a fee which was raised to 1s. by 14 September of that year. The gardens were patronized by the Dukes of York and Gloucester. Goldsmith's Mrs Hardcastle in *She Stoops to Conquer* commended the enterprise. Numerous concerts were given for the benefit of performing brothers who were members of a lodge of Freemasons which had been established at the Grotto. Typical of most was "Brother Neeves' Night" in August 1769: "The Vocal Parts by Brother Lowe, Miss Frowd, &c. First Violin and Solo, by Brother Smart."

The press reported that Thomas Finch died on 23 October 1770 and that he was buried in the churchyard at St George's, Southwark, although the registers of that church contain no such record. An account given by Mr Griffiths of Lant Street, the son of the undertaker who supposedly interred Finch, however, stated that he died on 28 September 1781 and that he was buried in Watlington, Oxfordshire; the registers of that parish church yield no record of the burial of Thomas Finch, although a William Finch was buried there on 22 March 1777. If the proprietor of the Grotto had, as reported by the papers, died in 1770, then probably the will of Thomas Finch which was made on 5 September 1761 belonged to him. It was proved at London on 22 November 1770 by Grace Finch, his widow, to whom properties unspecified were left. That Thomas Finch cut off at a shilling each his brother William Finch of Chatham, Kent, and his sister Elizabeth Finch Pratt of Deptford.

Findlay, Mr *d. 1799, prompter, actor, dancer.*

Mr Findlay (sometimes Finley) was an assistant prompter at Covent Garden Theatre from 1790–91 through 1798–99, at a salary of £1 per week. He was also the regular summer prompter at the Theatre Royal, Richmond, during that period. No doubt he was the Findlay who had been a boxkeeper at Brighton in 1787 and 1790.

On occasion, Findlay appeared on the stage in a very minor capacity. In 1789 at

Richmond he acted small roles in *The Beggar's Opera* and *The Author*. At Covent garden he regularly played one of the Waiters in *Harlequin's Treasure* in 1795–96 and on 7 June 1796 he performed a character in *The Way to Get Married*. He also appeared there in *Harlequin and Oberon* in 1796–97 and 1797–98 and in *The Genoese Pirate* in the latter year. His final part was a Recruit in *Harlequin's Chaplet* on 13 May 1799. He died soon after, "at an early age" (according to the *Authentic Memoirs of the Green Room*, 1804), and on 4 June 1800 Mrs E. Findlay shared in benefit tickets.

Mrs Findlay had first appeared on the stage at Richmond in 1798. After her husband's death she was "compassionately engaged" as a chorus singer at Covent Garden in 1800–1801 at £1 per week. She remained in the chorus at Covent Garden— "her petit figure rendering her incapable of representing any characters of consequence" —at least through 1808–9. In 1809 she signed a receipt at Covent Garden as Mrs. E. Findlay. She also sang at the Haymarket Theatre between 1801 and 1810. The Master Findlay who acted Pompey in *The Irish Widow* at the Haymarket on 9 April 1788 was probably the son of our subject.

Findlay, Mrs E. [*fl. 1798–1810*], *singer. See* FINDLAY, MR *d. 1799.*

Findlay, Master [*fl. 1788*], *actor. See* FINDLAY, MR *d. 1799.*

Findley, Mr [*fl. 1700–1706*], *booth operator, tumbler.*

Mr Findley (or Finley) and his wife Mary were active at the fairs at the end of the seventeenth century. Ned Ward in his *London Spy* (1699) discovered at Edward Barnes's Bartholomew Fair booth "Lady Mary as far outdoing the Dutch Frows [in rope dancing] as a lady of honour exceeds a milkmaid in dancing a borrie or minuet." Findley and Barnes operated a booth at the same fair in late August 1700 with "Lady Mary" as a star performer, and they presented rope dancing again at Mayfair and at Bartholomew Fair in 1701. Their bill for the latter called their troupe "Her Majesty's Company of Rope Dancers." Barnes offered his own rope dancing, Mrs Findley was advertised as "much improv'd . . . since the last Fair," and Mr Findley "entertained with such a variety of Tumbling . . . as was never seen in the Fair before." Lady Mary was probably the woman who inspired Steele to comment in the *Spectator* on 28 April 1711 that the "Pleasantry of Stripping almost Naked" on the stages of the legitimate playhouses was now being practised at Bartholomew Fair.

Barnes and Findley remained in partnership at May Fair, Bartholomew Fair, and Southwark Fair in 1702 and at May Fair in 1703, but Findley lost his partner a year later and ran his May Fair booth in 1704 with Mrs Barnes. Mrs Findley danced there that year, but by January 1705 she had died, apparently in a fall from the rope. The *Diverting Post* of 20 January contained "A Consolatory Epistle from the Earl of S——, to the Lord G——, in Imitation of the twenty-fourth Ode of the first Book of Horace, occasion'd by the Death of Lady Mary, the Famous Ropedancer." The poem lamented that "spritely, fair Miranda's gone" and remembered that her "Feet were conqu'ring as her Eyes, / Which doubly gave Delight." The poet said that in Lady Mary "Beauty and Mercy join'd," but now "No more she Breathes to Charm thy Heart, / Nor Touch the faithless Rope."

Mr Findley operated a booth at May Fair on 28 April 1705 and worked with the Widow Barnes and Evans on 1 May 1706, but after that his activity in London seems to have ceased.

Findley, "Lady Mary" *d. c. 1704, rope dancer. See* **FINDLEY, MR.**

Finell, Thomas *d. 1690, violinist, singer.*

Thomas Finell (or Fenell, Finall, Fynell) was a member of the Chapel Royal at least as early as 30 March 1661, when he was paid 4*s.* (with 8*d.* still due him) for singing at the funeral of Princess Mary, the King's eldest sister. In addition to being a singer Finell was a violinist, and on 20 May 1665 he was appointed to play the violin in the King's Musick, but without fee. He may have had to wait until 22 October 1667 for a salary for that post; on that date he was granted the place previously held by Robert Strong. On 15 February 1671 Finell replaced the deceased violinist John Atkins at 20*d.* daily plus livery.

The Lord Chamberlain's accounts frequently cited Finell in connection with service at the Chapel Royal, but he was also mentioned, on 28 June 1672, as a creditor of the musician Jeoffrey Banister: Thomas Finell of St Margaret, Westminster, was assigned the sum of £10. He accompanied the King to Windsor in the summer of 1674, played in the court masque *Calisto* on 15 February 1675, and went to Windsor again in 1675. On 22 November 1681 he and three other court musicians were suspended for neglecting "their duty in attending at y[e] play acted before his Ma[te] at Whitehall on Tuesday night [15 November, when *The Rival Queens* was performed by the King's Company]." The suspension was brief, for Finell was on duty at Windsor in the spring of 1682 and received £11 12*s.* 8½*d.* for his services. On 23 April 1685 he marched at the coronation of James II.

Thomas Finell died in March 1690 and was buried in the South Cloister of Westminster Abbey on 19 March; he was cited in the register as "one of the Core." It is possible that the Mary Finell who married David Webb at the Abbey on 24 April 1679 was Thomas Finell's daughter. *Grove's Dictionary of Music and Musicians* seems to have confused the singer-violinist Thomas Finell with the composer-organist of the same name. The Thomas Finell who was vicar choral of St Patrick's Cathedral, Dublin, in 1677, organist there from 1689 to 1694 (with the exception of 1691–92), and organist and vicar choral of Christ Church Cathedral from 1694 to 1698, may have been the son of the London singer and violinist. The Dublin musician was also a composer. He died in 1709.

Fineschi, Vicenzo [fl. 1787–1789], singer.

Engaged as the second tenor in serious opera and the second buffo in comic opera, Vicenzo Fineschi made his first appearance at the King's Theatre on 8 December 1787 as Sandrino in *Il re Teodoro in Venezia*. In anticipation of the event, he had advertised "Fineschi being hardly recovered from his late severe indisposition humbly hopes for the indulgence of the public, whom rather than disappoint, he would run any other danger." The piece was repeated on 12 January 1788; and on 15 January Fineschi sang Mynheer Vanderdur in *La locandiera*. On 4 March he performed Gelsomino in *La cameriera astuta*, on 15 May a principal role in *La Frascatana*, and on 26 May he had a benefit and presumably sang in *Gli schiava per amore*.

Fineschi was reengaged at the King's Theatre for 1788–89 at a salary of £150 for the season, in which he performed Corrado in *La cosa rara*, Arcade in *Ifigenia in Aulide*, Beraldo in *Il desertore*, Menghino in *La villana reconosciuta*, a character in *La buona figliuola*, Timagene in *La generosità d'Alessandro*, and Don Fausto in *La vendemmia*. His last performance, however, was at Covent Garden Theatre on 11 July 1789 as Almaviva in *Il barbiere di Siviglia*.

Finger, Gottfried b. c. 1660, instrumentalist, composer, impresario.

Gottfried (or Godfrey) Finger was born about 1660 in Olomouc, Moravia. He is said to have come to England about 1685, and the *Calendar of Treasury Books* contains a note of 5 July 1687 indicating that Finger was then a member of the Chapel Royal receiving £40 annually as an instrumentalist. On 19 December 1687, according to the Lord Chamberlain's accounts, he was paid as one of the court musicians who had attended the King at Windsor and Hampton Court the previous summer and fall. He was at Windsor again in the summer of 1688.

Finger's career as a composer began with the publication in 1688 of 12 sonatas for various combinations of strings. He continued composing, sometimes alone but occasionally in collaboration with such others as John Eccles and Daniel Purcell, to the end of the century. Much of his music was written for the stage. He wrote act tunes or songs for *Bussy D'Ambois* in 1691 (or perhaps a later revival), *Love for Love* and *The She-Gallants* in 1695, *The Husband His Own Cuckold* and *The City Bride* in 1696, *The City Lady* and *The Mourning Bride* in 1697, *Love at a Loss*, *Love Makes a Man*, and *The Pilgrim* in 1700, and *The Humor of the Age* and *Sir Harry Wildair* in 1701. He also wrote, at some point, act tunes for *The Wives' Victory*, an unidentified play.

In addition to tunes and songs for plays, Finger wrote, with Eccles, the music for the masque *The Loves of Mars and Venus* in 1696, and in 1700 he competed with Weldon, Eccles, and Daniel Purcell in a contest: each composed music for Congreve's masque *The Judgment of Paris*. According to *The London Stage*, Finger's music was heard at the Dorset Garden Theatre on 28 March 1701; he won fourth prize (Weldon won first). In May his opera *The Virgin Prophetess* was performed at Drury Lane, and in January 1703 music that he and Purcell wrote for *The Rival Queens* was heard at Lincoln's Inn Fields. Finger also composed several other works while

GOTTFRIED FINGER

engraving by Gribelin

he was in England, including a St Cecilia's Day ode in 1693.

It would appear that Finger left his post at court about 1689 to devote his time to composing. By the end of 1693 he was also involved in organizing concerts, at many of which his music was featured. The *London Gazette* of 20/23 November 1693 contained the following advertisement: "In York-Buildings on Monday next being the 27th Instant, will begin Mr Fingers Consort of Musick, and so continue every Monday night, beginning exactly at 8 of the Clock." His concerts, at which he may have played (though the advertisements did not mention his participation), continued until at least 17 February 1699, on which date he held a benefit at York Buildings.

Finger's humiliation at losing the 1701 music contest is said by Roger North to have caused his departure for the Continent. Finger objected to the fact that the judges were not professional musicians but members of the aristocracy; he "thought he was to compose musick for men and not for boys." Perhaps Finger stayed in London for the opening of *The Virgin Prophetess* in May 1701, but by the end of the year he was in Vienna. On 14 December 1701 George Stepney, Envoy to Vienna, wrote to Lord Halifax:

I thank you for your Eccles his Musick, wch. I suppose is got by this time to Hamburgh and will shortly be here, where Finger will see it performed to ye best advantage; He assures me notwithstanding the partiality which was shown by ye Duke of Somersett and others in favor of Welding and Eccles, Mr. Purcells Musick was the best (I mean after his own, for no Decision can destroy the Love we have for our selves).

By 1706 Finger was living in Breslau and was a chamber musician to the Court Palatine. He continued composing, one of his efforts being a portion of the opera *Sieg der Schönheit über die Helden*, which was performed in Berlin in December 1706. Finger was in Innsbruck in the fall of 1707, and in subsequent years he traveled to Neuburg-am-Danube, Heidelberg, and Mannheim. He was in the last city in 1717 and 1718, still composing. Grove states that Gottfried Finger was still alive in 1723, but his death date is not known.

A portrait engraving of Finger by S. Gribelin—a bust on a pedestal in a temple, with allegorical figures—serves as a frontispiece to the composer's *Sonatae XII*, 1688.

"Finland, The Tall Man from." *See* **"Tall Man from Finland, The."**

Finley. *See* **Findlay** and **Findley.**

Finney, Mr [fl. 1777–1797?], *house servant.*

Mr Finney, a house servant at Drury Lane Theatre, shared regularly in benefit tickets with other house personnel between 1777 and 1786. In the Lilly Library at Indiana University is a letter from J. P. Kemble to Westley (undated, but 1792 is suggested) requesting a draft to pay Finney "two guineas a week for services he undertook to do [for Drury Lane] theatre, which he has performed." Probably he was the same Finney who was paid "in full making £40 this season" by the Drury Lane treasurer on 12 June 1793. He received another £40 by "Mr Sheridan's Order" on 20 October 1795. A Mr Finney, perhaps the same man, shared in benefit tickets with house servants at Covent Garden Theatre on 6 June 1797. The Mrs Finney who shared in Drury Lane tickets in June 1787 was probably our subject's wife.

Finney, Mrs [fl. 1787], *house servant?*

Presumably the wife of the Drury Lane house servant Mr Finney (fl. 1777–1797?), Mrs Finney, perhaps also a house servant, shared in benefit tickets on 4 June 1787.

Finney, William *d. 1762, machinist, scene man.*

William Finney was a scene man at Covent Garden Theatre from as early as 1755–56 through 1757–58; he shared in benefits with other house personnel on 19 May 1756 and 19 May 1757. On 16 September 1758, Richard Cross, the prompter at Drury Lane, noted in his diary that Finney had gone to Dublin to work for Spranger Barry and Henry Woodward at their new theatre in Crow Street, where he received a benefit on 2 May 1760. On 16 February 1762 the *Dublin Journal* reported that William Finney, machinist at the Crow Street Theatre, had died "last week."

"Finnish Tall Man, The." *See* "TALL MAN FROM FINLAND, THE."

Fiorentina, Signora [*fl. 1755–1763*], *dancer.*

Signora Fiorentina was a member of Theophilus Cibber's troupe of unseasoned performers who appeared at the Haymarket Theatre in September 1755. On 1 September she was in *La Dance du village* with Settree and Walker, and on 11 and 15 September she was with them again in *Pierrot's Dance*. On 21 September 1761 a "Signora Florentina, a capital performer from the Opera House at Turin," offered a comic dance at a booth at Southwark Fair; she was very likely the same performer.

The Signora "Fiorentini" who danced in *The Bavarian Shoemakers* and *The Italian Robbers* at Drury Lane on 9 October 1762 was probably the same performer we have been following, though she was advertised as making her first appearance in England. During the 1762–63 season at Drury Lane she provided entr'acte dances and appeared in a *Masquerade Dance*, *The Witches*, *The Magician of the Mountain*, and *Phoebe*. Her last appearance may have been on 21 April 1763 when she danced in *The Witches*; the following day's bill indicated that she was dropped from the cast of *Phoebe*.

Fiorilli, Tiberio, called "Scaramouch" *1608–1694, actor, singer, manager.*

Tiberio Fiorilli was born in Naples on 9 November 1608. According to his earliest biographer, Angelo Constantini, he was the son of Silvio Fiorilli (or Fiorillo), a *commedia dell'arte* actor whose character was Captain Matamoros, and he had a brother who played Trappolino. There was, indeed, a Silvio Fiorilli who led a troupe of players in the early seventeenth century, and he had a son Giovanni Battista who acted Trappolino, but historians have questioned their relationship to Tiberio Fiorilli. In any case, about 1633 Tiberio married Isabella del Campo (some sources call her Lorenza-Elisabetta del Campo). She became an actress who went by her character name of Marinetta, just as Fiorilli came to be called Scaramouch. They went to Paris about 1639 or 1640, and Scaramouch supposedly charmed Louis XIII by quieting the bawling Dauphin with funny faces—only to get his lap saturated in the process. On 11 August 1644 Louis, the son of "Tiberio Fiorilly, comédien de la Royne, et d'Isabelle del Campo, sa femme," was baptized, with Cardinal Mazarin standing as godfather. Louis was Fiorilli's third son; others we know of were Silvio-Bernardo, who married Marie de Roussel de Lamy in 1666, and Charles-Louis, who became a canon of Troyes Cathedral.

Fiorilli acted at the Petit Bourbon in 1645 with the troupe that performed *La finta pazza* on 14 November, with scenes and machines by the famous Giacomo Torelli. In 1647 the company left Paris, but Fiorilli was back at the same playhouse in 1653, and in 1658 his troupe shared the theatre with Molière's company. Fiorilli's players left for Italy in July 1659, and word soon came back to Paris that Scaramouch

Harvard Theatre Collection

TIBERIO FIORILLI

engraving by Habert

had drowned in the Rhône. The poet Loret wrote a lamentation:

> . . . Scaramouch the Great is dead.
> A Man of an unrivalled Quality
> In the rare Art of Whimsicality,
> Who mimicked with a marv'lous Knack
> Both Woeful Will and Random Jack,
> Ignoramuses, Logicians,
> In brief, all Sorts and all Conditions;
> So that, the simple Truth t'express,
> This unapproach'd Resourcefulness
> In all Theatric Enterprize
> Excelled all his Contemp'raries
> (Blunden translation)

When the death report proved untrue, Loret wrote another poem to celebrate the resurrection of Scaramouch.

Fiorilli's troupe returned to Paris in 1661 and again shared a playhouse with Molière, this time the Palais Royal. Molière was a great admirer of the Italian comedian and is said to have studied him carefully.

Louis XIV, too, was impressed with him. Though Fiorilli's performances were chiefly mimetic, he was an able singer and guitarist and often performed with his dog and parrot, who "sang" trios with him. The visiting player was showered with gifts: in 1662 Fiorilli received one gift from the state treasury of 300 livres, another of 430 livres, and a grant of 600 livres for travel expenses to and from Italy. In 1664 he was again given money to travel to Florence, and in 1668, when he went again to Italy, Louis supplied him with 600 livres. Leaving his wife behind, Fiorilli returned to Paris in 1670 and soon took up with another woman. On 8 November 1673 "Tibère-François, fils de Tibère Fiorily, Napolitain, officier du roi, et de damoiselle Anne Doffan, sa femme," was baptized in Paris.

Charles II invited Fiorilli and his company to England, for though Londoners had not seen him perform, they were well acquainted with his fame on the Continent. As early as 1670 English plays made references to the great Scaramouch (Howard's The Woman's Conquest), and Wycherley paid tribute to him in The Gentleman Dancing-Master in 1672. The troupe's costumes, properties, scenery, and other goods were admitted duty free by an order dated 21 April 1673, and the comedians performed at court and at York House soon after that. On 22 August "Senior Scaramouchio" (for Fiorilli seems not to have been cited in any of the English records by his real name) begged leave of the King to take his players home, and on 12 September 1673 their goods were allowed to be exported free of duty. The King apparently provided his own private yacht, the Merlin. Before the company left the King had "prepared & deliuered vnto Scaramouchi and Harlekin vnto each of them a Medall & Chayne of Gold" and similar gifts for the four others in the troupe. The name of the actor who was Fiorilli's harlequin is not known, though

Domenico Biancolelli ("Dominique") had been in the company in Paris in 1659; there seems to be no proof that he ever appeared in England, however.

The following summer Fiorilli and his group were once more in England and played on a stage erected in St George's Hall, Windsor. On 1 June 1674 the troupe's goods were admitted duty free, and on 19 August they were shipped back to the Continent. A note in the Bulstrode papers dated 20 June 1675 tells us that Scaramouch was back again:

There is arrived Scaramouchy, ye famous Italien comedian with his crew, to act againe, & are to have ye King's Theatre in Whitehall for their use during their stay, and all people are allowed to come there & see them, paying as they doe at other houses, so y^t now a Papist may come to Court for halfe a crowne. This is not much lik'd by our other players, for it will half break both our houses.

On 24 July 1675 Andrew Marvell wrote to William Popple: "Scaramuccio acting dayly in the Hall at Whitehall, and all Sorts of People flocking thither, and paying their Mony as at a common Playhouse; nay even a twelve-penny Gallery is builded for the convenience of his Majesty's poorer Subjects." Evelyn did not like the break in tradition at all, though he admired Fiorilli; on 29 September 1675 he observed in his diary, "People giving monye to come in, which was very Scandalous, & never so before at Court Diversions: having seene him act before in Italy many yeares past, I was not averse from seeing the most excellent of that kind of folly."

In the spring of 1683 King Charles negotiated with Fiorilli to return once more. Nothing appears to have come of this, because, as the *Historical Manuscript Commission Seventh Report* makes clear, Fiorilli was concerned that the King still owed him £100 from a previous visit.

We have assumed that the Scaramouch so frequently mentioned in English govern-

ment documents, plays, prologues, and diaries during the 1670s and 1680s was, in fact, Tiberio Fiorilli. But the actor's biographer made no mention of any visits to London by Fiorilli, his real name was never cited in documents, and the company was referred to simply as the "Italian comedians" or the "Italian players."

Fiorilli was back in Paris in 1680 and in love with yet another woman. She was Marie-Robert Duval, by whom he had a daughter Anne-Elizabeth, baptized on 29 July 1681. The daughter married the painter Jean de Clermont in 1695. Fiorilli's wife died in Italy in 1687 (some sources suggest, surely incorrectly, 1639), and on 8 May 1688 the actor, then aged 80, married Mlle Duval. Fiorilli's last years were fraught with problems: his new wife robbed and cuckolded him, and his son Silvio (by his first wife, presumably) also robbed him. Madame Fiorilli was condemned to the convent at Chaillot on 29 October 1692 for her adultery.

Fiorilli stopped acting about 1690 or perhaps a year of two earlier, and he died on 7 December 1694. The actor was buried at St Eustache. He is said to have left all his wealth, nearly 100,000 crowns, to his son, the priest Charles-Louis. Fiorilli's burial certificate was signed by Silvio Fiorilli and Marc-Antoine Romagnesi. Angelo Constantini, called Mezzetin, wrote *The Birth, Life and Death of Scaramouch* (1695; modern edition 1924 in English by Cyril Beaumont) which contained a great deal of fancy interspersed with a few useful facts. Despite its flaws, the work is still the basic source of information on the greatest scaramouch of the seventeenth century.

Fiorilli was pictured as Scaramouch in an engraving by Nicholas Bonnart. Bonnart also made an engraving, after a portrait by Henri de Gissey, 1621, which was copied by Gervais and printed by Charles Delâtre in Paris in 1876. Other engravings include one by Habert in 1700, one by

Petrus Schenck, and one by Weyen in 1670. The Weyen engraving shows Fiorilli with a whip, instructing Molière.

Fiorillo, Federico *b. 1755, violinist, composer.*

Born at Brunswick, Germany, on 1 June 1755, Federico Fiorillo was educated in music by his father Ignazio Fiorillo (1715–1787), a Neapolitan mandolinist, lutenist, and composer who was chapel master in Brunswick. At first a mandolinist, Fiorillo later took up the violin and viola. He toured Poland and Russia in 1780, and in 1782 he was at the theatre in Riga, serving as a conductor, according to Grove, and as choirmaster, according to van der Straeten. Perhaps Sainsbury was more accurate in stating he was appointed *chef-d'orchestre.*

In 1784 Fiorillo traveled to Italy and then to Paris, where in 1786 he was a successful soloist on the violin at the Concert Spirituel and published some compositions. He came to London in 1788 where he played in Salomon's quartet and in the Concerts of Ancient Music from 1791. Although he made his last public appearance playing a viola concerto at the ancient music concert in 1794, Fiorillo evidently remained in London for several decades. From about 1805 to 1814 he composed music for such London ballets as *Le Voeu téméraire, La Siège de Troye,* and *Le Mariage secret* (1808). About 1815 he went to Amsterdam. By 1823 he was in Paris, where he had an operation, and then returned to London, where, according to van der Straeten, he "probably died soon after." But Fiorillo apparently was still alive when Sainsbury wrote the *Dictionary of Music* in 1824.

Fiorillo wrote quartets, symphonies, and many compositions for the violin, but only his *Etude pour violon formant 36 caprices* survives as "a work of high authority in the art of violin playing," according to Sainsbury, and as part of "the standard literature of the violin," according to van der Straeten.

The caprices were re-edited frequently in the nineteenth century and in 1855 Spohr added a second violin part for teachers.

Firbanch or Firbank. *See* FAIRBANK.

Firsk or Firske. *See* GRIST.

Firzi. *See* FERZI.

Fischar. *See* FISCHER, FISHAR, FISHER.

Fischer. *See also* FISHAR *and* FISHER.

Fischer, Johann Christian *1733–1800, oboist, composer.*

Born at Freiburg, Germany, in 1733, Johann Christian Fischer was to become a prominent member of an influential group of German musicians who eventually came to London and stimulated a mature taste for modern music. In the 1760s he was a member of the Elector of Saxony's court band at Dresden, which in its best days under the direction of Hasse, according to Dr Burney, "was regarded as the most judiciously arranged and the best disciplined in Europe." Eventually Fischer was employed in Frederick the Great's orchestra at Berlin, but he stayed only for a brief period, the wars in Germany having brought about diminishing support and opportunity for musicians in that country. Grove states that Fischer remained at Dresden until 1771, after which he went to Berlin, but by 1768 he was already in London, having arrived by way of Germany, France, and Holland where he had given concerts.

Taking lodgings with a peruke-maker named Stidman in Frith Street, Soho, Fischer made his musical debut in London playing the oboe in a concert at the Thatched House Tavern, St James's Street, on 2 June 1768. Playing the pianoforte at the same concert was Johann Christian Bach, who was at the time a co-promoter

By gracious permission of Her Majesty, Queen Elizabeth II

JOHANN CHRISTIAN FISCHER

by Gainsborough

with Karl Friedrich Abel of the famed subscription concerts at Spring Gardens. Abel had known Fischer from their years together in the Dresden band, so the launching of the latter's professional career at London was well assisted.

It was at the Bach-Abel concerts, and those at Vauxhall, that over the years Fischer was to become an attraction. He composed his own pieces for performance, an unusual concession by Bach and Abel, whose works were the dominating compositions at the concerts. By Burney's testimony, Fischer composed "in a style so new and fanciful, that in point of invention as well as tone, taste, expression, and neatness of execution, his piece was always regarded as one of the highest treats of the night, and heard with proportionate rapture." He enjoyed similar approbation over the years in the Professional Concerts, the Concerts of the Nobility, and the New Musical Fund Concerts. His continuing success, no doubt, persuaded Fischer to settle in London for good.

The first notice of Fischer's appearance in a London theatre was on 3 February 1769 when he played a solo on the oboe between the parts of the *Messiah* at the King's Theatre. A week later, on 10 February, he played at Covent Garden Theatre for a command performance of *Gideon* which was attended by their Majesties. During the remainder of the oratorio season at Covent Garden that spring he played regularly. Fischer's oboe concertos, in fact, became a regular fixture of oratorio performances at Covent Garden, Drury Lane, the Haymarket, and the King's from 1770 through 1776. He played for the first time at the Oxford Music Room on 18 November 1771. On 9 May 1774 he played at Hickford's Room. He was scheduled to appear in a concert given at the Society of Arts Exhibition Room in the Strand on 23 January 1776, but illness prevented him, so his place was filled by Barthélemon. He also gave concerts in Dublin between May and October 1771 and in 1776, at the Assembly Room, Prince's Street, Bristol, on 21 December 1773, 20 December 1774, and 19 December 1779, and at Bath in 1782.

Fischer's rendition of Handel's fourth oboe concerto at the Handel Memorial Concerts at Westminster Abbey and the Pantheon in May and June 1784 so impressed George III, according to Burney, the producer of the great event, that the King wrote of his pleasure in a note on his proof-sheets of Burney's *Account* of the commemoration.

On 5 June 1785 Fischer was recommended by Thomas Sanders Dupuis for admission to the Royal Society of Musicians. He was unanimously elected on 3 July 1785, and on 2 October of that year Dupuis signed the book of admission and paid the subscription in Fischer's behalf. In 1800, the year of his death, Fischer was serving as a Governor of the Society.

From as early as 1774 Fischer had been invited to participate in musical parties at court, and in 1780 was appointed chamber musician to Queen Charlotte at a salary of £180. A humorous story was told in the *Country Magazine* in March 1786 about Fischer's having become the victim of a practical joke at the hands of young Prince Adolphus during a concert at Windsor Castle. Just as Fischer was about to conclude one of his most elaborate cadences, the Prince, concealed under the music desk, "whipt the *oboe* out of his hands, and left the astonished musician in the attitude of playing, without an instrument. The figure of Fischer was so extremely ludicrous, and his expression of surprise so striking, that the whole company burst into a loud laugh, and the Royal Pair could not refrain from joining. . . ." So much disconcerted was the musician that after recovering his instrument, he retreated "with great precipitation." In her *Journals* Mrs Papendiek gave accounts of similar practical jokes played upon Fischer by members of the court.

On 21 February 1780 Fischer married Mary, the daughter of Thomas Gainsborough. The artist's apprehensions over the match proved to be well founded, for the couple soon separated, evidently without issue. In the credentials submitted by Fischer to the Royal Society of Musicians in 1785, it was stated that he was a married man but that he had no children at that date.

Perhaps because he was not appointed the Master of the King's Band upon the death of Stanley in 1786, a position for which he had had high expectations and for which he had competed with Burney and Parsons (the latter was appointed), Fischer left London in 1786 for several years. Mozart, who had been impressed by hearing Fischer in Holland some twenty years previously, wrote on 4 April 1787 of being very disappointed when he heard him again in Vienna and was highly critical of his musical execution and his compositions. Despite his severe judgment of him, Mozart arranged and played a set of variations upon a minuet which Fischer had written for an English court fête to mark the visit of the King of Denmark to England, and consequently the piece became a most popular composition.

By 1790 Fischer had returned to London to resume his concert activity and his appointment in the Queen's Band. Doane's *Musical Directory* in 1794 listed his address as No 40, Dean Street, Soho. Among his most important pupils were Kellner, Antonine Sallantin, William Shield, and Charles Suck. The oboist John Parke, who succeeded Fischer as a concert player at Vauxhall, credited him with stimulating his career, stating that when Fischer arrived in London the two principal oboists were using instruments which resembled a post-horn and that the German was responsible for effecting important changes. "The tone of Fischer was soft and sweet," wrote Parke, "and his execution at once neat and brilliant." The tone of Fischer's oboe was likened by A. B. C. Dario to that of a clarinet; Giardini claimed that it had "such an *impudence* of tone as no other instrument could contend with."

While playing a solo in a concert at the Queen's residence at St James's on the night of 29 April 1800, "after having executed his first movement in a style equal to his best performance during any part of his life" (according to Sainsbury), he was felled by a sudden stroke. Assisted from the apartment by Prince William of Gloucester, Fischer was conveyed to his house in Soho, but despite the aid of the King's physicians he died on the same night. At the end he expressed his wish that all his manuscript music might be accepted by the King.

Many of Fischer's compositions for oboe, flute, piano, and violin were published at Berlin and London, including concertos, duos, trios, quartets, divertimentos, and airs. A list of his music is found in the *Catalogue of Printed Music in the British Museum*. Pohl mentioned an arrangement of "God save great George our King," for four solo voices, chorus, and harp accompaniment, and a solo quartet and chorus for "The Invocation of Neptune."

A portrait of Fischer painted by his father-in-law Thomas Gainsborough was exhibited at the Royal Academy in 1780 and now hangs at Buckingham Palace. Thicknesse mentioned another portrait of Fischer by Gainsborough, "painted at full length . . . in scarlet and gold, like a Colonel of the Foot Guards," which was reported to have been exhibited for sale by a picture dealer in Catherine Street. A portrait by Gainsborough of the artist's daughter Mary, the wife of Fischer, was reproduced in a Christie's sales catalogue, dated 19 May 1908.

Fischer, Johann Ignaz Ludwig
1745–1825, singer.

According to his notice in the *Enciclopedia dello spettacolo,* Johann Ignaz Ludwig Fischer, who enjoyed a distinguished career as a *primo basso* on the Continent, sang in Salomon's concerts at London in 1794. We find, however, no corroborating evidence in concert notices or other sources.

Ludwig Fischer, as he was commonly called, was born on 18 or 19 August 1745 at Magonza where he received his early education from the Jesuits. By 1768 he was in the chapel choir of the Elector Karl August at Mannheim, and in 1772 he began singing important roles in the Court Opera in that city. By 1778, after appearing at Munich, he joined the Hofopera in Vienna with a large annual salary. Before his reported visit to London in 1794 he sang during the 1780s at Naples, Rome, Venice, and Berlin; in the 1790s he was at Dresden and Vienna, at Hamburg in 1801–2, and during the last years of his career, until 1816, at Vienna again and Berlin. He died in the latter city on 15 July 1825.

Fischer's wife, Barbara, née Strasser (b. 1758) also sang in Europe until she retired in 1789. They had four children who sang professionally on the Continent in the nineteenth century: Joseph (1780–1862), who married a contessa named Ottweiler; Josepha (b. 1782), whose married name was Vernier; Therese Wilhelmine (b. 1785), who married a baron named Walden; and Louise.

Fischer was the author of the drinking song "Im kuhlen Keller sitz ich hier." His autobiographical manuscript (which he kept until 1790) was published by H. Teinert in *Die Musik* (Vol. II), 1902. Additional information on Fischer's continental career and his children can be found in the *Enciclopedia dello spettacolo*.

Fischer, Ludwig. See FISCHER, JOHANN IGNAZ LUDWIG.

Fishar. See *also* FISCHER and FISHER.

Fishar, Arnold [*fl.* 1766?–1769], *dancer.*

An Arnold (Arnal) Fishar was a dancer at Covent Garden Theatre in 1767–68 and 1768–69. His salary in the former season, as listed by Jesse Foot in his *Life of Murphy* (where his name was given as Arnold Fishar, male dancer), was 6s. 8d. per day. On 27 May 1768 he received £1 9s. as his share of benefit tickets. On 5 November 1768 he signed his name as Arnal Fishar in a letter from Covent Garden performers to George Colman, the manager, which was printed in the *Theatrical Monitor*. Probably he was related to James Fishar, the principal dancer and ballet master at the same theatre at that time, and some of the dancing credited to the latter during those two years may actually have been done by Arnold Fishar. Either one of them may have been the Fishar who was a dancer at Liverpool in the summers of 1766 through 1769.

Fishar, James [*fl.* 1764–1780], *dancer, ballet master.*

James (sometimes Jacques) Fishar's name was first noticed in the London bills for 10 January 1764 when he danced a new piece called *Les Mattelots provençals* with Miss Auretti at the Haymarket Theatre. That dance, and another called *La Tambourine*, were repeated throughout the season. The following season he was engaged at Covent Garden, where he made his first appearance (wrongly called his first on the English stage) on 4 October 1764 in a new comic ballet *La Femme Maîtresse*. On the same evening he danced his *Les Mattelots provençals* with Signora Louisa Manesière, whom he later married. On 15 October he repeated *La Femme Maîtresse* and danced *La Tambourine*, and on 12 December he appeared in a new ballet *Rural Love* with Sga Manesière and others. On 21 January 1765 he and Miss Wilford danced a minuet in *Romeo and Juliet*.

Continuing as a principal dancer at Covent Garden, Fishar appeared in and trained dancers for such popular ballet and pantomime pieces as *Harlequin Doctor Faustus, The Rape of Proserpine, Harlequin's Jubilee, Mother Shipton,* and *Harlequin Sorcerer.* He also often performed specialty dances in such plays as *Macbeth, The Winter's Tale,* and *Henry VIII.* In 1767–68, Fishar's salary was £1 per week. In May 1768 he contracted with Covent Garden for a three-year period at £3 per year and 19*s.* 8*d.* per week, and a benefit. At his final benefit on 15 April 1774 he made a profit of £164 8*s.* 6*d.*

On 19 April 1775 the *Morning Chronicle* carried an advertisement for the publication of *Country Dances* by J. Fishar, "for ten years principal dancer and head teacher of all the dancing at the Theatre Royal, Covent Garden." Among the numerous young dancers who were introduced at Covent Garden under his instruction were Master Blurton, Miss Besford, Miss Capon, and Miss Parish. On 24 April 1773 Mr Miller, "Scholar to Fishar," danced a hornpipe for the first time, and a new grand ballet called *The Festival of the Black Prince* ("as performed at Paris by Fishar with universal applause") was shown. Either he or Arnold Fishar (fl. 1766?–1769) was probably the Mr Fishar who was a dancer at Liverpool in the summers of 1766 through 1769.

Fishar seems to have retired from active theatrical work after 1773–74, although he probably was the Fishar who gave a single performance of *The Scots Measure* at the Haymarket Theatre on 20 November 1775. His wife, the former Signora Manesière, with whom Fishar had lived and had "married . . . in her last illness" (according to Kemble's notes), died at Guildford on 7 August 1775 and was buried at St Mary's church in that city on 13 August. Fishar, himself, was still living at Guildford in 1780, and on 6 December of that year he was given a benefit ball there.

Fishar, Mrs James. *See* **MANESIERE, LOUISA.**

Fisher. *See also* **FISHAR** and **FISCHER.**

Fisher, Mr ₁*fl. 1706–1726*₁, *puppeteer.*

On 17 December 1726 *Farley's Bristol Newspaper* carried an announcement of the arrival at the Rose and Crown in Tucker Street of "the famous FISHER," who intended to present a performance of *Henry the Second of England, with the Death of Fair Rosamond* beginning on 26 December and continuing every night during the holiday season. The title role was to be played by a little boy and the rest of the roles by "moving Artificial Actors, the most to the life that ever was seen; they are Figures 5 Foot high, and move Heads, Eyes, Mouth, and all parts of their bodies to the Life, the like never seen upon any Stage in the Kingdom before. . . ." Fisher advertised that he had come to Bristol "after 20 Years Travels" and that he had had "the Honour to perform before His Royal Highness Prince George, and several Times at both Universities, and most of the Capital Cities [including London?] and Towns in England, and before most of the nobility in Great Britain, with a general Applause."

Fisher, Mr ₁*fl. 1796–1797*₁, *actor.* *See* **FISHER, MISS** ₁*fl. 1796–1804*₁.

Fisher, Mrs ₁*fl. 1752*₁, *actress.*
With Hallam's company at the New Wells, Lemon Street, a Mrs Fisher acted Desdemona in *Othello* on 16 November, Belvidera in *Venice Preserv'd* on 28 November, and Sylvia in *The Recruiting Officer* on 30 November 1752.

Fisher, Mrs ₁*fl. 1796–1797*₁, *actress.* *See* **FISHER, MISS** ₁*fl. 1796–1804*₁.

Fisher, Miss ₁*fl. 1796–1804*₁, *singer.*
A Miss Fisher performed with her parents at the Birmingham Theatre in the summer of 1797, when all three were billed as from the Royalty Theatre, London (pre-

sumably the previous season). She sang at the Royal Circus, London, between 16 May and 6 October 1800 and on 17 August 1801 and 8 October 1804.

Fisher, Mrs Alexander [*fl.* 1765–1782?], *actress.*

Mrs Alexander Fisher was a member of an Irish provincial company, managed by her husband and Knipe, which played at Belfast from 5 October 1765 through 10 March 1766. Prior to that engagement the company had been at Lurgan. Perhaps she had also been with her husband when he was playing with Elrington's company at Carmarthen in the 1750s and in Barry and Woodward's company at the Crow Street Theatre, Dublin, in 1759–60. Soon after a period of management by her husband at Dundas in 1769, she accompanied him with his itinerant company to France, Flanders, Denmark, and Russia. In 1771 Mr Fisher was superintendent of Empress Catherine's theatre at St Petersburg, and reportedly he offered Garrick 2000 guineas if the great actor would give four performances there, but Garrick refused.

On 22 April 1776 Mrs Fisher made her London debut at the Haymarket Theatre in the title role of *Isabella*, for her own benefit. Her son, Master P. Fisher, played Isabella's child. She also acted Catherine in the afterpiece *Catherine and Petruchio.* In announcing the performance, the *Morning Chronicle* of 30 March 1776 identified her as of Irish birth but as having acted chiefly in Russia and elsewhere in Europe. On 5 August 1776 the same newspaper reported that Mrs Fisher, "the celebrated heroine of Russia," was acting at Rotherhithe. Perhaps she was the Mrs Fisher who played the role of the Milliner in *The Temple Beau* at the Haymarket on 21 September 1782. Her husband, Alexander Fisher, who evidently did not act in London, should not be confused with the provincial managers in Norfolk, David Fisher (1729–1782) and his son David Fisher (1760–1832). The elder

David Fisher has sometimes been credited with the Russian management, but in his memoirs Charles Lee Lewes identified that manager as Alexander Fisher. W. J. Lawrence's notation in a manuscript now in the National Library of Ireland that Alexander Fisher was the father of the musician John Abraham Fisher (1744–1806) is without foundation. The musician's father was a Richard Fisher.

Fisher, Hugh *d. c. 1686, trumpeter.*

Hugh Fisher (or Fitchert) was one of four Dutchmen appointed trumpeters in ordinary to Charles II on 11 June 1660. Fisher received, according to a warrant in the Lord Chamberlain's accounts dated 23 December 1661, £60 annually. Though most of his career in the King's Musick was spent in London, from 26 August to 1 October 1663 Fisher attended the King at Bath at an extra fee of 5s. daily. On 23 February 1674 he was suspended temporarily for an unspecified misdemeanor, but he was still at court when James II came to the throne in 1685. By 23 April 1686 Hugh Fisher was dead, and his wife Jane, from the parish of St Martin-in-the-Fields, assigned to Charles Fisher (doubtless a relative) of St James, Westminster, £8 out of every £20 she received from the King for her late husband—his arrears in salary, no doubt.

Fisher, John Abraham 1744–1806, *violinist, composer, proprietor.*

John Abraham Fisher was born in 1744, at Dunstable, according to *The Dictionary of National Biography* and van der Straeten; at London, according to Sainsbury. A notation in the hand of W. J. Lawrence on a manuscript now in the National Library of Ireland states that he was the son of the provincial actors Mr and Mrs Alexander Fisher, but there seems to be no corroborating evidence for this claim. According to *The Dictionary of National Biography* his father, who is otherwise unidentified, was named Richard Fisher.

It is also said that Fisher was brought up in Lord Tyrawley's house. When Fisher, having studied with Pinto, made his debut at the King's Theatre on 25 January 1765 playing a solo on the violin for the benefit of the Musicians' Fund the bills announced that his appearance was by Tyrawley's permission. (The dates given by *The Dictionary of National Biography* and *Grove's Dictionary* for his debut are incorrect.) Fisher again played a violin solo at the King's on 23 January 1767. At that time he may have been a regular member of the band. No doubt he was the Abraham Fisher who signed the Admission Book of the Royal Society of Musicians in 1764; at some later date he was expelled for nonpayment of his subscription.

Although Fisher was a composer of sacred music, he was more widely known for his theatrical music. On 2 March 1767 he was paid £1 by Covent Garden Theatre for "tunes and use of the organ" in *Love in the City*, a new comic opera which had opened at that theatre on 21 February 1767 with a text by Bickerstaffe and the "Music compiled from Favourite airs of the most celebrated composers." At Covent Garden in 1769–70 he composed music for George Alexander Stevens's new opera afterpiece *The Court of Alexander*, which was first performed on 5 January 1770. At his benefit on 11 January Fisher received £82 5s. *The Freeholders Magazine* of that month judged that the airs "had uncommon merit" and pronounced Fisher "a young genius, who has hitherto been but little known in the musical world." He provided music for the new pantomime *Harlequin's Jubilee* which opened on 27 January and for which he was paid £26 5s. on 29 May 1770. On 21 April he played a concerto on the violin and accompanied Mrs Pinto, for her benefit, in Handel's song "Sweet Bird." He also played first violin at Marylebone Gardens in the summer of 1770. Later at Covent Garden Fisher set new songs for *Lionel*

and Clarissa on 8 November 1770 and wrote music for Craddock's new tragedy *Zobeide* on 11 December 1771 (for which he was paid £24 3s. on 28 January 1772).

On 27 February 1772, Fisher married Elizabeth Powell (d. 1780), the widow of the actor William Powell (d. 1769), at St Paul, Covent Garden. The marriage was originally intended for September 1771, but good taste dictated its postponement until after the raising of William Powell's monument at Bristol. (But the incorrect date of 19 September 1771, given by Winston in one of his manuscripts, has been often repeated, as has been the misconception that Fisher married one of Powell's daughters rather than his widow.) In the fifth edition of the *New Foundling Hospital for Wit* (1772), Mrs Powell was chided for her haste: "Or ere these sheets were old . . . married with a fiddler!" Though her maiden name was spelled Branston, Elizabeth may have been related to the Mr Branson who was a house servant at Covent Garden between 1767 and 1784 or to the Mrs Branson who acted at the same theatre during that period. As Mrs Powell, Elizabeth had acted at Bristol in 1766. She did not appear on the London stage, but at one time she worked in the wardrobe department at Covent Garden. By his marriage with Elizabeth Powell, Fisher had at least one child, Charles Langford Fisher, who was baptized at St Paul, Covent Garden, on 31 January 1774.

Through his wife, Fisher obtained a one-sixteenth share of Covent Garden Theatre which had been left to her by William Powell. Fisher took some active interest in the management and also remained involved in other musical and theatrical matters such as writing music for pieces at Sadler's Wells in 1772 (including *The Monster of the Woods*), playing at Marylebone Gardens in 1774, and performing with Giardini at the Ranelagh Regatta concerts in 1775. At Covent Garden he composed music for *The Sylphs* on 3 January 1774.

The reviewer in the *Westminster Magazine* of January 1774 called it "the worst Harlequin entertainment we remember to have seen" and damned the music as "very insipid and pilfered from other masters." Fisher was paid £42 for the music on 8 April 1774, and the piece was revived at the beginning of the next season, fitted up with a setting by Servandoni which must have been about the scene shop for years. But new scenery by Dahl, Carver, and Richards was provided for *The Druids*, a pastoral masque and pantomime, which first was performed on 19 November 1774 with music by Fisher.

Fisher's other compositions for Covent Garden in the 1770s included an overture for *Prometheus*, a pantomime, on 26 December 1775; *The Syrens*, a masque by Thompson, on 26 February 1776; an air for *The Seraglio* on 14 November 1776; the overture and music for *Harlequin's Frolicks* (an alteration of *Prometheus*) on 26 December 1776; new airs for *Lionel and Clarissa* on 3 October 1777; some music for *The School for Guardians* on 18 November 1777; the overture and music for *The Norwood Gypsies* on 25 November 1777; new music for the sacrifice scene in Act V of *Iphigenia* on 23 March 1778; additional airs for *The Tempest* on 13 May 1779; and the song "She that will now discover," sung by Mrs Morton in an entertainment called *A Fête* on 3 April 1781. During the 1770s Fisher occasionally played concertos on the violin at Covent Garden Theatre.

Maintaining his interest in sacred music as well, Fisher had matriculated at Magdalen College, Oxford, on 26 June 1777, and several weeks later on 5 July 1777 had been awarded the degrees both of Bachelor and Doctor of Music, his doctoral exercise having been an oratorio, *Providence*, performed several days earlier at the Sheldonian Theatre. The oratorio was given again at Freemasons' Hall, London, on 28 May 1778 for the benefit of the Middlesex Hospital, and then again in 1780.

Soon after Elizabeth Fisher died at Brompton on 7 May 1780, Fisher, evidently having lost interest in matters theatrical, disposed of his share in Covent Garden Theatre and went on a concert tour of the Continent, playing in France, Russia, and Germany. He was in Leipzig and Frankfurt in 1783. By 1784 he was in Vienna, where he married the singer and actress Anna Selina Storace (1766–1817), who was at the time engaged at the Imperial Theatre. The couple were not destined to live together for very long, for the marriage was tempestuous from the outset. By the end of that year, upon the Emperor's hearing of his cruel treatment of his new wife, Fisher was expelled from Austria. After her return to London Anna lived for many years with the singer John Braham (1777–1856), until he deserted her in 1816. She died on 24 August 1817, and in her will, drawn in her maiden name and dated 10 August 1797 while Fisher was still alive, she gave no indication of her marriage to the musician or even that he existed.

From Vienna Fisher went to Dublin. There he gave concerts at the Rotunda and supported himself by teaching. How long Fisher remained in Ireland is unclear. According to Lady Morgan's *Memoirs*, he left Dublin by 1788. Other sources, such as van der Straeten, suggest that he settled in Dublin and died there. In any event, the last 15 years of Fisher's life seem to have been uneventful professionally. Occasionally several of his airs were revived at Covent Garden, as on 2 May 1791 when tunes by him and other composers were played in *Alexander the Great*; on 2 October 1793 some of his music was played in *Harlequin's Chaplet*.

Fisher died in May or June 1806, either at Dublin or London.

As a musician, Fisher, according to van der Straeten, "Combined a brilliant technique with fiery temperament but also with a strong admixture of charlatanry." In person he was small and "exceedingly vain," and his affections included the employment of a servant in brilliant livery, who carried his violin in a richly gilded crimson case, while the master followed dressed, according to Pohl, "in a brown silk camelot coat bound with scarlet and ornamented with bright buttons." Diamond buttons fastened his knee breeches, and the costume was crowned by a very high, powdered, and perfumed headdress.

Among Fisher's printed music in the British Museum are the following songs: *The Favorite Cantata of Diana and Cupid, and a Collection of Songs sung . . . at Vaux Hall* (1770); *Diana and Acteon*, sung by Mr Vernon (1780?); *In vain I seek to calm to rest*, sung by Miss Cowper (1775?); *Just what you will*, sung by Mr Vernon (1775?); *The Morning Invitation* (1775?); *The Songs, Duetts and Chorusses in the Masque of the Druids* (1774); *The Songs, Chorusses, and Comic-Tunes in the Entertainment of the Sylphs* (1774); and *Vauxhall and Marylebone Songs*, sung by Vernon, Mrs Weichsell, and Dubellamy (1774). Other published works include: *Harlequin Jubilee . . . Set for the Harpsichord, Flute, or Violin* (1770); *The Overture of the Syrens . . . for Two Violins, Tenor & Bass, Two Hautboys, Two French Horns ad libitum* (1777); *The Music of the Epithalamium; consisting of Songs, Choruses, and a dead March, in Zobeide . . . adapted for the Harpsichord, Voice, Violin, and G Flute* (1771); *The Overture, Songs, Dances, &c. in . . . Harlequin's Museum* (1792) (*The London Stage* says the music was by Shields); *Six Duettos for two Violins* (1773?); *Seek ye the Lord*, an anthem sung by Dubellamy at Bedford Chapel and at Lincoln Cathedral (1775?); and *A Comparative View of the English, French, and Italian Schools. Consisting of Airs and Glees . . . Compos'd as Examples of their several manners during residence in those Countries* (1790?). Three of Fisher's violin concertos were published at Berlin in 1782. Fisher's autographed score for the opening scene of *Macbeth*

was sold from the Kitchiner Collection in 1839.

Fisher, Mrs John Abraham the first. *See* POWELL, MRS WILLIAM, ELIZABETH.

Fisher, Mrs John Abraham the second. *See* STORACE, ANNA SELINA.

Fisher, John Ernest [*fl.* 1784–1801], *singer.*

In 1794, John Fisher of No 38, Queen Street, Cheapside, was listed in Doane's *Musical Directory* as a bass singer, a member of the Cecilian Society, the Handelian Society, and the Academy of Ancient Music, a participant in the oratorios at Drury Lane Theatre, and a vocalist in the Handelian performances at Westminster Abbey. He was also described as engaged at Covent Garden Theatre, but incorrectly, for at that time he was employed by Drury Lane Theatre. In the subscription list of the New Musical Fund in 1794 his full name was given as John Ernest Fisher.

Fisher was listed by Burney among the vocal performers in the Handel Memorial Concerts at Westminster Abbey and the Pantheon in May and June 1784. He was regularly engaged as a singer in the Drury Lane chorus from 1793–94 through 1798–99, appearing numerous times in such pieces as *The Pirates, The Mountaineers, The Cherokee, Robinson Crusoe, Richard Coeur de Leon, Blue-Beard, The Captive of Spilburg*, and *Feudal Times*. In the summer of 1800 he was in the Haymarket company singing in the choruses of *Obi* and *What a Blunder*, but in early August he was dismissed by the stage manager because he "had sent a substitute to perform his business." The dismissal action was protested by Dr Arnold, then music director at the Haymarket, and Colman the manager assured him in a letter of 5 August 1800 that "Fisher shall continue in his situation." Fisher's name also appeared in the Haymarket bills for 1801.

Fisher, Joshua Bridges [*fl.* *1793–1819*], *actor, author.*

While still a youth, Joshua Bridges Fisher was a member of Colman's summer company at the Haymarket Theatre in 1793, playing a Scholar in *The Padlock* on 20 August and a Citizen in *The Surrender of Calais* on 27 August. The following summer at the Haymarket he played a Waiter in *The Suicide*, and Serv-

ants in *The Dead Alive, Tit for Tat*, and *She Wou'd and She Wou'd Not.*

In the fall of 1794 Fisher began an association with Drury Lane Theatre which was to last at least 25 years through 1818–19. He made his debut there on 2 October 1794 as Casimir in *Lodoiska*—"Benson being lame," noted the prompter William Powell on a copy of the playbill (at the British Museum), "Fisher went on as

Courtesy of the National Theatre, London

RICHARD SUETT as Diggery Duckling, WALTER MADDOCKS as Wat (or JOHN PURSER as Cymon), SARAH SPARKS as Miss Bridget Pumpkin, FRANCIS WALDRON as Sir Gilbert Pumpkin, MRS HENRY as Kitty Sprightly, VINCENT DE CAMP as Capt Charles Stanley, JOSHUA BRIDGES FISHER (second from right) as William, and George Bartley as Harry Stukely, in *All the World's a Stage*

by De Wilde

Casimir." Again on 13 November, True-man being ill, Fisher played Gustavus in the same piece. On 28 February 1795 he was a Servant in the premiere of Cumberland's *The Wheel of Fortune*, a role he repeated frequently during the remainder of the season. Throughout his years at Drury Lane he continued in a line of modest supporting roles such as a Servant in *The Recruiting Officer*, Prigg in *Harlequin Captive*, William in *The Man of Ten Thousand*, a Waiter in *The Plain Dealers*, Dina in *The Honey Moon*, a Servant in *The Chapter of Accidents*, a Gentleman in *The Chances*, Adam in *Catherine and Petruchio*, a Waiter in *A Bold Stroke for a Wife*, a Sailor in *Hamlet*, an unspecified character in *Fast Asleep*, and William in *All the World's a Stage*.

Fisher's salary at Drury Lane from 1796–97 through 1798–99 was £1 5s. per week. By 1802–3 it was £2 per week; it was raised in 1806–7 to £3 at which level it remained at least through 1813–14. On 6 July 1813 he signed his full name to a pay receipt.

In 1806 the *Authentic Memoirs of the Green Room* reported that Fisher was "confined to a very humble walk in the drama, though like many other stage-struck scribes, the *cacoethes ludendi* made him exchange the *quill* for the truncheon. He is a young and industrious man, and has occasionally adventured into the field of literature as a novelist, having a wife and family to support." Fisher's novel *Pathetic Tales* was published in 1808. His daughter performed at the Royal Circus, and on 6 June 1806 made her debut at Drury Lane as Little Pickle. His wife also performed at Drury Lane in the first decade of the nineteenth century; the account books record such payments as £4 3s. 4d. for 5 days to "Mr & Mrs & Miss Fisher" on 23 February 1805 and £4 per week to Mr and Mrs Fisher for 1805–6. On 7 March 1814 Fisher missed a performance because his wife was "on the point of death."

In addition to the roles cited above, in the nineteenth century Fisher also played, among others, the following: Guildenstern in *Hamlet*, Lorenzo in *The Duenna*, Fagg in *The Rivals*, Beaufort in *The Citizen*, Petit in *The Inconstant*, Buckle in *The Suspicious Husband*, Fabian in *Twelfth Night*, John in *The Man of the World*, Bushy in *Richard II*, and a Witch in *Macbeth*. A Drury Lane casting book dating from about 1815 assigns to Fisher a total of 40 parts for the season.

Fisher is depicted as the Servant in a painting by De Wilde of a scene from *All the World's a Stage* (as revived at Drury Lane on 12 March 1803). This painting had been titled as of "Quick and Mrs F. A. Henry," but the central male figure is not Quick but Francis Waldron. Now in the possession of the National Theatre, this painting is described in detail and its provenance given by Messrs Mander and Mitchenson in *The Artist and the Theatre*.

Fisher, Lawrence d. 1672, singer.

On 30 March 1661, according to the Westminster Abbey Muniments Precentor's Book, a number of the Gentlemen of the Chapel Royal were paid for singing at the funeral of Princess Mary; one Fisher attended, the notes say, expecting a place in the choir, but he lost it. That was probably Lawrence Fisher, described in the parish registers of Westminster Abbey as a "singing man." He was buried on 4 March 1672 in the East Cloister of the Abbey. Letters of administration of his estate were granted on 5 June 1672 to a creditor, his relict Elizabeth renouncing. Elizabeth Fisher appears to have married John Singleton, another court musician, on 19 February 1680.

Fisher, P. [fl. 1765–1776], actor.

Master P. Fisher, the son of the Irish actors Mr and Mrs Alexander Fisher, acted at Belfast with his parents in July 1765. He probably accompanied them on their professional tour of France, Flanders, Denmark, and Russia between 1769 and 1771. His name was announced in the bills for the role of Isabella's child when his mother made her London debut at the Haymarket in the title role of *Isabella* on 22 April 1776. That night at the end of the afterpiece *Catherine and Petruchio* Master Fisher delivered a "Humorous *Epilogue on Everybody*, to be spoke by Somebody, in the character of Nobody."

Fisher, Mrs Thomas. *See* ABRAMS, THEODOSIA.

Fishett, Mr [*fl.* 1798–1801], doorkeeper.

A Mr "Fitchett's" benefit tickets were accepted at Drury Lane on 9 June 1798; a Mr Fishett's tickets were accepted on 14 June 1800; and the account books for the theatre list a Mr Fishett as a doorkeeper in June 1800 and a Mr "Fisher" in that capacity in 1801. All the references may well be to the same employee, but it is impossible to tell what the correct spelling of his name was.

Fisin, James 1750–1847, pianist, violinist, composer.

By his own manuscript account (dated 28 December 1823) provided to Sainsbury and now in the University of Glasgow Library, James Fisin was born in Colchester; Fisin, however, neglected to provide a date. His obituary notice in the *Gentlemen's Magazine* for November 1847 stated he was 97 at the time of his death on 8 September 1847, thus placing his birth in 1750. He was early educated in music under Frederick Charles Reinhold. After leaving Colchester for London in 1776, Fisin was, in his own words, "placed under the auspices of the late Dr. Burney, from whom he experienced infinite advantages," and he also for many years was under the patronage of Sir Edward Walpole, "from whose exalted protection and benevolent attention he derived great benefit."

Fisin came to Burney's attention because of the interest of Thomas Twining, a resident of Colchester and a frequent correspondent with the great musicologist. Twining's letters to Burney about Fisin are preserved in the British Museum. In May 1776 Twining advised Burney that young Fisin was not succeeding in private practice at Colchester, having at that time only two scholars. By 7 October 1776, when Fisin had removed to London and was living at No 2, Bateman's Buildings, St Anne's, Twining again had written to Burney, this time to express his reservations about Burney's intentions to recommend the musician for a position at Newcastle: "I think he cannot possibly be qualified for the place you mention either as to playing or method of teaching." From yet another letter from Twining on 29 November 1776, it becomes clear that Burney nevertheless had made the recommendation. Since Twining had thought Fisin "pretty well qualified" for a position in a playhouse band when he had originally sought Burney's assistance, he suggests that Burney could save himself embarrassment with the authorities by indicating to them that he had been misled by Twining. In any event, Fisin was not appointed. On 24 January 1777, Twining wrote Burney, "I think just as you do about his failure at Newcastle. Moreover, I am persuaded that had he been elected, the people there would have been disappointed at his performance and he would have been uncomfortable." Fisin then took up a position in Beverly where Twining wished him success.

Little is known of Fisin's career between 1777 and 1782. On 2 June of the latter year, when James Simpson recommended him for membership in the Royal Society of Musicians, Fisin was described as a person who had "Studied & practic'd Music for a livelihood more than seven years & is not married plays the harsicor violin tenor &c & plays at the Pantheon and many other concerts." He was in the Society's list to play violin at the annual concerts at St Paul's for the benefit of the clergy in 1785 and regularly from 1790 through 1793. He had been one of the first violins in the Handel Memorial Concerts at Westminster Abbey and the Pantheon in May and June 1784. In 1787–88 he was paid £6 6s. for playing in the concerts of the Academy of Ancient Music. In 1791 he was still playing violin at the Pantheon. In 1794 he was listed in Doane's *Musical Directory* as a musician at the opera and as then living at No 49, Charlotte Street, Portland Place.

Failing health and a desire to leave London prompted Fisin in 1801 to remove to Chester where he taught and composed music. Again, Dr Burney, whose assistant he had been, was instrumental in obtaining the appointment. On 27 October 1800 Burney had written a long letter to his friend Frances Crewe in which he set out Fisin's terms and expectations (MS in the Berg Collection, New York Public Library):

. . . I have communicated the passage relative to a Chester Music-master to the person I had in my eye . . . . It is the worthy M^r. Fisin, whose character as a master has long been established in Chester by Miss Crewe's performance; & whose worthy & steady character I can answer for during more than 20 years. He told me 5 or 6 years ago, that he was tired of the bustle and fatigues of London. & wished for some quiet retreat in the Country. . . . He seemed ballancing – & doubtful, whether he c^d. pluck up courage to go so far from his connexions in Essex, where he spent his youth, & where he has still many friends. . . .

He is pleased to say, after other grateful Comp^{ts}. "It is now nearly 20 years since you took me under your protection . . . in the course of wch. time, I have been able to save a small sum of money wch. renders me a little independant of the world – and as I am a little *'declining into the vale of years'*, I sh^d. not wish to undertake a business where there was much riding to *distant* places in the Coun-

try; neither sh^d. I like to have anything to do wth. public Concerts; but I sh^d. not care how much my time was employed *in & near* Chester, in teaching. I think the terms are rather low, at a Guinea 12 lessons, according to the *times*. All the teachers ab^t. this Country, & at Norwich, have a Guinea for eight lessons.

Burney further reported that Fisin could not take up the Chester appointment until the spring of 1801. He remained there for three years before retiring to his native Colchester.

Fisin's published music included: *One Set of Canzonets*, dedicated to Miss Crewe; *One Set of Canzonets*, dedicated to Lady Vernon; *Three Sets of Canzonets*, dedicated to Mrs Wright; *Twelve Ballads*, dedicated to Mrs Norman; *Six Vocal Duets*, dedicated to Lady Hume; *Three Glees for four Voices*, dedicated to Sir George Smart; *The Seasons, or Vocal Year*, dedicated to the Princess Mary; *Judgment of Paris*, dedicated to the countess of Bridgewater; *Three Sonatas*, dedicated to Mrs Burney; *Three Sonatinas*, dedicated to Miss Graham; *Sacred Songs*; and a number of single pieces.

Fiske, Mr? [*fl.* 1795], *house servant?*
One Fiske, probably a house servant, was added to the Drury Lane pay list at 15s. per week on 25 April 1795.

Fitchert. *See* FISHER.

Fitchett. *See* FISHETT.

Fitz, Mr [*fl.* 1661], *actor?, singer?*
A prompt note in a Bodleian copy of *Aglaura* named a Mr Fitz, but what he did in the play is not clear. He may have been an actor playing a Lord, or he may have been a singer. If he was a singer, perhaps he was Theophilus Fitz, the court musician, who is known to have performed at the Bridges Street Theatre in 1664 – though he is not known to have been a singer. The prompt notes may concern a production of *Aglaura* by the King's Company at the

Vere Street Theatre; the work was performed there on 28 December 1661.

Fitz, Theophilus [*fl. 1645–1710*], *violinist, flutist.*

On 16 September 1645 the violinist Theophilus "Fitts" of the parish of St Margaret, Westminster, married Elizabeth Markes of St Mary Olave, Southwark. Their son Thomas, who also became a violinist, was probably born within a few years, and the couple had at least two daughters, Mary and Frances (later Mrs Edward Trimmer). Perhaps the Anne Fitz who was buried at Westminster Abbey on 30 May 1670 was also their daughter.

By 16 October 1660 Theophilus Fitz was a member of the King's Musick, earning a salary of 1*s.* 8*d.* daily plus an annual livery allowance of £16 2*s.* 6*d.* On 20 August 1661 he was appointed to the King's private music. Theophilus remained a faithful musical servant during the reigns of Charles II, James II, William III, and perhaps even of Queen Anne. He was, at any rate, still a member of the court musical establishment in 1710 and may have continued for a few years longer.

Like many royal musicians, Fitz frequently attended the monarch on trips outside London. He went to Portsmouth in 1662, Tunbridge and Windsor in 1663, Oxford and Hampton Court in 1665 and 1666, Tunbridge in 1666, Dover in 1670, Windsor in 1671, Hampton Court and Windsor in 1674, Windsor in 1675, Newmarket and Windsor in 1678, Windsor in 1679, 1680, 1681, 1682, 1686, and 1687, and Newmarket in 1689. For those trips he always received, though not necessarily on time, an extra fee of a few pence per day.

Theophilus Fitz was one of the court musicians who occasionally played at the public theatre. An order dated 20 December 1664 in the Lord Chamberlain's accounts reminded Fitz and others to wait upon Thomas Killigrew at the Bridges Street playhouse when he should require their services. And on 8 May 1677 Fitz and other court musicians petitioned against Charles Killigrew, Master of the Revels, for dismissing them from their attendance at the playhouse—presumably Drury Lane, though possibly the court theatre.

Fitz and his fellow royal musicians needed whatever extra income they could earn by performing in public or going on royal progresses, for their livery allowances were frequently in arrears. Fitz's wages at court as of 6 April 1665, when he succeeded to Stephen Strong's position, were still 1*s.* 8*d.* daily plus £16 2*s.* 6*d.* annually for livery; on 27 April he was given an additional position as a flutist "for life" at 1*s.* daily and, apparently, a second livery allowance; on 14 March 1667 he was chosen one of the violinists in the elite band of 12 within the regular group of 24, for which he received an additional but unspecified salary; by 9 January 1669 he was earning £46 10*s.* 10*d.* as a member of the wind instruments; and by 13 December 1679 he was getting a like amount as a violinist. But as of 25 February 1686 Fitz had not been paid his livery allowances for 1665, 1667, 1670, and 1679 through 1684. King James tried to pay some of the outstanding debts of Charles II, and on 21 September 1686 Fitz was granted £161 5*s.*

William III paid his court musicians less. On 25 March 1689 Fitz was receiving only £30 annually as his salary, but it is not clear whether that represented his total income or only half of it, for he still held positions in both the violins and the wind instruments. By 1697 his salary was up to £40, and there it appears to have remained at least to the end of the century.

Other references to Theophilus Fitz in the accounts show that on 3 September 1674 he and his son Thomas received £24 for violins; on 15 February 1675 they played in the court masque *Calisto*; and on 26 January 1685 they were ordered to practice at his majesty's theatre for a ball to be given there. Theophilus's son died in 1677, remembering his father in his will with a gift of £20 for mourning. Theophilus's musician friend John Goodwin died in 1693, leaving Fitz ("of Hampton") £5. No record of the death of Theophilus Fitz has been found. By 1710 he must have been quite old and near retirement, having devoted 50 years to the royal musical service.

Fitz, Thomas *d. 1677, violinist.*

Thomas Fitz, the son of Theophilus and Elizabeth Fitz, was probably born in the late 1640s, for his parents were married in September 1645, and by 2 December 1664 young Thomas was appointed a musician in ordinary for the violins in the King's Musick. On 16 November 1667 he succeeded to the place of the remarkable violinist Thomas Baltzar, who had recently died, at a salary of £110 annually, retroactive to 24 June of that year. On 27 March 1668 he was given, additionally it seems, the post of the deceased Richard Hudson, with (an extra fee?) £26 12s. 8d. Exactly a month later the Lord Chamberlain's accounts show that his salary was raised to £46 12s. 8d.

Thomas accompanied the King to Newmarket, Bagshot, Portsmouth, and Audley End for a period of 85 days in 1669, for which he received £21 10s. as a special stipend, and in May 1670 he attended the King at Dover. He was with the monarch again in the summer of 1671 at Windsor at 8s. daily, and in the fall of 1674 he went with him to Windsor and Newmarket again. In London on 15 February 1675 he played for the court masque *Calisto*, but another trip to Newmarket in March took him away from his chores at the royal chapel, and he was off to Newmarket yet again in the spring of 1676.

By early 1677 Thomas Fitz must have been very ill, for on 30 March of that year Edward Hooton was appointed to Fitz's post as violinist—but at no salary; he was

to have his fee at the death of Fitz. Similarly, John Twist was appointed on 10 April to another of Thomas's positions and had to wait "upon the death or other avoydance of Thomas Fittz, violin, deceased [*sic*]." Thomas finally died in early September 1677, and his salary from his various posts was quickly reassigned to Hooton and Twist. Fitz was buried at St Paul, Covent Garden, on 8 September 1677.

Thomas Fitz was probably about 30 when he made his will on 24 March 1676, and he apparently never married. His bequests included £100 to his mother, £100 to his sister Mary, and £200 to his sister Frances (Mrs Edward) Trimmer. He left £20 to each of his parents for mourning and £10 to his brother-in-law Edward Trimmer. To his godson Joseph Fashion the younger he gave £20. The rest of his estate he left to his friends Joseph Fashion the elder and William Fashion to distribute among his friends and relations. The elder and younger Joseph Fashion were, like Thomas Fitz and his father Theophilus, court musicians. The will was proved on 10 September 1677 by the elder Joseph Fashion, Fitz's executor.

Fitzgerald, Mr [*fl. 1778*], *dancer.*

A Mr Fitzgerald danced in Slingsby's ballet *The Savage Hunters* at Drury Lane Theatre on 9, 11, 21, 22, and 23 April 1778.

Fitzgerald, Mr [*fl. 1781–1782*], *actor.*

A Mr Fitzgerald, announced as from the Theatre Royal, Dublin, acted Fainwell in *The Artifice* on 16 October 1781 and Sancha in *Don Quixote in England* on 4 March 1782, both at the Haymarket Theatre.

Fitzgerald, Mrs, née Swan [*fl. 1707–1734*], *singer, actress.*

Mrs Fitzgerald, whose maiden name Chetwood said was Swan, acted in Dublin from 1707–8 to 1714, one of her known roles there being Camilluss in *The Spanish Wives*. Clark notes that she often took young men's roles. She was presumably the Mrs Fitzgerald who sang at Stationers' Hall in London on 6 April 1714 for her benefit, after which she returned to Dublin for almost two years.

She was in the Lincoln's Inn Fields troupe in London by 24 January 1716, when she and Leveridge sang "Since times are so bad" in *The Cobler of Preston*. In the following months she appeared as a solo singer, but Mrs Fitzgerald also played a Water Nymph in the first performance of *Presumptuous Love* on 10 March. The fall of 1716 found her again at Lincoln's Inn Fields, but on 31 December she made her first Drury Lane appearance, singing a new cantata. She participated in a concert at Stationers' Hall on 13 March 1717 and was given a benefit at Drury Lane on 6 June. She was again at Drury Lane in 1717–18, singing between the acts in October and November 1717 and later. On 19 March 1718 she performed at a concert at the Tennis Court (not James Street), and on 22 March she sang the Priestess of Isis in the masque in Act V of *The Lady's Triumph* at Lincoln's Inn Fields.

Her appearances in the years that followed were similarly sporadic. She was singing at Lincoln's Inn Fields in October 1718, was at Hickford's Room on 4 March 1720 and at Stationers' Hall on 9 February 1722 and 6 March 1723, apparently sang at the Haymarket Theatre in 1724–25, and certainly sang there, in Italian and English, on 24 February 1726. In August and September 1729 Mrs Fitzgerald sang at the Lee-Harper booths at Bartholomew and Southwark fairs, called Mrs Fitzgerald "Sr." to distinguish her from a second Mrs Fitzgerald who acted in August at Fielding's booth.

The London Stage reports Mrs Fitzgerald as singing at Goodman's Fields in 1729–30 though her only appearance there that season may have been on 3 June 1730 (according to Latreille). She sang there again on 1 October 1731, and she was probably the Mrs Fitzgerald who was Clymena in *The Fall of Phaeton* at the Lee and Harper booth at Bartholomew Fair on 23 August 1733. It was surely she who sang with Excell at Southwark Fair on 7 September 1734.

Fitzgerald, Mrs [*fl.* 1729–1732], actress.

On 23 August 1729 at Fielding's Bartholomew Fair booth a Mrs Fitzgerald acted a role in *Hunter* while another Mrs Fitzgerald (called "Sr." in the bill) sang at the Lee-Harper booth. The actress was probably the Mrs Fitzgerald who played Angelica in *The Constant Couple* at Goodman's Fields on 23 October 1730, though she was billed as from Drury Lane; she is not known to have performed at Drury Lane, and the other Mrs Fitzgerald (fl. 1707–1735) had not been at that theatre since 1718. Our subject acted Dorinda in *The Stratagem* at Goodman's Fields on 26 October 1730, and her last known role was Symphony in *The Blazing Comet* on 2 March 1732 at the Haymarket Theatre.

Fitzgerald, Frederick *d.* 1789, musician.

Frederick Fitzgerald, a musician, subscribed 10s. 6d. to the Drury Lane Theatrical Fund in 1775. Probably he was the Fitzgerald who was listed by Burney as a trumpet player in the Handel Memorial Concerts at Westminster Abbey and the Pantheon in May and June 1784. A notation in the Jerome manuscript at the Folger Shakespeare Library informs that he died on 13 June 1789.

In his will, made on 3 May 1789 and proved at London on 23 June 1789, Fitzgerald described himself as a musician of Duke's Court in the Parish of St Martin-in-the-Fields. To his children Frederick and Eleanor he left his household furniture, musical instruments, umbrella, pictures, fire irons, carpet and all other property, except four bedroom chairs, eight china plates, 15 cups, 22 saucers, and several other items which he left to his "ffriend Lucy Miners." Fitzgerald evidently was a widower. Probably he was related to William Fitzgerald (d. 1780), who also was a musician at Drury Lane.

Fitzgerald, Robert. *See* **JERROLD, ROBERT.**

Fitzgerald, William *d. 1780, bassoonist.*

William Fitzgerald was a principal bassoon player in the band at Drury Lane Theatre from as early as 1763 until his death. On 30 October 1771 he borrowed ten guineas from the theatre treasury. His salary was £2 per week from 1774–75 through 1776–77; by 1778–79 it was £2 10s. On 3 February 1771 at St Martin-in-the-Fields he married the singer Eleanor Radley, who died soon afterward at Richmond on 11 August 1772. The *Morning Post* on 6 May 1780 reported that William Fitzgerald had died on 4 May 1780. Probably he was related to Frederick Fitzgerald (d. 1789), a bassoonist at Drury Lane.

Fitzgerald, Mrs William, Eleanor, née Radley *d. 1772, singer, actress.*

Announced as "A Young Gentlewoman," Eleanor Radley made her stage debut at Richmond on 24 June 1767 as Nysa in *Midas*. On 1 August the bills named her for the part. In consequence of Mrs Arne's illness, Miss Radley made her first appearance at Drury Lane Theatre on 26 October 1768 as Leonora in *The Padlock* "and was well received," according to the prompter Hopkins. During that season she played Leonora a total of 49 times; she also performed Phillida in *Damon and Phillida*, Theodosia in *The Maid of the Mill*, Rhodope in *A Peep Behind the Curtain*, and Lucinda in *Love in a Village*. The

last-mentioned role she also acted at Covent Garden Theatre on 28 April 1769. On 2 May 1769 at Drury Lane she shared a benefit with Miss Rogers the dancer.

After playing in Richmond again in the summer of 1769, Miss Radley returned to Drury Lane for 1769–70, appearing as Leonora on 23 September 1769. She sang in *Romeo and Juliet* on 2 October and played Sylvia in *Cymon* on 4 October and Mademoiselle in *The Provok'd Wife* on 10 October. When Garrick opened his production of *The Jubilee* at Drury Lane on 14 October 1769, she was one of the Country Girls. Another country girl was Sophia Baddeley, who, according to Mrs Steele's *Memoirs* of that actress, became so pleased with Miss Radley that she gave her "all the jewels she wore, before she purchased her new set; and these could not amount to less than a hundred pounds." Miss Radley also received gifts of money and other valuables from her. That season she also acted Miss Jenny in *The Provok'd Husband*, the Milliner in *The Suspicious Husband*, a vocal part in *Macbeth*, Wishwell in *The Double Gallant*, Jenny in *Lionel and Clarissa*, Arsinoe in *Herod and Mariamne*, and on 31 March she sang a new song by Hook in Act IV of *The Double Falsehood*. She acted Ophelia for the first time on 2 May 1770 and Jessica in *The Merchant of Venice* on 29 May. Her last role of the season was as the title figure in *The Country Madcap in London* on 7 June.

After playing Lucinda in *Love in a Village* at the Haymarket Theatre on 20 September 1770, Miss Radley returned to Drury Lane where she continued in her usual line of ingenue roles, mostly in musical pieces, for two more seasons. On 29 November 1770 she played Daphne in *Daphne and Amintor* for the first time. On 3 February 1771 she married the Drury Lane musician, William Fitzgerald (d. 1780) at St Martin-in-the-Fields. For her benefit on 19 April, at which she had been too ill to perform, she was still called by her maiden name. When she played Jenny in *The Provok'd Husband* on 7 May 1771, she was billed as Mrs Fitzgerald, late Miss Radley.

In the "Poetical Essays" in the *Gentleman's Magazine* for January 1772, Mrs Fitzgerald was characterized as a "songstress of nature." During the earlier part of 1771–72 she was ill (or pregnant), and she did not appear until 14 December 1771, when she acted Patty in the premiere of Cumberland's *Amelia*, at which time the *Town and Country Magazine* for December 1771 congratulated her "on her return to the stage." After repeating Patty on 16 December she appeared infrequently as Sylvia in *Cymon* and Wishwell in *The Double Gallant*. When she played Leonora in *The Padlock* for her benefit on 15 May she suffered a deficit of £3 9s. Her last performance at Drury Lane was as Wishwell on 22 May 1772. Several months later at Richmond, on 11 August 1772, she died "of a Dropsy."

Fitzhenry, Mrs Edward, Elizabeth, née Flanagan, earlier Mrs John Gregory *d. 1790, actress.*

The actress Mrs Fitzhenry was born Elizabeth Flanagan, the daughter of the keeper of the Old Ferry Boat tavern at the lower end of Abbey Street in Dublin. A sentimentalized account of her by Samuel Whyte in the *Monthly Mirror* in August 1799, in which her name was incorrectly given as Mary Flannigan, claimed that she helped to support her aged father by needlework and embroidery and then spent her spare time reading plays. A manuscript in the Public Record Office, Dublin, gives her full name in a record of her marriage on 15 January 1742 to John Gregory, a lodger at Flanagan's tavern and the captain of a vessel trading to Bordeaux. They had not been long married when Gregory drowned and her father died as well, so Mrs Gregory was encouraged by her friends to turn to the stage. In his *History of the*

Theatres of London and Dublin (1761), Benjamin Victor took credit for auditioning her in Dublin in the role of Alicia in *Jane Shore* (with Bardin assisting as Hastings) and recommending her in a letter to Sparks in London.

Announced as "A Young Lady" making her first appearance on any stage, Mrs Gregory acted Hermione in *The Distrest Mother* at Covent Garden Theatre on 10 January 1754. In his diary the prompter Cross identified her by name and noted that she earned "Great Applause." Arthur Murphy gave her high praise in his account of her debut, which appeared in the *Gray's Inn Journal* on 12 January 1754:

On *Thursday* last the Audience was greatly surprised at the Appearance of a new Actress on this Stage, in the Character of *Hermione*; and it was universally agreed, that it was the best first Attempt they had ever known. This Actress came on without any previous Puffs to prejudice the Town in her Favour; a modest Prologue was spoke on the Occasion, in which she only begs to be endured, though she convinced every Body that she possesses all the Materials to form a great Actress; Her Person being tall and graceful; her Features well disposed, without any Disproportion, and her Voice clear, full and harmonious. She had not the pitiful Ambition to over do her Part, but her Elocution was perfectly natural, and the exertion of her Powers in some Passages shews what she is capable of, when her Fears have subsided. I am informed, she is so modest, that she does not expect that every Body shall be called a Scoundrel, a Pimp, a Rascal, an Hireling, a Coward, &c. that does not think her the best Actress, in the World. The same Advices add, that she does not desire to have a Letter addressed to her, full of scurrilous Abuse on every Person of Taste, whom the Scribler of it may dislike; nor does she plead her being a Gentlewoman to exempt her from being mentioned in the News-Papers. She will be proud to find herself mention'd with Approbation in the GRAY'S-INN JOURNAL, and she is ambitious to add to the Entertainment of the Public, by whom, it is hoped, she will be properly encouraged.

"Verses on the Young Lady who acted Hermione" were printed in the *Public Advertiser* on 19 January 1754:

> All was propriety, all was grace,
> We read the author's meaning in your
> face.
> Your elocution was both just and strong,
> Mix'd with due ease, and not an accent
> wrong,
> Such varied Musick in your voice we
> heard,
> That in the Tones both Taste and Sense
> appear'd.

A copy of "A Letter to Mrs Gregory upon her first Performance upon Ye Stage In the Character of Hermione," written by the actor William Havard and now in the Folger Shakespeare Library, praises her in general terms, speaks of her stagefright which a little "chill'd" her performance, commends her "unblemish'd reputation," and predicts a happy future for her as an actress. Havard also provided some specific criticisms and a caution:

> I must remark to you, Madam, that in ye Situation of Mind you here (at her grand exit) leave the stage, you can have no Regard to any Part of your Dress; so that the lifting up your Petticoat, in order to make your Exit the easier, prejudic'd your going off—But fear at a first appearance, & unacquaintance with the stage, may warrantly excuse. . . .
> Your natural Talents, as an actress, are great, your Person agreeable & striking, your Deportment easy, your Action proper; your Countenance significant, nay marking, and yr voice articulate, musical, & powerful—yet these Qualifications have been possessed before, and these Qualifications have been lost.

Mrs Gregory acted Hermione a total of ten times before the end of the season. On 23 March 1754 she played Alicia in *Jane Shore*, for the first time, and repeated the role on 28 March. On 19 January 1754, after she had acted Hermione for the fifth time, Murphy again championed her in the *Gray's Inn Journal*:

> Mrs. Gregory, who appeared here in the Character of *Hermione*, continues to rise in Reputation every Night, and never fails to draw a numerous Audience. I look upon it to be a peculiar Degree of Merit to adventure on the Stage unheard of and unknown, without Friends, and without any Kind of Party in her Favour; with these Disadvantages to extort the general Applause, and be in every Scene the most conspicuous Figure, tho' performing with practiced and experienced Players, is the Mark of an uncommon Genius. She is perfectly Mistress of graceful Deportment, natural and sensible Elocution, and a Conformity to Nature, without any Trick or Affectation. Every Cast of her Eye, every Attitude, and every Motion of her Arms throughout her Part, are all in Character, and there is no Reason to doubt, but she will be a very considerable Addition to the Theatre.

Despite Murphy's testimony to her "Mark of uncommon Genius," Mrs Gregory was not reengaged by Covent Garden. (Joseph Knight in *The Dictionary of National Biography* suggested that her "Irish accent impeded her success," but the praise specifically of her elocution, with "not an accent wrong," in the *Public Advertiser* makes that conjecture unlikely.) She was, instead, engaged by Sowdon and Victor at £300 for the Smock Alley Theatre, Dublin, where she made her debut on 1 November 1754 as Hermione and subsequently acted Zara in *The Mourning Bride*, Zaphira in *Barbarossa* and Volumnia in *Coriolanus*, earning herself the reputation of a first-rate actress in that company in 1754–55 and 1755–56. In the latter season she was paid £400. Testimonies to her potential continued to be raised in Dublin: "the prodigious Applause she has already met with is but an earnest of What, in some time, under good Instruction, she will deserve," wrote the anonymous author of *A Letter to Victor and Sowdon* (1775), but he cautioned her to "avoid becoming what the Painters call a *Mannerist*, let her study *Nature*, and she will certainly succeed to the Height of our Expectations."

On 5 January 1757 she returned to Covent Garden as Hermione to Mrs Woffington's Andromache. After repeating the role on 7 January, she acted Zara in *The Mourning Bride* on 14 January and Calista in *The Fair Penitent* on 21 February. *The Theatrical Examiner* (1757) reported that as Calista she deserved "the greatest encouragement . . . her rising strokes in acting proceed from natural feelings." She also performed Catherine in *Catherine and Petruchio* and Lady Macbeth for her benefit on 26 March 1757.

Mrs Gregory returned to act at Smock Alley in 1757–58, then again under the management of Thomas Sheridan, at a salary reported to have been £500 for the season. During the summer, she had married a lawyer, Edward Fitzhenry (who had been admitted to the Middle Temple on 7 November 1753), and when she appeared in Dublin on 24 October 1757 as Gertrude in *Hamlet* she was billed as Mrs Fitzhenry. On 27 October she acted Calista in *The Fair Penitent* and then continued throughout the season in an impressive line

Harvard Theatre Collection

ELIZABETH FITZHENRY, as Lady Macbeth

artist unknown

of capital roles: Lady Macbeth, Mrs Sullen in *The Stratagem*, Arpasia in *Tamerlane*, Alicia in *Jane Shore*, Hermione in *The Distrest Mother*, Lady Touchwood in *The Double Dealer*, Veturia in *Coriolanus*, Zara in *Osmyn*, Queen Elizabeth in *The Earl of Essex,* Zaphira in *Barbarossa,* Constance in *King John*, Cordelia, Lady Townly in *The Provok'd Husband*, Phaedra in *Phaedra and Hippolitus*, the Lady in *Comus*, Belvidera in *Venice Preserv'd*, Sigismunda in *Tancred and Sigismunda*, Lady Randolph in *Douglas*, Catherine in *Catherine and Petruchio*, Isabella in *Measure for Measure*, the title role in *Isabella*, Catherine in *Henry VIII*, Cleopatra in *All for Love*, Indiana in *The Conscious Lovers*, and Horatia in *The Roman Father*. She also acted for Mossop at Crow Street and Smock Alley, when he controlled both theatres in subsequent seasons. In 1761–62 she played infrequently and to slim houses. On 16 March 1762 Dr Thomas Wilson wrote from Dublin to Samuel Derrick at Bath: "Fitzhenry is praised to the Skies by the whole world, Every one is convinced that she has more merit than all the Actresses on the Stage put together—so well convinced of her merit, her excellence, so strongly engrav'd on their memories, that no one goes to see her.—She has done nothing this winter." On 17 March 1763, Mossop wrote to George Garrick that Mrs Fitzhenry's salary demands were so exorbitant and her characters by now were so few he could not think of engaging her for the following year. But he did. She also acted at Cork in September 1764.

In the fall of 1765 Mrs Fitzhenry returned to London to take up an engagement at Drury Lane Theatre, making her debut there on 15 October 1765 as Calista. Genest suggested that she had been brought in by Garrick "to curb" the troublesome Mrs Yates, whose friends suspected as much and received Mrs Fitzhenry cruelly. The *Universal Museum* in October 1765 reported that in the part of Calista "she is by no means a servile imitator of any other performer; whatever scenes she excels in, the merit is entirely her own." On 15 November she acted Hermione to Mrs Yates's Andromache, and on 6 December she acted Zara to Mrs Yates's Almeria in *The Mourning Bride*. When she again appeared as Zara on 20 January 1766, she was hissed a little. For her benefit on 9 April 1766 she acted Roxana (with an epilogue) in *The Rival Queens*. An unidentified critic (in a press clipping) commented on her slight improvement over the season:

Mrs. Fitz-Henry, on her first appearance, promised to arrive at excellence in a short time; but her improvements are slower than were then expected. There is a cast of parts suitable to her genius, and wherein she has merit; such as Hermione, Zara, &c. In Calista she supports the violence of her rage, where she tears the letter with great spirit; but afterwards fails in the distresses; and indeed in all characters of the tender or plaintive kind. Her action is too violent; and both that and her voice want that delicacy and tenderness which speaks to the heart. She does not promise to excel in Comedy, wanting an ease and genteelity which in polite characters is absolutely requisite. Would she modulate her voice, and regulate her action, it would add greatly to her excellence in Tragedy.

In 1766–67 Mrs Fitzhenry rejoined Mossop in Dublin where she continued to act through 1773–74. Evidently she then left the stage, with a daughter and son supported by a legacy from her husband, Edward Fitzhenry, who had died on 7 October 1772. A decade later she reappeared once at Smock Alley, on 12 March 1783; in the University of Cincinnati Library is a manuscript, evidently in the hand of James Winston, which indicates that she acted Mrs Sullen in *The Stratagem*, at a place unspecified, on 9 June 1788. Winston recorded her as "a beautiful woman & good figure."

Mrs Fitzhenry died at Ballinahallen, near Enniscorthy, County Wexford (not at Bath as erroneously reported in several sources), on 11 November 1790. Her death was reported by the *Gentleman's Magazine* in December 1790 and by the *Hibernian Journal* of 3 December 1790. In the year of her death the *Dublin Mirror* printed an epitaph:

Fitzhenry—indeed is a name
That dimly is found in the temple of
    fame
Like a meteor she blazes her fugitive fires
Appears on the scene, and, appearing,
    expires.

By most accounts Mrs Fitzhenry was an excellent actress, who evidently preferred the familiarity of the Irish environment to a greater fame in London. Although not an especially beautiful woman, like other tragic queens of her day she had the looks and manner which allowed her to command a scene and an audience. In *The Actor* (1755), John Hill praised her "sensibility" as Hermione, "a disposition to be affected by the passions which plays are intended to excite." She was "inferior to nobody" as Zara in *The Mourning Bride*, testified the *London Chronicle* (No 23, 1757), especially "in her manner of uttering the ironical sarcasms of Zara, which she delivers with a painful smile, and a kind of mortified pride." She had "an understanding that can frame just and lively ideas of a character"; and when once her imagination was impressed with that character, it seemed "to take entire possession of her." As Calista she played with "a wildness in her looks and the tones of her voice, as is very uncommon on the stage."

An engraving of her as Lady Macbeth, by an anonymous artist, is in the Harvard Theatre Collection.

Fitzherbert, Miss [fl. 1782], actress.

Miss Fitzherbert performed occasionally at the Haymarket Theatre in 1782, acting an unspecified character in *Love in a Ven-*

ture and Miss Rantipole in the *Tobacconist* on 21 March, Maria in *The Citizen* and Lady Lucy Pedant in *The Temple Beau* on 21 September, and Isabella in *Wit Without Money* on 25 November.

Fitzherbert, Richard [fl. 1785], trumpeter.

The Lord Chamberlain issued a warrant on 26 July 1785 appointing Richard Fitzherbert Serjeant Trumpeter.

Fitzherbert, William [fl. 1746–1747], singer.

William Fitzherbert was sworn a Gentleman of the Chapel Royal on 26 December 1746, according to a warrant in the Lord Chamberlain's accounts. His salary was to commence on 1 January 1747.

Flack. *See also* FALCK.

Flack, James Medlicot [fl. 1768–1770], assistant treasurer.

According to depositions given in July 1770 in litigation involving George Colman's management, James Medlicot Flack was an assistant treasurer at Covent Garden Theatre between 1768 and 1770.

Flack, John [fl. 1785–1798?], instrumentalist.

John Flack, the son of the musician John Casper Flack and his wife Mary, made his first appearance in public, announced as Master Flack, playing a violin solo at the end of Part I of the *Messiah* at Drury Lane Theatre on 16 March 1785. He was an instrumental performer at the concert of *Redemption*, from the works of Handel, at the King's Theatre on 24 February 1792, when his father also played. He was advertised with his father as playing in the Covent Garden Theatre oratorios on 20 February 1795, 12 February 1796, and 23 February 1798, and at a performance of the *Messiah* at the Haymarket on 15 January 1798.

By 1792 John Flack was the leader of the band at the Apollo Gardens. In 1794 Doane's *Musical Directory* listed him as a principal violinist and a player on the trombone, trumpet, and horn, with engagements at Drury Lane Theatre and the oratorios, so it is possible that some of the payments noted in the Drury Lane account books which we suggest were intended for John Casper Flack may have gone to his son. Doane also indicated that John Flack was a player in the performances at Westminster Abbey and at Apollo Gardens and in 1794 was living at No 8, Exeter Court, the Strand. Possibly John Flack, and not his father, was a member of the summer band at the Haymarket from 1804 through 1810.

John Flack is not known to have been a member of the Royal Society of Musicians, but a Mrs Flack (not his mother Mary who died in 1814) sent her thanks to the Society on 4 February 1827 for donations made to her.

Flack, John Casper 1748–1813, trombonist, composer.

The musician John Casper Flack was born in 1748; perhaps he was the son of John and Jane Flack, whose daughter Henrietta Maria was baptized at St George's Chapel, Hyde Park Corner, on 26 October 1742. By 1778–79 he was earning £2 per week as a horn player in the Drury Lane Theatre band, a position he held until at least 1807–8 and perhaps even until his death in 1813. By 1801 his salary was £2 8s. per week. The Drury Lane account books also record occasional extra payments to him for special services: £3 15s. on 8 December 1804 "For Sounding Signals in Matrimony" and £4 3s. on 15 April 1800 for "Repairing Carillons & binding music." He also played regularly for the spring oratorios and concerts of sacred music at the several theatres: at the King's Theatre in 1792 and 1793; at Covent Garden from 1794 through 1800; at the Haymarket in

1798; and at Drury Lane in 1794 when he, Eley, and Giornovichi were paid a total of £105 for their participation in the oratorios. His son, John Flack (fl. 1785–1798?), a violinist, also performed in some of those concerts. Either John Casper Flack or his son was a member of the summer band at the Haymarket from 1804 through 1810.

Flack was listed by Burney as one of the trumpet players for the Handel Memorial Concerts at Westminster Abbey and the Pantheon in May and June 1784. By 6 February 1785 he was a member of the Royal Society of Musicians, and he served the Society on the Court of Assistants regularly between 1794 and 1813. He played in the Society's annual concert at St Paul's in May 1789. In 1794 Doane's *Musical Directory* listed him as a player on the trombone, horn, and viola, a member of the Royal Society of Musicians, a participant in the Drury Lane oratorios and performances at Westminster Abbey, in the "Guards 1st Regiment," and as then living at No 40, Maiden Lane, Covent Garden. Flack was also a composer of divertimentos for winds.

He was buried at St Paul, Covent Garden, on 19 February 1813, aged 65. On 23 July 1813 the administration of his estate, valued at less than £600, was granted to his widow Mary Flack. On 7 November 1813 the Royal Society of Musicians agreed to grant Mary Flack her widow's allowance upon presentation of her marriage license. A Miss Flack, probably a daughter, notified the Society on 5 December 1813 that she was willing to allow Mrs Flack £20 per year "for the business" (unexplained), but by 2 January 1814 Mrs Flack had not agreed to the arrangement and her allowance was suspended. By September of that year Mary Flack had died and on 4 September 1814 the Society granted burial allowances for both her and her husband.

"Flame, Lady." *See* HAYWOOD, MRS VALENTINE.

Flanagan, Elizabeth. *See* FITZHENRY, MRS EDWARD.

Fleetwood, Mr [fl. 1746–1747], house servant?

A Mr Fleetwood shared a benefit with Wright, Reynolds, Green, Ockman, Elliott, and Miss Bennett at Drury Lane Theatre on 18 May 1747. Probably he was a house servant, and perhaps he was related to Charles Fleetwood, the former patentee of that theatre.

Fleetwood, Charles d. 1747, patentee, manager.

Charles Fleetwood was born a gentleman of an ancient and respectable family of Staffordshire. He was the only son of Thomas Fleetwood of Gerard's Bromley, by his wife the Hon Frances Gerard (d. c. 1735), daughter of Richard Gerard (d. 1680) of Hilderstone. Charles's paternal grandfather, Henry Fleetwood, was the youngest son of Sir Richard Fleetwood of Calwich, who had been made baronet in 1611 by James I. The name of Charles's father Thomas is found in a list of Roman Catholic nonjurors who refused to take oaths to George I in 1715. At that time Thomas Fleetwood estimated the annual incomes from his estates in Cheshire at £1349 5s. 1d. and in Staffordshire at £1236 9s. 11d.

At the age of 21, Charles Fleetwood inherited a landed estate reported to have been worth £6000 per year, presumably an ample living even for a person of excessive habits such as Fleetwood would prove to be. He was in his younger years a handsome man, elegant in manner and affable in personality. His amiability, especially, made him most attractive to persons of rank.

On 2 February 1734, the *Daily Courant* reported: "We are credibly inform'd, that Charles Fleetwood, Esq; of Bromley-Hall, in the County of Stafford . . . hath purchased all the shares of the Patentees of the Theatre in Drury-Lane." According to a press cutting (now in the British Museum), Fleetwood had purchased all the shares in the patent except the one-sixth belonging to Giffard of Goodman's Fields Theatre. The patent had been obtained at a very low price, for the seller, John Highmore, was anxious to extricate himself from one of the most difficult controversies over management in the English theatre to that date and one which stirred up an enormous amount of public attention and commentary. It concerned the rebellion of players of Drury Lane, led by Theophilus Cibber, against Highmore's managerial insolence. A band of the players defected to play at the theatre in the Haymarket in the fall of 1733, while some loyal non-seceders carried on under Highmore at Drury Lane. As Theophilus Cibber wrote about the rebellion in his *Two Dissertations on the Theatres* (1756), he had led the seceders to "a happy Asylum . . . protected by a generous Town, against, the despotic Power of some petulant, capricious, unskilful, indolent and oppressive Patentees."

Highmore's case at law was unsuccessful, and the right of the rebellious players to perform at the Haymarket was upheld. Among the few actors who remained loyal to Highmore were Kitty Clive and Charles Macklin, but they could not prevent a disastrous season for Drury Lane in 1733–34. When Highmore began to lose some £50 to £60 a week, he sold his shares to Fleetwood. The triumphant players returned to Drury Lane to a theatre controlled by yet another amateur, who in the words of Charlotte Charke in her play *The Art of Management* (1735), was "a Man of Fortune, who never appear'd but in a Side Box, or behind the scenes" before he became manager.

Fleetwood was sensible enough to appoint Macklin to supervise the artistic business of the theatre, but he himself kept an active control over the other management affairs. As Arthur Scouten points out in *The London Stage*, theatre historians, not fully appreciative of Fleetwood's daily supervision of the management, at least in his earlier years, have tended to dismiss him as an absentee proprietor. In the beginning the future of the players seemed promising, and it was reported in the press that Fleetwood intended to allow the players to share in the patent rather than "making a private Advantage to himself." Not in need of money himself, he was intending, it was said, "To leave a sort of Super-intendency over a Stage," which arrangement would result in "an useful Amusement to a Man of the best Quality in the Nation." A committee of actors, including Mills, Johnson, Miller, Mrs Heron, Mrs Butler, and Theophilus Cibber were, it was reported, to rent Drury Lane from Fleetwood for 15 years at £920 per year. But this arrangement did not come into being.

Eventually Fleetwood turned his head and heart to other concerns, and leaving the players to Macklin and the finances to his treasurer Pierson, he neglected the responsibilities of a patentee. Known as an inveterate gambler, he consorted with boxers and the other lowlife of the town. He was seized, wrote Tom Davies, with a "passion for low diversions, and took a strange delight in the company of the meanest of the human species." The players were offended when he began to populate the stage of Drury Lane with rope-dancers and freaks. Fleetwood had contributed to the erection of a monument to Shakespeare in Westminster Abbey in 1740, but he treated his own playwrights in a contemptuous manner. In a letter to Aaron Hill dated 3 February 1739, David Mallet complained of Fleetwood's neglect of his tragedy *Mustapha*, which was to be performed for the first time on the thirteenth of that month: "The manager (if that is a name for him) will not be at the expence of one shilling towards the dressing or decorating it. He even carries away the actors that are to play in it, from the rehearsals, to boxing matches at Totenham

Court where he himself presides as umpire." Aaron Hill, in a letter to Pope on 9 December 1738, had similarly complained that he could get no response from Fleetwood concerning the script of *Caesar* which the manager had had in hand for some time; and he wrote directly to Fleetwood requesting him to return "my *Caesar* . . . or act it" and criticizing the manager for the "disregard" with which he had been treated "for two or three Seasons, successively." Fleetwood did not produce the play. He also promised Samuel Johnson that his tragedy *Irene* would be produced at the beginning of the season of 1740–41, but the play was not produced until Garrick became manager some years later.

As a result of the great success enjoyed by Henry Giffard at Goodman's Fields Theatre in 1741–42 with the new star Garrick as his main attraction, the manager of the patent house put pressure upon the authorities to invoke the Licensing Act and to close down the competition. Then Fleetwood wooed Garrick to Drury Lane with an enormous salary.

Fleetwood now became more indolent and insolent, appropriating the profits from his theatre to his private amusements and taking large sums of money on loan from the treasurer Pierson, who also treated the actors with contempt to the point where they refused to play for his benefit on 7 April 1743. When Fleetwood discharged Shepherd, who had been attached to the house for many years, he made Shepherd take a benefit for the money that Shepherd owed him. Fleetwood also denied use of the house for the benefit of the under-actors, making it necessary for them to take Lincoln's Inn Fields Theatre for a night. The angered players, under the leadership of Garrick and Macklin, petitioned the Lord Chamberlain for a license to perform at the Haymarket Theatre and signed a pact not to return to Fleetwood unless all taking part in the revolt would agree. The Duke of Grafton, then the Lord Chamberlain,

met the petition with coldness and was much surprised, according to the account of Tom Davies, to learn that a person could earn £500 per year "merely by playing."

Both parties took their case to the public through a spate of pamphlets. In *The Case Between the Managers of the Two Theatres, and their Principal Actors* (1743), the players accused Rich and Fleetwood of forming a "cartel" to control the stage and to reduce salaries. Both managers were represented as grasping, tasteless and thoroughly dishonest. In *The Dramatic Congress. A Short State of the Stage under the Present Management* (1743), Chetwood also abused the managers for their cartel. The most devastating attack upon Fleetwood came in *Queries to be Answer'd by the Manager of Drury-Lane Theatre* (1743), which claimed that the manager overpaid harlequins at the expense of actors; that he had lowered the profession of acting; that he abused families of deceased performers to whom he owed money; that he refused to pay scenemen and supernumeraries, thereby having his scenes bare; that he refused to pay arrears to players he had discharged; that he owed great sums to tradesmen; and that he himself took in "between fifteen and sixteen Thousand Pounds" at the theatre in 1742–43, with a clear profit of near £3000. In his *Queries upon Queries* (1743), Fleetwood tried to answer the charges, article by article, but with little success, although he seemed confident in his position and his right, as patentee, to operate as he saw fit.

In the fall of 1743, Fleetwood began his season with players he had gathered from the provinces and the closed minor theatres. Eventually coming to financial distress, the rebellious players were obliged to return to the fold. Garrick, claiming it was in the interest of his fellows, capitulated in December, but Macklin held out and accused Garrick of reneging on their agreement. Caught in the middle, Garrick tried various

"The Theatrical Contest"

artist unknown

ways to bring about a resolution, even offering Macklin six guineas a week from his own pocket, but neither the manager nor Macklin would agree. This contention caused three more pamphlets to be published: *The Case of Charles Macklin, Comedian* on 5 December 1743, *Mr Garrick's Answer to Mr Macklin's Case* on 8 December, and *A Reply to Mr Garrick's Answer to The Case of Charles Macklin* on 12 December.

But even with most of his first-line players returning, Fleetwood could not survive the pitiful effects of his mismanagement. He was obliged to mortgage the patent for £3000 and to borrow £7000 against a lien on his costumes, scenes, and properties from Hutchinson Mure (1709–1794), a prosperous London merchant in the cabinet and upholstery business. When he tried to raise prices for pantomimes, the audiences rioted on 17 and 19 November 1744. It was said that the manager sent bullies with clubs into the pit to put down the public. In a pamphlet entitled *The Disputes with serving up old Pantomimes* (1744), Fleetwood was satirized as "Swifty-Timber," and it was reported that as a result of the riots the "theatre was most shockingly demolished, even to gutting of the Pit, and fleecing the boxes." In the frenzy of the first riot on the seventeenth, Horace Walpole rose in his box and denounced Fleetwood as "an impudent rascal."

Unable to continue his management, Fleetwood sold the patent to the bankers Richard Green and Norton Amber who paid him £3200 and guaranteed him £600 per year for life. The bankers set up James Lacy, a veteran stage-manager, in charge of the operation. The change-over occurred by 19 December 1744, on which date Macklin returned to Drury Lane. Several years later, in 1747–48, Garrick was to join with Lacy as co-patentee of the theatre and the venerable house would enjoy a long period of stability and success.

Ruined in fortune and in health (according to Benjamin Victor, his "Body was as much impaired by an excessive Gout, as his Fortune by his Misconduct"), Fleetwood went off to the Continent on his "wretched annuity."

Charles Fleetwood died in August 1747, at Châlon-sur-Saone, in Burgundy. In his will, drawn on 20 July 1743, he described himself as "now of Surry Street in the Parish of St Clements Danes." Previously he had lived in Catherine Street, Covent Garden. He left all his land, manors, and other property in Chester, Stafford, Middlesex, and Herts, to his wife Susanna and his two sons Charles and Thomas, in trust, to be sold to pay his mortgages. Administration of the estate was granted on 13 November 1747 to Charles Scrase, attorney on the behalf of Susanna Fleetwood, widow, then still residing at Châlon-sur-Saone. The will was proved at London on 22 April 1748 by his widow.

Fleetwood's wife Susanna was the daughter of Thomas and Grace Williams, of the parish of St James, Westminster. Reputedly she was an actress, perhaps the Miss Williams who performed in London between 1729 and 1738. The story told by Charles Howard, the Duke of Norfolk, in his *Thoughts, Essays, and Maxims*—that when a young man Fleetwood had been forbidden by his mother to marry a baronet's daughter of inferior fortune, a circumstance which broke his heart and started him on the road to dissipation—must be accepted with skepticism.

The Fleetwoods had three sons: Charles (d. 1784), who became an actor and is entered separately in this dictionary; Thomas, who was alive in 1743, but about whom little is known; and John Gerrard (d. 1776), born after 1743, who also became an actor and is entered separately. Mrs Fleetwood later married the painter and sometime scene designer for her late husband, Francis Hayman (1708–1776), at Petersham on 25 April 1752. By her marriage to Hayman, Fleetwood's widow was perhaps the mother of a daughter named Susannah, who proved the painter's will on 16 February 1776, thereby indicating that Mrs Hayman was dead by then. The child Susannah, however, may have been the issue of an earlier marriage by Hayman.

According to R. W. Buss, *The Fleetwood Family Papers* (1914), the portrait-engraving by Dixon usually said to be a picture of Charles Fleetwood cannot be of the patentee since the artist was not born until 1740; the caption describes the picture as "Sir Fopling arrested. Drawn from a late real scene" published by Bowles, 1769, some years after Fleetwood's death. The print shows a man who is holding a spyglass to his eye and who is being arrested by a bailiff. It was copied in an engraving by R. B. Parkes for an edition of Cibber's *Apology* in 1889. Buss suggests that the picture is really that of Fleetwood's eldest son, Charles. The patentee, however, is shown in a satirical print entitled "The Theatrical Contest," which was published on 24 October 1743; the print is described and explained in the British Museum *Catalogue of Political and Personal Satires* (No 2599).

Fleetwood, Mrs Charles, Susanna. *See* WILLIAMS, [SUSANNA?].

Fleetwood, Charles *d. 1784, actor.*
Charles Fleetwood was the eldest son of

"Sir Foppling Arrested," CHARLES FLEET-
WOOD, the younger?

by Dixon

Charles Fleetwood (d. 1747), who was the
patentee of Drury Lane Theatre between
1734 and 1746, by his wife Susanna, née
Williams. Information on the families of
his father and mother can be found in the
biography of the elder Charles Fleetwood.
The birthdate of Charles Fleetwood the
younger, as he was often called, is not
known, but he was alive when his father
drew his will on 20 July 1743, as was his
brother Thomas, about whom little is
known. A third brother, John Gerrard
Fleetwood, (d. 1776), who was born after
1743, also became an actor and is entered
separately in this dictionary.

On 22 June 1758, Richard Cross noted
in his prompter's diary that Young Fleetwood was to be among the new performers
engaged for the following season at Drury
Lane. Announced as making his first appearance on any stage, Fleetwood acted
Romeo on 28 September 1758; Cross
wrote in his diary that he was "receiv'd

with great and deserv'd Applause—he is
Son to our late Patentee." For his second
appearance as Romeo on 30 September,
there was "Great applause again"; Cross
added, "& he mended," presumably meaning he corrected some faults of the first
night. During his third appearance as
Romeo on 13 October, the novice made an
almost tragic error: "Mr Fleetwood in y^e
fight with Paris in ye last Act," wrote Cross,
"having a Sword by his Side instead of a
Foil, run Mr Austin [Paris] into the belly,
he lay some time but at last call'd to be
taken off—a Surgeon was sent for—No
harm, a small Wound, & he is recover'd."

Along with another young actor, William O'Brien, Fleetwood was being instructed by no less than the great actor-
manager himself, David Garrick. In a letter
to John Home on 19 October 1758, Garrick apologized for not having written
sooner, but said that he had been very
busy with his two pupils, Fleetwood and
O'Brien. On that evening, Fleetwood acted
Castalio and O'Brien Polydore in *The Orphan*, each for the first time. Fleetwood
next played Phocyas in *The Siege of Damascus* on 18 November, Octavius in *Antony and Cleopatra* on 3 January 1759,
and a role in *The Ambitious Step-Mother*
on 1 February. For his benefit on 17 April
1759, at which he cleared some £97, Fleetwood had the chance to play Hamlet opposite Mrs Cibber's Ophelia. To mark the
event, Garrick wrote and spoke a special
prologue upon Shakespeare and his works.
The anonymous author of the pamphlet
*A Letter to the Hon. Author of the new
farce, called The Rout* (1759) described
Fleetwood as a "promising actor" and took
Garrick to task for paying him only 50*s.*
per week.

Fleetwood began his second season at
Drury Lane on 25 September 1759 as
Romeo. Several nights later, on 2 October,
he acted Young Bevil in *The Conscious
Lovers*, for the first time according to the
bills. But probably he was the Fleetwood

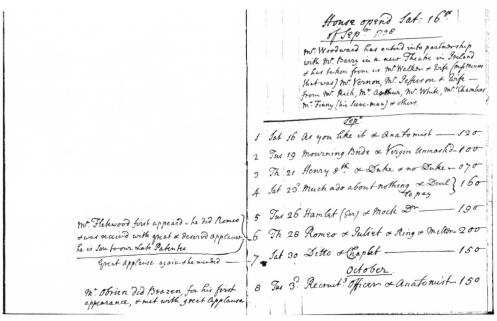

Opening from the "Prompter's Diary" of RICHARD CROSS, September 1758, noting the debut of CHARLES FLEETWOOD, the younger

who had acted the role at Plymouth the previous summer. His other roles at Drury Lane in 1759–60 included Castalio, the title role in *Comus*, Hamlet, Henrico in *The Desert Island*, Hardy in *The Funeral*, Etan in *The Orphan of China*, Valentine in *Love for Love*, Don Felix in *The Wonder*, and a role in *Marriage-à-la-Mode*. He also appeared several times to give the prologue to *Oroonoko*, although he had no role in that piece. Fleetwood's last performance at Drury Lane was as Romeo on 6 May 1760.

In the summer of 1760 Fleetwood joined the company at Jacob's Wells Theatre in Bristol, where he played Romeo and Hamlet. In manuscripts now at the British Museum, Reed noted for 9 September 1760 that "Mr Fleetwood quitted the stage." It was a premature notation, however, for Fleetwood became a member of the company at Crow Street, Dublin, in November of 1760 and remained for two seasons. But evidently Fleetwood's ambitions to live in

a better style than his wages for acting would allow finally prompted his decision to give up acting after 1761–62. Despite his promising beginning, he had not continued to please audiences, except as Young Bevil, a role which agreed with his natural personality. He was described by the *Monthly Mirror* in March 1799 as a person "elegant, handsome; with good understanding and education; he also possessed intrepidity with coolness . . . ." Such qualities served him to great advantage as a billiard player, "at which amusement he was, by all, allowed to be so excellent, that few would venture to hazard with him."

Sometime after his retirement from the stage Fleetwood became involved in commercial activities in India which brought him considerable fortune. On 8 December 1769 the *Public Advertiser* announced his departure for that country as a factor.

A letter dated 1 December 1772 which was published in the *Morning Chronicle* on

7 July 1773 stated that Fleetwood was acting in Bengal. In later years it was reported that he had died there, but perhaps more correct is Reed's contemporaneous information that Fleetwood died at Marylebone in London on 10 April 1784, his demise having been brought on by financial troubles and the threat of losing a brewhouse he had established.

According to R. W. Buss, *The Fleetwood Family Papers* (1914), Fleetwood had been married to a Mary Herdes, by whom he had two children, one of whom was named Charles. The registers of St Paul, Covent Garden, record the baptism of Frances Maria, daughter of Charles Fleetwood, Esq by Mary Herdes his wife on 18 February 1770, a date which falls several months after the *Public Advertiser* of 8 December 1769 had reported his departure for India. Perhaps Buss confused him with another Charles Fleetwood, or perhaps his family did not accompany him to the East. He is known to have been married to a young actress named Mary Simson (d. 1807), his second wife, if Mary Herdes was his first. Mary Simson was the sister of the actor and sometime soldier John Simson (who died in India about 1770); she, like her husband, had been an acting pupil of Garrick. After Fleetwood's death, she married about 1791 an actor at Belfast named White, with whom she lived for 16 years until her death on 22 January 1807. See her in these volumes as Mary Simson (d. 1807).

The portrait by Dixon thought to be of the elder Charles Fleetwood is possibly of this Charles Fleetwood.

Fleetwood, Mrs Charles, Mary. *See* SIMSON, MARY *d. 1807.*

Fleetwood, John Gerrard *d. 1776, actor.*

John Gerrard Fleetwood was the youngest of the three sons of Charles Fleetwood (d. 1747), who was the patentee of Drury Lane Theatre between 1734 and 1746, by his wife Susanna, née Williams. Information on the families of his father and mother will be found in the biography of the elder Charles Fleetwood. John Gerrard Fleetwood was born sometime soon after his father drew his will on 20 July 1743. His eldest brother, Charles Fleetwood (d. 1784), went upon the stage and is entered separately in this dictionary. The second brother, Thomas, who was born by 1743, remains little known.

Announced as a gentleman who had never before appeared on any stage, John Fleetwood acted the title role in *Oroonoko* on 17 April 1769 at Covent Garden Theatre, for the benefit of Robert Bensley. The *Town and Country Magazine* in April 1769 identified him as the son of the late patentee and brother to the gentleman who had appeared about nine years previously at Drury Lane. He appeared in London again, advertised as a young gentleman, this time at the Haymarket Theatre on 9 July 1770 as Lothario in *The Fair Penitent* (when he played the role again for his own benefit on 1 September the bills gave his name). As a member of Samuel Foote's company at the Haymarket that summer, Fleetwood also acted the Bastard in *King John* on 8 and 13 August and Polydore in *The Orphan* on 22 August.

Fleetwood hoped for an engagement at Drury Lane Theatre for the ensuing season, but it was not forthcoming. On 2 September 1770 David Garrick wrote to Fleetwood, at Prince's Court, near Story's Gate, Westminster, that a present engagement was impossible, and that it having been so hot at the Haymarket on the previous night (when Fleetwood acted Lothario) Garrick did not stay to see the performance. The great actor-manager advised Fleetwood to find an engagement in the provinces where he could more frequently play characters of consequence.

After several performances at the Haymarket the following spring (when he acted Oroonoko on 4 March 1771, Alcanor in *Mahomet* on 6 April, and Castalio in *The Orphan* on 20 April), Fleetwood took Garrick's advice and went to play with the company at Edinburgh, where he remained for two years. When he was seen by Sylas Neville in that city on 26 February 1772, Fleetwood proved better as Edgar in *King Lear* than the diarist had expected. At Edinburgh Fleetwood gained experience in a number of important roles, including — among others — Beverly in *All in the Wrong*, Chamont in *The Orphan*, Hotspur in *1 Henry IV*, Jaffeir in *Venice Preserv'd*, the title roles in *Henry VIII* and *Douglas*, Major Sturgeon in *The Mayor of Garratt*, Orlando in *As You Like It* and Ranger in *The Suspicious Husband*. He also acted at Glasgow in 1772, at Beverley and in Ireland in 1773, and at York for Wilkinson from 1773 to 1766.

While playing at York in February 1776 Fleetwood became ill but was well enough by 20 February to play Selim. On 7 March, however, his fall from a horse caused the postponement of a newly dressed performance of *The Distrest Mother*. Perhaps complications from his fall developed, for on 20 July 1776 Fleetwood died in Leeds, at no more than the age of 33. On 15 April 1777 administration of his unspecified estate was granted to his widow Margaret "Fletewood." In the order, Fleetwood was described as late of Leeds and York, "and an Esquire on half pay in the 73rd Regiment of Foot." Margaret Fleetwood had acted with her husband at Glasgow in 1772. Her name also appeared as a "renter" (of a box or concession?) at Drury Lane Theatre in 1794.

Fleming, Francis *d. 1777, musician.*
The Life and Extraordinary Adventures, the Perils and Critical Escapes of Timothy Ginnadrake was published in three volumes in Bath in 1771. In it the author, Francis Fleming (or Flemming), a Bath musician, provided odds and ends of information

By permission of the Trustees of the British Museum

FRANCIS FLEMING

engraving by Hibbart

about Bath and its society. His portrait, engraved by the Bath artist William Hibbart, served as a frontispiece. By 1774 Fleming was a musician in ordinary to the King, for that year he styled himself so when he gave his power of attorney to David Richard of Glanville Street, Rathbone Place. Glanville was a fellow musician and was empowered to collect Fleming's salary for him. According to the *Catalogue of Engraved British Portraits in the British Museum*, Fleming died in 1777.

"Flemish Hercules, The." *See* DUCROW, PETER.

"Flestrin, Quinbus." *See* SMART, CHRISTOPHER.

Fletcher, Mr [*fl. 1723–1724*], *house servant.*
Mr Fletcher, a house servant at Lincoln's

Inn Fields, shared benefits with two others on 29 May 1723 and 2 June 1724. The total receipts for the benefits were £138 16s. and £153 8s. 6d. respectively. Perhaps he was related to Mrs Manina Fletcher, the singer who spent most of her London career at Lincoln's Inn Fields, though she was not there during the period covered by his benefits.

Fletcher, The Misses [fl. 1794–1796], singers.

In 1794 Doane's *Musical Directory* listed three Misses Fletcher, all singers in performances at Westminster Abbey and all living in Birmingham. On 2 March 1796 one of them sang in a concert of sacred music at Covent Garden Theatre. A Miss Fletcher, perhaps the same one, sang in a similar concert there on 4 March, and on 16 March one of the sisters sang. Probably they were sisters of the musicians Thomas Fletcher (fl. 1762–1820) and William Fletcher (d. 1840?).

Fletcher, Maria, née Manina, later Mrs Seedo [fl. 1712–1733], singer.

The impresario Heidegger paid Signora Maria Manina £100 to sing in the operas at the Queen's Theatre in the spring of 1712. Her first known role there was Eucharis in *Calypso and Telemachus* on 17 May. The following season she probably sang Fedra in *Teseo* on 10 January 1713, and she was scheduled for but did not sing Almirena in *Rinaldo* on 24 March. The opera accounts show that Maria sang for Margherita de l'Épine's benefit on 25 April (Deutsch in his *Handel* says 28 April).

In late 1714 or early 1715 she married or formed an alliance with a Mr Fletcher (the music publisher J. D. Fletcher?), and as Signora Maria Fletcher or, sometimes, Mrs Manina Fletcher, she appeared at Lincoln's Inn Fields in 1715–16, offering entr'acte songs. There in 1716–17 she sang specialty songs, may have taken the title role in *Camilla* (and, if so, probably sang

in English), essayed her old role of Eucharis in *Calypso and Telemachus*, and sang Cleora in *Thomyris*. She seems not to have been a member of a theatrical company in 1717–18, though she sang at Hickford's Room in January and at York Buildings in March of 1718. She returned to Lincoln's Inn Fields in 1718–19, sang regularly between the acts, revived her old role of Cleora, had a vocal part in *Circe*, and, at her benefit on 25 April 1719, sang a new cantata by Pepusch.

Mrs Fletcher was again at Lincoln's Inn Fields in 1719–20 and 1720–21, but she was less frequently featured. Occasionally, as on 23 February 1720 and 3 March 1721, she appeared at Hickford's Room. Not until 1726–27 was she noticed again in London advertisements. That season she worked at Lincoln's Inn Fields at a salary of 10s. daily, but the bills rarely cited her. She sang Camilla on 19 November 1726, and at her benefit on 19 April 1727 she offered songs in Italian and collected £46 17s. in money and tickets—apparently before house charges.

Between 19 April and 29 September 1727 Mrs Fletcher married the musician Mr Seedo, and under her new married name she sang at Lincoln's Inn Fields from 1727–28 through 1731–32. During those seasons she performed between the acts and appeared in a few pantomime roles, such as Proserpine in *Harlequin Sorcerer*, Venus in *Apollo and Daphne*, a Spirit in *The Necromancer*, Proserpine in *The Rape of Proserpine*, Selima in *The Sultan*, and Cassiope in *Perseus and Andromeda*. At her benefit on 27 March 1728 she and other singers offered a "British Concert consisting of English & Scotch Ballads"; the receipts came to more than £140.

Mrs Seedo made few appearances after 1731–32. She sang Victory, Concord, and Peace in *Britannia* at the Haymarket Theatre on 16 November 1732 and Daphne in *Venus, Cupid, and Hymen* at Drury Lane on 21 May 1733. The last was a benefit for her husband, who had written the music; during the evening Mrs Seedo also offered some specialty songs. After the 1732–33 season she may have retired.

Fletcher, Thomas [fl. 1762–1820], trumpeter, lutenist, music seller, and publisher.

Thomas Fletcher was a partner with Francis Hodson in a music publishing shop at Cambridge from as early as 1762 to 1777 and probably beyond. Their names as publishers appeared on the imprint of *The Psalms of David . . . by I. Watts . . . A new edition, corrected* printed and sold by Collins and Johnson at Salisbury and also sold by Fletcher and Hodson at Cambridge in 1776.

Thomas Fletcher was perhaps the Mr Fletcher listed in 1794 in Doane's *Musical Directory* as a trumpeter, a member of the New Musical Fund, a participant in performances in Westminster Abbey, and a resident of Derby. His brother William Fletcher (d. 1840?) was listed in the same directory.

On 4 August 1811 Thomas Fletcher was recommended by Richard Godfrey Ashley for membership in the Royal Society of Musicians, and he was elected on 13 November 1811. He was on the list of musicians appointed by the Society to play in the annual concerts at St Paul's in 1812 and 1813. On 4 December 1814 he was elected a New Governor of the Society and on 3 December 1815 was elected an Old Governor. Thomas recommended his brother William for membership on 1 June 1817. The last notice of Thomas Fletcher known to us was in a request to the Society by William in 1820 that Thomas be allowed to substitute for him in the annual concert at St Paul's. The three Misses Fletcher who sang in the oratorios in 1796 probably were his sisters.

Fletcher, William d. 1840?, double bass player, violinist, music seller.

In 1794 Doane's *Musical Directory* listed William Fletcher as a double bass player, a member of the New Musical Fund, a participant in the Handel memorial performances in Westminster Abbey, and a resident of Birmingham. Little, however, is known of his professional life. From his music shop in Bull Street, Birmingham, Fletcher issued *Odes, Cantatas, Songs &c., Divine, moral, entertaining set to music by Mr. Pixell. Opera Seconda*, in 1775. About the same year he offered for sale, "Printed for W. Fletcher," *Three Duetts for two violins. Composed by Sigr. Benda*. In 1805 and 1815 he was named on the subscription list of the New Musical Fund.

On 1 June 1817 William Fletcher, presumably the same person (but possibly a son), was proposed for membership in the Royal Society of Musicians by his brother Thomas Fletcher (fl. 1762–1820) and was elected on 7 September 1817. His name was on the company list of the King's Theatre in 1818 as a violinist, a position he may have held over the years.

The Minute Books of the Royal Society of Musicians reveal that Fletcher had suffered a "paralytic affliction" (probably a stroke) by 1822, for on 3 March of that year he was granted £15 for temporary medical relief. In 1820, 1827, 1828, and 1829 he requested that a deputy be sent to play in his place at the annual charity concerts at St Paul's. On 2 March 1823 he had received another £15 from the society. Ten years later, on 6 April 1834, then noted as living in Birmingham, Fletcher was given another £3 for medical aid. He received payments of £10 on 1 June 1834 and on 7 December 1834, but on 5 April 1835 he was refused aid because his request came too soon after the last previous donation to him. A month later, however, on 3 May 1835 he was granted £10 after he suffered another attack of paralysis. Regular payments of £10, twice a year, went to him for another five years, with the last occurring on 3 May 1840.

The three Misses Fletcher who sang in oratorios in 1796 probably were his sisters.

Fletewood. *See* FLEETWOOD.

Fleuri, Mons ₍*fl. 1705*₎, *dancer.*
Advertised as newly arrived in England, Monsieur Fleuri danced at the Queen's Theatre in the Haymarket on 28 April 1705.

Fleuri, Nicholas *b. c. 1630, theorbo player.*
Born about 1630, Nicholas Fleuri mastered the theorbo and entered the service of the Duc d'Orléans. On 19 October 1663 he was sworn one of the French musicians in ordinary to Charles II, but it is not known how long his service in England lasted. He was still employed by the Duc d'Orléans in 1678.

Fleury, Mr ₍*fl. 1786*₎, *acrobat.*
Mr Fleury participated in a new dance called *The Country Wake*—with tumbling —at Astley's Amphitheatre on 24 July 1786. On the following 9 October he and others gave a tumbling exhibition at the same theatre.

Flight, William *d. 1791, assistant housekeeper, scene painter.*
William Flight was an assistant housekeeper at Covent Garden Theatre from as early as 1768 through 1776. In the transcript taken in July 1770 of a lawsuit brought against George Colman, Flight was also described as an assistant in the painting room and it was noted that recently his salary had been raised from 15s. to 16s. per week. He shared regularly in benefit tickets with other house personnel between 1769–70 and 1775–76, taking £2 18s. 6d. on 19 May 1770, £24 10s. on 25 May 1772, and £6 6s. 6d. on 28 May 1773.

William Flight's first wife, named Elizabeth, was dead by 1776. On 8 April 1776, described as a widower, he married Elizabeth Holdstock, spinster, of the Parish of St Matthew, Bethnal Green. No doubt he was the William Flight, from St Clement Danes, who was buried at St Paul, Covent Garden, on 15 September 1791.

The baptismal and burial registers of St Paul, Covent Garden, tell the sad tale of the early deaths of his children: William baptized 5 December 1762, buried 5 October 1765; George baptized 14 October 1764, buried 29 December 1764; Abliam baptized 4 February 1767, buried 9 February 1767; Elizabeth baptized 6 February 1770, buried 4 January 1771 (an earlier Elizabeth for whom there is no baptism registered was buried 5 October 1769); William Joseph baptized 29 April 1771, buried 29 February 1772; Elizabeth baptized 20 January 1777, no record of burial; William buried 18 May 1782, no record of baptism; and Louisa buried 24 February 1785, no record of baptism.

The registers of that church also contain numerous entries for the baptisms and deaths of the many children of Benjamin Flight (by his wives Frances and Elizabeth); he was probably William's brother and was buried on 25 July 1802.

Flin, Mr ₍*fl. 1784*₎, *dancer.*
A Mr Flin is in the bill for dancing with Laborie, the Simonet sisters and others after the burletta at Hughes's Royal Circus on 9 October 1784.

Flin, Mr ₍*fl. 1789*₎, *instrumentalist.*
Mr Flin was one of the instrumentalists in a concert of Handelian music directed by Dr Cooke at St Margaret, Westminster, on 27 May 1789.

Flingdon, Miss ₍*fl. 1767*₎, *performer.*
Miss Flingdon was one of several children who participated in eight performances of *The Fairy Favour* at Covent Garden beginning 31 January 1767. For her work she received £2 2s.

Flint, Miss. *See* FLINT, SARAH.

Flint, Sarah [*fl. 1790–1802*], *booth operator, puppeteer.*

When the excellent marionette manipulator and showman John Flockton made his will on 5 April 1794, a week before his death, he gave "unto my ffriend Sarah Flint who has for several years travelled with and assisted me in my professional Employment all and every the Stock and Apparatus and Articles used and employed by me in my said Employment." The following August Mrs Flint (always "the Widow Flint" in the playbills) joined with Mr and Mrs (Daniel?) Gyngell "at Flockton's original Theatre up the Greyhound Yard, Smithfield." Gyngell was a prestidigitator, singer, and player on the musical glasses, his wife was a singer, and Sarah Flint exhibited fantoccini. Another and principal feature of the show was the "Grand Musical Clock" which motivated "upwards of Nine Hundred Figures, at Work in their respective Trades and Callings."

Though Sarah Flint had been left the theatrical properties and mechanical figures, Ann Flockton Sturmer, John Flockton's niece and principal heir, and her husband and two children were in 1794 acting in a competitive booth at a theatre in Swan Yard. Sybil Rosenfeld in *The Theatre of the London Fairs* cites a Flint listed among the comedians in the Pie Powder Court Book in 1796 and 1798. We believe that person to have been Sarah. "The Widow Flint" and Gyngell were still in partnership on 21 July 1800. A bill of their performance of that date at the George Inn, Chiswick, survives. In 1802 Sarah (apparently alone) was presenting her marionettes at Sadler's Wells.

Flintoft, Luke *d. 1727, singer.*

Luke Flintoft was born in Worcester and took his B.A. from Queen's College, Cambridge, in 1700. From 1704 to 1714 he was priest vicar of Lincoln Cathedral, and on 4 December 1715 he was sworn a Gentleman of the Chapel Royal in London, replacing the deceased Andrew Trebeck. On 9 July 1719 Rev Luke Flintoft replaced Dr Mangey as reader of the Chapel at Whitehall, and about the same time he became a minor canon of Westminster Abbey. He was a singer of some ability and is said to have invented the double chant form.

Flintoft was in prison for debt in the spring of 1725, though in January 1726 he was able to subscribe half a guinea to become a member of the Academy of Vocal Music. He died on 3 November 1727 and was buried in the South Cloister of Westminster Abbey on 6 November. One of his creditors was granted administration of his estate on 23 November.

Flockton, Ann. *See* STURMER, ANN.

Flockton, John *d. 1794, puppeteer.*

John Flockton's puppets, or more properly, as he insisted, fantoccini, were a familiar sight at London's fairs and probably all over southern England for at least 35 years. He first came to notice, according to George Speaight's account in *The History of the English Puppet Theatre*, when in 1762 he took his show to Hickford's Great Room in Panton Street. Hogan in *Shake-*

Harvard Theatre Collection

JOHN FLOCKTON, in street pantomime

artist unknown

speare in the Theatre cites a theatre in the upper storey of a house in Rupert Street, Haymarket, managed by one Flockton. From 1776 through 1793 John Flockton brought his booth to Bartholomew Fair. He performed from time to time during the eighties at the Lyceum in the Strand, in 1787 at Leytonstone and Peckham, and in 1788 at Edmonton and Stourbridge Fair. Morley in *Memoirs of Bartholomew Fair* gives a typical Flockton fair bill of 1789:

Mr. FLOCKTON'S Most Grand and Unparallelled Exhibition. Consisting first, in the display of the Original and Universally admired ITALIAN FANTOCCINI, exhibited in the same Skilful and Wonderful Manner, as well as Striking Imitations of Living Performers, as represented and exhibited before the Royal Family, and the most illustrious Characters in this Kingdom. Mr. FLOCKTON will display his inimitable DEXTERITY OF HAND, Different from all pretenders to the said Art. To which will be perform'd an ingenious and Spirited Opera called THE PADLOCK. . . .

As he often did, in that performance Flockton employed live vocal performers, Signor Giovanni Orsi and Signora Vidina. "The whole," was "to conclude with his grand and inimitable MUSICAL CLOCK, at first view, a curious organ, exhibited three times before their Majesties," all for 1*s.*, or 6*d.* in the gallery. In the clock, according to Flockton's advertisement, were 900 moving figures at work at a variety of trades.

Flockton's fantoccini performed light opera, like *The Padlock, The Sailor's Return*, which was perhaps a sentimental comedy, and historical melodrama, like the *Rival Queens, or the Death of Alexander the Great*. His Newfoundland dog was trained to fight a marionette devil and, having bested him, to run off with him. But Flockton also presented real-life actors in his fair booths, at least near the end of his career. Sybil Rosenfeld cites one such performance in *The Theatre of the London Fairs*, that of 4 September 1790 in the George Yard, when the farce *Miss in Her Teens* was performed by Hicken, Jones, Potter, Nevit, Scowton, and Mrs and Miss Flint. They were "followed by tumblers from the Royal Circus, a Prussian strong man and his children's ballet."

The *Gentleman's Magazine* reported the death at Camberwell of Flockton, "of facetious memory," on 12 April 1794. He died possessed of £5000. His will was proved the same day by Robert Young, his executor, of St Leonard, Shoreditch.

The will provided that he should be buried in a leaden coffin in the churchyard of Saint Luke, Old Street. To his niece Ann Flockton "otherwise Sturmer" was to go "all that my ffreehold House with the Appūrts situate on the South Side of Old Street aforesaid known by the Name of Beckford's Head in the Occupation of James King . . ." and the leasehold of a house on the north side of Old Street, then in the possession of the widow Shakeshaft, as well as £50 in cash. He left his housekeeper Elizabeth Thorp £100 and "three handsome gowns of my late Wife's." But his most generous and interesting bequests were to his little family of performers and bespeak the earnestness with which he desired to have his art survive him: To "my man Henry Potter my own wearing apparel of all sorts" and £10. To "Joseph Potter, commonly called Joseph Flockton Son of the aforesaid Henry Potter all that my ffreehold Estate . . . on the South Side of Old Street . . . and in the Occupation of Thomas Bowan and also all that my ffreehold Estate situate at Peckham," the whole to be applied to the education of Joseph. Finally: "I give unto my ffriend Sarah Flint who has for several years travelled with and assisted me in my Professional Employment all and every the Stock and Apparatus and Articles used and employed by me in my said employment. . . ." As Flockton had hoped, after his death Mrs Flint carried on the enterprise for a number of years with the conjuror Gyngell. His niece Mrs Ann Flockton

Sturmer, with her husband, evidently operated a competing show.

An anonymous engraving titled "The Noted Flockton" shows him standing in a street with a pantaloon, a lady, and "Mr Punch."

Floid or **Flood**. *See* FLOYD.

Floranze, Mme   [*fl.* 1785–1788], *singer*.

Madame Floranze was a vocalist at Bermondsey Spa Gardens from 1785 to 1788.

Florence. *See* DE FLORENCE.

Florentina. *See* FIORENTINA.

Florio, Charles Haiman   *d. 1819*, *flutist, singer, composer*.

Charles H. Florio, usually called Florio Junior by his contemporaries to distinguish him from his father, the flutist Pietro Grassi Florio (d. 1795), was listed by Dr Burney as one of the tenor singers in the Handel Memorial Concerts at Westminster Abbey and the Pantheon in May and June 1784. Little is known of young Florio's musical education and early career. Probably he was trained by his father. A duet composed by Charles was sung by Mrs Bland and Miss Hagley at the end of Act II of *Twelfth Night*, performed by the Drury Lane company at the King's Theatre on 31 May 1792.

In 1794 Florio, then living in Queen Ann Street, was listed in Doane's *Musical Directory* as a pianist and tenor singer and a member of the Academy of Ancient Music and Salomon's Concerts. (The musician's middle name was given by Doane as "Haimon.") For the oratorios at Covent Garden Theatre on 7 and 21 March 1794 he was advertised as one of the principal vocal performers. Also singing on the same programs was the controversial diva Gertrude Elizabeth Mara, who soon left her husband, the violinist Giovanni Battista

Mara, and ran off to Bath with young Florio in the summer of 1794. Presumably Mara's last lover, Florio lived for many years in her shadow and was no match professionally for her substantial and flamboyant talents. It was this liaison presumably which drove Charles's father to drink and the grave in 1795.

The remainder of Florio's career was inconsequential but somewhat colorful. He accompanied Madame Mara to Dublin in the summer of 1796, having put aside his flute, according to the *Monthly Mirror*, "to warble" as Artaxerxes. While she continued a great success, Florio, despite his overblown billing in Dublin as the first singer at the Hanover Square Concerts, was hissed every night he appeared, a reception which evidently encouraged him to retire from professional singing.

The couple returned to a house in Brompton, where they brazenly defied public disapproval of their habits by taking the air together daily. On 11 August 1798 they were brought before Sir Richard Ford, magistrate at Bow Street, on charges of a violent assault upon their cook, Jane Aft. When the cook had attempted to move out of her position, Florio had threatened her with a knife and locked her in the kitchen, from which she had escaped, only to be caught in the garden and beaten by Florio and Madame Mara. The defendants denied the charges, but they were ordered to post bail and answer the complaint at the Sessions. Eventually the matter was settled out of court.

In the fall of 1798 Florio wrote the overture and music for a two-act opera, with book by Andrew Franklin, called *The Outlaws*, which was first given at Drury Lane on 16 October and ran a total of six performances. It was rumored at the time that some of the music was really furnished by Madame Mara. The piece was never printed (Larpent MS 1224) but the book of the songs was sold at the theatre. The account books show that Florio was paid £20 by

Drury Lane for his work. On 11 March 1800, *The Egyptian Festival*, another piece by Franklin with music by Florio, was premiered at Drury Lane, with Madame Mara in the principal role of Zemira. The production, which survived ten nights, was lavishly mounted with scenes by Greenwood and machinery, dresses, and decorations by Johnston. According to the *Monthly Mirror* in March 1800, with the exception of *Pizarro*, this was one of the "most magnificent spectacles the stage has for some time produced." Although Madame Mara's singing was pronounced by Dutton in the *Dramatic Censor* as "indisputable," her acting was called "an absolute libel on the profession," and her appearance in the piece was accounted for only as an intended compliment to the composer. On 29 May 1800 a new song by Florio was sung by Sedgwick for his benefit in the role of Firelock in *The Strangers at Home* at Drury Lane. Florio also wrote music for an anonymous operatic farce, *Who's the Rogue?*, at Covent Garden in 1801.

Published songs by Florio include *Ah will no change of Clime* (1795?), sung by Mrs Billington; *The Maid of the Rock* and *The Poor Recruit* (1795?), sung by Charles Dignum; *All I Wish in her obtaining* (1795?), a duet sung by Madame Mara and Mr Incledon in *Love in a Village*; *The Slaves beneath a fervid sky* (1800), a duet sung by Madame Mara and Mrs Bland in *The Egyptian Festival*; and *Se mi credi amato bene* (1800), a duet sung by Madame Mara and Signor Viganoni.

In 1801 Florio left London with Madame Mara for an extended visit to the Continent which took them to Paris first, to Berlin in 1803, and to Russia in 1807. At Moscow in 1808 Florio was arrested and sent to St Petersburg as a prisoner, having been mistaken by the police for another person named Richard Florio who had written a letter in French filled with invective against the government. When the error of identity was discovered, the musician was released and given a handsome present of money from Czar Alexander for his troubles and expenses.

Evidently an inveterate speculator, Florio made several trips back to London, once for an unsuccessful attempt to obtain a patent and another time to invest (with disastrous financial results) in pianofortes. His domestic affairs in Moscow became complicated when he impregnated one of Madame Mara's pretty servants. Although the servant and her infant were packed off to England by Madame Mara, the girl contrived to return to Moscow and take up residence in a suburb, where her affair with Florio resumed.

Florio died at Moscow early in 1819; toward the end of his days he had become mad and violent, refusing all food for three weeks because he was convinced that Madame Mara was giving him poison.

Florio, Pietro Grassi *d. 1795, flutist, composer.*

Leaving his position as a member of the Dresden band about 1756, the flutist Pietro Grassi Florio went to Paris and, early in the 1760s, found his way to London. Perhaps his earliest professional appearance in the English capital was at Drury Lane Theatre on 26 February 1762, when he played a concerto on the German flute in a program of musical pieces under the direction of Dr Arne. For a concert at the Haymarket Theatre on 16 March 1762 he again played a concerto. At Drury Lane again on 31 March he played after a performance of the *Messiah*. His other performances that season included concertos at the Haymarket on 22 April and 20 May.

Although he remained in London for more than 30 years, the record of Florio's musical activity is scant and sporadic. On very infrequent occasions he gave solo performances on the flute at the Haymarket Theatre, the dates for which included 11 March 1765, 4 March 1768, 15 February 1769, and 17 March 1773. In the latter half of the season 1766–67, he was engaged to play in *Cymon*, a romantic musical extravaganza concocted by Garrick and Michael Arne which was first performed at Drury Lane on 2 January 1767. On 2 February Florio was paid £21 for playing 20 nights in the piece, and on 22 May he received £7 7s. for another seven nights. He played in the oratorios at Covent Garden Theatre in February 1771, February and March 1776, and March 1778, and also at the King's Theatre on 15 February 1776 and 4 and 9 April 1778. Dr Burney listed Florio as one of the instrumental performers in the Handel Memorial Concerts given at Westminster Abbey and the Pantheon in May and June 1784.

By 1783 Florio was engaged as a flutist in the opera band at the King's Theatre, a position he seems to have retained on a regular basis through the 1790–91 season. He also appeared several times as a soloist in concerts at the Oxford Music Room in 1793. In 1794 (by which year he had retired) his address was listed in Doane's *Musical Directory* as No 9, Portland Street, St James's.

According to his brief obituary notice in the *Gentleman's Magazine* for July 1795, Florio had died in the previous month, indigent and broken-hearted, brought to his grave by his "propensity to drinking," which was said to have been increased by the scandalous escapades of his son Charles H. Florio with the singer Gertrude Elizabeth Mara. The elder Florio was given a decent burial by the members of the opera band, who had also made liberal subscriptions for his support during his last years.

About 1775 Florio published *New Instructions for the German Flute, including a description of a new-invented German-flute . . . play'd on by . . . Florio and Tacet*. Various sonatas, duets, trios, and quartets for German flutes and violins were also published by Florio.

Flower, Edmund [fl. 1666–1710], instrumentalist, singer?

Edmund Flower became a court musician at least as early as 24 November 1666, according to warrants in the Lord Chamberlain's accounts. Since he was apparently proficient on a variety of instruments, the accounts contain frequent references to him. On 30 June 1670 Flower was admitted to the King's private music as a musician in ordinary for the lute and theorbo, but without fee; not until Ambrose Beeland resigned his position on 19 March 1672 was Flower granted a salary—1s. daily plus £16 2s. 6d. annual livery, retroactive to 19 January. The following 3 April he was paid £12 for a tenor violin (i.e., viola), and a year later he was granted £15 for a theorbo. Oddly, the 1673 accounts show him waiting for the next vacant place in either the private or the wind music.

On 3 May 1676 Flower was appointed to replace William Howes in the wind instruments; on 5 March 1678 he received £15 for a double "sagbutt"; on 8 June he was admitted to the private music without fee; and on 27 September he was granted a place therein which had been vacated by John Lilly, then deceased (but Flower had to share his fee with Isaac Staggins). On 22 November 1679 he was given £14 for a lute; on 31 August 1685 he joined the private music of James II as a countertenor (though that assignment may have been for administrative purposes; there is no other indication that Flower was a singer); and he was appointed to the private music of William III on 20 July 1689.

The accounts also tell us of the ups and downs of Flower's financial life. By 13 December 1679 his salary had risen to £46 10s. 10d. His livery fee remained the same over the years, but he rarely received it on schedule during the reign of Charles II. On 21 September 1686 King James tried to pay off some of the royal debts, one of them being £112 17s. 6d. in livery fees owed to Flower. But on 2 April 1687 Flower and Henry Brockwell had to petition the Lord Chamberlain for £111 6s. 8d. due them from the King. By 25 March 1689 Flower's salary was down to £30 annually, but by 1697 it had been raised to £40.

Other entries in the accounts tell us of Flower's duties in the King's Musick. In many years between 1674 and 1691 he attended the royal family on trips out of London; on 15 February 1675 he was one of the regular band of 24 violins who supported the singers in the court masque *Calisto*; on 8 May 1677 he and other court musicians petitioned against Charles Killigrew, Master of the Revels, for dismissing their attendance at the playhouse—presumably Drury Lane, though possibly the court theatre; and on 26 January 1685 Flower was ordered to practise for a ball that was to be held at the court theatre.

Of Flower's personal life we get only glimpses. On 15 February 1684 the Lord Chamberlain received a petition from Rebecca Flower against Edmund Flower "upon promise of marriage"—but the accounts contain no further clarifying information. On 6 October 1691 Flower made William Brown, servant of the King's musicians, his lawful attorney; a similar power of attorney to Brown was made on 4 June 1698, when Flower was described as of Corsham, Wiltshire.

The accounts indicate that Edmund Flower continued in the royal musical service until at least as late as 1710. The occasional references to an "Edward" Flower in the accounts would seem to be errors for Edmund.

Floyd, Mr (*fl. 1660–c. 1673*), *actor.*
Mr Floyd was one of the minor actors in the troupe of John Rhodes at the Cockpit in Drury Lane; he usually acted "the Part of a Bawd and Whore," according to the prompter John Downes. Floyd joined Sir William Davenant's company at Lincoln's Inn Fields, but the only role there that is known for him was Monsieur Colemore in Boyle's *Henry V* on 13 August 1664 and subsequent dates. Downes listed Floyd as one of the players who died before the 1673–74 season. Printed plays of later dates sometimes listed players who were no longer active; for example, Floyd in 1676 was listed as playing Francisco in *Hamlet*—but when and where he acted the part is unclear. A Thomas Floyd married Jane Larke at St Paul, Covent Garden, on 14 June 1663, but there is no way of knowing whether or not Thomas was the actor.

Floyd, Mr (*fl. 1734*), *actor.*
At York Buildings on 8 July 1734 a Mr Floyd acted Stratocles in *Tamerlane.*

Floyd, Miss (*fl. 1787*), *actress.*
Miss Floyd, advertised as making her first appearance on that stage, acted at the Haymarket Theatre on 8 January 1787 as Rosetta in *Love in a Village*. Since she was not mentioned in any other London records, perhaps her previous experience was in the provinces.

Fly, Henry (*fl. 1784–1794*), *violist, bass player.*
The Reverend Henry Fly played tenor viol in the Handel Memorial Concerts at Westminster Abbey and the Pantheon in May and June 1784. Doane's *Musical Directory* of 1794 cited Fly as a violist and bass player living in Bread Street Hill. He was a member of the Chapel Royal choir and played also at St Paul's.

"Flying Boy, The" (*fl. 1732*), *aerialist.*
At the Haymarket Theatre on 8 May 1732, a little boy of 11 was to fly from the footman's gallery to the farthest part of the stage, "first with two Pistols, one in each Hand; a second Time with two Flags, and to make a small Stop in the Middle, and flourish them over his Head."

"Flying Mercury, The." *See* "LITTLE FLYING MERCURY, THE."

"Flying Phenomenon, The." *See* IRELAND, MR (*fl. 1799–1805*).

Fochetti, Vincenzo [1773–1783], *singer.*

On 23 October 1773 the managers of the King's Theatre announced that the bass singer Vincenzo Fochetti had been engaged for the comic operas that season. He made his debut on 7 December 1773 as a principal singer in *Il puntiglio amoroso.* His other performances at the King's that season included a role in *La contessina* on 11 January 1774 and Tagliaferro in *La buona figliuola* on 17 March; and he sang in a concert on 10 February. Fochetti also sang in *Il trionfo della costanza* at Hickford's Room on 9 May 1774.

Fochetti remained at the King's for another three seasons, singing Pilpatae in *Motezuma,* parts in *La marchesa giardiniera, I viaggiatori ridicoli,* and *La donna di spirito,* and Pasqualino in *La sposa fedele* in 1775; parts in *Il bacio* and *L'isola d'amore* and Don Fabrizio in *La Frascatana* in 1776; and parts in *Il geloso in Cimento, La schiava,* and *Alcina* in 1777. His last performance in London was as Don Fabrizio on 17 June 1777.

Fochetti also performed in operas at Dublin in 1776 and 1777, during which time he was "a constant and welcome guest" at the home of the young Michael Kelly's father. In his *Reminiscences* Kelly described him as "a powerful primo buffo, with a fine bass voice." He related meeting Fochetti subsequently in 1783 at Modena, his native city, where the singer had retired with a comfortable fortune and held a post in the Chapel Royal.

Foley, Mr [fl. 1744], *violinist.*

Mr Foley played a violin solo at the James Street Theatre on 10 December 1744.

Foley, Mr [fl. 1748–1770], *house servant.*

Mr Foley served at Drury Lane in several house capacities from 1748 through 1770, receiving yearly shared benefits. Usually the bills did not mention his duties, but in 1748 he was cited as a box lobby keeper, in 1749 a lobby doorkeeper, in 1750 a boxkeeper, in 1756 and 1760 a box lobby doorkeeper, in 1763 a doorkeeper, and in 1767 a lobby doorkeeper. A salary schedule dated 9 February 1765 listed him as a doorkeeper earning a salary of 1s. 6d. daily or 9s. weekly. His first notice was on 16 May 1748 and his last on 1 June 1770.

Foljambe, Godfrey [fl. 1671], *scenekeeper.*

A Lord Chamberlain's warrant dated 15 November 1671 named Godfrey Foljambe as one of the scenekeepers at the King's Company playhouse in Bridges Street.

Folkes, Mrs Martin. *See* BRADSHAW, LUCRETIA.

Follett, John d. 1790, *actor, singer, dancer.*

The elder John Follett was first named in London bills at Drury Lane on 4 December 1771 as a Messenger in *Timon of Athens,* a humble duty he repeated many nights throughout the season. But he had perhaps performed at the theatre obscurely before 4 December, for he repaid to the treasury a loan of £10 8s. 6d. on 10 December. He was one of the Officers in *Twelfth Night* on 10 December, and he walked in those two parts until 28 March 1772, when he was allowed to vary his repertoire with a mute Senator in *Timoleon.* His last part in his first season with Drury Lane was an anonymous Gentleman to the Duke in *The Chances.*

Follett must, then, have been ecstatic to find, when he joined the theatre in the Haymarket that summer, that he would be allowed to play parts which actually had names. They were few and small—Martin in the afterpiece *The Cooper* and Corydon in *Damon and Phillida* and (on the last night of the season) Jasper in *The Mock Doctor.*

Follett did not return to Drury Lane in the 1772–73 season (and may have been acting in a country company), but they remembered him at the Haymarket, and there in the summer of 1773 from 2 July until 20 September he was almost continuously employed, though adding to his slender repertoire only Argus in *The Contrivances*, Transfer in *The Minor*, a Sailor in *The Trip to Portsmouth*, Sir William in *Love in a Village*, and Old Whittle in *The Irish Widow*.

Returning to the Haymarket in April 1774, he played several of his old roles during the following summer and added Grumio and Biondello in *Catherine and Petruchio*, the Coachman in *The Devil to Pay*, Dr Catgut in *The Commissary*, Gibbet in *The Beaux' Stratagem*, Wingate in *The Apprentice* and unspecified parts in *The Duellist* and *The Nabob*. He played three nights of special actors' benefits in the rented Haymarket late in September 1774 and then again disappeared from the London bills.

In 1775 he was seen in London only twice, both times in special performances at the Haymarket, 21 September and 30 October. He was a part of the Richmond company in the summer of 1776.

The new management at Drury Lane signed Follett for the 1776–77 season. There in October he began his career as a pantomime performer with Scaramouch in *The Elopement* and one of the Justices in *Harlequin's Invasion*, both repeated several nights that season. He was also employed as a tenor voice in the chorus and a minor actor in farce. His salary for those efforts was £1 per week, and he was allowed to distribute benefit tickets for 15 May. That year he subscribed 10s. 6d. to the Drury Lane retirement fund. He assisted again at Richmond in the summer of 1777 but was otherwise unknown to the London area until 31 March 1778, when at the Haymarket there was a "Benefit for Follet, Smith & T. Smith, late of the Bear

Westminster-bridge. Tickets to be had of Follet, No 20, Little Wild-street, Lincoln's-inn-fields. . . ." In the performance of *A Bold Stroke for a Wife* Follett figured as Obadiah Prim, and Master Follett—John the younger—came on for the first time, playing the Quaker's Boy.

Follett was at Manchester in 1778, at Brighton in the summer of 1779, and with the Norwich company at Colchester on 12 August 1782 (acting in a production called *The Miniature Picture*). The Norwich Committee Books bear the entry on 13 September 1782: "Ordered That the Manager discharge Mr Follet and Son, and engage another Performer in Mr Follet's stead." On 3 October both the Folletts were playing at "Stirbich" Fair, near Cambridge.

After undiscoverable provincial journeys John Follett the elder turned up once again at the Haymarket, playing James in *The Miser* on 12 February 1785 (for the benefit of the comedian Richard Wilson, according to Decastro's *Memoirs*, though the bill did not show that). On 26 April following, for the benefit of Mrs Greville, he played Tester in *The Suspicious Husband*. On 8 January he played both Justice Woodcock in *Love in a Village* and Dr Julep in *The Devil Upon Two Sticks*, again at the Haymarket. He was by that time also playing in harlequinades at the Royal Circus. At the opening of the ill-starred (because illegal) Royalty Theatre on 20 June 1787 John Follett played Puff in the afterpiece *Miss in Her Teens*; on 3 July he was the Farmer in *Hobson's Choice*. On 1 January 1788 he played a part in *Thomas and Susan* and was also Pantaloon in *Harlequin Mungo*. On 29 April 1788 at the Haymarket he played Major Oakly in *The Jealous Wife* and on 30 September following at the same theatre essayed Puff, as well as Old Philpot in *The Citizen* and the Clown in *A Pantomimical Interlude*.

There followed a few more performances at the Royal Circus, in pantomime. But on 30 December 1789 the younger John Follett published a bill soliciting full support for his performance at the Lyceum, his father "having by an accident broke his Leg, which, after a long and painful illness, he has been obliged to have amputated; a circumstance that for ever deprives him of the support he could otherwise have professionally obtained." The *Authentic Memoirs of the Green Room* (1806) added the detail that Follett had broken his leg "going home at night to his lodgings in Rosemary-lane." He died on 15 January 1790.

Follett, John 1765–1799, *actor, singer, dancer.*

John Follett the younger was born in 1765. He was the son of the John Follett who in the 1770s and 1780s played small comic parts, sang in choruses, and danced in pantomimes in several London and provincial theatres.

The boy (whose mother was never mentioned in bills and accounts and may have died when he was a child) accompanied his father on his itinerant rounds. Jack, as he was invariably called, seems to have appeared for the first time in the part of the Quaker's Boy in *A Bold Stroke for a Wife* in a specially licensed benefit for his father and two friends at the Haymarket on 31 March 1778. He then accompanied his father on some provincial wanderings and may have played—as the senior Follett certainly did—at Manchester in 1778, Brighton in 1779, and with the Norwich company thereafter. The Committee Books of the Norwich Theatre bear a notice of 13 September 1782 ordering "That the Manager discharge Mr Follet and Son. . . ." A surviving bill of 30 July for the theatre at Richmond, Surrey, lists a "Follet, Jun," but no part is given. On 3 October both father and son were at "Stirbich" Fair near Cambridge. Young Jack was a Witch in *Harlequin Triumphant*. In the summer of 1785 he danced at Richmond.

Jack was a Printer's Devil in *The Devil Upon Two Sticks* in a benefit performance

Harvard Theatre Collection

JOHN FOLLETT, as Hercules

by G. Shepheard

for the Drury Lane prompter Harwood at the Haymarket on 8 January 1787, a night on which his father also performed, both in the mainpiece and the afterpiece. But if that activity was intended to curry favor with the Drury Lane management it evidently failed, for neither of the Folletts appeared there. Both played a few nights for John Palmer at the Royalty in 1787. They were second-line performers in pantomime at the Royal Circus (often called "Folliot"). Jack was seen in London patent theatres only on scattered occasions during the following two years: at the Royalty Theatre on 1 January 1788 as the Clown in *Harlequin Mungo*, on 9 April 1788 at the Haymarket as Sir Harry Beagle in *The Jealous Wife*, at the same theatre on 30 September as Harlequin in *A Pantomimical Interlude* and as Jeremy in *Barnaby Brittle*, and on 22 December as Mirvan in *Tamer-*

lane the Great. He had a single appearance, on 22 May 1789, at Drury Lane as Scaramouch in *Don Juan* for Robert Palmer's benefit.

Jack Follett's father died in January, 1790. The following fall, when Delpini left Covent Garden to assist Lord Barrymore at the Wargrave Theatricals, Follett was offered the place, signed articles, and entered upon a full season of singing and dancing. He essayed a "Principal" (but unspecified) character in *The Provocation* on 4 October and a dozen nights following, was the Clown in *Harlequin's Chaplet* on 15 November and following, and during the rest of the season added Grotesque in *A Picture of Paris*, Second to Lysimachus in *Alexander the Little*, an Indian Chief in *The Soldier's Festival*, and the title role in *Tippo Saib*.

Follett was now firmly established in the line he was to follow until his death — the utility harlequin, pierrot, clown, and scaramouch, singing, dancing, miming, and mastering the newest "tricks" furnished by the devisers of pantomime. His named roles after 1791 included Carrol in *Oscar and Malvina*, Clodpole in *Harlequin's Museum*, Clodpole in *Mother Shipton Triumphant*, Pierrot in *Harlequin and Faustus*, a Tradesmen in *Life's Vagrants*, the Squire in *The Tythe Pig*, Whalebone in *Lord Mayor's Day*, Don Quixotte in *Barataria*, Carter in *Love in a Village*, Isaac in *False Impressions*, Maon in *The Round Tower*, Scaramouchillo in *Harlequin and Quixotte*, and Lucifer in *Joan of Arc*.

In 1796 Follett took over the direction, with J. C. Cross, Thomas Haymes, and Thomas Rees, of the Richmond Theatre. When Follett and his wife were given a benefit at Covent Garden Theatre on 5 June 1797 they were living at No 46, Drury Lane. In the summer season of 1798 they were performing at the Birmingham Theatre.

Follett's powerful, muscular frame allowed him to perform astonishing feats of acrobatics. *The Thespian Dictionary* (1805) remembered that "He had a particular method of walking in a position in which his knees were so inverted as nearly to touch the stage, a striking proof of the strength of his muscles." He was a particular favorite of the royal family, and, according to the *Authentic Memoirs*, "From his open disposition and honest bluntness, he conciliated the good opinion of all his brother performers." He died on 12 January 1799 at 33 years of age and was buried at St Paul, Covent Garden, as "From St Martins," on 20 January. He had married the performer Mary Francis, daughter of Bodley William Francis and his wife Anne, on 23 June 1793. By her he had had at least four children.

There is an engraving of John Follett the younger as Hercules, by G. Shepheard, published by G. Rowe, 1794, and another, in the role of Maon in *The Round Tower*,

Harvard Theatre Collection

MR SIMPSON as Kildare and JOHN FOLLETT as Maon in *The Round Tower*

by Alvey

with Simpson as Kildare, engraved by W. C. Alvey and published by the engraver in 1797. A British Museum manuscript mentions a "Portrait swallowing a carrot before Geo 3rd," which we have not located; it pictures Follett as Phantom in *Fontainville Forest*.

Follett, Mrs John, Mary, née Francis

b. 1770, actress, dancer, singer.

Mary Francis, daughter of the performer and theatrical house servant Bodley William Francis and his wife Anne, was christened at St Paul, Covent Garden, on 2 December 1770. She grew up in a theatrical household, her older siblings, Sarah Thomas Bodley and William Bodley Francis, being well-known performers.

Mary's father somewhat wistfully pursued an acting career in summers at the Haymarket (but gave it up after a few years) and a parallel career, first as a dresser and then as a sub-prompter, at Covent Garden in the winters. Mary was probably in the theatre earlier than is shown by any London notice, but the first incontestable evidence of her performance was in the Covent Garden bill of 14 October 1782, when she played young Prince Edward in *Richard III*, repeated on 16 December. The next evidence came nearly a year later, on 13 October 1783, when she repeated the part, as she did again on 29 December following.

There are likewise some difficulties in separating the roles of the sisters Sarah and Mary in their late teens. However, we question the identification by *The London Stage* of Mary as the Miss Francis who played Fanny in *The Clandestine Marriage* at Hammersmith on 8 July 1785 (when she would have been not quite 15). That player was, more likely, Sarah, then 20. At any rate, appearances in the bills of the names of either sister were rare. Until the years of her early maturity Mary was usually to be found dancing or singing in chorus with others, or playing small comic

parts at the Haymarket or Covent Garden. One Miss Francis acted in York in 1785.

On 23 June 1793 Mary Francis ("of T. R. C. G. & Richmond," according to James Winston's jottings in the Folger Library) was married at St-Martin-in-the-Fields to the younger John Follett, clown and singer of Covent Garden and the Royal Circus. She played under her new name at Richmond, Surrey, in the summer of 1793, said Winston. On 8 September 1795 she took a benefit at Brighton. She was on the Richmond bills again in 1796, when her husband had a share in the management, and in the summers of 1797 and 1798 she was with him in the Birmingham Theatre, where she appeared alone in 1799, Jack Follett having died in January. She was on at Covent Garden in the winters through at least 1806–7.

She was often called "Folliot" (as was her husband) in the Covent Garden accounts during the season of 1793–94 and subsequently. Her salary that season and in 1794–95 and 1795–96, was £2 per six-day week. In 1796–97 it dropped to £1 10s. A Covent Garden pay list of 1798–99 at Harvard gives her £47 15s. for 191 nights and is endorsed "settled Mary Follett." The *Monthly Mirror* of June 1799 reported that her benefit for the year brought her £460, the large sum doubtless reflecting the audience's compassion for her widowhood. Another Harvard pay list, of 1806–7 gives her £57 10s. for the season and is endorsed by her.

In the early years of her marriage Mrs Follett had continued to figure frequently in pantomimes in bridesmaids, aerial spirits, shepherdesses, country girls and Irish peasants, priestesses, goddesses, and the like. But she also added some named parts in farce and comic opera: Nora in *Love in a Camp*, the title part in *Nina*, Malvina in *Oscar and Malvina*, the Duchess of Tuscany in *A Duke and No Duke*, Lucy Oakland in *Netley Abbey*, Belinda in *Modern Antiques*, Theodosia in *The Maid of the Mill*, Leonora in *Two Strings to Your Bow*, Corinna in *The Citizen*, Belinda in *The Ghost*, the Countess of Lindenberg in *Raymond and Agnes*, and Miss Clare in *Life's Vagaries*.

Mary and John Follett had at least four children. One, John, was born on 29 November 1797 and was christened at St Paul, Covent Garden, on 24 October 1804.

The death date of Mary Francis Follett is not known, but she may have been alive in 1819, for at the annual meeting of the Covent Garden Fund that year Fawcett, the treasurer, remarked that "the lovers of pantomime will not forget poor Follet; his children have been reared, and his widow provided with an annuity" by the Fund. A male Follett was on the house list at Drury Lane in 1811–12. There in 1812–13 he was named as a doorkeeper at 18*s*. per week and also as a "private boxkeeper," no salary specified.

Folliot. *See* **FOLLETT.**

Folteral. *See* **FOTTERAL.**

Fompré. *See* **DE FOMPRÉ.**

Fond. *See* **LA FOND.**

Fonesca, Emmanuel ₁*fl. 1664–1670*₁, *scenekeeper.*

The Lord Chamberlain's accounts contain a warrant dated 25 May 1665 describing Emmanuel Fonesca as a scenekeeper in the King's Company at the Bridges Street Theatre. *The London Stage* places Fonesca in the troupe in 1664–65, 1666–67, and 1669–70.

Fontain, John ₁*fl. 1794*₁, *musician.*

John Fontain was one of the subscribers to the New Musical Fund in 1794 and probably performed for that society.

Fontaine, Mons ₁*fl. 1775–1800?*₁, *dancer.*

Monsieur Fontaine, advertised as from

the opera at Paris, danced in *The Merry Peasants* at Drury Lane on 18 October 1775. The following 28 November he was in *The Maid of the Oaks*; on 12 December he danced in *The Sultan*; and on 19 December he participated in a comic dance between the acts. Perhaps the Fontaine who danced at the Crow Street Theatre in Dublin in 1790–91 and 1799–1800 was the same performer.

Fontenelle, Signor ₁*fl. 1773–1777*₁, *rope dancer.*

Signor Fontenelle performed as a rope dancer at Sadler's Wells in 1773. No doubt this person was the member of Signor Ferzi's company who performed at Birmingham in December 1776 as Signor Fontanella and at York as Fontanelli in March 1777. Advertised as from the Riding School at Westminster Bridge and also from Sadler's Wells, Fontenelle performed at Derby between 3 and 7 February 1777; one of his feats was a "Grand Italian Dance with Twelve Eggs." A Miss Fontanelli also did rope dancing at York in 1777.

Fontenelle, Louisa, later Mrs James Brown Williamson the second *1773?–1799, actress, singer.*

Announced as "A Young Lady" making her first appearance on any stage, Louise Fontenelle performed the role of Moggy in the premiere of O'Keeffe's comic opera *The Highland Reel* at Covent Garden Theatre on 6 November 1788. According to the *Thespian Dictionary* (1805) she had been introduced by William Woodfall the publisher to Harris the manager, who offered her an engagement for three years on the condition that either party could dissolve the agreement at the end of the first year. Her initial salary was £2 per week. Louisa's debut was, by most reports, an extraordinary success and for the seventh performance of the piece her name was given in the bills. The *European Magazine* in November 1788 reported her to be under 19 years of age (she was actually 15 if we credit the report that she was 26 at the time of her death in 1799), of middle stature and size, with a symmetrical face and expressive eyes. Her voice was good and she had performed with vivacity, comic effect, and perhaps too much spirit.

On the morning after her debut one newspaper predicted that "Miss Fontenelle, as a breeches figure, will rank with Jordan and Mrs Goodall," and after her second performance, on 10 November, another reviewer praised her as "one of the purest children of nature that ever trod the boards of a theatre." On 17 November 1788 the *Morning Chronicle* reported that *The Highland Reel* had brought greater houses to Covent Garden than any production since Mrs Inchbald's *Such Things Are* on 10 February 1787 and that Miss Fontenelle and Miss Reynolds (as Jenny) were receiving great applause. Effusive verses comparing Miss Fontenelle to Ann Catley were published on 21 November:

Harvard Theatre Collection

LOUISA FONTENELLE, as Moggy

engraving by Barlow

When Catley—Nature's darling child!
Quitted the stage belov'd—admired,
Euphrosyne no longer smil'd
And Juno's mirth at once expir'd.
The "Wanton God" had power no more;
The Jorum of its charms bereft;
Even Lucy did her loss deplore,
For ah! her equal was not left.
But Fontenelle wipes forth our tears,
Like Catley, full of whim and spirit,
The Heart revives when she appears
And owns how great her infant merit.
With sprightly air and mirthful glee
Blythe Moggy trips it o'er the stage,
Nature in Fontenelle shall see
The second Catley of the age.

Louisa's next role was as Sophia in the initial performance of another comedy by O'Keeffe, *The Toy*, on 3 February 1789. When she played Captain Macheath in *The Beggar's Opera* on 3 March, the *European Magazine* thought that the representation of a female Macheath was "disgusting" and

urged that her talents might be "more properly" employed. On 31 March she played an unspecified character in *Such Things Have Been* and on 30 April Mlle D'Epingle in *The Funeral*. For her benefit on 2 May 1789, at which she took receipts of £219 19s. (less house charges of £10,), she acted Roxalana (for that night only) in *The Sultan*, Moggy in *The Highland Reel*, and Priscilla Tomboy in *The Romp*. Benefit tickets were available from Louisa's mother at her house, No 271, Holborn. In his *Diary*, William Windham wrote that "Miss Fontenelle . . . is the best Romp we ever saw, Mrs Jordan alone excepted. . . . We are sorry to see her fall over the groove of the scene; but as practice is more forcible than precept, we hope it will teach her the truth of Friar Laurence's caution, 'they stumble who run fast.'"

Despite her excellent notices in that first season in London, Miss Fontenelle demonstrated a liveliness and forwardness on the stage so extravagant as to be damaging. "There perhaps never was a young Lady who came before the Public with more confidence," reported *The Secret History of the Green Room* (1792). But she was guilty of "Too much liveliness, and too many gestures, which were not always properly adapted," and she "jumped about the Stage, clapped her hands, shook her head, squalled, and stared, without the least regard to character or situation." Though she was prudent in private character, on stage the audience finally set her down "as the most impudent, nay, even indecent girl, that had ever been seen on the boards." Consequently the managers did not renew their option, and Miss Fontenelle went off in the summer of 1789 to act at Brighton and then joined the Edinburgh company in October 1789, where she remained for the winter season, playing such roles as Moggy in *The Highland Reel*, Phoebe in *Rosina*, Corinna in *The Confederacy*, Aura in *The Country Lasses*, Cherry in *The Beaux' Stratagem*, Hippolito in *The Tempest*, Lucy in *The Beggar's Opera*, and Miss Jenny in *The Provok'd Husband*, among others.

In the summer of 1790 she was engaged by Colman to replace Miss George at the Haymarket Theatre. After her first appearance, on 17 June 1790 as the Page in *The Follies of the Day*, she performed Nerissa in *The Merchant of Venice*, Wowski in *Inkle and Yarico*, Flora in *New Spain*, Aura in *The Farm House*, Nancy Lovell in *The Suicide*, Charlotte in *Who's the Dupe?*, Bloom in *The Basket Maker*, and Adeline in *The Battle of Hexham* — a variety of tomboy, ingenue, and breeches roles. She was reengaged at the Haymarket for three more summers, through 1793 (her salary the latter year was £8 per week), in a similar line of roles, such as Araminta in *The Young Quaker*, Madelon in *The Surrender of Calais*, Fringe in *The Agreeable Surprise*, Kate in *The Village Lawyer*, Miss Plumb in *Gretna Green*, and Dorothy in *All in Good Humour*. In comparing her perform-ances at the Haymarket to those of Miss George, *The Secret History of the Green Room* lamented a "falling off. — Miss Fontenelle is scarcely noticed; and the other was an uncommon favourite."

In January 1793 she returned to Edinburgh, where she remained until May of that year acting Adela in *The Haunted Tower*, Little Pickle in *The Spoiled Child*, Cowslip in *The Agreeable Surprise*, Jane in *Wild Oats*, Miss Leeson in *The School for Wives*, and others of a similar line. She also played some male roles, including Edward in *Every One Has His Fault*, Jack Bowline in *The Reprisal*, and Patrick in *The Poor Soldier*.

Louisa sang at Handy's Circus in Manchester in 1793. A Miss Fontenelle or Fontanelle acted at Brighton in July of 1789, 1790, and 1791, but she evidently was Ann Fontanelle, perhaps Louisa's sister. The Boston Public Library holds the manuscript of a prologue called "The Rights of Woman," spoken by Louisa at the Dumfries Theatre on 26 November 1792; it was written especially for her by the poet Robert Burns and is published in J. L. Robertson's edition of his works.

By September of 1795 she joined an English company in Hamburg, Germany, under the direction of James Brown Williamson (d. 1802), with whom she had acted at Edinburgh prompting Bellamy to versify in *The London Theatres* (1795):

> The sprightly FONTENELLE just
>   seen and gone,
> Now roams an alien to her native land,
> To gain in other realms the meed of
>   praise;
> Nor shall it be denied — Her private
>   worth,
> Her merit in a walk beyond her years,
> Her filial duty, and her guileless heart,
> Shall gain a just renown — denied her
>   here.

Bellamy's allusion to "filial duty" presumably implies that at least one of her parents was alive at that time.

Filial duty notwithstanding, Louisa was

soon after found in America with Williamson, now as his second wife. She made her first appearance on the American stage as Desdemona (to her husband's Othello) and Little Pickle in *The Spoiled Child* on 25 January 1796 in Boston. Manuscript letters (now in the Boston Public Library) from Williamson to the Trustees of the Federal Street Theatre indicate that while they arrived in Boston about the end of December 1795, probably directly from Hamburg, they could not have made their debuts at the Haymarket Theatre in January 1796, as both Clapp and Brown assert, since that theatre did not open until September of that year. Their debuts actually occurred at the Federal Street Theatre, which Williamson was to manage in the following season. Writing in the *Federal Orrery*, Robert Treat Paine, Jr, praised Louisa's performances as the finest and most brilliant yet seen in America. In his *Retrospections of America* John Bernard called her "A girl whose animal spirit" had led the actor Robert Merry to compare her "to brandy above proof!"

Now playing as Mrs Williamson she became a great favorite in Boston under her husband's management in 1796–97. The Williamsons played at Hartford in August and then joined John Joseph Leger Sollee's company at Charleston. They were back at the Federal Street Theatre in the fall of 1798, at a combined salary of $18.66 per week, but left in midseason after Williamson took $450 at his benefit on 26 December 1798 and headed for Charleston again. There she acted, among other roles, Sally in *Secrets Worth Knowing* on 23 January 1799, Portia in *The Merchant of Venice* on 4 February, Malvina in *Oscar and Malvina* on 1 March, and the breeches role of Sir Harry Wildair in *The Constant Couple* on 30 April. For her benefit on 13 March 1799 she offered the Charleston audience several favorite Scots songs.

After an illness of three days, she died unexpectedly at Charleston on 29 or 31 October 1799, at the age of 26. Out of respect, the theatre there was closed for a week. Her husband, who soon married the widow of Jones, a Charleston actor, died there on 26 March 1802. Williamson's third wife survived him only until November of that year.

A colored drawing by an unknown artist of Louisa Fontenelle as Moggy in *The Highland Reel* is in the British Museum. Another watercolor of her in the same role, done by A. Toedteberg in the nineteenth century, is in the Harvard Theatre Collection. The latter drawing is based on an engraving by Barlow and served also as the original for the engraving published by Toedteberg in his *Portraits of Actors*, 1893.

Fonthornoycts, Henricus [*fl.* 1711], *lutenist.*

On 20 December 1711, at Coachmakers' Hall, Henricus Fonthornoycts played on the French and arch lutes at a benefit concert for John and Thomas Baston.

Foote, Mr [*fl.* 1748], *exhibitor.*

In the *Daily Advertiser* on 20 October 1748, a person who styled himself as "Mr Foote the second, late arrived from Copenhagen," announced that he would exhibit his "Collection of Pictures" in Marshalsea Prison, Southwark, on every Thursday evening during the winter season. Some of the pictures were lately brought from New Zealand, others were done by the "present famous Mynheer Vandergoot," and one was an original of Monsieur Pantin from Paris. To be exhibited gratis was *The Murder of the Dragon of Wantley* and a "Sleepy Dance" by Count Tincture Laudanum from Goar. The advertisement was repeated on 27 October.

The notice obviously is suspect, perhaps part hoax, part truth. It capitalizes, in any event, on the *Auction of Pictures*, an entertainment brought on by Samuel Foote at the Haymarket Theatre in April 1748.

Foote, Mr [*fl.* 1786]. *See* FAWCETT, JOHN *1768–1837*.

Foote, Samuel *1721–1777, manager, playwright, actor.*

Samuel Foote, one of the most colorful, controversial, and consequential figures of the eighteenth-century English theatre, was baptized at St Mary, Truro, on 27 January 1721 (and not in 1720, the year usually given because of failure to transpose old style dating between 1 January and 24 March to the year ahead). He was the third surviving son and the last child of Samuel and Eleanor Foote of that city. His father was a lawyer and magistrate, who was a sometime mayor of Truro, an M.P. for Tiverton, a commissioner of the Prize Office, and a collector of fines. His mother, born Eleanor Dinely Goodere, was the daughter of the baronet Sir Edward Goodere of Hereford, who had married the granddaughter of the Earl of Rutland. Eleanor Goodere, also allied to the Dinelys

Harvard Theatre Collection

SAMUEL FOOTE

engraving by Blackmore, after Reynolds

of Charlton, Worcestershire, even to her old age displayed the wit and eccentricity of her aristocratic family, qualities which were to be found in abundant measure in Samuel Foote even as a child. There was also some hint of criminal insanity in her line: her brother Captain Samuel Goodere had his elder brother Sir John Goodere abducted and brought to his ship, the Ruby, off Bristol, and then strangled on 18 January 1741, in revenge for John's having disinherited him in favor of his sisters. Captain Goodere and his two accomplices were executed at Bristol on 20 April of that year.

Eleanor Foote was supposed to have been made comfortable by an inheritance from the murdered brother and probably she received money from her own husband's estate, but she, like her son Samuel, seems not to have been a prudent manager. Some years later she wrote to Samuel, "I am in prison for debt: come and assist your loving mother." Characteristically, Samuel sent his attorney to assist her and wrote "let us hope for better days."

Two of Samuel Foote's siblings died in infancy: Eleanor, born in April 1712, and Samuel (the first child of that name), born in November 1715. The eldest surviving brother, Edward Goodere Foote, baptized on 5 November 1716, failed to support himself as a clergyman, for which he had been educated, and eventually became dependent on Samuel for an annual pension of £60. Another brother, John, baptized on 14 April 1718, may have become rich in Jamaica; but it was also said that he changed his surname to Dinely in order to inherit his uncle's estate in Worcestershire, which John left to his son when he died in 1758.

After attending grammar school at Truro, where he exhibited an early bent for mimicry, Samuel Foote was accepted at Worcester College, Oxford, on 29 June 1737, at the age of 17, on the basis of his relationship through the Dinelys to the college's founder, Sir Thomas Cookes. Matriculating on 1 July 1737, Samuel applied himself more to pleasure and extravagance than to study but became, nevertheless, competent in Latin and Greek. In later years he was, according to a sketch of his life found in Arthur Murphy's papers, "ridiculously vain of his family and his classical knowledge, which was superficial. . . ." Foote had, however, a substantial native intelligence. His inclination to become quickly bored and his propensity to leave the college without permission—one time after a gambling spree he returned to Oxford in a rented carriage accompanied by two extravagantly uniformed footmen—finally resulted in the loss of his scholarship and his dismissal from the rolls on 25 February 1740.

Next Foote studied law at the Inner Temple, but although he lived in chambers there he never registered formally. Most of his time he spent wasting the money he was reported to have inherited about that time, establishing himself as a man of fashion and wit at the Grecian Coffee House and at the Bedford, where he mingled with theatrical folk. Dr Barrowby, as related by William Cooke, Foote's early biographer, described how Foote came

into the room dressed out in a frock suit of green and silver lace, bag wig, sword, *bouquet*, and point ruffles, and immediately joined the critical circle at the upper end of the room. Nobody knew him. He, however, soon boldly entered into conversation; and by the brilliancy of his wit, the justness of his remarks, and the unembarrassed freedom of his manners, attracted the general notice. The buz of the room went round, 'who is he? whence comes he?' etc; which nobody could answer; until a handsome carriage stopping at the door to take him to the assembly of a lady of fashion, they learned from the servants that his name was Foote, that he was a young gentleman of family and fortune, and a student of the Inner Temple.

Such magnificence was temporary. Soon the need for money prompted his first publication, the characteristically exploitative account of the family scandal: *The genuine Memoirs of the life of Sir John Dinely Goodere, Bart, who was murder'd by the contrivance of his own brother. . . . Together with the Life, history, tryal and last dying words of his brother Capt. Samuel Goodere. . . . By S. Foote, of Worcester-College, Oxford, Esq; and nephew to the late Sir John Dinely Goodere, Bart.*

The £20 which this long-titled first effort brought him hardly allowed Foote the life of a gentleman, so among other schemes, he joined partnership with a Mr Price—perhaps the notorious swindler Charles Price, known as "Old Patch"—for the brewing and selling of small beer, a venture that produced, according to Dr Johnson's anecdote, a brew so bad that the servants would not drink it. "Foote puffed off his small beer so well to the nobility," reported one newspaper after the failure of the partnership, "that it became as much in vogue as Mrs. Allen's closet. He soon, however, quarreled with his partner upon the small beer turning sour, and lost his credit as the greatest puffer and small beer brewer in Europe." But, in a sense, that reputation would soon be regained as the extraordinary puffer and purveyor of small-brew theatricals, the mimicking of actors, and the exploitation of topical fantastics in a distinct line of English entertainment.

Before venturing into the theatre, Foote tried marriage. On 10 January 1741 he wed Mary Hickes, a neighbor from Truro, at St Clement Danes, London. Seventeen at the time, described as very pretty, sensible to wit, and generally well-enough educated, Mary Hickes held the promise of a "good estate" for Foote. He went through her dowry quickly and on 13 November 1742 was confined for debt in Fleet Prison where she loyally lived with him. Among the numerous creditors set out in the "Statement of charges of debt against Samuel Foote" (the document is now at the Guildhall) were his own mother and the Viscountess Castlecomer. After a few months he was released but soon was recommitted on the same charges.

The passage of the bill for the relief of insolvent debtors won Foote his freedom on 7 September 1743. Soon after his release he began to treat his wife abusively and left her. Arthur Murphy and other friends persuaded him to take her in again. Because her carriage had overturned, she returned to his house with bruises, to which Foote assigned the names of geographical locations, the lumps upon her head called the "Islands of Scilly." Mrs Foote died at a date unknown, but, as Cooke wrote, "in good time for both parties; before age came on to incite a further distaste in her husband." Foote's callousness later prompted from his enemies the quatrain:

> Never drew drop of blood in all his life,
> Of Friend or Mistress—save his virtuous
>   Wife.
> What Kill his Wife?—He only lets her
>   starve.
> No more.—He cannot death for that
>   deserve.

There was no issue of the short-lived marriage. In his will, however, Foote mentioned two natural sons, Francis and George, evidently sired on one of his servants who then ran off with a bass-viol player at the Opéra when Foote took her to Paris. There may not be much truth in the anecdote that upon her obsequious return to Foote, he laughed, "What Madam! Have you not been basely violated? and do you want to run your gamut on me?" As Simon Trefman point out in *Sam. Foote, Comedian* (1971), Foote's relationships with women could tend to be "brutal and resounding with devastating repartee." The aloofness that seems to have characterized his attitudes towards the opposite sex later made him vulnerable to the charges of homosexuality which haunted his last years.

Desperation and destiny brought Foote to the stage. In the aftermath of the players' strike and subsequent settlement with Fleetwood the manager of Drury Lane, the actor Charles Macklin, feeling betrayed by Garrick and the other defecting players, refused to come back to work when the company began to act again on 8 December 1743. He formed an acting school, to which came the novice Foote, perhaps on recommendation of Francis Blake Delaval, a mutual friend of Macklin and Foote. While Macklin may have been serious about his school, it was also apparent that he was looking for a way of giving public performances without a patent. In the *Daily Advertiser* of 21 January 1744, Macklin announced his intention to present a "Concert of Music" at the Haymarket Theatre, after which would be offered *Othello*, gratis, the usual fiction for circumventing the Licensing Act.

On 6 February 1744, announced as a young gentleman making his first appearance on any stage, Foote acted Othello to Macklin's Iago. According to Kirkman's *Memoirs* of Macklin, "the performance for chasteness and spirit, exceeded the most sanguine expectations of Mr. Macklin's friends." The *Daily Advertiser* of 21 February reported that "the Gentleman who performed the character of Othello received Universal Applause," when he played it for the third night on 20 February (the second night was on 13 February). Those comments tend to deny the common belief that Foote was a dismal failure in his debut —an assumption perpetuated by Charles Lee Lewes, who wrote in his *Comic Sketches* (1804) that "His performance of Othello was such a masterpiece of burlesque that it never yet has been forgotten by those who saw it."

After additional performances at the Haymarket on 23 February and 2 March (making a total of five)—in the last of which the character of Othello was advertised to be "new dress'd, agreeable to the custom of his own Country"—Foote, still not named in the bills, played Othello at

Drury Lane Theatre on 10 March 1744, for the benefit of "a Gentleman under misfortunes." At the Haymarket again on 6 April (not on 2 March as stated in *The Dictionary of National Biography*) he tried Lord Foppington in *The Relapse* and spoke the epilogue, which may have been from his own pen. He repeated that role on 9 April and then returned to Drury Lane on 13 April to play it there. He ended his debut season back at the Haymarket on 26 April with Othello, now billed as being played by "a Citizen for his Diversion."

By autumn 1744 Foote was in Dublin for an engagement at the Smock Alley Theatre, where the star of the Irish actor Spranger Barry was now rising. Records are incomplete, but Foote acted Bayes in *The Rehearsal* on 25 October 1744 and remained at that theatre until 3 December, taking a benefit on 15 November as Lord Foppington. But soon the irrepressible Foote was impelled to strike out on his own. A letter now in the British Museum from an unknown writer, dated 20 February (1745), says, "The attention of the Publick has been lately taken up by the two rival Theatres; the old one in Smock Alley & a new one, under the direction of Mr. Foote, in Capel St.; but the last is in the greatest esteem at present, Mr. Foote having played Wildair, Bayes & Pierre five times each, to as crowded Audiences as ever were known. But it is talked he is going to leave the Kingdom to the regret of all people of taste here." In the light of the anonymous letter-writer's report, Robert Hitchcock's comment in *The Irish Stage* (1788) that Foote "brought a few crowded houses and was well received" would seem understated.

Evidently Foote's talents for the timing of an enterprise and as a crowd-pleasing performer matured simultaneously. Some notices have survived for performances at Capel Street in 1745 which reveal that Foote acted Sir Harry Wildair in *The Constant Couple* on 28 January, Tinsel in *The Drummer* on 8 February, Pierre in *Venice*

Harvard Theatre Collection

SAMUEL FOOTE, "Orator and Mimick"

artist unknown

Preserv'd and Fondlewife in *The Credulous Cuckold* on 9 February, Pierre again on the twelfth, Sir Harry on the eighteenth, Foppington on the twenty-fifth, and then on 4 March the title role in *Sir Courtly Nice*.

On the crest of that success Foote crossed the Irish Sea again, returning to London in time to take up an engagement at Drury Lane Theatre for the season of 1745–46. Had he come a season earlier Foote would have been a colleague of Garrick, but Garrick's dispute with James Lacy, then the manager at Drury Lane, had taken him to the rival Covent Garden house for that season and the next. Foote first appeared on 1 November 1745 as Sir Harry Wildair and then proceeded to play a series of comic roles, some of which he had acted at Dublin and which in earlier years had been associated with the career of Colley Cibber: Foppington, Sir Novelty Fashion in *Love's Last Shift*, Bayes, Dick in *The Confederacy*, Young Loveless in *The Scornful Lady*, Tinsel, and, for his benefit on 14 April 1746, Sir Courtly Nice. His performances totaled about 19 in all, indicating that he was not regarded as a regularly working actor in the company and was probably paid on a freelance basis. Whatever success he may have enjoyed must have been modest— there were no raves or acclamations for a promising new performer—and he was not to be found at Drury Lane the next season.

By the summer of 1746 Foote seemed ready to quit the stage, "not having the success he wanted in acting," according to his anonymous biographer in *Memoirs of . . . The English Aristophanes* (1788). He retreated to Cheltenham in August, where Garrick, in a letter to Francis Hayman on the eighteenth, described him as "full of Spirits, abounds in Pleasantry, Plays at Whist for five pounds a Rubber, wears lac'd Frocks with Shirts, & to the eternal Mortification of the Beaux Esprits he has renounc'd the Stage for Ever, & so (as Bayes says) farewell to Genius, humour & all that, *for damn him if he plays any more.*" A later biographer, John Forster (*Biographical Essays*, 1860), quotes Foote as having pondered, "If they won't have me in tragedy, and I am not fit for comedy, what the deuce am I fit for?" He was not

Opening of *A Treatise on the Passions,* by SAMUEL FOOTE

too many months away from his answer.

Foote found his calling as satirical writer and mimic in 1747. On 4 December 1746 he had played Othello again at the Haymarket under the familiar concert guise; evidently Foote had raised the temporary company and rented the theatre on his own. Early in 1747 came the publication of *A Treatise on the Passions, So far as they regard the Stage; With a critical Enquiry into the Theatrical Merit of Mr G[arric]k, Mr. Q[ui]n, and Mr. B[arr]y. The first considered in the Part of Lear, and the two last opposed in Othello.* It appeared anonymously, because Foote had insulting things to say about audiences and snide remarks about Garrick and his *Miss in Her Teens*. The main body of the work was solemn, a regulation examen of the passions and how they are to be acted; yet the essay does reveal some solid thinking about acting technique. In one passage about "ranters" he urged them to reform; otherwise he would bring them upon the stage and "force [them] to moderation"—a hint that his ideas for his mimic show were already percolating. But what started out as pleasant teasing ended up as somewhat malicious damning, especially of Garrick's propensity for interminable dying scenes. The whole of the *Treatise* reflected Foote's inability to resist capricious irony when objectivity— the mark of the truly comic writer—was demanded.

On 2 March 1747 his next critical work was advertised for imminent publication. It appeared on 27 March as *The Roman and English Comedy Consider'd and Compar'd. With Remarks on the Suspicious Husband and an Examen into the Merit of the present Comic Actors.* Here Foote was on surer ground, for he was writing about wit and comic acting. He admitted that Garrick was a far better actor than Colley Cibber, even in comedy, but defended a farcical style of acting which plays to the gallery's favor: "Don't Folks come to a Play to laugh? And if that End be obtained, what

matters it how? Has not he the most Merit, who pleases the most? Suppose Garrick has the Approbation of Twenty or Thirty Judges in the Pit, shall I give up my Fun, which makes the inhabitants of both the Gallerys my Friends, for his Humour?"

In April 1747 Foote began a publicity campaign to puff his forthcoming new entertainment, *The Diversions of the Morning; or, A Dish of Chocolate.* He cleverly —and transparently—sent an anonymous letter which was published in the *Daily Advertiser* on 20 April wherein Foote was threatened by horsewhipping if he carried out his plan to "take off" respected and well-known persons. It drew out Orator Henley, the eccentric speech teacher, in the *General Advertiser* on 21 April 1747: "*Foote a Fool.* Whoever attacks my Reputation, or Livelihood, is a mad Bull to me, and ought to be knocked down, prosecuted, etc. I hear I am to be hung up on Wednesday, at the Haymarket, by one Foote, a Fool."

Employing the concert cliché Foote advertised his opening for Wednesday, 22 April: "At the Theatre in the Hay-Market, this Day will be perform'd a Concert of Music. With which will be given Gratis a New Entertainment, call'd 'The Diversions of the Morning.'. . . To which will be added a Farce taken from 'The Old Batchelor,' call'd 'The Credulous Husband.' Fondlewife by Mr. Foote; Bellmour, Mr. Lee, Laetitia by Mrs Hallam." Those and the other performers, who included Shuter, Cushing, Costollo, Lee, Burton, and Miss Moreau, were all from the little Goodman's Fields Theatre, which had been operating outside the licensing laws in competition with the patent houses. While Foote had precedent, his venture was somewhat audacious, even though he did not sell tickets at the door, but at Mr Waller's, a bookseller in Fleet Street. It was a ploy which the patent managers were not inclined to tolerate, but there are conflicting accounts of what actually ensued after the first per-

formance. Some state that the second performance, presumably scheduled for the
next night, the twenty-third, was interdicted by the justice of the peace, Thomas
de Veil, at the instigation of James Lacy,
the Drury Lane co-manager. No advertisement appeared for a performance that
night, so either Foote had been warned
early enough that morning to cancel, or
he had no intention of playing anyway.
Before bringing on *The Diversions* again
he hit upon a compromise, which was to
perform in the afternoon and thereby
avoid direct confrontation with the patent
houses in the evening. The idea of the
matinee was not new. It dated back to
Jacobean times and was in vogue during
Pepys's day. But while other types of exhibitions and entertainments, such as prize
fights and fair shows, did occur at midday
during the 1740s, the practice begun by
Foote was novel in respect to indoor theatrical events. On Friday, 24 April, Foote
advertised that on the next day, Saturday
the twenty-fifth,

exactly at Twelve o'clock, at the New Theatre
in the Hay-Market, Mr. Foote begs the Favour
of his Friends to come and drink a Dish of
Chocolate with him; and 'tis hoped there will
be a great deal of good Company, and some
joyous Spirits; he will endeavour to make the
Morning as Diverting as possible. (Tickets
for the Entertainment to be had at George's
Coffee House, Temple Bar, without which no
Person will be admitted.)

Under the guise of inviting his friends
to take a dish of chocolate, Foote attracted
very large crowds and soon became encouraged enough to request via the press
on 28 April "that (to prevent confusion
at going out) the Ladies and Gentlemen
would pay for their Chocolate going in." In
earlier years Charlotte Charke had sold
tickets entitling her patrons to a pint of
ale, but Foote never intended anything
other than the fictitious "dish of Chocolate."
On 1 June he boldly abandoned the mati-

nees and reverted to the evening, changing
his "dish" as well: "At the request of several Persons who are desirous of spending
an Hour with Mr Foote, but find the Time
inconvenient, instead of Chocolate in the
Morning, Mr Foote's Friends are desir'd
to drink a dish of Tea with him, at half
an Hour after Six in the Evening." Foote
and his company continued to act at the
Haymarket through 6 June, giving in all
35 performances.

Foote's success had been uniquely and
skillfully manoeuvred. Even though what
he had done was forbidden by the Licensing
Act, he was clever enough to diminish the
threat to the incomes of the legitimate managers by beginning his operation at the
time of the season when benefit performances were given. In the future his programs would largely occupy the summers,
when the patent houses were closed. Perhaps it is not an overstatement to suggest
that Foote's ingenious device, begun in
April 1747, was a major landslide in the
steady eroding away of the Licensing Act,
one that led to the "minor theatre" phenomenon of the late eighteenth and early
nineteenth centuries.

The Diversions of the Morning as performed in 1747 was not published, save
for some revised excerpts combined with
others of Foote's pieces which were provided in later years by Cooke and Wilkinson. Clearly, however, it took the shape of
a satirical revue, consisting of take-offs of
notable persons and the satirical mimicry
of popular actors such as Quin, Delane,
Ryan, Mrs Woffington, Macklin, and Garrick. The epilogue provided additional opportunities to caricature the personalities
who frequented the Bedford Coffee House.

Foote returned to the Haymarket in the
autumn of 1747 to give a performance of
what he now called *Tea* on 4 November,
billed as the thirty-seventh performance,
suggesting that a thirty-sixth had taken
place after 6 June. (There are, however,
no bills extant for the Haymarket in July

or August.) The next performance of *Tea* occurred on 11 November 1747 at Covent Garden Theatre, where Rich, having lost his main attraction Garrick, who now was a Drury Lane patentee, no doubt hoped that Foote would be a bolstering factor. *Tea* was served some 13 times there through 2 February 1748, but without the success it had enjoyed the previous season at the Haymarket, no doubt because Foote was too inhibited by being obliged to leave out his imitations of the actors themselves. "His mimickry at Covent Garden," according to Wilkinson, "consisted of a whimsical teaching of stage pupils, the Puppets,—of Chevalier Taylor and a Dr Heberden." Foote's acting of Bayes in *The Rehearsal* on 23 and 24 November, Fondlewife in *The Old Bachelor* on 15 December, and Sir Novelty in *Love's Last Shift*, for his benefit and his last performance at Covent Garden that season on 2 February 1748, also caused little stir. On 6 February the publication of a set of satirical prints of Foote, one in the character of Instructor Puzzle from *Tea*, was announced in the *General Advertiser*. By then Foote was preparing for Dublin.

On 5 March 1748 Foote began morning performances of his *Dish of Chocolate* at the Capel Street Theatre. By 18 April, however, he was back at the Haymarket, with a new title if not a new format. Capitalizing on the trend for the numerous auctions of paintings prevalent in town that spring, Foote advertised that he would "exhibit for the Satisfaction of the Curious, a choice Collection of *Pictures*, all warranted *Originals*, and entirely new. The Auction to begin exactly at Twelve. Catalogues will be deliver'd at the Place of Sale, which Ladies and Gentlemen are desir'd to pay for at going in, and 'twill be allowed them in any Purchase they may make. The Sale will continue everyday till all the Catalogues are sold." Under the title of *Auction of Pictures* Foote's exhibition included "portraits" of Thomas de Veil,

the magistrate who had troubled his performance in the previous April and was now dead, and Henry Fielding, who had earlier expressed resentment of Foote and had taken Rich to task for allowing the mimic to use the Covent Garden stage. Fielding now opened his puppet show in Panton Street, advertised as Madam de la Nash's Breakfasting Room, and for several months the town enjoyed the satirical war on stage and in the broadsides between the two.

After 36 performances of the *Auction of Pictures*, ending on 16 June 1748, Foote perhaps traveled for part of the summer. He seems to have headed a company of London actors that played at summer's end in Hussey's booth, near the Hospital Gate, during Bartholomew Fair.

Foote did not resume his London presentations until the middle of the next theatrical season. Meanwhile, a person who styled himself "Mr Foote the Second" advertised on 20 October 1748 (and again on the twenty-seventh) that, "late arrived from Copenhagen," he would exhibit his "Collection of Pictures" in Marshalsea Prison, Southwark, to continue every Thursday evening during the winter. The notice is obviously suspect and perhaps a mere hoax; the pictures were said to have included some lately brought from New Zealand and some done by the "present famous Mynheer Vandergoot" and "Monsieur Pantin" from Paris. To be given gratis were *The Murder of the Dragon of Wantley* and a "Sleepy Dance by Count Tincture Laudanum from Goar."

At the Haymarket on 1 December 1748, Samuel Foote began what was to prove to be a most spirited season with his *Auction of Pictures*. On 5 December he added an "Oration in Praise of Sight, as at Edinburgh, Oxford, Cambridge, Dublin, Foreign Universities." The *Auction* was given some 18 times through 18 February 1749. The season also witnessed the delicious hoax of the Bottle Conjurer who promised to exhibit on 16 January at the Haymarket the amazing feat of putting himself into a common wine bottle and singing in it, all within sight of the audience. A gullible crowd paid from 7s. 6d. for stage boxes to 2s. for the gallery, but of course the Bottle Conjurer did not show up, prompting them to tear up the theatre. In the destruction "an excellent Bonfire was made of the Materials of Mr. Foote's Auction Room—Hats, Wigs, Swords, Snuffboxes &c were as plenty as the Pick Pockets could wish. . . ." On 18 January Foote published a letter in the *General Advertiser* denying any part in the hoax (which some years later was revealed as a scheme perpetrated by the Duke of Montague and the Duke of Richmond as the result of a wager between them over "the credulity of the English Nation"). Despite the loss he suffered, Foote resumed performances of his *Auction* on 25 January.

During that month of January a feud had erupted between Foote and the Drury Lane comedian Henry Woodward. It began when Foote introduced into his *Auction* on 7 January his mimicry of Garrick in the several roles of a poet, a Frenchman, and a drunken man in his *Lethe* which had been revived at Drury Lane on 2 January. Also taken off as the Fine Gentleman in that production was Woodward, who with Garrick's permission retaliated at Drury Lane by rewriting one of his speeches:

Sir, by Birth, Title, Travel, and Education, I lead the Fashions; I am principal Connoissour at all Auctions, except that of the Haymarket and there indeed is an impudent Fellow of an Auctioneer who makes nothing of me; but I' Gad I'll be even with him; for I intend to bribe Woodward the Actor, who has almost as much impudence as himself, and he shall treat him with the same Ease and Familiarity as he did in Dublin, where he drove him out of the Kingdom with a dish of his own Chocolate.

Woodward's last statement was a reference to their rivalry at Dublin in March 1748, when Woodward had concocted a piece called *Coffee* to oppose Foote's *Tea*. True to his threat, Woodward introduced his *Tit for Tat, or One Dish of his own Chocolate* as an afterpiece for his benefit at Drury Lane on 18 March 1749. A week earlier, on 10 March, Foote had written an open letter to Woodward in the *General Advertiser*: "Oh! ho! is it come?—What at your Irish tricks again?—No my dear, they won't do; I am too well establish'd here; . . . you defeat *me* in Ireland! Very likely; as if we did not know you!"

A packed house at Woodward's benefit brought him £286 (less house charges of £65). The *General Advertiser* on 21 March called it "the greatest audience that was ever seen there, and the *Dish of Chocolate* was receiv'd with uncommon applause." Cross the prompter described it in his "Diary" as "a bam, in mimickry upon Mr Foote." Woodward played *Tit for Tat* six more times through April.

Meanwhile Foote opened his new comedy *The Knights* at the Haymarket on 3 April 1749. With that two-act comedy (printed in 1754), his first dramatic effort, Foote was quite successful, playing 20 times (matinees and evenings) through 1 June. In it he acted Hartop, a young wastrel; and Shuter, another excellent comic, acted Sir Gregory Gazette. The first three performances also included at the end a cat-duet by Shuter and "Cat" Harris which spoofed the Italian opera—"The Company to be waited on by two Knights, from the Land's End, and a Brace of Cats from Italy. The Ladies and Gentlemen are desired to leave their Lapdogs and Spaniels at home because of the Cats." In the fourth performance, on 8 April, Foote took his revenge on Woodward: "The Company may depend upon having an Additional Treat of Chocolate, but vastly different from that lately distributed by Harry the Smuggler"; and for 15 April he brought back his *Auction* as afterpiece to *The Knights* with the announcement, "the Auctioneer will dispose of some Originals, particularly a Portrait of Harry the Smuggler, as he look'd at his Trial."

After his last performance of *The Knights* on 1 June 1749, Foote gave up his stage enterprises for over two years, evidently employing his time going through another inheritance. He seems to have spent most of the period at Paris with his closest friend Francis Blake Delaval. At one point Foote acted as marriage broker for Delaval in a bizarre scheme to gain the fortune of Lady Isabella Pawlett, a widow twice Delaval's age. The marriage indeed occurred on 8 March 1750, but Delaval discovered that most of her money was tied up in trusts. Foote settled for a much smaller broker's fee than the £12,000 he had anticipated, but for a while Lady Isabella sought solace from him, a circumstance which cooled his relationship with Delaval for several years.

While Foote was absent from the stage, Woodward took another swipe at him by announcing that in a revival of *Friendship in Fashion* to take place at Drury Lane in January 1750 he intended in the role of Malagene to mimic Foote. In protest Foote wrote to Garrick, but the manager replied (about 16 January) that he would not interfere with the feud and teasingly asked, "But shou'd he dress at you in the Play, how can you be alarm'd at it, or take it ill; the Character of Malagene (exclusive of some little Immoralities which can never be apply'd to you) is that of a very smart, pleasant, Conceited fellow, & a good Mimic. . . ." Still hoping to dissuade Woodward, on 20 January 1750 Foote placed an open letter to him in the *Daily Advertiser*, hypocritically protesting Woodward's method and warning vengeance. Foote seemed serious:

After so many defeats you have already suffer'd in the Mimical War between us . . . I was greatly surpris'd to hear that you again intended to provoke my future vengeance, by dressing me in the character of Malagene. . . . Whatever you may think, Mr W———d, these public exhibitions of par-

ticular persons by no means become the dignity of the stage, & though a disorder in my Finances may occasionally have urged me to some Pleasant attacks in this way, yet give me leave to say, I never was abandoned enough to think 'em justifiable. . . . Your intended attack on me . . . as the character you are to represent is . . . indeed not that of the most nice Morality; who knows but that . . . some may cry, "Tis he from head to Foot." As you are sensible this would be doing me great Injustice, & in my present circumstances might be particularly injurious to me, I expect you will alter the Design.

Woodward proceeded with his plan on 22 January but suffered an unexpected and extraordinary reversal. When he took off Foote as Malagene, "the Audience grew so outrageous that he was forc'd to desist," recorded Cross in his "Diary," and the fourth and fifth acts "were much hooted." When the play was given out for the next night, the audience called loudly for Garrick, but he being absent from the theatre, they "pull'd up the Benches, torn down yᵉ King's Arms," and would have done more damage had not the audience been informed that the play for the following night would be changed to *The Provok'd Husband*.

Whatever real animosity may have developed between Foote and Garrick over the Malagene affair was obviously patched up, for Foote's new farce *Taste* was given its premiere at Drury Lane on 11 January 1752, with a prologue written and delivered by Garrick as the Auctioneer. In his preface to the version published in 1752 (and dedicated to Delaval) Foote claimed to have written the piece for the benefit of James Worsdale, the painter, who had a hand in the writing of Lady Pentweazle, one of Foote's most durable characters. Worsdale, a clever mimic, also played the role.

The production of *Taste* was not carried off without incident. Anticipating that something unusual was bound to happen at a Footean event, the audience crowded the house early. They clamored for the farce to be played before the mainpiece, *The Revenge*, but since some of the actors had not yet arrived at the theatre, this request could not be complied with, so the audience sat impatiently through the first piece. Then came the surprise. Foote evidently had not intended to act in his play, but at the dress rehearsal on the previous night he had been unhappy with Yates's playing of Puff. On the morning of the premiere he persuaded Garrick "to prevail with Mr Yates to let 'em say he was sick," according to the prompter Cross's explanation in his diary, "that Mr Foote might have occasion to do the part." As Cross related it:

. . . Mr Garrick spoke y^e *Prologue* in the Character of an Auctioneer, with surprising Applause—when he had done, he made this Apology—Gents—a performer being taken ill, the Author, Mr Foote, is here, & will if you please, perform his part, this he spoke in a Hesitating manner, & was greatly applauded —the first Act went off well, & Mr Worsdale . . . play'd a Woman's part, & was greatly received—When Mr Foote came on—he made this Speech—Gent: I have left the Stage some time, nor have I any hopes of Profit from this Piece, but as a Performer is taken ill, I had rather appear my self, than have so many people, whom Curiosity has drawn together, be disappointed—Great Applause. . . .

Despite the enthusiastic reception of the first act, by the second act the audience found *Taste* dull, and by the end "hiss'd greatly," so that a great clamor went up when it was given out again for the next night. The management pondered their problem over Sunday and decided to advertise that "as ye Farce was not so well receiv'd" the author had withdrawn it for alterations. *Harlequin Ranger* was substituted for several nights until 21 January when *Taste* was brought back: "No alterations were made . . . but cutting out a little," wrote Cross, "& it was play'd with great Applause, & given out again with

great Clapping." The third night, the twenty-second, evidently went well enough, but at the fourth performance, on the twenty-fourth, "A little hissing during the farce, & at the End ye Audience call'd, no more &c.—& insisted upon another farce being given out wch Mr Blakes did—farewell *Taste*."

It was reported by *The Inspector* (No 271) that *Taste* had been the victim on the first night of "A party against it"; but the critic judged "There is, indisputably, more genuine Wit in it than in any piece of the kind ever produc'd among us; the characters are natural, tho many of them uncommon ones; their stile and sentiments are adapted to them with perfect propriety, and the incidents are not forced or crowded together upon the audience." The *Monthly Review* (January 1752) thought the subject was "abstract and singular," better for reading than for popular consumption in the theatre, an opinion which Foote concurred with in his published dedication. In the *Drury Lane Journal* for 16 January 1752, Bonnell Thornton summarized the event: "Tho' the house was very hot upon it, it met with a cool reception, and was reckon'd a Footy performance."

After the failure of *Taste*, Foote remained away from the theatre for another year, returning for the performance of his play *The Englishman in Paris*, which opened at Covent Garden on 24 March 1753 for the benefit of Macklin, his old acting coach. In a letter to Delaval written in April, Foote reported that the reception of the piece had exceeded his expectations, that Garrick had commented most kindly on it, but that upon the whole "it was damnably acted," especially by Macklin, as Buck, who did not know his lines or character. It was repeated only once more that season, on 24 April, for the benefit of Maria Macklin, the novice actress and daughter of Charles, who played Lucinda. Not until Foote himself played Buck the following season at Drury Lane did the play catch on; it became a mainstay of the repertory for some years.

After a holiday on the Continent in the summer of 1752, Foote returned to London to hear the rumor that he had been executed at Bordeaux for some crime. He lost little time in having his sport in a new prologue, written for him by Garrick, to *The Englishman in Paris*, for his reintroduction to the Drury Lane stage as Buck on 20 October 1753:

> . . . "Paper! boy." "Here, Sir, I am."
>   "What news today?"
> "Foote, Sir is advertised." "What! run
>   away?"
> "No, Sir; this week he acts at Drury
>   Lane."
> "How's that?" (cries feeble Grub).
>   "Foote come again!
> I thought that fool had done his devil's
>   dance;
> Was he not hang'd some months ago in
>   France?"

As Fondlewife in *The Old Bachelor* on 24 October, Foote drew high praise from Murphy in *Gray's Inn Journal* on 3 November 1753. Writing later in his *Dramatic Miscellanies* (1783–84), Thomas Davies, no admirer of Foote, remembered the performance: "In the course of the first scene he drew the attention of the audience, and merited, and gained much applause; but in the progress of the part, he forgot his exemplar [Colley Cibber] and degenerated into buffoonery." He played Sir Courtly Nice on 6 November, and Cross thought him and the whole play to be very indifferent.

For his first attempt at Ben in *Love for Love* on 16 January 1754 he received a temperate notice from his admirer Murphy (*Gray's Inn Journal*, 19 January), who found him very pleasant but unsure of himself in the new character. From the wings Cross was not impressed: "Foote could not sing ye Song in Ben, so said two or three times, I can't do it & upon a little Hissing,

said, Gentlemen, I have no talents for singing—ye whole play Hum." Davies thought he had murdered the role—"his Ben was as lifeless a lump of insipidity as ever a patient audience was presented with; it was not even a lively mistake of humour." After playing Brazen in *The Recruiting Officer* on 5 February, he appeared as Hartop in his own *The Knights* on the ninth; the farce was hissed, but played again on the twelfth to a small house of £80. He enjoyed a larger audience (£170) when he acted Fondlewife for his benefit, and last appearance of the season, at Drury Lane on 22 February, when tickets could be had of him at Mr Ray's, a woolendraper in Tavistock Row. A month later he was at Covent Garden playing Hartop for Mrs Bellamy's benefit on 28 March 1754.

After a repeat of *The Knights* at Covent Garden on 1 April, Foote retreated to his new residence in Blackheath, where he enjoyed a pleasant summer with Arthur Murphy as his guest and acting pupil. It was at Blackheath that Foote merrily duped Murphy into translating a piece from *Le Journal Littéraire* for *Gray's Inn Journal* (on 22 June 1754) which proved to have been a translation into the French of Johnson's original essay for the *Rambler*, No 190.

In 1754–55 Foote performed occasionally at Covent Garden, playing Fondlewife, Hartop, and Buck. On 18 March 1755 his *Taste* was revived there with him as Lady Pentweazle, for the benefit of Mrs Bellamy. It was acted again on 10 April for the benefit of Shuter who played Lord Dupe. Foote had intended to act Iago for Murphy's debut as Othello on 18 October 1754 but wisely reneged, leaving the role to Ryan. In December he was unable to curb the temptation to annoy his sometime friend Macklin. That actor had announced his retirement and set up a grandiose school of oratory in a tavern in Covent Garden. Despite the fact that Foote had played Buck at Macklin's benefit and presumed farewell performance at Drury Lane on 20 December 1753, he came to heckle Macklin's orations at the tavern with constant interruptions and challenges. On 16 December 1754, having rented the Haymarket once more, Foote began his comic lectures, aimed primarily at Macklin, under the title *A Writ of Inquiry will be Executed on the Inquisitor General*. During the six nights on which the *Writ of Inquiry* was presented at a profit of some £500 to Foote, Macklin's curiosity got the better of him and brought him to see for himself, but he became angry, yelled up to the stage, and was hooted by the house. Not too long afterward, goes one story, the two antagonists were reconciled in the street and went off to a tavern together.

Again engaged at Covent Garden on an occasional basis, Foote appeared on 3 February 1756 in *The Englishman Return'd from Paris*, his sequel to *The Englishman in Paris*. He had kept his scheme for this play secret for some time because he wished to get the jump on Arthur Murphy, who had conceived of the idea for a sequel and was at work writing it. In fact, until the discovery in recent years of Murphy's manuscript for his play at the Newberry Library, it was presumed that Foote had plagiarized Murphy's text, which was never published. He obviously stole the idea (yet it was a sequel to his own piece), but as Trefman points out "his plot and characters differ from Murphy's; his dialogue is superior and his story moves with more pace." Understandably, however, Murphy became incensed at Foote's duplicity; on 3 April 1756, at his own benefit, he brought out his sequel called *The Englishman from Paris*. The night brought Murphy £175. How much Foote took when his version was played for his benefit at Covent Garden on 8 March is not known. That season Foote also played several other times, as Fondlewife, Myrtle in *The Conscious Lovers*, Sir Paul Plyant in *The Double Dealer*, Hartop, and Lady Pentweazle.

Changing theatres yet again in 1756–57, Foote acted Fondlewife and Buck at Drury Lane on 14 October 1756, and Buck and Sir Paul in *The Double Dealer* on 29 October, but without great stir. When Foote played the same roles on 1 November, Cross noted that "Mr Foote brings sad houses." The night's receipts were £80. But matters improved with the premiere of one of his best and most enduring works, *The Author*, on 5 February 1757, with Foote in the role of Cadwallader, in which he mimicked a Mr Apreece, uncle of Francis Delaval. Actually Apreece had asked Foote to portray him on the stage but got more notoriety than he had hoped for and tried to suppress the play. On the day of the opening, Foote inserted into the *Public Advertiser*:

Whereas it has been represented to the Managers of Drury Lane that Mr Foote in his new Farce call'd the *Author*, intends introducing the Character of a Gentleman for whom he has the greatest esteem and regard, he thinks it incumbent upon him to assure the Public, that all the persons in that piece are fictitious and general.

At his benefit on 22 February 1757 when tickets could be had of him at the Whalebone Warehouse in James Street, Covent Garden, *The Author* brought him £135. That night he also acted Gomez in *The Spanish Fryar*. The *Monthly Mirror* of September 1799 published an additional scene to the farce, which Foote had intended to introduce at his benefit.

Foote played Hartop on 2 April but on 13 April was replaced by Yates as Cadwallader. Probably he had left London when the theatres closed for Holy Week on 4 April (on which day *The Knights* was published), bound for Dublin to appear at Smock Alley Theatre on 6 May in *The Englishman Return'd from Paris* and to give the prologue. There he also acted in *The Knights* on 9 and 16 May (for his benefit) and Fondlewife and Cadwallader on 23 May. (King evidently had acted the latter role when *The Author* was given on 13 May.)

He returned to Drury Lane in the autumn, but only briefly, to play Cadwallader and Sir Paul Pliant in October. After a performance of the former on 24 October he hurried off once more to Dublin, where between 18 November and 26 December 1757 he kept busy acting those roles and Buck, Fondlewife, Brazen, and Gomez. On 14 December he brought on his service of *Tea*—"In which will be introduced a Character of Mr. Puzzle's first Pupil, to be performed by a Young Gentleman, being his first Appearance on the Stage." The "Young Gentleman" was Tate Wilkinson, whom Foote had persuaded to accompany him to Dublin with promises of stardom. Wilkinson left behind an opportunity to play at Drury Lane, where he had impressed Garrick with an audition which consisted of imitations of actors, including Foote. On the journey Foote had tutored Wilkinson but had treated him somewhat callously. As he had promised, however, he got the young hopeful an interview with Sheridan, who allowed him to perform the Pupil in *Tea*. Although exceedingly nervous at the beginning, Wilkinson soon gained confidence and momentum so that by the end of the performance he took off Foote himself, to the glee and applause of the audience.

When not on the Smock Alley stage, Foote was filling his time with a bizarre activity. According to a letter in the *London Chronicle* of 17/19 January 1758, he had turned fortune-teller:

. . . He took it into his Head to take a private Lodging in a remote Part of the Town, in order to set up the lucrative Business of Fortune-Telling. After he had got his Room hung with Black, and got his dark Lanthorn, with some People about him that knew the People of Fashion who live in this City, he gave out Handbills, to let them know there was a Man to be met with at such a Place, who wrote down People's Fortunes, without asking them any Questions. As his Room was quite dark (the Light from his Lanthorn excepted) he was in less danger of being discovered. So that he went on with great Success for many days; insomuch that it is said he cleared at least Thirty Pounds a Day at half a Crown a Head.

There are, of course, hundreds of anecdotes about Foote, no doubt more than of any other eighteenth-century performer, including Garrick. But such a ruse was not beyond Foote.

Departing Dublin sometime after his last performances there as Sir Paul and Buck on 26 December 1757, Foote was back at Drury Lane to act Cadwallader again on 26 January (on which day *The Author* was published). Within a few days his life became complicated once more. Mr Apreece, the main butt of his satire in *The Author*, broke into Garrick's rehearsal on 30 January to complain. After a long argument, Garrick agreed to bring Foote to a meeting that evening at the Rose: "a great deal of abuse between him [Foote] and Aprice"; wrote Cross, "I don't know ye particulars, but it [the play] was order'd to remain at the bottom for Tuesday, but, as I hear, it is to be done no more." Cross heard correctly. *The Author* was given once more on Tuesday, 1 February, when Foote also acted Gomez in *The Spanish Fryar* and then was ordered off for the rest of the season by Garrick. Foote had no more to do at Drury Lane for the season, but on 9 March 1758 he played Buck in *The Englishman Return'd from Paris* at Covent Garden, for Mrs Bellamy's benefit.

Over the next several years Foote's life was comparatively without consequence if not without interest, and he was still without articles at either patent house. He freelanced again at Drury Lane in 1758–59, managing once more to ruffle feathers with a revival of *The Diversions of the Morning*, this time joined by Wilkinson as a comimic. In the *Diversions* he now introduced some kind of life-size puppets. The abuse brought down on Foote and Wilkinson by the wrath of the London actors was compensated for by the profits. Foote was also praised for his acting of Gomez on 14 November in the *London Chronicle* (14/16 November 1758), probably by Murphy):

Gomez is the representative of a character very common in human life; he is a mixture of archness, cowardliness, and covetousness; and nobody can show the part to more advantage than the agreeable Mr. Foote. His looks are so sly, his manner of speaking so bitter; and he is enabled by his great talent at mimickry to put on the odd fellow in his voice and gestures without such a ridiculous propriety, that it looks as if either he had been made for the part, or the part for him.

For his benefit at Drury Lane on 18 December 1758, he attempted Shylock for the first time but was not successful, although he netted £157. His intention to end the evening with a revival of *The Author* was thwarted by a last-minute order from the Lord Chamberlain obtained by Apreece, so *The Diversions* was substituted.

After a round of parties during the holiday season, Foote set off for Edinburgh. In order to make the journey he begged £100 from Garrick, through Wilkinson (because he would not ask Garrick directly). At that time, wrote Wilkinson, "birds of passage from London to Scotland were experiments unknown—for it was judged impossible for a London theatrical sunflower to survive the chillness of such a barbarous northern clime." His colleagues in London wondered that Foote would venture north, but he seems to have been very successful, arriving on 15 March 1759 and playing for the first time on 20 March in *The Author* at the Canongate Concert Hall. In addition he acted *The Diversions of the Morning*, *The Englishman Return'd from Paris*, Shylock, Gomez, Bayes, Sir Paul Plyant, and the Earl of Essex. On 30 March he gave what Dibdin termed "in all probability was the first morning performance of a play in Scotland." With a full purse Foote

was back in London by 21 April 1759 attending an afternoon gathering in celebration of Murphy's *The Orphan of China*, which was to open at Drury Lane that evening (it "went off with great applause" wrote Cross).

Fifteen years had now transpired since Foote had turned actor in January 1744. He had not enjoyed a full-time contract with a London house nor was one in prospect in the autumn of 1759. So he turned once more toward Dublin to join Barry and his old rival Woodward who had in 1758 set themselves up at the Crow Street Theatre in competition with Smock Alley. Before embarking, Foote made a pitiful exhibition of himself at the Haymarket on 9 November 1759. In a program advertised as *Comic Lectures* he left the audience numb; he stopped the presentation, and then on a darkened stage he sat at a table, with two candles for illumination, to read aloud his newest play, *The Minor*. The audience became even less responsive. Foote apologized, and, promising changes for the next performance, left the stage. The next morning he was on his way to Ireland.

This Irish venture was a failure, largely because he was overshadowed there by Wilkinson, who arrived in Dublin on 26 December 1759. Wilkinson had been allowed by Garrick to join Brown at Smock Alley, it seems, in a deliberately spiteful act more designed to injure Woodward, who had left Garrick to take up with Barry at Crow Street, than to hurt Foote. When Foote advertised his *Diversions* for 4 January, Wilkinson came out with his version of the same piece and imitated Foote. The pupil proved to be a greater attraction than the teacher. Despite Foote's appeal to Wilkinson that he was now suffering severe financial difficulties, Wilkinson would not relent. Foote experienced another setback on 28 January 1760, when *The Minor* failed at Crow Street, largely because of the unsatisfactory acting by Woodward of

Shift, the character through which Foote struck back at Wilkinson.

Returning to London in severe want of funds, Foote brought out *The Minor*, now lengthened from two to three acts, at the Haymarket on 28 June 1760. The company was made up mostly of novices, including the young Robert Baddeley who in the role of Sir William Wealthy was making his first appearance on the London stage and who, it was said, had been Foote's cook. A satire on George Whitefield and the Methodists, *The Minor* now proved to be a success, running for 35 nights through 30 August and creating a great furor of pro- and anti-Methodist letters and essays. Foote played three roles: Shift, in which he mimicked Wilkinson; Smirk, an impersonation of Abraham Langford, the auctioneer; and Mother Cole, the bawd, modelled after Mother Jennie Douglas, the London procuress. In the last, Foote delighted the audience with the dress, manner, and speech of the old woman. Among Foote's many good strokes was having Mother Cole mouth pieties as she tried to seduce the young hero by selling him one of her girls. For her remarkable conversion to Methodism, the bawd credited Mr Squintum, a character who never appeared on the stage in the play but hovered throughout. In the epilogue, however, Foote mimicked him. The satire on Whitefield, the Methodist preacher who had a cast in his eye, was obvious.

Watching the excitement created by *The Minor* during the summer, Garrick completed negotiations with Foote on 22 July to bring the satire on at Drury Lane in 1760–61. In early autumn, however, Lady Huntington, Whitefield's patroness, brought pressure to suppress the play, as did the Archbishop of Canterbury, to whom the Lord Chamberlain, the Duke of Devonshire, sent the play requesting him to specify the objectionable parts. But the Archbishop shrewdly reneged, realizing that Foote "would publish the play as *corrected*

Harvard Theatre Collection

SAMUEL FOOTE, as Mother Cole

engraving by Walker, after Dodd

and *prepared* for the press by his Grace the Archbishop of Canterbury." The premiere of the play at Drury Lane scheduled for 25 October was delayed by the closing of the theatres for three weeks because of the death of George II. In the interim, a letter signed Anti-Prophanus, probably by Dr Spence Madan, appeared entitled *A Letter to David Garrick, Esq.; Occasioned by the intended Representation of the Minor at the Theatre-Royal in Drury Lane*, which persuaded the Lord Chamberlain to eliminate the more offensive passages and the epilogue.

The Minor opened finally at Drury Lane on 22 November 1760. Just two nights later Covent Garden presented a pirated version of the play given to Rich by Wilkinson, who appeared in the same three roles being played by Foote at Drury Lane. Foote, hearing of the rival house's intentions, had gone across the road to assail its manager and threaten to "instantly produce," as Wilkinson quotes him, "your old stupid ridiculous self, with your three cats, and your hound of a mimic altogether, next week at Drury Lane," but Rich and Wilkinson persisted. All turned out well for Foote, for the most part, for he had the better of the competition and, to boot, Garrick was so infuriated with Wilkinson that he never again spoke to him. On 22 December Foote took his benefit, for which house receipts are not known.

During that season Foote also acted Lady Pentweazle in a performance of *Taste* on 6 April 1761, to which he provided a new additional act called *The Modern Tragedy*, a revision of the second act of Murphy's play of that name. It had been devised as a means of retaliating against Charles Churchill and Robert Lloyd for their recent poetic attacks in *The Rosciad* and *The Actor*. But the piece failed: "greatly hissed—and almost d——d," wrote Hopkins, now the Drury Lane prompter. Despite his earlier anger, he also played Buck in *The Englishman in Paris* at Covent Garden on 21 April for the benefit of Costollo, Stede, and Miss Pitt. At Drury Lane again on 25 April, Foote acted the Scotchman in the premiere of Joseph Reed's farce *The Register Officer*. In the printed edition that year Reed accused Foote of having stolen the character of Mrs Cole in *The Minor* from his Mrs Snarewell, an accusation which had been made earlier that year in the anonymously authored *An Additional Scene to The Minor*, published three months before the production of *The Register Office*. There was probably some truth to the charges, but in any event *The Register Office* failed: "A new farce wrote by one Reed, a ropemaker," wrote Hopkins, "brought out by Mr Foote—went off tolerable—hissed a little at the end." It was acted three other nights before the end of the season.

Finding that the Haymarket had already been leased by Reinhold and Gaudry for the summer of 1761, Foote and Murphy persuaded Garrick to let them have Drury Lane for the summer at a rental rate of one-fifth of their profits. They opened on 15 June 1761 with Murphy's *All in the Wrong*, with a new prologue written and delivered by Foote. On 2 July two more pieces by Murphy were introduced: *The Citizen*, with Foote as Young Philpot, and *The Old Maid*. The season was not a success; the company played only 23 of 48 nights planned, the managers each took only about £300 in net profits for the summer, and Foote had failed to live up to his agreement with Murphy to write three new plays to support the venture. In July Foote had advertised his house and gardens at Ellstree, near Edgeware, Hertfordshire, to let, "as he was engaged in town this Summer," and interested persons could inquire of him "on the Paved Stones, St. Martin's Lane."

The autumn did not begin well. On 16 October 1761 the *Public Advertiser* reported that "Mr Foote was robbed, at Bayswater, near Kensington Gravel Pits; as he was coming to town, by a single Highwayman, who appeared to be a very young fellow." *The Minor* was played at Covent Garden on 10 November, with Foote in his three roles, and he was paid £22 5s. 6d., representing one-quarter of the £89 2s. which was taken in over the house charges. At the same theatre on 12 January 1762 he brought out his new three-act comedy *The Lyar* (adapted from Corneille's *Le Menteur*), a piece he had been prevented from giving at the Haymarket at the end of the previous summer by the necessity to produce, by royal command, Richard Bentley's *The Wishes; or, Harlequin's Mouth Opened* on 27 July 1761 (in which he acted Distress, the Poet). *The Lyar* also failed, receiving only four performances that month, but in later years became a popular piece when it was supported by the grace of John Palmer in the leading role of Young Wilding. In that part Foote exhibited "a clumsiness of person, and an exuberance of *grotesque*," according to Cooke.

Until the late spring of 1762, Foote's career in the theatre, now 18 years old, had been sporadic and speculative. But now, although the future still held travail and even tragedy for him, his fortune changed. Continuity, at least, settled on his life when in this year he began a tenure as the summer manager at the Haymarket which was only interrupted 16 seasons later by his death. On 28 April 1762 he began his "Course of Lectures on English Orators" called *The Orators*, a concoction in three acts of caricature, topical satire, and mockery. Enormously successful, it ran for 38 performances. It played at noon until 4 May, when the time was moved to one o'clock; on 21 June, the patent houses having closed for the season, it was shifted to the evening.

The main target of Foote's mimickry in *The Orators* was Thomas Sheridan, who had given lectures on oratory at Pewterers' Hall between May 1761 and March 1762. Also provided were a mock trial of the Cock-Lane ghost, an imitation of the defense counsel in the infamous Elizabeth Canning case, and a satire of the Robin Hood Society, a debating club of which Foote became a member by 1764.

The most notorious piece of mockery in the performance of *The Orators* was Foote's caricature of the one-legged Dublin printer, George Faulkner, in the guise of Peter Paragraph. In an action for libel, Faulkner was awarded £300 when Foote returned to Dublin in the autumn of 1762, but Foote promptly retreated to London. Evidently he never paid the damages but did reimburse his Irish friends for the £400 in forfeited bail which they had posted on his behalf.

At the beginning of his 1763 summer season at the Haymarket, Foote burlesqued Faulkner and Irish justice in a new epilogue to *The Orators—The Trial of Samuel Foote, esq. for a Libel on Peter Paragraph*. He had already offered *An Address to the Public*, a mock suit for libel by Peter Petros against Aristophanes, which had been printed in the *Gentleman's Magazine* in January 1763, thereby giving stimulus to his nickname as the "English Aristophanes."

More significant that season, however, was the appearance of his extraordinarily successful two-act farce *The Mayor of Garratt* on 20 June 1763. With Foote as the ridiculous Major Sturgeon and Thomas Weston, then a young and unknown actor, as Jerry Sneak, the play ran for 24 consecutive nights, 36 in total that summer, and persisted as a popular vehicle well into the nineteenth century. This season, in which he also offered *The Minor, The Lyar, The Diversions, The Citizen,* and *The Englishman Return'd from Paris,* brought him some financial security that allowed him to remodel his houses in town and country and to invest £1200 in a set of silver plate.

Upon his return from his holiday in Paris in the autumn of 1763, Foote acted Major Sturgeon in *The Mayor of Garratt* at Drury Lane on 30 November. As Mrs Sneak, Mrs Clive was hissed, but the receipts were £170 5s. The play was given seven performances. On 5 December when Foote also acted Gomez in *The Spanish Fryar*, he took his benefit as an actor, but it is not clear if the figure of £64 4s. given by MacMillan in his *Drury Lane Calendar* was net. For his benefit as author on 9 December, the last performance of *The Mayor of Garratt*, he made £24 7s. 6d. above the house charges of £84. That was the last night Foote ever was to act in a winter patent house in London.

The next two summers went well. In 1764 Foote gave about 43 performances at the Haymarket, in 1765 about 53. The former season was bolstered by 17 performances of his new three-act comedy, *The Patron*, which opened on 13 June 1764

ROBERT BADDELEY as Major Sturgeon and SAMUEL FOOTE as Jacob Jollup in *The Mayor of Garratt*

engraving by Haid, after Zoffany

with Foote as Sir Thomas Lofty and Sir Peter Pepperpot, and the latter by *The Commissary*, a three-act satirical comedy which opened on 10 June 1765 with its author in the role of Zachary Fungus. Both pieces were laced with his usual personal satires and topical allusions.

In February 1766, now at the height of his prosperity and with his career on an even keel once more, Foote visited his friends, Lord and Lady Mexborough, at Cannon Park, in Hampshire, some 12 miles from London. On the third of February he was in high spirits, boasting among his elegant friends about his skill on horseback, when tragedy struck. Upon the urging of the company he mounted a high-spirited horse owned by the Duke of York, the honored guest of the party. Almost instantly the horse threw him, causing a double fracture of his leg. The eminent William Bromfield, surgeon to the royal household and the Duke of York's private physician, was obliged to amputate the leg. For so famous an accident, with such important consequences, it is odd that the contemporary reports and subsequent accounts have never definitely specified which leg was lost. It seems to have been the right one, if there is truth in the story told by Decastro in his *Memoirs* (1824) that shortly after the death of Thomas Weston in 1776 Foote said that "he had lost his right hand (meaning the death of poor Weston) as well as his right leg." According to the *London Chronicle* for 13 February 1766 the amputation was made three inches below his knee; but the author of *The English Aristophanes* and a reporter in the *Town and Country Magazine* (November 1777) indicated that the cut was made above the knee in order to accommodate the fitting of a wooden leg.

Complications from a burst artery continued to threaten his life for a week. On 13 February the *London Chronicle* reported that "Mr Foote is now supposed by his physicians to be out of danger." On that day David Garrick, the sometime target of Foote's stage burlesques, wrote him a warm letter of condolence and offered his assistance: "Should you be prevented from persuing any plan for y^r Theatre, I am Wholly at y^r Service, & will labour in y^r vineyard for you, in any Capacity, till you are able to do it, so much better for yourself." On 26 February Foote returned his gratitude in a letter which reveals his despair:

. . . the stage for me at present is a very distant object, for, notwithstanding all the flattery of appearances, I look upon my hold in life to depend upon a very slender tenure; and besides, admitting the best that can happen, is a mutilated man, a miserable instance of the weakness and frailty of human nature, a proper object to excite these emotions which can only be produced from vacant minds, discharged of every melancholy or pensive taint?

His enemies, of course, lost no time in pointing the moral in cruel comments and verses. Lines in the *London Chronicle* of 13/15 February 1766 were typical:

On an Unlucky Poet
What measure shouldst though [sic] *ever
     keep,*
Friend Sam! thy fate is such — —
A Foot too little now you are;
Before a Foote too much.

In an effort to offset some of the nastiness, Garrick composed "Upon Some Attempts, / (Weak, as inhuman) to jest upon Mr Foote's / late Accident," verses which were printed in the *London Chronicle* of 18/20 February 1766 (Garrick's autograph draft in the possession of Robert Eddison differs slightly):

The Ass once bold, threw out his heel,
To make the bed-rid Lion feel;
*   Cowards are ever rash:*
And so you think, *ye scribbling crew,*
Now Foote is down, that, valiant, you
*   Will give him* Dash *for* Dash.

O let your desperate folly rest,
Approach not with a ribald jest
*   Misfortune's sacred bed!*
Still you shall live in fear of him;
For tho' the Wit has lost a limb,
*   He has not lost his head.*

In physical stamina Foote soon proved to be as resourceful as in wit. Moreover, characteristically he turned his misfortune into advantage in several significant ways. In mid-March when being paid a visit by the conscience-stricken Duke of York, the recuperating Foote asked for his lordship's influence in securing a patent from the Crown for the Haymarket. The patent was not officially granted by the Lord Chamberlain until 5 July 1766, but Foote had already begun to make his plans for that summer's campaign. He had hoped for a patent without calendar limitations but received the right to open his theatre only from 15 May through 15 September, during the period when the winter houses were dark. (He had tried earlier to buy the patent to Covent Garden Theatre, but he and his backers could not raise the necessary £60,000, and it went to Colman and his associates in 1767.)

Purchasing two wooden legs, one for daily use and the other — "equipped with silk stockings and a polished shoe with a gold buckle" — for more formal occasions and for the stage, Foote opened the Haymarket on 18 June 1766 with *The Minor*, in which he acted Mother Cole. On 1 July he reintroduced *The Orators*, now being able to imitate Faulkner with greater authority. As Zachary Fungus in *The Commissary*, revived on 15 July, he mocked himself by riding a hobbyhorse onto the stage. He also played Major Sturgeon and acted the title role in *The Credulous Hus-*

band, an afterpiece concocted from *The Old Bachelor* for Weston's benefit on 21 August. Although he did not act a role, Foote revived Bullock's *Woman is a Riddle*, for the first time in 15 years, for Davis's benefit on 31 July. In August he had stiff competition from the King's Theatre, which had been rented by Spranger Barry's company from Dublin. Barry in serious drama attracted capacity crowds. The two managers tried to avoid conflict, and Foote accommodated by lending out actors and playing in *The Minor* for Barry at the King's on 20 August—a gesture which, Foote wrote to Wilkinson, had injured his health. He cut his season short, after 21 performances, on 21 August. In his *Recollections*, O'Keeffe described Foote's personal agony backstage as he leaned against the wall, propped on his one leg, while the false one was being fastened to his stump.

In 1767 Foote purchased the Haymarket Theatre from the executors of Potter, the carpenter who had originally built it in the 1720s. He refurbished and remodeled the building, adding an upper gallery. He also purchased a house in back of the theatre on Suffolk Street, part of which he converted for wardrobe space and part for his town living quarters. (Later, in 1772, he bought the adjacent house to facilitate passage behind the theatre.) In a grand gesture Foote entertained all the workmen on the stage of the Haymarket on 20 April 1767 with a dinner that consisted of "three large buttocks of beef, eight legs of mutton, greens, &c. and three barrels of porter: a band of music played all the time of the dinner." Healths were drunk to the Royal Family and to Foote, and after the banquet the leftovers were carried home by the workers to their wives and children.

About that time he was attacked by George Savile Carey in *Momus—a Poem or a Critical examination into the merits of the performers and comic pieces of the Theatre Royal in the Haymarket*:

See F—te *the foremost of the mimic race,*
Amuse the town with scandal and grimace,
While private characters each scene adorn,
Held up by him to meet the public scorn
. . . .
This maimed mimic, favour'd so by fate,
That he might still more truly imitate;
With self-vain zeal a stupid laugh to raise,
He with a low audacity conveys
His borrow'd puns, with a sarcastic face,
(Join'd by the meanest of the acting race)
Without restraint his dearest friends expose,—
But F—te and friendship are eternal foes.

The summer of 1767 was disappointing, but in the next season he introduced on 30 May 1768 his new three-act comedy *The Devil Upon Two Sticks*, in which he acted the lame Devil and Weston acted Dr Last. A parody on the medical profession and punctuated with Foote's topical satires, the piece contributed enormously to a summer's profit—reported to have been between £3000 and £4000, most of which Foote promptly lost in an orgy of gambling at Bath. (That year he also built a house in North End Village, Fulham, closer to town than his place at Blackheath.)

Some of his losses were recouped in November 1768 when *The Devil Upon Two Sticks* brought him crowded houses at Smock Alley, where he had gone to play for Mossop, first having had to borrow £100 for travel expenses. After wintering in Paris he returned to London in February 1769. That summer he bolstered his company with Thomas Sheridan and Sparks from Dublin. Nothing new came from his pen, but he had a hand in Bickerstaffe's farce *Dr Last in his Chariot*, adapted from Molière's *Le Malade imaginaire*, which opened on 21 June 1769 with Foote play-

By permission of the Trustees of the British Museum

THOMAS WESTON as Dr Last and SAMUEL FOOTE as Dr Hellebore (the President)
in *The Devil Upon Two Sticks*

engraving by Finlayson, after Zoffany

ing Ailwou'd. On the sixth night Foote announced to the audience his intention of
dropping the unsuccessful piece—"I have
got rid of my wife—I have got rid of my
complaints—and, thank God, I have now
got rid of this piece"—but was persuaded
by Bickerstaffe to give it another three
times.

If ever an event was tailored for Foote's
barbs it was the great Shakespeare Jubilee
that Garrick was preparing at Stratford
for early September 1769. He sharpened up
his wit with satirical reference to the Jubilee in a revival of *The Author* during the
summer, then maliciously announced his
intention of going to Stratford in preparation for a farce he would write called *The*
Drugger's Jubilee. He never wrote it, but
the anticipation of Foote's ridicule tor-
mented the already frantic Garrick. With
Macklin, Foote had lodgings secured by
Garrick at the Bear Inn in nearby Bridge-
town. He passed the three days of the fiasco
by "indulging in the sallies of that wit,"
wrote Davies, "which seemed to please
everybody by sparing nobody." The Jubilee
spawned numerous anecdotes and outrageous stories, and most of them seem to
have emanated from Foote's scorn. He applied the most famous criticism, perhaps,
when he introduced his "Devil's Defini-
tion" into a performance of *The Devil*
Upon Two Sticks at the Haymarket on 13
September 1769:

A Jubilee, as it hath lately appeared, is a public invitation circulated and arranged by puffing, to go posting without horses to an obscure borough without representatives, governed by a Mayor and Alderman who are no magistrates, to celebrate a great poet whose works have made him immortal by an ode without poetry, music without melody, dinners without victuals and lodgings without beds; a masquerade where half the people appear barefaced, a horse race up to the knees in water, fireworks extinguished as soon as they were lighted, and a gingerbread amphitheatre, which like a house of cards, tumbled to pieces as soon as it was finished.

When Garrick's version of the Jubilee procession became so enormously successful on the stage of Drury Lane, Foote put out about town his plan for a delicious parody in which, instead of the expensive and gaudy costumes employed by Garrick, his players would be in rags. One tattered fellow would approach the single figure of elegance who held a wand and wore enormous white gloves in mockery of Garrick's stewardship and speak the familiar lines

By permission of the Trustees of the British Museum

SAMUEL FOOTE and SARAH GARDNER, in *The Lame Lover*

artist unknown

written by the Poet Laureate, Whitehead, when Garrick had assumed leadership of his theatre in 1747: "A Nation's taste depends on you, / Perhaps a Nation's virtue too." Whereupon the Steward, flapping his arms, would respond: "Cock a doodle doo!"

By the intercession of a mutual friend, the Marquis of Stafford, Foote agreed to give up the idea. But he could not resist one more taunt, this time threatening to employ a pasteboard puppet with a mask of Garrick's face. His response to the query if the puppet was to be life-size was "Oh no—not much above the size of Garrick."

By the middle of the summer of 1770 Foote had completed negotiations to lease the new Theatre Royal at Edinburgh from David Ross for the ensuing winter season. Ironically, the theatre had opened the year before in Shakespeare Square on the very spot that Whitefield had used for about 20 years as his preaching ground. According to Dibdin, Foote had taken a three-year lease from Ross at a rental of 500 guineas per year. The report in the London press on 27 July 1770, that Foote had engaged "to give Mr. Ross 900 l. for the use of Edinburgh theatre with the wardrobe and appurtenances" was probably exaggerated. About the middle of September Foote set out for the north with 28 actors from his summer company, including Woodward, who had been persuaded to leave his engagement at Covent Garden. His plans included, according to the press notice, a stop at Newcastle, "where he will perform eighteen or twenty nights."

The Edinburgh venture began on 17 November 1770 with *The Commissary* and *The Lying Valet*. Foote is known to have acted Shylock on 3 December and Fondlewife on 3 January 1771. The performance of *The Minor*, with him as Mother Cole, on 24 November predictably brought down the wrath of the local clergy, their objections made all the more urgent by the recent death of Whitefield in Massachusetts in September 1770. On 2 December the

Rev James Bain preached against the play in a sermon published as *The Theatre Licentious and Perverted, or a Sermon for Reformation of Manners*, to which Foote replied with *An Apology for the Minor in a Letter to the Rev. Mr. Baine. To which is added the Original Epilogue.* A press clipping in the British Museum, hand-dated December 1770, reports: "The audience at Mr. Foote's Theatre at Edinburgh calling out repeatedly for the *Minor*, and not acquiescing to the first excuse, Mr Foote himself made his appearance, and in Latin intimated to the house, that the principal subject of ridicule having paid nature's great debt, he humbly submitted to their reflection, whether such an exhibition would be seemly."

In his *Memoirs* of Foote, Cooke indicated that although he managed to pay his expenses for the Edinburgh season, Foote did not make enough money to warrant the bother. But Foote's own testimony indicates the contrary. He returned south about mid-March and wrote to Garrick from his recently purchased home at North End Village, Fulham, about his problems with the actor Sowdon, his opinion of Woodward, and his substantial profit (letter, undated, in the Forster Collection, Victoria and Albert Museum):

. . . I can readily account for Sowdon's silence; he wanted I suppose to leave the door open for a re-union, but that can never happen; his summer salary joined to what I saved by his secession at Edinburgh, puts into my pocket three hundred pounds of the debt: it is not impossible but (from his calling for payment just at this time) that he may accompany Barry in his expedition to Ireland; I think Shuter's cant word for cash is cork; it has not only metaphorically, but literally been a useful jacket to Sowdon, on which he has often navigated with great success over the Irish seas.

I have wrote to Sowdon, desiring him to fix a place and a day in the next week to receive his money. By the last advice from Scotland, the balance in my favour was £1022.6.3 which with some little matter the last week will produce, closes the account. Woodward has taken a last night for himself [2 March 1771, as Bobadil in *Every Man in his Humour*], and offered the public a regale that would disgrace even Bartholomew Fair, cette homme la est bien charlatan. One of my bookeepers died about six weeks since, the recommendation of an honest man for the office is a favour done me. . . .

No doubt it was that letter to which Garrick was referring when he wrote to Boswell at Edinburgh on 18 April 1771 that "Our Friend Foote had convinc'd Me that he has brought from Scotland a ballance of above one thousand pounds." Boswell had written earlier, on 30 March, that Foote had "made a Very good Campaign of it here," and that Woodward "has been exceedingly admired & has been a great support to the House," but that Mrs Jewell, Foote's favorite, had failed—"her poorness of figure & aukward inanimate action disgust us much. . . ." In his reply, Garrick wrote that Foote's account differed: that he was much followed, "Woodward was deserted," and Mrs Jewell "was much approv'd of." (Mrs Jewell, née Ann Edwards, a former servant of Foote, had been trained by him; when she married William Jewell, Foote's treasurer, in 1768 she incurred Foote's displeasure.)

In any event, Foote decided to give up the enterprise in Edinburgh after his first season and sold his lease in 1771, at a loss, to West Digges. When Digges was arrested for debt, Ross (with Murphy as his solicitor) sued Foote to recover two years' rent. The case was settled finally on 26 May 1774, in Ross's favor. According to another Footean anecdote, when Foote paid Ross he inquired if the Scot would be returning north the cheapest way; Ross replied, "I shall travel on *foot*," to which Foote retorted, "I am heartily sorry for that, for I know no man who more richly deserves horsing."

The fine comedian Henry Woodward greatly bolstered the Haymarket company in the summer of 1771, his former bitter differences with Foote evidently now patched up, at least temporarily. On 26 June Foote brought out a new comedy, *The Maid of Bath*, inspired by young Elizabeth Linley, the beautiful singer of Bath who the previous year had been forced by her parents into a marriage contract with the elderly Sir Walter Long. Eventually the contract was broken (and later she married Richard Brinsley Sheridan), but Miss Linley's sad though temporary plight created sufficient stir in society for Foote to recognize the potential of its treatment on the stage. With Foote as the miserly and lustful Flint, Weston as Billy Button, Woodward as Sir Christopher Cripple, and Mrs Jewell as Miss Linnet, with a prologue written by Garrick and spoken by Foote, and with an epilogue by Cumberland delivered by Mrs Jewell, *The Maid of Bath* played 25 nights to crowded houses. The opening-night audience, graced by Dr Johnson, Colman, Garrick, Goldsmith, Sir Joshua Reynolds, and Lord Littleton, gave "much applause" and at one point stopped the play, reported the *Theatrical Intelligencer*, "and required one speech repeated." That summer Foote made his first appearance on 19 August 1771 as Don Lewis in *Love Makes a Man*.

In September 1771 the press reported that Foote had cleared £3700 for the summer and that he had "set out on a tour to Paris, accompanied by Mr. Woodward &c." That was probably the visit recollected by Harry Angelo, during which Foote gave memorable dinners at the Hotel d'Angleterre for his French friends and delighted his guests with a malicious imitation of Garrick.

In December 1771 the London papers reported that the Haymarket dressing room and green room areas had been completely torn apart to enlarge the stage to twice its size for the purpose of accommodating Woodward's new pantomimes the next summer. But Woodward did not return to the company in 1772 and Foote never staged pantomimes, so the report may have been false or a mistake for some work being done on a house recently bought by Foote next to his house on Suffolk Street.

The 1772 summer campaign was marked by the introduction on 29 June of *The Nabob*, Foote's three-act comedy about the unprincipled exploiters of the East India trade. After the season, Foote's petition to the King on 21 September 1772 for permission to remain open during the winter months went unheeded—as Foote reputedly told Lord Mansfield, the King had "paid no more attention to it than if all the people of England had petitioned him." Nevertheless, in the winter Foote introduced a most extraordinary and novel production of his "*Primitive Puppet Show*" called "*The Handsome Housemaid; or, Piety in Pattens.*" Maria Macklin wrote her father on 3 February 1773 that the town was "big with Expectation of Foote's Puppet Shew." Although everyone, including Roscius himself, expected the production to be devoted largely to ridicule at Garrick's expense, actually it turned out to be a most effective satire of sentimental comedy. The apprehensive Garrick, it seems, had negotiated with Foote some four days before the opening, according to Horace Walpole's letter to the Countess of Upper Ossory, "and by the secret article of the treaty is to be left out of the puppet show."

The piece opened at the Haymarket on 15 February 1773 to a swollen house: "The croud was so great before six o'clock . . . that the Haymarket was impassable for above an hour; the doors of the Theatre were broken open, and great numbers entered the house without paying anything for their admission," reported the *Gazetteer and New Daily Advertiser*; "Several hats, swords, canes, cloaks, &c. were lost among the mob; three ladies fainted away, and a girl had her arm broke in endeavouring to get into the pit." At seven the performance

Harvard Theatre Collection

"Foote, the Devil, and Polly Pattens"

artist unknown

began with a long "Exordium" by the mercurial Foote. Then the curtain rose to discover "a figure as large as life, who is supposed to speak the *prologue*, on the affected illness and stiffness of players." As reported by the *General Evening Post* (20/23 February 1773): "Previous to this matter, Mr. *Foote* begged permission of the audience, 'that he might sit there to explain the *Grecian Chorus*, if any part of it should be misunderstood by the audience.'—Addressing himself to the puppet, he begged 'his actions might go along with his words, or he might as well have one of the actors from the theatres.' " An illustration in the *Macaroni and Theatrical Magazine* (February 1773) of "Foote, the Devil and Polly Pattens," reveals fully-modeled, life-size figures, with strings or wires attached. The *Morning Chronicle* account on 16 February described the figures as "constructed with admirable skill, . . . all exceedingly well dressed, their actions managed with great adroitness, and their features made striking and expressive."

But what promised to be an event of extreme theatrical ingenuity turned into a fiasco on the opening night. The upper gallery, finding the entertainment too short and subtle, created a disturbance and tore up some benches in protest of its announced repetition:

. . . At length it was agreed that the contest relative to the repetition of the Puppet Shew should be decided by holding up of hands when three to one appeared in favour of it. The Gentlemen in the boxes, and the greatest part of the pit, behaved with uncommon candour and propriety; but, from the illiberal, unmanly conduct of the gallery, it seemed as if some of the persons there had come to the theatre, not in hopes of seeing a *primitive,* but a *modern* puppet-shew, and that they grew out of temper because Punch, his wife Joan, and little Ben the Sailor, did not make their appearance.

With revisions which included the introduction of songs and Punch, the show was given at noon on 6 March and then a total of 17 times through 16 April. Those performances are not listed in *The London Stage*.

The *Primitive Puppet Shew*, having appeared only a month before the premiere of *She Stoops to Conquer*, is now acknowledged as a significant contribution to anti-sentimentalism. Foote never bothered to publish it, but the manuscript in the Huntington Library recently has been brought out in a comprehensive study by Samuel N. Bogorad and Robert G. Noyes (*Samuel Foote's Primitive Puppet-Shew*, a monograph of *Theatre Survey*, Fall 1973).

The summer of 1773 at the Haymarket included Foote's new piece, *The Bankrupt*, which was first performed on 21 July with the author as Sir Robert Riscounter. After an otherwise uneventful but moderately successful season (in which he also brought on but did not act in *She Stoops to Conquer*, after its opening at Covent Garden), Foote went to Dublin in November, where he presented *The Maid of Bath*, *The Nabob*, and other pieces for Thomas Ryder at Smock Alley, but without special impact. In his Dublin lodgings one night his bed caught fire while he was reading by candlelight; only the swift action of Jewell in extinguishing the fire saved him, as he wrote to Garrick on 31 December 1773, from being "reduced to ashes." After a return to London for a brief period, he then went to play at Edinburgh, arriving by 11 February 1774 and departing by 4 March. According to a northern journal he received £250 for acting seven nights at Edinburgh. Later he wrote to Wilkinson that on the journey he had "encountered more perils than in a voyage to the Indies. Not to mention mountains, precipices, savage cataracts, and savage men, I was locked up for near a week in a village [Moffat], dirty, dismal, and desolate, by a deluge of snow." He promised to visit Wilkinson at York on his return journey, but not to act for him, determined that "All my campaigns shall end with this place, and my future opera-

tions shall be confined to my own principality."

At Foote's principality all was well in 1774. In June he had written a special prologue to be used by Yates in that actor's attempt to open a second theatre in Birmingham. *The Cozeners*, his new play, opening on 15 July 1774 with Foote as Aircastle and containing topical allusions to the troubles brewing in Boston, did well enough. The recent years had been his best in terms of productivity, success, and calm. But Foote, now 53, was getting weary. After the season of 1774 his thoughts turned to retiring, and from Paris he wrote to Garrick: "To tell you the truth I am tir'd with racking my brains toiling like a horse and crossing Seas and Mountains in the most Dreary Seasons merely to pay Servants' wages and Tradesmen's Bills." He had instructed Jewell "to discharge the Lazy Vermin of my Hall, and let my Hall too if he can meet with a proper tennant, help me to one if you can." Garrick's reply, if there was one, has not survived, but certainly he could appreciate Foote's state of mind, since he himself in the previous year had determined to "retreat from the Theatre" but had been prevented by the sudden death of his partner, James Lacy, on 25 January 1774.

On 12 December 1774 Garrick wrote to his brother George that Foote had returned from the Continent and was "in great Spirits," so his holiday must have helped to dispel his melancholy. After taking the waters at Bath in the company of George Colman, Foote returned to London to prepare for the summer of 1775. He would come to regret not having followed his earlier instinct to extricate himself from theatrical management, for his worst trials were waiting. The next and final two years of his life were to be shocked by the reverberations of his unfortunate confrontation with the Countess of Bristol and the public scandal of charges of homosexuality against him.

Elizabeth Chudleigh, an audacious and scandalous woman whose conquests were rumored to have included even George II, had married the Duke of Kingston in 1769 but had first found it necessary to obtain a suit of Jactitation of Marriage from Captain Augustus John Hervey, whom she had married 20 years earlier but from whom she had been separated for some time. He was the brother and heir to the Earl of Bristol. Hervey, it was said, for a bribe of £10,000 from the Duke of Kingston, had helped to wipe away all evidence of his marriage. When Kingston died in 1773 he left his estate to Lady Elizabeth, cutting off his eldest nephew Evelyn Meadows with £500. Disinherited, Meadows, although he could not break the will, sought revenge by bringing charges of bigamy against the Duchess. He secured an indictment on 10 December 1774. The Duchess retreated to Calais for eight weeks and then appeared before the Court of the King's Bench in May 1775. Eventually, after considerable legal maneuvering, the trial was set for 15 April 1776.

With an eye ever on the main chance, Foote wrote a play with the original title of *The Siege of Calais*, which he later changed to *A Trip to Calais*. Full of indiscretion and garrulity, the piece was a transparent attack on the Duchess through its main character Lady Crocodile. Intending it to be his chief attraction for the summer of 1775, he assured interest with his customary puffing, but when he submitted the play in July to the Lord Chamberlain, it was rejected for performance, obviously as the result of pressure from the Duchess. Unable to perform it without a license, the infuriated Foote threatened to publish the play, whereupon the Duchess called in Foote and offered a bribe, which he rejected. Cross letters were exchanged, and accusations filled the air and the press. Foote won the contest of wit with the Duchess, but he claimed that the suppression of the play lost him £3000 that summer. Moreover, he

was seriously damaged by charges that he had tried to extort £2000 from the Duchess to prevent his publishing the play. To make matters even worse, William Jackson, the Duchess's champion and publisher of *The Public Ledger*, inspired rumors that Foote was homosexual.

After a brief continental holiday, Foote, desperate for funds, went to play for a while at Smock Alley during the Christmas season. According to Thomas Snagg, an Irish player, Foote "took away a great deal of money and spoiled our other nights." On 18 January 1776 his friend Thomas Weston died from drink. Although deeply grieved, Foote must have welcomed at that perilous time the tribute paid to him by Weston in his will:

As from Mr Foote I derived all my consequence in life, and as it is the best thing I am in possession of, I would, in gratitude, at my decease leave it to the said Mr Foote, but I know he neither stands in need of it as an author, actor, or as a man; the public have fully proved it in the two first, and his good nature and humanity have secured it to him in the last.

After a trial of five days which began on 15 April 1776 before the House of Lords, Elizabeth Chudleigh was convicted of bigamy and lost her title as Duchess of Kingston. She was spared further humiliation by being allowed to retain her title as Countess of Bristol. William Jackson, however, continued his vicious attacks on Foote as a homosexual. When Foote opened his season on 20 May 1776 with *The Bankrupt*, he was distraught and unsure of his reception. For many years he had been a crowd pleaser, but he was too agitated to realize that his faithful gallery friends would not desert him. They roared and applauded their confidence for many minutes; then Foote stepped forward to address them:

It was not my intention, after the charge that has been made against me, to appear before the public till I had an opportunity of proving my innocence; but as this charge was made at the critical point of time when I usually opened my Theatre, and having engaged as good a set of performers for your amusement as I could procure, it was the unanimous advice of my friends, that I should open my house, in confidence that the public were too noble, and too just, to discard an old servant for a mere accusation.

I am ready to answer every charge which can be brought against me; and have pursued such legal steps to clear my reputation from the virulent attacks of a public paper as will speedily bring the writer to an issue in the court of King's Bench, which has this day made the rule absolute against the publisher.

I beg leave to return my thanks for the marks you have now given me of your humanity and justice: permit me to promise you, that I will never disgrace your protection.

It was a warm and encouraging scene, but within two months, on 8 July, John Sangster, one of Foote's servants, charged him with an attempted homosexual assault. With the assistance of Jackson, who probably encouraged Sangster to make the accusation, a warrant was sought for Foote's arrest. Forewarned, Foote posted bail in advance, but Sangster and Jackson secured another warrant by claiming a second assault on Sangster. Foote's lawyers had the case postponed until December.

Meanwhile, Foote tried to salvage his season with a revision of the suppressed *A Trip to Calais*, which he brought out on 19 August 1776 as *The Capuchin*. He played the title role, and Palmer acted Dr Viper, the character he had substituted for Lady Kitty Crocodile; Viper represented Jackson. Foote's anger was too personal; the critic of the *St James's Chronicle* of 17/20 August 1776 found Viper "ineffectual because it is a Portrait of a Man too low for Public Notice." Despite alterations *The Capuchin* closed after nine nights.

On 9 December 1776 at the Court of the King's Bench, Foote's attorneys, among them Arthur Murphy, shattered Sangster's

charges by proving that Foote had not even been in London on 1 May 1776, the day on which the accuser claimed the assault had occurred. Testifying to his absence were Mr and Mrs Jewell, the Haymarket actor Peirce, and Thomas Davies, bookseller and former actor. After seven hours of testimony, and a summation by Lord Mansfield, presiding, the jury, not even leaving the box but conferring for a few minutes, declared him not guilty. Murphy dashed from the court room to Foote's house in Suffolk Street where, as Cooke related the scene:

Foote had been looking out of the window, in anxious expectation. . . . Murphy, as soon as he perceived him, waved his hat in token of victory . . . ran up stairs to pay his personal congratulations; but alas! instead of meeting his old friend in all the exultation of high spirits on this occasion, he saw him extended on the floor in strong hysterics; in which he continued near an hour before he could be recovered to any kind of recollection of himself, or the object of his friend's visit.

By early October Foote had begun negotiations with George Colman for the leasing of his Haymarket patent. They came to terms by 18 October 1776, but the transaction was kept secret at Foote's request until after his trial. Although the press had guessed at the new manager's identity by the end of October, the lease was not conveyed until 16 January 1777. (The patent remained in Foote's name until his death, when it expired; thereafter Colman operated on an annual license procured from the Lord Chamberlain.) Foote was to receive an annuity of £1600 in quarterly installments, as well as £500 for his unpublished plays: *The Trip to Calais, The Nabob, The Capuchin, The Maid of Bath, The Devil Upon Two Sticks*, and *The Cozeners*. Foote was required to offer Colman first opportunity at any future plays he might write. He also bound himself to act at no other place but the Haymarket.

Foote was articled to perform only six nights for Colman in 1777. When he acted in *The Nabob* on 30 May, "his cheeks were lank and withered, his eyes had lost all their wonted intelligence," according to Cooke's description, "and his whole person appeared sunk and emaciated." On 6 June he acted in *The Devil Upon Two Sticks*, but then shaking and fainting fits kept him off the stage until 7 July, when he appeared as Mrs Cole in *The Minor* and Cadwallader in *The Author*. *The Nabob* was repeated on the eleventh and *The Minor* and *The Author* on the twenty-fifth. Foote's last appearances on the stage came on 30 July 1777, as Flint in *The Maid of Bath* and Major Sturgeon in *The Mayor of Garratt*. He was announced to play in *The Devil Upon Two Sticks* on 6 August, but he suffered another attack at rehearsal, and *Rule a Wife and Have a Wife* was substituted. Several of his obituary notices suggest he was then partially paralyzed from a stroke. Foote's *Piety in Pattens* was played, with live actors, six times during the summer, but he did not perform in it.

On doctor's orders Foote took sea-baths at Brighton. He seemed recovered enough when he returned to London in late September to share his table with friends. Advised to spend the winter in the south of France, he set out for Dover where he lodged at the Ship Inn on 20 October. The next morning he was in high spirits at breakfast, but a chill put him back to bed about eleven. When he began to tremble violently, the doctors wanted to bleed him, but he adamantly refused. He died about two o'clock on the afternoon of 21 October 1777.

Even after his death rumors persisted. The *European Magazine*, for example, reported that he had died of an overdose of laudanum, "taken either by mistake or design," although the reporter inclined to believe the latter. Some reports indicated that he had died at Calais, as if some sort of retribution had overtaken him. Garrick wrote to Lady Spencer, in a letter presumably dated 22 October 1777: "Mr Foote dy'd a few days ago upon his landing at Calais. He had much wit, no feeling, sacrific'd friends and foes to a joke, & so has dy'd very little regretted even by his nearest acquaintance."

Foote's body was taken from Dover by his faithful servant William Jewell to the house on Suffolk Street. On Monday evening, 3 November 1777, according to the Abbey Registers (and not on 27 October as given by Trefman), three coaches of mourners attended the body to Westminster Abbey, where it was buried by torchlight in a private ceremony in the West Cloister. The register gives his age as 55, although he was closer to 57. No monument was erected to him in the Abbey. A memorial tablet, however, was placed in the southwest corner of St Mary's Church, Dover, by Jewell:

Sacred to the Memory of Samuel Foote, Esq,
Who had a tear for a friend
And a hand and a heart ever ready to relieve
the distressed.
He departed this life Octr. 21st, 1777 (on his journey to France) at the Ship-Inn, Dover, Aged 55 Years.
This Inscription was plac'd here by his Affectionate Friend——Mr William Jewel.

Foote's will was proved on 22 October 1777, the very day following his death. It had been drawn on 13 August 1768; evidently never revised, much of it may have become obsolete, since Foote had leased away to Colman in 1776–77 many of the theatrical prerogatives bequeathed therein, and it is not clear how long, if at all, Colman was required to pay the £1600 annuity to the estate after Foote's death. For example, Foote had directed that "my Theatre Royal in the Haymarket and all my buildings thereto belonging with the payment of ten shillings and six pence every night that any theatrical or other performances shall be publickly exhibited to be paid nightly to my Treasurer Wm. Jewell which I give him for his own use during my term." He also gave Jewell the right to a rent-free benefit every year and the trustees were to take particular care that this provision should be written into any manager's contract, so perhaps Foote himself had negotiated those terms with Colman. Also to be written into any contracts with managers was the right of Jewell to sell wine, tea, and fruit at the theatre, without paying fees for the privilege.

To his executors William Fitzherbert of Tipington, Derby, and Archibald Hamilton of Fleet Street, he left £50 each. In addition, Fitzherbert was to have Zoffany's painting of Foote as Major Sturgeon, and Hamilton his gold-headed crutched cane. (Perhaps that was the gold-headed cane which the actor Charles Holland had be-

SAMUEL FOOTE, as Instructor Puzzle

artist unknown

queathed to Foote in 1769.) The remainder of his real and personal estate was bequeathed to "My two Natural Children ffrancis ffoote and George ffoote," equally upon their reaching majority. If both died before that, then Jewell was to receive £1000 with the residue's interest reserved for the natural life of Foote's widowed mother Eleanor Foote. Upon her death, his brother Edward Goodere Foote would receive the inheritance. After his death it would go to Jewell.

No other relatives were mentioned in the will. Several months after Foote's death, Garrick received a letter dated 31 December 1777 from Mrs Eleanor Naylor, whose husband had stopped her income for over eight months, so that she was now in Fleet Prison. Asking for financial aid, she reminded Garrick that she was the daughter of a man named Dinely, "brother to the late Mr Foote"; presumably the brother referred to was John Foote (b. 1718), mentioned in the beginning of this notice.

Soon after Foote's death biographical sketches, anecdotes, and collections of *bons mots* and witticisms began to appear in profusion. Most of them were as exaggerated in truth as were the zestful theatrical caricatures created by Foote himself. As every biographer of Foote has emphasized, his entire life was characterized, perhaps caricatured, by extravagance. He was dubbed "the Moliere of his age," "Beau Nasty," and "Proteus." Foote often referred to himself as "Captain Timbertoe."

His enemies thought him a mountebank but they feared him. His friends did not trust him but entertained a healthy respect for his talents and achievements. Macklin, who often felt Foote's barbs, called him "a mere mimeograph, in every sense of the word." Upon Foote's death Johnson wrote to Mrs Thrale: "He was a fine fellow in his way; and the world is really impoverished by his sinking glories." But the great wordsmith understood the real lexical meaning of Foote's entertainments. He told Boswell once: "Why, Sir, when you go to see Foote, you do not go to see a saint; you go to see a man who will be entertained at your house, and then bring you on a publick stage, who will entertain you at his house, for the very purpose of bringing you on a publick stage. Sir, he does not make fools of his company; they whom he exposes are fools already; he only brings them into action." Yet, upon hearing that Foote intended to caricature him as well, Johnson's reaction, while perhaps couched in more wit, was no less irate than most. He threatened to beat the mimic with an oak stick. Fear "restrained him," Johnson told Boswell after receiving the news that Foote had decided to refrain; "he knew I would have broken his bones. I would have saved him the trouble of cutting off a leg; I would not have left him a leg to cut off."

As an actor Foote was not especially successful or even talented. "In short," wrote Davies, "Foote was a despicable player in almost all parts but those which he wrote for himself." He was accused of always lowering comedy into farce, ever distorting and exaggerating. His short, fat, and flabby person did not allow him wide range; yet with a bright eye and an undeniable intelligence he was superb in the ridiculous characters of his own creation. Although full of buffoonery, he possessed the talent for isolating the most telling physical and psychological weaknesses of his subjects. While often guilty of overly vicious lashing, his keen eye for character and skill with witty dialogue allowed him to provide brilliant sketches of contemporary manners. As a mimic he was unequalled in his day, except perhaps by Wilkinson, whom he had taught.

Recent assessments of Foote as a minor dramatist have pointed out that his influence against the sentimental drama should not be underestimated nor should his literary style be underrated. "He is not, of course, truly an Aristophanes or a Moliere," writes Samuel N. Bogorad (*Samuel Foote's*

Primitive Puppet-Shew), "but he challenges our attention for extraordinary qualities."

In society he was often characterized as a cruel, heartless nuisance who thrived on giving pain to others. In *The Actor* (1764), Robert Lloyd castigated him:

> *But let the generous actor still forbear*
> *To copy features with a mimic's care!*
> *'Tis a poor skill which ev'ry fool can*
>   *reach,*
> *A vile stage custom honour'd in the*
>   *breach.*
> *Worse as more close, the disingenuous*
>   *art*
> *But shows the wanton looseness of the*
>   *heart.*
> *When I behold a wretch of talents mean,*
> *Drag private foible on the public scene,*
> *Forsaking Nature's fair and open road*
> *To mark some whim, some strange peculiar mode,*
> *Fir'd with disgust I loathe his servile*
>   *plan*
> *Despise the mimic, and abhor the man.*

One of his lifelong friends, Arthur Murphy, who seems to have held a true affection for him, began a biography of Foote, probably on the suggestion of Johnson, but abandoned the project. Among Murphy's papers, however, is found a bitter but perhaps objective sketch:

He was civil to your face, and seldom put you out of humour with yourself; but you paid for his civility the moment you were out of his company, and were sure of being made ridiculous; yet he was not as malignant as some men I have known; but his vanity and the desire he had of showing his wit made him run into satire and detraction. He loved titled men, and was proud of their company, though he gave airs of treating them with scorn. He was licentious and profligate, and frequently made a jest of religion and morality. He told a story very well, and added many pleasant circumstances of his own invention to heighten it, and could speak plausibly on grave subjects; but he soon grew tired of serious conversation, and returned naturally to his favourite amusement, mimickry, in which he did not excel; for he was coarse and unfair, and drew caricatures. But entertained you more than a closer mimick.

Murphy's portrait of him in the character of Dashwould in *Know Your Own Mind* (Covent Garden, 22 February 1777) was more gentle and generous; he had Bygrove respond to Sir John's remark that Dashwould had no harm in him: "No harm in him? . . . He has a wit to ridicule you; invention to frame a story of you; humour to help it about; and when he has set the town a laughing, he puts on a familiar air, and shakes you by the hand."

It was Sir Joshua Reynolds who was supposed to have said that "by Foote's buffoonery and broad-faced merriment, private friendship, public decency, and everything estimable among men were trod under foot." Most people saw Foote in that light —as selfish, egotistical, clever, and dangerous. Testimony could be heaped upon testimony. He seems to have enjoyed few true and close friends. There was a strong affection between him and Jewell. His dearest friend was Sir Francis Delaval. When he died on 8 August 1768, Foote "burst into tears, retired to his room, and saw no company for three days." Yet on the fourth day he could not suppress his quip on the dissection of his friend's head: "And what will they get there? I'm sure I have known poor Frank for these five and twenty years, and I could never find anything in it."

Foote's relations with Garrick fluctuated. Garrick's letters to him are full of respect, although sometimes taunting, and frequently sincerely affectionate. If Garrick was the superior conversationalist, then Foote was better at repartee, and it was said that Garrick feared his tongue more than any other in London. Foote knew Garrick's vulnerability, but most of his threats against him were intended to bait the great man and never materialized in direct lampoons. Foote, in a real sense, owed much to Garrick. Although Garrick seems not to have extended himself in helping Foote obtain his rights to summer productions, he did not use his enormous influence to deny him. He often gave Foote money and performed other favors for him. Wilkinson's statement that while they maintained the uneasy appearance of friendship they hated each other seems exaggerated, though if Foote envied Garrick that might be understandable. Garrick's success was immediate, enormous, and ever-increasing as actor, patentee, dramatist, socialite, and man of influence and renown. To each of these conditions Foote aspired; in each, despite constant struggle, he achieved incomplete success and acceptance.

It was even Foote's mischance to choose the wrong year in which to retire as patentee of the Haymarket, for the town and country had only just gone through the emotions of Garrick's farewells from the stage. "Poor Foote sighs his soul out for the loss of his *dramatic diadem*," wrote Henry Bate to Garrick on 11 June 1777; "is the man mad? Or does he think that mankind will be apt to make no distinction between the two *theatrical abdications* of 1776, and view one monarch retiring by his own choice, crowned with never-fading laurels, and the other driven to it by the reproaches of his own conscience, no *reckoning made 'with all his imperfections on his head.*' "

Most audiences delighted in Foote's impertinence, and wondered in anticipation of his next manoeuvre. Foote had a strong instinct for survival which seems to have caught their imagination. "One species of wit he has in an eminent degree, that of escape," said Johnson. "You drive him into a corner with both hands; but he's gone, Sir, when you think you have got him— like an animal that jumps over your head." The public seems to have been captivated by the man, who, as one biographer has put it, "lived in a blaze and died in a mist." Perhaps the best epitaph was provided by Edward Gibbon, who had a liking for London in the summer; he told his sister, "when I am tired of the Roman Empire I can laugh away the Evening at Foote's Theatre."

A long list of essays, tracts, attacks, counterattacks, and other polemical works which were occasioned by Foote's life and activities will be found in Arnott and Robinson's revised edition of Lowe's *Bibliographical Account of English Theatrical Literature* (1970). Lists of Foote's numerous publications are in Nicoll's *History of the English Drama 1660–1900* and *The Cambridge Bibliography of English Literature*. Editions of his collected plays were published in 1778, 1786, 1797, 1799, 1809, and 1830. In addition to numerous sketches and memoirs printed in the monthlies and prefaced to his collected works, biographies of Foote's life include the anonymous *Memoirs of the Life and Writings of Samuel Foote, Esq., the English Aristophanes: To Which are added the Bon-mots, Repartees, and Good Things Said by that Great Wit and Excentrical Genius* [1777]; *Wit for the Ton! The Convivial Jester, or Sam Foote's Last Budget opened. With Authentic Remarks on his Life and Writings* (1777); William Cooke, *Memoirs of Samuel Foote, Esq.* (1805); John Forster, *Samuel Foote* in *Historical and Biographical Essays* (Vol. II, 1858); Percy Fitzgerald, *Samuel Foote* (1910); Mary M. Belden, *The Dramatic Work of Samuel Foote* (1929); Simon Trefman, *Sam. Foote, Comedian* (1971). The personality of Samuel Foote also figures heavily in the many letters, memoirs, and books by and about such persons as Garrick, Johnson, the Colmans, Murphy, and Wilkinson. In the Huntington Library is a typescript by John Wells Wilkinson, entitled "The Life and Works of Samuel Foote." It consists of five volumes, treating Foote's life up to age 24; copies of that manuscript are in the British Museum and the Bristol University Library.

Portraits of Samuel Foote include:

1. By Jean François Colson, painting dated Paris 1769. In the National Portrait Gallery. This portrait was engraved by: S. Freeman as a plate to Mrs Inchbald's *Collection of Farces*, published by Longman, 1809; W. Reade, undated; W. Ridley as a plate to Parsons's *Minor Theatre*, 1794; C. Watson as frontispiece to W. Cooke's *Memoirs* of Foote, 1805; and an unknown engraver, published by Sherwood, Gilbert & Piper.

2. By Thomas Gainsborough, painting. This portrait was in the Wiltshire sale of 25 May 1867 but now is not traceable. According to E. K. Waterhouse, *Checklist of Portraits by Thomas Gainsborough* (Walpole Society, vol 33), "It was probably not the 30 × 25 formerly in the Booth Tarkington collection, Indianapolis, and with John Levy, New York, 1949—which was a picture of the early 1760's and did not represent Foote."

3. By Francis Hayman, pen, ink, and Indian wash drawing. In the British Museum. Foote is depicted with arms outspread, exclaiming "What is all this?" A crude engraving, by an unknown engraver, inscribed as "Drawn from the Life & Engraved in May's Buildings Covent Garden 1747," is in the Folger Shakespeare Library.

4. By C. Maucourt, painting, 1764. This portrait was put up for auction at Christie's on 5 March 1937 (lot 153) but was not sold. The owner at the time was A. S. Davis of South Kensington.

5. From the studio of Joshua Reynolds, painting. In the Garrick Club. The original belonged to Lady Burton and was painted about 1767. The Garrick Club portrait is evidently one of two studio replicas: one was owned by Caleb Whiteford and was sold at Christie's on 5 May 1810 to Lockyer for 50 guineas; the other was sold at Christie's on 15 March 1822 and was bought back by the owner, Penny, for 20½ guineas.

Engravings of the Reynolds in slight variations were done by: T. Blackmore, published by W. W. Ryland, 1771; Cooper as a plate to *Biographical Magazine*, published by Harrison, 1795; W. Greatbach twice, one undated, the other as a plate to *Bentley's Miscellanies*, 1837; T. Priscott, published by C. Dyer; S. W. Reynolds, published by Molteno & Graves, 1835; an unknown engraver as a plate to *Universal Magazine*, printed for J. Hinton; and an unknown engraver, with amorini holding garland, undated.

6. By George Romney, painting. At Knole. Copied from Reynolds.

7. By Thomas Worlidge, miniature on ivory. In the Victoria and Albert Museum.

8. By John Bacon, bust sculpture. Exhibited at the Royal Academy, 1778.

9. Engraved portrait by W. Arndt. Published in Berlin, 1796.

10. Engraved portrait by R. Brookshaw, after F. Cotes. Published by Haines & Brookshaw, Paris.

11. Engraved portrait by unknown artist. Published as frontispiece to *The English Aristophanes*, 1777.

12. Engraved portrait by unknown artist. Titled "Mr F——te, Orator and Mimick." This is a copy from A. Pond's etching of Ghezzi's caricature of the Italian singer Carnacci.

13. As Buck in *The Englishman Return'd from Paris*. Drawn and engraved by G. Smith. Published by C. Sheppard.

14. As Mrs Cole in *The Minor*. Black and colored chalk drawing by Francis Cotes. In the British Museum.

15. As Mrs Cole. Engraving by W. Walker, after Dodd. Published as a plate to *New English Theatre*, 1777.

16. As Mrs Cole. By anonymous engraver. Published as a plate to an edition of the play, by I. Wenman, 1777. A reverse engraving, vignette in rectangle, also appeared, undated.

17. As Mrs Cole. By anonymous engraver. Published by J. Smith and R. Sayer.

18. As Dr Hellebore (the President) with Thomas Weston as Dr Last in *The Devil Upon Two Sticks*. Painting by John Finlayson. In the National Theatre, London. This painting was done *en grisaille*, in preparation (?) for Finlayson's mezzotint of the picture in 1769, which was exhibited by him at the Society of Artists in 1770. It is a copy of the painting by John Zoffany described below.

19. As Dr Hellebore with Weston as Dr Last in *The Devil Upon Two Sticks*. Painting by Johann Zoffany, exhibited at the Society of Artists in 1769, at the British Institute in 1814 and 1840, at the New Gallery in 1891, and elsewhere, from the Collection of the Earl of Carlisle. It is now owned by the Hon George Howard at Castle Howard. See also above, No 18. Another painting attributed to Zoffany and sometimes titled "Foote and Weston in Dr. Last" is in the National Theatre, but the identification of the artist and the actors remains problematical. For a detailed discussion of this latter painting see Mander and Mitchenson, *The Artist and The Theatre*, No 33.

20. As Dr Hellebore. By anonymous engraver. Published by Smith and R. Sayer, 1769.

21. As Dr Hellebore. By anonymous engraver. Variant of No 20, printed for J. Smith and R. Sayer.

22. As Dr Hellebore. By anonymous engraver. No inscription. In the British Museum.

23. As Dr Squintum in *The Minor*, delivering the epilogue. Engraving by Cook, after D. Dodd. Published by Fielding & Walker, 1779.

24. As Fondlewife in *The Old Bachelor*. Colored drawing on vellum by J. Roberts. In the British Museum. Engraved by Thornthwaite as a plate to *Bell's British Theatre*, 1776 and 1795.

25. As Fondlewife. Engraving by W. Walker, after J. J. Barralet, as a plate to the *New English Theatre*, 1776.

26. As Gomez in *The Spanish Fryar*. By anonymous engraver. Published as a plate

to the *Hibernian Magazine*, November, 1777.

27. As Instructor Puzzle. By anonymous engraver. Undated.

28. As the Lecturer. By anonymous engraver. Published by I. Wenman, 1777.

29. As Major Sturgeon, with Robert Baddeley as Sir Jacob Jollup, in *The Mayor of Garratt*. Painting by Johann Zoffany. Owned by the Hon George Howard at Castle Howard. An engraving by J. G. Haid was published by Boydell, 1765. The figure of Sir Jacob Jollup was at one time believed to be that of Mr Hayes, who played the role in the first performance at the Haymarket on 20 June 1763. In the catalogue of the "Georgian Playhouse" exhibition at the Hayward Gallery in 1975, the painting is said to have been based on the performances given at Drury Lane between 30 November and 7 December 1763, when Baddeley played the role. A smaller version of the painting was owned by Mrs David Gubbay in 1931.

30. As Smirk in *The Minor*. By anonymous engraver. Undated.

31. As Sir Thomas Lofty in *The Patron*. Engraving by Taylor. Printed as a plate to an edition of the play published by Harrison, 1780.

32. As Zachary Fungus in *The Commissary*. Engraving by Terry. Printed as a plate to an edition of the play published by Harrison, 1779.

33. In a scene from the *Primitive Puppet-Shew*, titled "Foote, the Devil and Polly Pattens," depicting Foote with the life-size puppets. By anonymous engraver. Published as a plate to *Macaroni and Theatrical Magazine*, February 1773.

34. "Mr Foote and Mrs Gardner, in the Characters of two Serjeants at Law, with other droll Figures which form the first scene of the third Act of the Lame Lover." By unknown engraver. In the British Museum, as frontispiece to *Wit for the Ton! The Convivial Jester; or, SAM FOOTE's Last Budget Opened. The Lame Lover* was

first performed at the Haymarket on 22 June 1770; Foote acted Sir Luke Limp, and Sarah Gardner acted Mrs Circuit.

35. A crude oval engraving of Foote, with a foot below, appeared on the title page of a *Sodom and Anais, / A Satire / Inscrib'd to /* [here the picture] */ Esqr. / alias, the DEVIL upon two Sticks* (1777), the twenty-nine-page pamphlet by the Rev Jackson upon Foote as an alleged sodomite.

A painting attributed to Johann Zoffany, now at the National Theatre, at one time was believed to be of Foote, perhaps delivering a prologue or epilogue. It has been more recently retitled "A Gentleman (Captain Wilts?) in Masquerade Costume: The Times (1769)." For a discussion of this painting see Mander and Mitchenson, *The Artist and the Theatre*, No 41. Foote was also alluded to or depicted in a number of caricatures, some of which are described in the British Museum *Catalogue of Political and Personal Satires*.

Fopperwell, Mr ɪfl. 1775ɪ, *singer*.
On 30 October 1775 at the Haymarket Theatre a single performance was given of *Love in a Village* with Mr Fopperwell as Hodge.

Forbes, Elizabeth *d. 1807, actress*.
Mrs Elizabeth Forbes was a member of the company at Richmond in 1799, during which time she lived at No 26, South Street, Grosvenor Square. She signed her full name to articles of agreement with James Winston, the manager. Advertised as from Richmond, she acted at Dublin in 1799–1800 and then was at Shrewsbury in 1800, at Manchester in 1800 and 1801, and at Guernsey in 1802. At Plymouth, when she gained £16 at her benefit in the fall of 1802, she was described by the *Monthly Mirror* in December 1802 as having merit "of a very inferior kind," which caused her to be used less than expected. In a letter to that journal in January 1803, which she signed as Eliza Forbes, she contradicted the

criticism: "I performed upwards of *forty* characters, and those *all principal*, in three months, bills of which I still have by me. I have the *satisfaction* and *happiness* to *know* I left Plymouth *regretted* as an *actress*, and *esteemed* as a *woman*." In March 1805 she acted at Coventry. While touring with Anderson and Faulkner's company she died at Durham on 16 April 1807.

Forbes, Margaret, later Mrs William Miell [*fl.* 1765–1787?], *singer, actress.*

Mrs Margaret Forbes, who sang at Finch's Grotto Gardens, Southwark, in August 1765, made her stage debut at Drury Lane Theatre on 1 November 1768 as Arbaces in *Artaxerxes*, an opera written by her teacher Dr Arne. In his diary, the prompter William Hopkins commented that Mrs Forbes had "a small figure—a good voice, was well received, and went decently through the part." She repeated the role on 16 and 23 November and 7 December. During the summer of 1769 Mrs Forbes sang at Marylebone Gardens, singing at her benefit on 27 July in *Love and Innocence*; she also performed there for Mrs Pinto's benefit on 10 August and for Hook's benefit on 17 August. For her own benefit at the Haymarket Theatre on 14 December 1770 she played Camillo (with a song in character) in *The Mistake* and Leonora in *The Padlock*. Mrs Forbes acted at Norwich in the season of 1771–72 and the following summer returned to Marylebone Gardens, where she sang an *Ode* by Arnold and in *The Coquet* and *The Magnet*.

Sometime before 26 May 1773 Mrs Forbes began to live with William Miell (1753–1795), a northern actor who in 1768 had been at the Haymarket Theatre; on that date it was recorded in the Committee Books of the Norwich Theatre that Mr and Mrs Miell's application for an advance of £20 would be rejected unless they signed articles for 1773–74. The Miells, however, went to Dublin in 1773–74, she

making her debut at Smock Alley Theatre on 13 October 1773, announced as from Norwich. They returned to the latter city for 1774–75. She also acted at York in 1776–77 and 1777–78, at King's Lynn in 1776, and at Bath in the summer of 1778. "She had a powerful voice," according to Tate Wilkinson the York manager, "but not a temper that in harmony delighted."

The Miells evidently were never married by ceremony or license. William was buried at St Chad's, Shrewsbury, on 16 December 1795, at the age of 42. Probably the will of the William Miell who lived at Furnivall's Inn Court in the City of London in 1787 but who, according to a notation in the probate on 1 February 1797, was "late of Shrewsbury," belongs to the actor. In that will, made on 26 April 1787, William Miell left an unspecified estate in trust "to maintain educate and apprentice . . . the two infants William Benjamin Miell Who is now at the Reverend Mr Bowmans Academy and Amelia Miell Who is now with *my truly loving and unnatural wife* in Jermyn Street Saint James." Amelia no doubt was the daughter of William and Margaret Meill who was baptized at St Michael le Belfrey, York, on 22 May 1777. Administration of William Miell's estate was granted on 1 February 1797 to his son William Benjamin Miell who had obviously reached his majority by that date. Mrs Miell was not mentioned by Christian name in the probate nor was there any indication that she was still alive at the time of its registration.

Forcade, Miss [*fl.* 1750], *dancer. See* FORCADE, ANNE.

Forcade, Anne [*fl.* 1749–1750], *dancer.*

Miss Anne "Foulcade" and Master Maltere made their first appearance on any stage on 19 December 1749 at Drury Lane dancing *The Swedish Gardeners* and *The Wooden Shoe Dance*. Though there was a second Miss "Foulcade" who danced at the same house in 1750, it is probable that most of the citations refer to Anne. She was called Miss "Forcad" when she danced in *Comus* on 24 January 1750, so she was very likely the daughter of Leonard and Mary Ann Forcade, who had been married in London in 1735. Though the spelling of the surname of both parents and children varied in the playbills, we have chosen to use the spelling found in the Portuguese Embassy Chapel registers.

Anne Forcade appeared during the 1749–50 season at Drury Lane in a number of untitled specialty dances and was seen with Master Maltere in *La Sabotière*, with "The Little Swiss" in *The Black Joke*, and alone in a tambourin dance. At her shared benefit with three others on 1 May 1750 she was joined by Master Maltere and the second Miss Forcade (her sister, we would suppose) in a wooden shoe dance. Anne also performed *Les Fantasies de la dance* by herself and with young Maltere presented a louvre and minuet. At Drury Lane that season was a "Mrs Mimi" who was, we conjecture, her mother, Mary Ann Forcade.

Forcade, Leonard ₍fl. 1734–1735₎, performer.

Leonard Forcade (or Fourcade, Foulcade) was a member of Francisque Moylin's troupe when it performed at the Haymarket Theatre and Goodman's Fields in 1734–35, but his specialty is not known. Forcade married Mary Ann Joseph Desprez at the Portuguese Embassy Chapel on 19 March 1735. She was, it seems, the actress and dancer in the troupe who was usually called Miss or Mrs Mimi. Their marriage was witnessed by Charles Lesage, who was doubtless the elder of two actors named Lesage in the company, and by Louis Desprez, called de Verneuil, also a member of the troupe and probably the father or brother of the bride. Our guess is that the two Misses Forcade (or Foulcade) who

danced in England in 1750 were the fruits of the marriage.

Forcade, Mme Leonard, Mary Ann Joseph, née Desprez, called de Verneuil ₍fl. 1734–1750₎, actress, dancer.

In the entry of Monsieur de Verneuil in the fourth volume of this work we tentatively identified Mlle Mimi de Verneuil as the daughter of the de Verneuil couple who performed in Francisque Moylin's troupe in London in 1734–35. We have since found information in the marriage registers of the Portuguese Embassy Chapel which would seem to confirm our original conjecture, correct our notion that Mimi de Verneuil and Mimi "Fourçade" were two different people, and raise some new questions.

At the Chapel on 19 March 1735 Leonard Forcade married Mary Ann Joseph Desprez. Present as witnesses were other members of the French acting company: Charles Lesage and Louis Desprez "dit de Verneuill" and (his wife?) Maria Francisca. Louis Desprez, or de Verneuil, was probably the father or brother of the bride, and the theatrical advertisements citing Mimi de Verneuil very likely refer to Mary Ann Forcade before she was married. As was often the case in playbills of the time and with performers, designations of Miss and Mrs were not always consistent, and visiting foreigners sometimes complicated matters further by using their Christian names or stage names.

We conjecture, then, that our subject was the "Mrs Mimi" who acted Eliante in *Le Français à Londres* at the Haymarket Theatre on 9 December 1734, the "Miss Mimi" who was Angélique in *Le Joueur* on 13 December, the "Mrs Mimie" who played Isabella in *Arlequin balourd* and danced Pierrette in a chaconne on 27 December, the "Mrs Mimi" who in January 1735 was a Shepherdess in *Le Festin de Pierre*, Fatime in *Zaire*, and Dorimene in *Le Bourgeois Gentilhomme*, the "Miss

Verneuil" who danced *Pierrot and Pierrette* with the younger Lesage on 13 February, the "Miss Mimi Verneuil" who shared a benefit with Verneuil and Mrs Verneuil on 24 March, and the "Mrs Mimi Fourcade" who played Salomith in *Athalie* on 16 April. She was cited as Mrs Mimi Fourcade again on 2 June when the company concluded their engagement at the Haymarket with a grand ballet. The company played twice at the Goodman's Fields Theatre, on 23 May and 4 June.

On 9 November 1749 at Drury Lane a "Mrs Memi" danced in *The Savoyard Travellers*; on 27 and 28 November "Mlle Memi" was a Shepherdess in *Acis and Galatea*, a new dance entertainment; and the following season on 27 November 1750 "Mad Mimi" was a Bird Catcher in *The Bird Catchers*. That woman we take to have been our subject, because at Drury Lane in 1749 and 1750 were two young girls, Ann "Foulcade" (sometimes "Forcade") and another Miss "Foulcade." Those girls, both dancers, were, we would guess, the daughters of Leonard and Mary Ann Forcade, making their debuts, with their mother serving as chaperone and working at the theatre as a dancer. Leonard Forcade seems not to have been with them, or if he was he did not perform.

The new information from the Portuguese Embassy Chapel registers has helped clarify some matters, but it raises a question. The name Desprez has not otherwise been found in connection with any performer called de Verneuil, and the registers seem to identify the wife of de Verneuil as Maria Francisca rather than Marie-Louise, as Fuchs has it in his *Lexique* and as we conjectured in our de Verneuil entry. Until more information comes to light the matter must remain a mystery.

Forcer, Francis *c. 1650–1705, violinist, composer, impresario, dancing master.*

Francis Forcer was born about 1650. On 30 July 1673 he obtained a license to marry Jane Taylor of Worplesdon, Surrey; Forcer was then living in the parish of St Bartholomew by the Exchange and was said to be 23 years of age and a bachelor. (Or was our subject the "Franses Forster" who married a Mary Milles at St James, Clerkenwell, on 9 March 1672?) According to Forcer's will of 1705 he and his wife had a son Francis and a daughter who became Mrs Raynton (wife of the dancer Rainton who died in 1732?), and it is probable that the Denis Forcer, son of Francis and Jane, who was baptized at St Bride, Fleet Street, on 26 December 1679 was also their son.

Some of Forcer's songs were published in Playford's *Choyce Ayres and Dialogues* in 1679 and others in *The Theatre of Music* (1685–1687). In 1684 he was one of the four stewards for the St Cecilia's Day celebrations, and on 30 September 1686 he was probably the "Mr fforcell" who helped John Blow and Henry Purcell judge the quality of a new organ built by Bernard Smith for St Katherine Kree. Though Forcer was not a prolific or distinguished composer, he wrote some songs for *The Virtuoso* and *Abdelazer* in 1676 and *The Orphan* in 1680. Arundell in *The Story of Sadler's Wells* states that Forcer was also a dancing master (and, consequently, a fiddler) and formed a partnership with the impresario Sadler as early as 1684.

About 1697 Forcer and James Miles leased Sadler's Wells, the popular pleasure garden and spa in Islington. There they provided musical entertainment, as Sadler had done earlier. By 1699, however, Forcer seems to have given up his share in the management.

Forcer made his will on 20 January 1705. To his son Francis he left all his freehold property in Silver Street in Durham and his interest in two houses in Plow Yard, Fetter Lane, Holborn. To his daughter Mrs Raynton he bequeathed two silver salvers and a silver coffer, and to her son William he left a large silver tankard. He made his son Francis his executor and residuary legatee. Francis Forcer the elder died within a few months of making his will; it was proved on 30 April 1705.

Forcer, Francis c. 1677–1743, proprietor.

Francis Forcer was born about 1677, the son of the Restoration musician of the same name. His father was associated with James Miles in the operation of Sadler's Wells, the pleasure garden and spa, in the late 1690s. Young Forcer attended Merchant Taylor's School and Lincoln College, Oxford, and was called to the bar in 1703. His father died in 1705, making Francis his executor and residuary legatee as well as leaving him property in Holborn and in the city of Durham. Perhaps the younger Forcer was in some way concerned with Sadler's Wells before his father died, but not until the death of James Miles in 1724 did he become deeply involved. He had married Miles's daughter, the widowed Frances Tompkins; Miles left to her and her two sons, Henry and John Tompkins, most of his possessions. Miles had, from 1717, kept a booth at Stourbridge Fair, outside Cambridge, and in 1725 Forcer succeeded to it and perhaps also to Sadler's Wells.

In 1730 Forcer was granted a lease of the Wells by Thomas Lloyd, the ground landlord, and that year (his opening year, claims Arundell in *The Story of Sadler's Wells*) he offered patrons *The Prisoner's Opera*, among other musical entertainments, plus tumbling, vaulting, and rope dancing. In 1735 Forcer petitioned for a special clause in the Licensing Act (then being prepared) to allow his operation to continue. In his plea he boasted that the Wells had been a place of good reputation for over 40 years, that the amusements there consisted of music, rope dancing, and other activities of the body, and short pantomimes, all in dumb show. He noted that the Wells never opened until about the middle of March and continued only until the end of August—thus he was not in serious competition with the patent houses. He charged no admission and received money only for wine, liquor, and other beverages sold there. The petition was rejected.

In his *Roxburghe Revels* (1837) Haslewood quoted a dreadful poem, *New River* by William Garbott, written about 1742 and describing the Wells during Forcer's proprietorship:

> *Thro' Islington then glides my best lov'd*
> *theme,*
> *And Miles's Garden washes with his*
> *stream:*
> *Now F——r's garden is its proper name,*
> *Tho' Miles the man was, who first got it*
> *fame;*
> *And tho' it's own'd Miles first did make*
> *it known,*
> *F——r improves the same, we all must*
> *own.*

At the Wells patrons could sit under the shade trees, drink, smoke, fish, or watch the entertainment.

> *The famous Tumbler lately is come o'er,*
> *Who was the wonder of the other shore:*
> *France, Spain, and Holland, and High-*
> *Germany,*
> *Sweden, and Denmark, and fam'd Italy,*
> *His active feats did with amazement see,*
> *Which done by Man they thought could*
> *never be:*
> *Amongst the rest, he falleth from on*
> *high,*
> *Head foremost from the upper gallery,*
> *And in his fall performs a Somerset,*
> *The women shriek, in dread he'll break*
> *his neck,*
> *And gently on his feet comes to the*
> *ground,*
> *To the amazement of beholders round—*

By 1734, when Forcer made his will, he had acquired a freehold piece of waste ground which formed part of Mile End Green, and he had a copyhold estate in Ealing. The will, dated 17 December 1734, described Forcer as of the parish of St James, Clerkenwell. The Mile End Green property, Forcer stated, was still in mortgage for £500 to Robert Moreton and was in lease to the City of London for a yearly rent of £75. That property Forcer willed to his (second) wife Catherine during her life and to his only daughter Frances after Catherine's death. Forcer directed that his lease on Sadler's Wells, where he then lived, plus all the Wells' implements and household stuff, should be sold to pay off the mortgage on the Mile End Green property. To his daughter Frances (Mrs George Savage) he willed his copyhold estate in Ealing. He asked that John Bell and Thomas Besley serve as guardians to Frances, but this directive he later crossed out.

On 9 April 1743 after a few days illness, Frances Forcer died. The papers reported that he had been "a kind and indulgent Husband, a tender and loving Father, a generous Friend, and a Good Master [of the Wells]. In short he had all the necessary Qualifications to render a Person a Compleat Gentleman, which makes his death universally lamented by all those who had the pleasure of his Acquaintance. We hear the usual Diversions will be carried on by his Widow." Francis Forcer was buried on 13 April 1743 at St James, Clerkenwell, his name in the parish register being spelled "Forser" and his age given as 66. The amusements at Sadler's Wells were discontinued at his death but advertised as beginning again on 14 April, the day after his burial. Perhaps his widow Catherine did carry on as proprietress of the Wells, though the next known proprietor was John Warren.

Forcer is said to have been a tall, athletic gentleman, and he apparently carried on his work with great energy. To the Wells he attracted such performers as the tumbler Dominique (celebrated in Garbott's poem), Baudouin, Froment, Davenport and his wife, Mrs Woodward, Mr and Mrs Rayner, and the famous ropedancer Kerman.

The parish registers of St James, Clerkenwell, contain several references which probably concern the Sadler's Wells manager: on 5 November 1721 Elizabeth, the daughter of Francis and Frances Forcer, was baptized; perhaps she was the "Elizabeth Forser" of Red Lyon who was buried on 26 December 1722. On 8 August 1725 Mary Forcer of Sadler's Wells was buried, and on 28 August 1726 Frances Forcer was buried. The latter was probably Francis Forcer's first wife.

Forcer, Mrs Francis the second, Catherine [fl. 1743], *proprietress?*
See **Forcer, Francis** c. 1677–1743.

Ford. *See also* **Forde** and **Thornton, Henry F.**

Ford, Mr [fl. 1792], *actor.*
A Mr Ford played Heli in *The Mourning Bride* in a specially-licensed benefit performance for Silvester at the Haymarket Theatre on 26 November 1792.

Ford, Mrs [fl. 1671], *actress.*
Mrs Ford played the First Lady in *The Six Days' Adventure* at Lincoln's Inn Fields for the Duke's Company on 6 March 1671.

Ford, Ann, later Mrs Philip Thicknesse *1737–1824, musician, writer.*
Ann Ford was born in a house near the Temple, London, on 22 February 1737, the only child of Thomas Ford (d. 1768), clerk of the arraigns, and his wife, née Champion, who was the niece of the Queen's physician and also of the attorney-general of Jamaica.

How she acquired the musical knowledge to cultivate her formidable musical talents is not known. But by her late teens she was evidently an accomplished singer, viola da gamba player, and guitar player. Her Sunday amateur concerts at which she sang and played in company with eminent professionals like Dr Thomas Augustine Arne, were attended by the best society. On 2 October 1758 Mrs Frances Greville wrote to Dr Burney from Wilbury of an amateur performance of *Julius Caesar* in which Ann Ford participated:

> They introduced a procession of vestals to Mourn over Caesar's body . . . [O]ne of them Sang a Dirge divinely well. She is, I think, take her for [what] she is . . . the most pleasing singer I ever heard I dont dare say the best because I have not judgment enough to decide, but I know that I would rather hear her than any Italian I have yet heard. She is a Miss Ford, daughter of a sort of Lawyer in the city. Gordon, the Violoncello, & Barton [Garton?] the Harpsichord Man, accompanied her. . . .

Ann's father objected to her appearance in public, even as an amateur, and actually obtained a magistrate's warrant to confine her to his house. She finally escaped his tyranny and, on 18 March 1760 at the Haymarket Theatre, she gave the first of five subscription concerts, for which subscribers gave £1,500 (all according to Lydia M. Middleton in *The Dictionary of National Biography*; the concerts are not entered in *The London Stage*). Her despotic father attempted to thwart the concerts also by blocking the streets around the concert hall with Bow Street runners. But Lord Tankerville dispersed them by threatening to turn out a detachment of the Guards. Daily from 24 to 30 October 1761 Miss Ford was advertised to sing "English airs, accompanying herself on the musical glasses" in a large room, formerly Cocks's Auction Room, Spring Gardens. According to the *St James's Chronicle* for 3 December 1761 she had also performed occasionally on the musical glasses at Thomas Sheridan's lectures until that month, when she was succeeded by Miss Lloyd. On 2 November 1761 she published the only known method book for the musical glasses, *Instructions for Playing on the Musical Glasses, so that*

Bequest of Mrs Mary M. Emery, the Cincinnati Art Museum

ANN FORD (when Mrs Philip Thicknesse)

by Gainsborough

Any Person Who has the Least Knowledge of Music, or a Good Ear, May be Able to Perform in a Few Days if not in a Few Hours. The glasses used by Miss Ford were water-tuned and not the group of glasses of graded sizes which Benjamin Franklin (also probably in 1761) aligned closely together on a horizontal rod and called collectively the "Armonica."

In November 1761 Ann accompanied her friend Lady Elizabeth Thicknesse and that lady's husband the aristocratic adventurer and author Philip Thicknesse (1719–1792), to his purchased post as lieutenant-governor of Landguard Fort, Suffolk. Lady Elizabeth died on 28 March 1762, and on 27 September of that year Ann Ford became Thicknesse's third wife. She accompanied her husband in eight changes of

residence, in 1766 to Welwyn, Hertfordshire, then to Monmouthshire, then to Bath,
thence to self-imposed "exile" in Spain in
1776, again to Bath, to Sangate near Hythe,
to Paris in 1791 during the Revolution, and
back again to Bath. In the fall of 1792
Philip Thicknesse died in a coach on the
way with Ann from Paris to Boulogne and
was buried in the Protestant Cemetery at
Boulogne. Ann was arrested and confined
to a convent until 1794, when she was
freed. She returned eventually to England.
She lived her last 18 years with her friend
Sarah Cooper in a house in the Edgware
Road. She died at 86 on 20 January 1824.
A will signed on 15 February 1818 left to
her "unfortunate daughter Charlotte Wild
widow" an annuity of £40 and, by a codicil
of 16 November 1818, gave to Mary Ann
Vale, spinster, "now in service of Miss
Sarah Cooper," £10 per year "as a reward
for her most affectionate attention . . . for
more than twelve years." The sums were
to be "payable out of the profits of [the
sale of?] her dwelling house" in the Royal
Crescent, Bath. Her son John proved the
will on 10 February 1824.

Ann Ford Thicknesse published *Sketches
of the Lives and Writings of Ladies of
France* in three volumes (1778–1781) and
a novel, *The School for Fashion* (1800).
Her portrait was painted at Bath in 1760
by Thomas Gainsborough (whose patron
and biographer was her husband Philip),
and by one of the Hones. The Gainsborough is now in the Cincinnati Art Museum.
A pencil and watercolor by Gainsborough
—a study for his oil portrait—is in the
British Library. A study of Ann Ford holding a musical instrument, by Cipriani, is
in the Ashmolean Museum and a similar
study, by Hoare, is in the British Museum.

Ford, Elizabeth. *See* JOHNSON, MRS
JOHN.

**Ford, Harriet Ann, later Mrs John
Wilkinson** *b. c. 1754, actress, dancer.*

Harriet Ann Ford was born about 1754,
the fruit of an affair between Sarah Ford,
sometimes described as an actress (though
on no evidence now known), and Henry
Mossop the Irish actor. Sarah Ford was deserted by Mossop and in 1760 met George
Colman the elder. By 1761 she was living
with him and they were married in 1767.
According to the testimony of his theatrical treasurer William Jewell, George Colman treated Harriet "in every respect" like
his own son George, who had been born
in 1762.

At Drury Lane on 25 November 1762,
Miss Ford replaced Miss Froment as a Lilliputian in *The Witches*, and on 27 November she was specified as a "Lilliputian Columbine." On 27 January she appeared as
Grotilla in the afterpiece *Edgar and Emmeline.* At Drury Lane on 28 October 1763
Miss Ford replaced Miss Froment as a Lilliputian Columbine." On 23 November she
was on the bill as one of the fairies in *A
Midsummer Night's Dream*, which Colman
had had a share in altering. The alteration
displeased the audience but was a success
when, three days later (and even more
greatly altered), it was put on as *The Fairy
Tale.* Miss Ford joined the Misses Rogers
and Street and Master Clinton in the con-
cluding *Fairy Dance.* On 20 December Miss
Ford played Grotilla again. On 13 January
1764 the same trio, now identified as
"scholars to Gherardi," danced "A New
Comic Dance call'd the *Shepherdesses, or,
La Faux à Veugle*," and on 24 February
they danced *The Hunters.*

Such were Harriet's duties for the following four seasons at Drury Lane, through
1766–67—fairies and dwarfs, varied only
by the title part of *Queen Mab* on and after
26 December 1764, Agrippina in *All for
Love* on 22 March 1766, the Page in the
Orphan, and Prince Arthur in *King John*
on 23 September 1767 and several times
after 19 October 1767. Her pay in 1766–
67 was recorded as 20s. per week.

In 1768–69 Harriet joined the Covent

Garden company. There she came under the tutelage of the seasoned dancer Fishar and, with Master Blurton and Miss Besford, other youngsters, she danced a variety of creations such as *The Dutch Milkmaid* and *The Gardeners.*

After 1768–69 Harriet either left the stage or left London. An affidavit by William Jewell and Richard Jackson relative to some litigation by the younger George Colman spoke of "Harriet Ann the wife of John Wilkinson Gentleman . . . the only Daughter" of Sarah Ford Colman. Her husband should not be confused with Tate Wilkinson's son John.

Ford, [John?] [*fl.* 1671?–1675], singer.

A Mr Ford sang the role of America in the prologue to the court masque *Calisto* on 15 February 1675 for the entertainment of Charles II. Perhaps he was John Ford, a bookseller and stationer who specialized in musical publications at a shop at the Middle Temple Gate, Fleet Street, from 1671 to 1673.

Ford, Richard [*fl.* 1719?–1743], treasurer.

The London Stage lists Richard Ford as a numberer at the Lincoln's Inn Fields Theatre in 1729–30, though his first benefit came the following season on 26 May 1731 when he and Gwinn shared £139 15s. 6d. in receipts. Ford's shared benefits in the years immediately following brought in at least that much, the highest being £175 2s., which he shared with Salle's widow at Covent Garden on 4 May 1733. Perhaps our subject should be identified as the Richard Ford, bookseller and publisher, who was active from about 1719 to 1740 at the Angel in the Poultry, near Stocks Market.

By 1735–36 our Ford had become the Covent Garden treasurer at a yearly salary of £60 8s. 8d. and had lodgings in Brownlow Street, Longacre. After 1739–40 Ford left John Rich and Covent Garden to become a sharer in Henry Giffard's ill-fated venture at Lincoln's Inn Fields. His last notice was on 6 April 1743, when he shared a benefit with four others at that house.

Forde. *See also* FORD.

Forde, Miss [*fl.* 1784], actress.

A Miss Forde played some part unspecified in an anonymous new play *The Patriot* which was presented by a scratch company assembled under special license at the Haymarket Theatre on 23 February 1784.

Forde, Brownlow [*fl.* 1767?–1814], actor, playwright, clergyman.

Early sketches of Brownlow Forde's origins and education differ in some details. George Parker, writing in 1781, said that Forde "having met with some disappointment in the Church, had thrown by the Cassock to put on the Sock;—a whimsical exchange!" But William Upcott, in *A Biographical Dictionary of Living Authors* in 1816, offered the following account: "Forde, Brownlow, a native of Ireland, who studied medicine under Professor Cleghorn, after which he joined a company of strolling players, and closed his career by taking orders. It is said however that he retained so strong an inclination for his former profession as to play Scrub in the evening after having read prayers at Church."

William S. Clark in *The Irish Stage in the County Towns* places Forde at the Crow Street Theatre, Dublin, in 1767, but Faulkner's *Dublin Journal* of 5 April 1768 cited as his actual debut his appearance on 6 April as Scrub in *The Beaux' Stratagem*, advertised as "A Young Gentleman."

Forde made his first appearance in London in Samuel Foote's company at the Haymarket Theatre on 29 May 1769, playing the title part in *The Minor* and advertised as from Dublin. But when the farce was offered again, on 9 June, Davis replaced him in the part, as did Aickin later in the summer. Evidently Forde retreated to Ireland.

In his collected notes on the Dublin theatre Clark listed Forde as performing at the Smock Alley Theatre in 1771–72 and 1775–76, at Crow Street in 1776, at Fishamble Street in 1777, and at Crow Street again in 1777–78. But during the 1770s Forde also worked in the provinces. In November and December 1771, according both to Clark and to W. J. Lawrence's manuscript notations in the National Library of Ireland, Forde was with James Parker's Belfast company, and that year at Newry (which was on the Belfast theatrical circuit) George Stevenson published Forde's one dramatic effort, a farce entitled *The Miraculous Cure*, taken from Cibber's *The Double Gallant*. Forde's benefit bill of 4 December 1771 furnished his Dublin address, "Mr. Sloan's in Castle Street." In December 1772 and January 1773, says Clark, Forde was playing at Kilkenny and in April at Waterford. Lawrence says that he "was a printer and actor in Dublin in 1773."

Forde is traceable to Cork in July and October of the years 1776, 1777, and 1778. On 28 March 1780, advertised again as "from the Theatre-Royal, Dublin," he was at the Haymarket in the role of Lord Shamwell in *The Humours of Oxford*, a specially licensed performance for the benefit of Mrs Lefevre. The Lord Chamberlain's records show that in 1782 he was granted a license to put on plays and other entertainments at the Haymarket for a period not stated.

The *Hibernian Journal* of 4 February 1784 announced that Brownlow Forde had left the stage, had resumed his clerical obligations, and was preaching in London. One of the subscribers to the *Dramatic Works* of John O'Keeffe in 1798 was "The Rev. Brownlow Forde, L.L. D." Upcott noted that "A person of both his names succeeded Mr. Villette as ordinary of Newgate, but was dismissed from that office in 1814." George Parker testified that: "He

was polite, if possible, to a fault, but unfeignedly sincere."

Forde's wife was acting with him at Belfast in 1771. The *Hampshire Chronicle* reported her Portsmouth debut as 5 August 1782, when she was said to have been "from Dublin."

Fordham, John (*fl. 1656–1681*), *painter.*

With Thomas and John Stevenson, John Fordham painted the elaborate pageants for the Lord Mayor's Shows from 1656 through 1681.

Fordyce, Miss. See PERROTT, LADY MARGARET JEMIMA.

Foremantel. See FOURMANTEL.

Forester. See FORRESTER and FORSTER.

Foresyth. See FORSYTH.

"Forges." See HUBERT, ROBERT.

Forioso, Joseph (*fl. 1794–1799*), *acrobat.*

Joseph Forioso, an acrobat from England but a Neopolitan by birth, petitioned the authorities on 10 July 1795 for his troupe of acrobats to perform at the theatre in Valladolid, Spain. He stated that he had "had the honour to perform in various foreign kingdoms throughout Europe, in the present year in Madrid and at the present time in the city of Salamanca, gaining the approval of the highest dignitaries by the many skills of his famous and unsurpassed troupe of acrobats, in which is included his son commonly known as the Little Devil [*el Picolo Diablo*]." Permission was granted for him to perform in Valladolid from the beginning of August. In 1794 Forioso had paid his dues to the actors' guild, the Cofradía de la Novena.

The Picolo Diablo returned to Valladolid in the spring of 1799; the petition to perform, while not mentioning Forioso, did specify an acrobat known as the Celebrated Englishman (*el Famoso Inglés*).

Forioso is not known to us as a performer in London, but most of the tumblers and acrobats of that time, particularly those who did not perform in the patent houses, are anonymous. There were several performers in London who styled themselves as the Little Devil; the most famous of these was Paulo Redigé, whose father Jean Redigé had been a tumbler on the Boulevard du Temple in Paris. There seems to have been no connection between the Redigés and Forioso.

Forlivesi, Giuseppe   ₁*fl. 1788–1789*₁, *singer.*

The Italian tenor Giuseppe Forlivesi first sang in the opera at the King's Theatre on 5 April 1788 as Tito in *Giulio Sabino*. A month later, on 8 May, he sang Clistene in *L'Olimpiade*. Reengaged at the King's Theatre for 1788–89 at a salary of £541 13s. 4d. and a free benefit, Forlivesi sang the Prince of Spain in *La cosa rara* on 10 January 1789, Agamemnone in *Ifigenia in Aulide* on 24 January, Armondo in *Il disertore* on 28 February, Il conte d'Orneville in *La villana reconosciuta* on 24 March, Don Achille in *La vendemmia* on 23 May, and Alessandro in *La generosità d'Alessandro* on 2 June.

In his *General History of Music*, Dr Burney wrote of Forlivesi, who had sung in most of the great theatres of Italy, that he lacked power to be heard at a distance but that his tone was pleasing to those who could hear him—"The lower notes of his voice seem totally decayed; he has no shake; and though neither deficient in figure nor action, I am sorry truth obliges me to say, that he is one of the most uninteresting singers I have ever heard in an Italian serious opera."

Formantel or **Formentel**. *See* FOUR-MANTEL.

Forrest, Mr   ₁*fl. 1766–1768*₁, *numberer.*

A Mr Forrest was paid 2s. 6d. per day as a numberer at Covent Garden Theatre in 1766–67 and 1767–68. His function was to count the persons in the house to prevent fraud by the doorkeepers. Possibly he was related to Ebenezer and Theodosius Forrest, father and son, who were solicitors for Covent Garden Theatre, friends of John Rich, the manager, and sometime dramatic authors. Both solicitors are noticed in *The Dictionary of National Biography*.

Forrest Mr   ₁*fl. 1774?–1782*₁, *actor.*

A Mr Forrest acted Tom Errand in *The Constant Couple; or, A Trip to the Jubilee* at the Haymarket Theatre on 14 January 1782. After Act I of the afterpiece *The Irish Widow*, in which he acted the Nephew, Forrest and Groves rendered the song "How sweet are the Woodlands." A week later, on 21 January at the same theatre, Forrest played Capt Belmein in *The Beaux' Duel*. He was perhaps the Forrest who had acted at the Smock Alley Theatre, Dublin, in the summer of 1774.

Forrester. *See also* FORSTER *and* FOSTER.

Forrester, Mrs   ₁*fl. 1719–1737*₁, *actress, singer.*

Mrs Forrester (or Forester) acted Portia in *Julius Caesar* on 19 November 1719 at Lincoln's Inn Fields, and though she may have played other roles during the season, she was not cited in the bills again until her benefit on 17 May 1720, when she acted Alibech in *The Indian Emperor*. The following season she was named only for the role of Daraxa in *The Fair Captive* on 4 March 1721. Perhaps she spent the ensuing seasons touring, for the next mention of her in London was not until 1 December 1729 when she played Betty in *The Emperor of the Moon* at Lincoln's Inn Fields. At her shared benefit with Mrs Clarke on 23 May

1730 she took the title part in *Flora* and sang an Irish song in *2 Don Quixote*. Then she played Mrs Squeezum in *Rape Upon Rape* at the Haymarket Theatre on 23 June, Lucilla in *The Fair Penitent* on 7 July, and Colombine in *The Amorous Adventure* on 17 July. On 1 August she turned up at Tottenham Court and later that month worked for Reynolds at Bartholomew Fair.

Mrs Forrester's 1730–31 season at Lincoln's Inn Fields brought her out as Goody Costive in *Sylvia*, Betsy in *The Gamester*, an Attendant on Circe in *Orestes*, Pallas in *The Judgment of Paris*, and, for her shared benefit with Mrs Vincent on 7 May 1731, Polly in *The Beggar's Opera*. The ladies split respectable gross receipts of £125 1s.

The career of Mrs Forrester at Lincoln's Inn Fields and, from 1732 on, at Covent Garden, continued through 1736–37. She was rarely assigned important leading parts, but she obviously found her niche in the troupe. Among her characters over the years were Myrtilla in *The Provok'd Husband*, Jenny in *The Beggar's Opera*, Phillida in *Damon and Phillida*, Dainty Fidget in *The Country Wife*, Penelope in *Tunbridge Walks*, Polly in *The Stage Coach*, Pindress in *Love and a Bottle*, Regan in *King Lear*, Thais in *Timon of Athens*, Jenny in *The Lottery*, Betty in *The Contrivances*, and a Peasant in *Apollo and Daphne*. She also played the Queen in *Hamlet*, at least once, at a special performance at the old Lincoln's Inn Fields playhouse in April 1736.

She ventured to Bartholomew Fair on 24 August 1734 to act Queen Eleanor in *Fair Rosamond*, but otherwise she was content to stay at the patent house and act in London only during the regular seasons. Her salary in 1735–36 was a modest 3s. 4d. daily or £28 13s. 4d. for 172 nights. She received no benefit. After the 1736–37 season she seems to have left the stage.

Forrett, Mr ₍fl. 1798₎, *musician*.
When the *Messiah* was performed at the

Haymarket Theatre on 15 January 1798 an instrumentalist named Forrett participated.

Forster. *See also* **FORRESTER** and **FOSTER.**

Forster, Mr ₍fl. 1800–1807?₎, *actor*.
Advertised as "A Gentleman," Mr Forster made his first appearance on 29 August 1800 playing Prince David in *Cambro-Britons* at the Haymarket Theatre. Possibly he was the Mr Foster or Forster who played small parts at the Royal Circus from 1803 to 1807, but certain identification is impossible.

Forster, Mrs ₍fl. 1796–1804?₎, *actress*.
At the Haymarket Theatre on 22 February 1796 a Mrs Forster played Leonora in *The Mourning Bride*. Perhaps she was the Mrs "Forrester" who acted at Sadler's Wells, playing an Attendant in *The Old Man of the Mountains* and an Amazon in *The British Amazons* in 1803. That actress also performed at the Wells in March 1804.

Forster, Miss ₍fl. 1791₎, *performer*.
A Miss Forster performed an unspecified role in *The Magic Grot* at Sadler's Wells on 3 October 1791.

Forster, William ₍fl. 1786?–1838?₎, *violinist, violoncellist, trombonist*.
William Forster (or Foster) was listed in Doane's *Musical Directory* of 1794 as a violinist living in the Strand. That would suggest that he was probably the musical-instrument maker, music seller, and publisher William Forster the younger listed in Humphries and Smith's *Music Publishing in the British Isles* as having had a shop at No 348, the Strand, near Exeter 'Change, from 17 July 1786 (the day after his marriage) to 1803. From 1803 to 1816 he was at No 22, York Street, Westminster; then he held forth at No 87, the Strand, until 1821, after which he moved to No 41, Lisle

Street, until 1824. He published a catalogue of music about 1800. His father had been a musical-instrument maker, music seller, and publisher (but not a performer) from about 1762 to his death in 1808. Perhaps also related to the elder and younger Forsters was the oboist William John Forster.

Doane stated that William Forster played for the New Musical Fund and in the Handel performances at Westminster Abbey. He was probably the Forster who was in the Drury Lane Theatre band in 1799 and the years immediately following, though the account book entries could refer to William John Forster, who was also employed at that playhouse. The Forster who performed at the Haymarket Theatre in the summers from 1804 through 1810 may have been either William or William John, though William, who was clearly of a younger generation, was certainly at that theatre in 1815 and 1816. In 1815 the Haymarket accounts listed William as a violoncellist and trombonist at a salary of £1 16s. weekly. William Forster was on the Court of Assistants of the New Musical Fund in 1815.

Perhaps our subject was the Forster who was elected a member of the Royal Society of Musicians on 4 January 1824 and served as one of the Society's governors as early as January 1826, though that man may well have been a third-generation Forster. His name, variously spelled, appeared in the Society's Minute Books again in 1827, 1829, 1831 through 1835, 1837, and 1838. From 1832 onward he was often cited as having received a donation, so by that time he was probably retired.

Forster, William John *d. 1811, oboist.*

William John Forster (or, almost as frequently, Foster) was recommended for membership in the Royal Society of Musicians by John Parke on 3 August 1777. Forster was described as an oboist and a married man with no children. He was admitted on 2 November. Perhaps he was related to William Forster the musical-instrument maker, music seller, and publisher (but not performer) who was active in London from about 1762 until his death in 1808, and to his namesake son, who was similarly employed from 1786 to 1824 and was, we believe, the violinist, violoncellist, and trombonist William Forster. William John Forster would appear to have been of about the same generation as the elder William Forster. William John may have been the William Forster who, according to Reed's "Notitia Dramatica," became the husband (perhaps in name only) of the actress, singer, and flutist Ann Fields on 9 January 1786.

Our subject performed frequently at the theatres in London. He accompanied Mrs Bannister in "Sweet Echo" at the Haymarket Theatre on 27 June 1783 and subsequent dates through 12 June 1788. On the last date Mrs Forster also performed. William John was also mentioned occasionally in playbills as an accompanist for vocalists at Drury Lane Theatre, as on 4 October 1787 and 26 September 1789, when he and Mrs Crouch entertained with "Sweet Echo." He was at the Haymarket on 7 March 1794 in the oratorio band, on 4 March 1795 in the band for *The Thespian Panorama*, on 16 August 1797 as accompanist for Mrs Atkins in "The Nightingale," on 9 August 1798 as accompanist for Mrs Bland in "Sweet Echo," and on 26 August 1800 when he joined Mrs Mountain in the same song. He was probably the Mr Foster listed as a band member at Drury Lane in 1801 and again on 16 September 1807 at £2 weekly.

In addition to his theatrical performing Forster also played in the Handel Memorial Concerts at Westminster Abbey and the Pantheon in May and June 1784 and in the St Paul's concerts in 1785 and 1790 through 1798. Perhaps he was the Mr Forrester who wrote the words for Smether-

gill's *Moggy Macbride*, published about
1790 as sung by Mrs Forrester at Islington
Spa. Ann Field Forster had died in 14 July
1789. But, as has been indicated, there is no
certain proof that the Forster who married
or gave his name to Ann Field was our
subject. We know that William John
Forster had a wife in 1777 and left a widow
in 1811.

In 1794 our Forster was Secretary to
the Royal Society of Musicians and was living in Hall Staircase, Temple. The Society
minutes show that on 6 March 1796 property belonging to the Society which was in
Forster's custody was insured for £200. The
Society minutes show that William John
Forster died in 1811. A general meeting
was called on 7 April 1811 to elect a new
secretary, and on 6 May Forster's widow
was granted a pension of 2½ guineas
monthly. On 7 July £8 was paid for
Forster's funeral, which apparently took
place in Lambeth. Mrs Forster, on 3 March
1822, was listed in the minutes as receiving
a grant of £2 16s., having attained 60 years
of age; on 2 January 1825 it was reported
that she had died.

Forster, Mrs William ₁John?₁. *See*
FIELD, ANN.

Forsyth, Mrs ₁*fl. 1726–1729*₁, *singer.*
Advertised as one "who never appeared
in Publick before," Mrs Forsyth sang songs
from operas at the Haymarket Theatre on
29 April 1726. The following 6 May at
Lincoln's Inn Fields she was again announced as making her first appearance;
there she sang with Mrs Davis and Mrs
Grimaldi in Italian and English. She appeared on 17 March 1727 at the Haymarket and on 28 March 1729 at Hickford's Music Room, each time singing for
her own benefit.

Fort, Mr *d. 1797, performer?*
The *Hibernian Journal* of 17 January
1798 reported the drowning in December

1797 of Mr and Mrs Fort and other members of a troupe headed for Astley's Amphitheatre Royal in Dublin. They were on
the packet *Viceroy*, out of Liverpool, and
went down in the Irish Sea. Fort and his
wife had probably worked at Astley's Amphitheatre in London.

Fort, Mrs *d. 1797, performer?* *See*
FORT, MR.

Forti, Giuseppe ₁*fl. 1758–1759*₁,
dancer.
According to the 1758 edition of *Attalo*,
Giuseppe Forti was one of the dancers who
participated; it is likely he performed on
11 November 1758 at the King's Theatre
when the opera was presented. He danced
at the King's again on 16 January 1759,
and on 22 May he and his wife were given
a charity benefit to help them recoup their
losses when the ship with their costumes on
it was seized by the French.

Forti, Signora Giuseppe ₁*fl. 1757–
1759*₁, *dancer.*
Signora Giuseppe Forti danced at the
King's Theatre in 1757–58, appearing on
10 January 1758 and subsequent dates. On
12 April she danced a piece called *She
Wou'd and She Wou'd Not* with Gallini
for his benefit at Covent Garden. Except for
her shared benefit with her husband in the
spring of 1759 at the King's, she seems not
to have done any dancing in 1758–59
worthy of notice in the bills.

"Fortissimo, Signor" ₁*fl. 1790*₁,
equestrian.
The 22 July 1790 bill for the Royal
Circus advertised that "Signor FORTISSIMO
(commonly called ATLAS) will display
his unparalleled exhibition accompanied
by the whole of his Troop."

"Fortnight Actor, The." *See* ELLIS-
TON, ROBERT WILLIAM.

Fortunelli [*fl. 1771–1772?*], *clown.*
A clown named Fortunelli (or Fortunelly) performed on the slack rope at Astley's Amphitheatre about 1771 or 1772.

Fosbroke, Mr [*fl. 1776*], *scene painter?*
According to Carola Oman in her *Garrick* (1958), a scene painter from Drury Lane Theatre named Fosbroke worked at Sir Watkin William Wynn's private theatre in North Wales in 1776. The only person of that name known to have been employed at Drury Lane at that time was Thomas Fosbrook (sometimes Fosbroke), the box bookkeeper and numberer.

Fosbrook, Henry [*fl. 1794–1800*], *ticket taker.*
Henry Fosbrook, who was no doubt related to the box bookkeeper and housekeeper Thomas Fosbrook (d. c. 1830) as a brother or son, was a ticket taker at Drury Lane Theatre from 1794–95 to 1799–1800. On 5 June 1795 he shared in benefit tickets with a number of other house servants, as he also did on 15 June 1796, when his share amounted to £7 15s. 6d., and on 9 June 1798, when his share was £11 5s. 6d. and his name was given in full in the account book. In 1795–96 his salary was 1s. 4d. per day. An entry in the account book for 9 July 1800 indicates that on that day he was "discharg'd."

Fosbrook, Thomas *d. c. 1830, numberer, box bookkeeper, housekeeper.*
Thomas Fosbrook was employed in positions of high responsibility in the house at Drury Lane Theatre for at least 32 years from 1766 to his retirement in 1808. Possibly the William Fosbrooke whose estate was granted to his widow Hester by the Consistory Court at London on 3 June 1775 was his father. Fosbrook was a numberer (he counted heads in the audience to check against ticket receipts) at 15s. per week between 1766–67 and 1776–77. By the

latter season he was a box bookkeeper and by 1782–83 he was also a housekeeper, positions he retained for the remainder of his career. Although his regular salary probably never rose above several pounds per week, from his office near the stage door, where he took reservations for seats, Fosbrook was in a traditionally lucrative position in respect to gratuities for services and favors rendered. His annual benefits, moreover, were almost always substantial, testifying to his popularity and bringing him a very comfortable living. In round figures, he took £173 in 1777, £141 in 1778, £200 in 1779, £179 in 1780, £196 in 1781, similar amounts through the 1780s, £369 in 1792, £322 in 1793; in his last years his benefits brought him £293 in 1800, £289 in 1802, £266 in 1803, £133 in 1804, £240 in 1805, and £125 in 1806. Occasionally he suffered a deficit benefit as on 13 May 1776 (£61), 17 May 1784 (£82), 16 May 1785 (£48), 17 May 1786 (£65), and 1796 (£68). He retired at the end of 1807–8 with, according to Gilliland's *Dramatic Mirror* in 1808, "a handsome fortune."

The Drury Lane account books record regular and numerous payments to him of large sums of money which he disbursed to persons in his departments and to various tradesmen for services to the theatre. He also received regular summer payments for salary and expenses as custodian of the dark house: £30 on 1 October 1782, £26 2s. 9d. on 23 October 1782, £56 8s. 4d. on 15 November 1786, and £53 18s. 1d. on 27 December 1791 are typical.

Garrick regarded Fosbrook as a trusty employee and often called upon him to carry out special favors or to serve as an emissary. When he sold the theatre to Sheridan, Linley, and Ford, the great actor took care to secure Fosbrook's position with the new managers. According to Gilliland's account, at any rate, Garrick called Fosbrook on the stage in the presence of the new proprietors and said, "here is a person I wish to recommend to you—I know his

The SEVENTY-NINTH NIGHT.

At the Theatre Royal, Drury Lane,

This prefent MONDAY, Dec. 27, 1790,

The HAUNTED TOWER.

Lord William by Mr. Dignum,
The Baron by Mr. Baddeley, Edward by Mr. Bannifter Jun.
Lewis by Mr. Suett Robert by Mr. Hollingfworth,
Charles by Mr. Fox, Hugo by Mr. Moody,
De Courcy by Mr. Whitfield, Martin by Mr. Williames,
Lady Elinor by Mrs. Crouch, Adela by Signora Storace,
Cicely by Mrs. Bland, Maud by Mrs. Booth.

With (1ft. Time) a Pantomime partly new and partly compiled, called, The

FAIRY FAVOUR;

OR, HARLEQUIN ANIMATED.

The New Scenes defigned and executed by Mr. *Greenwood.*
The Compiled Part, taken from the favourite Pantomimes of

QUEEN MAB,	The WITCHES,
The ELOPEMENT,	MERCURY HARLEQUIN,
FORTUNATUS,	LUN's GHOST,
The GENII,	HARLEQUIN from the MOON, &c.

Harlequin by Mr. BANKS,
Pantaloon by Mr. Burton, 'Squire Sapfcull by Mr. Hollingfworth,
Clown by Mr. Fairbrother, Scaramouch by Mr. Harris,
Punch by Mr. Hamoir, Mezetin by Mr. Bidotti, Pero by Mr. Kirk,
Watchmen by Meffrs. Chapman, Maddocks, Jones, Webb,
Chairmen by Meffrs. Phillimore, Haymes,
Surgeon Cauftic by Mr. Fawcett, Bandage by Mr. Lyons, Waiter by Mr. Benfon,
Statuary by Mr. Bland, Gardener by Mr. Bourk,
Fifherman by Mr. Alfred, Mandarine by Young Grimaldi,
Colombine by Mifs BLANCHET,
Queen Mab by Mifs DE CAMP.
To conclude with a DANCE of

Fairies and Pantomimic Characters,

By Mr. Hamoir, the Young D'Egvilles
Mifs Blanchet, Mifs De Camp.
. BOOKS of the Songs with a Defcription of the Pantomime to be had at the
Theatre.
The Pantomime being partly compiled,

HALF PRICE WILL BE TAKEN.

NO MONEY TO BE RTEURNED.

Places for the Boxes to be taken of Mr. FOSBROOK, at the Theatre
The Doors to be opened at a Quarter paft Five, to begin at a Quarter paft Six

To-morrow, SHE WOU'D and SHE WOULD NOT,

Folger Shakespeare Library

Playbill, Drury Lane Theatre, 27 December 1790
"Places for the Boxes to be taken of Mr. FOSBROOK"

honesty and worth, and while you continue to treat him well, you will find him a useful and valuable acquisition to your property—I will answer for him." Fosbrook rode in the tenth coach of Garrick's funeral procession in January 1779.

Fosbrook and his wife were each left £5 for mourning rings by the Drury Lane actor John Purser in his will dated 26 April 1808. In an autograph notebook now at the Folger Shakespeare Library, James Winston noted for 1830 that Fosbrook was then "deceased." His wife (fl. 1794–1808) also worked as a housekeeper in the theatre; the Henry Fosbrook (fl. 1794–1800) who was a ticket taker at Drury Lane was probably his son or brother.

Fosbrook, Mrs Thomas *fl. 1794–1808*, *housekeeper.*

Mrs Thomas Fosbrook, the wife of the box bookkeeper and housekeeper at Drury Lane Theatre, was a concession renter at that theater by 1794. By 26 June 1799 she was working as a housekeeper, for on that date she was paid £6 13*s.* 9*d.* for aprons and dusters. The account books listed her as a housekeeper in 1801–2 at a salary of £1 4*s.* per week, and in 1802–3 at £1 13*s.* 4*d.* per week. She was left £5 for a mourning ring by the actor John Purser in his will made on 26 April 1808.

Fossan. *See* **RINALDI.**

Fossett. *See* **JOSSETT.**

Foster. *See also* **FORRESTER** and **FORSTER.**

Foster, Mrs [*fl.* 1772], *singer.*
A Mrs Foster sang at Marylebone Gardens in 1772.

Foster, Benjamin [*fl.* 1672], *musician.*
Benjamin Foster was one of a number of musicians ordered apprehended on 2 October 1672 for playing music without a license.

Foster, Emmanuel [*fl.* 1768–1769], *manager, actor.*
Emmanuel Foster managed a booth at the Stourbridge Fair at Cambridge in the fall of 1768. In September and early October his troupe offered *George Barnwell* and a (probably) pirated version of *The Padlock.* On 28 February 1769 the Mr Foster who played the Duke in *Othello* at the Haymarket Theatre in London was very likely Emmanuel. He was back at Stourbridge, according to the Cambridge *Chronicle*, in September and early October 1769 with *The Recruiting Officer, The Maid of the Mill, Polly Honeycomb, The Suspicious Husband, Midas, Love in a Village, The Citizen,* and *Jane Shore.* A puff in the paper called Foster's offerings "Theatrical Oratorios" and claimed they had met "with great applause from very polite and crouded

audiences, and the Performers in general [are] reckoned the best that have been at Stirbitch Fair." The author of the praise was probably Foster himself.

Fotteral, James [*fl.* 1769–1805], *actor.*
Little is known of James ("Jemmy") Fotteral, despite his career of over 35 years on the Irish and English stages. He was at Smock Alley Theatre, Dublin, in 1770–71, 1773–1775, 1781–82, 1784–1786; at Crow Street in the summer of 1775 and in 1778–1780; at Belfast in 1770, 1771, 1772, and 1787; at Kilkenny and Newry in 1771; at Cork in 1769, 1775, 1781, 1783, and 1785; and at Hull in 1787.

At the Haymarket Theatre on 29 August 1777, announced as "A Gentleman from the Theatre Royal, Dublin," making his first appearance on the London stage, Fotteral acted the title role in *Henry VIII.* In identifying him the *London Chronicle* misspelled his name as "Fotheril." On September 1777 at the Haymarket he performed the Manager in the specialty piece called *The Occasional Prelude.* Evidently he acted Lockit in *The Beggar's Opera* on 6 October (although the bills listed Edwin for the role), for the *Morning Chronicle* the following day reported that "Mr Fotteral's Lockit was infinitely more in character than his King in Henry VIII."

Fotteral also acted at Derby from October 1777 to January 1778, and in July 1793 he performed at the Town Hall, Abergavenny, for the benefit of Mr and Mrs Taylor. In October 1795 he was a leading man at Swansea and was reckoned a good actor there. The *Thespian Dictionary* (1805) stated that he was a favorite of the gallery gods at Smock Alley and Crow Street, who often competed with him in noisemaking. Among his few good portrayals was the dancing master in *The Son-in-Law.* John Bernard described Fotteral as a notorious gambler who was always shabby and penniless.

Fouks, [Mr?] [*fl. 1790*], *house serv-ant?*

A person named Fouks, presumably male, was added to the pay list of Drury Lane Theatre at 1*s*. 6*d*. a day on 3 October 1790.

Foulcade. *See* FORCADE.

Foulis, John [*fl. c. 1750–1793*], *composer, violinist, music copyist.*

The earliest records of the musician John Foulis (or Fowlis) date about 1750, when two of his songs were published: *The Confession* and *The Maid's Prayer*. By 14 September 1767 he was earning 6*s*. 3*d*. daily as a member of the orchestra at Covent Garden, and a notation in the theatre's books on 29 May 1770 shows that he was also paid for copying music. He was still at Covent Garden on 29 May 1780 when he was paid £101 17*s*. for music copying.

Beginning 16 November 1781 the Drury Lane accounts show regular and frequent payments to Foulis ranging from 4*s*. 6*d*. to £9 3*d*. The books rarely give any indication of the amount of work Foulis did for the sums he was paid, though on 26 March 1789 he received £7 18*s*. 6*d*. for "Copying of a new Farce." The last mention of him in the accounts was on 1 March 1793.

During his Drury Lane years Foulis was also the copyist and librarian for Vauxhall Gardens in 1790 and 1791. It was his duty, apparently, to compile the "List" or program, display it in the Gardens, and communicate it to the newspapers. Foulis may have retired after the 1792–93 theatrical season; the Minute Books of the Royal Society of Musicians show what appears to have been a gift of 10 guineas to Foulis on 7 July 1793.

Related to our subject may have been Andrew Foulis of Glasgow, a printer who brought out an edition of Ramsay's *The Gentle Shepherd; a Pastoral Comedy* in 1788 and again in 1796. The Foulis printings contained the music for the songs; the 1788 edition was sold in Edinburgh and London and the 1796 by Andrew Foulis himself in Glasgow.

Foulstone, John [*fl. 1784–1794*], *singer, bass player?*

John Foulstone (or Foulston) sang tenor in the Handel Memorial Concerts at Westminster Abbey and the Pantheon in May and June 1784. Doane's *Musical Directory* of 1794 listed him as a bass (player, presumably) and a tenor who lived in Forbes's Passage, Swallow Street; he was a participant in the oratorios at Drury Lane Theatre and the Abbey and in concerts presented by the Portland Chapel Society.

Fourcade. *See* FORCADE.

Fouriere. *See* FERRERE.

Fourmantel, Catherine [*fl. 1758–1760*], *singer.*

Catherine Fourmantel was a popular singer by 8 May 1758 when John Baker visited Ranelagh Gardens with friends and entered in his *Diary* "Miss Fromantel sang." In July following was published the collection *Ten Favourite Songs Sung by Miss Fromantel at Ranelagh, Music by Mr Oswald*. She returned to Ranelagh in the summer of 1759, when she lived with her mother in Meard's Court, Soho.

When, how, or where Miss Fourmantel met Laurence Sterne is as uncertain as her origins. Twelve letters from Sterne, in which she was to gain fame as "Dear Kitty," date from the winter of 1759–60 when she was living with her mother in the Stonegate, York, and singing at the Assembly Rooms. (Her benefit concert there was 15 February 1760.) The letters came into the possession of Mrs Henry Weston, the daughter of a friend of Catherine's. From Mrs Weston stems a romantic story, thought by Lewis Perry Curtis, a modern editor of the letters, to be apocryphal: Catherine was a descendant of the "Berenger de Fourmantels," aristocratic Protestants who had fled France after the revocation of the Edict of Nantes and who were forced to sacrifice extensive properties in Santo Domingo. But Curtis himself suggests some relationship to a Jean Berenger de Formantel, who appeared as a witness to the marriage of Emanuel du Seret and Emée Reid on 7 February 1734 at the French Chapel in Leicester Fields, and also to Charles (d. 23 June 1763) and Mary Fourmantel of Old Bond Street and to Richard Berenger (1720–1782), Gentleman of the Horse to George III.

The *Public Advertiser* for 7 April 1760 noted that Kitty had failed to find an engagement at Ranelagh for the following summer. But, possibly through Sterne's influence, she was hired, and the verses to at least one of the songs in *A Collection of New Songs Sung by Mr. Beard, Miss Stevenson, and Miss Fromantel at Ranelagh*, published on 28 August 1760, were penned by Sterne.

A letter from Sterne to "Dear Kitty" on 1 January 1760 is of special interest. It is laudatory of *Tristram Shandy*, recently published, and directs her to copy the praises out in her own hand and send them to some influential person, unnamed but apparently understood. Curtis believes the person to have been David Garrick, for on 27 January 1760 Sterne mentioned that Garrick "had actually spoke well of my Book."

According to Mrs Weston's story Kitty Fourmantel went mad after being jilted by Yorick, had to be placed in a private asylum, and was the model for the mad Maria of Moulines in Sterne's *Sentimental Journey*. Certainly she was the inspiration for the "dear, dear Jenny" of *Tristram Shandy*.

Fourner, Mons ₁fl. 1741₁, *dancer*.
Advertised as never having appeared there before, Monsieur Fourner danced at Goodman's Fields Theatre on 14 September 1741. He was not mentioned again.

Fouzi. *See* **Fuozi.**

Fowell. *See* **Powell.**

Fowler, Mr ₁fl. 1726–1727₁, *house servant*.
Though his specific duties are not known, Mr Fowler was apparently a house servant at Lincoln's Inn Fields in 1726–27. His name appeared in the accounts for that season, usually in connection with the issuing of tickets to the brothers John and Christopher Rich. It is probable that Fowler was one of the office staff.

Fowler, Mr ₁fl. 1794–1795₁, *carpenter*.
A Mr Fowler was paid 19s. per week as a carpenter by Covent Garden Theatre in 1794–95.

Fowler, Miss ₁fl. 1787–1794₁, *actress*.
Miss Fowler, the daughter of the provincial actor Thomas Fowler (1739–1797) and his wife (fl. 1766–1787), acted with her mother at the Red Lion Inn, Stoke Newington, in late March 1787, playing a Maid in *She Stoops to Conquer* on the twenty-ninth, Gipsey in *The Beaux' Stratagem* on the thirtieth, and a vocal part in *Romeo and Juliet* on the thirty-first. Perhaps she was the Miss Fowler who performed with Sarah Baker's company at Bartholomew Fair in 1794.

Fowler, Mrs Thomas ₁fl. 1766–1787₁, *actress*.
Mrs Thomas Fowler passed most of her theatrical career in the provinces with her husband. As members of Roger Kemble's company they acted at Coventry in August 1766 at Worcester in January 1767, and at Derby in February 1769 and November 1771. Probably she performed at Dublin in 1781–82, at Edinburgh in 1781 and 1783, at Norwich in 1790–91, and perhaps at Shrewsbury in the 1790s, all places

at which her husband is known to have played.

The first of her known sporadic appearances in London was on 11 February 1777 when she played Hostess Quickly in *Henry IV* at the Haymarket Theatre. At the China Hall, Rotherhithe, on 3 June 1778, she acted Nell in *The Devil to Pay*, and on 10 June she sang in the funeral procession in *Romeo and Juliet*. Several years later she played with a company at the Crown Inn, Islington, appearing as Rose in *The Recruiting Officer* on 15 March 1781, Kitty Pry in *The Lying Valet* on 27 March, the Duchess of York in *Richard III* on 30 March, Florella in *The Orphan* and Madge in *The King and the Miller of Mansfield* on 5 April, and Dorcas in *The Mock Doctor* on 9 April. In 1782 she performed on two nights at the Haymarket: Lady Darling in *The Constant Couple* on 14 January and Mrs Guzzle in *Don Quixote in England* and the Duchess of York in *Richard III* on 4 March. On 17 September 1784 she again played the latter role at the Haymarket. Her last appearances in London were at the Red Lion Inn, Stoke Newington, in March 1787 when she acted her previous roles of Florella and Madge and of Lady Sneerwell in *The School for Scandal*, Dorcas in *Thomas and Sally*, Mrs Hardcastle in *She Stoops to Conquer*, Gymp in *Bon Ton*, Lady Bountiful in *The Beaux' Stratagem*, Lady Capulet in *Romeo and Juliet*, and Ursula in *The Padlock*. Also appearing at the Red Lion was Miss Fowler, presumably her daughter. It is not known if Mrs Fowler was still alive when her husband, Thomas Fowler, who evidently never acted in London, was buried at St Chad's, Shrewsbury, on 9 January 1797, aged 58.

Fowlis. *See* FOULIS.

Fox, Mrs *d. 1790, actress, singer.*
A Mrs Fox played an unspecified role in *The Poor Soldier* at Richmond, Surrey, on 11 September 1786. She was probably the Mrs Fox who acted several times at the Haymarket Theatre in 1787, playing Lucinda in *Love in a Village* on 8 January, Louisa Dudley in *The West Indian* on 12 March, and Young Lady Lambert in *The Hypocrite* on 30 April. She then joined the company at John Palmer's new Royalty Theatre where she acted Celia in *As You Like It*, the inaugural production, on 20 June 1787. During the summer at that theatre she appeared in *Hero and Leander* (Reeve's song *Come, come my sweet love*, as sung by her and Arrowsmith in that piece, was published 1787), as Daphne in *Apollo Turn'd Stroller*, Hope in *Hobson's Choice*, and in a principal role in *The Birth-Day*. In 1789–90 she was engaged at Drury Lane for 5s. per day where her roles were a Bacchant in *Comus*, Teresa in *The Island of St Marguerite*, Mrs Cooper in *The Beggar's Opera*, and Columbine in *Harlequin's Frolicks* (she played this latter role some 21 times between 26 December 1789 and 1 March 1790).

Mrs Fox's last performance at Drury Lane was in *Comus* on 20 May 1790. She died later in the year at or near Birmingham, according to a notation by John Philip Kemble. Her name was taken off the paylist on 12 February 1791, and her salary from the beginning of the season, amounting to £26, was "Return'd" in the receipts ledger. This Mrs Fox should not be confused with Mrs Joseph Fox (née Eleanor Candler), who evidently did not act in London.

Fox, Mrs Charles James, Elizabeth. *See* ARMSTEAD, MRS.

Fox, George 1762–1794, violinist.
When George Fox was recommended by Charles Linton for membership in the Royal Society of Musicians on 2 November 1783, he was described as 21 years old, single, and a violinist in the Covent Garden Theatre band. Fox was on the Society's list

to play in the annual May concerts at St Paul's in 1785, 1789, 1791, and 1793. He had also been among the first violins in the Handel Memorial Concerts at Westminster Abbey and the Pantheon in May and June 1784. Probably he was the Fox for whose benefit a concert was given at the Crown and Anchor Tavern on 6 April 1789.

Fox remained a member of the Covent Garden band until 17 May 1794, when his name was removed from the paylist because he had died. His salary had been 6s. 8d. per night.

Fox, Hannah. *See* WALKER, MRS THOMAS [fl. 1794].

Fox, John [fl. 1790–1803], *prompter.*
According to Joseph De Castro's *Memoirs* (1824), John Fox was a prompter at Astley's Amphitheatre, probably in the 1790s, before Philip Astley gave up his management. He may have been related to the burletta singer at Astley's between 1785 and 1795. In his *Memoirs*, the younger Charles Dibdin referred to him as "the late Mr T. Fox," who was stage manager at Astley's Amphitheatre when it burned in 1793. We assume that the "T" is the editor's misreading of "J" in the manuscript.

Fox, Joseph *d. 1791, actor, manager, singer.*
Joseph Fox, who had a theatrical career of at least 33 years in London, Brighton, and elsewhere, made his first appearance in London on 25 September 1758 at Covent Garden Theatre as Fenton in *The Merry Wives of Windsor.* He evidently went to play in Dublin for the remainder of the season. By the end of November 1759 he was back in London, this time engaged at Drury Lane Theatre, where he made his debut on 1 December 1758 as a Slave in *Oroonoko*, an anonymous role which he acted some eight times by the end of the month. On 31 December he played a small role in *Harlequin's Invasion*, which he re-

peated some 25 times. He also performed Zimventi in *The Orphan of China*, Watchall in *A New Way to Pay Old Debts*, Essex in *King John*, a vocal part in *Romeo and Juliet*, Angus in *Macbeth*, Darby in *Jane Shore*, and a Servant in *The Jealous Wife*. On 3 May 1760 he shared benefit tickets with Royall.

Continuing at Drury Lane every season (except 1765–66) through 1767–68 without special notice, Fox filled numerous journeyman roles, a selection of which includes Blunt in *The London Merchant*, Smart in *The Minor*, a Footman in *All in the Wrong* and another in *The School for Lovers*, Mat in *The Beggar's Opera*, Burgundy in *King Lear*, a Courtier in *Elvira*, Rosencrantz in *Hamlet*, Montano in *Othello*, Spinoza in *Venice Preserv'd*, Trickit in *The Register Officer*, and a Knight in *The Countess of Salisbury*. His salary from 1764–65 through 1766–67 was 4s. 3d. per day, or £1 5s. per week.

For the season 1768–69 Fox changed theatres, appearing on 26 September 1768 in a vocal part in *Romeo and Juliet* at Covent Garden. There he had a regular engagement through 1779–80, playing over those 12 years a number of small parts. In his first season there, 1768–69, for example, he filled Jupiter and Damaetas in *Midas*, a minor role in *Macbeth*, Sir Ardolph in *The Countess of Salisbury*, McMorris in *Henry V*, a minor role in *The Roman Father*, Stanmore in *Oroonoko*, Catesby in *Jane Shore*, and Sir John Loverule in *The Devil to Pay*. By 1777–78, when his salary was £2 per week, after playing numerous footmen and officers and walking in countless processions, his situation had improved little and he was acting Simon in *The Commissary*, Decoy in *The Miser*, a Friar in *The Duenna*, the Music Master in *Catherine and Petruchio*, Jupiter in *Midas*, Corrigidor in *She Wou'd and She Wou'd Not*, Foigard in *The Stratagem*, and Bardolph in *Henry V*.

On 26 March 1781 Fox made his first

appearance at the Haymarket Theatre as Don Diego in *The Padlock*. His son William Fox made his London debut as Leander in the same performance. The elder Fox also acted roles in musical pieces and broad comedies at the Jacob's Wells Theatre in Bristol in the summer of 1763 and at the Bristol Theatre Royal in 1773, 1774, 1775, and in 1787–88, 1788–89, and 1789–90. On 30 August 1782 he had acted Hastings and his wife had played Mrs Hardcastle in a performance of *She Stoops to Conquer* given at the theatre in Ostend, Belgium.

In 1780 Fox gave up his engagement at Covent Garden, no doubt with hopes of finding greater opportunity and income elsewhere. By that year, probably, he was already the keeper of the Shakespeare Tavern and Coffee House in Bow Street, Covent Garden, a proprietorship he retained until about a year before his death, when he passed it to a Mr Williames. That establishment had declined daily under Fox's management, according to *The Secret History of the Green Room* (1795), because he "really took pains to drive away customers."

An earlier enterprise by Fox had begun in 1777 when he took a lease of the North Street Theatre, Brighton, from its builder Samuel Paine, at 60 guineas per annum for 15 years. The theatre opened on 1 July 1777 with *Jane Shore* for its first season with Fox as lessee. Fox operated the theatre every summer and early fall through 1790, usually with a working manager in his employ. Griffiths managed for him in 1778; Buckle managed from 1782 through 1787. Fox, himself, usually acted in the company as well. In his earlier years as lessee he suffered through a variety of disputes over an agreement which granted to Paine, the lessor, an annual charge-free benefit and free admission for himself and family for all occasions. When Fox tried to collect "incidental expenses" of the benefit—which were not specifically excluded in the agreement—Paine, in revenge, descended upon

the theatre with all his children and relations, taking the best seats *gratis,* much to Fox's financial disadvantage. Legal arbitration settled that Paine had to pay £20 per year for half the benefit expenses. Finally Fox decided to build another theatre in Duke Street, which he opened in July 1791 under a new license granted by the magistrate of Lewes, where he also had a theatre. But before the year was out, Fox died at Brighton on 7 December 1791.

In his will, made on 15 October 1791—when he was "Sick in Body but of Sound and disposing Mind"—Fox left to his wife Eleanor the unexpired leases of his theatres at Brighton and Lewes and the profits thereof after payment of his debts, as well as all his remaining estate and effects. He had married her at St Paul, Covent Garden, on 4 April 1769, at which time she was registered as Eleanor Candler, widow, of the parish of St Marylebone. Fox recommended in his will that the management of the two theatres should be put into the hands of James Wild, the prompter at Covent Garden, for a salary of two guineas per week. He also directed that his sister Mary Fox should be appointed housekeeper at one of the theatres at a salary of £20 per year and that Richard Thomas should be retained as boxeeper. The will was proved by his executors Eleanor Fox, Stephen Ponne (a builder at Brighton), and James Charles Mitchell (gentleman) at London on 12 September 1792 (a fourth named executor, Richard Kent, brickmaker of Brighton, had since died).

Fox had died, however, with debts amounting to £2700, including a mortgage of £1600 held by Hewitt Cobb, an attorney of Clement's Inn. Mrs Fox was given a benefit at Brighton on 21 August 1792 which brought her £80. Cobb allowed her an annuity of £100 which he subsequently reduced to £75, paid to her until her death at Bath on 13 June 1798. She was buried at St James's Church, Bath, on 27 June 1798. Although she probably acted in the provinces, and certainly at Ostend in 1782, Mrs Fox never appeared on the London stage. After her death, her orphans were given a benefit on 11 September 1798 in Brighton, where they were living at No 17, Black Lion Street. Cobb continued to pay the annuity to the daughter Eleanor ("Nelly") Fox who shared it with another sister and brother William Fox (d. 1803). By the late 1790s the latter was already an established provincial actor and had played for a season (1790–91) at Drury Lane. Eleanor Fox married a Mr Brown by 1805. Cobb bought up all the shares and became owner of the theatrical property.

The identity of Joseph Fox's third surviving child, the other daughter, is not known to us. Joseph and Eleanor Fox had two other children who died young: William, who was buried at St Paul, Covent Garden, on 24 January 1777, and Henrietta, who was buried there on 2 December 1778.

Fox, T. *See* **Fox, JOHN.**

Fox, Thomas *d. 1796, singer.*

Thomas Fox was probably the Mr Fox who sang at Sadler's Wells on 7 and 24 May 1784 and who appeared in burlettas and other musical pieces at Astley's Amphitheatre between 1785 and 1796. Roles at Astley's for which his name was announced in the newspaper advertisements included a part in *Cupid Pilgrim* on 27 October 1785, the King of Clubs in *The Marriage of the Knave of Hearts* on 24 July 1786, Gripe in *Love from the Heart* on 4 September 1786, a role in *A Sales of English Beauties at Grand Cairo* on 17 September 1786, Cardinal Wolsey in *The King and the Cobbler* on 6 May 1791, a Countryman in *The Tythe Sheaf* in July 1791, a Corporal in *Bagshot Heath Camp* in August 1792, a character in the pantomime *La Forêt Noire* on 31 January 1793, the Lord of the Manor in *The Reasonable Wife* on 22 August 1795, and Sir Toby in *The Magician of the*

THOMAS FOX

by Jenner

Rocks on 16 May 1796. Perhaps this singer was related to the John Fox who was prompter at Astley's about that time.

According to the British Museum's *Catalogue of Engraved British Portraits*, the ballad singer Thomas Fox died in 1796. His portrait was engraved by I. Jenner and published by the engraver in that year.

Fox William *d. 1803, actor, singer.*

William Fox, the son of the actor Joseph Fox (d. 1791) by his wife Eleanor Candler Fox (d. 1798), made his first appearance in London at the Haymarket Theatre on 26 March 1781 as Leander in *The Padlock*. His father acted Don Diego in the same performance. Young Fox passed most of the following decade in the provinces: he was in Wilkinson's company at York in 1786, with his father's company at Bath in 1787, and with Masterman's company at Swansea in 1789. Although his name did not appear in the Drury Lane bills in 1789–90, he shared in benefit tickets with minor actors at that theatre on 2 June 1790. When his father opened his new theatre in Duke Street, Brighton, in July 1790, William was a member of the company.

He was engaged at Drury Lane for 1790–91, making his first appearance of the season as Frederick in *As You Like It* on 27 October 1790. He then played a Gentleman in *Isabella* on 7 December, Calippus in *The Grecian Daughter* on 14 December, William in *No Song No Supper* on 15 December, Charles in *The Haunted Tower* on 22 December, and the Boatswain (with a song) in *Don Juan* on 23 December. On 1 January 1791 he acted Ismael in the first performance of Cobb's comic opera *The Siege of Belgrade*, a role he had performed some 32 times by the end of the season. He also acted Trophonius in the premiere of Hoare's comic opera *The Cave of Trophonius* on 3 May 1791. At the end of the season he was one of several actors discharged from Drury Lane.

At Brighton again in the summer of 1791, Fox acted Young Fashion in *The Man of Quality* and Ferdinand in *Nootka Sound* at his benefit. He was probably the Fox who acted at Liverpool in September 1791 and at Newcastle on 5 December 1791 (his first appearance there in eight years, according to the *Newcastle Courant*, 3 December 1791). He was with Stephen Kemble's company at Edinburgh when the season began on 21 January 1793, playing Acres in *The Rivals*. There among other roles, Fox played Crabtree in *The School for Scandal*, the title role in *The Farmer*, Gregory Last in *The Volunteer*, the Host in *The Merry Wives of Windsor*, Nicholas in *The Midnight Hour*, and Trudge in *Inkle and Yarico*. In the 1794 season at Edinburgh he was seen as the Duke of Buckingham in *Richard III*, Jabal in *The Jew*, Ramirez in *The Castle of Andalusia*, Rosencrantz in *Hamlet*, and Zeydan in *Such Things Are.*

A notation in a manuscript now at the Folger Shakespeare Library, dated 19 February 1795, announced that "Young *Fox* of Brighton" had a new comedy in three acts which Colman was to produce at the Haymarket Theatre the ensuing summer, under John Bannister's "Sanction," but the Haymarket bills for that summer reveal no such piece, nor does Nicoll list a play by Fox. Curiously enough, another manuscript entry, this one at the Public Record Office, indicates that a Mr Fox was granted a license for plays and entertainments at the Haymarket for 14 March 1796; however, *The London Stage* shows no bills for the Haymarket for that or any date proximate.

Fox passed the remainder of his career as an itinerant. When he played at Wolverhampton in February 1799, taking almost £60 at his benefit, the *Monthly Mirror* for that month reported that "our old favourite, who has trod this stage several seasons," had lost "none of his popularity." He was at Worcester in 1801, and back at Wolverhampton in December–January 1801–2, again referred to as "our favourite low comedian."

Little more than the indication that he was popular in the provinces survives as testimony to William Fox's acting. In the *Theatric Tourist,* James Winston told an amusing story about Fox's hairdressing in one instance: "When the tax on hair powder first came up, it was exceedingly unpopular at Brighton, insomuch that persons using it, subjected themselves to public insult, Mr. Fox, the late manager's son, having a character to perform, which rendered powder necessary, applied it to one side of his head, and not the other . . . ; being interrogated as to the reason of the oddity, he replied, that he did it to please both parties."

William Fox died, probably at Worcester, soon after he made his will in that city on 2 March 1803. He left his property to his wife and executrix Mary (née Mandevill) whom he had married at Edinburgh.

No children were mentioned in his will, which was proved by his widow at London on 4 April 1803. For information on William Fox's parents and sisters, and his annuity share from his father's theatres, see Joseph Fox (d. 1791).

Foxall, Mr *[fl. 1735–1737], house servant?*

Mr Foxall's benefit tickets were accepted on 3 June 1735, 28 May 1736, and 20 May 1737 at Drury Lane. He was probably one of the house servants.

Foxwell, Mr *[fl. 1745], house servant?*

Mr Foxwell's benefit tickets were accepted at the Goodman's Fields Theatre on 1 May 1745. He was probably a house servant.

Foxwell, Sarah *[fl. 1729], actress.*

Sarah Foxwell played Dolly Trull in a performance of *The Beggar's Opera* given by a "Lilliputian Company" at Lincoln's Inn Fields on 1 January 1729.

Foy, Mr *[fl. 1790–1793], violinist.*

A Mr Foy, violinist, was on the list of musicians appointed by the Royal Society of Musicians to play at the annual concerts at St Paul's each May from 1790 through 1793. Perhaps he was related to the violinist James Foy (d. 1820) of Dorsetshire.

Fraizer. *See* **Frazier.**

France, Mons *[fl. 1785], acrobat.*

Monsieur France (a pseudonym?) was one of the tumblers who performed at Astley's Amphitheatre on 7 April 1785.

Francel. *See* **Frantzel.**

Frances. *See also* **Francis.**

Frances, Mrs *[fl. 1729], actress.*

A Mrs Frances had an unspecified role in

Hunter at Fielding's booth at Bartholomew Fair on 23 August 1729.

"Francesina, La," stage name of Elisabetta Duparc *d. 1778, singer, dancer.*

Elisabetta Duparc, called "La Francesina" (or "Francescina"), was French by birth but was trained in Italy. Details of her continental career are not known. On 15 November 1736 she was in England, singing before the Queen at a private recital in Kensington. After the singing was over, "*Francesina* performed several dances to the entire satisfaction of the court."

On 23 November she appeared at the King's Theatre in the Haymarket as a member of Porpora's opera company, singing Laodice in *Siroe*. She followed that with Argia in *Merope*, Barrene in *Demetrio*, Servilla in *Tito*, and Cresua in *Demofoonte*. In 1737–38 she sang Rosimiri in *Arsace*,

Harvard Theatre Collection

"LA FRANCESINA" (Elizabeth Duparc)

engraving by Faber, after Knapton

Courtesy of Music and Letters

"LA FRANCESINA" and
GEORGE FRIDERIC HANDEL

artist unknown

Clotile in *Faramondo*, Isifile in *La conquista del vello d'oro*, Sallustia in *Alessandro severo*, Climene in *Partenio*, and Romilda in *Serse*. In 1738–39 she sang Michael in *Saul* and the first soprano part in *Israel in Egypt*, and she may have participated in *Jupiter in Argos*.

With Handel at Lincoln's Inn Fields in 1739–40 she sang in a St Cecilia's Day concert, was Galatea in *Acis and Galatea*, sang in *L'Allegro, il Penseroso, ed il Moderato*, and took the lead in *Esther*. In Handel's final opera season at that theatre she sang Rosmene in *Imeneo*, the title role in *Deidamia*, and a part in Veracini's *A New Eclogue*. She was not heard again in London until 10 February 1744 at Covent Garden when she sang the title role in *Semele*. That spring she also sang Dalila in *Samson*, Asenath in *Joseph and His Brothers*, and (at the King's Theatre) a role in *Alceste*. In 1744–45 she sang the title role in *Deborah*, Iola in *Hercules*, and Nitocris in *Balshazzar* at the King's Theatre and ap-

peared at a benefit for "decay'd" musicians at Covent Garden. For her efforts in 1744–45 at the King's she was paid £400. Her only known appearance during the 1745–46 season was at Covent Garden on 14 February 1746 when *The New Occasional Oratorio* was presented.

"La Francesina" seems not to have sung in London again until 11 January 1752, when she participated in a concert at the Great Room in Dean Street, Soho. Dr Burney did not value her highly as a singer, but she was clearly a favorite of Handel, under whose tutelage she is said to have improved considerably over the years. She died, according to the *Catalogue of Engraved Portraits in the British Museum*, in 1778.

George Knapton painted her portrait and J. Faber made a mezzotint engraving of it in 1737. An anonymous artist drew Elisabetta with Handel about 1745; that red chalk picture was owned in 1935 by Harry Stone of New York.

Franche, John Ernest   ₍fl. 1794₎, *musician.*

John Ernest Franche was a subscriber to the New Musical Fund in 1794. An A. C. Franch, possibly a relative, was an honorary member of the society in 1805.

Franchi, Angelo   ₍fl. 1783–1785₎, *singer.*

Angelo Franchi made his first London appearance at the King's Theatre on 16 December 1783 as Monsieur Floran in *L'albergatrice vivace*. He followed that with Masotto in *I rivali delusi* on 6 January 1784, Narbale in *Il trionfo d'Arianna* on 17 January, Leango in *L'eroe cinese* on 17 February, Lelio in *La schiava* on 24 February, a role in *Demofoonte* on 4 March, Marchese Roberto in *Le gelosie villane* on 15 April, a role in *Issipile* on 8 May, and Gracinto in *Le gemelle* on 12 June.

His schedule in 1784–85 was not so

heavy. He sang Il Conte di Ripaverde in *Il curioso indiscreto*, a role in *Demetrio*, Monsieur de Crotignac in *Il pittore parigino*, Amasi in *Netteti*, a vocal role in an heroic ballet based on *Macbeth*, and a role in *La finta principessa*. His salary for the season was £250. He made his last appearance in England on 10 May 1785 in *Il pittore parigino*.

Francis. *See also* FRANCES.

Francis, Mr [*fl.* 1751], *actor.*

Mr Francis was a member of the summer company acting at Richmond and Twickenham in 1751. At Richmond he played Friendly in *A Bold Stroke for a Wife* on 22 June, Sullen in *The Beaux' Stratagem* and Corydon in *Damon and Phillida* on 6 July, Butler in *The Drummer* on 13 July, Brazen in *The Recruiting Officer* on 29 July, Rosano in *The Fair Penitent* on 3 August, Claudio in *Much Ado About Nothing* and both Sir Dilberry Diddle and Tearthroat in *Diversions of the Morning* on 24 August, one of the Carriers in *Henry IV* on 26 August, and one of the Bravoes in *The Inconstant* on 31 August.

At Twickenham he was Horatio in *The Wife's Relief* on 9 July, Friendly in *The Schoolboy* on 16 July, and the Prince in *Romeo and Juliet* on 27 August. Despite that flurry of activity in 1751, Francis seems not to have played in London or its suburbs again.

Francis, Mr [*fl.* 1794], *equestrian.*
Thomas Frost in *Circus Life and Circus Celebrities* (1875) cited a Mr Francis, equestrian, at the Royal Circus in 1794. He is otherwise unknown.

Francis, Mrs [*fl.* 1794–1795], *dresser.*
During the season of 1794–95 Mrs Francis, a dresser, was paid 17*s.* per week at Covent Garden Theatre.

Francis, Master. *See* BLAND, GEORGE.

Francis, Miss [*fl.* 1719–1723], *dancer, actress.*

Miss Francis danced a "new Passacaille" at Lincoln's Inn Fields Theatre on 19 March 1719, a number which she repeated on 27 April. She was a student of Kellom Tomlinson, and when he published *The Art of Dancing* in 1734 he remembered her as "*Miss* Francis, *who, on the Theatre Royal in* Little Lincoln's-Inn-Fields, *performed the* Passacaille de Scilla, *consisting of above a thousand Measures or Steps, without making the least Mistake; but she left me in the midst of her Improvement.*"

She was a regular feature at the theatre in the spring and summer of 1719, and in August and September she danced at Bartholomew and Southwark fairs. She remained a member of the Lincoln's Inn Fields troupe through the 1722–23 season, regularly appearing as an entr'acte entertainer. Most of the bills gave no titles for her dances, though we know she performed the *French Peasant* with Newhouse and a similar dance with Sandham; she appeared with Delagarde's two sons; and for her benefit on 19 May 1721 she offered some new dances and attracted a house worth £146 17*s.* 6*d.*

On 23 November 1721 she tried her hand at acting a small part: the Page in *The Orphan*, but that was evidently her only attempt at acting. Except for an appearance at Richmond on 20 August 1722 and a return to the fairs in August and September of the same year, she confined her activity to Lincoln's Inn Fields.

Francis, Bodley William *d. 1780, actor, house servant.*
An actor named Francis appeared in a cast among several other debutants at the Haymarket on 1 September 1764, playing Downright in *Every Man in His Humour*. The name did not appear again until the Haymarket bill of 18 June 1766, when one Francis played one of the Constables in Foote's *The Minor*, a performance which

he repeated several times during that summer season. Francis shifted that same season to Barry's summer company at the King's Theatre to play Ternon in *Venice Preserv'd* on 13 and 15 August and 10 September.

Was that the Francis who acted at the Haymarket in the summer of 1772? He had been preceded that season by Miss Francis, as the Boy in *The Contrivances*, an afterpiece on 10 July. He made his bow in an unspecified part in *The Rehearsal* on 10 August, repeated it on 24 August, and bowed out for the season as the Lord Mayor in *Richard III* on 17 September, a night on which little Miss Francis made her second appearance as the Duke of York. Francis played on 18 June 1773 his unspecified role in *The Rehearsal*, on 6 August (replacing Osborne) Margin in *The Bankrupt*, on 11 August an unspecified part in *The Minor*, on 27 August another in *A Trip to Portsmouth*, on 3 September still another in *The Orators* (on that night Miss Francis played Dicky Drugger in *The Pantheonites*), and ended his activities on 14 September 1773 in *The Bankrupt* (part unspecified but probably Margin again). He figured but once in the summer season of 1774, on 27 June in an unspecified part in *The Rehearsal*. "For this night only," on 21 September 1774 a company played for a special benefit *The Duellist*. "Frances" was listed in a role not given in the bill. Again, on the bill at the Haymarket on 15 May 1775 his role was concealed. He played only three times the next summer season at the Haymarket: in *The Rehearsal* on 2 August 1776 (Miss Francis was also present), Furnish in *The Miser* on 18 September 1776, and Wat Dreary in *The Beggar's Opera* on 20 September. After that his acting in London is not recorded again until a season of at least 14 nights, probably more, of a pickup company at the Windsor Castle Inn, King Street, Hammersmith, 17 June–27 July 1785. He played only Frederick in *The Wonder* on 17 June, so far as

the bills show. His daughter Sarah was briefly in the company.

Parallel with the Haymarket actor's sporadic and rather modest attempts was the career of a Francis at Covent Garden, who apparently never acted there but served the theatre in one auxiliary capacity or another from 1760 through 1777. The Covent Garden aide began as a dresser in 1760–61 as 1s. per night. He always shared benefits or was allowed to "give out" benefit tickets along with several other minor people of the house staff. But by 1767 he may have achieved a position of some trust. He was the subject of the Covent Garden account-book entry of 17 February 1767: "Paid Wm Francis for writing parts £5 3d." Ten years later, on 27 November 1777: "Paid Francis for writing parts £2 11s." That chore was usually an important function of one of the prompter's assistants. That person seems without a doubt to have been the Bodley William Francis identified as late of Covent Garden Theatre by the *Morning Chronicle* of 4 March after his death on 2 March 1780.

A reasonable conclusion would seem to be that the Covent Garden house servant Bodley William Francis unsuccessfully sought to fashion an acting career summer after summer, subduing his ambition and accepting minor parts at the Haymarket. This hypothesis seems strengthened by several linked facts: "Sarah Daūgr of Bodly William Francis by Anne his wife" was christened at the "actors' church," St Paul, Covent Garden, on 3 April 1765. Sarah fashioned a fairly successful career, which is traceable in London through 1792–93. It seems obvious that she began it in the juvenile parts at the Haymarket in 1771 under the guidance of her father.

Bodley William Francis had another, better known, daughter on the stage. She was Mary, christened on 2 December 1770 at St Paul, Covent Garden. She married John Follett the younger in 1793. A son of Bodley William Francis, Thomas Bodley Francis, christened on 4 September 1768, grew up to play in the Covent Garden Theatre band before he died at 34. From several indications it is probable that the "William Bodley son of Bodley William Francis by Anne his wife" christened at the family church on 5 October 1766 was the William Francis who acted in England and America, dying in Philadelphia in 1827.

Bodley William Francis (which he is called in every one of the parish register notices concerning his family except that of his death, where the given names are reversed) was buried at St Paul, Covent Garden, on 8 May 1780.

Francis, Dolly or **Dorothea.** *See* JOR-DAN, DOROTHY.

Francis, Mrs [**Francis, Sarah?**] [*fl. 1792?–1801?*], *actress.*

The actress who was introduced anonymously to the London public at Covent Garden Theatre on 7 June 1798 (the last night of the season) in the title part in *Rosina* was identified in the June *Monthly Mirror* as Mrs Francis and as being from the Royalty Theatre. She was very likely the Mrs Francis who was said to be from the Theatre Royal, York, when she joined Macready's company at Birmingham in December 1797. "Mrs Francis," thought an anonymous critic, "certainly has merit, but her deportment possesses a confidant assurance tending to create disgust."

There is some doubt whether she was the Mrs Francis who played Jacintha in *The Suspicious Husband* at the Smock Alley Theatre, Dublin, in 1792 (however, Macready was in that cast). A Mrs Francis played Miranda in *The Tempest* in Manchester in 1793. Very likely our subject was the woman mentioned in the Christ Church, Harrogate, baptismal register on 16 September 1798, on which date a daughter of Francis and Sarah Francis, "comedians," was christened. She was per-

haps also the Mrs Francis who first appeared at Edinburgh on 27 June 1801 at the Theatre Royal as Kathleen in *The Poor Soldier* and Mrs Candour in *The School for Scandal.*

Francis, Mary. *See* FOLLETT, MRS JOHN.

Francis, Sarah *b. 1765? actress, singer, dancer.*

Sarah Francis was christened at St Paul, Covent Garden, on 3 April 1765. She was the daughter of Bodley William and Anne Francis. Her father, her sister Mary, and her brothers William Bodley and Thomas Bodley Francis were all at some time London performers.

Sarah must have been the Miss Francis who was the Boy in *The Contrivances* at the Haymarket on 10 July 1772. Her father was there in Foote's company that season but did not play that night. She was given the traditional debut role for children, the little Duke of York in *Richard III*, for her second appearance, on 17 September.

Her father was a minor functionary of the Covent Garden theatre during the winter season, and she repeated her small role in *The Contrivances* on 28 May 1773. She carried the part to the Haymarket on 2 August. She helped introduce Francis Gentleman's new and short-lived farce *The Pantheonites* on 3 September, repeating on 9 September.

In 1774 little Miss Francis secured only two nights of work at the Haymarket, both in some unspecified part in *The Rehearsal*. In 1775 she played two parts in *The Rehearsal*. On 5 March 1776 at Covent Garden she was carried on the bills as a substitute for Miss Anne Pitt—a strange opportunity for an eleven-year-old girl—as Margery in *The Syrens*.

For the next few years Sarah acted small parts, sometimes named and sometimes not. She also sang, but nearly always in choruses, and danced, but always with more than one partner. She was not seen often in any capacity. In 1776–77 she was little Lord William in *The Countess of Salisbury* and one of the Lilliputians in *Lilliput* at Covent Garden. In 1777–78 she added only the Child in *Isabella*; in 1779–80 she added the Boy in *Henry V* and a "Principal Character" in *The Touchstone* at Covent Garden and, in September at the Haymarket, Prince Edward in *Richard III*.

In 1780–81, listed for the first time among the dancers, and drawing £1 5s. per week pay, she cavorted with Aldridge, Langrish, Jackson, and Miss Besford in *Sports of the Green*, danced in minuets, quadrilles, and cotillions and swelled choruses and crowds. On 10 May 1781 she was for the first time shown as being authorized benefit tickets. That summer at the Haymarket she was Lucinda in *Love in a Village* for the first time, danced in *The Life and Death of Common Sense*, and began her curiously varied series of roles in *The Beggar's Opera* as Jemmy Twitcher. (The June 1781 edition of Dublin's *Hibernian Magazine* published "partners of my toils and pleasures" by W. Jackson, a "vaudeville to *The Lord of the Manor*," as sung by a Miss Francis with other singers, all of whom were at that period in Ireland —Ryder, Johnson, and Mrs Richards.)

In 1782–83 Miss Francis appeared only once in the bills—on 22 October 1782 as Betty Doxey in *The Beggar's Opera*—but probably sang in the choruses. She was paid £1 5s. weekly. During the season a Miss M[ary] Francis was distinguishable from her sister in the bills the two times Mary played, both times as Prince Edward in *Richard III*. The summer of 1783 saw Sarah, then 18, back at the Haymarket to sing and dance in *Harlequin Teague*, perform Jemmy Twitcher, depict one of the Actresses in *The Manager in Distress*, and add Dorcas in *Thomas and Sally*.

She was not in the Covent Garden bills in 1783–84 yet she shared in tickets on 15

May 1784, so she must have contributed something. She was perhaps the Francis on the company list at York in 1785–86. She was classed as a singer on the Covent Garden list in 1784–85 but was in the bills only on 26 November 1784, singing the "Solemn Dirge" accompanying Juliet's funeral procession.

In the summer of 1785 Sarah returned to the Haymarket to play several old parts and add the inconsiderable role of Miss Barnavag in *A Beggar on Horseback*. She also played on 17 June in a pickup company of more experienced actors at the Windsor Castle Inn, King Street, Hammersmith, where she was a chambermaid in *The Jealous Wife*, and she very likely took other parts there. Her father turned up at Hammersmith for his last recorded performance. She returned on 8 July to play the more interesting part of Fanny in *The Clandestine Marriage*.

In 1785–86 at Covent Garden Sarah was one of the Bacchants in *Comus*, a Lady in *Which is the Man?*, Betty Doxey, and assisted, with a good many others, in Shield's invention "a Roman Ovation" inserted into Act V of *Catherine and Petruchio*.

Grown now into young womanhood Sarah settled down into her pattern of singing medium size parts in musical comedies and ballad operas, acting then in occasional farces, dancing in pantomime and entr'acte, at Covent Garden in the winter and Haymarket in the summer. But the *Oracle* for 15 October 1789 reported that she was among several persons discharged from the Haymarket company "In consequence of the management . . . having devolved on young Colman. . . ." And indeed, she was not on the list at the Haymarket in 1790 or ever again. (She may have spent the summer of 1790 in Ireland, for a song, "To speer my love, with glances fair," hesitantly dated 1790? by the *Catalogue of Printed Music in the British Museum*, was published at Dublin.)

She had been earning £1 10s. per week at Covent Garden in 1789–90, but in 1790–91 she was raised to £2 and began to be employed much more frequently. She was evidently a quick study and a dependable understudy because, although her repertoire was not wide, she often assumed roles at a few hours' notice—as, for instance, 27 January 1791 when she took Lucinda in *Love in a Village* ("Mrs Mountain being confin'd"). But she never found the security of constant first- or second-rate roles, her very versatility perhaps making against her. She was to the end of her career still very likely to be found in a chorus greeting the "Grand Triumphal Entry of Alexander into Babylon" in *Alexander the Great*, with two dozen other voices singing the "Solemn Dirge" accompanying Juliet's funeral march, and the like, dancing as a "Pantomimical Character," as she did in Bonnor and Merry's new pantomime *The Picture of Paris*, or walking as a Female Prisoner in *The Crusade* spectacle.

Sarah Francis was last recorded as playing on 12 June 1793, at Covent Garden, as Stella in *Robin Hood*. Her parts, in addition to those named above, included: Trusty in *The Provok'd Husband*, Grace in *Separate Maintenance*, the original Charlotte in James Cobb's *English Readings*, Serina in *The Orphan*, Charlotte in *The Intriguing Chambermaid*, the Colonel's Lady in *Tippoo Saib*, Fanny Goodwin in *The Brothers*, the Milliner in *The Suspicious Husband*, a Shepherdess in *Cymon*, Arabella in *The Author*, Coach Passenger in *Ways and Means*, Maid of Honour in *Chrononhotonthologos*, Donna Anna in *Don Juan*, the original Betty in *Thimble's Flight from the Shopboard*, Emai in *The Death of Captain Cook*, Nora in *Love in a Camp*, and Mrs Coaxer in *The Beggar's Opera*.

Francis, Thomas Bodley *1768–1802, instrumentalist.*

Thomas Bodley Francis, son of the actor (and house servant) Bodley William Francis and his wife Anne, was christened 4 September 1768 at St Paul, Covent Garden.

When he was proposed for membership in the Royal Society of Musicians on 6 December 1789 he was certified by Griffith Jones to have "Studied music under Mr [Walter] Clagget for five years and upwards and has made it his livelihood three years prior to that—plays the Violin, Tenor, Violoncello and Double Bass—for the latter he is engaged at Covent Garden and the Haymarket Theatres. Is a single Man, one and twenty years of age." He was balloted for on 7 March 1790, secured 12 yeas against one nay, and signed the membership book. The Governors of the Society assigned him to play double bass at the annual concerts for the benefit of the clergy at St Paul's Cathedral every May from 1790 through 1798. He was himself a Governor in 1797 and 1798.

He was named as one of 27 "Principal Instrumental Performers" in a band of 200 musicians supporting the solo singers and chorus at Covent Garden on 20 February 1795 in *A Grand Selection of Sacred Music, From the Works of Handel*. He was occasionally named in the bills advertising the Ashleys' oratorios at Covent Garden, and in other musical events until after the turn of the century.

"Thomas Bodily Francis aged 34 years" was buried at St Paul, Covent Garden, on 14 August 1802. A notation of 5 September in the Minute Books of the Royal Society of Musicians recorded payment of £8 to pay for his funeral. On 16 September 1802 administration of his property, worth under £20 was granted to Matthew Little, a creditor, "Mary Follett, natural and lawful sister & next of kin renouncing."

Francis, William Bodley *1766–1827, actor, dancer, ballet master, singer.*

William Bodley Francis was born to the actor and house servant Bodley William

Harvard Theatre Collection

WILLIAM BODLEY FRANCIS, as Sir George Thunder

engraving by Longacre, after Neagle

Francis and his wife Anne, probably around the first of October 1766. He was christened on 5 October in St Paul, Covent Garden. His brother Thomas Bodley Francis was a musician, and his sisters Sarah and Mary were both on the stage. Unlike his father and siblings, his record of London performance is slight, consisting of one short summer season in an irregular company at the little theatre in the Windsor Castle Inn in King Street, Hammersmith. Furthermore, it is not certain how much of that one season he shone, inasmuch as many of the bills are lost and those which are left make much use of "&c." He is thought to have played Frederick in *The Wonder: A Woman Keeps a Secret* on 17 June 1785. Even that is questionable, for the name Francis opposite the character is a manuscript notation on the playbill in the New York Public Library Theatre Collection, with the printed name of the actor Murray deleted. It is conceivable that our subject

was the William Francis, bachelor, who married Eleanor Slater, spinster, on 15 February 1786, at St Marylebone Church. There were Slaters acting at that period.

William Bodley Francis went on to some distinction as harlequin, ballet master, and actor in the English provinces and in America. He was likely the Mr Francis who was at Edinburgh's Theatre Royal, Shakespeare Square, between 22 December 1787 and 8 March 1788, playing the following parts: Balthazar in *Romeo and Juliet*, Beau Trippet in *The Lying Valet*, Cudden in *The Agreeable Surprise*, Dapper in *The Citizen*, a Footman in *The Devil to Pay*, Francis in *The Brothers*, the French Lover in *Mother Shipton*, an Indian in *Inkle and Yarico*, Lounge in *The Young Quaker*, Lovelace in *Three Weeks after Marriage*, the Nephew in *The Irish Widow*, Osric in *Hamlet*, a Prisoner in *Such Things Are*, Seaton in *Macbeth*, Stanmore in *Oroonoko*, and Vane in *The Chapter of Accidents*. He may have been the Mr Francis recorded by Kathleen Barker as playing a principal character in *The Royal Naval Review* in Merchant Taylors' Hall in Bristol on 28 November 1789.

The Thespian Mirror . . . of the Theatres Royal, Manchester, Liverpool, and Chester (1793) talked briefly of "Francis the pantomime motley hero," who, though "seldom exciting profound admiration," gave to his roles "his utmost endeavours." It was thought that "His Bagatelle [in O'Keeffe's *The Poor Soldier*] proves him possessed of merit."

Seilhamer in his *History of the American Theatre* said:

William Francis had been the *Harlequin* at Manchester and Birmingham since 1787, and was noted for the skill with which he prepared pantomimic ballets for the stage and superintended their production. Mr. Wignell saw a specimen of his work in the "Enchanted Wood" at the Haymarket in 1792, and engaged him for similar services in Philadelphia.

(Francis's pantomime *The Enchanted Wood* had been given six performances in July and August 1792.) A Mr and Mrs Francis played at Crow Street, Dublin, in the summer of 1792. As Seilhamer observed, William Francis is liable to be confused with another dancer who went by that name in America, but whose real name was Francis Menzius or Mentges, and who danced before the Revolution and not after.

Because of progressive gout in legs and feet Francis abandoned pantomime parts which required him to dance and worked into a varied line of other characters which, Dunlap remembered, he played "respecably."

His first advertised Philadelphia performance was on the opening night of Wignell and Reinagle's New Theatre in Chestnut Street, 17 February 1794, as one of the *banditti* in *The Castle of Andalusia*. Mrs Francis was Doiley in the afterpiece *Who's the Dupe*. His first and second named parts were on 19 February—Sampson in *Isabella* and William in *Rosina*. For the rest of the Philadelphia season, which ran until 18 July 1794, he was kept busy in old men, eccentrics, rustics, foreigners, servants, and dialect characters. He played Peter in *The Dramatist*, Tipple in *The Flitch of Bacon*, the Drunken Cook in *The Lying Valet*, Hodge in *Love in a Village*, Tom in *The Jealous Wife*, Moses in *The School for Scandal*, Snarl in *The Village Lawyer*, Rundy in *The Farmer*, Pedro in *Isabella*, Dr Rosy in *Saint Patrick's Day*, Jack in *The Sailor's Landlady*, Tag in *The Spoiled Child*, Spruce in *The School for Wives*, Simkin in *The Deserter*, Coupee in *The Virgin Unmask'd*, Rossano in *The Fair Penitent*, the Music Master in *Catherine and Petruchio*, Arcas in *The Grecian Daughter*, Charley in *The Highland Reel*, David in *The Rivals*, John in *The Agreeable Surprise*, Jasper in *Miss in Her Teens*, Ratcliff in *Richard III*, Rosencrantz in *Hamlet*, Lubin in *La Forêt noire*, Sir Wil-

liam Wealthy in *The Quality Binding*, Antonio in *The Duenna*, William in *As You Like It*, the Apothecary in *Romeo and Juliet*, Watty Cockney in *The Romp*, the Drummer in *The Battle of Hexham*, Perez in *The Mourning Bride*, Jack Mainstay in *Embargo*, Peterson in *Gustavas Vasa*, Bob in *The Woodman*, Bundle in *The Waterman*, Hippy in *How to Grow Rich*, Ben Hassan in *Slaves in Algiers*, Frill in *The Prisoner at Large*, the First Gentleman in *Cymbeline*, Apoxem in *The Devil Upon two Sticks*, Paul Perry in *Ways and Means*, Hippolito in *The Tempest*, and Harlequin in *The Birth of Harlequin*. Surely his time at Manchester had been well employed, or he was an exceedingly quick study. He was doubtless the Francis who played similar parts in Charleston from 29 September 1794 to 7 February 1795.

Parts like those were his lot until the end, in 1821, of his long career with the Philadelphia company. He accompanied the troupe to New York, Baltimore, Washington, and Alexandria. Mrs Francis acted during all those years and at all those places, gradually progressing from soubrettes and then the frilly young women of sentimental comedy to portly matrons. She had received her first experience in Manchester and had never acted in London.

William Francis died on 12 May 1827, and was buried in the grounds of Christ Church, Philadelphia. The age stated in his inscription, 64 years, was off by three years and is perpetuated in Grove and elsewhere. W. B. Wood in his *Recollections* gave Francis's age at death as 69.

Mrs Francis (born 1766) survived her husband until 1834.

William Bodley Francis was pictured as Sir George Thunder in *Wild Oats* in a painting by John Neagle. The picture is now in the Players Club in New York. It was engraved by J. B. Longacre and published by A. R. Poole in Philadelphia in 1826. Francis was also depicted as "Sir Absolute" (Sir Anthony Absolute in *The*

Rivals?), with other performers, in an engraving by T. Johnston.

Francisco, Signor. *See also* FRANKLYN, MR, and GALLI, FRANCESCO.

Francisco, Signor [*fl. 1699*], *singer.*
On 25 December 1699 Sir John Vanbrugh wrote to the Earl of Manchester from London: "We have the Emperors Crooked Eunuch here, Francisco. They give him a hundred and twenty Guineas for five times. He has sung Once and was well likt." Signor Francisco was presumably singing at one of the theatres, perhaps Lincoln's Inn Fields, to which Vanbrugh referred in other parts of the same letter.

Francisco, Mr [*fl. 1728*], *dancer.*
At the Haymarket Theatre on 20 March 1728 a dancer named Francisco performed with Signora Violante.

Francisco, Signor [*d. 1741*]. *See* GOODSENS, FRANCISCO.

Francisco, Signor [*fl. 1744–1763?*], *dancer, acrobat, bell ringer.*
Signor Francisco appeared as a dancer and tumbler at the Stoke's Croft Theatre in Bristol in February and March 1744, November 1745, and March 1746 as a member of Dominique's troupe of entertainers. The company was advertised as from Sadler's Wells in London, and Francisco had presumably performed there with the troupe. He was, perhaps, the Francisco who appeared at the New Concert Hall in Edinburgh on 26 February 1752.

According to a bill for the Orchard Street Theatre in Bath, Francisco had also appeared at some point at Covent Garden Theatre in London:

The celebrated Sig. FRANCISCO, who performed at the Theatre Royal in Covent Garden in the Entertainment of Harlequin Sorcerer, will ring eight Bells, namely, two on his head, two in each hand, and one on each Foot, rising, changing and falling them with unparalleled Dexterity. He also plays several Tunes on them with the greatest Exactness, and is allowed the greatest Curiosity of the kind in the world.

That bill was dated only "Tuesday, June 21." June 21 fell on a Tuesday in 1757 (the first year it did so after the Orchard Street Theatre opened in 1750), and *Harlequin Sorcerer* had been performed at Covent Garden in the early months of 1757 (though the cast was not listed in the bills).

Francisco and Rayner were said to have been coming to Manchester from Sadler's Wells in London and from Preston Guild in the fall of 1762 for a four-week engagement. In May and June 1763 a Mr Franklin of Covent Garden, a pantomime performer, appeared with Mathews at Coopers' Hall in Bristol. His billing sounds very much like Francisco's: he and Mathews performed "Equilibres on the Wire," and at the performances on 23, 24, and 25 May 1763 in Bristol a bell-ringing exhibition was advertised, not unlike that of Francisco's in the previous decade—but the performer was not mentioned. Francisco could have changed his name (perhaps his name was Franklin to begin with) after the death in 1758 of a Mr Franklyn whose specialty was, again, the bell-ringing act.

Francisco, Mr [*fl. 1776*], *actor.*
On 16 September 1776 at the Haymarket Theatre a Mr Francisco played one of the two Master Taylors in *The Taylors.*

Francisque. *See* MOYLIN, FRANCISQUE.

Franck, Anthony [*fl. 1661–1662*], *trumpeter.*
Two warrants in the Lord Chamberlain's accounts dated 19 December 1661 stated that John Baker was appointed to replace Anthony Franck as a trumpeter in the

King's Musick, but another warrant in 1662 listed Franck as a musician in ordinary.

Franck, Johann Wolfgang b. c. 1641, impresario, composer.

Johann Wolfgang Franck was born about 1641 and from 1665 to 1679 he served at the court of the Margrave of Anspach. He was a court musician and, from 1673, director of the court music and court theatre. He composed several operas and other works while there and continued throughout his career to write operas and songs. His *Die drey Tochter Cecrops* (1679) is the earliest German opera that has survived in full score.

Franck killed one of his court musicians in a rage of jealousy in January 1679 and decided that desertion to Hamburg was the better part of valor. There he continued his successful career as a composer and, from 1682 to 1685, served as music director of the Hamburg Cathedral.

By 1690 Franck was in London, organizing concerts with Robert King. On 10 October 1690 the *London Gazette* noted that "Mr Franck's Consort of Vocal and Instrumental Musick will be performed to-morrow, being Friday the 10th instant, at the Two Golden-Balls at the upper-end of Bow-Street, Covent Garden, at 7 in the Evening, and next Wednesday at the Outropers-Office on the Royal Exchange, and will be continued all the ensuing Winter." On 19 February 1691 the same paper announced that "The Consort of Musick, lately in Bow Street, is removed next Bedford Gate in Charles Street, Covent Garden, where a room is newly built for that purpose." Franck and King's advertisements appeared regularly in 1690–91 and 1691–92. On 17 September 1691 they announced that they were enlarging their music room, and by the following March they had dubbed their place the "Vendu." They attracted a very elegant auditory, the most notable being the Ambassador from Morocco and his entourage.

The *Gentleman's Journal* in May 1693, when Franck was apparently working without his partner King, noted that "We have had lately a Consort of Music, which as it pleased the most nice and judicious lovers of that art, would doubtless have had your Approbation; I only speak of the Notes which were by Mr. Franck; As for the words I [Peter Motteux] made 'em in haste." In June Franck held a concert at York Buildings; in November he was operating in Charles Street; but by June 1694 he seems to have given up promoting concerts.

Franck may have remained in London at least until January 1696, when his music for *Love's Last Shift* was heard at Drury Lane. Many of the songs Franck composed while in London appeared in Motteux's *Journal* between May 1692 and May 1694 and in Franck's *Remedium Melancholiae* in 1690. The latter was advertised as being sold by the author, who was then living at Mr Bond's the barber in Lothbury. Other plays for which Franck provided music were *Timon of Athens* and *The Loves of Mars and Venus* (in revivals; the original music had been composed by Finger and Eccles). Grove cites a number of Franck's works, as does the *Catalogue of Printed Music in the British Museum*.

Franck may have died in London, though the date of his death is not known. He was still remembered in 1719 in D'Urfey's *Wit and Mirth*, for that collection contained lyrics of several songs that had been set by Franck.

Franco, Francesco [fl. 1668–1669], performer?

The London Stage lists Francesco Franco "detto Torangin" as a member of the King's Company in 1668–69. A warrant in the Lord Chamberlain's accounts dated 30 November 1668 cites Franco but does not indicate his duties in the troupe. Perhaps he was a performer.

François, Mr *[fl. 1799–1800]*, *scene painter?*

The Drury Lane accounts cite one François on 13 and again on 18 May 1799 for payments of £1 5*s*. He was apparently a scene painter. His benefit tickets were accepted at the theatre on 14 June 1800.

Francolino, Grimaldo *[fl. 1726–1727]*, *dancer, strong man.*

On 21 September 1726 an Italian troupe arrived in London to perform at the King's Theatre beginning 28 September. At the opening performance was presented "a Dance call'd the King of Morocco's Diversions, by Signor Grimaldo Francolino of Malta, and his most surprizing Activity and Strength in a Dance on his Knees with a wonderful heavy Machine upon his Head, never yet attempted by any one before." On 6 April 1727 the papers noted that "Signor Grimaldo Francolino of Malta, Operator for the Teeth, being on his Departure, will perform for this Time only some of his wonderful Dances; particularly one within [*sic*] a Dark Lanthorn."

This performer may have been John Baptist Grimaldi (d. 1760), Joe Grimaldi's great-grandfather, or related to him. The facts that Francolino was from Malta and associated with dentistry lend great weight to a likely connection, since the Grimaldis had roots in Malta and practised dentistry.

Frank, Master *[fl. 1770–1771]*, *actor.*

At the Haymarket Theatre on 27 September 1770 Master Frank and Miss Rose (age five) offered imitations of Mr and Mrs Cadwallader, characters in *The Author*. At the same house on 4 April 1771 Master Frank spoke an occasional prologue before *The Distrest Mother*, played Cadwallader, and spoke an original prologue to *The Author* in imitation of Foote.

Franket, Bernard *[fl. 1786]*, *dog trainer.*

The Bristol papers reported on 29 July 1786 that Bernard Franket and Michael and John Malizia, all Neopolitans, had been arrested for parading the streets with dancing dogs and had been flogged as vagrants at St Peter's Hospital. The Malizias had come from London, where their trained dogs had been performing at Astley's Amphitheatre, and it is likely that Franket was one of their troupe.

"Franki." *See* **DAVENPORT, FRANCES,** and **FRANKS.**

Franklin, Mr *[fl. 1763]*. *See* **FRANCISCO, SIGNOR.**

Franklin, Mrs, née Leary *[fl. 1786–1821]*, *singer, organist?*

Mrs Franklin was a popular soprano concert singer steadily and long employed at Vauxhall Gardens, where she appeared first in the summer of 1786 and through 1792 as Miss Leary. She was married by the summer of 1793. Doane's *Musical Directory* of 1794 listed her address as No 234, Piccadilly, and declared her also a performer in the concerts of the Academy of Ancient Music and the Anacreontic Society. She was living at the same address on 7 April 1798(?), when she had a benefit performance at Willis's Rooms, King Street, when Salomon led the band and Viganoni, Rovedino, Dignum, and Signora Angelleli sang, with Masi at the piano, Holmes on the bassoon, Miss Deysarque playing the harp, and Master Pinto on the violin. On 7 April 1802, by which time she was living at No 109, Queen Street, Golden Square, she had another benefit, at which Spagnioletti was leader, again at Willis's. The Crown and Anchor Tavern was the site of her benefit of 11 April 1804. Brooks, from Bath, led the band, and the singers Incledon, Townsend, Dignum, Mrs Mountain, and Miss Correy assisted. By 2 February 1808 Mrs Franklin was resident at No 14, Great Castle Street, Cavendish Square.

Mrs Franklin appears to have been active occasionally up to 1821. The *Catalogue of Printed Music in the British Museum* lists over 30 songs by James Hook, published "as sung by" Mrs Franklin at Vauxhall.

Franklin, [Robert Henry?] [1769–1802?], *actor, manager?*

A Mr Franklin played Old Norval in *Douglas* at the Haymarket Theatre on 23 April 1798 at a benefit for the widow and children of Sir Richard Perrott. It was the actor's only performance in London, apparently, and he was the only actor named Franklin playing in London at any time in the century. The afterpiece on the bill that night was *The Irishman in London*, in which he may also have participated, but the cast was not listed in the bill.

It is possible that the appearance at the Haymarket was a compassionate gesture on the part of the provincial actor-manager Robert Henry Franklin (1769–1802). In fact, the single appearance would necessarily indicate either an amateur or a provincial actor—and the rest of the company, led by the younger John Palmer, were professionals.

Robert Henry Franklin acted and managed at Derby, Sheffield, York, and elsewhere in the 1790s. Tate Wilkinson in *The Wandering Patentee* in 1795 said:

Mr. FRANKLIN made his appearance at Hull in Sir Lucius O'Trigger. That gentleman, without any compliment, has a natural turn for the muses, and has wrote many little pieces deserving of much approbation; particularly, when a boy, he more than assisted in the writing the romance of "Allan Fitzherbert." His merit as a comedian appears to be in the lower comic Irish characters, but he likes to play Marplot, Ranger, &c.; and what practice, aided by strong inclination, may do, I am not prophet enough to tell. His behaviour is that of a gentleman; and his educa-

tion, I believe, demands it from him as a just debt. He surprised all the hearts of the young ladies at Stamford (when in Mr. Pero's company) to such a degree, that he, with his Dublin persuasive argument, most honourably has taken to wife a lady of very respectable connections and fortune, and by his and her endeavours to avoid all superfluous expences, will I hope always make their pot boil.

If the Franklin who acted in London in 1798 was, in fact, Robert Henry Franklin, it is probable he had an important role in *The Irishman in Dublin*. The character of Old Norval would have been out of his line, but the *Monthly Mirror*, reporting on him at Stafford in November 1801, indicated that he occasionally took roles in serious plays: "Mr. Franklin, in comedy, is capable enough—his tragedy, however, is very indifferent."

When he made his will on 13 June 1802 he left in trust with his partner (after 1796) Thomas Shaftoe Robertson and his brother John Franklin for the benefit of his son Robert Augustine Franklin the "right title and interest in the company of Comedians known by the name of Robertson and ffranklin's company usually performing in the City of Lincoln, the towns of Boston Grantham and Spalding, the city of Peterborough and the town of Newark in Nottingham, the town of Wisbeck in the Isle of Ely . . . the town of Huntington and the town of Northampton. . . ." The will, made in Peterborough, Northampton, was proved in London on 8 September 1802.

According to the *Gentleman's Magazine* in 1793, Franklin had married a Miss Forster (or Foster), probably at Stamford, on 3 August of that year. The *Stamford Mercury* of 17 May 1799 reported that Mrs Franklin died on 13 May.

Franklin, Thomas [fl. 1786–1794], *equestrian, manager.*

On 25 April 1786 the bill for the Equestrian Amphitheatre in Union Street, Whitechapel, listed (Thomas) Franklin as one of

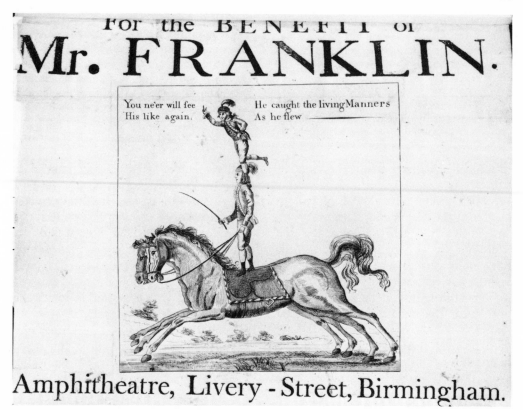

For the BENEFIT of

Mr. FRANKLIN.

You ne'er will fee His like again.

He caught the living Manners As he flew

Amphitheatre, Livery - Street, Birmingham.

By *permission of the Board of the British Library*

Benefit ticket, THOMAS FRANKLIN

artist unknown

the equestrians. At Bristol on 25 April 1788 in "a large commodious yard at the back of the Angel, in the Borough Walls, leading from Redcliff-street to Thames-street" was presented riding, rope-dancing, and other entertainments by a group of performers from Astley's and Hughes's riding schools in London, but called "[Benjamin] Handy's Troupe" in the advertisements. Featured were "the celebrated Mr. Franklin," "the Child of Promise" (Mary Ann Handy), Signora Riccardini (Mrs Handy), and Benjamin Handy, all equestrians. By March 1790 Franklin and Handy had become partners and were again in Bristol, building a new riding school and ring for performance behind the Full Moon in North

Street, St Paul's. Construction was delayed, and the planned opening on 8 March was postponed to the twenty-second. Meanwhile the two men offered riding lessons to ladies and gentlemen of Bristol.

Even though they had so recently erected an arena, on 10 May 1790 Franklin and Handy announced plans for a more elaborate riding school and performance ring, saying that as soon as 500 guineas (of a total of 1000 needed) should be subscribed construction would commence. They noted that they would be in attendance six months of the year to teach riding to Bristolians and to break horses for them. They performed in their old circus at Bristol through May and then departed to perform elsewhere. They returned to Bristol in August.

On 6 March 1792 the pair were once more in Bristol, this time performing at their new amphitheatre and riding school in Limekiln Lane, "elegantly illuminated with patent lamps, and a good band of music." But on 28 May Franklin and Handy announced the dissolution of their partnership. After they parted they became friendly competitors, often following one another at the amphitheatre in Bristol. During that period when Franklin worked with Handy he is known to have performed with Handy's daughter; one bill, in 1788 at Bristol, said: "The CHILD of PROMISE will, for this Evening, ride on Mr. *Franklin*'s Shoulders, Without the Assistance of Hand or Rein, having nothing to keep her up but her perpendicular Balance, and which is allowed to be the greatest balance ever attempted."

Franklin was back in Bristol with a troupe in April 1793, operating at the amphitheatre in Limekiln Lane for a fortnight. Either before or after that in 1793 he appeared at the Royal Circus in London. De Castro in his *Memoirs* said that Thomas Franklin formed a partnership with Handy and Charles Hughes and operated the Circus. It was "in a complete state of ruin for want of repair, with little or no accommodation for the public. However, by their spirited exertions, they drew rather tolerable houses, and by dint of economy and diligent industry, they were no losers . . . nor any great gainers; and the following Easter or Whitsuntide [1794] they opened it again, with very little or no better success." De Castro said that Franklin "afterwards" went to America, and there died.

Franklyn. *See also* FRANCISCO.

Franklyn, Mr *d. 1758, dancer, clown.*
Mr Franklyn performed at Sadler's Wells on 9 October 1756, his specialty being a dance with bells attached to his head, hands, and feet. He performed triple peals

and "bob-majors" by jerking his arms and legs and nodding his head. He was advertised as the "twelve-bell man," though a year later, on 2 November 1757 at the Haymarket Theatre, he presented a dance using "Eight Hand Bells" as part of "Mrs Midnight's" (Christopher Smart's) *Medley Concert*. Perhaps he was the Mr Franklyn who was a clown at the Orchard Street Theatre at Bath about that time. A Signor Francisco performed at Bath on the same bill, offering a very similar entertainment; Francisco was scheduled to appear in Manchester in 1762 after playing at Sadler's Wells.

Franklyn drowned off the Scottish coast in late October 1758. He, Theophilus Cibber, Michael Maddox, and other performers set out from Parkgate for Dublin on 27 October, and the ship went down that day or the next.

Franks, Mr ₁fl. 1794–1797₁, *trombonist.*
Doane's *Musical Directory* of 1794 identified Mr Franks (or Franki) as a trombonist living in Charles Street, Westminster. He played at Ranelagh Gardens and in the Handel performances at Westminster Abbey, and he was a regular member of the band at the Covent Garden Theatre. The bills at Covent Garden mentioned Franks as an instrumentalist in oratorio performances in March 1794, February 1796, and March 1797, and the account books cited him in February 1796 and March 1797.

Frano. *See* DE FRANO.

Fransdorf. *See* FRENSDORF.

Frantzel, Signor ₁fl. 1754–1755₁, *dancer.*
Signor Frantzel (or Francel) was advertised as an Italian dancer recently arrived from the Court of "Bareith" (Bayreuth) in Germany when he and Signora

Balbi appeared in England in November
1754. They gave their first performance
on 18 November at Covent Garden; the
next day they danced *L'Hôte du village*.
On 4 January 1755 they were in a pas de
quatre and a *Peasant Dance*, and on 16
April they shared a benefit at which
Frantzel offered a solo *Drunken Peasant*
and joined Signora Balbi in a comic minuet.
Tickets for the benefit were available from
Frantzel at the Golden Ball in Bow Street,
Covent Garden.

Frasi, Signor [fl. 1751–1756], *singer.*
Signor Frasi was doubtless related to
Giulia Frasi and, like her, was a singer. On
30 April 1751 at Hickford's Music Room
in Brewer Street he was one of the singers
at little Marianne Davies's benefit. At the
King's Theatre in the Haymarket on 30
April 1753 Frasi was one of the soloists
in a concert for the benefit of indigent
musicians and their families. He sang at
another such benefit at the same theatre on
5 April 1756, on which occasion Giulia
Frasi also performed.

Frasi, Giulia [fl. 1742–1772], *singer.*
Of Signora Giulia Frasi's continental
career nothing is known beyond the fact
that her teacher was named Brivio. In the
fall of 1742 she joined the opera company
at the King's Theatre in the Haymarket,
her first role there being Mahobeth in the
pasticcio Gianguir on 2 November. She
then sang Emira in *Mandane* on 4 December,
a role in *Enrico* on 1 January 1743,
Roxana in *Temistocle* on 22 February,
songs at a benefit for "decay'd" musicians
and their families on 30 March, and Nerena
in *Sirbace* on 5 April. Grove states that she
also sang in Galuppi's *Alessandro in Persia*,
though no cast was listed when that *pasticcio*
was performed on 13 November 1742.

Signora Frasi returned to the King's
Theatre in 1743–44 to sing Tassile in
Roxana, Garzia in *Alfonso*, Ernesto in
Rosalinda, Timotele in *Aristodemo*, and

GIULIA FRASI

artist unknown

Olinto in *Alceste*. As she had done in 1743
and continued to do for many years, Signora
Frasi sang at the benefit for destitute
musicians in the spring of 1744. On 4 April
she appeared at the Haymarket Theatre to
sing for Russell's benefit.

Through the 1761–62 season Giulia Frasi
sang in London every season in operas,
oratorios, recitals, and benefit concerts at
the King's, the Haymarket, Covent Garden,
Drury Lane, Hickford's Music Room, the
Chapel of the Foundling Hospital, Haberdashers'
Hall, the Great Room in Dean
Street, Soho, the Long Room in Hampstead,
and the Swan and the Castle taverns. An
able, though not first-rate, singer, she kept
herself busy over the years, despite Handel's
opinion that she lacked diligence (when
she told him she planned to learn thorough
bass in order to accompany herself, Handel,
according to her teacher Dr Burney, exclaimed,
"Oh—vaat may ve not expect!").

But she apparently learned much while singing for Handel in his oratorios.

Among the many roles in operas and oratorios which she essayed were Quintus Flaminius in *Il trionfo della continenza*, Clearchus in *Antigono*, Lucilla in *Lucio Vero*, Silvia in *La ingratitudine punita*, the First Israelite Woman in *Judas Maccabaeus*, the title part in *Susanna*, the First Harlot in *Solomon*, the title role in *Theodora*, Iphis in *Jephtha*, Semira in *Artaserse*, Sabina in *Tito Manlio*, Beauty in *The Triumph of Time and Truth*, Egle in *Zenobia*, Emira in *Solimano*, and Nitocris in *Balshazzar*. She also sang in *Acis and Galatea*, *Samson*, *L'Allegro ed il Penseroso*, *Alexander's Feast*, the *Messiah*, and many other works by Handel.

In March 1745 Signora Frasi was living in Great Pulteney Street, Golden Square, but by March 1752 she had moved to Gerrard Street, where she lived for many years.

She appeared at Ranelagh Gardens in 1751 and 1752, at the oratorio performances in Oxford in 1754 and 1756, and at the Three Choirs Festival from 1756 through 1764, meanwhile continuing her busy regular schedule. But by 1762 her appearances became less frequent, and after a solo benefit at the Great Room in Dean Street on 21 April 1762 she did not perform again in London until she appeared about 1764 at Haberdashers' Hall. Richard John Samuel Stevens recalled (he thought) the latter concert 50 years later: "I now remember her person, She was a short fat woman and had a remarkably clear voice; and (which attracted my notice considerably) she had on a pair of very fine brilliant ear-rings." She sang in *Esther* at Covent Garden on 6 March 1767, in the *Messiah* at Haberdashers' Hall on 10 December (perhaps that was really the concert Stevens remembered), in *Judas Maccabaeus* at the Haymarket on 18 April 1769, as Artabaces (for the first time) in *Artaserse* at the King's for her benefit on 1 June, and in *Judas Maccabaeus* at the Hay-

market for her benefit on 4 May 1770. Those were typical of her sporadic performances during her later years.

In January 1772 the *Gentleman's Magazine* printed a poem that cited the major performers of the time, alphabetically: "F was a Frasi, whose singing delights." But she is not known to have been singing at that late date. Burney said she had a smooth, chaste style but little feeling. Lysons noted that "she pronounced our language in singing with a more distinctive articulation" than did the native English. Giulia Frasi is said to have lived extravagantly and in her later years she was driven into debt and died destitute in Calais. Musgrave's *Obituary* lists John Frasi, a brother of the singer, who was an embroiderer in St Martin's Street. He died in January 1795 at the age of 65.

Giulia Frasi was pictured in a mezzotint engraving by an anonymous artist. Written at the bottom of the Harvard copy of the engraving is a note: "Mr Kitchin who published this print under the Title of the 'Musical Lady' Inform'd me that it was intended for Signora Frasi."

Frasier. *See* **FRAZIER**.

Fratanzanti. *See* **FRATESANTI**.

Fratelli, Signor [*fl.* 1733], *musician*.
At Lincoln's Inn Fields on 7 May 1733 a benefit concert was held for the violoncellist Lancetti; among the performers was a Signor Fratelli.

Fratesanti, Signor [*fl.* 1743–1744], *singer, organist?*
Signor Fratesanti was probably the singer to whom Horace Walpole referred on 17 November 1743 in a letter to Horace Mann: "they have got a dreadful bass, who, the Duke of Montagu says he believes, was organist at Aschaffenburgh." Lady Hertford wrote to Lord Beauchamp that at the King's Theatre in the Haymarket for the opera

season of 1743–44 was "a bass from Italy whose name is Fratanzanti." Deutsch in his *Handel* cites the Walpole *Letters* as identifying the singer who portrayed Clito in *Rossane* on 15 November 1743 as Signor*a* Fratesanti; but the role was written for and had been previously sung by a bass, and the bulk of the evidence would suggest that the singer in question was a man.

No further references were made during the season to a Signora Fratesanti, but Signor Fratesanti sang Pelagio in *Alfonso* on 3 January 1744, Selvaggio in *Rosalinda* on 31 January, at a benefit for "Decay'd" musicians on 28 March, Ippomedonte in *Aristodemo* on 3 April, Fenico in *Alceste* on 24 April, and at a concert at Hickford's on 16 May.

Fratesanti, Signora. *See* FRATESANTI, SIGNOR.

Frazier, Mr [fl. 1743–1755?], *actor*.
A Mr Frazier played Marshall in *The Triumphant Queen of Hungary* at the Godwin-Adam booth at Bartholomew Fair on 23 August 1743. Perhaps he was the actor "Frasier" who acted the Miser in *The Imprisonment of Harlequin* at the New Inn, without Lawford's Gate, Bristol, on 20 May 1751. Further, a Mr Frasier acted Sackbut in *A Bold Stroke for a Wife* on 2 October 1755 at Widow Yeates's "Large Theatrical BARN facing the Boarding-School in CROYDON. . . ."

Frazier, Mr [fl. 1791], *porter*.
Mr Frazier, a porter at Drury Lane, was cited three times in the account books in October 1791. His salary appears to have been 9s. weekly.

Freake, John George [fl. 1739–1763], *violinist, composer*.
John George Freake (or Freek, Freeks) became one of the original subscribers to the Royal Society of Musicians on 28 August 1739, by which time he was considered

a professional musician. His first known public appearance and earliest musical compositions, however, date from the late 1740s. His *XII Solos for a Harpsichord, Violin, German Flute, &c.* was published in 1746; other similar compositions were printed in 1755.

On 9 December 1748 at the Haymarket Theatre he played first violin at a benefit concert for Waltz. Freake put on two concerts for his own benefit there on 23 and 26 March 1750. He held a benefit at the Great Room in Dean Street, Soho, on 5 March 1753, played in the *Messiah* at the Chapel of the Foundling Hospital in May 1754 for 15s., and performed again there on 27 April 1758 for the same fee. *Mortimer's London Directory* of 1763 cited Freake as a violinist living in Rathbone Place.

Frederic. *See also* FREDERICK.

Frédéric, Mons [fl. 1781–1792], *dancer*.
The dancer advertised as Frédéric was a member of the corps de ballet at the Opera in Paris from 1781 to 1784 and again from 1786 to 1789. The *Petit almanach des grands spectacles de Paris* (1792) called him the "Petit prodige du Nord transplante en France," but where he was born is not known.

Frédéric was in London on the roster of the King's Theatre in the season of 1784–85, receiving a total of £160. Between 18 December and 28 June he danced a varied repertoire of *divertissements entr'acte* and figured in various ballets such as *Le Parti de chasse d'Henry IV*, *Le Tuteur trompé*, *Le Jugement de Paris*, *A la plus sage; ou, La Vertu récompensée*, *Il Convitate de Pietro*, and the "Heroic Ballet" *Macbeth*.

Frederic, Mr [fl. 1784], *actor*.
A Mr Frederic appeared in some part unspecified in *The Fair Refugee* and as Sprightly in *The Author* at a specially

licensed performance by a casual company at the Haymarket Theatre on 10 February 1784.

Frederic, Mme. *See* BIRT, MISS S.

Frederic, Miss   [fl. 1767–1775?], singer.

A Miss Frederic, a pupil of Dr Thomas Augustine Arne, and thus probably a juvenile, sang one of the treble parts—along with Mrs Michael Arne and six choir boys—in a performance of glees taken from the collection of the Noblemen's and Gentlemen's Glee and Catch Club, in the Rotunda at Ranelagh Gardens on 12 May 1767. On 28 July 1768 at Marylebone Gardens Dr Arne furnished music for a comic interlude of two acts called *Capochio and Dorinna*, in which Capochio was played by a Master Brown (whose benefit night it was) and Dorinna by "Miss Fredric." She was very likely the "Miss Frederick" who sang Lucinda in *Love in a Village* for the benefit of Jacobs at the Haymarket on 30 October 1775.

Frederica, Mrs   [fl. 1745], singer.

The Latreille manuscript in the British Museum lists "Mrs Frederika" for a principal but unspecified role in the opera *La incostanza delusa* at the Haymarket on 9, 16, 23 February, 2, 9, 16 March and 6 April 1745. *The London Stage* gives "Mrs Frederica" no performance on 8 February at the Haymarket and gives no casting for 9 March and subsequently except Signoras Frasi and Galli as "first singers." Those sources agree that 6 April was Mrs Frederica's benefit night. Latreille gives her address as a "house in Sherrard S[t]. facing Queen S[t]. near Golden Square."

Frederica, Miss. *See* FREDERICK, CASSANDRA.

Frederick. *See also* FREDERIC.

Frederick, Mr   [fl. 1792–1804?], actor, dancer?, singer?

The only metropolitan London appearance of Mr Frederick was at Richmond in the late summer of 1792. A clipping in the Richmond Library, hand dated 26 September 1792 reveals that Mr Frederick "of the Theatre Royal, Birmingham" had been engaged for the remainder of the season. His employment at Birmingham is confirmed by bills in the Birmingham Public Library. He had evidently come to Birmingham from York. On his debut at York on 12 April 1792 he was said to have come from the Edinburgh company.

His manager at York, Tate Wilkinson, has left in *The Wandering Patentee* a brief account of Frederick, the only one extant:

On Thursday, April 12 [1792], a young gentleman, whose name was FREDERICK, almost a novice to the stage, (having only acted twice the character of Oroonoko at Edinburgh) appeared in that unfortunate prince: His action was unembarrassed and good; his voice remarkably pleasing, but *not* powerful; and his figure, though particularly neat, was deficient in height; of course Oroonoko, Alexander, &c. he should avoid, but there are many parts in which, I think when ripened by time, experience, and assiduity, he will rank as a gentleman of consequence on the stage. His behaviour is remarkably polite; he is the son of a gentleman in London; has made the tour of Paris, and has had a good education. How his *papa* likes his wild-goose chase I know not. The said young gentleman I recommended to Mr. Yates, my company being full, and on the first hearing him repeat before Mr. Siddons and others, at Birmingham, he was instantly engaged; and, though so young a proficient, he was entrusted with several of the first characters, which he performed to the satisfaction of the manager Mr. Yates and the public. He not only lost his benefit at Birmingham that summer, but was a considerable sufferer as to his apparel, &c. owing to the dreadful calamity of a fire, which consumed not only the theatre, but the tavern adjoining, where Mr. Frederick lodged, who had very nearly lost his life, being brought naked from his bed in flames. . . .

Mr. Frederick, after that misfortune, acted a few parts at Richmond in Surrey, in August, 1792, under the direction of Capt. [George] Wathen, and is now [1795], I believe, figuring away as a hero in tragedy at the Norwich theatre. . . .

Frederick was at Norwich by 1793, with Mrs Frederick (who was not recorded at Richmond). He may have been the Frederick who acted Sandy in *The Highland Reel* at Charleston in December 1797 and who played at Philadelphia from 24 April through 8 June 1798. He or another of that name offered solo readings and songs at Portland, Maine, in June 1800, advertising himself as being from the Charleston and New York theatres. It is possible, though not likely, that ours was the Frederick listed at various times during the Covent Garden season of 1803–4 among both the chorus singers and the dancers.

Frederick, Mme. *See* BIRT, MISS S.

Frederick, Miss   [*fl.* 1780–1784], actress.

A Miss Frederick (not Miss Frederic[k] the singer) played Clara in the anonymous new comedy *The Detection* which was brought out by special license at the Haymarket on 13 November 1780. The bill noted that she was onstage for the first time. On 23 February 1784, in identical circumstances—an anonymous new comedy, *The Patriot*—Miss Frederick made her second attempt, in a part unspecified.

Frederick, Cassandra, later Mrs Thomas Wynne   *b. c. 1744, singer, harpsichordist, organist.*

At the Haymarket Theatre on 10 April 1749 was given "For the Benefit of Miss Cassandra Frederick, a Child of Five years and a half old and a Scholar of Mr. Paradies [Pietro Domenico Paradisi, 1707–

1791], a Concert of Vocal and Instrumental Musick." The child would "perform on the Harpsichord several lessons of Scarlatti and other Great Masters, and also a Concerto of Mr. Handels." Signoras Frasi and Galli were to contribute vocal airs, and tickets could be had "of Mr. Frederick in Wardour St Soho, near Meard's Court." Carl Ferdinand Pohl, writing in *Grove's Dictionary*, thinks Cassandra "was undoubtedly older" than the bills claimed she was at the time of that early appearance. Yet the claim was insisted upon a year later when, on 29 March 1750, at Hickford's Room in Brewer Street, "For the Benefit of Miss CASSANDRA FREDERICK, *a Child of Six and a Half Old*" and still "a *Scholar of Mr. PARADIES*," a concert was given and the beneficiary played on the harpsichord "two Concertos of Mr. *Handel's*."

Deutsch in his *Handel* excerpts a passage from a letter of 14 April 1750, sent by Philip Dormer Stanhope, Fourth Earl of Chesterfield, to his godson the King's Resident at the Hague, Solomon Dayrolles—a passage which Deutsch believes may have referred to Cassandra: "I could not refuse this recommendation of a *virtuoso* to a *virtuoso*. The girl is a real prodigy. . . . The great point is to get the Princess of Orange to hear her, which she thinks will *make her fortune*. Even the great Handel has designed to recommend her there; so that a word from your Honour will be sufficient." (Anne, Princess of Orange, had been Handel's pupil, as had Chesterfield's wife.) A benefit concert and ball was held for "Miss Cassandra Frederica" on 29 November 1751 at the Assembly Room at St Augustine's Back in Bristol. She played the harpsichord.

But it was not as an instrumentalist that Miss Fredericks was to make her mark, although she certainly exercised her talents on the keyboard on other occasions. When next her name showed in a London bill it was as one of Handel's young singers, in the role of Daniel in the oratorio *Bel-*

shazzar at Covent Garden on 22 February 1758. She sang Storgé in *Jeptha* on 1 March, perhaps the Israelite Man in *Judas Maccabaeus* on 3 March, and some part in *Messiah* at the Chapel of the Foundling Hospital on 27 April. She was paid £4 4s. for singing in the *Messiah*.

Cassandra was called "Miss Frederica" when she sang in Thomas Augustine Arne's *Alfred the Great* at Covent Garden on 1 February and 23 March 1759. No roles were distributed by the bills. But she was "Miss Frederick" again in the extant bills of the spring of 1760 and until the end of her career. On 18 January 1760 in the Great Room in Dean Street, Soho, she sang an unspecified part in *Judas Maccabaeus*. At the same locale on 14 February she joined other vocalists and some other instrumentalists in a *Charlottenburg Festegiante* and on that occasion both sang and played "Between the First and Second Part a Concerto on the Organ." There on 13 March she assisted in a performance of the opera *L'isola disabitata*, with Signora Calori, Tenducci, and Quilici, for the latter's benefit. One of the ancillary "Entertainments" was "a *Concerto* on the Harpsichord, the composition of Sg Paradies," by Cassandra. On 27 March she sang in another performance of *L'isola disabitata* at the Haymarket, and on 29 April, at Hickford's Room, in still another, for the "Benefit of Signora Laura Rosa" who had lost her salary "by the late Failure at the Opera House."

On 21 January 1761 Cassandra Frederick, Quilici, Tedeschino, and Signoras Passerini and Eberardi were the vocal principals in the oratorio *Isaac* at the Great Room, Dean Street, Soho. On 12 March at the King's Theatre she was in the stellar company of singers like Miss Brent, Beard, Signora Frasi and Miss Young and instrumentalists like Cervetto, Vincent, and Baumgarten when she sang Ciampi's *Di nobil alma* and *Verdi prati* from Handel's *Alcina*. The concert was for the benefit of the "Fund for the Support of Decayed Musicians."

Those are the last engagements known for Cassandra Fredericks, unless she should be identified with the singing Miss Frederic (or Frederick) of 1767–1789, and / or the actress of c. 1775–1784. But both identifications are unlikely, for reasons adduced in those entries.

The *Catalogue of Printed Music in the British Museum* lists a song, *While with a gentle smile you strove*, as sung by "Miss Cassandra Frederick with a gentleman." The conjectured publication date is 1770, which is probably too late. Pohl says that "she married Thomas Wynne, a landowner in South Wales, and exercised considerable influence on the musical education of her nephew [Joseph, Count] Massinghi." Cassandra's sister had married Tommaso Mazzinghi, a wine merchant and theatre pit musician, Joseph's father.

Frederika. *See* FREDERICA.

Fredric. *See* FREDERIC.

Freeburg. *See* FRIBOURG.

Freek or **Freeks.** *See* FREAKE.

Freeman, Mr *d. c. 1726, porter.*
The account books for the Lincoln's Inn Fields Theatre cited Mr Freeman frequently from 25 September 1724 through 16 September 1726. He was a porter and received a daily salary of 5s. He died in late 1726 or early 1727, for by 1 February 1727 the accounts refer to his wife as "Freeman, porter's widow."

Mrs Freeman was first mentioned in the accounts on 26 November 1726, when she was listed with the porters and paid 5s. for five days' work. In February 1727 she was given a widow's pension, though the books do not make it clear how much she was granted. On 14 June 1727 she was still receiving 1s. for her work at the theatre.

Judging by the references to her, she may have worked in the theatre office, issuing tickets.

Freeman, Mr [*fl.* *1735–1756*], *actor.*

A group of players at York Buildings on 19 March 1735 performed *Othello* with a Mr Freeman in the title role. At Lee's booth at Tottenham Court on 28 May Freeman played Sir George in *The Drummer*, and on 17 July, back at York Buildings, he shared a benefit with Stone and acted Young Fashion in *The Relapse*. In 1735–36 Freeman appeared with Fielding's troupe at the Haymarket Theatre as the Constable in *The Recruiting Officer*, Goosequill in *The Rival Milliners* (Miss Freeman, possibly his daughter, played Molly Wheedle), Colonel Promise in *Pasquin*, Clerimont in *The Female Rake*, and Jupiter and a Manager in *Tumble-Down Dick*. He also had a solo benefit at Lincoln's Inn Fields, on 3 March 1736, at which he acted Memnon in *Busiris*.

Freeman turned up again in London in 1742–43 at Lincoln's Inn Fields to act Thomas in *The Virgin Unmask'd*, the Shoemaker in *The Relapse*, Scale in *The Recruiting Officer*, Slango in *The Honest Yorkshireman*, Norfolk in *Richard III*, the Coachman in *The Devil to Pay*, Burgundy in *King Lear*, the Lover in *Bickerstaff's Unburied Dead*, Dumain Junior in *All's Well that Ends Well*, Robin in *The Beggar's Opera*, and Snap in *Love for Love*. On 23 August 1743 at Godwin and Adams's booth at Bartholomew Fair Freeman played the King of France in *The Triumphant Queen of Hungary*.

He was at Goodman's Fields in the spring of 1745, though only two parts are known for him: Alonzo in *The Tempest* and List in *The Miser*. On 8 September 1746 he acted Don Guzman in *The Fate of Villainy* at Warner's Southwark Fair booth. It is possible that the Mr Freeman who played Archer in *The Beaux' Stratagem* at Canterbury on 27 July 1756 was our sub-

ject, and if so, he was the husband of the Mrs Freeman who performed from 1743 to perhaps 1758.

Freeman, Mr [*fl.* *1765–1770*], *actor.*

A Mr Freeman acted Montano in *Othello* at the Haymarket Theatre on 10 January 1770. Perhaps he was the Freeman who had acted with Parsons' company at Derby in September 1765 and later with a company at Edinburgh in 1769. In the latter city played Harry Beagle in *The Jealous Wife* on 13 March 1769, and Dicky in *The Constant Couple* and Captain Slang in *The Absent Man* on 23 March. The Mrs Freeman who acted Eliza in *Burletta* at Edinburgh on 15 April 1769 was no doubt his wife. Probably he was the Freeman who acted at Glasgow from 20 January through 30 March 1770.

Freeman, Mr [*fl.* *1774?–1798?*], *box inspector, actor?*

A Mr Freeman was a box inspector at Drury Lane Theatre from as early as 1776–77, when his salary was 12*s.* per week, through 1789–90 when it was 9*s.* per week. Possibly he was the Freeman whose name was listed as a supernumerary on the Drury Lane account book for 1774–75. In the Drury Lane Fund Book (now at the Folger Library) James Winston noted "1798 Mr. Freeman fr 1794"—presumably meaning that Freeman paid a subscription in 1798 for 1794.

Freeman, Mr [*fl.* *1778–1809?*], *actor.*

A Mr Freeman, announced on the bills as "A Gentleman" making first appearance on any stage and identified by name in the *Public Advertiser* on 7 April 1778, acted Chamont in *The Orphan* at the Haymarket Theatre on 9 April 1778, for a benefit he shared with Massey. Tickets could be had of Freeman in Vine Street, Piccadilly. He, or another actor of the same name, played Flint in *The Detection* and Nat Forge in

The City Association at the Haymarket on 13 November 1780. In the summer of 1783 at the same theatre he acted the character of Reviving Death in *Harlequin Teague* 14 times between 30 June and 3 September; and he had the same role there in July 1785. In Christmas week of 1793 a Mr Freeman performed five times as Beadle in *Harlequin Peasant* at the Haymarket. An actor of that name was at Belfast in 1788 and 1789 (with a Mrs Freeman), at Manchester in 1790 (with Mrs Freeman), at Exeter in 1794, and at Liverpool in 1797. (Possibly this person was Samuel Thomas Foote [1761–1840], the actor who performed early in his career at Plymouth as Mr Freeman, his real name; assuming the name of Foote in 1795, he developed a considerable reputation in the provinces and managed the theatres at Plymouth and Exeter in the late 1790s.) A Mr Freeman was being paid £1 5*s*. per week at Covent Garden from 1801–2 through 1803–4 and £1 10*s*. from 1805–6 through 1808–9.

Freeman, Mrs ₁*fl. 1726–1727*₁, *house servant. See* **FREEMAN, MR** *d. c. 1726.*

Freeman, Mrs ₁*fl. 1734–1741*₁, *actress.*

Mrs Freeman played Lady Grace in *The Provok'd Husband* at the Haymarket Theatre on 7 June 1734, but on 14 June she switched to the role of Lady Wronghead. She repeated that part at Lincoln's Inn Fields on 20 August. In July 1735 she was at Lincoln's Inn Fields again, playing Lucy in *The London Merchant* on the eleventh, Lady Wronghead on the sixteenth, and Lady Charlot in *Squire Basinghall* and Mrs Squeamish in *The Stage Mutineers* on the twenty-third. A year later, on 26 June 1736, she played Mrs Peachum in *The Beggar's Opera* at the Haymarket.

It is most probable that she was the Mrs Freeman who turned up in the fall of 1741 playing a Countrywoman in *Harlequin the Man in the Moon* at Southwark Fair on 14 September and Lucy in *George Barnwell* at the James Street Theatre on 9 November.

Freeman, Mrs ₁*fl. 1743–1758?*₁, *actress, dancer, singer.*

Advertised as never having appeared on any stage before, Mrs Freeman played Edging in *The Careless Husband* at Lincoln's Inn Fields Theatre on 3 March 1743, sharing a benefit with Dukes and distributing tickets at the Rainbow Coffee House in Fuller's Rents. On the following 11 May she danced a minuet with Froment at Drury Lane. Her 1743–44 season in London brought her out as a singer at the James Street playhouse on 16 March 1744 and as Doll Tearsheet in *The Captive Prince* at May Fair on 3 May.

Mrs Freeman joined Theophilus Cibber's company at the Haymarket Theatre to play the Maid in *The Mock Doctor* on 29 September 1744, after which she appeared as Isabella in *The Conscious Lovers* and possibly Charlotte in *The Prodigal*. She moved to the Goodman's Fields Theatre on 26 December to act Lucy in *The Recruiting Officer*, and on 4 February 1745 she played Lucy in *The Beggar's Opera*. Perhaps she was the Mrs Freeman who acted at Norwich from about 1744 to 1758 and the Mrs Freeman who, with her husband, performed at Canterbury on 27 July 1756, appearing as Mrs Sullen in *The Beaux' Stratagem*.

Freeman, Mrs ₁*fl. 1789?–1792*₁, *singer.*

A Mrs Freeman sang in concerts at Bermondsey Spa Gardens in the summer of 1792. Perhaps she was the Mrs Freeman who with her husband (fl. 1778–1809?) performed at Belfast in 1788 and 1789 and at Manchester in 1790. At the latter city she was reviewed as "an excellent singer."

Freeman, Miss *[fl. 1736]*, *actress.*

On 19 January 1736 at the Haymarket Theatre a Miss Freeman played Molly Wheedle in *The Rival Milliners*. When the play was published in 1737 Miss Freeman was not listed for the role, though a Mr Freeman (her father?) was named for the part of Goosequill.

Freeman, Miss *[fl. 1779]*, *actress.*

A Miss Freeman acted Lucinda in *The Prejudice of Fashion* and Fidelia in *The Foundling* at the Haymarket Theatre on 22 February 1779. Perhaps she was the daughter of the Mr Freeman (fl. 1778–1809?) who acted at that theatre occasionally between 1778 and 1793.

Freeman, John *c. 1666–1736, singer.*

John Freeman the singer was born about 1666 and first came to notice as a performer in June 1690 in *The Prophetess* at the Dorset Garden Theatre. Another John Freeman, an actor, was also in the company; he had started his career about 1675 in Dublin and was playing mature roles by the 1680s. About 1691 Purcell's *Sound Fame* from *Dioclesian* (the second title of *The Prophetess*) was published, with John Freeman mentioned as the singer. On 2 May 1692 Freeman sang in *The Fairy Queen* at Dorset Garden, and on 22 November of that year he participated in the St Cecilia Day festival. He was in *The Prophetess* again on 10 January 1694 and sang in *2 Don Quixote* in late May. One of the two John Freemans played Pedro Rezio in the latter production.

After the United Company split in 1695 Freeman the actor worked at Lincoln's Inn Fields while Freeman the singer performed at Drury Lane and Dorset Garden with Christopher Rich's company. During the last five years of the seventeenth century the singer appeared in *The Indian Queen*, *Bonduca*, *Brutus of Alba*, *Phaeton*, *Victorious Love*, *The Island Princess*, *Achilles*, and *The Grove*. The only time a specific role was cited for him was on 29 April 1700 when he was Janus in the masque in *The Pilgrim*. During that same period he also sang a birthday song for the Duke of Gloucester (Purcell's "Who can from joy refrain," on 24 July 1695) and participated in a benefit recital for Daniel Purcell at York Buildings on 7 June 1698. Two songs printed about 1700 mentioned Freeman: Croft's *How Severe is my Fate*, which Freeman sang at York Buildings, and Daniel Purcell's *Thus Damon Knock'd at Celia's Door*, from *The Constant Couple*.

On 6 December 1700 John Freeman was sworn a Gentleman of the Chapel Royal extraordinary—that is, without fee until a position became vacant. Upon the death of Nathaniel Vestment, Freeman and Humphry Griffith, on 5 September 1702, were appointed to share the vacant post. On 23 December of that year, upon the death of Moses Snow, Freeman and Griffith were granted full positions. Freeman was also a member of the choirs of Westminster and St Paul's and is said to have possessed a fine tenor voice.

Freeman's theatrical activity virtually ceased after he joined the Chapel Royal, though he was cited in some published songs and may have made occasional appearances at the playhouses. He was mentioned as the singer of Daniel Purcell's *Glory, our Martial Paradice* from *2 Massaniello* (c. 1715), Purcell's *Come all away* from *The Grove* (c. 1715), and some songs in the *Wit and Mirth* collection (1719). On 11 January 1723 at Buckingham House Freeman sang in a concert.

Of his personal life not much is known. His wife Avis died at the age of 60 in 1732; she was buried in Westminster Abbey on 6 November of that year. John Freeman died at 70 on 10 December 1736 and was buried in the West Cloister of the Abbey on 14 December. He left no will, and administration of his estate was granted on 19 January 1737 to Elizabeth Freeman, spinster, John's "natural and lawful" daughter. Freeman was described in the administration as of the parish of St Andrew, Holborn. His daughter married the organist and composer James Kent (1700–1776).

Freeman, John [*fl. c. 1675–1710*], *actor.*

There were evidently two John Freemans active in the late seventeenth and early eighteenth centuries, one an actor and one a singer. The actor began his career in Dublin about 1675, two of his roles there being Beelzebub in *Belphagor* and Montano in *Othello*. On 8 December 1680 Freeman was a member of the Duke's Company in London and acted a Fecialian Priest in *Lucius Junius Brutus* at the Dorset Garden Theatre. There he also played the Old Jew in *2 The Rover* in January 1681 and Sebastian in *The False Count* in October (according to Robert Hume and Judy Milhous). For the United Company he acted one of the two Gentlemen in *The Jovial Crew* at Drury Lane in December 1683, the Doctor in *The Devil of a Wife* at Dorset Garden on 4 March 1686, the Hermit in *The Libertine* about 1686–87 at one of the two United Company houses, and Scrapeall in *The Squire of Alsatia* on 3 May 1688 at Drury Lane.

Freeman ran into legal troubles, some of which were recorded in the Lord Chamberlain's accounts. On 23 May 1688 Charles Killigrew and Thomas Davenant were ordered to pay out of Freeman's salary a debt he owed to one Alexander Blayer. The debt was still in litigation on 10 August 1689 and was still not paid as of 12 November 1690. On 5 November 1693 Mary Barrow sued Freeman for a debt; on 22 December 1694 James Illingworth, a butcher, sued him for a debt; and on 20 July 1696 the same man sued him for unpaid rent. The following August Freeman was arrested, but on some unspecified technicality the arrest was declared false and Freeman was released by the end of the month.

Freeman's performing career continued despite his troubles. About 1688–89 he acted in *Othello*, and before the United Company split in 1695 he was seen as Proculus in *Valentinian*, Cavagnes in *The Massacre of Paris*, Colonel Wellman in *The Widow Ranter*, Captain Tilbury in *Madam Fickle*, Sir Richard Mounchensey in *The Merry Devil of Edmonton*, a Persian Magi in *Distress'd Innocence*, Nevill in *Edward III*, Oswell in *Alphonso*, Bluster in *The Scowrers*, Old Merriton in *Love for Money*, Henry III in *Bussy D'Ambois*, Strain Conscience in *Win Her and Take Her*, Roderic in *The Rape*, Petruchio in *The Traytor*, Ding-boy in *The Volunteers*, Sir Charles Romance in *The Richmond Heiress*, Pedro in *The Fatal Marriage*, Briomar in *The Ambitious Slave*, and perhaps Pedro Rezio in *2 Don Quixote*. The singer John Freeman was also in the troupe from June 1690, appearing in musical productions.

When Thomas Betterton led many of the older players away from Drury Lane to Lincoln's Inn Fields in 1695 Freeman the actor went with him. On 30 April of that year he played Buckram in *Love for Love* at the new company's opening. With Betterton from 1695 till the opening of the new Queen's Theatre in the Haymarket in 1705 Freeman acted such roles as Freeman in *She Ventures and He Wins*, Compasse in *The City Bride*, Acmat in *The Royal Mischief*, Sanchio in *Rule a Wife and Have a Wife*, Perez in *The Mourning Bride*, Lyonell in *The Innocent Mistress*, Fabian in *Boadicea*, Lord Dacres in *Queen Catherine*, Casca in *Julius Caesar*, Memnon in *Xerxes*, Sir Peter Pride in *The Amorous Widow*, Worcester in *Henry IV*, the Provost in Gildon's adaptation of *Measure for Measure*, Pedro in *The Fatal Marriage*, Mirza in *The Ambitious Step-Mother*, Omar in *Tamerlane*, Haly in *Abra Mule*, Sir Thomas Valere in *The Gamester*, and Renault in *Venice Preserv'd*.

Freeman's first role at the Queen's Theatre was Ephialtes in *Ulysses* on 23 November 1705, but he acted there only for the 1705–6 season, playing that role and Metaphrastus in *The Mistake*, Aventius in *The Faithful General*, and Gomez in *Adventures in Madrid*. His name was not mentioned in cast lists again until 25 February 1710, when he probably acted Scruple in *The Fair Quaker of Deal* at Drury Lane. There also on 11 March he played Sir Edward Hartford in *The Lancashire Witches*. On 28 August he acted Sulpitious in *Caius Marius* at Pinkethman's playhouse in Greenwich, where he also played Creon in *Oedipus*, Don Alvarez in *The Mistake*, Dinant in *Aureng-Zebe*, and, on 30 September 1710—the last notice of him—his old role of Omar in *Tamerlane*.

Freeman, John (fl. 1686–1732), *scene painter.*

John Freeman the history painter, who was commissioned in 1686 to do a staircase wall at Belvoir Castle, was looked upon as a rival of Isaac Fuller in his day. Freeman went to the West Indies, survived an attempt there on his life, and returned to England. It is said that in his later years he painted scenery at the Covent Garden Theatre; that would indicate that he was still active when that new playhouse opened in 1732. None of his work seems to have survived.

Fremble. *See also* FRIMBLE.

Fremble, Master (fl. 1742), *performer.*

At Woodburn's booth at Southwark Fair on 16 September 1742 there was dancing and singing by Master Fremble, Miss Crozier, and Mme Debon.

Fremont. *See* FROMENT.

French, Mrs (fl. 1776–1779), *actress.*

A Mrs French was paid £1 per week as an actress at Drury Lane Theatre in 1776–77, and on 9 October 1779 she was paid six days' salary at 3s. 4d. per day. In 1776 she subscribed 10s. 6d. to the theatre's retirement fund. Possibly she was related to the family of scene painters named French who worked at Drury Lane during that period.

French, Daniel (fl. 1732?–1751), *actor, manager.*

The Mr French who played a Countryman in *The Metamorphosis of Harlequin* on 4 August 1732 at the booth in Cherry Tree Garden, near the "Mote," at Tottenham Court, was probably Daniel French. A Mrs French played the Hostess in the same work. On 25 March 1734 "for his Diversion," Daniel French of Hampstead acted Hob in *Flora* at Covent Garden. He popped up again on 27 March 1735 at Goodman's Fields in the same role, and he played Timothy Peascod in *The What D'Ye Call It* at Covent Garden on 8 April.

On 2 April 1736 he acted Hob again, at Lincoln's Inn Fields for his benefit, and he was Robin in *The Walking Statue* at Covent Garden on 15 March 1737 for Walker's benefit. He played Hob once more on 6 May 1737 at Lincoln's Inn Fields, preceded by Teague in *The Committee*—for his benefit. Those sporadic appearances of French may have been attempts to stay ahead of his creditors; his performances were usually heralded in the papers by doggerel verses beseeching the interest of the public in his financial plight.

At Drury Lane on 24 April 1740 benefit tickets for French were accepted, as they were at Covent Garden on 1 April 1741. He turned up on 10 May 1744 at the Haymarket Theatre playing the Cook in *The Miser*, and in 1748 he opened an amphitheatre in Tottenham Court Road and performed *The Country Wake*. The evening consisted of "cudgle-playing, boxing, wrestling" and the play. On 21 November 1751 Dan played Hob again for his benefit at the Haymarket, and a poem appeared:

Poor Dan is crept
To Friends in debt
And fain would he get out
Now tries a way
And by a play,
To bring the thing about.
Then buy my Tickets
'Twill cure my rickets
Make me again firm stand;
I swear by my star
You shall have them at par,
And I'll no more bubble the land.

Indeed, that was the last that was heard from Daniel French of Hampstead.

French, Mrs [Daniel?] [fl. 1732], actress.

Mrs French played the Hostess in *The Metamorphosis of Harlequin* on 4 August 1732 at "the Great Theatrical Booth in the Cherry-Tree Garden near the Mote" at Tottenham Court. She was doubtless the wife of the Mr (Daniel?) French who acted a Countryman in the same production.

French, George 1755–1817, violinist, composer, band leader.

Born in 1755 the son of a musician at York, for many years George French was the leader of the band at the York Theatre and for the circuit which included Hull, Leeds, Wakefield, and Doncaster. He was playing at York by 1770, for on 12 May of that year he and his father were articled there for another year at £2 2s. per week. On 30 May 1776 his father was discharged but George was kept on at a weekly salary of £1 7s. with the responsibility of writing out all the music scores "that his father used to do." At Leeds in the summer of 1788 he suffered a broken arm.

In 1794, Doane's *Musical Directory* listed French as a violinist and composer at the York Theatre and as a member of the New Musical Fund, an affiliation which suggests that French participated in London concerts. He was named on the subscription lists of the New Musical Fund in 1805

and 1815; in the latter year he was living at Hull. While still an active musician he died at Wakefield on 23 September 1817. The Mrs French who acted at York and Hull between 1790 and 1801 was no doubt his wife. She died at York on 23 March 1841, aged 80.

French, Gregory [fl. 1784–1815], violinist.

Gregory French was no doubt the Mr French listed by Burney as a second violinist in the Handel Memorial Concerts at Westminster Abbey and the Pantheon in May and June 1784 and the G. French, violinist, who was paid £4 4s. for performing in the concerts of the Academy of Ancient Music in 1787–88. In 1794, Doane's *Musical Directory* listed Gregory French as a violinist, a member of the New Musical Fund, a performer in the Handel performances at Westminster Abbey and the Pantheon and as then living at No 5, Water Street, Bridewell Precinct. In January 1798 French played in the oratorios at the Haymarket Theatre. In 1805 he was named as a member of the Court of Assistants on the subscription list of the New Musical Fund. In 1815 he was still listed as a subscriber to that fund.

French, John d. 1776, scene painter.

In 1763 John French of No 7, Clement's Inn, was listed in *Mortimer's London Directory* as "Scene Painter to the Theatre-Royal, in Drury-Lane." In an announcement of the opening of the new theatre at Richmond, Surrey, in August 1765 French of Drury Lane was referred to as the painter of the new scenery. About that time at Drury Lane, French painted a setting for *Harlequin's Invasion* that contained a transparent back scene behind which visionary figures could pass to create an effect of enchantment. Lighting effects provided by the elder Angelo consisted of screens covered with colored moreen, which when lighted in front reflected various colors onto the stage and setting. Probably French's work for this pantomime was in connection with its revival on 16 November 1765 after Garrick returned from the Continent, but it may also have been for the original production on 31 December 1759.

French was "an artist of no mean talent," but one, in the opinion of Angelo, not very liberally rewarded by Garrick. The account books, however, show substantial payments to him from 1766 to 1776: £353 12s. in 1766–67; £413 4s. in 1771–72; £392 19s. 6d. in 1772–73; £193 17s. 9d. in 1773–74; £304 15s. in 1774–75; and £532 2s. 6d. in 1775–76. Those payments may have been intended to cover materials as well as labor. In March of 1768 he submitted a bill for £138 12s., through Garrick, for painting scenes for the theatre in Calcutta.

Although Benjamin Wilson served as artistic advisor to Garrick for the Shakespeare Jubilee in 1769, French was the leader of a team of painters sent by the manager to Stratford to do huge transparent paintings. His chief assistant was Porter, a Sadler's Wells painter who had specialized in spectacular displays. French also was in charge of painting and decorating the Rotunda for the Jubilee. But he was fond of his cups, and George Garrick, who supervised the preparations in Stratford for his brother, had difficulty in keeping him on the job unless drink was provided in the painting rooms.

At Drury Lane French worked with Carver from 1770, executed some of De Loutherbourg's designs from 1773, and painted with Thomas Greenwood from 1774. His brother, Samuel French (d. 1803?), and another relative, Thomas French (1737–1808), also assisted in the scene shop during the 1770s, and it is not always possible to discern their individual contributions to productions. John French's work included scenes, particularly that of a pagan temple, for a revival of *King Arthur* on 13 December 1770 (with a winter-prospect by Carver) and the painting of De Loutherbourg's

designs for *Alfred* on 9 October 1773, *Electra* on 15 October 1774, *The Maid of the Oaks* on 5 November 1774, and *Queen Mab* on 11 November 1775. He also painted scenes for the Theatre Royal, Bristol, particularly palace wings for *King Arthur* in 1775.

In 1772, French found himself in financial distress; declaring bankruptcy, he sold off his collection of continental paintings and some of his own designs and also put his premises on Bow Street up for rent. The following notice appeared on 27 May 1772:

To be sold by auction by John Riley, on the premises in Bow-street, Covent-garden, by order of the assignees, tomorrow, the well-chosen collection of Italian, French, Flemish, and Dutch pictures, prints, etchings, drawings, ornaments, designs, books of perspective of that celebrated artist Mr. John French, scene-painter to Drury-lane house, a bankrupt; consisting of upwards of 250 old pictures, 3000 prints, amongst which are a great number of capital paintings, and finest impressions of the most esteemed masters of the Italian, French, Flemish, and Dutch Schools.

To be viewed till the sale, which will begin at twelve.

Catalogues at the place of sale, and of Mr. Riley, No. 71, Longacre.

The prints will be sold next Thursday and Friday evenings at six.

Note, The house to be lett.

John French worked at Drury Lane until his death on 10 December 1776. In his will, made two weeks earlier on 28 November 1776, he described himself as a painter of Catherine Street in the parish of St Mary le Strand and left £10 for mourning to his brother Samuel French. The fact that he did not make a similar bequest to Thomas French, also a painter at Drury Lane, suggests that Thomas was not his brother, and perhaps was not even related. John left the remainder of his estate to his wife and executrix Isabella French, who proved the will at London on 2 January 1777. (The administration of the estate of a John French granted to his widow Elizabeth on 16 October 1776, sometimes cited for the painter, refers to some other person.)

In January 1778 John French's widow, claiming to be under unfortunate circumstances, through the good offices of the painter John Bromley tried to recover money due her late husband from Drury Lane, but the new manager Sheridan was unresponsive.

Isabella French was John's second wife, for the death of an earlier wife had been reported in the *Public Advertiser* on 26 October 1765. Perhaps the wedding of John French and Connada Rosa, of St. James, Westminster, at St George's Chapel, Hyde Park Corner, on 8 June 1749 refers to his earlier marriage.

The Miss French who occasionally performed children's roles at Bristol in 1783–84 may have been John's daughter, but more likely she was the child of Thomas French.

French, Nathaniel   [*fl. 1674–1689*], *violinist.*

The Lord Chamberlain's accounts first cited Nathaniel French as a member of the King's Musick in 1674, when he replaced Thomas Purcell and received £16 2s. 6d. annual livery. On 20 November 1682 he was appointed to the King's private music, again as a replacement for the deceased Purcell. French accompanied the King and Queen to Windsor and Hampton Court from mid-August to early October 1685.

On 10 July 1686 French, describing himself as from the parish of St Martin-in-the-Fields, appointed the musician Nicholas Staggins his lawful attorney. French and Staggins had attended the King at Windsor from mid-May to October that year. On 10 November 1687 French assigned £25 12s. of his pay to a tradesman named Thomas Cooke—further indication that he may have been in financial straits. French was reap-

pointed to the King's private music under James II and attended the King at Windsor in the summer of 1687. Under William III French's annual salary was £30, but after 25 March 1689 the name of Nathaniel French disappeared from the records.

French, Samuel   *d. 1803?, scene painter.*

Samuel French was paid 5s. per day as a scene painter at Drury Lane Theatre between 7 December 1771 and 17 October 1773. His name is not again found in the account books until 5 October 1776 when he received £5 16s. 8d. for one month's work. Similar payments to Samuel French continued until the middle of 1777–78, in which year, according to one of Sheridan's letters, his salary was £120 for the season. His specific work is unknown, but probably he was the "French Jun." who painted scenes with Leroy and Greenwood for *Harlequin's Invasion* on 1 January 1777. Either he or Thomas French did some work at Covent Garden Theatre in 1781 for which that theatre paid £9 19s. 6d. on 17 January and £26 11s. 6d. on 23 June.

Many of the payments recorded in the Drury Lane account books up to the middle of 1778 were made to both Samuel and Thomas French, but then Samuel's name as a specific entry disappeared. We assume that subsequent payments to French then refer to Thomas French, perhaps a relative, but neither his father nor his brother. Samuel was the brother of the scene painter John French who left him £10 for mourning by his will of 1776. John did not mention Thomas French in his will.

Possibly the administration of the estate of Samuel French, late of Clarges Street, Piccadilly, which was granted to Peace French, widow and relict, on 27 December 1803 referred to the scene painter.

French, Thomas   *1737–1808, scene painter.*

Thomas French was a scene painter at

Drury Lane Theatre between 1771 and 1794 whose name first appeared in the account books in October 1771 when he was being paid 8s. per day. His assignees were paid £60 9s. on 27 February 1772 for the balance of his account with his managers. His name is next found in the accounts in 1776–77 for the modest monthly salary of £10, a figure he was paid through 1779–80. On 11 March 1788 he received £5 18s. for "Setting a Picture," and he received payments on account of £12 12s. on 15 December 1780, £11 3s. on 11 June 1781, £10 10s. on 26 April 1794, and £7 7s. on 10 May 1794. Either he or Samuel French did work at Covent Garden in 1781 for which that theatre paid £9 19s. 6d. on 17 January and £26 11s. 6d. on 23 June. Little is known of his specific work in London except that with Greenwood, Malton, Capon, and others he painted new scenery for the production of *Macbeth* which was the first dramatic offering at the new Drury Lane Theatre on 21 April 1794.

In 1774 he exhibited four pictures (a storm, a magician's cell, and two small landscapes) at the Free Society of Painters in London, at which time he was living at No 6, Scroop's Court, Holborn.

Thomas French may have been related to John and Samuel French, scene painters at Drury Lane in the 1770s as well, but he was not old enough to have been their father and he seems not to have been their brother. When John left £10 for mourning to his brother Samuel in 1776, he made no mention of Thomas in his will.

Most of Thomas French's identifiable work was done at Bristol and Bath, where he was a scene painter for many years. He chiefly resided at Bath, his address in 1800 being No 1, Cottage Crescent. His scenery at Bristol, described in the pages of the *Farley's Bristol Journal*, included settings for *The Count of Narbonne* in April 1782, in which "the appearance of lightening through the church window had an astonishing effect"; *The Necromancer* on 18 Oc-

tober 1782, in which he created transitions from a cavern to a kitchen, from summer to winter, and to an exact copy of a moonlight scene of the eruption of Mt Vesuvius taken on the spot by Wright of Derby ("best exhibition of painting that has ever been produced here"); and *Poor Vulcan* on 14 February 1783, which had scenes of a blacksmith's forge and a celestial territory.

French's scenes for *Andalusia* in February 1784 received special praise, his views of Bristol and environs for *Brystowe; or Harlequin Mariner* in October 1788 drew "bursts of applause," and his settings (done with his son Thomas) for *The Castle Spectre* in April 1798 possessed "some of the most striking and effective scenery" that the reporter had ever seen. With his son Thomas, who seems not to have worked in London during the eighteenth century, he also did scenery at Bristol for *Blue-Beard* in May 1799 and *Pizarro* in October 1799 and at Bath for *A Tale of Mystery* in January 1803. The younger Thomas painted scenery with Capon, Grieve, and Marchbanks for the production of *Richard III* which opened the New Beaufort Square Theatre at Bath in October 1805. The Miss French who performed children's roles at Bristol in 1783–84 was probably the elder Thomas's daughter.

Thomas French died in Bath on 5 September 1803 at the age of 66. Administration of his estate (about £100) was granted to his widow, Mary French, on 12 November 1803. Probably she was the Mrs French who was granted a quarterly annuity of £6 from the Drury Lane Theatrical Fund on 25 March 1809.

"French Boy and Girl, The." *See* MECHEL.

"French Rose, The." *See* VESTRIS, GAËTAN APPOLINE BALTHAZAR.

Frensdorf, Mr [fl. 1767–1773], *cheque taker.*

Mr Frensdorf (or Fransdorf) was a cheque taker at Covent Garden Theatre earning, as of 14 September 1767, 2s. daily. His benefit tickets were admitted each spring through 28 May 1773, but the accounts show that on several such occasions he received only half value for his tickets. He was most successful in May 1769, but he only made a pitiful £6 11s. 6d.

Freudenfeld, Auguste [fl. 1726–1727], clarinetist.

On 25 March 1726 Auguste Freudenfeld the clarinetist shared a benefit concert at Hickford's Music Room with Francis Rosenberg; the pair held a similar benefit there a year later, on 15 March 1727.

Friar. See FRYER.

Fribourg, Mr [fl. 1726–1735], boxkeeper, concessionaire.

As early as 5 September 1726 a Mr Fribourg (or Freeburg) began advertising himself as a boxkeeper at the Haymarket Theatre. One of his notices, which he ran in the papers several times, said that "All Persons that want Places or Boxes to be kept, are desir'd to send to Mr. Fribourg's at the Snuff-shop under the Play-house." He was still active in 1734–35 when his typical advertisement stated that "Places for the Boxes may be taken at Mr. FRIBOURG's, Merchant of Rappee-Snuff, at the [Haymarket] Theatre."

Fribourg, Mr [fl. 1748], dancer.

A Mr Fribourg was one of the dancers at Phillips's booth at Southwark Fair on 7 September 1748 who participated in a Grand Dance of Furies. Perhaps Fribourg was one of two brothers called Fribourg who danced at the Opéra Comique in Paris that year; their real names were François and Joseph Bertind.

Frichot, Louis Alexandre 1760–1825, serpent player, inventor.

Louis Alexandre Frichot (or, in error, Frishot), the musician and instrument inventor, was born at Versailles in April 1760, the son of a cook who served the Duke of Burgundy. In the early 1790s he fled to England because of the Revolution, and in 1793 he was playing the serpent for the Society of Ancient Music. His unusual instrument was described in 1825 in the Quarterly Musical Magazine and Review:

About thirty years ago there came to England a Frenchman, of the name of Frichot, who played an air with variations, of rapid execution, and containing very difficult chromatic passages. His instrument was a long tube, terminated by a globe about 7 or 8 inches in diameter. . . . It was in serpentine form, but the bends were not more than a foot in extent. The tube gradually increased in size from the mouthpiece to the globe. Its tone was round and pure, resembling the lower notes of the bassoon, but deeper and of greater volume.

The instrument was an early bass horn and gained sufficient interest to be manufactured by George Astor in London before the end of the eighteenth century.

Frichot returned to France after the Peace of Amiens and finally settled in Lisieux, apparently his wife's native town. There he taught music and invented the basse-trompette, which was patented in 1810. Frichot died at Lisieux on 9 April 1825.

Frick, Philipp Joseph 1740–1798, organist, armonica player, composer, pianist.

Philipp Joseph Frick (or Frike) was born in Würzburg, Germany, on 27 May 1740. He became organist to the Margrave of Baden, spent several years traveling, visited Russia, and then came to England about 1780. Though he was proficient on the organ and piano and played the latter in public, his specialty was the glass armonica, on which he performed in London with great success. Because of his health he had to give up the armonica in 1786; he devoted the rest of his life to teaching, composing, and writing. One of his works was *A Treatise on Thorough-bass*, published in 1786.

In London Frick lived at No 24, Blanford Street, Manchester Square. Haydn included him in his list of notable musical people in London in 1792. Philipp Joseph Frick died in London on 15 June 1798.

Frickler, Mr ₍fl. 1766₎, clarinetist.

Mr Frickler was one of the instrumentalists who played at Marylebone Gardens in 1766. Though the advertisements were not specific, it is probable that he was a clarinetist.

Friend, Mr ₍fl. 1744–1745?₎, actor.

A Mr Friend played Foigard in *The Beaux' Stratagem* at May Fair on 7 June 1744. Perhaps he was the Mr "Friendly" who acted Freeman in *A Bold Stroke for a Wife* on 14 November 1745 at Goodman's Fields Theatre.

Friend, John 1730–1798, singer.

When the countertenor John Friend died in 1798 he was said to have been 68, so we may place his birth in 1730. He was probably the Mr Friend who married the sister of Sir Thomas Robinson, Bart., sometime director of the entertainments at Ranelagh Gardens. Sir Thomas's will, dated 13 November 1775 and proved on 10 March 1777, left £50 to his sister Mrs Friend, £50 to her sons William, Robert, and John, and £50 to her daughter Mrs Campbell.

John Friend sang in the Handel Memorial Concerts at Westminster Abbey and the Pantheon in May and June 1784. Doane's *Musical Directory* of 1794 described Friend as a principal alto of the Chapel Royal, a participant in the Westminster Abbey concerts, and a member of the St Peter's and Windsor choirs. Friend was then living at No 2, Little George Street, Westminster.

John Friend died on 25 December 1798 and was buried with great ceremony on 31 December in the West Cloister of the Abbey. The funeral service was sung by the choirs of Westminster, St Paul's, and St James's. His will, dated 15 December 1798 and proved by his relict Jane on 24 January 1799, included bequests to his son John of Durham Cathedral and his three daughters Mary and Sarah Friend and Grace Burrows of the Haymarket, stationer. If John Friend was the man who married Sir Thomas Robinson's sister earlier in the century, some of Friend's children cited in Sir Thomas's will may have died before 1798.

Friend, John ₍fl. 1775?–1799₎, singer.

The younger John Friend, son of the countertenor John Friend and his wife Jane, may have been the man of that name mentioned in the will of Sir Thomas Robinson on 15 November 1775. Sir Thomas left £50 to John, the son of his sister Mrs Friend.

John Friend performed at the Oxford Meeting in 1793 and in 1794 was listed in Doane's *Musical Directory* as a principal tenor in the Windsor and Durham choirs and a participant in the Handelian concerts at Westminster Abbey in London. On 24 January 1799 he was one of the principal singers in a performance of the *Messiah* at the Haymarket Theatre. The same day he sang at the theatre, his father's will was proved: John, his mother, and his three sisters were named legatees.

Friendly, Mr ₍fl. 1745₎. See FRIEND, MR ₍fl. 1744–1745?₎.

Friendly, Mr ₍fl. 1770₎, actor.

Mr Friendly played Bellmour in *Jane Shore* and Young Wilding in *The Citizen* on 16 November 1770 at the Haymarket Theatre. On the following 19 December he acted Alonzo in *The Mourning Bride* at the same house.

Frier. *See* FRYER.

Frighton. *See* WRIGHTON.

Frike. *See* FRICK.

Frimble. *See also* FREMBLE.

Frimble, Mrs [*fl.* 1755–1756], actress.

Mrs Frimble played Mrs Prim in *A Bold Stroke for a Wife* on 2 October 1755 at Widow Yeates's "Large Theatrical BARN Facing the Boarding-School in CROYDON." She was Industrious Jenny in *Adventures of Half an Hour* on 3 September 1756 at the Swan Inn at Bartholomew Fair, and on the following 20 September at Bence's Southwark Fair booth she acted Estifania in *The Intriguing Captains.*

Frimbley, Mr [*fl.* 1789–1799], actor.

Mr Frimbley played Campley in *Inkle and Yarico* at the King's Head, Southwark, on 16 September 1789. At the White Hart, Fulham, he acted the role again and added Rigdumfunnidos in *Chrononhotonthologos* on 9 November, and on 11 November at the same tavern he was Villiard in *The Foundling* and Sailor in *The Shipwreck.* Frimbley was heard from again on 15 May 1799 when it was advertised that at the Old Crown, Highgate, he would act Glenalvon in *Douglas* and Darby in *The Poor Soldier.* Performances were to be given on Monday, Wednesday, and Friday, but it is not clear how long the run lasted. Tickets for the entertainment were to be had from Frimbley at the Old Crown.

Mrs Frimbley, presumably his wife, played Lady Randolph in *Douglas* and Kathleen in *The Poor Soldier.* She may have been the Hannah Frimbley whose aunt, Mary Palmer, left her a small bequest in her will dated 4 March 1812 and proved 16 March 1814.

Frimbley, Mrs [*fl.* 1799–1814?], actress. *See* FRIMBLEY, MR.

Frisby, Mr [*fl.* 1756], actor.

A Mr Frisby played Jack the Drawer in *Adventures of Half an Hour* on 3 September 1756 at the Swan Inn at Bartholomew Fair. He is not known to have been related to the (Richard) Frisby of earlier years, though it is remarkable that the Frisby of 40 years before played the same role in the same play.

Frisby, Mr [*fl.* 1785–1788], singer, actor.

Mr Frisby sang in *Cupid Pilgrim* on 27 September 1785 at Astley's Amphitheatre. He had an unspecified role in a burletta on 5 October. Perhaps he was the "comic wag" Frisby who was a member of Mrs Baker's troupe in Kent in 1788.

Frisby, Juliana. *See* SIMPSON, MRS JOHN.

Frisby, [Richard?] [*fl.* 1715–1733], actor.

A young actor named Frisby (or Frisbe) played Roi Gomez in *Don Carlos* at Drury Lane on 17 June 1715. At Lincoln's Inn Fields he was a Drawer in *Adventures of Half an Hour* when it received its first performance on 19 March 1716, and Frisby shared a benefit with Rogers on 11 May when *The Spanish Fryar* was presented.

An actor named Frisby—possibly the same person—was a member of the Smock Alley troupe in Dublin in 1721–22 and 1722–23, one of his known roles there being Perolto in *The Rival Generals* in March 1722. Perhaps the actor in question was Richard Frisby who, according to Sybil Rosenfeld's *Strolling Players*, performed at Norwich beginning in 1726. His wife had joined the Norwich troupe in 1725 and had then been described as having come from Dublin. The Frisbys were active in Norwich through 1733 at least, and Miss Frisby (their daughter, one assumes) acted there fairly regularly from 1736 to 1751. Richard Frisby in 1730 altered Cibber's *Damon and Phillida* for performance in Norwich.

Frith, Edward *1771–c. 1831?, violinist, violist, organist.*

Edward, the son of Edward Frith, an excise officer, and his wife Lydia, was baptized at St Saviour, Southwark, on 13 January 1771. By 1794 the younger Frith was a violinist, violist, and organist living at No 183, Upper Thames Street. At that time he was a participant in the oratorios at Westminster Abbey, played at Astley's Amphitheatre, and was the organist at St James, Garlickhithe. On 6 March 1796 he was recommended for membership in the Royal Society of Musicians and described as a married man with no children. In addition to his position at St James's, Frith was organist of Whitchurch, Little Stanmore, Middlesex. He was admitted to the Society on 5 June. From 1797 through 1806 he usually participated in the Society's annual St Paul's concerts in May, playing either the violin or viola.

Frith was not very active in the Society after 1806, though he occasionally attended meetings. On 3 April 1831 he was granted £40 annually and £5 for medical care because of a paralytic affliction which had plagued him for a year and a half. It is likely that he died not long after that, for the Society minutes make no further mention of him.

Frodsham, Mr [*fl. 1777–1791*], *actor.*

A Mr Frodsham acted the Prince of Wales in *Henry IV* at the Haymarket on 11 February 1777. Perhaps he was the same Mr Frodsham who 14 years later played Constant in *The Humours of Sir John Brute* and Leicester in *King Henry II* at the same theatre on 26 December 1791. Possibly he was a son of Bridge Frodsham (1734–1768) and his wife Isabella, who were actors at York for many years; if so, he was the brother of Sarah Frodsham who acted at the Haymarket in the 1780s and later in the provinces as Mrs Reily.

Frodsham, Sarah, later Mrs Reily and then Mrs George Inchbald *b. 1761, actress.*

Sarah Frodsham was born in 1761, probably at York, where her father Bridge Frodsham (1734–1768) and her mother Isabella Frodsham were actors for many years. Her father was a celebrated provincial actor, who is noticed in *The Dictionary of National Biography*, and whose playing of Hamlet was regarded by Tate Wilkinson to have been inferior only to those of Garrick and Barry. Sarah began acting at the age of eight at York when on 22 April 1769 she gave an "Address to Ladies" for her mother's benefit. With her sister, Miss F. Frodsham, who had been acting since 1768, Sarah played regularly at York through 1776, and she or her sister acted Nysa in *Midas* at Norwich on 15 June 1775. Sarah made her debut at the Crow Street Theatre, Dublin, on 30 June 1777, announced as "A Young Lady," age 16; she also played at Cork in the summer of 1778, at King's Lynn in 1779, and later at Manchester.

On 4 July 1783, she made her debut at the Haymarket Theatre as Rosalind in *As You Like It*. After repeating Rosalind on 9 July, she played Dinah Primrose and spoke the epilogue to *The Young Quaker* some 19 times between 26 July and 15 September. At the Haymarket the following summer, she acted as "Mrs Riley," having married a provincial actor named Reily (sometimes Riley) who was also in the Haymarket company at that time. Her only role at the Haymarket in 1784 was Dinah Primrose. During the following two summers, 1785 and 1786, she frequently played Bloom in *I'll Tell You What*, after which she evidently did not appear again in London.

She played at Cambridge in 1786, at

Manchester in 1787, and at Norwich in 1788–89, and also at Bath and Lincoln. In September 1792 she married George Inchbald (d. 1800), an actor who was the son of the actor Joseph Inchbald (1735–1779) and the stepson of Elizabeth Inchbald (1753–1821), actress and author. Evidently Sarah did not continue to act as Mrs Inchbald.

Fromantel. *See* **FOURMANTEL.**

Froment, Miss. *See* **SUTTON, MRS.**

Froment, John Baptiste L. ⟨*fl.* 1739– 1777⟩, *dancer, choreographer, dancing-master.*

John Baptiste L. Froment (for so he signed himself in 1770, though printers sometimes spelled his name Fremont and Frument), danced the role of a Haymaker in *Harlequin Shipwrecked* at Drury Lane on 10 March 1739. He was also in an *Ethiopian Dance* on 15 May and subsequent dates but was not cited for any other dance assignments during his first season. In 1739–40 he danced again at Drury Lane in his old parts and in *The Double Dealer*, but he also appeared at Covent Garden on 4 December 1739 as an Infernal in *Perseus and Andromeda* and on 12 February 1740 as a Swain in *Orpheus and Euridice.* On 13 September 1740 he turned up at Sadler's Wells, and on 4 December he danced at the Aungier Street Theatre in Dublin. He made his last appearance of the season at Aungier Street on 7 March 1741 and then returned to London.

On 14 September 1741 he was at Sadler's Wells again, but on 28 September he appeared at the Goodman's Fields Theatre dancing *Les Bergères* with Mme Duvall. At that playhouse in 1741–42 he also danced in *The Imprisonment, Release, Stratagems, and Marriage of Harlequin* and offered *The Italian Peasants*, a new comic dance with Miss Scott, and a minuet with Mlle August. On 21 May 1742 he shared a benefit with two others. In 1742–43 he was dancing at Drury Lane in *Les Amant volages, Comus,* and *French Peasant,* and he also appeared in a solo *Scotch Dance* and a minuet with Mrs Freeman. On 14 May 1743 he was granted a solo benefit.

Froment went off to Scotland, appearing in Edinburgh in 1743 with Thomas Este's company. There on 3 April 1745 he was given a benefit, his address being advertised as at his school in Bailie Fife's Close. By the 1747–48 season he was back in London dancing at Covent Garden as a Huntsman and Zephyrus in *Apollo and Daphne.* At his shared benefit (with two others) on 28 April 1748 he danced *Pigmalione* and a minuet and louvre with Mme Dumont. His affiliation with Covent Garden lasted through 1750–51, during which time he danced such numbers as a *Scotch Measure* and a *Highland Reel* and appeared as an Infernal in *Perseus and Andromeda* and an Aerial Spirit and Pluto (Punch) in *Merlin's Cave.* In addition to what he may have earned at his shared benefits, Froment was paid (in 1749–50 at least) £1 10s. weekly.

His name disappeared from the bills in London until 17 June 1757 when he turned up at the Haymarket Theatre in Theophilus Cibber's troupe dancing in *Blind Man's Buff, Les Bergères, Les Paysans,* a *Dutch Dance,* and *The Marine Boys Marching to Portsmouth* — or at least some of those numbers. He was at the Haymarket in September and October and again in December and in January 1758, appearing occasionally with Mlle Dulisse or Mme Dulisse in specialty dances. For his solo benefit on 25 January 1758 he danced the title part in *Pigmalione* with Mlle Dulisse.

Once again Froment's name disappeared from the London bills, but he was given a solo benefit at Drury Lane on 6 May 1761, at which he performed a louvre and minuet with one of his young female scholars and played a solo on his "Little Violin." It is probable that at that time he held an important position in the Drury Lane Company, perhaps as ballet master, for in 1761–62 his name again failed to appear until benefit time when, on 12 May 1762, he was given a solo benefit at which he danced with Miss Froment, age six, *Les Charactères de la dance*, a louvre, and a minuet. We may guess that Miss Froment was his daughter, though the bill only specified that she was his scholar and was making her first appearance.

Perhaps Froment was working at one of the patent houses during the years that followed, but it is more likely that he devoted his time to teaching and made only those occasional public appearances which suited him. In the summer of 1767, for instance, he danced at the Haymarket Theatre, offering a hornpipe, *The Italian Peasant*, and a new tambourin. On 31 August, according to Sylas Neville's manuscript diary, Barry had to announce that Mrs Dancer was ill and could not perform; the gallery patrons hissed and cried, "Off Off" as "little" Froment, with equanimity danced to pacify them.

By 1770 Froment was living in Lambeth. On 2 May 1771 he danced a louvre and minuet with Miss Froment at her benefit at the Haymarket; on 24 April 1773 he reappeared with her at Drury Lane, by which time she had become Mrs Sutton. For her he composed a new *Turkish Dance*. On 20 April 1774 he again danced a louvre and minuet with Mrs Sutton at her benefit, and he did the same in April 1775, 1776, and 1777. Perhaps by 1777 Froment was living at her house at No 8, Great Wild Street, Lincoln's Inn Fields. On 4 September 1777 at the Richmond Theatre Froment again danced with Mrs Sutton, but after that his name disappeared from the theatrical bills.

Frompe. *See* DE FOMPRÉ.

Front, Mr ₁*fl.* 1776₁, *actor.*
Mr Front played Paris in *The Jealous Wife* at the Haymarket Theatre on 2 May 1776.

Frost, Mr ₁*fl.* 1781–1794?₁, *actor.*
Mr Frost acted at the Crow Street Theatre in Dublin in 1781, but by 17 September 1784 he was in London, playing Ratcliff in *Richard III* at the Haymarket Theatre. In the summer of 1785 Frost performed at Brighton, and at Abingdon, south of Oxford, on 9 January 1789 he played the first Planter in *Inkle and Yarico*. He was at the Haymarket again on 7 March 1791, this time acting Sir Jealous Traffic in *The Busy Body*. Possibly he was the Mr Frost who was in the circus in Limekiln Lane, Bristol, in early March 1794.

Frost, Mrs ₁*fl.* 1733₁, *actress.*
Mrs Frost played Moll Hackabout in *The Harlot's Progress* on 28 September 1733 in "a large commodious Room in Artichoke Yard at Mile-End, during the Time of the Fair."

Frost, Henry *c. 1631–1696, singer.*
The Henry Frost who was a tenor in the Chapel Royal at the coronation of Charles II on 23 April 1661 was very likely the Henry Frost of St Martin-in-the-Fields, gentleman and bachelor, age about 30, who married Margaret Smart of Lambeth, Surrey, on 30 December 1661. The couple wed with the consent of Margaret's father, for Margaret was only about 15. The parish registers of St Margaret, Westminster, which contain so many entries concerning court musicians, record a number of baptisms of children of a Henry and Margaret Frost: John on 10 May 1666, Frances on 17 June 1672, William on 23 June 1674, and Henry on 13 April 1676.

Henry Frost was mentioned frequently in the Lord Chamberlain's accounts. He was exempted from paying the subsidies levied by Parliament in 1661; he accompanied the King to Windsor in the summers of 1671, 1674, 1675, and 1678; he was reappointed to the Chapel Royal by James II on 23 April 1685; he was one of the witnesses of the musician Richard Hart's will on 26 December 1689; and in 1689 he was again appointed to the Chapel Royal under William and Mary.

Presumably he was the Henry Frost of St James, Westminster, who wrote his will while "indisposed in body" on 12 March 1695, leaving his daughter Frances and sons William and John 10*s.* each "in full barr of all claims against my estate." He left his wife Margaret the rest of his estate. The will was proved by Mrs Frost on 2 July 1696.

Froud, Miss ₁*fl. 1768–1769*₁, *singer.*
Miss Froud sang at Marylebone Gardens in 1768 and at Finch's Grotto Gardens in August 1769. Among the published songs which cited her as the singer were *My Laddie is gang'd far away* (1768), *The Milk Maid* (1769), and *The Tim'rous Lover* (1769), all of which she offered to audiences at Marylebone Gardens.

Froud, Charles ₁*fl. 1734–1763*₁, *organist, violinist.*
In 1734 Charles Froud (or Frowd) was one of several musicians who competed for the post of organist at St Michael, Cornhill. He lost to Kelway, and it is not known whether or not he tried for a different post. In 1739 when the Royal Society of Musicians was formed, Froud became an original subscriber. He played second violin in a performance of *Acis and Galatea* on 1 April 1758 at the Great Room in Dean Street, Soho, and on the following 27 April he was one of the violinists in the *Messiah* at the Chapel of the Foundling Hospital. *Mortimer's London Directory* of 1763 listed Froud as an organist and teacher of the harpsichord who lived in King Street, Bloomsbury.

Frudd, Mr ₁*fl. 1784*₁, *violinist.*
Mr Frudd of Nottingham played first

violin in the Handel Memorial Concerts at Westminster Abbey and the Pantheon in May and June 1784.

Frument. *See* **FROMENT.**

Fry, Mr ₁*fl. 1794*₁, *singer?*
Doane's *Musical Directory* of 1794 listed a Mr Fry, of Crayford, Kent, as a tenor (singer, presumably) who participated in the Handel performances at Westminster Abbey.

Fry, William ₁*fl. 1775*₁, *musician.*
As of 20 August 1775 William Fry was a member of the band at Drury Lane.

Fryar, Mr ₁*fl. 1745–1750?*₁, *house servant?*
Mr Fryar's benefit tickets were accepted at Drury Lane on 9 May 1745, 7 May 1746, and 12 May 1747. He was apparently one of the house servants. Perhaps he was the hosier named Fryar who was paid £6 12*s.* by Drury Lane on 3 January 1750.

Fryer, Mr ₁*fl. 1794*₁, *singer?*
Doane's *Musical Directory* of 1794 listed a Mr Fryer of York as an alto (singer, presumably) in the Handelian concerts at Westminster Abbey.

Fryer, Margaret, later Mrs Vandervelt *c. 1635–1747, actress, dancer.*
"Peg" Fryer may have been born about 1635. Possibly she was the actress who played the Old Widow in *Love and Honour* at Lincoln's Inn Fields on 21 October 1661 and subsequent dates, and perhaps she was the "Pegg" who acted Nell in *Ignoramus* with the Duke's Company at court on 1 November 1662. Montague Summers suggested that Sir Charles Sedley's mistress "Pegg" in 1668 was Peg Fryer, but it is more likely that the woman in question was Margaret Hughes. There are many references in the parish registers of St Giles in the Fields in the 1660s and 1670s to the

surname Fryer, and one in 1674 in the registers of St Margaret, Westminster—some of them referring to a Margaret Fryer and some to Elizabeth. It is impossible to tell whether or not any of those refer to the actress.

Peg Fryer married a Mr Vandervelt and kept a tavern in Tottenham Court Road, but she returned to the stage on 11 January 1720 at Lincoln's Inn Fields to play Widow Rich in *The Half-Pay Officers*, heralded as "Peg Fryer, it being the first time of her Appearing on any Stage since the Reign of King Charles II." The bill said she was 85 years old and would also dance a "Bashful Maid and Irish Trot." In the 1720 edition of the play she was called Mrs Vandervelt in the cast list and was praised in the preface:

the part of Mrs. Fryer is in an old play called *Love and Honour,* which she acted when she was young, and which was so imprinted in her memory, she could repeat it every word; and it was to an accidental conversation with her, this Farce owed its being; she acted with so much spirit and life, before two or three persons who had some interest with the house, that we judged it would do upon the stage; she was prevailed upon to undertake it; upon which this Farce was immediately projected and finished in 14 days.

The prologue to the odd compilation of Shakespeare and Shirley (with some original bits pieced in) stated that

Tonight strange means we try your
*   smiles to win,*
And bring a good old Matron on the
*   scene:*
Kindly she quits a calm retreat to show
What acting pleased you fifty years ago.
When you behold her quivering on the
*   stage,*
Remember, 'tis a personated age:
Nor think, that no remains of youth she
*   feels,*
She'll show you, e're she's done—she has
*   it in her heels.*

Whincop in his *English Dramatic Poets* said of the performance:

Peg Fryer was 85. Her character in the Farce was that of a very old woman; she went through it very well, but when, the Farce being done, she was brought upon the stage again to dance a jig, which had been promised in the bills, she came tottering in, as if ready to fall and made two or three pretended offers to go out again, but all on a sudden, the music striking up the Irish Trot, she danced and footed it away as nimbly as any wench of 25 could have done.

The "Bashful Maid" she danced in the ensuing Farce, *Hob's Wedding.* Peg also acted Mrs Amlet in *The Confederacy* on 28 March 1720 at Lincoln's Inn Fields. Whincop claimed that she turned to tavern-keeping after, not before, her 1720 stage appearances. In any case, she returned to the stage again in 1723; the *Weekly Journal* of 26 January that year said:

At the New Theatre, right over against the Opera House in the Hay-Market, on Monday January 28, will be acted the *Half-pay Officers*, with *Hobb's Wedding*; the Widow Rich performed by the celebrated Peggy Fryar, aged 71, for her benefit, who dances the bashful Country Maid and the Irish Trot, and played but one [*sic*] Since the days of King Charles, and taught three Queens to dance.

Peg Fryer died in November 1747 at the incredible age, according to the *Scots Magazine* in 1786, of 117; if true, that would place her birth date in 1630 rather than 1635. The notices of 1723 would suggest a birth date in 1652, but if she was acting at the Restoration, she may have been born in the mid-1630s.

Fulford, Mr [*fl.* 1736–1737], *actor.*
Mr Fulford (or Fulfort) played Bonniface in *The Stratagem* on 8 October 1736 for his first appearance at Covent Garden. He had apparently acted elsewhere, though

there are no records of his previous activity. On 9 December he played the Captain in *The Scornful Lady*; on 29 December he was Mixem in *A Woman's Revenge*; and on 13 May 1737 he shared a benefit with two others and acted Driver in *Oroonoko*. Mrs Fulford, presumably his wife, acted Widow Lackit at his benefit. She was probably the Mrs Fulford who performed at Norwich in 1738–39. No further trace of Mr Fulford has been found.

Fulford, Mrs [*fl.* 1737–1739], actress. See FULFORD, MR.

Fullam, Michael 1758–1826, actor, manager.

Michael Fullam, who spent his entire career in the provinces outside the London area except for one summer at Richmond, Surrey, in 1791, was born in 1758, according to W. J. Lawrence's notes at the National Library of Ireland, and in St Catherine's parish, Dublin, according to the *Hibernian Magazine* (May 1804). If indeed born in 1758, he could not have been the adult Irish actor named Fullam who performed at the Crow Street Theatre, Dublin, in 1767, at Belfast in 1768, at Limerick in 1771, and occasionally at Kilkenny between 1771 and 1773. The older actor, no doubt, was Michael's father, and the Mrs Fullam who performed with him at the above places was Michael's mother.

Michael Fullam was probably the person of that name who acted at Belfast in February 1780, when for his benefit on the tenth he performed Sir Benjamin Dove in *The Brothers*. A week earlier, on 3 February, Juliet was played by Mrs Fullam, no doubt his wife. Perhaps he was the Fullam who had acted in the previous summer of 1779 at the New Theatre, Birmingham.

After acting at Exeter in the 1780s, and no doubt in Ireland as well, Michael Fullam played at Brighton in July 1790 and in May and June 1791, when his name was given as "Fulham." Later that summer he

Harvard Theatre Collection

MICHAEL FULLAM, as Justice Woodcock

artist unknown

acted at Richmond, as noted above, and then performed at Kilkenny in 1792, 1793 (when he also managed the company), 1795, and 1799. In the last-mentioned year at Kilkenny he gave special performances for his fellow Masons. He also appeared at Waterford in February and March 1793 and at Limerick in 1799 and 1800. From 1797–98 through 1799–1800 he was a member of the company at Crow Street, where he also acted in the nineteenth century.

His full name was given in the *Dramatic Register*, which listed his death date incorrectly as 24 February 1825. He died in January 1826, and his will was listed in the index of wills at the Four Courts, Dublin, that year. The records of that registry, however, were destroyed by fire in 1922, so his will is lost. His wife had acted at Brighton in 1791, at Plymouth in 1792, and at Norwich between 1793 and 1796, as well as at Belfast in 1800. In his *Irish Stage in the County Towns*, William S. Clark conflated the career of Michael Fullam with that of his father and that of his wife with that of his mother.

An engraved portrait by G. Shea of Michael Fullam was published as a plate to the *Hibernian Magazine*. He was also depicted by an unknown engraver as Justice Woodcock, with an unidentified actress in the character of Rosetta, in *Love in a Village*.

Fuller, Mr [*fl. 1800*], *house servant?*
On 14 June 1800 a Mr Fuller's benefit tickets were accepted at Drury Lane. Possibly he was one of the house servants.

Fuller, Isaac *1606–1672, scene painter.*
Isaac Fuller was born in 1606 and studied painting in Paris under François Perrier about 1630. It is likely that Fuller

Victoria and Albert Museum

ISAAC FULLER

self-portrait

was at Oxford in 1641 while Charles I held court there, that he worked in Paris from about 1645 to 1650, and that he returned to Oxford, where he did much of his work in the 1650s and early 1660s. In the chapel at Wadham College he painted a picture of the Children of Israel gathering manna, and at Magdalen College he painted the Last Judgment as an altar piece. To the Irish Parliament he presented 15 pictures of the "Escape of Charles II. after the battle of Worcester." He etched some plates for a drawing book, *Un libro da disegnare* (1654), and with Tempesta and Henry Cooke he etched plates for the "Moral Emblems" by Cesare Ripa.

On a visit to Oxford in 1664 John Evelyn saw "the Picture on the Wall over the Altar at All-Soules, being the largest piece of Fresco Painting (or rather in Imitation of it, for tis in oyle [of turpentine]) in England, & not ill design'd, by the hand of one Fuller: yet I feare it will not hold long, & seemes too full of nakeds for a Chapell. . . ." The fresco Evelyn saw represented the Resurrection and was, indeed, replaced about 1705. Fuller also painted some portraits while at Oxford. Walpole thought "his pencil was bold, strong, and masterly" in portraits, but he found Fuller extravagant in his manner and a wretched painter of historical compositions.

In London Fuller executed wall paintings in a number of taverns: the Crown in Smithfield, the Mitre in Fenchurch Street, the "Corner House" in Soho Square, and the Sun behind the Royal Exchange. Unfortunately, none of Fuller's wall paintings in London or Oxford has survived.

For the production of Dryden's *Tyrannick Love* at the Bridges Street Theatre in the spring of 1669 the King's Company contracted with Fuller on 14 April to paint "a new Scene of an Elysium." According to testimony given at a trial a year later, the players planned to perform the play by the end of April, and Fuller agreed to have the scenery painted in two weeks. He did not complete the work until the end of June, said the players, and the painting was done "very meanly and inconsiderably." The actors had paid Fuller £40 on account but claimed damages of £500 for the loss of patronage they suffered. The play was not performed until 24 June, by which time many playgoers would have left London for the summer.

Fuller told a different story. He claimed that Dryden and Mr Wright, a joiner who worked for the King's Company, had originally proposed the work to him at a time when Fuller was "lying sick at his own house." A few days later the painter went to the theatre to discuss the matter with the players, and then the contract was drawn up. Fuller claimed in court that he had not agreed to paint the scenery in a fortnight, for that would have been impossible; the work took him about six weeks, and he felt that "no painter in England could have finished the same and have done the work So well . . . in So Short a Space." The scene painter Robert Streeter testified to Fuller's skill and speed at painting and pronounced the scenery "excellently well done." Fuller described to the court how for three weeks while he worked on the Elysium scene he "did not put off his Clothes but lay upon a pallet-bed in the Room and rose up to work as Soon as he could See." He claimed that the players were well satisfied with his work at the time he presented it to them. When he received no further payment for his painting, Fuller went to court to sue Charles Hart and Michael Mohun, the leading actors in the troupe. At the trial in Guildhall in Easter term 1670 Fuller won his case and was to be paid £335 10s. After that discouraging relationship with the players, Fuller may not have attempted theatre work again.

Isaac Fuller died of dissipation on 17 July 1672 in Bloomsbury Square. Lely is said to have lamented "that so great a genius should besot or neglect so great a

talent." Fuller left three sons: Isaac, Nicholas (who became a coach painter), and Mathew. The parish registers of St Andrew, Holborn, contain the baptismal record for Mathew, dated 5 July 1661. The parents were cited as Isaack and Elizabeth Fuller of Shoe Lane. When Fuller died in 1672 he was living in the parish of St Giles in the Fields; a note in the registers there indicates that he was "caryed away" on 18 July, and the St Andrew registers list his burial on the same day, noting him as a "paynter" from Southampton Buildings in St Giles's parish.

In 1670 Fuller painted a self-portrait at the request of the owner of the Mitre Tavern; it is a work which, it is said, Fuller painted when he was drunk. It is now at the Bodleian Library, Oxford, and variants of it are at the National Portrait Gallery and at Queen's College, Oxford. The version at Queen's College shows Fuller with a boy, said to be his son. A related drawing is at the Victoria and Albert Museum. Engravings of Fuller's self-portrait were made by T. Chambers and J. Jackson. A wash drawing of Fuller by G. Vertue is at the Huntington Library.

Fuller, [John?] [fl. 1737–1776?], house servant.

From the spring of 1737 through that of 1743 (with the exception of 1740) Mr Fuller's benefit tickets were accepted at Drury Lane Theatre. The first mention of him was on 27 May 1737 and the last on 23 May 1743. Since he was often listed with other members of the house staff, Fuller was probably one of the house servants. From 1743 to 1776 John Fuller —possibly the Fuller who had been employed at Drury Lane—operated a bookselling and publishing business at the Dove in Creed Lane, then in Paternoster Row, then at the Bible and Dove in Ave Mary Lane, and finally in Blowbladder Street, Cheapside. Information on Fuller's business activities was compiled by Humphries and Smith for their *Music Publishing in the British Isles*.

Fuller, William [*fl.* 1663–1670], *rope dancer.*

On 22 February 1663, along with Jacob Hall and Thomas Cosby, William Fuller was sworn one of the "Valters & Dancers on ye Rope and other agillity of Body" to Charles II. Fuller and Hall set up a rope dancing booth near the Maypole in the Strand on 26 March 1667, and the pair still had a troupe in 1669. It is very likely that the following entry in the St Margaret, Westminster, parish register concerns Fuller the rope dancer: On 27 February 1670 William Fuller and his wife Jane baptized a son Salvator Jacob Fuller.

Fullerton, Mr [*fl.* 1729], *house servant?*

On 10 July 1729 a Mr Fullerton's benefit tickets were accepted at the Haymarket Theatre. Perhaps he was one of the house servants.

Fullwell. *See* FULWELL.

Fullwood, Mr [*fl.* 1733–1745], *boxkeeper.*

Mr Fullwood (or Falwood) was a boxkeeper at the Haymarket Theatre and shared a benefit with his brother Mason Mr Lee on 23 April 1733. He was not cited in the bills the following two seasons, but on 21 May 1736 his benefit tickets were accepted at Drury Lane. He was similarly noticed each spring thereafter through 8 May 1745, though his duties at Drury Lane were never specified. Possibly he was the Charles Fullwood whose daughter Elizabeth was buried at St Paul, Covent Garden, on 4 October 1722.

Fullwood, Thomas [*fl.* 1794], *singer.*

Thomas Fullwood of No 94, Bunhill Row, sang bass for the Choral Fund, the Handelian Society, and in the oratorios performed at Drury Lane, according to Doane's *Musical Directory* of 1794.

Fulton, Mr [*fl.* 1785–1790], *violinist.*

The Minute Books of the Royal Society of Musicians cite a Mr "Futton" as a violinist who played at the St Paul's concerts on 10 and 12 May 1785. The notation was surely a scribal error for "Fulton," for a violinist of that name played at the St Paul's concerts on 18 and 20 May 1790.

Fulwell, Mr [*fl.* 1745–1747], *dancer.*

Mr Fulwell (or Fullwell) danced one of the Demons in *The Tempest* on 14 February 1745 and subsequent dates at Goodman's Fields. On 1 May his benefit tickets were accepted. Though he was not mentioned in the bills the following season, he shared a benefit with Owen on 24 March 1747.

Fuozi, Mlle [*fl.* 1786], *dancer. See* FUOZI, ANTONIO.

Fuozi, Antonio [*fl.* 1784–1789], *dancer.*

Antonio and Eleanor Fuozi (or Fouzi, Fuse, Fusi, etc.) were dancers from Bologna. They performed at the King's Theatre in 1784–85 for a season salary of £150. With them that season was a Mlle Fuozi, presumably their daughter, who made her first English appearance at the King's on 18 December 1784 in a new divertissement. On 4 September 1786 Mlle Fuozi danced at Astley's Amphitheatre, and in 1786–87 she and her sister were employed at Drury Lane for £1 each weekly. One of the girls was named Elena, and perhaps she was the Mlle Fuozi who danced *The Village Archers* with Ferrere on 24 February 1787.

Though the Fuozi girls seem not to have continued their careers in London, Antonio and Eleanor remained active in the late 1780s. Signora Fuozi appeared at the Royal

Circus in the fall of 1786, the spring of 1787, and May 1789; she danced at Astley's in 1788 and at the Royalty Theatre and in Norwich in 1790. Signor Fuozi performed at the Royal Circus in a ballet called *The Morris Dancers* on 12 May 1789.

Fuozi, Signora Antonio, Eleanor [*fl.* 1784–1790], *dancer. See* FUOZI, ANTONIO.

Fuozi, Elena [*fl.* 1784–1787], *dancer. See* FUOZI, ANTONIO.

"Furioso, Signor" [*fl.* 1737–1738], *actor, singer.*
When *The Dragon of Wantley* was performed at the Haymarket Theatre on 16 May 1737 the title role was taken by "Sig Furioso (his other Name to be conceal'd)." The bill added facetiously that "The Dragon was intended to have charm'd the City at Stationer's Hall; but from a Punctilio very common to Singers, he insisted on exerting his Musical Faculty at the Haymarket." Over a year later, on 5 September 1738, the same performer played the Spanish Giant in *Merlin* at Lee's booth at Southwark Fair.

Furkins, Mr [*fl.* 1797–1814?], *carpenter.*
A Mr Furkins, probably the son of William Furkins the boxkeeper, served the Covent Garden Theatre as a carpenter from as early as 25 May 1797, when he was first mentioned in the bills. He was very likely the Furkins who was a member of the Covent Garden company in 1813–14.

Furkins, William [*fl.* 1767–1797], *boxkeeper.*
William Furkins was a boxkeeper at Covent Garden from at least as early as 14 September 1767, when he was noted on a pay list as receiving 2s. daily (*The London Stage* lists him as "Parkins"), to as late as 25 May 1797, when he was last mentioned in the bills as one of those house servants whose benefit tickets would be accepted. His salary seems to have remained the same throughout his 30 years of service. The Furkins who was a carpenter at the theatre at the end of the eighteenth century was probably William's son.

Furnival, Miss [*fl.* 1745–1747?], *actress.*
A Miss Furnival made her first appearance on any stage—according to the bill—on 6 November 1745 at Drury Lane playing Indiana in *The Conscious Lovers*. On 14 November she was seen as Amanda in *The Relapse* and on 11 December as Amanda in *Love's Last Shift*. Perhaps that ended Miss Furnival's career, though *The London Stage* lists her as a member of the Covent Garden company in 1746–47. No roles are known for her for that season, but *Mrs* Furnival acted at Covent Garden when Mrs Cibber was too ill to perform.

Perhaps Miss Furnival was a daughter of Mr and Mrs Thomas Furnival, and she may have been a sister of the Miss Furnival who made her first appearance on any stage at Smock Alley, Dublin, on 29 May 1740 playing the title role in *The Virgin Unmask'd*. There is a possibility that the two Misses Furnival cited were one and the same, but the girl who appeared in Dublin is said to have become Mrs Thomas Carmichael on 1 February 1741.

Furnival, Thomas *d. 1773, actor.*
Thomas Furnival was probably the Furnival who shared a benefit with his wife at the Theatre on St Augustine's Back in Bristol on 4 September 1728. In London he was first noticed on 30 November 1730 when he played Constant in *The Coffee-House Politician* and Lord Truetaste in *The Battle of the Poets* at the Haymarket Theatre. He followed that performance with a full and busy season at the same playhouse, acting Sciolto in *The Fair Penitent*

on 7 December, a role in *The Merry Masqueraders* on 9 December, Lodovico in *Othello* on 17 December, Sparkish in *The Author's Farce* on 23 December, the King in *The Generous Freemason* on 28 December, Sullen in *The Stratagem* on 15 January 1731, Lorenzo in *The Spanish Fryar* on 18 January, a role in *The Spendthrift* on 20 January, Townly in *The Provok'd Husband* on 10 February, a role in *The Indian Empress* on 17 February, Valentine in *Love for Love* on 26 February, a role in *Lupone* on 15 March, Sir Jasper in *The Cobler of Preston* on 17 March, Squire ap Shinken in *The Welsh Opera* on 22 April, and Sir Robert Holland (and the prologue) in *The Fall of Mortimer* on 12 May. He played Thorowgood in *The London Merchant* on 8 September at Southwark Fair to conclude his rather spectacular first season in London. But the names of Thomas and Elizabeth ("Fanny") Furnival dropped from London bills after that, and it is likely that they went off to the provinces. A Mrs Furnival is known to have acted at York in 1736.

The Furnivals reappeared in London in the spring of 1737: on 5 May at Drury Lane they shared a benefit with Macklin when *The Provok'd Husband* was performed. Mrs Furnival acted Lady Townly, but Thomas seems not to have participated. In 1737–38 and 1738–39 both Furnivals were active at Drury Lane. Thomas played such parts as Alphonso in *The Spanish Fryar*, Douglas in *1 Henry IV*, Aristander in *The Rival Queens*, Tanais in *Tamerlane*, Hotman in *Oroonoko*, and the Master of the Madhouse in *The Pilgrim*. Though he received no benefits during those seasons, Mrs Furnival did, giving her (and presumably his) address as next door to the Blackamoor's Head in Exeter Street, near the Strand.

The Furnivals then went to Ireland, where Thomas made his first Smock Alley appearance on 29 May 1740 as Moneses in *Tamerlane*. A Miss Furnival, presumably

Thomas and Fanny's daughter, made her first stage appearance the same night; on 1 February 1741 she became Mrs Thomas Carmichael. Fanny Furnival acted in Dublin from 1740–41 through 1745–46, but Thomas returned to London by the fall of 1744, and the careers of the pair followed separate courses after that.

Furnival played Brabantio in *Othello* at the Haymarket on 22 September 1744 with Theophilus Cibber's company and stayed on to act Montague in *Romeo and Juliet*, Humphrey in *The Conscious Lovers*, Steward in *The Prodigal*, and Phoenix in *The Distrest Mother*. On 12 December he moved to the Goodman's Fields Theatre to act the title role in *The Miser*. He followed that appearance with Balance in *The Recruiting Officer*, Prospero in *The Tempest*, Ford in *The Merry Wives of Windsor* for his benefit on 28 March 1745, and Colonel Manly in *Woman is a Riddle*.

He remained with the Goodman's Fields troupe in 1745–46 and 1746–47 playing a very heavy schedule that included some of his old parts plus such new ones as Elder Wou'dbe in *The Twin Rivals*, Carlos in *Love Makes a Man*, Simon Pure in *A Bold Stroke for a Wife*, Heartwell in *The Old Bachelor*, Sir George in *The Drummer*, Hamlet (on 27 November 1745), Aboan in *Oroonoko*, Iago in *Othello*, the King in *1 Henry IV*, Dumont in *Jane Shore*, Sempronius in *Cato*, Tressel in *Richard III*, Clause in *The Royal Merchant*, Chaplain in *The Orphan*, Trusty in *The Funeral*, Scandal in *Love for Love*, Worthy in *The Recruiting Officer*, Tamerlane, Barnwell Senior in *The London Merchant*, Manly in *The Provok'd Husband*, Coupler in *The Relapse*, Sealand in *The Conscious Lovers*, Macduff in *Macbeth*, Horatio in *Hamlet*, Charles in *The Careless Husband*, and Drawcansir in *The Rehearsal* (for his benefit on 23 March 1747). Between these two seasons, on 20 October 1746, he acted with others from Goodman's Fields at Southwark. Mrs Furnival returned to London that fall, but she was engaged by Drury Lane.

Furnival's appearances in 1747–48 and 1748–49 were sporadic. On 4 April 1748 he turned up at the New Wells, Lemon Street, to play Balance in *The Recruiting Officer*; on 27 February 1749 he was there again acting Careless in *The Committee*; on 1 June 1749 he shared a benefit with Sherman at the Haymarket Theatre where Foote's troupe was playing; and on 23 August 1749 he acted Amphitryon in *The Descent of the Heathen Gods* at Bartholomew Fair.

From about 1750 to 1755 Furnival acted at Bath, and he was probably the "Furnevall" in Roger Kemble's company at Bath from 18 September 1767 to 31 May 1768. Thomas Furnival died there in 1773 (at an advanced age, according to Penley's *The Bath Stage*). He was buried at St James's, Bath, on 12 February 1773. Despite his few seasons of feverish activity in London in the 1730s and 1740s and the wide range of roles he attempted, Thomas Furnival seems to have been ignored by the critics.

Furnival, Mrs Thomas, Elizabeth, "Fanny", later Mrs Roger Kemble the first? [*fl.* 1728?–1752], *actress, singer.*

Mrs Thomas Furnival, better known to her contemporaries as "Fanny", was probably the Mrs Furnival who appeared in Bristol with her husband in 1728 at the Theatre on St Augustine's Back. The pair performed in London at the Haymarket Theatre in 1730–31, Fanny's first known role being Lady Grace in *The Provok'd Husband* on 10 February 1731. She went on to play a part in *The Indian Empress* on 17 February, Mrs Frail in *Love for Love* on 26 February, Elvira in *The Spanish Fryar* on 12 March, a part in *Lupone* on 15 March, and Betty in *The Welsh Opera* on 22 April. She was probably the "Miss" Furnival who acted Lucy in *The London*

Merchant at Southwark Fair on 8 September 1731, after which Fanny and Thomas apparently left London.

Chetwood in his *General History* (1749) stated that Fanny was acting in York in 1736 and was there seen by a person of high station who arranged for the actress's Drury Lane debut. Chetwood, the prompter at that house, apparently sponsored a revival of *The Scornful Lady* on 17 March 1737 with Mrs Furnival in the title role, in which, according to him, she acquitted herself well. She played Mrs Sullen in *The Stratagem* on 12 April and, for her shared benefit with her husband and Macklin on 5 May, Lady Townly in *The Provok'd Husband*. As Chetwood told the story, Fanny had no chance to act tragic roles at Drury Lane, since they were already assigned to others, so the noble person who brought her to London from York advised her to try Dublin.

Fanny did not take the advice immediately. The following season at Drury Lane, 1737–38, she played Mrs Sullen again and then Portia in *Julius Caesar*, one of Clytemnestra's Attendants in *Agamemnon*, and, for her shared benefit with Woodward on 8 May 1738, Millamant in *The Way of the World*. Her benefit bill stated that she was living next door to the Blackamoor's Head in Exeter Street, near the Strand. In 1738–39 she acted, among other new parts, the Duchess of Suffolk in *Lady Jane Gray*, Clarissa in *The Confederacy*, Hypolita in *She Wou'd and She Wou'd Not*, Goneril in *King Lear*, Narcissa in *Love's Last Shift*, and Lady Fidget in *The Country Wife*.

Mrs Furnival acted at the Smock Alley Theatre in Dublin beginning in 1739–40. Through the summer of 1742 she played such parts as Lady Lurewell in *The Lottery*, Mrs Sullen in *The Beaux' Stratagem*, Hermione in *The Distrest Mother*, Laetitia in *The Old Bachelor*, Monimia in *The Orphan*, Amanda in *Love's Last Shift*, Jane Shore, Lady Froth in *The Double Dealer*, Hippolito in *The Tempest*, Almeria in *The*

Mourning Bride, Angelica in *Love for Love*, Queen Elizabeth in *Richard III*, Lady Lurewell in *The Constant Couple*, Sylvia in *The Recruiting Officer*, Rosalind in *As You Like It*, Isabella in *The Fatal Marriage*, Millwood in *The London Merchant*, Hamlet, Calista in *The Fair Penitent*, Portia in *The Merchant of Venice*, Belvidera in *Venice Preserv'd*, Imoinda in *Oroonoko*, Cordelia in *King Lear*, Andromache in *The Distrest Mother*, Lady Macbeth, Indiana in *The Conscious Lovers*, Lady Townly in *The Provok'd Husband*, Semandra in *Mithridates*, Berinthia in *The Relapse*, Lady Betty in *The Careless Husband*, Miranda in *The Busy Body*, and Gertrude in *Hamlet*. During that period she also toured and is known to have acted in Belfast on 7 January 1741.

In 1742–43 and 1743–44 Mrs Furnival acted at the Aungier Street Theatre in Dublin, playing many of her old roles and also appearing as Mrs Page in *The Merry Wives of Windsor*, the lead in *The Scornful Lady*, Eudocia in *The Siege of Damascus*, Viola in *Twelfth Night*, Lady Jane Gray, Phillis in *The Conscious Lovers*, Paulina in *A Winter's Tale*, Phaedra in *Amphitryon*, Alicia in *Jane Shore*, Emilia in *Othello*, Marwood in *The Way of the World*, the title role in *The Prude*, Athenais in *Theodosius*, Lappet in *The Miser*, and Victoria in *Love and Loyalty*. She was with the United Company in 1744–45, again playing some of her old parts but also acting Aurelia in *The Twin Rivals*, Marcia in *Cato*, and Leonore in *The Revenge*. In 1745–46 the company began the season at Aungier Street, but moved to Smock Alley on 5 December 1745.

Sheldon, in *Thomas Sheridan*, estimated Mrs Furnival's salary in 1743–44 as about 30*s*. nightly at Smock Alley and £3 weekly at Aungier Street. Fanny's husband left Ireland about 1744, and the pair seems not to have been reunited, at least professionally.

During the 1745–46 season at Smock Alley Mrs Furnival had a rencounter with George Anne Bellamy, who recorded the incident (probably with exaggeration) in her *Memoirs*. For a production of *All for Love* in which George Anne was cast as Cleopatra and Mrs Furnival as Octavia, George Anne had a fancy costume given her by the Princess of Wales. Jealous of George Anne's notices, Fanny made off with the dress and had it let out to fit her. George Anne's Irish servant discovered the theft and the

blood of her great forefathers boiled within her veins, and without any more ado, she fell tooth and nail upon poor Mrs. Furnival. So violent was the assault, that had not assistance arrived in time to rescue her from the fangs of the enraged Hybernian nymph, my theatrical rival would probably have never had an opportunity of appearing once in her life adorned with real *jewels*.

George Anne thereupon sent to Mrs Furnival for the jewels; Fanny, encouraged by the presence of her paramour Morgan (of whom we know nothing else), sent word to George Anne that she could have them after the play. Mrs Bellamy wanted to play Cleopatra with her diadem, "that indispensible mark of royalty," and the remarkably perceptive audience somehow understood all that had taken place and cried out, "No more Furnival!" Fanny "very prudently called fits to her aid, which incapacitated her from appearing again"; Mrs Elmy finished the part for her.

Advertised as from Dublin, Mrs Furnival was at Drury Lane on 10 November 1746, replacing Mrs Macklin as Lady Macbeth to Spranger Barry's Macbeth. On 5 December she acted Emilia in *Othello*. During the rest of her season at Drury Lane (while her husband was playing at Goodman's Fields), Mrs Furnival played Pulcheria in *Theodosius*, Octavia in *All for Love*, Lady Upstart in *The Artful Husband*, Gertrude in *Hamlet*, and Portia in *Julius Caesar*. She also acted Alicia in *Jane Shore* at Covent Garden for £5 5*s*. per performance, replacing the ailing Mrs Cibber. Perhaps Mrs Furnival was active at Drury Lane throughout the 1747–48 season, but her only mention in the bills was on 27 April 1748 when she was scheduled to play Millwood in *The London Merchant*—but the play was not performed. Chetwood wrote in 1749 that Mrs Furnival was in England that year but that she would be better remembered in Dublin, especially for her Alicia, Hermione in *The Distrest Mother*, Lady Macbeth, and Zara in *The Mourning Bride*.

Lee Lewes wrote in his *Memoirs* of Mrs Furnival's activity in Canterbury in 1752 when she was the leading lady in Smith's troupe. Roger Kemble joined the company, and

formed a very tender connexion with the celebrated Fanny Furnival, who was then performing there. The lady was struck with Roger's nose and athletic make; . . . In return for his tender affection she flattered him with the promise of making an actor of him, and no woman on the British stage was better qualified for giving instructions in theatricals, at that time Ann. Dom. 1752. She was far superior to any of her predecessors, possessing an elegant figure, an uncommon share of beauty, a perfect knowledge of every part she undertook and an execution scarcely excelled by any actress of that day, Mrs Pritchard and Mrs Cibber excepted. . . . It is singular that under all the disadvantages of private character, she was invited to the first families in every town the company visited, in consequence of her being a polite and agreeable companion, and superior in merit to all her theatrical sisters.

According to Lewes, Fanny spent seven weeks drumming the role of Kite in *The Recruiting Officer* into Kemble's head, to little avail. "So coldly was he received in it, that notwithstanding Mrs Kemble [i.e., Fanny] was Smith's principal support, he could not be prevailed upon to allow her husband encouragement." Whether or not the couple actually married is debatable.

While in Smith's troupe Fanny (billed as Mrs Kemble, or frequently, as Mrs Campbell) is known to have played Mrs Wisely in *The Miser*, Arpasia in *Tamerlane*, Queen Elizabeth in *Richard III*, Horatia in *The Roman Father*, Belvidera in *Venice Preserv'd*, and Jane Shore. She also sang in *Romeo and Juliet* and provided entr'acte songs. After the 1751–52 season the pair left—for Coventry say some sources, for Birmingham say others. In any case, Fanny apparently rejected Kemble for another man; Roger went on to marry Sarah Ward and sire one of the most famous acting families in history, and Fanny Furnival disappeared from theatrical records.

Furrs, Mr [*fl.* 1707], *actor.*
A Mr Furrs acted Sir Paul Squelch in *The Northern Lass* at Drury Lane on 26 December 1707.

Furzer. *See* FUOZI.

Furzi. *See* FERZI.

Fuse, Fusi, Fussi, Fusy. *See* FUOZI.

Futton. *See* FULTON.

Fuzzi. *See* FUOZI.

Fynell. *See* FINELL.

= G =

Gabriel, Mr *[fl. 1778], puppeteer.*

Mr Gabriel, in partnership with Antonio Ambroise and Ballarini, presented ombres chinoises at the Great Room in Panton Street from January to May 1778.

Gabriel, C. *[fl. 1794], singer.*
Doane's *Musical Directory* of 1794 listed C. Gabriel as a bass who lived in Old Street and sang with the Cecilian Society.

Gabriel, F. *[fl. 1794], singer.*
Doane's *Musical Directory* of 1794 listed F. Gabriel as a tenor who lived in Old Street and sang with the Cecilian Society.

Gabrielli, Adriana. *See* **FERRARESE, SIGNORA.**

Gabrielli, Caterina *1730–1796, singer.*
Caterina Gabrielli was born on 12 or 13 November 1730 in Rome, the daughter, it is said, of a cook—hence her nickname "La Coghetta" (variously spelled). Caterina studied under Garcia in Rome and Porpora in Naples. Her earliest stage appearances may have been in Lucca in 1747. She sang in Naples in 1750 and, in the fall of 1754, in Venice, was Ermione in *Antigono*. By 1755 she was in Vienna, where she stayed for six years—with occasional trips elsewhere—performing and polishing her talent with study under Metastasio and Gluck. While in Vienna she sang in several of Gluck's works, notably *La danza*, *L'innocenza giustificata*, *Il re pastore*, and *Tedide*. She visited Parma in 1759 to appear in Traetta's *Ippolito ed Aricia*, after which she

sang in several of his other operas: *Tindaridi*, *Enea e Lavinia*, *Zenobia*, *Alessandro nell'Indie*, and *Armida*.

After leaving Vienna in 1761 Signora Gabrielli performed in Milan, Turin, Naples, and Palermo, establishing herself as a singer of the first rank. Garrick heard her in Naples on 23 December 1763 and wrote the following day to George Colman that "the famous *Gabrielli* pleas'd me much; she has a good person, is y^e best Actress I ever saw on an Opera Stage, & has y^e most agreeable voice I ever heard; she sings

Harvard Theatre Collection
CATERINA GABRIELLI
artist unknown

more to yᵉ ear, than to yᵉ heart—" On 5 February 1764 he elaborated his thoughts in a letter to Dr Burney:

I have heard the famous Gabrielli, who has indeed astonishing powers, great compass of voice and great flexibility, but she is always yᵉ same, and though you are highly transported at first with her, yet wanting that nice feeling of yᵉ passions (without which everything in yᵉ dramatic way will cease to entertain) she cannot give that variety and that peculiar Pleasure which alone can support the tediousness of an Opera—in short, the Musick, vocal and instrumental, has lost its nature, and it is all dancing on yᵉ slack rope, and tumbling through yᵉ hoop . . .

Signora Gabrielli became known for her eccentric behavior which, in time, caused as many people to find her contemptible as found her dazzling. She demanded exorbitant fees (5000 ducats when she went to Russia in 1771, for example), frequently missed performances due to actual or faked indispositions, forgot engagements, and sang well only when the spirit moved her. Leopold Mozart wrote in March 1770 that Signora Gabrielli was known to be "an extremely conceited fool who besides squandering all her money does the most idiotic things." On the other hand, some people found her one of the most stunning coloratura sopranos of the eighteenth century; fellow singers were occasionally staggered by her overwhelming stage presence and vocal abilities; and audiences all over Europe were attracted to her performances.

After spending three years in St Petersburg, Signora Gabrielli came to London for one season. Her first appearance was on 10 November 1775 at the King's Theatre in the title part in *Didone abbandonata* (a performance planned for 7 November had been canceled because of the illness of two singers, one of them probably Caterina). Dr Burney recorded his impressions: "The celebrated singer, La Gabrielli, made her first appearance upon the opera stage last

Saturday. She had frequently disappointed the public by deferring the opera, after it was promised; but she had only heightened expectation by this coquetry; and the crowd to see and hear her, was prodigious." At her first entrance

she appeared at the most distant part [of the stage], and marched forward quite close to the orchestra, amidst the most violent acclamation of applause. She has a pretty figure, rather short, but charmingly proportioned; her face is also very pretty. She still looks very young, is rather plump and is perfectly graceful. She walks extremely well, and has great dignity in her air. Her voice is feeble, but sweetly toned. She has great powers of execution; but she is no Agujari!

Her chief excellence, Burney thought, was "the rapidity and neatness of her execution," though he felt Cecilia Davies was as good. But Signora Gabrielli had

an elegance in the finishing her musical periods or passages; and, an accent and precision in her divisions, not only superior to Miss Davis, but to every singer of her time. As an actress, though of low stature, there were such grace and dignity in her gestures and deportment, as caught every unprejudiced eye; indeed, she filled the stage and occupied the attention of the spectators so much, that they could look at nothing else while she was in view.

In conversation Burney found her intelligent and well-bred, and he felt that by the time she had reached England she had subdued most of her "freaks and espiegleries." Mount-Edgecumbe in his *Reminiscences* did not agree. He went to a performance of *Didone*, but

all I can recollect of it [was] the care with which she tucked up her great hoop as she sidled into the flames of Carthage. Another opera she acted here was La Vestale, which I likewise saw performed, but on that night Catterina *chose* to be indisposed, and to make her sister Francesca take her part; the latter was a miserable performer whom she carried every where to act as the seconda donna, and occasionally as her *double*.

During Signora Gabrielli's 1775–76 season she sang, in addition to Dido, a role in *La Vestale* on 6 February 1776, songs at the benefit concert for indigent musicians on 15 February, Amarilli in *Le ali d'amore* on 29 February, Marcia in *Caio Mario* on 20 April, and Berenice in *Antigono* on 18 May.

Londoners were fascinated with her eccentric behavior. When she left the theatre after a performance, Lady Edgecumbe said, "First goes a running footman; then the sister [Francesca]; then the Gabrielli; then a page to hold up her train; then a footman; and then a man out of livery with her lap dog in her muff!" "But," asked Mr Brudenal, "where is Lord March all this time?" "O," Lady Edgecumbe replied, "he, you know, is *Lord of the Bedchamber*." Indeed, Caterina left behind innumerable lovers wherever she went, and sometimes the only way to persuade her to sing with full energy was to plant her current lover in the audience where she could see and sing to him. But even that did not always work, as Patrick Brydone wrote in his *Tour through Sicily and Malta* (1773–1776), and often, if she took the whim, she would sing her arias "*sotto voce*, that is, so low, that they can scarcely be heard."

Horace Walpole was disappointed in Signora Gabrielli. He wrote to Sir Horace Mann in Florence on 8 December 1776: "Tell me truly, is or has the Gabrielli been a great singer? She has, at least, not honoured us but with a most slender, low voice. Her action is just, but colder than a vestal's. However, as you know, she carries the resemblance no further."

After the 1775–76 season Caterina left England. Wolfgang Amadeus Mozart wrote his father on 19 February 1778 and was sharply critical:

Those who have heard Gabrielli are forced to admit that she was adept only in runs and roulades; she adopted, however, such an unusual interpretation that she won admiration; but it never survived the fourth time of hearing. In the long run she could not please, as people soon got tired of coloratura passages. Moreover, she had the misfortune of not being able to sing. She was not capable of sustaining a breve properly, and as she had no *messa di voce*, she could not dwell on her notes; in short, she sang with skill, but without understanding. (*Anderson translation.*)

Signora Gabrielli made some appearances in Lucca, Milan, and Venice between 1778 and 1782. Burney said that she retired to Bologna, but Grove places her retirement in Rome. She died in Rome on 16 February 1796.

She was pictured in a large group of singers in an engraving after A. Fedi, published between 1801 and 1807. On 1 May 1776 A. Hamilton published a satirical print showing two bust portraits in frames illustrating "Histories of the Tête-à-Tête annexed: or, Memoirs of Lord B——u, and Signora G–b––lli." The nobleman in question was Edward Hussey Montagu, Earl of Beaulieu. A reversed version of the engraving was published the same year by T. Walker.

The *Enciclopedia dello spettacolo* contains details of Signora Gabrielli's continental career.

Gabrielli, Francesca [fl. 1756–1776], *singer*.

Francesca Gabrielli was the sister of the more famous Caterina Gabrielli and, like her, a singer. Her first known role was Tamiri in *Il re pastore* in Vienna on 8 December 1756. Francesca followed her sister almost everywhere, according to Mount-Edgecumbe, serving as Caterina's substitute on occasion, but she was, he said, "a miserable performer." In London at the King's Theatre she sang Camilla in *La sposa fedele* on 31 October 1775, Selene in *Didone ab-*

bandonata on 10 November, Lucinda in *La buona figliuola* on 12 December, Clarice in *Il bacio* on 9 January 1776, a part in *La Vestale* on 6 February, a part in *Le ali d'amore* on 29 February, Rodope in *Caio Mario* on 20 April, and a part in *Antigono* on 18 May.

Gabrielli, Tomaso *[fl. 1708–1712]*, *harpsichordist.*

Tomaso Gabrielli, frequently cited in Vice Chamberlain Coke's papers at Harvard as "Il Bolonese" or "Tomaso," played harpsichord or cembalo at the Queen's Theatre in the Haymarket from 1708 to 1712—and perhaps earlier and later. About 1708 he was receiving 30s. nightly for his efforts. He was among the opera house musicians who played a concert at the Duchess of Shrewsbury's in Kensington about 1710.

Gaches, John James *[fl. 1688–1713]*, *singer.*

John James Gaches, from Deptford, was sworn a Gentleman of the Chapel Royal in ordinary on 8 November 1688. Though nothing else is known of the singer's musical life, the parish registers of St Paul, Covent Garden, contain several references to his children. On 13 April 1702 Raimund, the son of "James" Gaches from St Giles, was buried at St Paul, Covent Garden; on 1 February 1703 Rebecca, the daughter of John-James "Gash" from St Giles, was buried at the same church. Gustavus "Gachus," the son of "Jo: Jam," was buried on 20 December 1706; Gustanah, daughter of John James Gash of Deptford, was buried on 3 October 1711; and a second Gustavus was buried on 26 August 1713. Gaches was identified in the last instance as from Lambeth.

Gacomozzi. *See* GIOCOMAZZI.

Gadbury, Mr *[fl. 1728]*, *musician?*
A benefit concert for Mr Gadbury was held at York Buildings on 13 March 1728.

He was probably a musician and may have been a descendant of Richard Gadbury, the Restoration singer.

Gadbury, Richard *d. 1680, singer.*
Richard Gadbury was sworn a Gentleman of the Chapel Royal on 16 March 1674 as a replacement for the deceased John Wilson. Gadbury was a countertenor from Windsor and attended the King there from 1 July to 11 September 1675 for 6s. daily. Gadbury died at Windsor on 18 January 1680.

Gaetan. *See* VESTRIS.

Gaetani, Signor *[fl. 1726]*, *dancer.*
Signor and Signora Gaetani were dancers in an Italian troupe which came to London in the fall of 1726. The group began performing at the King's Theatre in the Haymarket on 28 September.

Gaetani, Signora *[fl. 1726]*, *dancer.*
See GAETANI, SIGNOR.

Gaetano, Sieur. *See* ROSSIGNOL.

Gagneur family *[fl. 1769–1770]*, *tumblers.*
In September 1769 Mr Le Gagneur and his five children performed tumbling acts at Sadler's Wells. They returned to that theatre in September 1770. While working at the Wells the Gagneur family introduced a "new-invented Tumble called the Tranplain"—an early trampoline act.

Gaine, Mr *[fl. 1792–1797]*, *house servant?*
The Drury Lane account books contain a notation dated 7 January 1792 to the effect that a Mr Gaine, probably a house servant, was dropped from the company roster. He had been earning 4s. 2d., presumably weekly. On 17 December 1797 the accounts have a cryptic "–1" entry for

Gaine, probably an indication of his having been paid 1*s.*

Gair, Thomas [*fl. 1739–1743*], *musician.*

Thomas Gair was an original subscriber to the Royal Society of Musicians when it was formed on 28 August 1739. He shared a benefit at Lincoln's Inn Fields on 15 March 1743 and may have participated in the musical part of the performance.

Galari. *See* CALORI.

Gale, Mr [*fl. 1735–1745?*], *actor.*

On 7 April 1735 Mr Gale played Plume in *The Recruiting Officer* at the Great Booth on Bowling Green at Southwark. He is said to have received a solo benefit at Drury Lane on 21 December 1742, though *The London Stage* does not list it. Perhaps he was the Mr "Cale" who acted at Norwich in 1745.

Gale, Mr [*fl. 1760–1767*], *billsticker.*

Mr Gale was a billsticker at Covent Garden earning 2*s.* daily as of 22 September 1760. By 14 September 1767 his salary had dropped to 1*s.* 6*d.* daily.

Gale, Mrs [*fl. 1723*], *actress.*

Mrs Gale played Gipsey in *The Stratagem* on 14 March 1723 at the Haymarket Theatre.

Galenali. *See* GALERATI.

Galeotti, Vincenzo, stage name of Vincenzo Tomasselli 1733–1816, *dancer, choreographer.*

Born at Florence in 1733, Vincenzo Galeotti, whose real surname was Tomasselli, was originally intended for medicine, but, drawn to the stage, he became a student of the ballet master G. Angiolini. Galeotti's long and distinguished career began in Venice in 1759 and took him to principal theatres throughout Europe. For

Royal Theatre, Copenhagen

VINCENZO GALEOTTI

attributed to Viertel

some time he was with Noverre's company, in which he met his future wife, the dancer Antonia Guidi (c. 1735–1780). By 1754 he was with her in Copenhagen, where much of his career was spent, and by 1765 he was a leading choreographer for the theatres in Venice. At the Teatro Regio in Turin in 1767 he created ballets for Bertoni's *Tancredi* and Gluck's *Don Juan.*

Accompanied by his wife, Galeotti engaged with the King's Theatre in London for 1769–70 as a featured dancer and ballet master. He composed the new dance in which Signora Guidi made her English debut on 6 February 1770, and on 22 February he made his own debut dancing with her. They performed in his dances for *Il disertore* on 19 May and for *Orfeo*, for their benefit, on 24 May.

Galeotti continued as ballet master at the King's for a total of three seasons, through 1771–72. He also danced occasionally. In his last season he and his wife performed in *A Venetian Dance*, which he had adapted for the opera *Carnovale di Venezia*, on 14 January 1772.

The Galeottis returned to Italy in 1772 to perform in Milan, Venice, and Genoa. In 1775 he became associated with the Royal Opera at Copenhagen, where he spent most of the remainder of his career choreographing numerous ballets, the details of which may be found under his name in the *Enciclopedia dello spettacolo* and in M. H. Winter's, *The Pre-Romantic Ballet* (1974). His wife died at Copenhagen in June 1780. Galeotti died there on 16 December 1816, after a long career in which he had made influential contributions to the choreography of Italian dancing, especially in the evolution of character and costume, in about 30 ballets which received over 2000 performances. A portrait of Galeotti, attributed to Viertel, is in the Royal Theatre of Copenhagen.

Galeotti, Signora Vincenzo, Antonia, née Guidi [*fl. c. 1735–1780*], *dancer. See* **GUIDI, ANTONIA.**

Galerati, Catterina [*fl. 1711?–1721*], *singer.*
Vice Chamberlain Coke's papers at Harvard suggest that the singer Catterina Galerati was involved in opera productions at the Queen's Theatre as early as 1711, though the first mention of her in the bills was in 1714. On 9 January 1714, described as "newly come from Italy," Signora Galerati sang Silvio in *Dorinda*. She followed that with the title role in *Creso* on 27 January, the title role in *Arminio* on 4 March, and Vitige in *Ernelinda* on 3 April. She was given a benefit on 17 April. During her

second season, 1714–15, she added to her list of parts Goffredo in *Rinaldo* and the title role in *Lucio Vero*.

Signora Galerati returned to England in 1720 to sing Amulio in *Numitore* and Tigrane in *Radamisto* in April. In 1720–21 she was Agenor in *Astarto*, Fraarte in *Radamisto*, Mitrane in *Arsace*, Lucio Tarquinio in *Muzio Scevola*, and Miceno in *Ciro*. Her last appearance in England may have been on 28 June 1721 in *Astarto*. Signora Galerati sang both soprano and contralto roles.

Galia. *See* **GALLIA.**

Galindo, Mrs P. *See* **GOUGH, CATHERINE.**

Galiotti. *See* **GALEOTTI.**

Galla. *See* **GALLI.**

Gallant, Mr [*fl. 1717–1739*], *house servant.*
Mr Gallant worked at Lincoln's Inn Fields and, from 1732 on, at Covent Garden for at least 22 years, his first mention in the bills being on 3 June 1717 when he shared a benefit. His position was pit doorkeeper, though on occasion he served as a boxkeeper—probably when the pit and boxes were laid together. Over the years he shared benefits, usually with two or three others, and the accounts show that the shared benefit receipts normally ran over £100 and, on one occasion, in the spring of 1732, came to £161 14s. 6d. Gallant's last notice in the bills was on 28 May 1739 when he shared a benefit with three others.

Gallarini, J. [*fl. 1794–1799*], *musician.*
J. Gallarini worked at Drury Lane as a musician, an account book entry there on 14 April 1794 noting him as receiving £13 12s. 6d. weekly and citing him as "opera." In August 1799 Gallarini was instrumental in the negotiations between the singer

Damiani and the King's Theatre proprietor Taylor.

Gallet, Sébastien *1753–1807, dancer, choreographer.*

Sébastien Gallet was born in 1753, according to the *Katalog der Porträt-Sammlung der K.U.K. General Intendanz der K.K. Hoftheater*, Vienna. The *Enciclopedia dello spettacolo* says that Gallet was born about 1753, that he became a student of Noverre, that he danced in *Persée* at Versailles on 17 May 1770, and that by 1775 he was working in Vienna, presenting his master's ballets.

On 7 November 1776 Gallet and one of his regular partners, Mlle Dupré, made their first appearance in England, dancing *The Double Festival*, a work by Gallet, at Drury Lane Theatre. He also contributed a serious ballet, *The Triumph of Love*, in which he danced. Both pieces were introduced into a performance of *The Maid of the Oaks*. The evening was something of a disaster. Some of the costumes had not been brought to the theatre; the first dance had to be postponed until later in the play; and when it was finally presented, not all of the dancers had their proper dresses. The prompter Hopkins noted in his diary:

They were all very confused – the Music also was not perfect. Gallet went on, and spoke in French to the Audience, and told the Band that he wished they had any Heads [*sic*]. In the first Dance Mlle Dupré fell down, and a little after Gallet fell down, but [they] did not hurt themselves, and the Dance went on – and even with all these Disadvantages was much applauded.

Later in the season, on 4 January 1777, Gallet's *Dance of Spirits* was worked into *The Tempest*, apparently with better results.

Gallet's first-season salary of £400 was raised to £500 in 1777–78. The account books show payments to Mrs Gallet as well, though her name did not appear in any playbills. She was probably one of the mi-nor dancers in the troupe. Gallet's 1777–78 season brought forth more of his choreography: a dance called *Rural Grace*, in which he performed, and three dances introduced into *Cymon* – a *Dance of Cupids*, a *Dance of Daemons*, and a grand ballet.

He left England and made his official debut at the Académie Royale de Musique on 6 August 1782 in a divertissement in Act III of *Roland*. He continued working on the Continent until 1796, when he returned to England to serve as the ballet master for the opera company at the King's Theatre. His first ballet there was *Appolon berger* on 27 December. From then through 1803 Gallet produced a number of dance works, often in collaboration with the composer Cesare Bossi, the leader of the theatre's band. Among them were *Les Délassements militaires*, *L'Heureux Retour*, *Le Trompeur trompé*, *Le Rendez-vous*, *Ariadne et Bacchus*, *Eliza*, *Le Triomphe de Thémis*, *L'Offrande à Terpsichore*, *La Chasse d'amor*, *Constance et Alcidonis*, *Les Rivaux généreux*, *Les Scyths*, *La Vengeance de l'amour*, *Enée et Didon*, *Le Déserteur*, *La Fête de Venus*, *La Fôret enchantée*, *La Foire de Batavia*, *Laurette*, and *Vologeso*.

Perhaps his greatest triumph, however, was *Pizarre*. The *True Briton* on 8 February 1797 called it "Magnificent perhaps beyond parallel on a British stage, but it is considerably too long, as it was past twelve before it was concluded." The *Morning Chronicle* the following day disagreed on the length: the work was "perhaps the only Ballet we ever saw from which we would not wish a single scene to be removed." What may have been the last of Gallet's ballets, *Vologeso*, was performed at the King's Theatre on 26 April 1803.

Gallet retired to Vienna, where he died on 10 June 1807.

Gallet, Mme Sébastien *fl. 1776–1777, dancer?*

On 5 October 1776 "Mrs" (Sébastien) Gallet, Mr Preto, and Mr Higgins were

paid £3 13 s. by the Drury Lane management; the accounts do not make clear what
the money was for or if it was a total sum
for all three. For the period 9 June to 19
July 1777 Mr and Mrs Gallet (he was the
ballet master) were paid £41 18s. 4d.,
which amount consisted of their salary in
full and a benefit. There is no record of Mrs
Gallet's performing, but she may have been
a minor member of the dancing chorus.

Galli, Signor d. 1799, musician?

Nothing is known of Signor Galli beyond the fact that, according to the *Monthly
Mirror* of March 1799, he died at a very
advanced age and was the husband of the
singer Caterina Ruini Galli. The fact that
from 1792 to her death in 1804 Signora
Galli was given grants by the Royal Society of Musicians would seem to indicate
that her husband was a professional musician and a member of the Society. There is
no evidence to confirm that conjecture,
however, and the Society may have helped
support Signora Galli simply because she
had been one of Handel's favorite singers.

Galli, C. [fl. 1710], violinist.

In the papers of Vice Chamberlain Coke
at Harvard is a note dating about November or December 1710 concerning musicians at the Queen's Theatre in the Haymarket. C. Galli, a violinist, was apparently
replaced at the opera house by "Echel" —
that is, Eccles.

Galli, Caterina Ruini 1723–1804, singer, composer.

Information concerning Caterina Ruini
Galli's age at her death assures us that she
was born in 1723, but her place of birth
and her early years are unknown. Burney
said only that she came to England from
Italy. The first record of her in England
was on 4 December 1742, when she sang
Idrenus in *Mandane* at the King's Theatre.
During the rest of the season the mezzo-
soprano sang a role in *Enrico* on 1 January

1743, Lisimachus in *Temistocle* on 22 February, and Astarbus in *Sirbace* on 5 April.
She also joined other performers to sing for
the benefit of indigent musicians on 30
March 1743.

Signora Galli became one of Handel's
earliest students in 1744 and sang in many
of his works. On 2 March 1744 she was
Phanor in his *Joseph and His Brethren* at
Covent Garden; at the Haymarket on 9
February 1745 she sang a leading character
in *L'incostanza delusa;* and at Covent Garden in April she participated in the oratorio
performances. At Covent Garden on 1
April 1747 she sang the Priest and the
Israelite Man in *Judas Maccabaeus* (she frequently took male parts); at the King's she
was Vologesus in *Lucio Vero* on 14 November 1747 and Alessandro in *Rossane* on
8 March 1748. During the same season she
sang Othniel in *Joshua* on 9 March 1748
and the title part in *Alexander Balus* on 23
March at Covent Garden.

In 1748–49 she sang Joacim in *Susanna*
and the title role in *Solomon* at Covent
Garden, participated in the benefit for indigent musicians at the King's, and sang in
concerts at the Haymarket and Hickford's
Music Room. In 1749–50 she appeared as
Irene in *Theodora* at Covent Garden, in
Solomon at Drury Lane, and at a concert at
the King's.

About 1750 was published a song composed by Signora Galli, *When first I saw
thee graceful move*, which she (probably)
had sung at the "publick Gardens." During
the period from 1750 to 1754 she usually
performed at the benefit for "Decay'd" musicians and their families, and she made occasional appearances at the Haymarket and
Covent Garden and at concerts, opera performances and oratorios. She was heard as
Storage in *Jeptha* and sang in *Alexander's
Feast* and *Acis and Galatea*, and on 15 May
1754 she earned £4 14s. 6d. for singing in
the *Messiah*. After that the bills stopped
mentioning her, though she must have continued performing until 1757, for on 26

February 1773 she was advertised as returning to the stage after 16 years to sing in the *Messiah* at the Haymarket Theatre.

Caterina Galli then set forth on a remarkably active new career, and for two seasons she sang regularly at the King's and made occasional appearances elsewhere. At the King's she appeared as Aricato in *Lucio Vero*, Teutile in *Montezuma*, and in unspecified parts in *Antigono, Nitteti, Artaserse, L'Olimpiade, Armida, Alessandro nell'Indie, La Marchesa giardiniera, I viaggiatori ridicoli, La diffesa d'amore,* and *Piramus and Thisbe.* Fanny Burney later remembered her as "squalling Galli," and, indeed, by the 1770's Signora Galli's voice was gone. In 1775–76 she rarely sang. She was in *La Vestale* at the King's and sang in a concert there that season, but then she once more left the London stage.

Caterina became a companion of Martha Ray, an amateur singer and mistress of the fourth Earl of Sandwich. James Hackman, who was hopelessly in love with Miss Ray, shot her in a jealous rage as she was leaving the Covent Garden Theatre with Signora Galli on 7 April 1779, according to Mount-Edgecumbe.

By the 1790s Caterina Galli and her husband (about whom very little is known) were in extreme poverty. On 1 July 1792 the Royal Society of Musicians paid 10 guineas to Signora Galli, which would suggest that her husband may have been a professional musician and a member of the Society. It is not clear why she rather than her husband should have been involved in the transaction, unless he was ill.

Several early sources stated that Signora Galli sang in an oratorio in 1796 at the age of 75, and perhaps she did, though the records do not show her returning to the stage until 3 March 1797 when she sang "He was despised" in a performance of the *Messiah* at Covent Garden. The bill claimed that she had sung it under Handel's direction in 1741, but that statement is incorrect, at least as to the year; she is not known to

have sung in the *Messiah* when it was first performed in Dublin in 1742 nor in London in 1743 when oratorio performances began under Handel's direction.

The *Monthly Mirror* in March 1797 criticized the organizers of the oratorios for employing Signora Galli in her dotage:

In the name of decency and common humanity, why exhibit a poor emaciated worn out old woman, merely to excite risibility. If she has exhausted her faculties in the service of the public, that public, ever grateful to those who through a long life have endeavoured to please, never yet withheld its support on proper application. But we suspect the manager has other motives than charity to the oppressed for introducing upon the stage an old lady of 75, whom we recollect 35 years ago, in the Italian Operas, performed castrato characters in male attire, and she was at that time thought a respectable singer. We are sorry to hear Handel's divine compositions so barbarously murdered.

Mount-Edgecumb was more compassionate. He said in his *Musical Reminiscences* that after the killing of Miss Ray, Signora Galli

fell into extreme poverty, and at the age of about seventy, was induced to come forward to sing again at the oratorios. I had the curiosity to go, and heard her sing, "He was despised and rejected of men" in the Messiah. Of course her voice was cracked and trembling, but it was easy to see her school was good; and it was pleasing to observe the kindness with which she was received, and listened to; and to mark the animation and delight with which she seemed to hear again the music in which she had formerly been a distinguished performer. The poor old woman had been in the habit of coming to me annually for a trifling present; and she told me on that occasion that nothing but the severest distress should have compelled her so to expose herself, which after all did not answer its end, as she was not paid according to her agreement.

Signora Galli nevertheless sang in the oratorios throughout March 1797, and on 2 April she offered her services to the Royal Society of Musicians for their annual benefit; her offer was referred to the concert committee and must have been turned down, for there is no record of her participating in anything the rest of the year. On 1 July 1798 she thanked the Society for a benefaction of £10 10s. that had been sent to Madame Mara, apparently for Signora Galli's use.

Caterina Galli sang once more, at Covent Garden on 15 March 1799 "in her 77th year, and in greatest distress," said the bill. She again chose "He was despised." Her distress was not only financial: the *Monthly Mirror* in March 1799 reported that Signor Galli had died at an advanced age. His "widow, once celebrated in the musical world, with difficulty defrayed the expense of his interment."

On 7 July 1799 Signora Galli thanked the Royal Society of Musicians for a benefaction of £5 5s., as she did again for unspecified grants in 1800, 1801, and 1802. On 3 July 1803 the minutes of the Society show that Signora Galli was being given £21 annually in two installments. The last grant was made in July 1804. Caterina Ruini Galli died in Chelsea on 23 December 1804 at the age of 81 and was buried on 30 December at Chelsea Old Church. On 6 January 1805 the Society granted £5 for her funeral expenses.

Galli, Cornelio ₁fl. 1682₁, *singer.*

Born in Lucca, the Italian singer Cornelio Galli became a member of Queen Catherine's Chapel in London during the Restoration period. He was, according to Berenclow, a very accomplished artist. Galli was in London in 1682, but when he came and when he left remain a mystery.

Galli, Francisco ₁fl. 1669–1688₁, *harpsichordist, bassoonist?*

Several references in Restoration documents to a Signor Francisco seem to concern the harpsichordist Francisco Galli. On 30 November 1669, according to the Lord Chamberlain's accounts, the musician Robert Strong was paid £52 for two double curtolls (bassoons) which he delivered to Signor Francisco for the Queen's service. Possibly Francisco Galli played the bassoon, though Robert Strong was a violinist, not a bassoonist, so the two musicians may only have been serving as intermediaries in the transaction.

Evelyn wrote on 2 December 1674 of hearing "Signor Francisco on the Harpsichord, esteem'd on[e] of the most excellent masters in Europe on that Instrument. . . ." Galli was in England at the time of the Popish plot and faced persecution because of his Catholicism, but the threat passed. He was in the service of Mary of Modena during the reign on James II. The last mention of him in the accounts was on 20 October 1688, when he was to be paid for going to Windsor from 24 July to 20 September of that year.

Gallia, Maria Margherita, ₁née Lucca?₁, later Signora Giuseppe Fedeli Saggione ₁fl. 1696?–1734₁, *singer.*

Maria Margherita Gallia may have been born Lucca (or *in* Lucca?), and there is a slight possibility that she was the "Italian Woman" brought to London by Thomas Betterton for performances at the Lincoln's Inn Fields Theatre about December 1696. The first certain notice of her in London, however, was on 1 June 1703 at Lincoln's Inn Fields when she sang entr'acte music. She was said to be just arrived from Italy and making her first English appearance. The songs she offered were by her future husband, Giuseppe Fedeli Saggione. Signora Gallia then appeared at York Buildings on 20 and 28 April 1704. She had a benefit recital there on 16 November 1704, after which she married Saggione and may have gone to the Continent.

She was still advertised as Maria Margherita Gallia when she sang Eurilla in *The Temple of Love* at the Queen's Theatre in the Haymarket on 7 March 1706. Grove reports that documents formerly owned by Julian Marshall indicate that Signora Gallia was paid £700 for the season, but only the role of Eurilla is known for her, and the Coke papers at Harvard never show her receiving more than £200. Signora Gallia was Dorisbe in *Arsinoe* at the Queen's on 18 February 1707, sang the title role in *Rosamond* at Drury Lane on 4 March, and held a benefit concert at York Buildings on 4 April.

As Signora Saggione she sang Eurilla in *Love's Triumph* at the Queen's on 20 March 1708; she held a benefit concert at York Buildings on 29 March 1710; and she sang Clizia in *Teseo* at the Queen's on 10 January 1713. After that the soprano seems to have given up performing and turned to teaching. On 25 September 1722 Lord Percival wrote to Alexander Pope that "Sagioni formerly known here by the name of Maria Gallia is lately return'd, & sings to [Brigadier Hunter's] judgment extreamly well. She is not engaged to the Hay market [i.e., the King's Theatre, formerly the Queen's], & probably will perform at Drury lane upon moderate encouragement, for she is come with a view of maintaining her Self by Schollars." She seems not to have returned to the stage. Years later, on 17 September 1734, Pope wrote of visiting Dr Arbuthnot at Hampstead where he found, among others, "Mrs Saggione."

Several sources suggest that Maria Gallia was the sister of Margherita de l'Épine, but Grove contends that there seems to be no evidence to support the conjecture.

Galliard, Benjamin [fl. 1794], violinist.

Doane's *Musical Directory* of 1794 listed Benjamin Galliard of Charles Street, Middlesex Hospital, as a violinist who played in the performances at Westminster Abbey and for the New Musical Fund.

Galliard, Johann Ernst c. 1666?–1747, oboist, composer.

Johann Ernst Galliard was born in Celle, Germany, the son of a perukemaker, but his birthdate is not certainly known. Some historians suggest c. 1687, Grove says c. 1680, and one source (which says Galliard died at 81) would lead us to believe he was born about 1666. Since the musician's death date has been given, in error, as 1749 (it was 1747), we must be skeptical of the vital statistics that have been reported.

Grove tells us that Galliard studied music under the director of the Hanover concerts, Farinelli, and under Steffani and Marschall. Farinelli was, presumably, Giovanni Battista (Jean Baptiste Farinel), who was Konzertmeister to the Elector of Hanover about 1680 and remained there at least until 1714, when the Elector became George I of England. Agostino Steffani went to Hanover in late 1688 or early 1689 (which would argue in favor of 1666 as a likely birthdate for Galliard); in his *History* Hawkins cited a manuscript note in a catalogue of Galliard's works which said Galliard was 15 or 16 in 1702, when he studied under Farinelli and Steffani (which would argue for a birthdate in the 1680s). According to Galliard's own notes, on 22 June 1704 at Hanover he wrote an air for Farinelli.

Galliard came to England, according to Grove, about 1706, and was appointed chamber musician to Prince George of Denmark. Earlier sources say Galliard was given the post on the Continent and came to England when the Prince was married, and Galliard's name was listed as a member of the royal musical establishment in the Lord Chamberlain's accounts in 1702. He was then described as one of the royal musicians being paid by the Hon Spencer Compton. At some point Galliard was appointed to the sinecure post of organist at Somerset House. He learned English quickly and well and composed a number of pieces to English words, including anthems sung at St Paul's and by the singers of the Chapel

Royal on victorious occasions. About 1710, with Dr Maurice Greene, Bernard Gates, and the gentlemen and boys of the Chapel Royal, Galliard formed the Academy of Ancient Music, an organization which flourished for many years.

In his *Journal to Stella* on 8 February 1712 Swift commented on a musician:

I dined to-day in the city; this morning a scoundrel dog, one of the queen's musick, a *German*, whom I had never seen, got access to me in my chambers by Patrick's folly, and gravely desired me to get an employment in the customs for a friend of his, who would be very grateful; and likewise to forward a project of his own, for raising ten thousand pounds a year upon *Operas*: I used him civiller than he deserved; but it vexed me to the pluck—

Galliard may well have been the person referred to, for he was, indeed, about to set forth on an operatic career.

In 1712 Galliard composed the music for Hughes's opera *Calypso and Telemachus*. The work was first performed at the Queen's Theatre in the Haymarket on 17 May of that year, with Galliard, perhaps, playing oboe in the band. He was certainly an oboist at the theatre in 1713 and probably continued his employment there for some years. The Treasury records show that in 1714–15 Galliard's income also included a pension as an ex-member of the Prince of Denmark's music. Money came to him, too, for music he wrote for John Rich's pantomimes and other productions at the Lincoln's Inn Fields Theatre. He set the music for the masque in Theobald's *The Lady's Triumph* in 1718, for *Circe* in 1719, for *The Necromancer* and *Jupiter and Europa* in 1723 (for *The Necromancer* music, or at least part of it, he was paid £15 15*s.* on 1 January 1724), for *Harlequin Sorcerer* (later called *The Rape of Proserpine*) in 1725, for *Apollo and Daphne* in 1726, and for *The Royal Chace* in 1736.

Perhaps during most of those years Galliard, in addition to composing music for

Rich's spectacles, played in the theatre band. The accounts show that in connection with *The Rape of Proserpine*, for instance, Galliard was paid £2 14*s.* for providing a hand organ for the production, and he was called in the accounts "Gillier," a member "of the Musick." He was also busy composing a formidable work scored for 24 bassoons and four double basses, as well as hymns, songs, violin solos, and works for violoncello and for bassoon. He also appeared regularly at concerts: on 28 February 1722, for example, he had a benefit at which a new cantata of his composing was performed, with Galliard accompanying Mrs Barbier on the oboe, and on 31 March 1740 at Hickford's Music Room he played an oboe solo he had composed.

In May 1724 Galliard was one of many London composers satirized in the *Session of Musicians*, wherein the various composers come before Apollo to be judged who is best (Handel won, of course):

> *His Fate, soft* G[a]ll[ia]rd *with Care attends,*
> *In Sounds and Praise they still prov'd equal Friends.*
> *Shewing his Hautboy and an* Op'ra *Air,*
> *He gently whisper'd in his Godship's Ear:*
> *So oft he was distinguish'd by the Town,*
> *That without Vanity, he claim'd the Crown.*
> *The God replied—your Musick's not to blame,*
> *But far beneath the daring Height of Fame;*
> *Who wins the Prize must all the Rest out-strip,*
> *Indeed you may a Conjurer equip;*
> *I think your Airs are sometimes very pretty,*
> *And give you leave to sing 'em in the City.*

Dr Burney later agreed with that tepid praise. He thought Galliard was "an excellent contrapuntist; but with respect to his compositions in general, I must say, that

I never saw more correctness or less originality in any author that I have examined, of the present century, Dr Pepusch always excepted."

On 7 January 1726 at the Crown Tavern in the Strand, Galliard, Wesley, Pepusch, Greene, King, Gates, and others formed the Academy of Vocal Music. The Children of St Paul's sang, everyone had bread and wine, and a decision was made to meet fortnightly. By 1729 there were 69 subscribers, but the Academy may not have continued much past 26 May 1731, the last entry in their Minute Books. Possibly John Ernst Galliard, as he came to be called in England, was the Mr "Galliardy" who built a theatre in Fulham in 1732 and, on 13 November of that year, presented the scholars from his school in Terence's *Eunuchus*. But the production seems to have been a non-musical event, and our subject's career appears to have been chiefly musical.

Galliard became one of the original subscribers to the Royal Society of Musicians on 28 August 1739. One of the last musical events of his career was a benefit held at the Lincoln's Inn Fields Theatre on 11 December 1744 (the last known performance at that house). His *Love and Folly* "Intermix'd with the Choruses to the Tragedy of Julius Caesar" and called a Serenata was performed (the play in question was the Duke of Buckingham's, not Shakespeare's). Also performed was Galliard's concerto grosso for 24 bassoons.

Galliard is reported to have died on 18 February 1747 at Chelsea at the age of 81 (earlier in the 1740s he had been living in Rathbone Place near Soho Square). He left behind a collection of printed music from the first half of the eighteenth century. Included were some of his own works; an incomplete opera on the Orestes story was one of the more interesting pieces. The collection was sold by auction a few months after Galliard died; most of it is now in the Henry Watson Music Library in Manchester. Administration of Galliard's estate

was granted in March 1747, but neither the administration nor Galliard's will has been located. In addition to works already cited, Galliard composed a little opera called *Pan and Syrinx* in 1717, *The Nuptial Masque* in 1734, new music for *Oedipus* in 1736, and *The Happy Captive*, an English opera with a text by Theobald, in 1741. Perhaps Galliard's most popular work was the song, "With early horn," in *The Royal Chace*. In 1743 Galliard translated Tosi's *Observations*, a valuable source of information on eighteenth century music and musicians.

Galli-Bibiena, Carlo   *1728–1787, scene painter.*

According to Luigi Lanzi's *Storia pittorica della Italia* (1825) Carlo Galli-Bibiena, a third-generation member of the famous family of scenographers that worked for royalty throughout Europe in the eighteenth century, arrived in London in 1760 and remained for three years, supposedly decorating stage settings. Although Lanzi reported that "at the court of London [Carlo] rejected many offers to take up his residence in that city," he failed to provide any record of the designer's activities. We are unable to find any mention of Carlo Galli-Bibiena in contemporary English chronicles during those years. Perhaps he had been summoned to London in connection with the coronation of George III or for the festivities attending the monarch's marriage to Charlotte in September 1760. Since the new queen had been the Princess of Mechlenberg, it is not unlikely that an artist of Carlo's reputation at the German courts would have been so employed.

Possibly Carlo was the designer of the settings for Cocchi's *La speranze della terra*, an opera given at the King's Theatre on 4 June 1761, according to the title page of the edition printed at London in that year. (The performance is not listed in *The London Stage*.) It was presented in celebration of the King's birthday and was repeated on 19 September 1761 with new "Dances,

From the collection of Kalman A. Burnim

Scene design by CARLO GALLI-BIBIENA

Scenes, Illuminations, Dresses and other Decorations." One of the stupendous staging effects noted in the libretto recalls Carlo's transparent setting for *L'uomo* at Bayreuth in 1754:

. . . The Field of Battle disappears, when the Temple of FATE is discovered, supported by many transparent Columns, with Symbols, alluding to His Majesty. . . . At the same time, in the most elevated part, opposite to the Theatre, appears a Globe of thick Clouds, which, (dispersing) discovers to the Eye of the Spectators, various propitious Genii, who sing in praise of His Majesty.

Born in Vienna probably in 1728 (some sources give 1725), Carlo was the son of Giuseppe Galli-Bibiena (1696–1757), the "first theatrical engineer" of the Hapsburg court and the greatest scenic artist of the century. Carlo spent his youth as an apprentice to his father, witnessing the magnificent spectacles staged under Giuseppe's

direction. Obviously experiencing little difficulty in securing an influential position for himself, Carlo entered the service of the Margrave Friedrich at Bayreuth in 1746. With his father in 1748 he completed the sumptuous decorations of the new Bayreuth Opera House, which still stands as a monument to the Baroque Age. In connection with the festivities attending the wedding of Princess Frederike to Duke Karl Eugen von Württenburg, Carlo designed the settings for the operas *Ezio* and *Artaserse* with which the house was inaugurated in September 1748.

During the 1750s Carlo divided his time between the courts of Bayreuth and Brunswick. At the outbreak of the Seven Years War in 1756, he went to live in Rome. In 1758 he returned for a brief time to Bayreuth, then traveled through France and the Netherlands, and then perhaps arrived in London in 1760. At the conclusion of the war he was appointed by Frederick the

Great to occupy his father's former position at Berlin for an annual stipend of 2400 thaler. In that city in 1765 he designed settings for *Leucippe* and *Achille in Sciroe*, but lacking his father's enormous talents Carlo did not find favor with Frederick and was discharged in 1766, whereupon he traveled again, this time to Denmark, Sweden, Spain, Italy, and Russia. During that period productions designed by him included *Cerere placata* at Naples in September 1772 and *Birjer Jarl* at Stockholm in 1774. His settings for the latter piece, given in the Great Gallery of the Stockholm Palace, still survive at the Drottningholm Court Theatre. Little is known of his work at St Petersburg, where he was engaged by Catherine the Great at an annual salary of 2000 rubles. He left Russia by 1778 and settled in Italy, his father's native country. Carlo died in Florence in 1787.

Carlo was, it seems, the least talented of his illustrious family. His designs did not exhibit the skill or genius of his father's, but neither did the work of any other designer of the period. In the *Enciclopedia dello spettacolo* may be found information on the Galli-Bibiena family.

Several notices later in the century raise the possibility of another and unknown member of the family having worked in London. In January 1780 an Italian puppet troupe under the management of Signor Micheli, presenting shows at No 22, Piccadilly, announced:

This, and Every Evening During this week, will be presented a new Comic Opera in two Acts, called 'Ninnette à la Cour; or, the Fair Nancy at Court.'. . . . To which will be added a new Entertainment, in One Act, called 'Harlequin's Love-Triumph, by the Magic Art' . . . . In which Harlequin will take his Flight round a room 60 Feet long and 49 Feet wide, in a manner truly surprising and never before exhibited in Europe. The whole of the Scenery and Machinery entirely new. The public is acquainted by the Manager that this valuable edifice is just imported from Italy; and is,

in small Compass, the exact Model of the superb Theatre Nuova at Bologna, and the Scenery are the Painting of the celebrated Bibbiena.

In February 1791 a season in Savile Row was presented by Martinelli, who had worked the Piccadilly puppets in 1780. The scenery for those performances was announced as having been painted by Rebecca, Capon, and Bibiena. The first two, of course, enjoyed well-known London careers.

By 1780, the year of the first puppet show with which the family name was associated, all of the known Galli-Bibienas, except Carlo, were dead, including Antonio (d. 1774) who in 1763 had designed the theatre at Bologna referred to in the puppet-show advertisement. By 1791, the year of the second notice, Carlo, too, was dead.

Gallini, Giovanni Andrea Battista
1728–1805, dancer, dancing master, choreographer, impresario.

Giovanni Andrea Battista Gallini was born at Florence on 7 January 1728. The short entry by J. M. Rigg in *The Dictionary of National Biography* has him emigrating to England "about 1753, in which year he made his debut at the Opera House, Haymarket, as a dancer," but Antoine de Léris, in the *Dictionnaire portatif des théâtres* (1754), places him in the company of L'Académie Royale de Musique as late as July 1754.

Gallini once boasted that he had come to England with only a half-crown piece in his pocket. Rigg's account notes that he "achieved a remarkable and rapid success, so that the next season [1754–55] he was appointed principal dancer, and soon afterwards director of the dances, and finally stage manager of that theatre." Nalbach, in *The King's Theatre*, says only that Gallini was "the leader of the dance company . . . in the years before he assumed the management of the theatre."

Harvard Theatre Collection

GIOVANNI GALLINI

engraving by Bretherton

But the first mention given him in the bills, according to *The London Stage*, was when, at Covent Garden Theatre on 17 December 1757, he joined Miss Hilliard "in a Pantomime Ballet call'd *The Judgment of Paris*" and a comic ballet, *The Sicilian Peasants*, both of which were repeated several times during the season. He was placed at the head of the 17 featured dancers assisting at the revival of the "dramatic opera" *The Prophetess*, on the Covent Garden bill for 1 February 1758. He was awarded single billing on 13 March, when he gave "a *New Dance*, adapted to the Comedy" *The Sheep Shearing*. On 5 April he and Miss Hilliard were featured in a "Masquerade Scene" introduced into *The Provok'd Husband* and on 12 April, on the occasion of his benefit he appeared once more in *The Judgment*

of Paris, performed again in *The Sicilian Peasants* (this time with Miss Capdeville), presented an unnamed "new dance" with Mrs Granier and Miss Liviez, joined Signora Forti in a ballet exercise called *She Wou'd and She Wou'd Not*, and topped off the evening in "A *Minuet* by Gallini and a Gentlewoman." For those exertions he received £70 9s., after the house charges of £63.

Gallini went over to the *corps de ballet* at the King's Theatre under Vaneschi's management in the fall of 1758, where he was shortly denominated "Director of Dances." Arthur Murphy, in the *London Chronicle* for 18/21 November 1758, believed

that Signor Galini is universally allowed to be one of the finest dancers in Europe; but at the King's Theatre, where he at present performs, he not only gives us the strongest proofs of his executive powers, but also of his skill in designing, by having composed three of the prettiest ballets I ever saw; and for plot, movement, humour, and, if I may make use of the expression, gesticulated wit, they are equal I believe, to any of those which Lewis the Fourteenth himself was so fond of.

Murphy added a long paragraph particularizing the beauties of one of the ballets. Gallini remained in that situation, drilling his small group of dancers, devising ballets, and dancing himself, through the opera season of 1762–63. He was also accepting pupils (Drury Lane, 14 September 1761: "dance by Master Roger and Miss Capitani, scholars to Gallini") and on 3 March 1762 he published *A Treatise on the Art of Dancing*, which went into three editions in the next decade.

When Signora Mattei gave over the opera management to Giardini and Signora Mingotti in 1763–64, Gallini went back to Covent Garden. His appearance in the ballet *Venus Reveng'd* on 22 December 1763 was advertised as his first performance there in six years. He danced Hymen in "a New

Masque" on 20 January 1764 and figured in several other evenings, but he does not seem to have been employed fully. In 1765–66 he was re-engaged at the opera by Crawford, Gordon, and Vincent but his name was seen in few bills. After that season he never again appeared as a dancer on the roster of a London theatre. His activities for the next few years are not known.

Many of the most important details of Gallini's personal life and his continental experiences are unknown or hard to place in time. He is said to have been awarded the knighthood of the Order of the Golden Spur by the Pope, who was delighted by his dancing. Afterwards, he insisted on the addition "Sir" and was usually indulged by

his acquaintances, although his title had no standing in England.

He was a popular figure and successful both professionally and socially. He was much in demand in fashionable households as a dancing master, and in that capacity he visited the residence of the Earl of Abingdon, where his agreeable personality captivated the Earl's eldest daughter, Lady Elizabeth Peregrine Bertie. No record has been found of their marriage, but it seems to have been acknowledged by her family, and she had assumed the name Gallini by 13 October 1766, when she gave birth to twin sons.

Gallini was energetic and ambitious. When, in 1778, R. B. Sheridan and Thomas Harris purchased the King's The-

---

The grand pathetic of the ſerious ſtile of dancing is not what every one enters into. But all are pleaſed with a brilliant execution, in the quick motion of the legs, and the high ſprings of the body. A paſtoral dance, repreſented in all the pantomime art, will be commonly preferred to the more ſerious ſtile, though this laſt requires doubtleſs the greateſt excellence : but it is an excellence of which few but the connoiſſeurs are judges ; who are rarely numerous enough to encourage the compoſer of dances to form them entirely in that ſtile. All that he can do is to take a great part of his attitudes from the ſerious ſtile, but to give them another turn and air in the compoſition ; that he may avoid confounding the two different ſtiles of ſerious and half-ſerious. For this laſt,
it

it is impoſſible to have too much agility and briſkneſs.

The comic dancer is not tied up to the ſame rules or obſervations as are neceſſary to the ſerious and half ſerious ſtiles. He is not ſo much obliged to ſtudy what may be called nature in high life. The rural ſports, and exerciſes ; the geſtures of various mechanics or artificers will ſupply him with ideas for the execution of charraĉters in this branch. The more his motions, ſteps, and attitudes are taken from nature, the more they will be ſure to pleaſe.

The comic dance has for objeĉt the exciting mirth; whereas, on the contrary, the ſerious ſtile aims more at ſoothing and captivating by the harmony and juſtneſs of its movements;
by

From *A Treatise on the Art of Dancing,* by GIOVANNI GALLINI atre for £22,000 they mortgaged the property for £12,000. Gallini purchased the mortgage, expecting to acquire the shares of the hard-pressed Sheridan. But Sheridan sold to William Taylor. Taylor over-extended himself in remodelling the theatre in 1782 and while he was jailed for debt saw his part in the theatre sold at auction to Harris. Gallini bought it from Harris. While Gallini was in France in 1783 engaging performers, Taylor's lawyers found a flaw in the sale, and Taylor (though still in jail) resumed control, operating through a board of trustees. Complicated litigation and furious pamphlet warfare ensued, the most incensed and circumstantial issuing from three members of the King's Theatre —W. Allen, T. Luppino, and H. Reynell— in *The Case of the Opera House Disputes Fairly Stated* (1784).

The Lord Chamberlain finally squeezed Taylor out by the simple expedient of refusing his trustees a license to perform operas and awarding a license to Gallini— to whom Taylor was consequently forced to sell. But the theatre was still under debt, Gallini also had incurred the Lord Chamberlain's suspicions (as an exchange of letters in the Public Record Office shows), and he was finally forced to furnish security, to consent to having a receiver-treasurer appointed, and to certify the amounts he proposed to pay performers. Gallini became proprietor of the King's Theatre in the fall of 1785 and retained effective control until the theatre burned on 17 June 1789. Gallini was, according to Wilkinson and others, under-insured, which fact alone would seem to have been enough to exculpate him from the suspicion of arson which was nevertheless hinted at in the *Times*. (Edward W. Brayley in *Historical and Descriptive Accounts of the Theatres of London* [1826] said that in 1790, on his deathbed, Pietro Carnevale, once deputy acting manager at the opera, confessed that he had set fire to the theatre out of jealousy of his successor Ravelli. But Brayley's account may rest on rumor.)

Gallini had not been a stranger to trouble during his managership. He had apparently done his best to procure talented continental singers and dancers, but they were the cause of strife and destruction. *The Final Farewell* (1787) celebrates one of his recruiting forays:

> *Welcomed by hautboys, fiddles, flutes and*
> *   drums,*
> *Posting from Italy, GALLINI comes!*
> *He comes, the cheapest bargains having*
> *   made,*
> *For who so nice a judge in his trade?*
> *Cou'd ever manager like him engage?*
> *He brings—'the finest performers of the*
> *   age!'—*
> *And though he proved unlucky at Ver-*
> *   sailles,*
> *His grand negociation seldom fails;*
> *And though forbidden,—ladies do not*
> *   droop!*
> *'Tis thought VESTRIS [junior] will join*
> *   Gallini's troop.*

Vestris did join, but despite Gallini's best efforts and the acquisition of a few dancers like Didelot, Duquesney, Saulnier, and Mlle Adelaide, there was general critical and audience dissatisfaction with the dancing. The *World* of 2 February, reporting the performance of 31 January, was devastating: "The Dance, if such it can be called, was like the movements of heavy Cavalry. It was hissed very abundantly," but, conceded that writer, "Gallini has the excuse of not having been able to get better dancers." On 7 February

At the conclusion of the last dance hostilities commenced by hissing and hooting from the pit and boxes . . . the dancers, however, were not dismayed, but continued their evolutions, though the noise was so great that they derived but little aid from the music. At last a body of malcontents, among whom were several *stars* and *ribbons,* sallied from the pit and took possession of the stage, from which they drove the light-heeled troops, and immediately began to perform a *ballet tragique.*

A description of the destruction of the theatre ("till they had demolished everything they found that was moveable") followed. A clipping dated only 1789, in the Daly Collection at the Huntington Library, gives a supplementary version of the affair:

On Saturday night last as soon as the opera was over, Mr. Gallini and Mr. Noverre appeared on the stage both together, but Mr. Noverre getting the start of Mr. Gallini, began addressing the audience in French, that new dancers were just arrived, but that Mr. Gallini would not allow him the proper things to bring the dancing forward; by this time the stage was filled with gentlemen, if you could call them such, and without their hats, on which one of them attempted to throw Mr. Gallini headlong backwards into the orchestra; but some of the musicians seeing him falling, jumped up and threw him forward, else certainly he must have been killed on the spot; on recovering himself, though old as he is, knocked down his assailant, who lay sprawing [sic] upon the stage, on which the uproar became general; ladies screaming out, others crying off, off! enough, enough! while in the bustle Moriga kept dancing round Gallini, crying out, you Old Dog, give me my money, where be my money, I can get no porter; and Delpini in the midst trying to support his Old Master. By this time the patent lamps began to suffer, by kicking them in pieces, the glass cutting several musicians in the face, the oil running down their cloaths, the stands overturning in the orchestra, and the side lamps and the oil running about the stage; while several in the first gallery were not behind hand in stripping the seats of their coverings, and the uproar continued till near twelve o'clock.

On 10 February, by way of the playbill: "Mr Gallini respectfully informs the Nobility, Subscribers, and Gentry that he sent a person to Paris on Monday last to engage the best capital Female Dancer that can be got; and if a good Man Dancer is to be procured, he is very ready to engage him. . . ." He acquired a few dancers of both sexes

later in the spring, but nearly all were gone before the 1789–90 season began.

Immediately after the burning of the King's, Gallini entered into partnership with a young law student and enthusiast for theatre named Robert Bray O'Reilly. They secured a temporary license to perform operas at the Haymarket Theatre and Covent Garden in the season of 1789, meanwhile seeking permission to erect a permanent house in Leicester Fields. Nalbach details the intricate and bizarre events which followed and which may be summarized: Taylor took a lease of the site of the destroyed King's Theatre, planning an opposition opera; O'Reilly purchased a site in Leicester Fields, but Gallini refused to help pay for it, hoping to freeze him out of the license, which excluded Gallini; Gallini and Taylor joined forces, but Gallini later assigned his share to Taylor, who then employed Michael Novosielski to rebuild the King's Theatre on the old location (despite new operatic competition from O'Reilly, who employed James Wyatt to remodel the Pantheon as an opera house).

But Gallini had other affairs to occupy him during the whole period of his association with opera. On 28 June 1774 Gallini had joined with Johann Christian Bach and Karl Friedrich Abel in the purchase of a large house on the east side of Hanover Square. In its garden they had erected and joined to the house a room 95 by 30 feet. The Hanover Square Rooms opened on 1 February 1775 with one of Bach and Abel's subscription concerts, already a successful enterprise. The following spring masquerades and balls were also introduced. From the beginning the rooms made money. On 12 November 1776 Gallini bought the one-half interest owned by his partners. Bach and Abel continued to hold their concerts at the rooms, however, until 1782. Thereafter a group of musicians, organized under the title "Professional Concerts," began playing in the Rooms. The violinist Salomon also instituted concerts there and in 1804 the Concert of Ancient Music was moved to the Rooms for a rent of £1000 per year.

During much of that time Gallini also lived at the Hanover Square address but was so anxious to derive income from the property that he left himself scarcely any room for amenities. He died a rich man, despite the immense losses he had incurred. His wife had brought him the manor of Hampstead Norris and another at Yattenden (where he erected a mansion in the Italian style) in Berkshire, the assembly rooms had made money, he had prospered as a teacher of dancing, and evidently he had invested well. His will was signed "in good health" on 15 December 1804. He "died very suddenly at his appartments in Hanover St . . . at or about nine o'clock" on 5 January 1805, according to the affidavit of Edward Prendergrass and William Alexander Hay who authenticated his signature on 2 February 1805.

One of the trustees named in Gallini's will was his brother-in-law the Earl of Abingdon. Gallini left a freehold estate in trust for his son Francis, entailing it so it could not be liquidated. A recently purchased house, No 76, Berkeley Street, he left to his two daughters, Bess and Louisa Gallini. His three freehold estates in Hanover Square (on lease to Lord Chesterfield and other noblemen) defined as "assembly rooms, with stables & coach house & yard and 2 houses adjoining," were to be retained, and the income from the rentals used to defray the costs of educating the children of his son Francis until they reached the age of 25. After that, the continuing rentals were to be divided equally among them. The furniture, carriage and horses, with moneys unspecified in the Bank of England and lifehold annuities in the hands of Mons Perrignan, banker at Paris, were to go to Gallini's children in equal shares. Gallini left a legacy of £200 to his brother Ulbardo, a Franciscan in a monastery in Florence. Among other beneficiaries

was a witness to Gallini's will, Edward Prendergrass of Duke's Street, Manchester Square, who received £50. Gallini left £25 to his "assistant Mr. Hobart." The sum of £50 went to another assistant, Mr Sidonry (?). Annuities of £10 went to each of his two servants, the coachman Wood and his wife. His trustees, Lord Abingdon, a Mr Wickham (?), and a Mr Noble, a banker of Pall Mall, each was rewarded for his stewardship with £100.

S. H. H., writing in *Notes and Queries* in 1860, recalled that Gallini's two daughters "built and endowed the handsome Roman Catholic chapel in Grove Road, St. John's Wood, called 'Our Lady's Chapel,' together with two wings; one a residence for themselves, and the other for the priest, the Very Rev. Canon O'Neil. The remains of the two ladies lie in the vaults beneath the chapel."

A mural tablet inscribed to the memory of Gallini and his wife was placed in Yattenden church.

A portrait engraving of Gallini by C. Bretherton was published on 10 August 1781.

Galliotti. *See* **GALEOTTI.**

Gallot, Mr [*fl.* 1784–1794], *violinist.*
Mr Gallot played second violin in the Handel Memorial Concerts at Westminster Abbey and the Pantheon in May and June 1784. Doane's *Musical Directory* of 1794 listed him as a resident in Leicester Street, Swallow Street, and as a participant in oratorio performances at the Abbey and at Drury Lane Theatre.

Gallot, Mr [*fl.* 1794], *singer.*
Doane's *Musical Directory* of 1794 listed Mr Gallot of Leicester Street, Swallow Street, as a bass who sang in the Handel performances at Westminster Abbey and the oratorios at Drury Lane.

Gallot, Mr [*fl.* 1795–1801], *singer.*

Mr Gallot was a tenor who sang in the general chorus at Drury Lane from as early as 30 October 1795, when he was in *The Cherokee*, through the 1800–1801 season. During that period he was a Soldier in *The Prisoner* and *The Captive of Spilburg*, a Villager in *The Honey Moon* and *Feudal Times*, a Janizary in *Blue-Beard*, a Peasant in *Richard Coeur de Lion* and *Blue-Beard*, a member of the Horde in *Lodoiska*, and part of the general chorus in *The Cherokee*, *The Pirates*, and *Mahmoud*. He was probably related to the other musical Gallots of the time, and the wife of one of them may have been the Mrs "Galot" who thanked the Royal Society of Musicians on 2 February 1823 for a donation.

Galloway, Mr [*fl. 1794*], *music copyist?*

The Drury Lane accounts for 1794 show a payment of 13*s*. 12*d*. (*sic*) to one Galloway "for an Opera"—which suggests that he may have been a music copyist. He may have been (or have been related to) Daniel or William Galloway, who were active in London music life in the early nineteenth century. Daniel and William were partners in a music selling and publishing firm at No 12, Great Pulteney Street, about 1814 to 1816; they had additional premises at No 37, Great Pulteney Street. Daniel continued alone at the latter address from about 1816 to 1819. William was in business for himself, adding the sale of musical instruments to his activity, at No 21, Wigmore Street, from about 1819 to 1828 and at No 4, Lower Seymour Street, from 1828 to 1831.

Gally. *See* **GALLI.**

Galori. *See* **CALORI.**

"Gamba Di Ferro." *See* **GRIMALDI, JOHN BAPTIST** [*fl. 1740–1742*].

Gambarini. *See* **DE GAMBARINI.**

Gambellon, Mr [*fl. 1728*], *dancer*.

Mr Gambellon played an Egyptian in Mrs Violante's "Dramatick Entertainment of Dancing in Grotesque Characters" called *The Rivals* at the Haymarket Theatre on 21 February 1728 and subsequent dates that season.

Gamble, John *d. 1687, violinist, cornetist, composer.*

John Gamble was a student of Ambrose Beeland, one of the violinists in the King's Musick under Charles I and Charles II. In July 1658 Anthony à Wood noted in his diary:

A. W. entertain'd two eminent musitians of London, named John Gamble and Thomas Pratt, after they entertain'd him with most excellent musick at the meeting house of William Ellis. Gamble had obtain'd a great name

VERA EFFIGIES IOANNIS GAMBLE PHILOMUSICI
This to the Graver owes ; But read and Find— T. Cross sculpsit   By his owne hand , a most Harmonious Mind. I.S.

By permission of the Board of the British Library

JOHN GAMBLE

engraving by T. Cross

among the musitians of Oxon for his book before publish'd, entit. "Ayres and Dialogues to be sung to the Theorbo-Lute, or Bass-viol" [1656; second volume 1659].

One of the poems prefacing Gamble's book was by John Tatham:

> *Here, thou hast play'd the* Cunning
>   Chymist, *fixt*
> Mercurial-*Notes to* Words, *so aptly mixt,*
> *So wedded to each Accent, sense, and*
>   *Feet;*
> *They like two* Bodies *in one* Center
>   *meet* . . . .

At the Restoration Gamble became a member of the King's Musick, replacing William Lanier, and about 1660 (Grove says 1662) he composed music for the City pageant *Aqua Triumphalis* by Tatham. The pageant, on barges, entertained the King and Queen as they came from Hampton to Whitehall. At court Gamble received £16 2s. 6d. annually as a livery fee—though it was rarely paid on time—plus an unspecified salary. A Lord Chamberlain's warrant dated 23 September 1662 stated that Gamble replaced Jerome Lanier, deceased; that may have been a second post awarded Gamble or a correction of Lanier's Christian name.

On 4 July 1663 Gamble and others were paid for attendance on the King at Windsor; how much each received was not stated in the accounts, but 15 men were paid a total of £30. During those early years Gamble was cited simply as a member of the wind instruments, though from later sources we know he also played violin and cornet. His yearly salary as a cornetist was £46 10s. 10d., and he supposedly received further pay as a violinist.

Gamble lost everything he owned in the Great Fire of 1666 and was imprisoned for a debt of £120. His poverty is understandable: the King owed him £221 10s. 4½d. in back salary for the years 1663, 1664, and 1665. The accounts show that he bor-

rowed money in 1666, was still owed £46 10s. 10d. by the Crown in 1669, and assigned his unpaid livery fee in 1672 to one Joseph Parrot, probably to get a loan.

On 4 July 1674 Gamble was one of several court musicians ordered to report to Monsieur Cambert at the theatre in Whitehall to practice for a concert to be presented before the King at Windsor. Gamble was at Windsor in the summer of 1674, played violin in the court masque *Calisto* on 15 February 1675, and journeyed to Windsor again in July 1675. His financial status improved not a whit: in 1675 he still owed livery for 1667; in 1675 and 1676 he borrowed frequently from the Crown (Charles seems to have had money to lend but none to pay his debts); and on 13 December 1676 Gamble appointed John Spicer of St Martin-in-the-Fields his lawful attorney—probably to receive Gamble's salary and pay his debts. Gamble at that time described himself as from the parish of St Giles in the Fields. On 18 August 1683, still in debt, Gamble wrote another power of attorney, to Robert Strong (the court musician, most likely). That document is in a British Museum copy of his *Ayres and Dialogues.*

John Gamble died in 1687 and was buried at St Bride, Fleet Street, on 30 November of that year. In the parish register is a marginal note reading, "at the 2 black posts Salisbury Court," which may have been the musician's address. Gamble had made his will on 30 June 1680, describing himself then as of St Bride's parish and calling himself "crazed and infirme of body." He left his grandson John Gamble, a servant to Mr (Robert?) Strong in 1680, £20 out of sums owed Gamble by the King. To his grandson Gamble also left all his books of music. To the rest of his kindred, unnamed, he bequeathed 12d. each if demanded. The remainder of his estate, which was doubtless small, Gamble left to his wife Elizabeth. She proved the will on 3 December 1687.

Since we know that Gamble lived in St Giles's parish in 1676, the following entry in the parish registers of St Giles in the Fields probably concerned him: Elizabeth, daughter of John "Gambell," was buried on 30 April 1672. The registers of St Margaret, Westminster, which contain many references to court musicians, cited the baptism of a John Gambell, son of John and Alice, on 17 June 1661. If that referred to the musician, he must have had a first wife who died before 1680.

A portrait of John Gamble engraved by T. Cross served as a frontispiece to Gamble's *Ayres and Dialogues* in 1656. An engraved copy of the portrait by W. Richardson was published on 1 March 1793.

Games, Andrew [fl. 1696], *musician*.
Andrew Games was appointed a musician in ordinary without fee in the King's Musick on 18 December 1696 but seems not to have succeeded to a salaried post.

Gandell, John [fl. 1794], *violist?, flutist*.
Doane's *Musical Directory* of 1794 listed John Gandell of No 40, Lime Street, Fenchurch Street, as a flutist and tenor (violist, supposedly, though he may have been a singer). Gandell performed for the Handelian Society and in the performances at Westminster Abbey.

Gandry. *See* **GAUDRY.**

Gang, Mr [fl. 1735], *dancer*.
Mr Gang and Miss Rogers danced a Mezzetin Man and Woman in *The Necromancer* at Covent Garden on 26 September 1735. The production ran through December.

Ganlers, Mr [fl. 1661], *musician?*
On 22 October 1661 the Westminster musicians who made up the Corporation of the Art and Science of Musick met at the house of Mr Ganlers in Durham Yard in the Strand to organize themselves after the Restoration. Ganlers was presumably a professional musician; the Marshal of the group was Nicholas Lanier, Master of the King's Musick under Charles I.

Ganning. *See* **CAMPBELL, MISS, LATER MRS J. GUNNING.**

Ganthony, Joseph *d. 1795, violinist, bass player, composer*.
Joseph Ganthony wrote a few light songs during the 1760s and 1770s which became popular at London's pleasure gardens. The *Catalogue of Printed Music in the British Museum* lists some of his published works. In 1775–76 Ganthony was playing (violin, presumably) in the band at Drury Lane. In May and June 1784 a Mr "Granthony," probably our subject, played double bass in the Handelian performances at Westminster Abbey and the Pantheon.

By 1787 Ganthony was in Ireland. He subscribed 1s. 1d. to the Irish Musical Fund on 1 January of that year, though by 1 April he had withdrawn his name. On 7 October 1792 the Royal Society of Musicians in London entertained a petition from Ganthony asking for relief, but on 4 November the plea was rejected. Ganthony was still in Dublin at the time, and the Royal Society of Musicians launched an investigation to determine Ganthony's exact financial situation. Meanwhile, on 2 December 1792, they made him a temporary grant of two guineas per month.

Doane's *Musical Directory* of 1794 listed Ganthony as a violinist, a member of the Royal Society of Musicians, and a resident of Dublin. Some time in early 1795 Joseph Ganthony died. The Society received the news on 5 April, and on 3 May they voted to send five guineas to Dublin for Ganthony's funeral expenses. In most of the transactions involving Ganthony in the 1790s the Society's representative was a Mr Callcott—possibly John Wall or William Callcott. On 1 March 1801 Ann

Ganthony, Joseph's widow, was granted by the Society £2 12s. 6d. monthly.

"Gapatoona, Signora" [fl. 1754], singer.

Christopher Smart, under the name of "Mrs Midnight," presented entertainments at the Haymarket Theatre in April and May 1754 which featured, among others, a singer masquerading as "Signora Gapatoona." She was in *The Adventures of Fribble* beginning on All Fool's Day, sang in a concert on 22 April, and shared a benefit with "Timbertoe" on 2 May.

"Gapatoono, Signor" [fl. 1753], singer?

"Signor Gapatoono," a pseudonym concocted by Christopher Smart for some performer who appeared in his entertainments, was probably a singer. He appeared in *The Old Woman's Concert* on 13 March 1753 and shared a benefit with Master Benjamin Hallett on 10 April. Gapatoono was hailed as "first cousin to Farinelli," the famous male soprano, and he was perhaps related to the female of the species, Signora Gapatoona, who appeared in Smart's productions in 1754.

Garani-Morichelli, Mme [fl. 1790], singer.

Beginning in March 1790 there are records of concerts in the Hanover Square Rooms, mostly organized by Johann Peter Salomon. Among the singers participating was Mme Garani-Morichelli, doubtless a relative of Signora Anna Morichelli, who sang in London in 1794 and 1795.

Garbutt, Mr [fl. 1800–1803], house servant?

On 13 June 1800 tickets delivered by Mr Garbutt for admission to Drury Lane were accepted; he was probably one of the house servants. Mr Garbutt was still in the company in the 1802–3 season. The Drury Lane accounts contain mentions of a Mrs Garbott in June 1800 and a Miss Garbett on 17 June 1801; if variant spellings are taken into account, one may suppose those were Mr Garbutt's wife and daughter.

Garbutt, Mrs [fl. 1800], mantua-maker.

Mrs Garbutt (or Garbott) was a mantua-maker who was mentioned in the Drury Lane account books in June 1800. Since a Mr Garbutt was on the theatre staff and a Miss Garbett was cited in the books on 17 June 1801 for a payment of £1 4s. for two weeks' salary, we may guess that Mrs Garbutt was on the theatre payroll and not an outside supplier.

Garcia, Signor [fl. 1785], clown, dancer, rope dancer.

At Astley's Amphitheatre on 27 September 1785 Signor Garcia was one of several figure dancers. The following 8 October he performed on the slack rope (for the first time, the bill stated), and at his shared benefit on 14 October he served as a clown and performed "The Humorous Trick of the Roasted Pig, on the Slack Rope." On that occasion the bill referred to him as Signor "Garse."

Gard. See GARDEN and GUARD.

Garde. See DELAGARDE.

Gardel. See also GUIARDELE.

Gardel, [Agathe?] [fl. 1769–1770?], dancer.

On 5 September 1769 the *Public Advertiser* reported that Signora Gardel had been engaged as one of the principal dancers at the King's Theatre for the coming season. Her name, however, is not on any of the extant bills. Possibly that person was Agathe Gardel (sister of Pierre Gabriel Gardel), who danced at the Paris Opéra in 1767.

Gardel, Pierre Gabriel *1758–1840, dancer, ballet master, choreographer, violinist, composer.*

The French dancer Pierre Gabriel Gardel (sometimes called *Gardel cadet*) was born at Nancy on 4 February 1758. He was the son of Claude Gardel (d. 1774), ballet master at the courts of Württemberg and Mannheim and at Nancy, by his wife Jeanne-Louise Dartenay Gardel (who was still living in 1776). Pierre's brother Maximilien Léopold Philippe Joseph Gardel (1741–1787), called *Gardel aîné*, had a long career as a dancer and choreographer at the Paris Opéra where he succeeded Noverre as ballet master in 1781. A sister Agathe Gardel also was a dancer there beginning in 1767.

Pierre Gardel first danced small roles at

Harvard Theatre Collection
PIERRE GABRIEL GARDEL
lithograph by Ducarme, after Midy

the Paris Opéra in 1771. In 1772 he appeared in *Castor et Pollux*, and on 23 September 1773 he was much admired in a pas de deux with Dorival in *L'Union de l'Amour et des Arts*. Other ballets in which he performed in those early years included *Azolan, Iphigénie en Aulide, Orphée*, and *Sabinus* in 1774; *Céphale et Procris* and *Philémon et Baucis* in 1775; *Les Romans* in 1776; and *La Chercheuse d'esprit* in 1778.

In 1781–82 Gardel enjoyed success at the King's Theatre, London, in a dancing company headed by Noverre. He made his debut on 17 November 1781 in a *Divertissement Dance* and a new ballet *Les Amants réunis*, both composed by Noverre, and danced with Mlle Baccelli, Nivelon, Mlle Théodore, Simonet, and others. Other ballets by Noverre in which Gardel was featured that season were *Le Triomphe de l'amour conjugal, Rinaldo and Armida, La Rosière de Salency*, and *Medea and Jason*. For his benefit on 9 May 1782, by desire of the Prince of Wales, he danced in Noverre's *Mirsa*, a new ballet taken from an American anecdote. In the concert scene of that ballet, Gardel executed a concerto on the violin. As Alexander in Noverre's *Apelles and Campaspe*, first played on 5 June, he gave his last performance of the season on 29 June 1782.

Upon his return to the Paris Opéra Gardel was awarded a pension of 4800 livres. In 1787 he succeeded his brother as *maître des ballets*, a post he held until 1828. He returned to London for a brief period in the spring of 1788 to dance at the King's Theatre with his first wife, Anne Jacqueline Coulon (fl. 1787–1792). On 21 February 1788 the dances included a *Pas de Russe* composed by Gardel and danced by Vestris and Mlle Hilligsberg. At his wife's benefit on 3 April (when tickets could be had of her at No 8, Great Suffolk Street, Charing Cross) Gardel danced "the celebrated *Pas de Quatre of Panurge*," with Mlle Coulon, Mlle Hilligsberg, and Vestris.

Harvard Theatre Collection

PIERRE GABRIEL GARDEL, as Télémaque

engraving by Prud'hom, after Coeuré

Two days later it was reported in the *General Advertiser* that "The dance between Gardel and Vestris on Thursday is everywhere talked of, in the highest terms of admiration. Such excellence no audience ever before witnessed."

At Paris Gardel danced in numerous pieces until an accident about 1795 ended his career as a performer. He continued to choreograph ballets, among which were *Les Sauvages* (in collaboration with his brother) in 1786; *Télémaque dans l'île de Calypso* and *Psyché* in 1790; *Le Jugement de Paris* in 1793; *La Dansomanie* in 1800 (in which he played the violin); *Paul et Virginie* in 1806; and *Alexandre chez Apelle* in 1808. He also was occupied in the management of the Opéra between 1782 and 1793 and directed its school of dancing.

Among his last ballets was *La Servante justifée* in 1818, after which he arranged incidental dances for other choreographers.

He died in Montmartre, Paris, on 18 October 1840.

After the death of his first wife Anne Jacqueline Coulon, Gardel had married Marie Elizabeth Anne Boubert, the daughter of a royal musician. She danced at Paris and London under the names Mlle Miller and Miss Millard (1770–1833).

Gardel was also a fine musician, having practiced under Imbault and Gavinie. His taste in choosing music for the dance was excellent and he composed ballet music. As a ballet master he occasionally collaborated with such excellent musicians as Mehul, Cherubini, Kreutzer, and Catel.

Additional information on Pierre Gardel's continental career may be found in Campardon's *Académie royale*, M. H. Winter's *The Pre-Romantic Ballet*, and the *Enciclopedia dello spettacolo*.

Carrée's engraved portrait, after Dutertre, of Gardel in *Thémistocle* was published in *Costumes et Annales des Grandes Théâtres de Paris* (1786). A portrait engraved by Ducarme, after Midy, was published by Blaisot in *Galerie Universelle*. A lithograph portrait by Englemann was printed at Paris in 1828. An engraving by Prud'hon, after Coeuré, of Gardel as Télémaque was published in *Galerie Theatrale*, 1873.

Gardel, Mme Pierre Gabriel the first. *See* COULON, ANNE JACQUELINE.

Gardel, Mme Pierre Gabriel the second. *See* MILLARD, MARIE ELIZABETH ANNE.

Garden, Mr [*fl.* 1779–1784], *actor.*

On 8 March 1779 at the Haymarket Theatre a Mr "Gard," apparently not William Gard of Covent Garden, played Bauldy in *The Gentle Shepherd*. The following 10 May a Mr Garden, very likely the same actor, was an Officer in *Douglas* at the same house. Garden acted Bauldy in *The Gentle Shepherd* at the Haymarket on 9 February 1784, and a Mr Gardin, again probably the same person, played in *The Reprisal* there on 23 February.

Gardener. *See* GARDINER *and* GARDNER.

Gardi, Signora [*fl. 1773*], *singer.*
Signora Gardi was hired in the fall of 1773 to sing both serious and comic parts in operas at the King's Theatre in the Haymarket. The bills mentioned her only as a participant in *Il puntiglio amoroso*, which opened on 7 December and was performed periodically during the month.

Gardin. *See* GARDEN.

Gardiner. *See also* GARDNER.

Gardiner, Mr [*fl. 1743–1750*], *boxkeeper.*
A Mr Gardiner was a boxkeeper at Covent Garden Theatre from as early as 1743–44 through 1749–50, regularly sharing in end-of-season benefits with other house servants. On 15 May 1747 he was paid £10 "for his attendance at the boxes this season." On 21 April 1750 his name was taken off the theatre's paylist.

Gardiner, Mr [*fl. 1750–1757*], *dancer, choreographer.*
A Mr Gardiner was a chorus member at Covent Garden Theatre from 1750–51 through 1753–54. His name was first noticed in the bills on 30 October 1750 as one of the Infernal Spirits in the pantomime *Perseus and Andromeda*, an assignment he repeated many times during the season. He also danced a Polonese in *Apollo and Daphne* and an Aerial Spirit and Neptune in numerous performances of *Merlin's Cave*. "Gardner" shared a benefit on 4 May 1751.
In 1751–52 he danced those roles again as well as a Demon in *The Necromancer*. On 16 and 27 April 1754 (the latter for his benefit) Gardiner danced with Mlle

Camargo, the sister of the famed French *prima ballerina*. In 1756–57 he was at Drury Lane Theatre, making his first appearance there on 13 October 1756 with Mrs Vernon in a new serious dance called *The Shipwreck, or, The Distressed Lovers* after Act II of *The Gamester* and a new comic dance titled *The Press Gang, or The Sailor's Farewell* after Act IV. Those dances, composed by Gardiner himself, were repeated throughout the season.

Gardiner, Mr [*fl. 1794*], *singer?*
In 1794 a Mr Gardiner was listed in Doane's *Musical Directory* as a tenor (singer, or violist?) who participated in the Handel performances at Westminster Abbey and who lived at No 9, Chesterfield Street, Marylebone.

Gardiner, Mrs [*fl. 1726?–1731*], *house servant?*
A "Widow Gardiner" shared benefit receipts of £109 17s. (before house charges) with Wilcocks and Mines at Lincoln's Inn Fields Theatre on 25 May 1731. Possibly she was the "Mrs Gardner" who had been paid 16s. for an unspecified service by the same theatre on 2 March 1726.

Gardiner, Mrs G., Sarah, née Arne *d. 1808, singer.*
Sarah Arne was the daughter of the composer and singer Michael Arne (c. 1740–1786), probably by his third wife Ann Arne, née Venables (fl. 1772–1820), a singer of little distinction whom he married on 1 May 1773. Sarah's health had been worn down in caring for her father during his last illness in 1786, but eventually she recovered to have a modest career on the stage, which she began as a chorus singer at Drury Lane Theatre in 1793–94 at a salary of £2 15s. per week. Her name appeared in the bills for the role of Marietta in *The Pirates* for its first performance on 16 May 1794 and for the subsequent per-

formances in that season. In the following season she again appeared in *The Pirates* and sang in the chorus for *The Cherokee*.

At Drury Lane on 6 February 1795, announced as a young lady making her first appearance on any stage, she played Polly in *The Beggar's Opera*. She is identified in a notation by Kemble on a playbill: she acted "very badly." Obviously she made no great impression, for she passed most of the remainder of her career in the chorus. Her other known roles included Dorinda in *The Honey Moon* on 7 January 1797, Katharina in *Don Juan* on 11 May 1798, Margaritone in *The Italian Monk* on 30 May 1798, a pastoral Nymph in *Comus* on 18 June 1798, Honoria in *Love Makes a Man* on 26 December 1798, and Angelica Goto in *The Shipwreck* on 10 June 1800.

Miss Arne's salary in 1796–97 was £1 10s. per week, at which level it remained through 1807–8, her last season at Drury Lane.

In the summer of 1800 she was performing at Birmingham, playing Fatima in *Blue-Beard* in a "chastened impressive manner." The press reported that "the young Lady's performance in the different characters she has appeared in, has been so diffidently, yet correctly supported, as to have rendered her a very general favourite." She had also played at Margate in the summer of 1797.

Sometime in the summer of 1803 she married a Mr G. Gardiner, and from the onset of the season 1803–4 was billed as Mrs Gardiner. Perhaps she was the Mrs Gardner whose name was listed in the Haymarket Theatre accounts as a chorus member in the summers from 1804 through 1808, although there seem to have been at least three persons by the name of Gardner or Gardiner singing in the London theatres at this period.

According to Moody's notation in a notebook of the Drury Lane Theatrical Fund (now in the Garrick Club), Mrs Gardiner ("dau. of Michael Arne") died on 3 December 1808. She was buried at St Martin-in-the-Fields on 10 January 1809.

Gardiner, William Nelson *1766–1814, actor, scene painter, engraver, bookseller.*

William Nelson Gardiner was born on 11 June 1766 in Dublin, the son of John Gardiner ("*crier* and *fac-totum*" to Judge Scott) and his wife Margaret, née Nelson, a pastry cook in Henry Street. The facts of his early life and career are set forth in a brief memoir that Gardiner wrote on the last day of his life, 8 May 1814. Displaying an early talent for drawing, Gardiner was put to study in the academy of Sisson Darling. Before he was ten, his mother died and his father went into the service of Sir James Nugent of Donore, Westmeath. As Gardiner wrote, he soon found himself his "own master." He learned to play the violin, the dulcimer, and the German flute, and also had the opportunity while living

By permission of the Trustees of the British Museum

WILLIAM NELSON GARDINER

artist unknown

with his father at Donore to ride, fish, and hunt.

After spending three years at the Royal Dublin Academy, where he won a silver medal, Gardiner came to London, finding his first employment with a Mr Jones in the Strand whose trade was making "reflecting mirrors" and profile shadow-portraits. Gaining little profit or pleasure from that work, he soon joined an actor named Davis, one of Samuel Foote's performers, in a theatrical venture at Mile End. In his memoir Gardiner provided no date for that association, but it was probably about 1778–79. Gardiner claimed to have been a scene painter at Mile End and to have acted, "playing generally comedy, occasionally tragedy, and was thought to have some, though I believe, very little merit." The group was broken up by the intervention of the Lord Chamberlain.

Gardiner was also a member of a company of actors that performed at the Crown Inn, Islington, in February, March, and April 1780. The name of a Mr "Gardner" is in the surviving bills for Tressel in *Richard III* and Harlequin in *The Death and Restoration of Harlequin* on 6 March 1780, Tybalt in *Romeo and Juliet* on 13 March, Major Bedford in *The Deuce is in Him* on 17 March, Barnwell in *The London Merchant* and the Serjeant in *The Camp* on 27 March, and Archer in *The Beaux' Stratagem* on 5 April.

Gardiner claimed that his last role was Darby in *The Poor Soldier* at the Haymarket Theatre, but his name cannot be found in any bills of that piece provided by *The London Stage*. Perhaps Gardiner was referring to some performance at the Haymarket for which the bills are lost.

Because, he wrote, it was "not suiting the state either of my finances or my stomach," Gardiner abandoned acting and resumed work as a profile-shade maker under a Mr Beetham in Fleet Street. Soon he met Captain Francis Grose, the antiquarian, who found him a position as an assistant to

R. Godfrey, the engraver of the *Antiquarian Repertory*, from whom Gardiner said he "learned little." As a consequence of taking his engraving of his "original" design (which he later confessed to having stolen from Cipriani) of "Shepherd Joe" in *Poor Vulcan* to Messrs Sylvester and Edward Harding, owners of a shop in Fleet Street, Gardiner was employed by them for many of their publications. He also worked for Bartolozzi and exhibited paintings at the Royal Academy in 1787, 1792, and 1793. As an engraver, Gardiner ranked himself "inferior only to Bartollozzi, Schiavonnetti, and Tomkins," all of whom did engravings of theatrical persons.

Gardiner's name appears on some theatrical engravings, such as portraits of James Fearon as Captain Driver in *Oroonoko* (1790), John Philip Kemble (1797), Charles Macklin as Sir Pertinax Macsycophant in *The Man of the World* (1786), and John Quick (1789), all after S. Harding. Gardiner also drew the caricature portrait of Charles Frederick Abel (1787) which is reproduced in this dictionary (I, 4). He made engravings for *Shakespeare Illustrated, The OEconomy of Human Life, The Biographical Mirror, The Memoirs of Count de Grammont*, and other works.

Gardiner left England for a while in the early 1790s and went to Dublin, where he squandered his money. Soon he returned to London, taking lodgings at Mr Good's, a stationer in Bond Street, and determined to study for the clergy. Dr Farmer helped him gain admission to Emmanuel College, Cambridge. Hoping to receive a fellowship available to Irish students, Gardiner transferred to Benet College, where he took his degree in 1797. He lingered some five years at Cambridge, never receiving the fellowship, and eventually abandoned his hopes for holy orders. He returned to London to work again for Harding, copying portraits from oil to watercolors.

About 1802 he opened a bookshop in Pall Mall, assisted by a Miss Seckerson—a "very respectable and interesting young woman"—with whom he was "united" but not married. But he was, as he wrote, dogged by the same "ill fortune" which had followed him through life.

A vigorous Whig, he expressed his political views with abandon. Thomas Frognall Dibdin introduced him under the character of "Mustapha" in his *Bibliomania*. Gardiner responded with bitterness in his sales catalogues, and Dibdin in his *Bibliographical Decameron* again referred to him in an uncomplimentary way.

Gardiner developed a considérable knowledge of rare books. His business might have prospered, but the deaths of Miss Seckerson and their child were shocks from which he never recovered. He became filthy in dress and eccentric in behavior, living his last years as a recluse.

On the evening of 8 May 1814 Gardiner hanged himself in his Pall Mall shop. The coroner returned a verdict of insanity. Gardiner left behind the manuscript memoir—misdated May 9—which was printed in the *Gentleman's Magazine* for June 1814. In its conclusion he wrote: "I have seen men on every side of me, greatly inferiors in every respect, towering above me . . . while I have been forsaken and neglected, and my business reduced to nothing. It is, therefore, high time for me to be gone."

A portrait of Gardiner was made by an anonymous engraver.

Gardner. *See also* **GARDINER.**

Gardner, Mr [*fl.* 1775], *proprietor.*
According to Joseph Haslewood in *Roxburghe Revels* (1837), in 1775 a Mr Gardner was the proprietor of Acton Wells, where he held assemblies and public breakfasts by subscription.

Gardner, Mr [*fl.* 1778–1792], *house servant.*
A Mr Gardner was a house servant at Drury Lane Theatre from 1778–79 through 1791–92, regularly sharing in benefit tickets with other house servants each year.

Gardner, Mr [*fl.* 1792], *actor.*
A Mr Gardner acted Garcia in *The Mourning Bride* and the President in *The Apprentice* in a specially licensed performance at the Haymarket Theatre on 26 November 1792.

Gardner, Miss [*fl.* 1767]. *See* **GARDNER, MRS WILLIAM.**

Gardner, James [*fl.* 1788–1800], *stage manager, actor, singer.*
By 1788 James Gardner was serving as stage manager and leading actor in a touring company in Kent operated by Mrs Sarah Baker. The company made regular visits to Canterbury, Rochester, Maidstone, and Tunbridge Wells. At Canterbury on 5 April 1797, Gardner acted Hamlet; he was praised for his Reginald in *The Castle Spectre* in June 1798 at Maidstone, where he also played Dr Pangloss in *The Heir at Law*. The *Thespian Magazine* for April 1794 stated that Gardner was "over 50 years of age."

Thomas J. Dibdin tells an amusing story in his *Reminiscences* (1827) about Gardner and Mrs Baker, whose company Dibdin had joined in 1788. One night while playing Gradus in *Who's the Dupe?* Gardner forgot his lines in the middle of a speech in which he affected the speaking of Greek. Mrs Baker, whose "practice in reading had not been very extensive," was serving as prompter:

he cast an anxious eye towards the prompteress for assistance; Mrs. B. having never met with so many syllables combined in one word, or so many such words in one page as the fictitious Greek afforded, was rather puzzled, and hesitated a moment; when Gardner's distress increasing by the delay, he rather angrily, in a loud whisper, exclaimed, "Give me the word, Madam." The lady replied, "It's a hard

word, Jem."—"Then give me the next."—
"That's harder."—"The next?"—"Harder still."
Gardner became furious; and the manageress,
no less so, threw the book on the stage, and
left it, saying,—"There, now you have 'em all,
you may take your choice."

Dibdin characterized Gardner as "the
stage manager, who played all the heroes,
Falstaff, and the violoncello, set accompani-
ments for the orchestra, taught the singers,
and sometimes copied the parts: he was a
gentlemanly man of some education, without the slightest objection to a second bottle
at seasonable hours, or a third at any time."

Gardner made his London debut at the
Haymarket Theatre as Old Dornton in *The
Road to Ruin* on 29 June 1799, a role he
repeated on 3 July. The *Monthly Mirror* in
July 1799 pronounced him a mediocre actor
who "commenced his theatrical career at
too late a season of his life." Gardner in the
fall of 1799, with the assistance of his old
friend Dibdin, procured an engagement at
Covent Garden Theatre at a salary of £2
10*s.* per week, making his debut there on
18 September as Lockit in *The Beggar's
Opera*, a character which he "creditably sustained" in the judgment of the *Monthly
Mirror* that month. Next he acted Gratiano
in *Othello* on 4 October, the Jailor in *The
Way to Get Married* on 25 October, a
Witch in *Macbeth* on 28 October, and
Kilderkin in *The Flitch of Bacon* on 13
November. In the premiere of Thomas
Knight's comic opera *The Turnpike Gate*
on 14 November, Gardner played Old May-
thorn, a role he repeated some 16 times that
season. He also sang in the chorus of Infernal Spirits in Thomas Dibdin's new
pantomime *The Volcano* on 23 December
(and 25 other dates) and played Bluff in
Abroad and at Home on 11 January 1800,
a Shepherd in *Joanna* on 16 January, a
Friar in the chorus of *Raymond and Agnes*
on 10 February, a Coachman in *The Devil
to Pay* on 17 March, a Porter in *The Belle's
Stratagem* on 27 March, and Sir Toby Fuz

in *A Peep Behind the Curtain* on 5 April.
Soon thereafter he returned to Mrs Baker's
company at Tunbridge Wells; he died
there, according to Dibdin, at a date unknown.

Gardner, Luke. *See* GARDNER, WIL-
LIAM *d. 1790.*

Gardner, William [*fl.* 1702], *drummer.*
A document among the Lord Chamberlain's papers in the Public Record Office
places William Gardner as one of four
drummers in the royal musical establishment as of about 1702.

Gardner, William *d. 1790, actor.*
Although the career of the London actor
William Gardner spanned three decades,
very little is known of his life beyond the
numerous tertiary roles which he supported. Often he was called "Luke" by his
contemporaries, and his surname was sometimes in the bills as Gardener or Gardiner,
but his correct name was William Gardner,
which he used in signing letters and in legal
documents. On 5 November 1768 he signed
as William Gardner on a letter from some
Covent Garden Theatre actors to George
Colman which was printed in the *Theatrical
Monitor*, and he signed thus again on a
letter from some Haymarket Theatre actors
which appeared in the *Morning Herald* on
8 September 1783. His full name was also
recorded on a license granted to him from
the Lord Chamberlain to give a special winter performance at the Haymarket on 30
December 1782.

Advertised as "Mr Gardiner," he made
his first recorded appearance on the London
stage at Drury Lane Theatre (rented for
the summer by Foote) on 2 July 1761,
when he acted an unspecified role in *The
Citizen*, a part he played six other times
during July and August. He also acted an
unspecified role in *The Wishes* at Drury
Lane on 27 July (and three other times)

and Sir Richard Wealthy in *The Minor* on 7 August.

The ensuing winter season he joined the company at Covent Garden, where his name was first seen in the bills, as "Gardner," on 11 December 1761 for the role of Mouldy in *2 Henry IV*. No doubt he had already performed other very minor roles there, for on 14 November 1761 his name was entered on the pay list for 2*s.* 6*d.* per day or £1 10*s.* per week, beginning on 31 October. Gardner continued to play Mouldy for numerous performances throughout the season; his other small roles included Essex in *King John*, Tyrrel in *Richard III*, Heartwell in *The Old Maid*, Charles in *The Busy Body* (on 17 April 1762 for a benefit he shared with many other personnel), Marcellus in *Hamlet*, and a part in *The Lyar*. In the following season, 1762–63, his situation at Covent Garden did not improve. He continued in many of the roles mentioned above and added Slap in *The Intriguing Chambermaid*, Warwick in *2 Henry IV*, Seyton in *Macbeth*, Dennis in *As You Like It*, and Don Manuel in *Love Makes a Man*. On 14 May 1763, when he shared a benefit with Lewis, Redman, Widow Collins, and others, he acted Kite in *The Recruiting Officer*.

Gardner continued in the business of a journeyman actor at Covent Garden for a total of 11 seasons, through 1773–74, playing dozens of bits, walk-ons, and minor supporting parts. Only occasionally did he have a chance to act a character of even the second rank, and very rarely of the first line, such as Alonzo in *The Mourning Bride* on 17 October 1763, Richmond in *Richard III* on 3 May 1765, Horatio in *Hamlet* on 18 September 1765, the Bastard in *King Lear* on 19 December 1765, Shylock in *The Merchant of Venice* on 13 May 1772 (for a benefit shared with R. Smith at which each suffered a deficit of £15 6*s.* 6*d.*), Sir Charles Marlow in the premiere of *She Stoops to Conquer* on 15 March 1773, and Cymbeline on 12 November 1773.

During that period Gardner also acted at the Haymarket Theatre under Foote's management, making his first appearance there on 10 June 1765 as Bridoun in the first performance of the manager's comedy *The Commissary*. Playing the role of Mrs Mechlin that evening was a young actress, Sarah Cheney, whom Gardner married sometime during the summer and who, as Mrs Gardner, then acted at Covent Garden with him through 1773–74. That first summer at the Haymarket Gardner played the farce and light comedy roles of Sir Jacob Jollop in *The Mayor of Garratt*, Captain Loveit in *Miss in Her Teens*, Charles in *The Busy Body*, Sir Richard in *The Minor*, Johnson in *The Rehearsal*, and unspecified parts in *The Orators* and *The Patron*.

Gardner seems to have enjoyed a more substantial number of feature roles at the Haymarket, where he acted every summer (except 1766) through 1772, than was his lot at Covent Garden. Indeed, when he played Acasto in *The Orphan* on 22 August 1770, the *Town and Country Magazine* for that month suggested that the managers of the winter house should cast him in better roles which "we are inclined to think he might fill with success." While still filling small business at the Haymarket, Gardner also played Bruin in *The Mayor of Garratt*, Pinchwife in *The Country Wife*, Kent in *King Lear*, and Sciolto in *The Fair Penitent*. On 20 September 1771 he acted Shylock for the first time (a role, as noted above, which he played again at Covent Garden the following May) at a benefit for his wife, who made her first attempt as Portia.

Gardner's engagement of ten years at Covent Garden ended after the season of 1773–74. He was not at the Haymarket the summer before or the summer after that season, although on 30 September 1774 at that theatre he made an appearance as Henry in *Richard III* for the benefit of Mrs Williams and Mrs Weston. For several years he made only very occasional appearances in London, acting Almada in

By Permiſſion of the LORD CHAMBERLAIN.

For the Benefit of Mr. GARDNER.

Theatre-Royal, Hay-Market,

On MONDAY, December 30, 1782,
Will be performed, A TRAGEDY, called

The Fair Penitent.

Lothario, by a GENTLEMAN,
(Being his firſt Appearance on the Stage.)
Sciolto, by Mr. GARDNER.
Altamont, by Mr. WETHERHEAD.
Roſſano, Mr. SPENCER.
And Horatio, by Mr. USHER.
Lavinia, Mrs. KING.
Lucilla, Miſs PAINTER.
And Caliſta, by a LADY,
(Being her firſt Appearance on the Stage.)
After the Play, the fourth Act of

The Merchant of Venice.

Antonio, by Mr. USHER.
Baſſanio, by the GENTLEMAN,
Who plays LOTHARIO.
Duke, by Mr. ROBERTS.
Gratiano, by Mr. WETHERHEAD.
And Shylock, by Mr. GARDNER.
Neriſſa, by Miſs PAINTER.
And Portia, by the LADY,
Who plays CALISTA.
To which will be added,

The Examination of Dr. Laſt before the College of Phyſicians.

(From the DEVIL upon TWO STICKS.)
The Devil, Mr. COOKE,   Secretary, Mr. ROBERTS.
Dr. Calomel, Mr. BOON.   Dr. Camphire, Mr. CORNE.
And Dr. LAST, by

SirJefferyDunſtan,

The preſent worthy Mayor of Garrat.
(Being his firſt Appearance on the Stage.)
Mr. GARDNER having unavoidably been obliged to poſtpone his Night from
the 26th to the 30th, he thinks it his Duty to inform his Friends that,
Tickets delivered for the 26th will be taken.
⁎ Places to be had of Mr. RICE at the Theatre.
The Doors to be opened at Five, and to begin at a Quarter paſt Six.

Sᵗ JEFFERY   DUNSTAN

The preſent Worthy MAYOR of GARRAT
in the Character of Dᵗ Laſt in the Devil upon Two Stick

Braganza at Drury Lane on 3 November 1775 and 19 March 1776 (he was paid £5 5s. on 20 April 1776) and Dactyl in *The Patron* at the Haymarket on 29 July 1776. Gardner performed at Richmond in the summer of 1775, at Brighton in 1777, at Manchester in 1778, and at Cambridge in 1779. At Drury Lane on 24 and 25 January 1780 he was called in to read the role of Casca in *Julius Caesar* as a last-minute substitute for the indisposed Aickin.

He did not have an engagement at a winter house in London between 1774–75 and 1784–85, although he was in the town to act at the Haymarket again regularly in summer from 1778 through 1789, the last summer of his life. At the Haymarket on 30 December 1782, by permission of the Lord Chamberlain, Gardner gave himself a benefit (originally scheduled for the twenty-sixth but postponed) in which he performed Sciolto in *The Fair Penitent* and Shylock in *The Merchant of Venice* (Act IV only). In the afterpiece, *Dr Last's Examination before the College of Physicians*, the title role was acted by Sir Jeffery Dunstan, "the present Worthy Mayor of Garratt," announced as making his first appearance on any stage. Dunstan was a notorious beggar about town and, from an engraved picture of him on the unusual bill for this performance, seems to have been a dwarf.

After an absence of 11 years, Gardner returned to a regular engagement at Covent Garden in 1785–86, at a salary of £2 per week, making his reappearance on 21 September 1785 as the Lord Mayor in *Richard III*, an assignment which was a portent of his continuing humble status. In fact his roles over the final years of his career con-

Folger Shakespeare Library

Playbill, Haymarket Theatre, 30 December 1782

Benefit for WILLIAM GARDNER

sisted mainly of even less consequential characters. In his first season back, for example, he filled the stage in such roles as the Player King in *Hamlet*, Don Quixote in *Barataria*, Northumberland in *1 Henry IV*, Smith in *The Rehearsal*, a Soldier in *The Grecian Daughter*, Alquazil in *The Choleric Fathers*, the Prince and Tybalt in *Romeo and Juliet*, Ratcliffe in *Jane Shore*, the Duke Senior in *As You Like It*, the Adjutant in *Love in a Camp*, Stukely in *The West Indian*, Fulvio in *The Bird in a Cage*, and the Jeweller in *Timon of Athens*. In 1789–90, his final year at Covent Garden, when his salary was still £2 per week, he was still playing most of those roles, as well as Siward in *Macbeth*, the Duke in *Othello*, Plunder in *The Lady of the Manor*, and Farmer Stubble in *The Farmer*.

Gardner's last performance was as the Physician in *King Lear* on 11 January 1790. Thereafter other names appeared in bills for his usual roles. No doubt he suffered illness for several months, and on 4 May 1790 he died.

Gardner had been estranged from his wife Sarah Gardner since 1777, in which year they were reported to have "a growing family." There are conflicting testimonies as to who had been the unfaithful partner. She was in America at the time of William Gardner's death and did not return to London until 1795.

Gardner, Mrs William, Sarah, née Cheney [*fl.* 1763–1795], *actress, playwright, lecturer.*

Playing in the early part of her career under her maiden name, Miss Cheney, the actress Sarah Gardner made her first appearance at Drury Lane Theatre on 1 October 1763 in the role of Miss Prue in *Love for Love*. In his manuscript diary the prompter Hopkins wrote of her debut: "a Pretty Figure, play'd with Spirit, very Awkward, & Speaks too much at the top of her Voice." After repeating Miss Prue on 6

October and 3 and 11 November, she acted Rose in *The Recruiting Officer* on 13 January 1764. Engaged at Drury Lane for the following season at 6*s.* 8*d.* per day, or £2 per week, she acted Miss Prue again on 20 October 1764 and Philotis in *The Frenchified Lady Never in Paris* on 11 April 1765. On 10 June 1765 at the Haymarket Theatre she was the original performer of Mrs Mechlin in Foote's comedy *The Commissary*, a role she played numerous times throughout the remainder of the summer season.

Sometime during the same summer she married William Gardner (d. 1790), a journeyman actor at Covent Garden Theatre, who was also a member of Foote's company and had played Bridoun in *The Commissary*. In the fall she joined her husband at Covent Garden, now acting as Mrs

Harvard Theatre Collection

SARAH GARDNER, as Lady Macbeth

artist unknown

Gardner, making her debut there on 19 October 1765 as Polly in *Polly Honeycombe*. On 19 November she acted her favorite role of Miss Prue. She played Belinda in *The Man of Mode* on 15 March 1766 and Jenny Private in *The Fair Quaker of Deal* on 15 April, and on 26 April she was the original Fanny in the first performance of Thomas Hull's afterpiece *All in the Right*. The next season at Covent Garden she acted very seldom, her roles being Doll Tearsheet in *2 Henry IV* on 6 October 1766 and Jenny Private on 19 May 1767. On 5 November 1768 she, with other Covent Garden performers, signed her full name on a letter sent to Colman. In an inventory of July 1769 her wardrobe at Covent Garden was valued at a very modest £6.

Mrs Gardner remained a member of the company at Covent Garden through 1773–74, playing for the most part a comparatively small repertory of broad comic roles. In 1767–68, when her salary was 5*s.* per day, she acted Megra in *Philaster* on 2 January 1768, Flora in *The Wonder* on 6 May, and Flora in *She Wou'd and She Wou'd Not* on 11 May. Her other roles at Covent Garden during this period included: Betty in *The Sister*, Jenny in *The Knights*, Termagant in *The Upholsterer* in 1768–69; the Landlady in *Man and Wife*, Altea in *Rule a Wife and Have a Wife*, Lucy in *The Brothers*, Biddy in *Miss in Her Teens* in 1769–70; Mrs Cadwallader in *The Author*, the Fine Lady in *Lethe*, Lady Dove in *The Brothers*, a principal role in *The Modern Wife* in 1770–71; Miss Sterling in *The Clandestine Marriage*, Lady Wou'dbe in *The Fox*, Maria in *Twelfth Night*, Queen Fadladinida in *Chrononhotonthologos*, the Nurse in *Romeo and Juliet* in 1771–72; and Mrs Fulmer in *The West Indian* in 1773–74.

For her roles at Covent Garden she received little critical favor. For her performances as Lady Wou'dbe in *The Fox* (Jonson's *Volpone*, revived at Covent Garden on 26 November 1771 after 20 years), the

St James's Chronicle accused her of *"o'erdoing Termagant, or out-heroding Herod."* Her portrayal of Mrs Fulmer in *The West Indian* was "so *outre* & peculiar to herself" that the *Covent Garden Magazine* (1773) did not know what to make of it. "Her gait resembled the sidling of a ship, without ballast, in a gale of wind," wrote the critic, and the audience showed its taste by hissing. Evidently the management of Covent Garden shared the view of the critic that "the less she is seen the better," for she was not reengaged after that season.

It was as a regular member of Foote's summer companies at the Haymarket, however, that Mrs Gardner achieved some reputation. After her first summer there in 1766 she returned in 1767 to play Kitty Pry in Garrick's *The Lying Valet* and Foote's *The Commissary* on 4 June 1767. On 8 June she acted Kitty in Foote's farce *The Lyar*, and during the season also played Maria in *The Citizen*, Miss Harlow in *The Old Maid*, Cherry in *The Stratagem*, the Nurse in *Romeo and Juliet*, a Lady in *The Taylors*, the Fine Lady in *Lethe*, Regan in *King Lear*, Lady Wronghead in *The Provok'd Husband*, Mrs Slammekin in *The Beggar's Opera* (in which she introduced the business of pretending to get drunk), Lady Manlove in *The School Boy*, Jenny in *The Knights,* and Patch in *The Busy Body*. On 29 May 1767 she was surely the "Miss" Gardner who played Tag in *Miss in Her Teens*. In *Momus*, a poem published that year by an anonymous writer, Mrs Gardner was accused of obvious attempts "to catch the manner of a *Pope* or *Clive*."

Mrs Gardner stayed with Foote at the Haymarket until the manager's death in 1777, playing a variety of roles similar to those already cited. In original performances of Foote's plays she acted Margaret in *The Devil Upon Two Sticks* on 30 May 1768, Mrs Circuit in *The Lame Lover* on 22 June 1770, Mrs Matchem in *The Nabob* on 29 June 1772, and Mrs Simony in *The Cozeners* on 15 July 1774. Having seen a performance of *The Author* on 14 September 1771, Sylas Neville found Mrs Gardner "as great an oddity" in Mrs Cadwallader as Foote was in Cadwallader. On 20 September 1771 she and her husband made their first appearances as Portia and Shylock. She acted soubrettes for part of the season at Bristol in 1773, and on 27 April 1776, after a two-year absence she reappeared at Covent Garden for the night to perform a new character in an interlude taken from *The Register Office.*

At the Haymarket in 1776 Mrs Gardner acted Mrs Sullen in *The Beaux' Stratagem* for the first time on 23 September. As Mrs Hardcastle in *She Stoops to Conquer* on 9 June 1777 she was severely criticized by one newspaper reviewer for throwing her arms about "like the wings of a windmill," and Colman, the manager after Foote's death, was entreated to "use some means to prevent Mrs Gardner's *bouncing* & *bawling.*" By that time, it seems clear, Mrs Gardner had degenerated into a blowzy and brash actress. She had once given pleasure, even in the *outré* characters which she now overplayed, but, according to the *Theatrical Biography* (1775), having had Foote for a teacher she had picked up his mannerisms, and she did not have his genius. Her voice lost its softness and her person its grace. By 1772 she had become tiresome in the view of Francis Gentleman in *The Theatres*, with "Billingsgate in every line."

During the summer of 1777 Mrs Gardner suffered the tribulations of having her three-act comedy *The Advertisement; or, A Bold Stroke for a Husband* produced at the Haymarket on 9 August. (The text was never printed but is in Larpent MS 13L at the Huntington Library.) Her difficulties with Colman over the acceptance of *The Advertisement* and with the players over its preparation are related in a bulky foolscap volume of her writing which was found in a small cupboard in a wall in Old Court House, Colyton, Devon, where presumably Mrs Gardner had at some time lived. Among the manuscripts discovered in Devon (and reported in detail in *Theatre Notebook,* VII and VIII) is Mrs Gardner's own copy of the play, with a preface which sets forth her grievances and the abuses she claims to have suffered because of the failure of the actors to learn their lines. Drunk upon his entrance, John Edwin had had to read his part, and his conduct had drawn hisses. "The performers, who had evidently agree'd to damn the play," wrote the authoress, "now grew alarm'd, and were afraid that the rod of correction would be extended to more than Edwin," so they had set about studying their parts backstage during the performance. Mrs Gardner herself in the role of the Widow had played well, except for nervousness for her piece. Although she accused Colman of neglecting the play, it seems that he had agreed to have it performed provided Mrs Gardner would make the arrangements for its playing, including the obtaining of the license; and he had disclaimed any further responsibility, allowing her the evening's receipts for her benefit in order to rid himself of the troublesome woman.

By 1777 Mrs Gardner was estranged from her husband, who presumably had neglected her and her children. The *Morning Post* of 10 August 1777 reported that she lived in "a retired and humble manner," attentive to "a growing family," but John Bernard, who knew her later in Dublin, characterized her in his *Retrospections* as "a lady of extravagant habits," who, though a married woman, was "fond of very singular adventures." He admitted that she was a "chambermaid actress of great merit."

After the summer of 1777 at the Haymarket, Mrs Gardner acted in a specially licensed performance of Hitchcock's *The Coquette* at that theatre on 9 October 1777, and then evidently was gone from London for almost four years. Early biographers

Harvard Theatre Collection

SARAH GARDNER as Lady Plyant and
JOHN PALMER as Careless

engraving by Walker, after Dodd

place her in the West Indies from 1777 until 8 August 1781 when, they say, she was Mrs Cadwallader in *The Author* at Kingston, Jamaica, announced as being from Covent Garden Theatre. Yet a Mrs Gardner appeared at the Haymarket as Dogwood in *A Wife to be Lett* and in an unspecified role in *The Sharper's Last Shift* on 22 January 1781. Either the biographers or the Haymarket playbills are in error, or there was at this period another Mrs Gardner acting in London.

By the summer of 1782 Mrs Gardner was back in London, playing Mrs Cadwallader at the Haymarket on 13 August, when she was announced—somewhat incorrectly—as making "her first appearance on any stage these five years." Several

nights later, on 16 August 1782, she acted Mrs Metaphor, the leading character in a farce called *The Female Dramatist* (Larpent MS 29.M) which has often been attributed to her but which the younger George Colman claimed to have written.

Mrs Gardner's subsequent engagement at the Capel Street Theatre, Dublin, in 1783 led to another quarrel with a management over one of her plays. In a letter to the *Freeman's Journal* on 18 March 1783 she complained that the managers had broken their promise to perform one of her comedies and, moreover, that she could not get her salary. The Capel Street house was in so sorry a state, according to the *Biographia Dramatica* (1812), that the production would have brought her little fame or money. She resorted to delivering at the theatre a "Course of humorous, entertaining, political and satyrical Lectures, never before exhibited," which included a selection entitled "On Myself," and which brought her a polite and large audience. She was a difficult and canny woman, and according to Bernard she arranged a mock illness and "funeral" to elude her creditors in Dublin. On 30 October 1783 the *Public Advertiser* announced that Mrs Gardner was at the time "giving lectures on Heads, etc., at Liverpool. And she is said to pick up a good many Half Crowns."

Soon she again crossed the ocean. The January 1785 issue of the *Cornwall Chronicle* in Jamaica announced that "Mrs Gardner, the celebrated actress and Mr Mahon, a vocal performer of eminence, from the Covent Garden Theatre are arrived in this Island." The only surviving record of her activities was of a benefit she took at Kingston on 15 April 1786, when she played Papillion in *The Lyar* and offered an "Occasional Prelude" written by herself—"in the writing and performance thereof, she equally proved the strength of her genius and abilities, in the comic, satiric and initiative veins"—and an epilogue, also presumably of her composition:

For me, whate'er may be my future lot,
Your gen'rous favours ne'er will be for-
got,
To all my friends, around—above—be-
low—
A frank return of Gratitude I owe.
My cordial thanks await you to receive;
For what is life, without the means to
live?
For this your goodness warmly shewn
to me,
Long may this gen'rous Isle be bless'd
and free.

Eventually Mrs Gardner found her way to the North American mainland, but her professional activities there are little known. By April 1789 she was giving concerts of vocal and instrumental music, with entertainments which probably included her "lectures," at McCrady's Long Room in Charleston, South Carolina. On 17 November 1789 she made her first appearance in New York, at the City Tavern, in "an entertainment rhetorical and oratorical, entitled Fashionable Raillery or the Powers of Eloquence Displayed in a Spirited and humorous Touch on the Times," a program she claimed to have performed 47 nights in Dublin and with "equal success" in Jamaica and Charleston. Several months later on 30 December 1789 she received a benefit at the John Street Theatre in New York, having announced in a letter to the press that "she was deceived in Charleston by a plausible scamp, brought north, stripped of every penny and left helpless."

Announced as making her first appearance since her return from the West Indies, Mrs Gardner appeared at the Haymarket Theatre in London on 22 April 1795, for Everard's benefit. The first piece of the evening was *Mrs Doggrell in Her Attitudes; or, The Effects of a West India Ramble*, which she had written (never published, Larpent MS 1101) and in which she and Everard appeared. She also performed Mrs Heidelberg in *The Clandestine Marriage* and Mrs Cadwallader in *The Author*. After that evening Mrs Gardner was not heard from again. Her husband William Gardner, who remained in London during her many years of absence, had died on 4 May 1790.

Among Mrs Gardner's manuscripts found in the Old Court House in Colyton were, in addition to *The Advertisement* and its lengthy preface, a comedy in five acts called "The Loyal Subject," a farce in one act called "Charity" (with short preface and prologue)—"Founded on Facts and perform'd by Gentlemen for their amusement"—as well as 20 miscellaneous sets of verses and "An Open Letter to the Prime Minister on Certain Aspects of the American War and Suggestions upon Taxation." Also in the cupboard was an account book of a village store for the years 1810–1813, suggesting the possibility that Mrs Gardner ran a shop after she left the stage.

Mrs Gardner is depicted as Lady Plyant, with John Palmer as Careless, in a scene from *The Double Dealer* which was engraved by Walker, after Dodd, as a plate for the *New English Theatre*, 1777, and in *Macbeth*, by an anonymous engraver as a plate to the *Hibernian Magazine*, April 1778. There is no record of her appearance in either play in London. An engraving of "Mr Foote and Mrs Gardner, in the Characters of two Serjeants at Law, with the other droll Figures which form the first scene of the third Act of the Lame Lover," was published as frontispiece to *Wit for the TON! The Convivial Jester; or, SAM FOOTE's Last Budget Opened* (1777?). *The Lame Lover*, in which Mrs Gardner acted Mrs Circuit, was first played at the Haymarket on 22 June 1770.

Gardoner. *See* GARDINER *and* GARDNER.

Gare, Mr *[fl. 1779], acrobat?*

At Sadler's Wells on 5 April 1779 Mr Richer, "Baptiste Gare," and Signora Mariana presented "New and Capital Exhibitions"—acrobatic feats, apparently. The bill very likely was in error in naming Baptiste Gare as one person; Baptiste was probably Jean Baptiste Dubois and Gare another person. A year earlier, on 11 May 1778, a bill for the Wells cited Richer, "Mynheer Baptiste," Master Gare, and Signora Mariana as presenters of undescribed exhibitions. Master Gare (unless he was in fact our subject) was presumably Mr Gare's son.

Gare, Master [fl. 1778], acrobat. See **GARE, MR.**

Garee, John [fl. 1710–1712], musician.

John Garee (or Geree), probably a musician, was given benefit concerts at Couch's Drawing Room on 24 February 1710 and at Stationers' Hall on 11 January 1711 and 7 February 1712.

Garelli, Giovanni [fl. 1791–1794], singer.

Giovanni Garelli's first recorded appearance in London was on 17 February 1791 at the Pantheon as Carlo in *Armida*. On 14 April he sang Imaro in *Idalide*, and on 2 June he was Marco Fabio in *Quinto Fabio*. He had been hired to sing first parts in both serious and comic operas. Smith's *Italian Opera in London* lists Garelli as a second *buffo* at the Pantheon and the Haymarket during the 1791–92 season, but the singer's only notice in opera bills was on 19 April 1792 when he sang for the elder Bannister's benefit with the Drury Lane troupe at the King's Theatre.

In 1792–93 and 1793–94 Garelli was at the King's, singing such parts as Nardone in *Le contadine bizzarre*, Biaggino in *Don Giovanni*, Maccabruno in *La bella pescatrice*, Mitrani in *Il capriccio drammatico*, Valerio in *Il burbero di buon cuore*, and Vespone in *La serva padrona*. His last appearance seems to have been on 8 July 1794 when he sang Mitrane in *Semiramide*.

"Gargantua Pantagruel." See **CHETWOOD, WILLIAM RUFUS.**

Gariboldi, Stefano d. 1790, bass viol player.

When Stefano Gariboldi was recommended for membership in the Royal Society of Musicians in 1779, he was described as a performer on the double bass at the Pantheon Theatre, a participant in Mr Hammell's concerts, and a teacher of several instruments. He had a wife and grown children, but they were not in England. He was admitted to the Society on 4 June 1780. In 1783 he played at the King's Theatre in the Haymarket; in May and June 1784 he participated in the Handel concerts at Westminster Abbey and the Pantheon; in May 1785 he played at the Society's St Paul's concert; and on 27 February 1789 at Covent Garden he was one of the instrumentalists in a performance of the *Messiah*. Gariboldi died in 1790, and on 4 April of that year the Royal Society of Musicians granted £8 for the musician's burial expenses.

Garland, [Halhed?] [fl. 1765–1776], numberer, actor?, singer?

A Mr Garland was a numberer at Drury Lane receiving, as of 9 February 1765, 15s. weekly, the highest rate paid any of the theatre's house servants. It seems likely that he was the Halhed Garland who, with Benjamin Victor and Thomas Evans, witnessed the Drury Lane patentee James Lacy's will on 20 May 1768.

During the 1775–76 season at Drury Lane a Mr Garland, possibly the same person, acted a number of small parts. On 9 November 1775 he played a Drawer in *Old City Manners*, and during the season he appeared as a Servant in *The Blackamoor Wash'd White*, a Servant and a Gentleman Hunter in *The Runaway*, Alguazile in *She Wou'd and She Wou'd Not*, and the Third Gardener in *The Rival Can-*

didates. He was also in *The Rehearsal*, had a vocal part in *Romeo and Juliet*, and appeared in *The Man of Quality* and *The Genii*. His benefit tickets were accepted on 24 May 1776. Garland subscribed 10*s*. 6*d* to the Drury Lane fund in 1776, but the accounts show that he left the theatre at the end of the 1775–76 season. Perhaps the same Garland was with Roger Kemble at Carmarthen the following fall: a Mr Garland played Beau Clincher in *The Constant Couple* there on 20 September 1776.

Garland, William Wayte [*fl.* 1772–1787], *actor*.

On 14 August 1772 the *Whitehall Evening Post* reported that William Wayte Garland, a harlequin, was acting at the English theatre in St Petersburg. According to *Faulkner's Dublin Journal* on 22 October, Garland was scheduled to act at Smock Alley the following day, and he was hailed as from Covent Garden in London. The Govent Garden bills make no mention of Garland in the early 1770s, though he may have been playing small parts. Garland continued at Smock Alley in 1773–74.

A Mr Garland, very possibly William Wayte, played harlequin and extra parts at Bristol in 1775, and the *Morning Chronicle* in London on 9 September 1776 reported that a "Garland of Deptford" was playing at the China Hall, Rotherhithe. There on 25 September Garland acted the Earl of Surrey in *Henry VIII*, and on 14 October he played Young Philpot in *The Citizen* and Garcia in *The Mourning Bride*.

Harvard has a manuscript letter from Thomas Hull of Covent Garden to a Mr Garland (presumably the Garland who had played at Rotherhithe) dated 17 August 1778. Hull told Garland that the Covent Garden roster was already full for the 1778–79 season but that if Garland would accept 30*s*. weekly and play harlequin characters he could have an engagement. Garland appeared on 14 October 1778 as one of the principal characters (unspeci-

fied) in *The Medley*, which ran periodically through April 1779. He was also in *The Norwood Gypsies* on 22 October 1778 and was one of several whose benefit tickets were accepted on 29 April 1779.

The *European Magazine* in July 1787 reported that William Wayte Garland, the Covent Garden harlequin, had married a Miss Riley.

Garman, Mr [*fl.* 1776?–1801], *equilibrist?*, *dancer*, *actor*.

During the time of the fair in March 1776 in Bristol at Merchant Taylors' Hall in Broad Street "the little POLANDER" exhibited "his amazing Performances upon Chairs, a Ladder, &c. the same as performed at Sadler's-Wells" in London. He was identified as Master Garman when he received a benefit night at Astley's Amphitheatre in London on 7 September 1779. He was surely related to the performer (Peter? Francis?) Garman, who was active during the last half of the eighteenth century. Master Garman was in the Sadler's Wells troupe as of 16 September 1785, and we take him to have been the "Garman Junior" who appeared there as a Sailor in *Sans Culottes* in 1793 and a Wild Boar in *William Tell* on 12 May 1794.

As Mr Garman he danced and acted at Drury Lane Theatre from 1794 to 1801. His first notice was on 20 December 1794, when he was one of the minor members of the cast of *The Cherokee* (in January 1795 he was cited as playing one of the Indians). Other assignments Garman received over the years were similar: a Gipsy in *Harlequin Captive*, a Shepherd in a dance called *The Triumph of Love*, a Peasant in *Richard Coeur de Lion*, a Villager in *The Scotch Ghost* (a dance), a "Principal Savage" in *Robinson Crusoe*, a Slave in *Blue-Beard*, Jemmy in the dance *Moggy and Jemmy*, a Vassal in *Feudal Times*, Gabriel in *Catherine and Petruchio*, a Slave in *The Egyptian Festival*, and a solo hornpipe dancer in *The Beggar's Opera*. Garman's salary during most of his stay at Drury Lane was £1 weekly.

Garman, Mons [fl. 1793], pyrotechnist.

A puff in a Bristol paper of 16 February 1793 told of the pyrotechnists Mons Garman and Carr, previously with Astley in London. Their fireworks were to be an adjunct to Handy's circus performances in Limekiln Lane. There is no record of Garman's activity in London.

Garman, Master [fl. 1746], dancer.

Master Garman danced at Sadler's Wells in April 1746, as did (Peter? Francis?) Garman. They were probably son and father.

Garman, [Peter? Francis?] [fl. 1742–1797], clown, actor, dancer, tumbler.

At the St Germain fair in 1742 a rope dancer and tumbler named "German" performed in the *Grande troupe étrangère* under the direction of Restier and the elder Lavigne, according to the *Dictionnaire des théâtres*. On 3 February he played Sancho Panca, a servant of Colombine's father, in *A trompeur, trompeur et demi*, and on 15 February he was the Dutch peasant Yorès in *Diable boîteux*. In the company was a female rope dancer from London named German and identified by Campardon in *Spectacles de la foire* as Mlle Frédérick. Leathers in *British Entertainers in France* spells her name "Germain," calls her Frederica, and says she was the sister of the rope dancer.

The same woman, probably, advertised as Mme Garman, entertained at the theatre in Stoke's Croft, Bristol, in July 1743 with a tumbling act. She shared a benefit with the troupe leader Dominique on 12 March 1744 and later that month performed a rope dance "with Rolls on her Ankles, and also with two Flags, in Jack Boots." She was with the company that month in Salisbury and returned with Dominique to Bris-

tol in February 1746. That month the manager was at pains to assure Bristolians that his performers were not all French, as had been rumored; Mme Garman, he noted, was from Amsterdam. At her benefit on 25 February she danced on the slack rope.

Mr Garman may have performed in Bristol and Salisbury, too, but his name has not been found in any advertisements. He did, however, dance at Sadler's Wells in London in April 1746 (as did Master Garman, who may have been his son). Garman performed on the stiff rope at Derby on 3 August 1750, and he exhibited "feats of activity" at Sadler's Wells in 1751. Mrs Garman appeared on 26 February 1752 at the New Concert Hall in Edinburgh, and Mr Garman served Sadler's Wells as a clown, rope dancer, and tumbler off and on through 1781. He was a tumbler at Astley's Amphitheatre from 1780 through 1785 and appeared in spectacle productions at Sadler's Wells from 1788 to 1797.

In 1756–57 and 1757–58 the Garmans had appeared at the Smock Alley Theatre in Dublin. Miss Kiza Garman danced there in 1756–57 and later performed in London, first as Miss Garman and then as Mrs Invill. On 2 June 1760 Mrs Garman played Colombine in *Harlequin Hussar* at the Haymarket Theatre in London, and a bill for Sadler's Wells in 1762 spoke of Mr Garman rope dancing with two boys and then two men tied to his feet. "Carman" danced Apollo (Mezzetin) in *The Royal Chace* at Covent Garden Theatre on 12 May 1766.

Arundell in *The Story of Sadler's Wells* says Garman's first name was Peter, but other sources cite him as Francis. It is possible that there were two Garmans, but the bills do not provide sufficient information to clarify the matter. Francis Hayman painted a picture of the Sadler's Wells manager Rosamon and several of his performers in 1754, but the picture has been lost. Garman was one of the group.

Garman, Mrs [Peter? Francis?], **called Mlle Frédérick** [fl. 1742–1760], *dancer, tumbler*. *See* GARMAN, [PETER? FRANCIS?].

Garman, Kiza. *See* INVILL, KIZA.

Garner, Mr [fl. 1751]. *See* GARDINER, MR [fl. 1750–1757].

Garnet, Mrs [fl. 1715–1721], *actress*.
The first notice in the bills of Mrs Garnet was on 24 May 1715, when she acted the Eunuch in *Valentinian* at Lincoln's Inn Fields. She played two other roles there before moving to Drury Lane for the rest of her career: Secret in *The Doating Lovers* on 23 June 1715 and the Maid in *The Cobler of Preston* on 24 January 1716.

Mrs Garnet's first recorded part at Drury Lane was Betty Frisk in *The Country Wit* on 12 July 1716, after which there was no mention of her until 25 February 1717, when she played Zara at the premier of *The Sultaness*, though she may have been acting bit parts regularly. From 1717–18 through 1720–21 at Drury Lane Mrs Garnet appeared in such new parts as Hillaria in *Love's Last Shift*, Jenny in *The Play is the Plot*, Flora in *Love in a Vail*, Betty Jiltall in *Love for Money*, Ruth in *The Committee*, Lydia in *Love in a Wood*, Charmian in *All for Love*, Emilia in *The Man of Mode*, Lady Graveairs in *The Careless Husband*, Araminta in *The Old Bachelor*, Fainlove in *The Tender Husband*, Lucy in *Oroonoko*, Statilia in *The Bondman*, Epicoene in *The Silent Woman*, Julia in *The Fatal Marriage*, Florinda in *The Rover*, Mrs Frail in *Love for Love*, Mrs Termagant in *The Squire of Alsatia*, and Leonora in *The Mourning Bride*. Though she seems to have begun building a very respectable repertoire, after the 1720–21 season Mrs Garnet apparently left the stage.

Garney. *See* CARNE.

Garnier, Miss [fl. 1785], *dancer*.
Miss Garnier participated in a pantomime dance and a piece called *Harlequin's Exhibition of the Times* at Astley's Amphitheatre on 27 September 1785. Possibly she was the Mlle Grenier who danced at the King's Theatre in 1787–88, but there is not sufficient evidence to make a certain identification.

Garrard, Mrs [fl. 1787–1792?], *singer*.
A bill for the Royal Circus dated 1787 listed Mrs Garrard as a participant in a burletta called *The Boarding School*. Perhaps she was the Mrs Garrard who performed in 1792 at the new theatre in the market place in Ashby.

Garrard, Francis [fl. 1673–1677], *violinist, wind instrumentalist*.
On 13 November 1673 Francis Garrard was admitted to the King's Musick as a musician in ordinary for the violin, but without fee. On 16 September 1677 Garrard replaced Edward Hooton in the wind instruments, and on the following 24 December he replaced the deceased John Mason at a daily wage of 1s. 8d. plus livery.

Garrat, Miss [fl. 1760], *dancer*. *See* GARRAT, SAMUEL.

Garrat, Samuel [fl. 1760–1794], *singer*.
The Mr Jarrut (or Janiot, Jarratt) whose name appeared in the Covent Garden accounts in 1760 and the Drury Lane accounts in the mid-1770s was very likely Samuel Garrat. On 30 May 1760 the Covent Garden accounts show a payment of £21 to him for his daughter's dancing during the season, which entry suggests that she was probably a minor. Then he was cited in the Drury Lane accounts in 1774–75 and, as a member of the singing chorus ("treble") at £2 weekly, in 1776–77. Doane's *Musical*

Directory of 1794 stated that Samuel Garrat was an alto singer, a member of the Handelian Society, and a participant in the Handel concerts at Westminster Abbey and the oratorios at Drury Lane. His address was given as No 6, Snow's Fields, Southwark. There is a possibility that the actress Mrs Garrett, who performed in 1787, was a relative. And perhaps the Miss Garrat of 1760 was the Miss Jarratt, who made her official debut at Drury Lane in November 1772.

Garrelli, Mons [fl. 1737], actor.

Monsieur Garrelli (or Gurrelli) played Pantaloon in *Le Mariage forcé* at Covent Garden on 8 April 1736. The troupe was made up of foreign actors who had just come over from the Continent, augmented by some of the Covent Garden regulars. The experiment was apparently not successful, for no second performance was given, nor did the visiting players act in London again. The income for the night, however, was £131 18s.

Garrett, Mrs [fl. 1787], actress.

Mrs Garrett acted with the summer company at the Haymarket Theatre from June to September 1787, but her only known part was Penelope in *The Romp* on 26 June.

Illustrations

VIEWS AND DRAWINGS OF PROVINCIAL THEATRES

Harvard Theatre Collection
Andover Theatre
from Winston's *The Theatric Tourist*, 1805

Harvard Theatre Collection
Bath Theatre
from Winston's *The Theatric Tourist*, 1805

Harvard Theatre Collection
Birmingham Theatre
from Winston's *The Theatric Tourist*, 1805

Harvard Theatre Collection
Brighton Theatre
from Winston's *The Theatric Tourist*, 1805

Harvard Theatre Collection
Chichester Theatre
from Winston's *The Theatric Tourist,* 1805

Harvard Theatre Collection
Edmonton Theatre
from Winston's *The Theatric Tourist,* 1805

Harvard Theatre Collection
Exeter Theatre
from Winston's *The Theatric Tourist*, 1805

Harvard Theatre Collection
Grantham Theatre
from Winston's *The Theatric Tourist*, 1805

Harvard Theatre Collection
Lewes Theatre
from Winston's *The Theatric Tourist*, 1805

Harvard Theatre Collection
Liverpool Theatre
from Winston's *The Theatric Tourist*, 1805

Harvard Theatre Collection
Maidstone Theatre
from Winston's *The Theatric Tourist,* 1805

Harvard Theatre Collection
Manchester Theatre
from Winston's *The Theatric Tourist,* 1805

Harvard Theatre Collection
Margate Theatre
from Winston's *The Theatric Tourist,* 1805

Harvard Theatre Collection
Newbury Theatre
from Winston's *The Theatric Tourist,* 1805

Harvard Theatre Collection
Newcastle Theatre
from Winston's *The Theatric Tourist,* 1805

Harvard Theatre Collection
Norwich Theatre
from Winston's *The Theatric Tourist,* 1805

Harvard Theatre Collection
Plymouth Theatre
from Winston's *The Theatric Tourist,* 1805

Harvard Theatre Collection
Portsmouth Theatre
from Winston's *The Theatric Tourist,* 1805

Harvard Theatre Collection
Reading Theatre
from Winston's *The Theatric Tourist*, 1805

Harvard Theatre Collection
Richmond Theatre
from Winston's *The Theatric Tourist*, 1805

Harvard Theatre Collection
Southampton Theatre
from Winston's *The Theatric Tourist*, 1805

Harvard Theatre Collection
Tunbridge Wells Theatre
from Winston's *The Theatric Tourist*, 1805

Harvard Theatre Collection
Winchester Theatre
from Winston's *The Theatric Tourist,* 1805

Harvard Theatre Collection
Windsor Theatre
from Winston's *The Theatric Tourist,* 1805

ELEVATION OF THE THEATRE ROYAL, LIVERPOOL.

Engraved from the Original Drawing (same size) by Robert Chaffers, taken 12th May 1773.

This Theatre was built in Williamson Square at the Expense of the Corporation & opened under the Authority of a Patent,
on Friday June the 5th 1772 with the Play of Mahomet & an occasional Prologue written by the Elder Colman.

The celebrated John Palmer of Drury Lane Theatre & Manager of the Royalty died upon this Stage while performing the Character of the Stranger, August 2nd 1798.

London — Published 4th June 1822 by Robert Wilkinson, N°.725 Fenchurch Street.

The Theatre Royal, Liverpool, in 1773
from Wilkinson's *Londina Illustrata*, 1819–25

T Thwaites delin.   _Pétro sculp._

"_Such Pray'rs ne'er fail, when so devoutly given,_"
"_But swiftly fly on Angels wings to Heav'n!_"

Folger Shakespeare Library
The Sunderland Theatre stage, with James Cawdell
from Cawdell's _Miscellaneos Poems,_ 1785

Theatre-Royal, Richmond,

OPEN EVERY

Monday, Wednesday, and *Friday,*

For the remainder of the Seafon.

This present MONDAY, JULY 22, 1799,

Will be performed (for the fecond Time) a favourite New PLAY, call'd

Lovers Vows:
Or, The NATURAL SON.

Tranflated from the German of KOTZEBUE.

(Which can only be performed once more, on account of the Novelties in preparation.)

Frederick   by   Mr.   J O H N S O N,

(Who performed Wilford *at this Theatre, laft Seafon, and twice at the Theatre-Royal, Covent-Garden, with univerfal Approbation.)*

Count Caffell (Firft Time)   by   Mr.   N E V I L L E,

Annault   by   Mr.   W I L L I A M S,

Verdon   by   Mr.   N O B L E,

Cottager   by   Mr.   J.   K E L L Y,

Farmer   by   Mr.   B A R R E T T,

Huntfmen   by   Meff.   B L U R T O N   and   B R A W N,

And Baron Wildenham (Firft Time)   by   Mr.   C L I F F O R D.

Amelia   by   Mrs.   B A R R E T T,

Country Girl   by   Mifs   W A L L A C K,

And Agatha   by   Mrs.   N E V I L L E.

To which will be added, (by Defire) a Mufical Piece, call'd

The P U R S E.

Theodore   by   Mr.   N O B L E,

The Baron   by   Mr.   W I L L I A M S,

Will Steady   by   Mr.   J O H N S O N,

And Edmund   by   Mrs.   B A S T E R.

(Being her Firft Appearance at this Theatre.)

The Page   by   Mifs   W A L L A C K,

And Sally   by   Mifs   C R O W.

BOXES 4s.   PIT 2s.   GALLERY 1s.

Doors to be Opened at Six, to begin precifely at Seven o'Clock. *Vivant Rex & Regina.*

Places for the Boxes to be Taken of Mr. B. BUDD, at the Stage Door of the Theatre.

N. B. No Perfon can be admitted behind the Scenes.

The univerfally admired PLAY of

P I Z A R R O,

(Tranflated from the German of *Kotzebue,* & adapted to the Englifh Stage by *R. B. Sheridan,* Ffq. M. P.)

Will be brought forward as foon as the fuperb new Scenery, Dreffes, Decorations, Banners, Trophies, &c. &c. can be compleated, on which (at a great Expence) the different Artifts are now bufily Employed.

Folger Shakespeare Library

Playbill for the Richmond Theatre, 22 July 1799

For the BENEFIT of

La Chevaliere D'EON,

And Positively the last Time of her Performing here.

THEATRE-ROYAL, CHELTENHAM.
TUESDAY, September, 22, 1795, will be presented,
Cumberland's favorite Comedy, of

THE JEW.

Sheva, (the *Jew*) Mr. SHUTER.
Sir Stephen Bertram, Mr. VILLARS.
Frederic, Mr. DARLINGTON. Charles Ratcliffe, Mr. SMITH.
Jabal, (the *Jew's Man*) Mr. HARVEY.
And Eliza Ratcliffe, Mrs. CARLETON.

TO WHICH WILL BE ADDED

All the World's a Stage

Sir Gilbert Pumpkin, Mr. VILLARS.
And Diggory Duckling, Mr. SHUTER.

Miss Bridget Pumpkin, Mrs. VILLARS. Jenny, Mrs. BUTLER,
And Kitty Sprightly, Mrs. CARLETON.

END OF THE SECOND ACT
THE CELEBRATED
CHEVALIERE D'EON,
WILL MAKE A GRAND

Assault D'armes,

Or, A True Representation of an

ATTACK and DEFENCE,

In Single Combat, Sword in Hand,
With an ENGLISH GENTLEMAN,
A Professor in the ART of FENCING.

(Agreeable to the best and most approved Method now practised by the first Masters in Europe.)

Wherein every Skill and Dexterity in the Science of *Excrime* will be displayed.
MADEMOISELLE D'EON will on that occasion appear in ARMOUR with a Casque and Plume of Feathers; the Dress she Fenced in at Ranelagh; before the PRINCE of WALES, and many of the Royal Family.

End of the Play. The favorite Comic Song, of the RUSHLIGHT,
To be Sung by the GENTLEMAN, who Fences with the Chevaliere.

To the LADIES and GENTLEMEN of CHELTENHAM.

CHARLOTTE GENEVIEVE LOUISE D'EON, formerly known by the title of Chevalier D'EON, Knight of the Royal Military Order of St. Louis, Minister Plenipotentiary from France to the Court of Great-Britian, &c. residing thirty-three years in Brewer-Street, Golden Square, LONDON; and in 1777, was by judgment of the Court of King's Bench, and by special order of the French King, obliged to resume her female dress, and was restored to the name, title, and condition of Mademoiselle D'EON DE BAUMONT, in her native Country; but not being able since the Revolution in France, during the epoch of this war, to draw the Pensions which had been granted to her by the late kings of France, LOUIS XV. and XVI. for her political and military services; sustaining a loss of 15,000 Livres per Annum, and being prevented from receiving the revenues of her Estates at Tonnerre, in Burgundy; besides having had the misfortune to be frustrated in the receipt of the sum of 6000 pounds sterling, deposited by the late king of France in the hands of an English noble lord, for her support in England:—She lost her Estate and Fortune with cool and philosophic Resignation.

Thus circumstanced, and waiting the restoration of Peace, she at the age of SIXTY-EIGHT embraced the resource of her skill and long experience in the science of her arms, to *Cut her Bread with her Sword;* and instead of idly looking up for support from those, who in her prosperity were her *Professed Good Friends,* she relies on the Liberality of BRITONS at large to protect an unfortunate Woman of Quality from the "*Stings and Arrows of outrageous Fortune,*" in a Foreign Country, and in "*the Vale of Years.*"

To begin precisely at 7 o'Clock.----Boxes 3s.----Pit 2s.----Gallery 1s.
Tickets and Places to be had at the Theatre, and of Mademoiselle D'EON, N°. 107.

Folger Shakespeare Library
Playbill for the Cheltenham Theatre, 22 September 1795

Harvard Theatre Collection
Lord Barrymore's theatre at Wargrave

Trustees of the British Museum
A provincial performance of Hamlet, 1772
engraving by R. St G. M.

Comedy in the Country, 1807
engraving by Rowlandson

Folger Shakespeare Library
The Shakespeare Jubilee at Stratford-on-Avon, 1769
drawing by an anonymous artist

68) a. Act 4th Seen 4th — Grimaldi's House.

Call W. 12 V.

Call Enter Grimaldi: Marone:

Mar: 'Tis the most I can gather, — pansa stands firme to his first
Examination; — And Bianca, more and more clears her Lady.

Grim: Nor can any thing please me better; ~~first~~ that my freind's
gott up agen.

Mar: Would I coud say as much of Roderigo.

Grim: ffor why man.

Mar: He's broke, And run away.   *ready to ring for y. Trap*

Grim: What? — He that dark'nd all our Starres! — Impossible.

Mar: Too true. —

Grim: Yet, how you magnifi'd him!   *Drum r. to thunder*

Mar: His great dealings, And punctual payments; might have
Cheated any man, as well as me

Gri: was the summe Considerable?   *Call Roderigo*

Mar: 200000 Duckats at least.

Grim: 'Tis a wonder no more follow him: ffor it is often with
Merchants, as Nine-pinns; — Hitt but your first and second
right; — And tis odds, but two parts in three Tumble:

Mar: That I'me afraid shall I, for one; — He owes me ten thousand
Duckats; And when I went to his Lady this morning; She told
me, he had left her a Beggar.

Grim: And yet you know, — He was Wise, prudent, vertuous; —
And once your Glory, that he call'd ye freind! — And shall a
little dirt part ye? — Come. — yo.r Credit, will sett him up.

Mar: If it woud to the Gallows, I'de venture as much more.

Grim: Your freind? — You woud'nt sure?

Mar: My freind? — A very Rogue; — A meer cheating, beggarly
Banknrupt Rascal.

Folger Shakespeare Library

Page from the manuscript promptbook for Wilson's *Belphegor*,
Smock Alley Theatre, Dublin, c.1670s